Quantum Information and Computation

Quantum Information and Computation

Editors

Shao-Ming Fei
Ming Li
Shunlong Luo

MDPI • Basel • Beijing • Wuhan • Barcelona • Belgrade • Manchester • Tokyo • Cluj • Tianjin

Editors
Shao-Ming Fei
Capital Normal University,
Beijing, China

Ming Li
China University
of Petroleum,
Qingdao, China

Shunlong Luo
Chinese Academy of Sciences,
Beijing, China

Editorial Office
MDPI
St. Alban-Anlage 66
4052 Basel, Switzerland

This is a reprint of articles from the Special Issue published online in the open access journal *Entropy* (ISSN 1099-4300) (available at: https://www.mdpi.com/journal/entropy/special_issues/quantum_information_computation).

For citation purposes, cite each article independently as indicated on the article page online and as indicated below:

LastName, A.A.; LastName, B.B.; LastName, C.C. Article Title. *Journal Name* **Year**, *Volume Number*, Page Range.

ISBN 978-3-0365-7202-4 (Hbk)
ISBN 978-3-0365-7203-1 (PDF)

© 2023 by the authors. Articles in this book are Open Access and distributed under the Creative Commons Attribution (CC BY) license, which allows users to download, copy and build upon published articles, as long as the author and publisher are properly credited, which ensures maximum dissemination and a wider impact of our publications.

The book as a whole is distributed by MDPI under the terms and conditions of the Creative Commons license CC BY-NC-ND.

Contents

About the Editors vii

Shao-Ming Fei, Ming Li and Shunlong Luo
Quantum Information and Computation
Reprinted from: *Entropy* 2023, 25, 463, doi:10.3390/e25030463 1

Hongting Song and Nan Li
Quantumness and Dequantumness Power of Quantum Channels
Reprinted from: *Entropy* 2022, 24, 1146, doi:10.3390/e24081146 5

Daipengwei Bao, Xiaoqing Tan, Qingshan Xu, Haozhen Wang and Rui Huang
Robust Self-Testing of Four-Qubit Symmetric States
Reprinted from: *Entropy* 2022, 24, 1003, doi:10.3390/e24071003 17

Yuan Zhai, Bo Yang and Zhengjun Xi
Belavkin–Staszewski Relative Entropy, Conditional Entropy, and Mutual Information
Reprinted from: *Entropy* 2022, 24, 837, doi:10.3390/e24060837 35

Qing-Hua Zhang and Ion Nechita
A Fisher Information-Based Incompatibility Criterion for Quantum Channels
Reprinted from: *Entropy* 2022, 24, 805, doi:10.3390/e24060805 51

Pu Wang, Zhihua Guo and Huaixin Cao
Quantum Incoherence Based Simultaneously on k Bases
Reprinted from: *Entropy* 2022, 24, 659, doi:10.3390/e24050659 67

Yu Guo
When Is a Genuine Multipartite Entanglement Measure Monogamous?
Reprinted from: *Entropy* 2022, 24, 355, doi:10.3390/e24030355 81

Junjun Duan, Lin Zhang, Quan Qian and Shao-Ming Fe
A Characterization of Maximally Entangled Two-Qubit States
Reprinted from: *Entropy* 2022, 24, 247, doi:10.3390/e24020247 97

Lihua Yang, Xiaofei Qi and Jinchuan Hou
Quantum Nonlocality in Any Forked Tree-Shaped Network
Reprinted from: *Entropy* 2022, 24, 691, doi:10.3390/e24050691 107

Shuquan Ma, Changhua Zhu, Dongxiao Quan and Min Nie
A Distributed Architecture for Secure Delegated Quantum Computation
Reprinted from: *Entropy* 2022, 24, 794, doi:10.3390/e24060794 125

Xiaodong Fan, Quanhao Niu, Tao Zhao and Banghong Guo
Rate-Compatible LDPC Codes for Continuous-Variable Quantum Key Distribution in Wide
Range of SNRs Regime
Reprinted from: *Entropy* 2022, 24, 1463, doi:10.3390/e24101463 141

Ximing Hua, Min Hu and Banghong Guo
Multi-User Measurement-Device-Independent Quantum Key Distribution Based on GHZ
Entangled State
Reprinted from: *Entropy* 2022, 24, 841, doi:10.3390/e24060841 155

Shanqi Pang, Hanxiao Xu and Mengqian Chen
Construction of Binary Quantum Error-Correcting Codes from Orthogonal Array
Reprinted from: *Entropy* **2022**, *24*, 1000, doi:10.3390/e24071000 . . . . **169**

Kai Li, Ming Zhang, Xiaowen Liu, Yong Liu, Hongyi Dai, Yijun Zhang and Chen Dong
Quantum Linear System Algorithm for General Matrices in System Identification
Reprinted from: *Entropy* **2022**, *24*, 893, doi:10.3390/e24070893 . . . . **181**

Chuanmei Xie, Zhanjun Zhang, Jianlan Chen and Xiaofeng Yin
Quantum Correlation Swapping between Two Werner States Undergoing Localand Nonlocal Unitary Operations
Reprinted from: *Entropy* **2022**, *24*, 1244, doi:10.3390/e24091244 . . . . **195**

About the Editors

Shao-Ming Fei

Prof. Dr. Shao-Ming Fei. Research interests: quantum information, quantum computing and mathematical physics. Worked in Institute of Physics, Chinese Academy of Sciences as an associate researcher in 1993 at the Institute of Mathematics, University of Bochum, Germany, as an Alexander von Humboldt visiting scholar in 1994 and at the Institute of Applied Mathematics, University of Bonn, Germany, in 1999. Since 2001, he has been worked in School of Mathematical Sciences, Capital Normal University, as a full professor. He has published more than 450 papers in journals, including *Physical Review Letters*, *Nature Communications* and *NPJ Quantum Information*, and had served as editorial board members of journals such as *Scientific Reports*, *Entropy* and *Science China Physics, Mechanics, and Astronomy*.

Ming Li

Prof. Dr. Ming Li is a visiting scholar at the Max Planck Institute for Mathematics in the Science in Leipzig. Currently, he is the vice President of the School of Science, China University of Petroleum (East China). His research interests include quantum entanglement detection and measurement, fidelity of quantum teleportation, quantum nonlocality and Bell inequality, quantum coherence theory, quantum computing, and quantum machine learning algorithm design. In recent years, he has published more than 70 papers in journals such as *Physical Review Letters* and *Physical Review A*. He has served as a guest deputy editor of *Entropy*.

Shunlong Luo

Prof. Dr. Shunlong Luo is currently the director of the Institute of Applied Mathematics, Academy of Mathematics and Systems Science, Chinese Academy of Sciences. He was a plenary speaker of the 8th International Congress on Industry and Applied Mathematics (2015). His research interests include probability and statistics, quantum theory, and information theory.

Editorial

Quantum Information and Computation

Shao-Ming Fei [1,*], Ming Li [2,*] and Shunlong Luo [3,*]

[1] School of Mathematical Sciences, Capital Normal University, Beijing 100048, China
[2] School of Science, China University of Petroleum, Qingdao 266580, China
[3] Academy of Mathematics and Systems Science, Chinese Academy of Sciences, Beijing 100190, China
* Correspondence: feishm@cnu.edu.cn (S.-M.F.); liming3737@163.com (M.L.); luosl@amt.ac.cn (S.L.)

Quantum technology can break through the bottleneck of traditional information technology by ensuring information security, speeding up computation, improving measurement accuracy, and providing revolutionary solutions to some issues of economic and social development. The theory of quantum information and computation provides guarantee on the development of quantum technology. This Special Issue is intended to investigate some basic features and applications of quantum information, including but not limited to complementarity, quantum algorithms, quantum coherence, quantum correlations, quantum measurement, quantum metrology, quantum uncertainties, and quantum information processing.

The works in this Special Issue can be divided into two categories: basic theory of quantum information, and quantum information processing and algorithm designs. We start with the former.

A quantum channel usually changes the quantum features of the system, such as causing decoherence of quantum states and destroying quantum correlations. Characterizing quantum channels from the information perspective has yielded fruitful results. In [1], Song and Li propose a framework to qualitatively and quantitatively characterize quantum channels from the perspective of the amount of quantumness in ensembles that a quantum channel can induce. They investigate the dynamics of quantumness in ensembles and propose quantumness power and dequantumness power to characterize quantum channels. If a channel reduces the quantumness for all the ensembles at all times, it is a completely dequantumness channel. The relationship with Markovian channels is also studied through several examples. The work illustrates new properties of quantum channels from the perspective of the information flow in terms of quantumness brought by the interaction between the system and environment. The results can be directly generalized to arbitrary dimensions and other measures of quantumness.

Quantum verification has been highlighted as a significant challenge on the road to scalable technology. In addition to the tomography of a quantum state, self-testing is a device-independent approach to verifying that the previously unknown quantum system state and uncharacterized measurement operators are, to some degree, close to the target state and measurements (up to local isometries) based only on the observed statistics, without assuming the dimension of the quantum system. Previous studies focused on bipartite states and some multipartite states, including all symmetric states, but only in the case of three qubits. Bao et al. [2] give a criterion for the self-testing of a four-qubit symmetric state with a special structure and provide a robustness analysis based on vector norm inequalities. Bao et al. also generalize the idea to a family of parameterized four-qubit symmetric states through projections onto two subsystems.

The Belavkin–Staszewski (BS) relative entropy is an enticing and crucial entropy used to process quantum information tasks, which can be used to describe the effects of possible noncommutativity of the quantum states (the quantum relative entropy does not work well for this case). Katariya and Wilde employed the BS relative entropy to study quantum channel estimation and discrimination. Bluhm and Capel contributed a strengthened

data processing inequality for BS relative entropy. This property was first established by Hiai and Petz. Bluhm et al. presented some results on weak quasi-factorization for BS relative entropy. Fang and Fawzi studied quantum channel capacities with respect to the geometric Rényi relative entropy. In [3], Zhai et al. define two new conditional entropy terms and four new mutual information terms by replacing quantum relative entropy with BS relative entropy. Some basic properties of the newly introduced entropies are investigated, especially in classical-quantum settings. In particular, the authors of [3] show the weak concavity of the BS conditional entropy and obtain the chain rule for the BS mutual information. Finally, the subadditivity of the BS relative entropy is established; i.e., the BS relative entropy of a joint system is less than the sum of its corresponding subsystems with the help of some multiplicative and additive factors. Meanwhile, a certain subadditivity of the geometric Rényi relative entropy is also provided.

One of the fundamental phenomena in quantum physics is the impossibility of simultaneous realization of two quantum operations. The Heisenberg uncertainty principle and the no-cloning theorem are two famous incarnations for such phenomena. Generally, two (or more) quantum operations, such as measurements, channels, or instruments, are called compatible if they can be seen as the marginals of a common operation. Otherwise, they are called incompatible. The concept of incompatibility of quantum channels has been proposed in terms of the input–output devices. In [4], Zhang and Nechita present a new incompatibility criterion for quantum channels based on the notion of (quantum) Fisher information. The power of this incompatibility criterion is further discussed in different scenarios. The authors of [4] present the analytical conditions for the incompatibility of two Schur channels. They also investigate the incompatibility structure of a tuple of depolarizing channels by comparing the newly introduced criterion with the known results from asymmetric quantum cloning.

As an important resource in many quantum information tasks, quantum coherence is a feature of quantum systems rooted in the superposition principle. Since the coherence of quantum states depends on the choice of the reference basis, it is natural to study the relationship among the coherence with respect to different bases. Wang et al. [5] study quantum incoherence based simultaneously on k bases. They firstly define a correlation function m(e,f) of two orthonormal bases e and f, by which the relationships between sets I(e) and I(f) of incoherent states are investigated. They show that I(e) = I(f) if and only if the rank-one projective measurements generated by e and f are identical. They also provide a necessary and sufficient condition for the intersection I(e)∩I(f) to include a state except the maximally mixed state. In particular, if two bases e and f are mutually unbiased, then the intersection has only the maximally mixed state. The authors then introduce the concepts of strong incoherence and weak coherence of a quantum state with respect to a set B of k bases and propose a measure for the weak coherence. They prove that in two-qubit systems there exists a maximally coherent state with respect to B for k = 2 but not for k = 3.

Entanglement is a quintessential manifestation of quantum mechanics and is often considered to be a useful resource for tasks such as quantum teleportation or quantum cryptography. Genuine multipartite entanglement is an important type of entanglement that offers significant advantages in quantum tasks compared to bipartite entanglement. The distribution of entanglement is believed to be monogamous, i.e., a quantum system entangled with another system limits its entanglement with the remaining others. There are two methods used in this research. The first one is to analyze monogamy relations based on bipartite entanglement measure, and the second one is based on multipartite entanglement measure. In [6], Guo explores the complete monogamy of a genuine multipartite entanglement measure (GMEM). Guo firstly studies the framework for unified/complete GMEM according to the unified/complete multipartite entanglement measure. He finds a way of inducing unified/complete GMEM from any given unified/complete multipartite entanglement measure. It is shown that any unified GMEM is completely monogamous, and any complete GMEM that is induced by the given complete multipartite entanglement measure is completely monogamous. In addition, the previous GMEMs are checked under this framework. It turns out that the genuinely multipartite concurrence is not a good candidate for GMEM.

Entanglement detection is a basic problem in quantum theory. A powerful tool is the so-called positive partial transpose (PPT) criterion, proposed by Peres. PPT condition is not only necessary but also sufficient for the separability of qubit–qubit, qubit–qutrit, or qutrit–qubit systems. Rana shows that all eigenvalues of any partially transposed bipartite state fall within the closed interval $[-1/2, 1]$. In [7], Duan et al. study a family of bipartite quantum states for which the minimal eigenvalues of the partially transposed states are $-1/2$. For a two-qubit system, the authors of [7] find that the minimal eigenvalue of its partially transposed state is $-1/2$ if and only if the two-qubit state is maximally entangled. They also show that this result does not hold in general for two-qubit systems when the dimensions of the underlying space are larger than two.

The second category of the works in this Special Issue focuses on quantum information processing and algorithm designs.

Since the multi-locality in quantum networks features several independent sources under joint measurements, one can obtain stronger correlations throughout the whole network. Such networks were first observed in a bi-local network. Since then the nonlocality of various quantum networks has been explored, including chain-shaped networks, star-shaped networks, triangle networks, and tree-tensor networks. In [8], Yang et al. consider the nonlocality of any forked tree-shaped networks, where each node shares an arbitrary number of bipartite sources with other nodes in the next "layer". Yang et al. derive Bell-type inequalities for such quantum networks in terms of all $(t_n - 1)$-local correlations and all local correlations, where t_n denotes the total number of nodes in the network. The authors of [8] also derive the maximal quantum violations of these inequalities and the robustness to noise in these networks.

In recent years, quantum computing has been extensively studied from theory to practice. Noisy intermediate-scale quantum (NISQ) computers may not have the capability to deal with large-scale quantum information processing. Delegating computations to the companies that offer quantum computing may be a better choice to access quantum computers. In [9], Ma et al. propose a distributed secure delegated quantum computation protocol, which allows clients to delegate their private computation to several quantum servers. Ma et al. show that their protocol can guarantee unconditional security of the computation under the situation where all servers, including the third party, are honest but curious, and they are allowed to cooperate with each other.

As an important application of quantum theory, quantum key distribution (QKD), which allows two users to share a secure key privately, is one of the options to combat the lack of safety in communication caused by the increasingly developed quantum computation. Bennett and Brassard present the first QKD protocol. In [10], Fan et al. propose a design rule of rate-compatible low-density parity-compatible codes which covers all potential signal-to-noise ratio with a single check matrix. By such codes, high-efficiency continuous-variable quantum key distribution information reconciliation is achieved.

There exist various loopholes in practical systems through which eavesdroppers can attack the QKD process. Lo et al. present a measurement-device-independent quantum key distribution (MDI-QKD) protocol to prevent attacks on measurement devices and enhance the communication distance between two users. In [11], Hua et al. propose a flexible multi-user measurement-device-independent quantum key distribution (MDI-QKD) scheme based on a GHZ entangled state. Hua's scheme can distribute quantum keys among multiple users while being resistant to detection attacks. Hua et al. then present simulation results which show that the secure distance between each user and the measurement device can reach more than 280 km, while reducing the complexity of the quantum network. Hua et al. also present a method to expand the scheme to a multi-node, multi-user network, which can further enhance the communication distance between the users at different nodes.

In quantum information processing, errors are inevitable. Quantum error-correcting codes (QECCs) are invented to ensure the implementation of quantum communication and quantum computing. Pang et al. [12] draw support from the Hamming distance and minimal distance of orthogonal arrays to study the relationship between uniform states and binary QECCs. They provide new methods to construct pure quantum error-correcting codes. By using these methods, several infinite series of quantum error-correcting codes including some optimal ones are constructed.

A large number of practical problems often boil down to solving a system of linear algebraic equations, such as elasticity in engineering and science, circuit analysis, geodesy, heat conduction, vibration, etc. Many effective numerical methods, such as spline interpolation, least-squares fitting, generalized Newton method for solving nonlinear equations, method for calculating the coefficients of Newton–Cotes quadrature formula, finite difference method, and finite element method for solving numerical solutions of partial differential equations, are also finally converted into problems of solving linear equations. Zhang et al. in [13] provide a modified quantum scheme to obtain the quantum state corresponding to the solutions of linear system of equations with less machine running time than the existing quantum algorithms. The authors of [12] also investigate the problem of finding solutions to a linear system with a sparsity-independent and non-square coefficient matrix.

Quantum entanglement swapping is a highly significant technology in quantum entanglement repeaters, which are generally employed to realize long-distance quantum entanglements in many quantum information processing tasks. In [14], Xie et al. discuss the problem of quantum correlation (QC) swapping between two Werner-like states by performing Bell measurements on the middle node and taking into account the measurement-induced disturbance (MID) and ameliorated MID.

Conflicts of Interest: The authors declare no conflict of interest.

References

1. Song, H.; Li, N. Quantumness and Dequantumness Power of Quantum Channels. *Entropy* **2022**, *24*, 1146. [CrossRef] [PubMed]
2. Bao, D.; Tan, X.; Xu, Q.; Wang, H.; Huang, R. Robust Self-Testing of Four-Qubit Symmetric States. *Entropy* **2022**, *24*, 1003. [CrossRef] [PubMed]
3. Zhai, Y.; Yang, B.; Xi, Z. Belavkin–Staszewski Relative Entropy, Conditional Entropy, and Mutual Information. *Entropy* **2022**, *24*, 837. [CrossRef] [PubMed]
4. Zhang, Q.-H.; Nechita, I. A Fisher Information-Based Incompatibility Criterion for Quantum Channels. *Entropy* **2022**, *24*, 805. [CrossRef] [PubMed]
5. Wang, P.; Guo, Z.; Cao, H. Quantum Incoherence Based Simultaneously on k Bases. *Entropy* **2022**, *24*, 659. [CrossRef] [PubMed]
6. Guo, Y. When Is a Genuine Multipartite Entanglement Measure Monogamous? *Entropy* **2022**, *24*, 355. [CrossRef] [PubMed]
7. Duan, J.; Zhang, L.; Qian, Q.; Fei, S.-M. A Characterization of Maximally Entangled Two-Qubit States. *Entropy* **2022**, *24*, 247. [CrossRef] [PubMed]
8. Yang, L.; Qi, X.; Hou, J. Quantum Nonlocality in Any Forked Tree-Shaped Network. *Entropy* **2022**, *24*, 691. [CrossRef] [PubMed]
9. Ma, S.; Zhu, C.; Quan, D.; Nie, M. A Distributed Architecture for Secure Delegated Quantum Computation. *Entropy* **2022**, *24*, 794. [CrossRef] [PubMed]
10. Fan, X.; Niu, Q.; Zhao, T.; Guo, B. Rate-Compatible LDPC Codes for Continuous-Variable Quantum Key Distribution in Wide Range of SNRs Regime. *Entropy* **2022**, *24*, 1463. [CrossRef]
11. Hua, X.; Hu, M.; Guo, B. Multi-User Measurement-Device-Independent Quantum Key Distribution Based on GHZ Entangled State. *Entropy* **2022**, *24*, 841. [CrossRef] [PubMed]
12. Pang, S.; Xu, H.; Chen, M. Construction of Binary Quantum Error-Correcting Codes from Orthogonal Array. *Entropy* **2022**, *24*, 1000. [CrossRef] [PubMed]
13. Li, K.; Zhang, M.; Liu, X.; Liu, Y.; Dai, H.; Zhang, Y.; Dong, C. Quantum Linear System Algorithm for General Matrices in System Identification. *Entropy* **2022**, *24*, 893. [CrossRef] [PubMed]
14. Xie, C.; Zhang, Z.; Chen, J.; Yin, X. Quantum Correlation Swapping between Two Werner States Undergoing Local and Nonlocal Unitary Operations. *Entropy* **2022**, *24*, 1244. [CrossRef] [PubMed]

Disclaimer/Publisher's Note: The statements, opinions and data contained in all publications are solely those of the individual author(s) and contributor(s) and not of MDPI and/or the editor(s). MDPI and/or the editor(s) disclaim responsibility for any injury to people or property resulting from any ideas, methods, instructions or products referred to in the content.

Article

Quantumness and Dequantumness Power of Quantum Channels

Hongting Song [1] and Nan Li [2,3,*]

[1] Qian Xuesen Laboratory of Space Technology, China Academy of Space Technology, Beijing 100094, China
[2] Academy of Mathematics and Systems Science, Chinese Academy of Sciences, Beijing 100190, China
[3] School of Mathematical Sciences, University of the Chinese Academy of Sciences, Beijing 100049, China
* Correspondence: linan@amss.ac.cn

Abstract: Focusing on the dynamics of quantumness in ensembles, we propose a framework to qualitatively and quantitatively characterize quantum channels from the perspective of the amount of quantumness in ensembles that a quantum channel can induce or reduce. Along this line, the quantumness power and dequantumness power are introduced. In particular, once a quantum dynamics described by time-varying quantum channels reduces the quantumness for any input ensembles all the time, we call it a completely dequantumness channel, whose relationship with Markovianity is analyzed through several examples.

Keywords: quantumness in ensembles; quantum channel; quantum Markovianity; non-commutativity

Citation: Song, H.; Li, N. Quantumness and Dequantumness Power of Quantum Channels. *Entropy* **2022**, *24*, 1146. https://doi.org/10.3390/e24081146

Academic Editors: Shao-Ming Fei, Ming Li and Shunlong Luo

Received: 10 July 2022
Accepted: 14 August 2022
Published: 18 August 2022

Publisher's Note: MDPI stays neutral with regard to jurisdictional claims in published maps and institutional affiliations.

Copyright: © 2022 by the authors. Licensee MDPI, Basel, Switzerland. This article is an open access article distributed under the terms and conditions of the Creative Commons Attribution (CC BY) license (https://creativecommons.org/licenses/by/4.0/).

1. Introduction

As natural generalizations of transition matrices in stochastic analysis, quantum channels are completely positive and trace-preserving maps. A quantum channel usually changes the quantum features of the system, such as causing the decoherence of quantum states [1,2] and destroying the quantum correlations [3–6]. Characterizing quantum channels from the information perspective has received fruitful results. The entangling power [7], decorrelating capability [8], cohering and decohering power [9–14], and quantumness-generating capability [15] of quantum channels have been studied.

In this work, we propose a framework to qualitatively and quantitatively characterize quantum channels by analyzing the dynamics of quantumness in ensembles. A quantum ensemble $\mathcal{E} = \{(p_i, \rho_i), i \in \mathcal{I}\}$ is represented by a family of quantum states together with a probability distribution specifying the probability of the occurrence of each state [16]. It arises naturally in quantum mechanics and statistical physics, and is a fundamental and practical object in quantum information, especially in quantum measurement and quantum communication [17–23]. As long as the involved quantum states are not commutative, the quantum ensemble possesses a certain intrinsic quantum feature, which is named as quantumness in quantum ensembles. It plays a central role in quantum cryptography and other various quantum information processing tasks. Various measures of quantumness have been proposed from different perspectives, such as that via commutator [24,25], that based on no cloning and no broadcasting [19], that defined from the perspective of accessible information [24], and that via relative entropy [26] and coherence [27,28].

In general, the quantumness in a quantum ensemble will change after performing a quantum channel. It is natural to investigate the maximal amount of quantumness that a quantum channel can introduce or reduce. In this work, by virtue of the quantumness measure based on commutators [24] that is easy to calculate, we study the characterization of quantum channels from the perspective of quantumness power and dequantumness power, which quantify the maximal amount of quantumness that a quantum channel can induce and reduce, respectively. Comparing with the result in Ref. [29] where the quantumness of the channel is defined as the minimum average quantum coherence of the state space after the dynamics, quantumness power defined here is the maximal amount of the non-commutativity between the states that can be generated after the channel. The properties and calculation process of quantumness power and dequantumness power have been analyzed. We call a quantum dynamics described by a quantum channel a completely dequantumness channel if it reduces the quantumness in ensembles all the time. Through several significant examples, the relationship between the completely dequantumness channel and quantum Markovian channel is analyzed. It is worth mentioning that although we mainly focus on the qubit channels, without loss of generality, the result can be directly extended to qudit cases.

The paper is organized as follows. In Section 2, we briefly review the measure of quantumness adopted in this work. Quantumness power and dequantumness power of the quantum channel with their modified versions are introduced in Section 3. We give the definition of the completely dequantumness channel and investigate its relationship with quantum Markovianity through several significant examples in Section 4. We conclude with a summary in Section 5.

2. Measure of Quantumness

Based on the direct connection between the quantumness of an ensemble and the non-commutativity among its constituent states, the quantumness of the quantum ensemble $\mathcal{E} = \{(p_i, \rho_i), i \in \mathcal{I}\}$ can be naturally quantified via the commutator as [24]

$$Q(\mathcal{E}) = -\sum_{i,j} p_i p_j \mathrm{tr}[\rho_i, \rho_j]^2, \quad (1)$$

where $[\rho_i, \rho_j] = \rho_i \rho_j - \rho_j \rho_i$ stands for the commutator, which is anti-Hermitian. This measure is easy to calculate. We remark that in Refs. [30,31] the authors also used the Hilbert–Schmidt norm of the commutators between two density operators to quantity the non-commutativity between these two density operators.

For the two-qubit case, by virtue of the Bloch representation of the state, the expression of $Q(\mathcal{E})$ for ensembles with only two ingredients such that $\mathcal{E} = \{(p, \rho_1), (1-p, \rho_2)\}$ can be further derived. Here $p \in (0,1)$, $\rho_i = \frac{1}{2}(\mathbf{1} + \vec{r}_i \cdot \vec{\sigma})$, $i = 1, 2$ with $\mathbf{1}$ the identity operator, $\vec{r}_i = (r_{ix}, r_{iy}, r_{iz})$ the Bloch vector of the state ρ_i, and $\vec{\sigma} = (\sigma_1, \sigma_2, \sigma_3)$ the vector of the Pauli matrices. Then, it can be calculated that

$$Q(\mathcal{E}) = p(1-p)|\vec{r}_1 \times \vec{r}_2|^2 = p(1-p)(r_1^2 r_2^2 - (\vec{r}_1 \cdot \vec{r}_2)^2).$$

Here $r_i^2 = |\vec{r}_i|^2$, $\times$ and $\cdot$ denote the outer and inner product of the vectors, respectively. The Bloch vector of state ρ_i can be given as $\vec{r}_i = r_i(\sin \theta_i \cos \phi_i, \sin \theta_i \sin \phi_i, \cos \theta_i)$ with $r_i \in [0,1]$, $\theta_i \in [0, \pi]$, and $\phi_i \in [0, 2\pi)$, then

$$Q(\mathcal{E}) = p(1-p) r_1^2 r_2^2 (n_1^2 + n_2^2 + n_3^2), \quad (2)$$

with

$$\begin{aligned} n_1 &= \sin \theta_1 \sin \theta_2 \sin(\phi_1 - \phi_2), \\ n_2 &= \sin \theta_1 \cos \phi_1 \cos \theta_2 - \cos \theta_1 \sin \theta_2 \cos \phi_2, \\ n_3 &= \sin \theta_1 \sin \phi_1 \cos \theta_2 - \cos \theta_1 \sin \theta_2 \sin \phi_2. \end{aligned} \quad (3)$$

Recently, a modified version of this measure is proposed in Ref. [15] as

$$Q'(\mathcal{E}) = -\sum_{i,j} \sqrt{p_i p_j} \mathrm{tr}[\sqrt{\rho_i}, \sqrt{\rho_j}]^2,$$

which is proved to bear some nice properties, such as the positivity, unitary invariance, subaddtivity, concavity under probability union, convexity under state decomposition, and increasing under fine graining.

For simplicity in calculation, we adopt the measure in Equation (2) in the following. It is worth mentioning that all the work derived here can be directly generalized to other measures.

3. Quantumness and Dequantumness Power

After a quantum channel Λ, which is a linear, trace-preserving completely positive map, the ensemble $\mathcal{E} = \{(p_i, \rho_i), i \in \mathcal{I}\}$ evolves to $\Lambda(\mathcal{E}) = \{(p_i, \Lambda(\rho_i)), i \in \mathcal{I}\}$. By analyzing the dynamics of quantumness in ensembles, we can characterize the quantumness power and dequantumness power of the quantum channel. To be specific, the quantumness power of a quantum channel is defined as the maximal amount of quantumness that it generates over all input ensembles $\mathcal{E}$. Its expression is given as

$$C(\Lambda) = \max_{\mathcal{E}} \left(Q(\Lambda(\mathcal{E})) - Q(\mathcal{E}) \right),$$

which quantifies the ability to induce quantumness. If we only focus on the initial commutative ensembles, we can get another definition of quantumness power which we denote as C' with expression

$$C'(\Lambda) = \max_{\{\mathcal{E}:\, Q(\mathcal{E})=0\}} Q(\Lambda(\mathcal{E})).$$

Similarly, we can define the dequantumness power of a quantum channel as the maximal amount by which the quantumness of the ensemble is reduced when it passed through the channel, i.e.,

$$D(\Lambda) = \max_{\mathcal{E}} \left(Q(\mathcal{E}) - Q(\Lambda(\mathcal{E})) \right).$$

When we only consider the initial ensembles with the maximal quantumness, we can obtain a modified version

$$D'(\Lambda) = \max_{\{\mathcal{E}:\, Q(\mathcal{E})=Q_{\max}\}} \left(Q(\mathcal{E}) - Q(\Lambda(\mathcal{E})) \right)$$
$$= Q_{\max} - \min_{\{\mathcal{E}:\, Q(\mathcal{E})=Q_{\max}\}} Q(\Lambda(\mathcal{E})).$$

Here $Q_{\max}$ denotes the maximal amount of quantumness in a quantum ensemble for a given Hilbert space, which is dependent on the space dimension.

We remark that in [32], the quantumness of a quantum channel is defined as the maximal quantumness (non-commutativity) between the output states of the quantum channel for any two maximal-quantumness states, which can be formally expressed as

$$\max_{\{\mathcal{E}:\, Q(\mathcal{E})=Q_{\max}\}} Q(\Lambda(\mathcal{E})).$$

Note that another difference in the motivation is that we start from the quantumness in ensembles rather than any two quantum states.

From the definition, we can obtain the following properties.
(1) $C(\Lambda) \geq C'(\Lambda)$ and $D(\Lambda) \geq D'(\Lambda)$.
(2) $C'(\Lambda) = 0$ is equivalent to that Λ is a commutativity preserving channel.
(3) $C(U) = 0$ and $D(U) = 0$, where U is the unitary operation.
(4) $C(\Lambda_1 \circ \Lambda_2) \leq C(\Lambda_1) + C(\Lambda_2)$ and $D(\Lambda_1 \circ \Lambda_2) \leq D(\Lambda_1) + D(\Lambda_2)$.
(5) $C_2(\Lambda) \leq C_n(\Lambda) < 2C_2(\Lambda)$ and $D_2(\Lambda) \leq D_n(\Lambda) < 2D_2(\Lambda)$, where $C_n(\Lambda)$ and $D_n(\Lambda)$ represent the quantumness and dequantumness power defined on the ensembles with less than n ingredients, respectively.

Proof. Since the first four properties can be directly verified from the definition, we only prove the property (5) as follows. For simplicity, we just give the proof of the quantumness power, with the case of the dequantumness power similarly derived.

For ensembles having two ingredients $\mathcal{E}_2 = \{(p, \rho_1), (1-p, \rho_2)\}$, the quantumness power is

$$C_2(\Lambda) = \max_{\mathcal{E}_2}\left(Q(\Lambda(\mathcal{E})) - Q(\mathcal{E})\right) = \max_{p,\rho_1,\rho_2} 2p(1-p)\left(\text{tr}[\rho_1,\rho_2]^2 - \text{tr}[\Lambda(\rho_1),\Lambda(\rho_2)]^2\right)$$

$$= \frac{1}{2}\max_{\rho_1,\rho_2}\left(\text{tr}[\rho_1,\rho_2]^2 - \text{tr}[\Lambda(\rho_1),\Lambda(\rho_2)]^2\right) \triangleq \frac{1}{2}H.$$

For ensembles with less than n constitutes denoted by $\mathcal{E}_n$, the quantumness power is

$$C_n(\Lambda) = \max_{\{\mathcal{E}_2,\cdots,\mathcal{E}_n\}}\left(Q(\Lambda(\mathcal{E}_n)) - Q(\mathcal{E}_n)\right) = \max_{k=2,\cdots,n}\max_{\mathcal{E}_k}\left(Q(\Lambda(\mathcal{E}_k)) - Q(\mathcal{E}_k)\right)$$

$$= \max_{k=2,\cdots,n}\max_{\{(p_i,\rho_i),i=1,\cdots,k\}} \sum_{i\neq j} p_i p_j \left(\text{tr}[\rho_i,\rho_j]^2 - \text{tr}[\Lambda(\rho_i),\Lambda(\rho_j)]^2\right)$$

$$\leq \max_{k=2,\cdots,n}\max_{\{p_i,i=1,\cdots,k\}} \sum_{i\neq j} p_i p_j H = \max_{k=2,\cdots,n}\max_{\{p_i,i=1,\cdots,k\}} (1 - \sum_i p_i^2)H$$

$$\leq \max_{k=2,\cdots,n}(1 - \frac{1}{k})H < 2C_2(\Lambda),$$

meanwhile $C_n(\Lambda) \geq C_2(\Lambda)$, then we can directly get that

$$C_2(\Lambda) \leq C_n(\Lambda) < 2C_2(\Lambda), \quad n \geq 2.$$

□

From this property, we can obtain that the calculation of quantumness power and dequantumness power can be restricted to the ensembles with two ingredients. In the following, focusing on one particular channel, the explicit calculation process is given.

Example 1. *For amplitude damping channels the Kraus operators of which are* $E_0 = \begin{pmatrix} 1 & 0 \\ 0 & \sqrt{1-\lambda} \end{pmatrix}$ *and* $E_1 = \begin{pmatrix} 0 & \sqrt{\lambda} \\ 0 & 0 \end{pmatrix}$, *we can calculate the quantumness power and dequantumness power as follows.*

Through this channel, the Bloch vectors of the states in the ensemble $\mathcal{E}_2 = \{(p, \rho_1), (1-p, \rho_2)\}$ change from $r_i(\sin\theta_i\cos\phi_i, \sin\theta_i\sin\phi_i, \cos\theta_i)$ to

$$\vec{r}_i = \left(r_i\sin\theta_i\cos\phi_i\sqrt{1-\lambda}, r_i\sin\theta_i\sin\phi_i\sqrt{1-\lambda}, \lambda + (1-\lambda)r_i\cos\theta_i\right).$$

From Equation (2), we can obtain the quantumness of this evolved ensemble as

$$Q(\Lambda(\mathcal{E}_2)) = p(1-p)(1-\lambda)\left[\lambda^2(h_1^2 + h_2^2) + r_1^2 r_2^2(n_2^2 + n_3^2)\right.$$
$$\left. + r_1^2 r_2^2(1-\lambda)n_1^2 + 2\lambda r_1 r_2(n_3 h_1 + n_2 h_2)\right], \quad (4)$$

where n_i are the same to the ones in Equation (3), and

$$h_1 = r_1\sin\theta_1\sin\phi_1 - r_2\sin\theta_2\sin\phi_2 + r_1 r_2(\cos\theta_1\sin\theta_2\sin\phi_2 - \sin\theta_1\cos\theta_2\sin\phi_1),$$
$$h_2 = r_1\sin\theta_1\cos\phi_1 - r_2\sin\theta_2\cos\phi_2 + r_1 r_2(\cos\theta_1\sin\theta_2\cos\phi_2 - \sin\theta_1\cos\theta_2\cos\phi_1).$$

The quantumness power restricted to the ensembles with two ingredients is

$$C_2(\Lambda) = \max_{p,r_i,\theta_i,\phi_i}\left(Q(\Lambda(\mathcal{E}_2)) - p(1-p)r_1^2 r_2^2(n_1^2 + n_2^2 + n_3^2)\right).$$

Since the optimization is very complicated, we only show the numerical result as the blue solid line in Figure 1.

If we only focus on the initial ensembles without quantumness, i.e., $Q(\mathcal{E}_2) = 0$, which means r_1 (or r_2) $= 0$ or $n_1 = n_2 = n_3 = 0$, we can get the expression of the modified quantumness power as

$$C_2'(\Lambda) = \lambda^2(1-\lambda), \qquad (5)$$

whose proof is left in the Appendix A. The difference between these two measures is shown in Figure 1. $C_2(\Lambda) > C_2'(\Lambda)$ when $0 \leq \lambda < \lambda_c$ and $C_2(\Lambda) = C_2'(\Lambda)$ when $\lambda_c < \lambda \leq 1$, where $\lambda_c \approx 0.75$.

Similarly, we can get the expression of dequantumness power as

$$D_2(\Lambda) = \max_{p,r_i,\theta_i,\phi_i} \left(p(1-p)r_1^2 r_2^2 (n_1^2 + n_2^2 + n_3^2) - Q(\Lambda(\mathcal{E}_2)) \right).$$

Noting $\max_{p,r_i,\theta_i,\phi_i} Q(\mathcal{E}_2) = \frac{1}{4}$ with $p = \frac{1}{2}$, $r_1 = r_2 = 1$ and $\sin\theta_1 \sin\theta_2 \cos(\phi_1 - \phi_2) = -\cos\theta_1 \cos\theta_2$, the modified dequantumness power is

$$D_2'(\Lambda) = \max_{\theta \in [0,\pi]} \frac{1}{4}\Big[1 - (1-\lambda)\big[(2\lambda^2 - 2\lambda + 1) \\ \pm 2\lambda^2 \sin\theta \cos\theta + 2\lambda(1-\lambda)(\cos\theta \pm \sin\theta)\big]\Big].$$

As shown in Figure 2, $D_2(\Lambda) = D_2'(\Lambda)$ in this case.

From this example, we can obtain that $C(\Lambda)$ can be strictly larger than $C'(\Lambda)$, which means that the maximum may not be achieved at the free case just like the cohering power [14]. Though $D_2(\Lambda) = D_2'(\Lambda)$ in this case, we conjecture this equality may fail in certain cases. But we have not found the counterexample satisfying $D_2(\Lambda) > D_2'(\Lambda)$ yet.

Meanwhile, we can obtain that the channel with higher quantumness power does not necessarily have stronger or weaker dequantumness power. The relationship among them is complicated. For example, $C_2(0.25) > C_2(0.99)$ while $D_2(0.25) < D_2(0.99)$, $C_2(0.5) > C_2(0.1)$ and $D_2(0.5) > D_2(0.1)$.

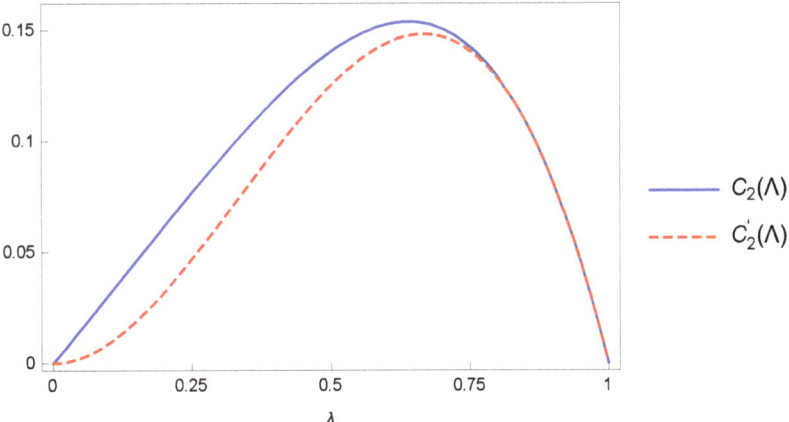

Figure 1. The graphs of C_2 and C_2' for the amplitude damping channel.

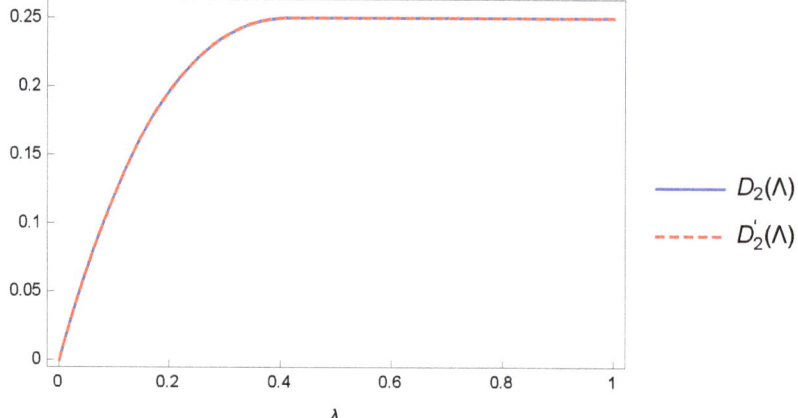

Figure 2. The graphs of D_2 and D'_2 for the amplitude damping channel.

4. Completely Dequantumness Channel and Its Relationship with Quantum Markovianity

In this section, we consider a quantum channel as a quantum evolution Λ_t. If for all the quantum ensembles, the channel reduces the quantumness all the time, we call this channel as the completely dequantumness channel. For these channels, we always have

$$\frac{d}{dt}Q(\Lambda_t(\mathcal{E})) \leq 0, \quad \forall \mathcal{E}, \; \forall t \geq 0.$$

The completely dequantumness channel can be verified to satisfy the following properties:

(1) The quantumness power of the completely dequantumness channel is always 0, while the inverse is not always true.

(2) To verify whether a channel is a completely dequantumness channel or not, we only need to verify whether the inequality $\frac{d}{dt}Q(\Lambda_t(\mathcal{E})) \leq 0$ holds or not for all the ensembles with two ingredients.

Proof. We only give the proof of property (2) since the first one can be verified directly from the definition. If the channel reduces quantumness for all ensembles $\mathcal{E} = \{(p_i, \rho_i), i \in \mathcal{I}\}$, we can directly obtain that for the ensembles with two ingredients $\mathcal{E} = \{(p, \rho_1), (1-p, \rho_2)\}$, the inequality $\frac{d}{dt}Q(\Lambda_t(\mathcal{E})) \leq 0$ holds.

Conversely, if for all the ensembles with two ingredients, the inequality holds, then by virtue of the definition in Equation (1), for the general ensembles with arbitrary numbers of ingredients, we can obtain that $\frac{d}{dt}Q(\Lambda_t(\mathcal{E})) = -\sum_{i,j \in \mathcal{I}} p_i p_j \frac{d}{dt} \text{tr}[\Lambda_t(\rho_i), \Lambda_t(\rho_j)]^2 \leq 0$. □

For open quantum systems, the definition of completely dequantumness channel (dynamics) reflects the information flow of quantumness from the quantum system to the environment. Since the information loss is a typical feature of Markovianity, it is natural to investigate the relationship between the completely-dequantumness property of a quantum dymamics and its Markovianity.

It is worth mentioning that there are various criteria proposed to qualitatively or quantitatively characterize quantum non-Markovianity from different perspectives, such as divisibility [33–36], the distinguishability of states [37,38], fidelity [39], correlations [35,40,41], Fisher information [42–44], and Rényi entropy [45]. Among these, a criterion that can fully characterize the non-Markovianity of a quantum dynamics [33] is using the appearance of negative decoherence rates in the canonical form of the master equation

$$\frac{d\rho_t}{dt} = -\frac{i}{\hbar}[H(t), \rho_t] + \sum_{k=1}^{d^2-1} \gamma_k(t) \left[L_k(t) \rho_t L_k(t)^\dagger - \frac{1}{2}\{L_k(t)^\dagger L_k(t), \rho_t\} \right],$$

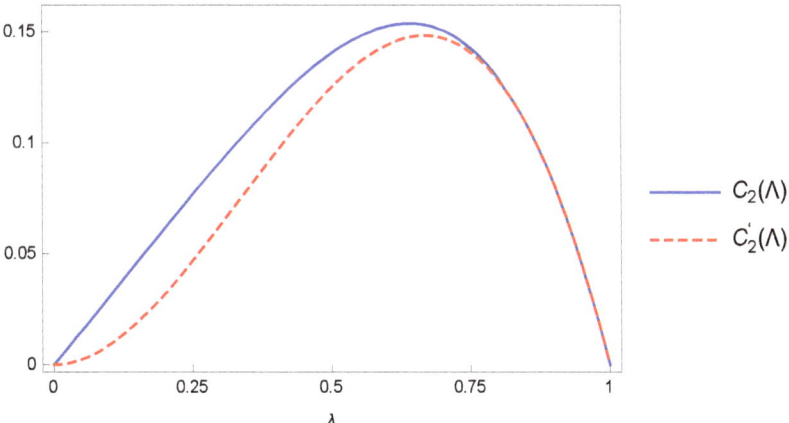

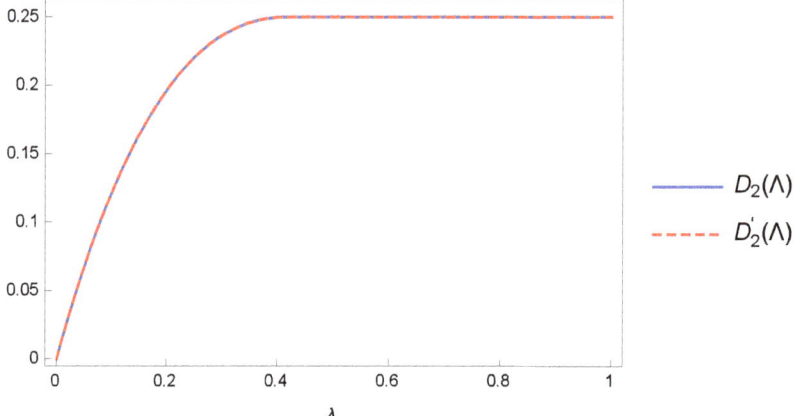

where the $L_k(t)$ form an orthonormal basis set of traceless operators, i.e., $\text{tr}L_k(t) = 0$, $\text{tr}L_j(t)L_k(t)^\dagger = \delta_{jk}$, and $H(t)$ is Hermitian. In this sense, a time-local master equation is Markovian if and only if the canonical decoherence rates are positive at any time, i.e.,

$$\gamma_k(t) \geq 0, \quad \forall t \geq 0, \quad k = 1, \cdots, d^2 - 1. \tag{6}$$

More importantly, the authors in Ref. [33] give an example of a master equation that is non-Markovian for all times $t \geq 0$, but to which nearly all proposed non-Markovian measures do not work. For this reason, we will adopt this criterion for Markovianity.

To make a comparative study between the completely-dequantumness property and the Markovianity, we focus on phase damping dynamics, amplitude damping dynamics, and random unitary dynamics.

4.1. Phase Damping Dynamics

Consider the qubit dynamics $\Lambda = \{\Lambda_t : t \geq 0\}$ with $\rho_t = \Lambda_t(\rho)$ described by the differential equation

$$\frac{d\rho_t}{dt} = \gamma_t(\sigma_z \rho_t \sigma_z - \rho_t),$$

where $\int_0^t \gamma_s ds \geq 0$ and σ_z is the Pauli-z spin matrix.

This dynamics is actually a phase damping channel and can be presented as $\Lambda_t(\rho) = E_0 \rho E_0^\dagger + E_1 \rho E_1^\dagger$ with Kraus operators $E_0 = \text{diag}(1, \sqrt{1-\lambda_t})$ and $E_1 = \text{diag}(0, \sqrt{\lambda_t})$, where $\lambda_t = 1 - e^{-4\int_0^t \gamma_s ds}$.

The Bloch vectors of the evolved states are

$$\vec{r}_i(t) = r_i(\sqrt{1-\lambda_t}\sin\theta_i\cos\phi_i, \sqrt{1-\lambda_t}\sin\theta_i\sin\phi_i, \cos\theta_i).$$

The quantumness of evolved ensemble $\Lambda_t(\mathcal{E}) = \{(p, \Lambda_t(\rho_1)), (1-p, \Lambda_t(\rho_2))\}$ turns out to be

$$Q(\Lambda_t(\mathcal{E})) = p(1-p)r_1^2 r_2^2 [(1-\lambda_t)^2 m_1 + (1-\lambda_t)(m_2 + m_3)],$$

with $m_i = n_i^2$ given in Equation (3), and the derivative is

$$\frac{dQ(\Lambda_t(\mathcal{E}))}{dt} = -p(1-p)r_1^2 r_2^2 \left[2(1-\lambda_t)m_1 + m_2 + m_3\right] \frac{d\lambda_t}{dt} \propto -\gamma_t.$$

From above, we can obtain that for all quantum ensembles,

$$\frac{dQ(\Lambda_t(\mathcal{E}))}{dt} \leq 0 \text{ if and only if } \gamma_t \geq 0.$$

It can be directly verified from the definition of Equation (6) that $\gamma_t \geq 0$ is just the condition that the channel Λ_t is Markovian, which is also in accordance with the results revealed by the measures based on the quantum trace distance (BLP-Markovianity) [37], dynamical divisibility (RHP-Markovianity) [35], quantum mutual information (LFS-Markovianity) [41], and quantum Fisher information [43] (see Refs. [41,43] and references therein). This implies that for the phase damping dynamics, it is completely dequantumness if and only if it is Markovian.

4.2. Amplitude Damping Dynamics

Consider the qubit dynamics $\Lambda = \{\Lambda_t : t \geq 0\}$ with $\rho_t = \Lambda_t(\rho)$ satisfying the following master equation

$$\frac{d\rho_t}{dt} = -\frac{i}{2}s_t[\sigma_+\sigma_-, \rho_t] + \gamma_t(\sigma_-\rho_t\sigma_+ - \frac{1}{2}\{\sigma_+\sigma_-, \rho_t\}),$$

where $\{\cdot,\cdot\}$ denotes the anti-commutator, $\sigma_\pm$ are the atomic raising and lowing operators, respectively, and $s_t = -2\Im\frac{\dot{G}_t}{G_t}$, $\gamma_t = -2\Re\frac{\dot{G}_t}{G_t}$. Here G_t satisfies the equation $\dot{G}_t = -\int_0^t f_{t-s}G_s ds$ with initial condition $G_0 = 1$, and f_t is the reservoir correlation function.

This dynamics is actually an amplitude damping channel. We can directly obtain the Bloch vectors of the evolved states in ensemble $\Lambda_t(\mathcal{E})$ as

$$\vec{r}_i(t) = \Big(r_i|G_t|\sin\theta_i\cos(\phi_i+\delta_t), r_i|G_t|\sin\theta_i\sin(\phi_i+\delta_t), 1-|G_t|^2(1-r_i\cos\theta_i)\Big).$$

Here δ_t is the argument of G_t. The derivative of quantumness of this evolved ensemble can be calculated as

$$\frac{dQ(\Lambda_t(\mathcal{E}))}{d|G_t|^2} = p(1-p)\Big[k_{12}(t)f_{12}(t) + 2|G_t|^2 r_1^2 r_2^2 \sin^2\theta_1 \sin^2\theta_2 \sin^2(\phi_1-\phi_2)$$
$$+ k_{21}(t)f_{21}(t) - 2r_1 r_2 \sin\theta_1 \sin\theta_2 \cos(\phi_1-\phi_2)l(t)\Big],$$

where

$$k_{ij}(t) = r_i \sin\theta_i(1-|G_t|^2(1-r_j\cos\theta_j)), \quad i,j=1,2,$$
$$f_{ij}(t) = r_i \sin\theta_i(1-3|G_t|^2(1-r_j\cos\theta_j)), \quad i,j=1,2,$$
$$l(t) = 1 - 2|G_t|^2(2-r_1\cos\theta_1-r_2\cos\theta_2) + 3|G_t|^4(1-r_1\cos\theta_1)(1-r_2\cos\theta_2).$$

We define

$$h(|G_t|) \triangleq \min_{p,r_i,\theta_i,\phi_i} \frac{dQ(\Lambda_t(\mathcal{E}))}{d|G_t|^2}$$

and plot it in Figure 3. From the figure, we can easily get that $h(|G_t|) < 0$ when $|G_t| > \frac{1}{4}$, which implies that

$$\frac{dQ(\Lambda_t(\mathcal{E}))}{dt} \leq 0, \forall \mathcal{E} \Leftrightarrow |G_t| \leq \frac{1}{4} \text{ and } \frac{d|G_t|}{dt} \leq 0.$$

If $|G_t| > \frac{1}{4}$, we can always find particular ensemble whose quantumness increases during the evolution.

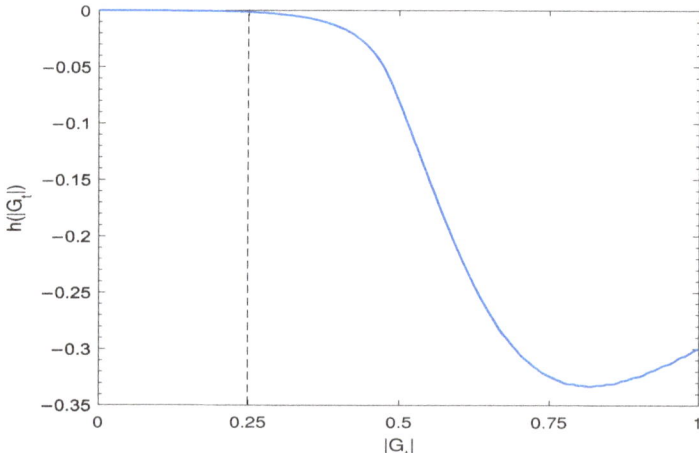

Figure 3. $h(|G_t|)$ as a function of $|G_t|$.

It can be directly verified from the definition of Equation (6) that the amplitude damping channel is Markovian if and only if $\gamma_t = -\frac{2}{|G_t|}\frac{d|G_t|}{dt} \geq 0$, i.e., $\frac{d|G_t|}{dt} \leq 0$, which is also in accordance with the result revealed by the measures based on the quantum trace distance (BLP-Markovianity), quantum mutual information (LFS-Markovianity), and quantum Fisher information (see Refs. [41,43,46] and references therein). Based on this observation, we know that Markovianity does not imply completely dequantumness. It means that there exists a Markovian channel that can induce quantumness for some ensembles.

4.3. Random Unitary Dynamics

Consider the qubit dynamics $\Lambda = \{\Lambda_t : t \geq 0\}$ with $\rho_t = \Lambda_t(\rho)$ described by the master equation

$$\frac{d\rho_t}{dt} = \sum_{i=1}^{3} \gamma_i(t)(\sigma_i \rho_t \sigma_i - \rho_t),$$

where $\gamma_i(t)$ are suitable real functions of time, and σ_i are the Pauli spin matrices. This dynamic is actually a random unitary dynamic and can be written in the following equivalent form

$$\Lambda_t(\rho) = \sum_{i=0}^{3} p_i(t) \sigma_i \rho \sigma_i.$$

Here $p_0(t) = (1 + \sum_{j=1}^{3} \lambda_j(t))/4$ and $p_i(t) = \lambda_i(t)/2 + (1 - \sum_{j=1}^{3} \lambda_j(t))/4$ with $\lambda_i(t) = e^{2 \int_0^t (\gamma_i(s) - \sum_{j=1}^{3} \gamma_j(s)) ds}$.

The Bloch vectors of the evolved ensemble $\Lambda_t(\mathcal{E})$ can be derived as

$$\vec{r}_i(t) = r_i(\lambda_1(t) \sin \theta_i \cos \phi_i, \lambda_2(t) \sin \theta_i \sin \phi_i, \lambda_3(t) \cos \theta_i),$$

and the quantumness measure is

$$Q(\Lambda_t(\mathcal{E})) \propto \lambda_1^2(t) \lambda_2^2(t) m_1 + \lambda_1^2(t) \lambda_3^2(t) m_2 + \lambda_2^2(t) \lambda_3^2(t) m_3.$$

From this expression, we can obtain that

$$\frac{d}{dt} Q(\Lambda_t(\mathcal{E})) \leq 0, \forall \mathcal{E} \Leftrightarrow \frac{d}{dt} \lambda_i(t) \lambda_j(t) \leq 0, i \neq j,$$

which is equivalent to $\gamma_1(t) + \gamma_2(t) + \gamma_3(t) + \gamma_j(t) \geq 0$ for all $j = 1, 2, 3$.

Recall that it has been verified that the random unitary dynamics is Markovian by the definition of Equation (6) if and only if $\gamma_i(t) + \gamma_j(t) \geq 0$ for all $i \neq j$, $i, j = 1, 2, 3$ [47], which is consistent with the result revealed by the measures based on the quantum trace distance (BLP-Markovianity) [48]. From the above, we get that Markovianity implies the completely dequantumness, while the inverse is not always true.

In summary, for several significant quantum channels, we have derived the conditions for the dynamics to be completely dequantumness, and compare them with the Markovian conditions. Their relationships are illustrated in Table 1.

Table 1. Relationship between completely dequantumness (CDQ) and Markovianity.

Channel	Completely Dequantumness	Markovianity	Relationship
Phase Damping	$\gamma_t \geq 0$	$\gamma_t \geq 0$	CDQ $\Leftrightarrow$ Markovianity
Amplitude Damping	$\|G_t\| \leq \frac{1}{4}$ and $\frac{d\|G_t\|}{dt} \leq 0$	$\frac{d\|G_t\|}{dt} \leq 0$	CDQ $\not\Rightarrow$ Markovianity
Random Unitary	$\gamma_1(t) + \gamma_2(t) + \gamma_3(t) + \gamma_j(t) \geq 0$	$\gamma_i(t) + \gamma_j(t) \geq 0, i \neq j$	CDQ $\not\Leftarrow$ Markovianity

From the table, we find that the completely dequantumness channel is related with Markovian channel, while they are different. There exists the Markovian channel, which induces quantumness for some ensembles. Meanwhile, there are also some completely dequantumness channel that are non-Markovian.

5. Conclusions

In this work, we mainly investigate the dynamics of quantumness in ensembles, and propose quantumness power and dequantumness power to characterize quantum channels. Once the channel reduces quantumness for all the ensembles at all times, we call it the completely dequantumness channel, whose relationship with the Markovian channel is studied through several examples. This work illustrates new properties of quantum channels from the perspective of the information flow in terms of quantumness brought by the interaction between the system and environment. It is worth mentioning that although we only focus on the qubit case and one special quantumness measure, the results can be generalized to arbitrary dimensions and other measures of quantumness.

There are still some problems to be further investigated. (1) From Ref. [49], we can obtain that the commutativity-preserving channels cannot increase the quantumness of ensembles, which means the quantumness power is zero for the unital qubit channel. Can we find any non-unital qubit channel without quantumness power? (2) Whether the convex combination of completely dequantumness channels is still completely dequantumness? Suppose Λ and Φ are two completely dequantumness channels, we need to check whether $\alpha\Lambda + (1-\alpha)\Phi$ is a completely dequantumness channel or not. Since quantumness of ensembles plays an important role in quantum communication and quantum cryptography, this work is expected to be helpful in guiding quantum information tasks.

Author Contributions: The authors contribute equally to the work. All authors have read and agreed to the published version of the manuscript.

Funding: This research was funded by the National Natural Science Foundation of China (Grants Nos. 11605284, 11775298, 61833010), the Youth Innovation Promotion Association of CAS (Grant No. 2020002), and the National Key R&D Program of China (Grant No. 2020YFA0712700).

Acknowledgments: The authors are very grateful to Shunlong Luo for his helpful suggestions and to the referees for helpful comments.

Conflicts of Interest: The authors declare no conflict of interest.

Appendix A

Here we give the proof of Equation (5). From the definition of the modified quantumness power, we only need to focus on the ensembles without quantumness. By Equation (2) we know that for an ensemble $\mathcal{E} = \{(p, \rho_1), (1-p, \rho_2)\}$ such that $Q(\mathcal{E}) = 0$, it holds that

$$r_1(\text{or } r_2) = 0 \quad \text{or} \quad n_1 = n_2 = n_3 = 0.$$

Towards these two cases, we calculate the quantumness of the ensemble $\mathcal{E}$.

(i) For the case that $r_i = 0, i = 1$ or 2, without loss of generality, we assume $r_1 = 0$, then from Equation (4) it follows that

$$Q(\Lambda(\mathcal{E})) = p(1-p)\lambda^2(1-\lambda)r_2^2 \sin^2\theta_2 \leq \frac{1}{4}\lambda^2(1-\lambda),$$

and the upper bound can be achieved by the ensemble $\mathcal{E}_0 = \{(\frac{1}{2}, \rho_1), (\frac{1}{2}, \rho_2)\}$ with $\rho_1 = \frac{1}{2}$, and $\rho_2 = \frac{1}{2}\begin{pmatrix} 1 & e^{-i\phi} \\ e^{i\phi} & 1 \end{pmatrix}$, $\forall \phi \in [0, 2\pi)$.

(ii) For the case that $n_1 = n_2 = n_3 = 0$, from Equation (4) it follows that

$$Q(\Lambda(\mathcal{E})) = p(1-p)\lambda^2(1-\lambda)(r_1^2\sin^2\theta_1 + r_2^2\sin^2\theta_2 - 2r_1r_2\sin\theta_1\sin\theta_2\cos(\phi_1 - \phi_2))$$
$$\leq p(1-p)\lambda^2(1-\lambda)(r_1^2\sin^2\theta_1 + r_2^2\sin^2\theta_2 + 2r_1r_2|\sin\theta_1\sin\theta_2|)$$
$$= p(1-p)\lambda^2(1-\lambda)(r_1|\sin\theta_1| + r_2|\sin\theta_2|)^2 \leq \lambda^2(1-\lambda),$$

and the upper bound can be achieved by the ensemble $\mathcal{E}_0 = \{(\frac{1}{2}, \rho_1), (\frac{1}{2}, \rho_2)\}$ with $\rho_1 = \frac{1}{2}\begin{pmatrix} 1 & e^{-i\phi_1} \\ e^{i\phi_1} & 1 \end{pmatrix}$ and $\rho_2 = \frac{1}{2}\begin{pmatrix} 1 & -e^{-i\phi_2} \\ e^{i\phi_2} & 1 \end{pmatrix}$, $\forall \phi_i \in [0, 2\pi), i = 1, 2$.

Combining these two cases, we get that the modified quantumness power of the amplitude damping channel Λ is

$$C_2'(\Lambda) = \max_{\{\mathcal{E}_2 : Q(\mathcal{E}_2) = 0\}} Q(\Lambda(\mathcal{E}_2)) = \lambda^2(1 - \lambda).$$

References

1. Schlosshauer, M. Decoherence, the measurement problem, and interpretations of quantum mechanics. *Rev. Mod. Phys.* **2005**, *76*, 1267. [CrossRef]
2. Joos, E.; Zeh, H.D.; Kiefer, C.; Giulini, D.; Kupsch, J.; Stamatescu, I.-O. *Decoherence and the Appearance of a Classical World in Quantum Theory*; Springer: New York, NY, USA, 2003.
3. Yu, T.; Eberly, J.H. Finite-time disentanglement via spontaneous emission. *Phys. Rev. Lett.* **2004**, *93*, 140404. [CrossRef] [PubMed]
4. Maziero, J.; Céleri, L.C.; Serra, R.M.; Vedral, V. Classical and quantum correlations under decoherence. *Phys. Rev. A* **2009**, *80*, 044102. [CrossRef]
5. Bellomo, B.; Franco, R.L.; Compagno, G. Non-markovian effects of the dynamics of entanglement. *Phys. Rev. Lett.* **2007**, *99*, 160502. [CrossRef]
6. Mazzola, L.; Piilo, J.; Maniscalco, S. Sudden transition between classical and quantum decoherence. *Phys. Rev. Lett.* **2010**, *104*, 200401. [CrossRef] [PubMed]
7. Zanardi, P.; Zalka, C.; Faoro, L. Entangling power of quantum evolutions. *Phys. Rev. A* **2000**, *62*, 030301(R). [CrossRef]
8. Luo, S.; Fu, S.; Li, N. Decorrelating capabilities of operations with application to decoherence. *Phys. Rev. A* **2010**, *82*, 052122. [CrossRef]
9. Wang, L.; Yu, C. The roles of a quantum channel on a quantum state. *Int. J. Theor. Phys.* **2014**, *53*, 715–726. [CrossRef]
10. Mani, A.; Karimipour, V. Cohering and De-cohering power of quantum channels. *Phys. Rev. A* **2015**, *92*, 032331. [CrossRef]
11. García-Díaz, M.; Egloff, D.; Plenio, M.B. A note on coherence power of N-dimensional unitary operators. *arXiv* **2015**, arXiv:1510.06683.
12. Zanardi, P.; Styliaris, G.; Venuti, L.C. Coherence-generating power of quantum unitary maps and beyond. *Phys. Rev. A* **2017**, *95*, 052306. [CrossRef]
13. Zanardi, P.; Styliaris, G.; Venuti, L.C. Measures of coherence-generating power for quantum unital operations. *Phys. Rev. A* **2017**, *95*, 052307. [CrossRef]
14. Bu, K.; Kumar, A.; Zhang, L.; Wu, J. Cohering power of quantum operations. *Phys. Lett. A* **2017**, *381*, 1670–1676. [CrossRef]
15. Li, N.; Luo, S.; Mao, Y. Quantumness-generating capability of quantum dynamics. *Quantum Inf. Process.* **2018**, *17*, 74. [CrossRef]
16. Long, G.L.; Zhou, Y.F.; Jin, J.Q.; Sun, Y.; Lee, H.W. Density matrix in quantum mechanics and distinctness of ensembles having the same compressed density matrix. *Found. Phys.* **2006**, *36*, 1217. [CrossRef]
17. Fuchs, C.A. Just two nonorthogonal quantum states. *arXiv* **1998**, arXiv:9810032v1.
18. Fuchs, C.A.; Sasaki, M. The quantumness of a set of quantum states. *arXiv* **2003**, arXiv:0302108v1.
19. Horodecki, M.; Horodecki, P.; Horodecki, R.; Piani, M. Quantumness of ensemble from no-broadcasting principle. *Int. J. Quantum Inf.* **2006**, *4*, 105. [CrossRef]
20. Oreshkov, O.; Calsamiglia, J. Distinguishability measures between ensembles of quantum states. *Phys. Rev. A* **2009**, *79*, 032336. [CrossRef]
21. Zhu, X.; Pang, S.; Wu, S.; Liu, Q. The classicality and quantumness of a quantum ensemble. *Phys. Lett. A* **2011**, *375*, 1855. [CrossRef]
22. Ma, T.; Zhao, M.J.; Wang, Y.K.; Fei, S.M. Non-commutativity and local indistinguishability of quantum states. *Sci. Rep.* **2014**, *4*, 6336. [CrossRef] [PubMed]
23. Piani, M.; Narasimhachar, V.; Calsamiglia, J. Quantumness of correlations, quantumness of ensembles and quantum data hiding. *New J. Phys.* **2014**, *16*, 113001. [CrossRef]
24. Luo, S.; Li, N.; Fu, S. Quantumness of quantum ensemble. *Theor. Math. Phys.* **2011**, *169*, 1724. [CrossRef]
25. Li, N.; Luo, S.; Mao, Y. Quantifying quantumness of ensembles. *Phys. Rev. A* **2017**, *96*, 022132. [CrossRef]
26. Luo, S.; Li, N.; Sun, W. How quantum is a quantum ensemble. *Quantum Inf. Process.* **2010**, *9*, 711. [CrossRef]
27. Mao, Y.; Song, H. Quantumness of ensembles via coherence. *Phys. Lett. A* **2019**, *383*, 2698. [CrossRef]
28. Naikoo, J.; Banerjee, S. A study of coherence based measure of quantumness in (non) Markovian channels. *Quantum Inf. Process.* **2020**, *19*, 29. [CrossRef]
29. Shahbeigi, F.; Akhtarshenas, S.J. Quantumness of quantum channels. *Phys. Rev. A* **2018**, *98*, 042313. [CrossRef]
30. Iyengar, P.; Chandan, G.N.; Srikanth, R. Quantifying quantumness via commutators: An application to quantum walk. *arXiv* **2013**, arXiv:1312.1329.
31. Ferro, L.; Fazio, R.; Illuminate, F.; Marmo, G.; Vedral, V.; Pascazio, S. Measuring quantumness: From theory to observability in interferometric setups. *Eur. Phys. J. D* **2018**, *72*, 1. [CrossRef]

32. Naikoo, J.; Banerjee, S.; Srikanth, R. Quantumness of channels. *Quantum Inf. Process.* **2021**, *20*, 32. [CrossRef]
33. Hall, M.J.; Cresser, J.D.; Li, L.; Andersson, E. Canonical form of master equations and characterization of non-Markovianity. *Phys. Rev. A* **2014**, *89*, 042120. [CrossRef]
34. Wolf, M.M.; Eisert, J.; Cubitt, T.S.; Cirac, J.I. Assessing non-Markovian quantum dynamics. *Phys. Rev. Lett.* **2008**, *101*, 150402. [CrossRef] [PubMed]
35. Rivas, Á.; Huelga, S.F.; Plenio, M.B. Entanglement and non-Markovianity of quantum evolutions. *Phys. Rev. Lett.* **2010**, *105*, 050403. [CrossRef]
36. Hou, S.C.; Yi, X.X.; Yu, S.X.; Oh, C.H. Alternative non-Markovianity measure by divisibility of dynamical maps. *Phys. Rev. A* **2011**, *83*, 062115. [CrossRef]
37. Breuer, H.-P.; Laine, E.-M.; Piilo, J. Measure for the degree of non-Markovian behavior of quantum processes in open systems. *Phys. Rev. Lett.* **2009**, *103*, 210401. [CrossRef]
38. Breuer, H.-P. Foundations and measures of quantum non-Markovianity. *J. Phys. B* **2012**, *45*, 154001. [CrossRef]
39. Rajagopal, A.K.; Usha Devi, A.R.; Rendell, R.W. Kraus representation of quantum evolution and fidelity as manifestations of Markovian and non-Markovian forms. *Phys. Rev. A* **2010**, *82*, 042107. [CrossRef]
40. Alipour, S.; Mani, A.; Rezakhani, A.T. Quantum discord and non-Markovianity of quantum dynamics. *Phys. Rev. A* **2012**, *85*, 052108. [CrossRef]
41. Luo, S.; Fu, S.; Song, H. Quantifying non-Markovianity via correlations. *Phys. Rev. A* **2012**, *86*, 044101. [CrossRef]
42. Lu, X.-M.; Wang, X.; Sun, C.P. Quantum Fisher information flow and non-Markovian processes of open systems. *Phys. Rev. A* **2010**, *82*, 042103. [CrossRef]
43. Song, H.; Luo, S.; Hong, Y. Quantum non-Markovianity based on the Fisher-information matrix. *Phys. Rev. A* **2015**, *91*, 042110. [CrossRef]
44. Naikoo, J.; Dutta, S.; Banerjee, S. Facets of quantum information under non-Markovian evolution. *Phys. Rev. A* **2019**, *99*, 042128. [CrossRef]
45. Song, H.; Mao, Y. Dynamics of Rényi entropy and applications in detecting quantum non-Markovianity. *Phys. Rev. A* **2017**, *96*, 032115. [CrossRef]
46. He, Z.; Mao, Y.; Zeng, H.-S.; Li, Y.; Wang, Q.; Yao, C. Non-Markovianity measure based on the relative entropy of coherence in an extended space. *Phys. Rev. A* **2017**, *96*, 022106. [CrossRef]
47. Chruściński, D.; Wudarski, F.A. Non-Markovianity degree for random unitary evolution. *Phys. Rev. A* **2015**, *91*, 012104. [CrossRef]
48. Chruściński, D.; Wudarski, F.A. Non-Markovian random unitary qubit dynamics. *Phys. Lett. A* **2013**, *377*, 1425. [CrossRef]
49. Li, N.; Luo, S.; Song, H. Monotonicity of quantumness of ensembles under commutativity-preserving channels. *Phys. Rev. A* **2019**, *99*, 052114. [CrossRef]

Article

Robust Self-Testing of Four-Qubit Symmetric States

Daipengwei Bao, Xiaoqing Tan *, Qingshan Xu, Haozhen Wang and Rui Huang

School of Information Science and Technology, Jinan University, Guangzhou 510632, China; baodaipengwei@stu2020.jnu.edu.cn (D.B.); xuqingshan1008@stu2018.jnu.edu.cn (Q.X.); wanghz0125@163.com (H.W.); huang6666@foxmail.com (R.H.)
* Correspondence: ttanxq@jnu.edu.cn

Abstract: Quantum verification has been highlighted as a significant challenge on the road to scalable technology, especially with the rapid development of quantum computing. To verify quantum states, self-testing is proposed as a device-independent concept, which is based only on the observed statistics. Previous studies focused on bipartite states and some multipartite states, including all symmetric states, but only in the case of three qubits. In this paper, we first give a criterion for the self-testing of a four-qubit symmetric state with a special structure and the robustness analysis based on vector norm inequalities. Then we generalize the idea to a family of parameterized four-qubit symmetric states through projections onto two subsystems.

Keywords: Bell inequality; self-testing; symmetric states; device independent

Citation: Bao, D.; Tan, X.; Xu, Q.; Wang, H.; Huang, R. Robust Self-Testing of Four-Qubit Symmetric States. *Entropy* **2022**, *24*, 1003. https://doi.org/10.3390/e24071003

Academic Editors: Giuliano Benenti, Shunlong Luo, Ming Li and Shao-Ming Fei

Received: 16 May 2022
Accepted: 18 July 2022
Published: 20 July 2022

Publisher's Note: MDPI stays neutral with regard to jurisdictional claims in published maps and institutional affiliations.

Copyright: © 2022 by the authors. Licensee MDPI, Basel, Switzerland. This article is an open access article distributed under the terms and conditions of the Creative Commons Attribution (CC BY) license (https://creativecommons.org/licenses/by/4.0/).

1. Introduction

In recent years, quantum technology has developed rapidly and is expected to gain new real-world applications in communication, simulation, sensing, and computing [1–4]. Quantum devices promise to effectively solve some problems that are difficult to deal with in the classical field [5,6]. However, it also brings a thorny problem. How do we verify the solutions? The task of ensuring the correct operations of quantum devices in terms of accuracy of output is known as quantum verification [7], which is attracting more attention.

A common quantum state verification technology was quantum state tomography (QST) [8] in the past. It has been implemented in systems with few components, but unfortunately, it becomes unfeasible for larger systems because the complexity grows exponentially with the system size. To solve this problem, another alternative technique called self-testing [9] was proposed. These two techniques could be used to verify the quantum systems.

Self-testing is a device-independent approach to verifying that the previously unknown quantum system state and uncharacterized measurement operators are to some degree close to the target state and measurements (up to local isometries) based only on observed statistics, without assuming the dimension of the quantum system. The device-independent (DI) approach [10] is important in practical quantum communications. One of the main applications of self-testing is quantum key distribution (QKD) [11,12], which is of great interest because of its high security. For the users, the quantum key distribution system is purchased from the device providers. However, if a device provider deliberately creates a "dishonest" quantum device, which does not perform key distribution according to the correct protocol, then the key distribution performed with such a device will be insecure. Therefore, it is imperative to test the trustworthiness of quantum cryptographic devices. Fortunately, based on the idea of self-testing quantum systems, it is possible to design device-independent quantum cryptography protocols. For example, in the device-independent QKD protocols, even if the device provider is not trusted, the user can still ensure that the keys generated by the device are secure. The essence is that the user self-tests the quantum device and uses its output as the key under the condition that the test is passed, and the key must be trusted in this case. In addition to quantum key distribution, various protocols, such as random number generation [13], and entanglement witness [14], have been designed in a device-independent framework so far.

Let us consider a scenario where N distant observers share an unknown N-partite quantum state $|\Psi\rangle$. Each party can perform uncharacterized measurements $\{M_{a_i}^{x_i}\}$ on the state with their quantum devices, where i marks different parties, x_i marks different measurement settings for party i, and a_i marks the corresponding measurement outcomes. In a device-independent scenario, the process of measuring an unknown quantum state can be viewed as a black box for the N observers: they can only query their devices with possible measurement settings x_i, and to any query, the black box produces a corresponding outcome. As we do not assume the dimension of the quantum system, the dimension of the Hilbert space is not fixed. Without loss of generality, we assume that the unknown state is pure. There is no loss of generality because an extra system can be added to some of the parties, if necessary, to purify the state, and the purification of the state can be included in the black boxes. Similarly, we can further assume that the measurement operators are projective without loss of generality, as an auxiliary system in some known state can be added to the measured system to replace a general POVM on this system by a projective measurement on the extended system [9]. According to the postulates of quantum mechanics [15], the data they observe are given by

$$p(a_1, a_2, \cdots, a_N \mid x_1, x_2, \cdots, x_N) = \langle \Psi | M_{a_1}^{x_1} \otimes M_{a_2}^{x_2} \otimes \cdots M_{a_N}^{x_N} | \Psi \rangle, \qquad (1)$$

which is referred to as a *correlation* [16] based on the quantum nonlocality [17] of entangled states [18]. As the possibility to self-test quantum states and measurements usually relies on quantum nonlocality, only the entangled states can be device-independently verified by self-testing techniques. The self-testing problem consists of deciding if the knowledge of the *correlation* allows us to deduce the structure of the unknown quantum system.

Symmetric states [19] have been found useful in many quantum information tasks, such as measurement-based quantum computation (MBQC) [20], as they are not too entangled to be computationally universal. Due to the important role of symmetry in the field of quantum entanglement, it is important to explore the properties of symmetric states.

This paper is organized as follows. The basic definitions and preliminaries are given in Section 2. In Section 3, we prove analytically that a particular symmetric four-qubit state can be self-tested and give bounds that are robust to inevitable experimental errors. In addition, we show the self-testing of a family of parameterized four-qubit symmetric states, which are superpositions of four-qubit Dicke states through projections onto two subsystems in Section 4, and we give the conclusions in Section 5.

2. Basic Definitions and Preliminaries

In this section, we present the definitions of self-testing [21] and give the known results as several lemmas, which may be used as building blocks for our work.

Definition 1 (Self-testing). *A known correlation allows for self-testing the state $|\Psi'\rangle$ and measurements $\{M'^{x_i}_{a_i}\}$; if any state and measurements $|\Psi\rangle$ and $\{M^{x_i}_{a_i}\}$ reproduce the correlation, there exists a local isometry Φ such that*

$$\begin{aligned}\Phi(|\Psi\rangle) &= |junk\rangle \otimes |\Psi'\rangle, \\ \Phi(M_{a_1}^{x_1} \otimes M_{a_2}^{x_2} \otimes \cdots \otimes M_{a_N}^{x_N} |\Psi\rangle) &= |junk\rangle \otimes (M'^{x_1}_{a_1} \otimes M'^{x_2}_{a_2} \otimes \cdots \otimes M'^{x_N}_{a_N} |\Psi'\rangle), \end{aligned} \qquad (2)$$

where the state $|junk\rangle$ is an auxiliary state which will be traced out and thus not taken into consideration.

The currently known self-testing protocols are mainly tailored for bipartite states [22–26]. We first review two-qubit self-testing. As given in [23,24], all pure two-qubit

entangled states can be self-tested by observing the maximum violation of the tilted CHSH inequality [27]

$$\mathcal{B}(\alpha, A_0, A_1, B_0, B_1) \equiv \alpha A_0 + A_0(B_0 + B_1) + A_1(B_0 - B_1) \leq 2 + \alpha, \quad (3)$$

where $0 \leq \alpha < 2$ and A_i and B_i are observables with outcomes ± 1. The maximal violation is given by $b(\alpha) \triangleq \max_\phi \langle \phi | \mathcal{B}(\alpha, A_0, A_1, B_0, B_1) | \phi \rangle = \sqrt{8 + 2\alpha^2}$.

Lemma 1. *Any pure two-qubit states in their Schmidt form $|\Psi_\theta\rangle = \cos\theta |00\rangle + \sin\theta |11\rangle$ can be self-tested by achieving the maximal quantum violation of the tilted CHSH inequality Equation (3). The corresponding measurements A_i and B_i for two distant parties, Alice and Bob, are set as*

$$\begin{aligned} A_1 &= \sigma_z, B_1 = \cos\mu\sigma_z + \sin\mu\sigma_x, \\ A_2 &= \sigma_x, B_2 = \cos\mu\sigma_z - \sin\mu\sigma_x. \end{aligned} \quad (4)$$

Here, $\sin 2\theta = \sqrt{\frac{4-\alpha^2}{4+\alpha^2}}$ and $\mu = \arctan\sin 2\theta$.

Especially for the maximally entangled two-qubit states in the form $\frac{|00\rangle + |11\rangle}{\sqrt{2}}$, there exist another two criteria [25].

Lemma 2 (Mayers–Yao criterion). *Consider five unknown dichotomic measurements $\{X_A, Z_A; X_B, Z_B, D_B\}$. If the following statistics are observed*

$$\begin{aligned} \langle \Psi | Z_A Z_B | \Psi \rangle &= \langle \Psi | X_A X_B | \Psi \rangle = 1, \\ \langle \Psi | X_A Z_B | \Psi \rangle &= \langle \Psi | Z_A X_B | \Psi \rangle = 0, \\ \langle \Psi | Z_A D_B | \Psi \rangle &= \langle \Psi | X_A D_B | \Psi \rangle = \frac{1}{\sqrt{2}}, \end{aligned} \quad (5)$$

then up to a local isometry, the state $|\Psi\rangle$ is self-tested into the maximally entangled two-qubit state $\frac{|00\rangle + |11\rangle}{\sqrt{2}}$, and the measurements are the suitable complementary Pauli operators.

Lemma 3 (XOR game). *Consider four unknown operators $\{A_0, A_1, B_0, B_1\}$ with binary outcomes ± 1 and let $E_{xy} \equiv \langle \Psi | A_x B_y | \Psi \rangle = \cos\alpha_{xy}$. The state $|\Psi\rangle$ can be self-tested into the maximally entangled two-qubit state $\frac{|00\rangle + |11\rangle}{\sqrt{2}}$ by winning the binary nonlocal XOR game defined by the figure of merit $\sum_{(x,y)\in(0,1)^2} f_{xy} E_{xy}$ if it satisfies $\alpha_{00} + \alpha_{10} = \alpha_{01} - \alpha_{11}$. The coefficients f_{xy} are constructed by*

$$\begin{pmatrix} f_{00} \\ f_{01} \\ f_{10} \\ f_{11} \end{pmatrix} = \begin{pmatrix} \sin^{-1}\alpha_{00} \\ -\sin^{-1}(\alpha_{00} + \alpha_{10} + \alpha_{11}) \\ \sin^{-1}\alpha_{10} \\ \sin^{-1}\alpha_{11} \end{pmatrix}. \quad (6)$$

However, the self-testing of multipartite scenarios has not been fully explored. In this paper, we work on the four-qubit symmetric entangled states.

Definition 2 (Symmetric states). *Symmetric quantum states preserve invariance under any permutation of their subsystems. We say that an n-partite state $|\Psi\rangle$ is symmetric if $P|\Psi\rangle = |\Psi\rangle$ for all $P \in S_n$, where S_n is the symmetric group of n elements. The n-qubit Dicke states $|S_{n,k}\rangle$ are typical examples of symmetric state, which are the equally weighted sums of all permutations of computational basis states with $n - k$ qubits being $|0\rangle$ and k being $|1\rangle$:*

$$|S_{n,k}\rangle = \binom{n}{k}^{-1/2} \sum_{\text{Permutation}} \underbrace{|0\rangle|0\rangle\ldots|0\rangle}_{n-k} \underbrace{|1\rangle|1\rangle\ldots|1\rangle}_{k}. \quad (7)$$

Let $|\Psi\rangle$ be a state vector in an N-fold tensor product space $S_1 \otimes \cdots \otimes S_N$, where $\dim S_1 = \cdots = \dim S_N = d \geq 2$ and $N \geq 3$. As the generalization of the Schmidt decomposition given in [28], if $d = 2$, any multipartite states can be written in the expansion as

$$|\Psi\rangle = \sum_{i_1, i_2, \cdots, i_N \in \{0,1\}} t^{i_1 i_2 \cdots i_N} |i_1\rangle |i_2\rangle |i_3\rangle \cdots |i_N\rangle, \tag{8}$$

where some coefficients satisfy

$$t^{011\cdots 11} = t^{101\cdots 11} = \cdots = t^{111\cdots 10} = 0, \tag{9}$$

and the rest $2^N - N$ orthogonal product states

$$\{|\overbrace{000\ldots00}^{N}\rangle, |\overbrace{000\ldots01}^{N-1}\rangle, \cdots, |1\overbrace{0\ldots00}^{N-1}\rangle, \cdots, |00\overbrace{1\ldots11}^{N-2}\rangle, \cdots, |\overbrace{11\ldots100}^{N-2}\rangle, |\overbrace{111\ldots11}^{N}\rangle\} \tag{10}$$

can be seen as a set of local bases. To characterize the symmetric multi-qubit states, we only need to make the rest coefficients have properties

$$t^{000\cdots01} = t^{00\cdots010} = \cdots = t^{100\cdots00},$$
$$\vdots \tag{11}$$
$$t^{001\cdots11} = t^{0101\cdots1} = \cdots = t^{11\cdots100}.$$

3. Self-Testing of a Four-Qubit Symmetric State

In this section, we focus on a four-qubit symmetric state with a special structure by using the known results. In the case of $N = 4$, as given in Equation (10), the set of local bases is

$$\{|0000\rangle, |0001\rangle, |0010\rangle, |0100\rangle, |1000\rangle, |0011\rangle,$$
$$|0101\rangle, |0110\rangle, |1001\rangle, |1010\rangle, |1100\rangle, |1111\rangle\} \tag{12}$$

3.1. Self-Testing of a Specific Four-Qubit Symmetric State

The specific four-qubit symmetric state we consider is

$$|\Psi'_1\rangle = \frac{1}{2\sqrt{2}}(|0000\rangle + |0011\rangle + |0101\rangle + |0110\rangle + |1001\rangle + |1010\rangle + |1100\rangle + |1111\rangle)_{ABCD}, \tag{13}$$

which is shared by four distant observers, Alice, Bob, Charlie and David.

Rewrite the state as

$$|\Psi'_1\rangle = \frac{1}{2\sqrt{2}}[\sqrt{2}|00\rangle_{AB} \otimes \frac{1}{\sqrt{2}}(|00\rangle + |11\rangle)_{CD} + \sqrt{2}|01\rangle_{AB} \otimes \frac{1}{\sqrt{2}}(|01\rangle + |10\rangle)_{CD}$$
$$+ \sqrt{2}|10\rangle_{AB} \otimes \frac{1}{\sqrt{2}}(|01\rangle + |10\rangle)_{CD} + \sqrt{2}|11\rangle_{AB} \otimes \frac{1}{\sqrt{2}}(|00\rangle + |11\rangle)_{CD}]. \tag{14}$$

The concept of partial measurements [29] is involved in our scheme, which appears very often in reality. A similar approach for quantum nonlocality chracterization is given in [30], where quantum imcompatibility is used to characterize nonlocality. According to the partial measurement postulate given in [29], if any two parties, without loss of generality, e.g., Alice and Bob, each measure in the σ_z basis, the remaining two parties share a maximally entangled two-qubit state $\frac{|00\rangle + |11\rangle}{\sqrt{2}}$ conditioned on the outcome "00" and "11", respectively, which can be self-tested combining Lemma 2.

We construct the local isometry Φ as Figure 1. Here, H is the usual Hadamard gate. Obviously, if $Z_i = \sigma_z$, $X_i = \sigma_x$, we can extract the essential information on the unknown state into auxiliary systems. Inspired by this, Z_i and X_i should act analogously to the Pauli operators on $|\Psi_1\rangle$ to guarantee the feasibility of the protocol. However, in order to make the protocol device-independent, we cannot directly consider Z_i and X_i of each party as Pauli operators, but should construct them with the measurements $\{M_{a_i}^{x_i}\}$ properly. We sum the result up as below.

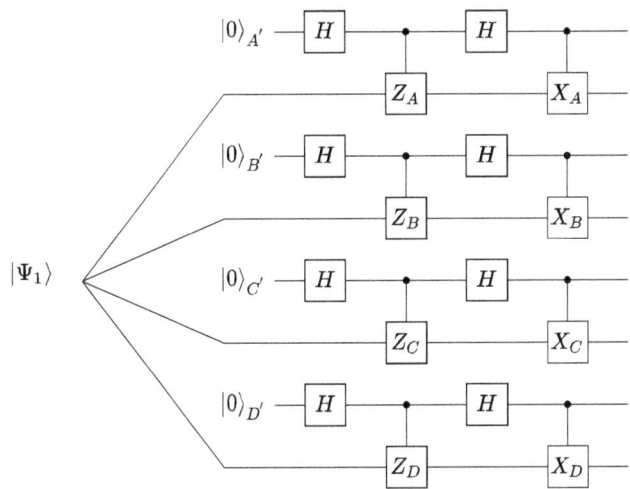

Figure 1. Swap circuit of the isometry Φ to self-test the target state $|\Psi_1'\rangle$.

Result 1. *Consider four spatially separated parties, Alice, Bob, Charlie and David, each performing three measurements $\{X_s, Z_s, M_s\}$ ($s \in \{A, B, C, D\}$) with binary outcomes on an unknown shared quantum state $|\Psi_1\rangle$. The target symmetric state $|\Psi_1'\rangle$ is self-tested if the statistics are observed as the following:*

$$\langle P_A^0 P_B^0 P_C^0 P_D^0 \rangle = \langle P_A^0 P_B^0 P_C^1 P_D^1 \rangle = \langle P_A^0 P_B^1 P_C^0 P_D^1 \rangle = \langle P_A^0 P_B^1 P_C^1 P_D^0 \rangle$$
$$= \langle P_A^1 P_B^0 P_C^0 P_D^1 \rangle = \langle P_A^1 P_B^0 P_C^1 P_D^0 \rangle = \langle P_A^1 P_B^1 P_C^0 P_D^0 \rangle = \langle P_A^1 P_B^1 P_C^1 P_D^1 \rangle = \frac{1}{8}, \quad (15)$$

$$\begin{cases} \langle P_i^0 P_j^0 X_k X_l \rangle = \langle P_i^0 P_j^0 Z_k Z_l \rangle = \frac{1}{4} \\ \langle P_i^0 P_j^0 X_k M_l \rangle = \langle P_i^0 P_j^0 Z_k M_l \rangle = \frac{1}{4\sqrt{2}}, \\ \langle P_i^0 P_j^0 X_k Z_l \rangle = 0 \end{cases} \begin{cases} \langle P_A^1 P_B^1 X_C X_D \rangle = \langle P_A^1 P_B^1 Z_C Z_D \rangle = \frac{1}{4} \\ \langle P_A^1 P_B^1 X_C M_D \rangle = \langle P_A^1 P_B^1 Z_C M_D \rangle = \frac{1}{4\sqrt{2}}, \\ \langle P_i^1 P_j^1 X_k Z_l \rangle = 0 \end{cases} \quad (16)$$

where $(i, j, k, l) = \{(A, B, C, D), (A, C, B, D), (A, D, B, C), (B, C, A, D), (B, D, A, C), (C, D, A, B)\}$ and $P_s^0 \triangleq P_{Z_s=+1} = \frac{1+Z_s}{2}$, $P_s^1 \triangleq P_{Z_s=-1} = \frac{1-Z_s}{2}$, where $s \in \{A, B, C, D\}$ are projectors for the Z_s measurement.

Proof. To begin with, the output after the isometry given in Figure 1 is

$$|\tilde{\Psi}_1\rangle = \Phi(|\Psi_1\rangle |0000\rangle_{A'B'C'D'})$$
$$= \sum_{a,b,c,d \in \{0,1\}} X_A^a X_B^b X_C^c X_D^d P_A^a P_B^b P_C^c P_D^d |\Psi_1\rangle |abcd\rangle. \quad (17)$$

Observation Equation (15) implies that

$$\langle P_A^0 P_B^0 P_C^0 P_D^0 \rangle + \langle P_A^0 P_B^0 P_C^1 P_D^1 \rangle + \langle P_A^0 P_B^1 P_C^0 P_D^1 \rangle + \langle P_A^0 P_B^1 P_C^1 P_D^0 \rangle$$
$$+ \langle P_A^1 P_B^0 P_C^0 P_D^1 \rangle + \langle P_A^1 P_B^0 P_C^1 P_D^0 \rangle + \langle P_A^1 P_B^1 P_C^0 P_D^0 \rangle + \langle P_A^1 P_B^1 P_C^1 P_D^1 \rangle = 1, \quad (18)$$

and thus $P_A^a P_B^b P_C^c P_D^d |\Psi_1\rangle = 0$ for other eight projectors. Based on the fact that $\langle \psi | \phi \rangle = 1$ implies $|\psi\rangle = |\phi\rangle$, observation of Equation (16) implies

$$\begin{cases} P_i^0 P_j^0 X_k |\Psi_1\rangle = P_i^0 P_j^0 X_l |\Psi_1\rangle, P_i^0 P_j^0 Z_k |\Psi_1\rangle = P_i^0 P_j^0 Z_l |\Psi_1\rangle \\ P_i^0 P_j^0 X_k |\Psi_1\rangle \perp P_i^0 P_j^0 Z_k |\Psi_1\rangle, P_i^0 P_j^0 X_l |\Psi_1\rangle \perp P_i^0 P_j^0 Z_l |\Psi_1\rangle \\ P_i^0 P_j^0 M_l |\Psi_1\rangle = \dfrac{P_i^0 P_j^0 X_l |\Psi_1\rangle + P_i^0 P_j^0 Z_l |\Psi_1\rangle}{\sqrt{2}} = \dfrac{P_i^0 P_j^0 X_k |\Psi_1\rangle + P_i^0 P_j^0 Z_k |\Psi_1\rangle}{\sqrt{2}} \end{cases}, \quad (19)$$

and

$$\begin{cases} P_A^1 P_B^1 X_C |\Psi_1\rangle = P_A^1 P_B^1 X_D |\Psi_1\rangle, P_A^1 P_B^1 Z_C |\Psi_1\rangle = P_A^1 P_B^1 Z_D |\Psi_1\rangle \\ P_A^1 P_B^1 X_C |\Psi_1\rangle \perp P_A^1 P_B^1 Z_C |\Psi_1\rangle, P_A^1 P_B^1 X_D |\Psi_1\rangle \perp P_A^1 P_B^1 Z_D |\Psi_1\rangle \\ P_A^1 P_B^1 M_D |\Psi_1\rangle = \dfrac{P_A^1 P_B^1 X_D |\Psi_1\rangle + P_A^1 P_B^1 Z_D |\Psi_1\rangle}{\sqrt{2}} = \dfrac{P_A^1 P_B^1 X_C |\Psi_1\rangle + P_A^1 P_B^1 Z_C |\Psi_1\rangle}{\sqrt{2}} \end{cases}. \quad (20)$$

Obviously, we have $(P_i^0 P_j^0 M_l)^2 |\Psi_1\rangle = P_i^0 P_j^0 M_l^2 |\Psi_1\rangle$. Since $X^2 = Z^2 = M^2 = I$, we have $P_i^0 P_j^0 |\Psi_1\rangle = \dfrac{P_i^0 P_j^0 (X_k + Z_k)^2 |\Psi_1\rangle}{2} = \dfrac{P_i^0 P_j^0 (X_l + Z_l)^2 |\Psi_1\rangle}{2}$. Hence, we obtain the following anti-commutation relation

$$P_i^0 P_j^0 X_k Z_k |\Psi_1\rangle = -P_i^0 P_j^0 Z_k X_k |\Psi_1\rangle$$
$$P_i^0 P_j^0 X_l Z_l |\Psi_1\rangle = -P_i^0 P_j^0 Z_l X_l |\Psi_1\rangle \quad (21)$$

for all $(i,j,k,l) = \{(A,B,C,D), (A,C,B,D), (A,D,B,C), (B,C,A,D), (B,D,A,C), (C,D,A,B)\}$, and similarly,

$$P_A^1 P_B^1 X_C Z_C |\Psi_1\rangle = -P_A^1 P_B^1 Z_C X_C |\Psi_1\rangle$$
$$P_A^1 P_B^1 X_D Z_D |\Psi_1\rangle = -P_A^1 P_B^1 Z_D X_D |\Psi_1\rangle. \quad (22)$$

All these properties of the operators will help to reduce the output Equation (17). By using Equation (21), $X_C X_D P_A^0 P_B^0 P_C^1 P_D^1 |\Psi_1\rangle$ is equal to $P_A^0 P_B^0 P_C^1 P_D^1 X_C X_D |\Psi_1\rangle$. As $P_A^0 P_B^0 X_C |\Psi_1\rangle = P_A^0 P_B^0 X_D |\Psi_1\rangle$ shown in Equation (19), this term becomes $P_A^0 P_B^0 P_C^0 P_D^0 |\Psi_1\rangle$. We can simplify the other five terms similarly. For the last term, we can obtain $P_A^1 P_B^1 P_C^0 P_D^0 |\Psi_1\rangle$ using Equations (20) and (22), which can also be simplified to $P_A^0 P_B^0 P_C^0 P_D^0 |\Psi_1\rangle$. As a reminder, there are eight terms equal to zero. Hence, the output Equation (17) is reduced to

$$|\tilde{\Psi}_1^*\rangle = P_A^0 P_B^0 P_C^0 P_D^0 |\Psi_1\rangle (|0000\rangle + |0011\rangle + |0101\rangle + |0110\rangle + |1001\rangle + |1010\rangle + |1100\rangle + |1111\rangle) \quad (23)$$

and can be normalized into the form of $|junk\rangle \otimes |\Psi_1'\rangle$, here $|junk\rangle = 2\sqrt{2} P_A^0 P_B^0 P_C^0 P_D^0 |\Psi_1\rangle$. □

3.2. Robustness Analysis Based on the L_2 Norm

In this section, we give the analysis of robustness based on the vector norm inequality. Result 1 relies on the observation of Equations (15) and (16) exactly; however, which may be impossible in actual experiments due to the inevitable deviation from the ideal case. Suppose each observation in Equations (15) and (16) admits a deviation at most ϵ around the ideal value. We say that the self-testing of $|\Psi_1'\rangle$ is robust [31] if the isometry still extracts a state close to it and satisfies

$$\| |\tilde{\Psi}_1\rangle - |junk\rangle \otimes |\Psi_1'\rangle \| \leq f(\epsilon), \quad (24)$$

where $f(\epsilon) \to 0$ when $\epsilon \to 0$.

We show that

$$\| |\Psi_1\rangle - |junk\rangle \otimes |\Psi'_1\rangle \| \leq f(\epsilon) = 265.98\epsilon + 348.45\epsilon^{\frac{3}{4}} + 94.87\epsilon^{\frac{1}{2}} + 60.70\epsilon^{\frac{1}{4}} \quad (25)$$

in Appendix A, which proves the robustness of Result 1.

4. Self-Testing of a Family of Parameterized Four-Qubit Symmetric States

In this part, we consider a more general state

$$|\Psi'_2\rangle = \frac{1}{\sqrt{8+4t^2}}[|0000\rangle + t(|0001\rangle + |0010\rangle + |0100\rangle + |1000\rangle) + |0011\rangle \\ + |0101\rangle + |0110\rangle + |1001\rangle + |1010\rangle + |1100\rangle + |1111\rangle]_{ABCD} \quad (26)$$

where $t > 0$ and $t \neq 1$. The parameterized state is a superposition of W state, GHZ state and $|S_{4,2}\rangle$ state, where the ratio of the coefficient of GHZ state and $|S_{4,2}\rangle$ state is a constant value, which is equal to $\frac{1}{\sqrt{3}}$. Rewrite the states as

$$|\Psi'_2\rangle = \frac{1}{\sqrt{8+4t^2}}[\sqrt{2+2t^2}\,|00\rangle_{AB} \otimes \frac{1}{\sqrt{2+2t^2}}(|00\rangle + t|01\rangle + t|10\rangle + |11\rangle)_{CD} \\ + \sqrt{2+t^2}\,|01\rangle_{AB} \otimes \frac{1}{\sqrt{2+t^2}}(t|00\rangle + |01\rangle + |10\rangle)_{CD} \\ + \sqrt{2+t^2}\,|10\rangle_{AB} \otimes \frac{1}{\sqrt{2+t^2}}(t|00\rangle + |01\rangle + |10\rangle)_{CD} \\ + \sqrt{2}\,|11\rangle_{AB} \otimes \frac{1}{\sqrt{2}}(|00\rangle + |11\rangle)_{CD}]. \quad (27)$$

Denote

$$|\psi_1\rangle = \frac{1}{\sqrt{2+2t^2}}(|00\rangle + t|01\rangle + t|10\rangle + |11\rangle)_{CD}, \\ |\psi_2\rangle = \frac{1}{\sqrt{2}}(|00\rangle + |11\rangle)_{CD}. \quad (28)$$

The state $|\psi_1\rangle$ in its Schmidt form is

$$|\psi_1\rangle = \cos\beta\,|0'\rangle_C|0'\rangle_D + \sin\beta\,|1'\rangle_C|1'\rangle_D, \quad (29)$$

where $\cos\beta = \frac{1+t}{\sqrt{2+2t^2}}$, $\sin\beta = \frac{|1-t|}{\sqrt{2+2t^2}}$. Here, $\{|i'\rangle_C\}, \{|i'\rangle_D\}, i \in \{0,1\}$ are the corresponding new bases for C and D. (See detail in Appendix C).

If $t = 1$, $|\psi_1\rangle$ is not an entangled state and the lack of nonlocality may result in the failure of the self-testing. Following the framework of [32], we intend to divide the four parties into two parts, and one of them performs local measurements on $|\Psi_2\rangle$. If we divide $ABCD$ randomly into groups that each have two parties, for example, AB and CD, as a result, the projection measurements may collapse the state shared by the remaining parts into some unknown pure bipartite entangled states. Then the remaining two parts should check whether the projected state they share violates maximally Equation (3) for the appropriate α. Without loss of generality, if A and B perform the measurement in the σ_z bases, $|\psi_1\rangle$ and $|\psi_2\rangle$ should be self-tested by C and D, respectively, and simultaneously conditioned on the outcomes "00" and "11".

Following the result given in Lemma 1, $|\psi_1\rangle$ can be self-tested by reaching the maximal violation of the tilted CHSH Bell inequality

$$b(\alpha) = \sqrt{8+2\alpha^2} = \frac{2\sqrt{2}(t+1)}{\sqrt{1+t^2}}, \quad (30)$$

where $\alpha = 2\sqrt{\frac{1-\sin^2 2\beta}{1+\sin^2 2\beta}}$ and the optimal measurement are set as Lemma 1 with $\tan\mu = \frac{1-t^2}{1+t^2}$. Meanwhile, $|\psi_2\rangle$ is still a maximally entangled two-qubit state under the same transformation of bases

$$|\psi_2\rangle = \frac{1}{\sqrt{2}}(|0'0'\rangle + |1'1'\rangle)_{CD}, \qquad (31)$$

and hence, we can use the same measurement settings as $|\psi_1\rangle$. As the definition given in Lemma 3, $\alpha_{00} = \mu, \alpha_{01} = -\mu, \alpha_{10} = \frac{\pi}{2} - \mu, \alpha_{11} = -\frac{\pi}{2} - \mu$, and thus it will satisfy the condition $\alpha_{00} + \alpha_{10} = \alpha_{01} - \alpha_{11}$.

Define

$$f(t) = \begin{cases} 0, & t < 1 \\ 1, & t > 1 \end{cases}. \qquad (32)$$

Then $|\psi_1\rangle$ can be self-tested by winning the XOR game and we give the criterion to self-test $|\Psi'_2\rangle$ as the following Result 2.

Result 2 (See proof in Appendix B). *Consider four spatially separated parties, Alice, Bob, Charlie and David, each performing five measurements with binary outcomes denoted as $A_i, B_j, C_k, D_l (i,j,k,l \in \{0,1,2,3,4\})$ on an unknown shared quantum state $|\Psi_2\rangle$. The target state $|\Psi'_2\rangle$ is self-tested if the statistics are observed as the following*

$$\begin{cases} \langle P_A^0 P_B^0 P_C^0 P_D^0 \rangle = \langle P_A^0 P_B^0 P_C^1 P_D^1 \rangle = \langle P_A^0 P_B^1 P_C^0 P_D^1 \rangle = \langle P_A^0 P_B^1 P_C^1 P_D^0 \rangle = \langle P_A^1 P_B^0 P_C^0 P_D^1 \rangle \\ = \langle P_A^1 P_B^0 P_C^1 P_D^0 \rangle = \langle P_A^1 P_B^1 P_C^0 P_D^0 \rangle = \langle P_A^1 P_B^1 P_C^1 P_D^1 \rangle = \dfrac{1}{8+4t^2} \\ \langle P_A^0 P_B^0 P_C^0 P_D^1 \rangle = \langle P_A^0 P_B^0 P_C^1 P_D^0 \rangle = \langle P_A^0 P_B^1 P_C^0 P_D^0 \rangle = \langle P_A^0 P_B^1 P_C^0 P_D^0 \rangle = \dfrac{t^2}{8+4t^2} \end{cases}, \qquad (33)$$

$$\begin{cases} \langle P_M^0 P_N^0 \mathcal{B}(\alpha, Q_0, Q_1, R_2, R_3) \rangle = \dfrac{t^2+1}{2t^2+4}\sqrt{8+2\alpha^2} \\ \langle P_M^0 P_N^0 Q_0 (R_2 - R_3) \rangle = 0 \\ \dfrac{\langle P_M^0 P_N^0 R_2 \rangle}{2\sin\mu} - \dfrac{\langle P_M^0 P_N^0 R_3 \rangle}{2\sin\mu} = (-1)^{f(t)} \langle P_M^0 P_N^0 R_1 \rangle \end{cases}, \qquad (34)$$

$$\begin{cases} \sum_{i\in(0,1), j\in(2,3)} f_{ij} \langle P_A^1 P_B^1 C_i Q_j \rangle = \dfrac{2}{(2+t^2)\sin 2\mu} \\ \langle P_A^1 P_B^1 C_0 (D_2 - D_3) \rangle = 0 \\ \dfrac{\langle P_A^1 P_B^1 D_2 \rangle}{2\sin\mu} - \dfrac{\langle P_A^1 P_B^1 D_3 \rangle}{2\sin\mu} = (-1)^{f(t)} \langle P_A^1 P_B^1 D_1 \rangle \end{cases}, \qquad (35)$$

$$\langle P_M^0 P_N^0 P_Q^0 P_R^0 R_0 \rangle = \dfrac{t}{4t^2+8}, \qquad (36)$$

where $(M,N,Q,R) \in \{(A,B,C,D), (A,C,B,D), (A,D,B,C), (B,C,D,A), (B,D,A,C), (C,D,A,B)\}$, $P_s^0 \triangleq P_{Z_s=+1} = \dfrac{1+Z_s}{2}, P_s^1 \triangleq P_{Z_s=-1} = \dfrac{1-Z_s}{2}$, *where* $s \in \{A,B,C,D\}$ *are projectors* for the Z_s measurement and $\sin\mu = \frac{|1-t|}{\sqrt{2+2t^2}}, \cos\mu = \frac{1+t}{\sqrt{2+2t^2}}$. At the same time, we find a proper construction of the local isometry Φ, where Z_s and X_s are based on the measurement settings

$$
\begin{aligned}
Z_A &= A_1 = (-1)^{f(t)} \frac{A_2 - A_3}{2\sin\mu}, & X_A &= A_0 = \frac{A_2 + A_3}{2\cos\mu}, \\
Z_B &= B_1 = (-1)^{f(t)} \frac{B_2 - B_3}{2\sin\mu}, & X_B &= B_0 = \frac{B_2 + B_3}{2\cos\mu}, \\
Z_C &= C_1 = (-1)^{f(t)} \frac{C_2 - C_3}{2\sin\mu}, & X_C &= C_0 = \frac{C_2 + C_3}{2\cos\mu}, \\
Z_D &= D_1 = (-1)^{f(t)} \frac{D_2 - D_3}{2\sin\mu}, & X_D &= D_0 = \frac{D_2 + D_3}{2\cos\mu},
\end{aligned}
\tag{37}
$$

and thus makes the protocol device-independent. In addition, each party may need another fifth measurements $A_4 = Z_A X_A, B_4 = Z_B X_B, C_4 = Z_C X_C, D_4 = Z_D X_D$ to obtain the observation of Equation (36). Since $\sigma_Z \sigma_X = i\sigma_Y$, the fifth measurements are feasible in practical experiments.

5. Conclusions

In this paper, we propose schemes to self-test a large family of four-qubit symmetric states. The target states we focus on are the superposition of the four-qubit Dicke states.

We first present a procedure for self-testing of a particular four-qubit symmetric state with a special structure, and this procedure makes use of the self-testing of the maximally entangled two-qubit state $\frac{|00\rangle + |11\rangle}{\sqrt{2}}$. At the same time, we prove that this protocol is robust against inevitable experimental errors based on norm inequality. In addition, we propose an approach to self-test a one-parameter family of four-qubit pure states through projections onto two systems. Here in our work, only the simplest Pauli measurements are used, which is quite helpful in the experiments.

It would also be of interest to work on a more general state with two parameters by using the swap method and semidefinite programming (SDP) [26] in the form

$$|\Psi\rangle = \cos\theta\cos\rho\,|GHZ\rangle + \cos\theta\sin\rho\,|S_{4,2}\rangle + \sin\theta\,|W\rangle, \tag{38}$$

where $\theta \in [0, \frac{\pi}{2}], \rho \in [0, \frac{\pi}{2}]$, which may provide better robustness than the analytical bounds. What is more, our work could potentially be generalized to a higher dimension scenario. These are reserved for our future work.

Author Contributions: Methodology, validation, investigation, resources, writing—original draft preparation, D.B.; writing—review and editing, project administration, funding acquisition, supervision, X.T.; discussion, Q.X., H.W. and R.H. All authors have read and agreed to the published version of the manuscript.

Funding: The research was partly funded by the Natural Science Foundation of Guangdong Province of China under Grant No. 2021A1515011440, the Major Program of Guangdong Basic and Applied Research under Grant No. 2019B030302008, the National Natural Science Foundation of China under Grant No. 62032009, and the Outstanding Innovative Talents Cultivation Funded Programs for Doctoral Students of Jinan University under Grant No. 2021CXB007.

Informed Consent Statement: Not applicable.

Conflicts of Interest: The authors declare no conflict of interest.

Appendix A. Proof of the Robustness

In this section, we give the proof of Equation (25) based on the L_2 norm. Rewrite the norm Equation (24) as

$$
\begin{aligned}
\| \,|\tilde{\Psi}_1\rangle - |junk\rangle \otimes |\Psi_1'\rangle \, \| &= \| \,|\tilde{\Psi}_1\rangle - |\Psi_1^*\rangle + |\Psi_1^*\rangle - |junk\rangle \otimes |\Psi_1'\rangle \, \| \\
&\leq \| \,|\tilde{\Psi}_1\rangle - |\Psi_1^*\rangle \, \| + \| \,|\Psi_1^*\rangle - |junk\rangle \otimes |\Psi_1'\rangle \, \|.
\end{aligned}
\tag{A1}
$$

Obviously, we need to find the upper bounds for $\| |\tilde{\Psi}_1\rangle - |\Psi_1^*\rangle \|$ and $\| |\Psi_1^*\rangle - |junk\rangle \otimes |\Psi_1'\rangle \|$ respectively. Suppose each observation in Equations (15) and (16) has a deviation at most ϵ around the ideal value. Then we can obtain some inequalities, for instance

$$\frac{1}{8} - \epsilon \leq \langle P_A^0 P_B^0 P_C^0 P_D^0 \rangle \leq \frac{1}{8} + \epsilon, \quad \langle P_A^0 P_B^0 X_C X_D \rangle \geq \frac{1}{4} - \epsilon, \quad \langle P_A^0 P_B^0 Z_C Z_D \rangle \geq \frac{1}{4} - \epsilon,$$
$$\langle P_A^0 P_B^0 X_C Z_D \rangle \leq \epsilon, \quad \langle P_A^0 P_B^0 X_C M_D \rangle \geq \frac{1}{4\sqrt{2}} - \epsilon, \quad \langle P_A^0 P_B^0 Z_C M_D \rangle \geq \frac{1}{4\sqrt{2}} - \epsilon. \quad (A2)$$

In addition, for convenience and rigorous of the derivation, we assume that

$$\langle P_A^0 P_B^0 P_C^0 P_D^1 \rangle \leq \epsilon, \langle P_A^0 P_B^0 P_C^1 P_D^0 \rangle \leq \epsilon, \langle P_A^0 P_B^1 P_C^0 P_D^0 \rangle \leq \epsilon, \langle P_A^1 P_B^0 P_C^0 P_D^0 \rangle \leq \epsilon,$$
$$\langle P_A^0 P_B^1 P_C^1 P_D^1 \rangle \leq \epsilon, \langle P_A^1 P_B^1 P_C^0 P_D^1 \rangle \leq \epsilon, \langle P_A^1 P_B^0 P_C^1 P_D^1 \rangle \leq \epsilon, \langle P_A^1 P_B^1 P_C^1 P_D^0 \rangle \leq \epsilon, \quad (A3)$$

which may not direct the observation statistics. We can now write

$$\| (P_A^0 P_B^0 X_C - P_A^0 P_B^0 X_D) |\Psi_1\rangle \|$$
$$= \sqrt{|\langle \Psi_1| P_A^0 P_B^0 X_C X_C P_A^0 P_B^0 + P_A^0 P_B^0 X_D X_D P_A^0 P_B^0 - 2 P_A^0 P_B^0 X_C X_D P_A^0 P_B^0 |\Psi_1\rangle |}$$
$$= \sqrt{|\langle \Psi_1| P_A^0 P_B^0 X_C X_C P_A^0 P_B^0 |\Psi_1\rangle + \langle \Psi_1| P_A^0 P_B^0 X_D X_D P_A^0 P_B^0 |\Psi_1\rangle - 2 \langle \Psi_1| P_A^0 P_B^0 X_C X_D P_A^0 P_B^0 |\Psi_1\rangle|} \quad (A4)$$
$$\leq \sqrt{\frac{1}{4} + 4\epsilon + \frac{1}{4} + 4\epsilon - 2(\frac{1}{4} - \epsilon)} = \sqrt{10\epsilon} = \epsilon_1,$$

and similarly,

$$\| (P_A^0 P_B^0 Z_C - P_A^0 P_B^0 Z_D) |\Psi_1\rangle \| \leq \sqrt{10\epsilon}. \quad (A5)$$

In addition,

$$\| P_A^0 P_B^0 \frac{X_C + Z_C}{\sqrt{2}} |\Psi_1\rangle \|$$
$$= \sqrt{\frac{1}{2} |\langle \Psi_1| P_A^0 P_B^0 X_C X_C P_A^0 P_B^0 + P_A^0 P_B^0 X_D X_D P_A^0 P_B^0 + 2 P_A^0 P_B^0 X_C Z_C P_A^0 P_B^0 |\Psi_1\rangle|} \quad (A6)$$
$$\leq \sqrt{\frac{1}{2}[\frac{1}{4} + 4\epsilon + \frac{1}{4} + 4\epsilon + 2(\epsilon + \sqrt{10\epsilon(\frac{1}{4} + 4\epsilon)})]} = \sqrt{\frac{1}{4} + 5\epsilon + \sqrt{10\epsilon(\frac{1}{4} + 4\epsilon)}},$$

where $\langle \Psi| P_A^0 P_B^0 X_C Z_C P_A^0 P_B^0 |\Psi_1\rangle \leq \epsilon + \sqrt{10\epsilon(\frac{1}{4} + 4\epsilon)}$ from

$$\langle \Psi_1| P_A^0 P_B^0 X_C Z_C P_A^0 P_B^0 |\Psi\rangle - \langle \Psi_1| P_A^0 P_B^0 X_C Z_D P_A^0 P_B^0 |\Psi_1\rangle \leq \sqrt{10\epsilon(\frac{1}{4} + 4\epsilon)} \quad (A7)$$

by using the Cauchy–Schwarz inequality [33] and Equation (A5). Hence, we obtain

$$\| P_A^0 P_B^0 M_D |\Psi_1\rangle - P_A^0 P_B^0 \frac{X_C + Z_C}{\sqrt{2}} |\Psi_1\rangle \|$$
$$= \sqrt{|\langle \Psi_1| P_A^0 P_B^0 M_D M_D - \sqrt{2} P_A^0 P_B^0 (M_D X_C + M_D Z_C) |\Psi_1\rangle + \| \frac{P_A^0 P_B^0 X_C + P_A^0 P_B^0 Z_C}{\sqrt{2}} |\Psi_1\rangle \|^2 |} \quad (A8)$$
$$\leq \sqrt{\frac{1}{4} + 4\epsilon + \frac{1}{4} + 5\epsilon + \sqrt{10\epsilon(\frac{1}{4} + 4\epsilon)} - 2\sqrt{2} \times (\frac{1}{4\sqrt{2}} - \epsilon)}$$
$$= \sqrt{(9 + 2\sqrt{2})\epsilon + \sqrt{10\epsilon(\frac{1}{4} + 4\epsilon)}} = \epsilon'.$$

Since the norm of the projectors is equal to 1, we have

$$
\begin{aligned}
&\|P_A^0 P_B^0 (M_D)^2 |\Psi_1\rangle - P_A^0 P_B^0 M_D \frac{X_C + Z_C}{\sqrt{2}} |\Psi_1\rangle \| \\
\leq& \|P_A^0 P_B^0 M_D\|_\infty \|P_A^0 P_B^0 M_D |\Psi_1\rangle - P_A^0 P_B^0 \frac{X_C + Z_C}{\sqrt{2}} |\Psi_1\rangle \| \\
\leq& \|P_A^0\|_\infty \|P_B^0\|_\infty \|M_D\|_\infty \|P_A^0 P_B^0 M_D |\Psi_1\rangle - P_A^0 P_B^0 \frac{X_C + Z_C}{\sqrt{2}} |\Psi_1\rangle \| \\
=& \|P_A^0\|_\infty \|P_B^0\|_\infty \|P_M^0 - P_M^1\|_\infty \|P_A^0 P_B^0 M_D |\Psi_1\rangle - P_A^0 P_B^0 \frac{X_C + Z_C}{\sqrt{2}} |\Psi_1\rangle \| \\
\leq& \|P_A^0\|_\infty \|P_B^0\|_\infty (\|P_M^0\|_\infty + \|P_M^1\|_\infty) \|P_A^0 P_B^0 M_D |\Psi_1\rangle - P_A^0 P_B^0 \frac{X_C + Z_C}{\sqrt{2}} |\Psi_1\rangle \| = 2\epsilon'.
\end{aligned}
\quad (A9)
$$

Similarly,

$$
\|P_A^0 P_B^0 \frac{X_C + Z_C}{\sqrt{2}} M_D |\Psi_1\rangle - P_A^0 P_B^0 (\frac{X_C + Z_C}{\sqrt{2}})^2 |\Psi_1\rangle \| \leq 2\sqrt{2}\epsilon', \quad (A10)
$$

which implies

$$
\begin{aligned}
&\|P_A^0 P_B^0 |\Psi_1\rangle - P_A^0 P_B^0 (\frac{X_C + Z_C}{\sqrt{2}})^2 |\Psi_1\rangle \| \leq (2 + 2\sqrt{2})\epsilon' \\
\Longrightarrow& \|P_A^0 P_B^0 X_C Z_C |\Psi_1\rangle + P_A^0 P_B^0 Z_C X_C |\Psi_1\rangle \| \leq 2(2 + 2\sqrt{2})\epsilon'.
\end{aligned}
\quad (A11)
$$

Finally, since

$$
\begin{cases}
\|P_A^0 P_B^0 Z_C X_C |\Psi_1\rangle - P_A^0 P_B^0 Z_C X_D |\Psi_1\rangle \| \leq \sqrt{10\epsilon(\frac{1}{4} + 4\epsilon)} \\
\|P_A^0 P_B^0 X_D Z_C |\Psi_1\rangle - P_A^0 P_B^0 X_D Z_D |\Psi_1\rangle \| \leq \sqrt{10\epsilon(\frac{1}{4} + 4\epsilon)}
\end{cases}
\quad (A12)
$$

$$
\Longrightarrow \|P_A^0 P_B^0 Z_C X_C |\Psi_1\rangle - P_A^0 P_B^0 X_D Z_D |\Psi_1\rangle \| \leq 2\sqrt{10\epsilon(\frac{1}{4} + 4\epsilon)}. \quad (A13)
$$

Similarly,

$$
\|P_A^0 P_B^0 X_C Z_C |\Psi_1\rangle - P_A^0 P_B^0 Z_D X_D |\Psi_1\rangle \| \leq 2\sqrt{10\epsilon(\frac{1}{4} + 4\epsilon)}, \quad (A14)
$$

therefore we can obtain

$$
\begin{aligned}
&\|P_A^0 P_B^0 X_D Z_D |\Psi_1\rangle + P_A^0 P_B^0 Z_D X_D |\Psi_1\rangle \| \leq 2(2 + 2\sqrt{2})\epsilon' + 4\sqrt{10\epsilon(\frac{1}{4} + 4\epsilon)} \\
=& 2(2 + 2\sqrt{2})\sqrt{(9 + 2\sqrt{2})\epsilon + \sqrt{10\epsilon(\frac{1}{4} + 4\epsilon)}} + 4\sqrt{10\epsilon(\frac{1}{4} + 4\epsilon)} \\
\leq& 2(2 + \sqrt{2})(10\epsilon)^{\frac{1}{4}}(\frac{9 + 2\sqrt{2} + 2\sqrt{10}}{\sqrt{10}}(\epsilon)^{\frac{1}{2}} + 1) + 4(\frac{\sqrt{10}}{2}(\epsilon)^{\frac{1}{2}} + 2\sqrt{10}\epsilon) = 2\epsilon_2.
\end{aligned}
\quad (A15)
$$

Hence, we obtain

$$
\begin{cases}
\|P_i^0 P_j^0 X_k |\Psi_1\rangle - P_i^0 P_j^0 X_l |\Psi_1\rangle \| \leq \epsilon_1 \\
\|P_i^0 P_j^0 Z_k |\Psi_1\rangle - P_i^0 P_j^0 Z_l |\Psi_1\rangle \| \leq \epsilon_1 \\
\|P_i^0 P_j^0 X_k Z_k |\Psi_1\rangle + P_i^0 P_j^0 Z_k X_k |\Psi_1\rangle \| \leq 2\epsilon_2 \\
\|P_i^0 P_j^0 X_l Z_l |\Psi_1\rangle + P_i^0 P_j^0 Z_l X_l |\Psi_1\rangle \| \leq 2\epsilon_2
\end{cases}
\quad (A16)
$$

and

$$\begin{cases} \|P_A^1 P_B^1 X_C |\Psi_1\rangle - P_A^1 P_B^1 X_D |\Psi_1\rangle\| \leq \epsilon_1 \\ \|P_A^1 P_B^1 Z_C |\Psi_1\rangle - P_A^1 P_B^1 Z_D |\Psi_1\rangle\| \leq \epsilon_1 \\ \|P_A^1 P_B^1 X_C Z_C |\Psi_1\rangle + P_A^1 P_B^1 Z_C X_C |\Psi_1\rangle\| \leq 2\epsilon_2 \\ \|P_A^1 P_B^1 X_D Z_D |\Psi_1\rangle + P_A^1 P_B^1 Z_D X_D |\Psi_1\rangle\| \leq 2\epsilon_2 \end{cases}, \quad (A17)$$

where $(i,j,k,l) = \{(A,B,C,D), (A,C,B,D), (A,D,B,C), (B,C,A,D), (B,D,A,C), (C,D,A,B)\}$. In addition, we have

$$\begin{aligned}
&\|X_D P_A^0 P_B^0 P_C^0 P_D^1 |\Psi_1\rangle |0001\rangle + X_C P_A^0 P_B^0 P_C^1 P_D^0 |\Psi_1\rangle |0010\rangle \\
&+ X_B P_A^0 P_B^1 P_C^0 P_D^0 |\Psi_1\rangle |0100\rangle + X_A P_A^1 P_B^0 P_C^0 P_D^0 |\Psi_1\rangle |1000\rangle \\
&+ X_B X_C X_D P_A^0 P_B^1 P_C^1 P_D^1 |\Psi_1\rangle |0111\rangle + X_A X_C X_D P_A^1 P_B^0 P_C^1 P_D^1 |\Psi_1\rangle |1011\rangle \\
&+ X_A X_B X_D P_A^1 P_B^1 P_C^0 P_D^1 |\Psi_1\rangle |1101\rangle + X_A X_B X_C P_A^1 P_B^1 P_C^1 P_D^0 |\Psi_1\rangle |1110\rangle \| \\
\leq & \|X_D P_A^0 P_B^0 P_C^0 P_D^1 |\Psi_1\rangle |0001\rangle\| + \|X_C P_A^0 P_B^0 P_C^1 P_D^0 |\Psi_1\rangle |0010\rangle\| \\
&+ \|X_B P_A^0 P_B^1 P_C^0 P_D^0 |\Psi_1\rangle |0100\rangle\| + \|X_A P_A^1 P_B^0 P_C^0 P_D^0 |\Psi_1\rangle |1000\rangle\| \\
&+ \|X_B X_C X_D P_A^0 P_B^1 P_C^1 P_D^1 |\Psi_1\rangle |0111\rangle\| + \|X_A X_C X_D P_A^1 P_B^0 P_C^1 P_D^1 |\Psi_1\rangle |1011\rangle\| \\
&+ \|X_A X_B X_D P_A^1 P_B^1 P_C^0 P_D^1 |\Psi_1\rangle |1101\rangle\| + \|X_A X_B X_C P_A^1 P_B^1 P_C^1 P_D^0 |\Psi_1\rangle |1110\rangle\| \\
= & |\langle P_A^0 P_B^0 P_C^0 P_D^1 \rangle| + |\langle P_A^0 P_B^0 P_C^1 P_D^0 \rangle| + |\langle P_A^0 P_B^1 P_C^0 P_D^0 \rangle| + |\langle P_A^1 P_B^0 P_C^0 P_D^0 \rangle| \\
&+ |\langle P_A^0 P_B^1 P_C^1 P_D^1 \rangle| + |\langle P_A^1 P_B^0 P_C^1 P_D^1 \rangle| + |\langle P_A^1 P_B^1 P_C^0 P_D^1 \rangle| + |\langle P_A^1 P_B^1 P_C^1 P_D^0 \rangle| \leq 8\epsilon.
\end{aligned} \quad (A18)$$

With a similar derivation in [34], we have $|\langle P_A^0 P_B^0 Z_C \rangle| \leq \epsilon_1 + \epsilon_2$ and $|\langle P_A^0 P_B^0 Z_D \rangle| \leq \epsilon_1 + \epsilon_2$, which implies that

$$\begin{aligned}
&\|P_A^0 P_B^0 (1+Z_C)(1+Z_D)\| \\
=& 2\sqrt{\langle P_A^0 P_B^0 \rangle + \langle P_A^0 P_B^0 Z_C \rangle + \langle P_A^0 P_B^0 Z_D \rangle + \langle P_A^0 P_B^0 Z_C Z_D \rangle} \\
\leq & 2\sqrt{\frac{1}{4} + 4\epsilon + \epsilon_1 + \epsilon_2 + \epsilon_1 + \epsilon_2 + \frac{1}{4} + \epsilon},
\end{aligned} \quad (A19)$$

and thus

$$\|\frac{(1+Z_A)(1+Z_B)(1+Z_C)(1+Z_D)}{4\sqrt{2}}\| = \|\frac{P_A^0 P_B^0 (1+Z_C)(1+Z_D)}{\sqrt{2}}\| \\ \leq \sqrt{1 + 10\epsilon + 4(\epsilon_1+\epsilon_2)} \leq 1 + 5\epsilon + 2(\epsilon_1+\epsilon_2). \quad (A20)$$

We now can write

$$\begin{aligned}
\| |\tilde{\Psi}_1\rangle - |\Psi_1^*\rangle \| &\leq 8 \times (\epsilon_1 + \epsilon_2) + 8\epsilon = 8(\epsilon_1 + \epsilon_2 + \epsilon), \\
\| |\Psi_1^*\rangle - |junk\rangle \otimes |\Psi_1'\rangle \| &\leq 5\epsilon + 2(\epsilon_1 + \epsilon_2),
\end{aligned} \quad (A21)$$

which implies

$$f(\epsilon) = 13\epsilon + 10(\epsilon_1 + \epsilon_2) = 265.98\epsilon + 348.45\epsilon^{\frac{3}{4}} + 94.87\epsilon^{\frac{1}{2}} + 60.70\epsilon^{\frac{1}{4}}. \quad (A22)$$

Appendix B. Proof of the Self-Testing of a Family of Parameterized Four-Qubit Symmetric States

Observation Equation (33) implies that

$$\langle P_A^0 P_B^0 P_C^0 P_D^0 \rangle + \langle P_A^0 P_B^0 P_C^0 P_D^1 \rangle + \langle P_A^0 P_B^0 P_C^1 P_D^0 \rangle + \langle P_A^0 P_B^1 P_C^0 P_D^0 \rangle + \langle P_A^1 P_B^0 P_C^0 P_D^0 \rangle$$
$$+ \langle P_A^0 P_B^0 P_C^1 P_D^1 \rangle + \langle P_A^0 P_B^1 P_C^0 P_D^1 \rangle + \langle P_A^0 P_B^1 P_C^1 P_D^0 \rangle + \langle P_A^1 P_B^0 P_C^0 P_D^1 \rangle + \langle P_A^1 P_B^0 P_C^1 P_D^0 \rangle \quad \text{(A23)}$$
$$+ \langle P_A^1 P_B^1 P_C^0 P_D^0 \rangle + \langle P_A^1 P_B^1 P_C^1 P_D^1 \rangle = 1,$$

and thus $P_A^a P_B^b P_C^c P_D^d |\Psi_2\rangle = 0$ for other four projectors.

For convenience, we use $(M, N, Q, R) = (A, B, C, D)$ as an example to prove Result 2. Define the operators for party C and D as

$$X_C = C_0, Z_C = C_1, Z'_C = C_0, X'_C = C_1,$$
$$X_D = D_0, Z_D = D_1, Z'_D = \frac{D_2 + D_3}{2\cos\mu}, X'_D = \frac{D_2 - D_3}{2\sin\mu}. \quad \text{(A24)}$$

The maximal violation of the tilted CHSH inequality as Equation (34) implies

$$P_A^0 P_B^0 Z'_C |\Psi_2\rangle = P_A^0 P_B^0 Z'_D |\Psi_2\rangle, \quad \text{(A25a)}$$
$$P_A^0 P_B^0 Z'_C X'_C |\Psi_2\rangle = -P_A^0 P_B^0 X'_C Z'_C |\Psi_2\rangle, \quad \text{(A25b)}$$
$$P_A^0 P_B^0 X'_C (I + Z'_D) |\Psi_2\rangle = \frac{1}{\tan\beta} P_A^0 P_B^0 X'_D (I - Z'_C) |\Psi_2\rangle. \quad \text{(A25c)}$$

Then we have

$$P_A^0 P_B^0 X_C |\Psi_2\rangle = P_A^0 P_B^0 X_D |\Psi_2\rangle,$$
$$P_A^0 P_B^0 X_C Z_C |\Psi_2\rangle = -P_A^0 P_B^0 Z_C X_C |\Psi_2\rangle \quad \text{(A26)}$$

by Equations (A25a) and (A25b). The observation of Equation (34) implies

$$P_A^0 P_B^0 Z'_C |\Psi_2\rangle \perp P_A^0 P_B^0 X'_D |\Psi_2\rangle, \quad \text{(A27)}$$

and combined with the relation Equation (A25a) from the tilted CHSH inequality, we have

$$P_A^0 P_B^0 Z'_D |\Psi_2\rangle \perp P_A^0 P_B^0 X'_D |\Psi_2\rangle. \quad \text{(A28)}$$

We can write the $Z_D |\Psi_2\rangle$ in the subspace of $P_A^0 P_B^0$ as

$$P_A^0 P_B^0 Z_D |\Psi_2\rangle = (-1)^{f(t)} P_A^0 P_B^0 X'_D |\Psi_2\rangle \quad \text{(A29)}$$

by Equation (34) and thus we can define the vector $X_D |\Psi_2\rangle$ orthogonal to $Z_D |\Psi_2\rangle$ as

$$P_A^0 P_B^0 X_D |\Psi_2\rangle = P_A^0 P_B^0 Z'_D |\Psi_2\rangle. \quad \text{(A30)}$$

From Equations (A25a) and (A25c), we obtain

$$P_A^0 P_B^0 Z'_D X'_D |\Psi_2\rangle = -P_A^0 P_B^0 X'_D Z'_D |\Psi_2\rangle. \quad \text{(A31)}$$

Hence, we obtain

$$P_A^0 P_B^0 X_D Z_D |\Psi_2\rangle = P_A^0 P_B^0 Z'_D X'_D |\Psi_2\rangle = -P_A^0 P_B^0 X'_D Z'_D |\Psi_2\rangle = -P_A^0 P_B^0 Z_D X_D |\Psi_2\rangle. \quad \text{(A32)}$$

Similarly, we obtain the following relations

$$P_M^0 P_N^0 X_Q |\Psi_2\rangle = P_M^0 P_N^0 X_R |\Psi_2\rangle,$$
$$P_M^0 P_N^0 X_Q Z_Q |\Psi_2\rangle = -P_M^0 P_N^0 Z_Q X_Q |\Psi_2\rangle, \quad \text{(A33)}$$
$$P_M^0 P_N^0 X_R Z_R |\Psi_2\rangle = -P_M^0 P_N^0 Z_R X_R |\Psi_2\rangle$$

for all $(M, N, Q, R) = \{(A, B, C, D), (A, C, B, D), (A, D, B, C), (B, C, A, D), (B, D, A, C), (C, D, A, B)\}$. The maximal violation of the XOR game Equation (35) implies

$$P_A^1 P_B^1 Z_C' |\Psi_2\rangle = P_A^1 P_B^1 Z_D' |\Psi_2\rangle,$$
$$P_A^1 P_B^1 X_C' |\Psi_2\rangle = P_A^1 P_B^1 X_D' |\Psi_2\rangle,$$
$$P_A^1 P_B^1 Z_C' X_C' |\Psi_2\rangle = -P_A^1 P_B^1 X_C' Z_C' |\Psi_2\rangle, \quad \text{(A34)}$$
$$P_A^1 P_B^1 Z_D' X_D' |\Psi_2\rangle = -P_A^1 P_B^1 X_D' Z_D' |\Psi_2\rangle.$$

We can use a similar method as above and obtain

$$P_A^1 P_B^1 X_C |\Psi_2\rangle = P_A^1 P_B^1 X_D |\Psi_2\rangle,$$
$$P_A^1 P_B^1 X_C Z_C |\Psi_2\rangle = -P_A^1 P_B^1 Z_C X_C |\Psi_2\rangle, \quad \text{(A35)}$$
$$P_A^1 P_B^1 X_D Z_D |\Psi_2\rangle = -P_A^1 P_B^1 Z_D X_D |\Psi_2\rangle.$$

At last, the observation Equation (36) implies that

$$P_M^0 P_N^0 P_Q^0 P_R^0 X_R |\Psi_2\rangle = t P_M^0 P_N^0 P_Q^0 P_R^0 |\Psi_2\rangle \quad \text{(A36)}$$

for all $(M, N, Q, R) = \{(A, B, C, D), (A, C, B, D), (A, D, B, C), (B, C, A, D), (B, D, A, C), (C, D, A, B)\}$.

We construct the local isometry similar to Figure 1: just replace $|\Psi_1\rangle$ with $|\Psi_2\rangle$. The output after the isometry is

$$|\tilde{\Psi}_2\rangle = \Phi(|\Psi_2\rangle |0000\rangle_{A'B'C'D'})$$
$$= \sum_{a,b,c,d \in \{0,1\}} X_A^a X_B^b X_C^c X_D^d P_A^a P_B^b P_C^c P_D^d |\Psi_2\rangle |abcd\rangle. \quad \text{(A37)}$$

By using Equation (A26), $X_D P_A^0 P_B^0 P_C^0 P_D^1 |\Psi_2\rangle$ is equal to $P_A^0 P_B^0 P_C^0 P_D^0 X_D |\Psi_2\rangle$. Combining with Equation (A36), one can simplify this term to $t P_A^0 P_B^0 P_C^0 P_D^0 |\Psi_2\rangle$. The third to fifth terms share a similar simplification process.

In addition, $X_C X_D P_A^0 P_B^0 P_C^1 P_D^1 |\Psi_2\rangle$ is equal to $P_A^0 P_B^0 P_C^0 X_C P_D^0 X_D |\Psi_2\rangle$ and then can be replaced by $P_A^0 P_B^0 P_C^0 P_D^0 |\Psi_2\rangle$ using Equation (A33). Terms from the seventh to eleventh are similar. For the last term, we can obtain $P_A^1 P_B^1 P_C^0 P_D^0 |\Psi_2\rangle$ using Equation (A35), which is then the same as the eleventh term. We remind that there are four terms equal to zero. Finally, the output is reduced to

$$|\Psi_2^*\rangle = P_A^0 P_B^0 P_C^0 P_D^0 |\Psi_2\rangle (|0000\rangle + t|0001\rangle + t|0010\rangle + t|0100\rangle + t|1000\rangle$$
$$+ |0011\rangle + |0101\rangle + |0110\rangle + |1001\rangle + |1010\rangle + |1100\rangle + |1111\rangle), \quad \text{(A38)}$$

which can be normalized to the form $|junk\rangle \otimes |\Psi_2'\rangle$, here $|junk\rangle = \sqrt{8 + 4t^2} P_A^0 P_B^0 P_C^0 P_D^0 |\Psi_2\rangle$. Then the unknown state $|\Psi_2\rangle$ is self-tested as $|\Psi_2'\rangle$, which proves that Result 2 holds with the required observations Equations (33)–(36). The protocol is also robust by a norm-inequality-based analysis similar to the Result 1 and the detailed derivation process is omitted here.

Appendix C. Relations between Pauli Operators and the Unknown Measurements

In this section, we give details of the relations between Pauli operators and the unknown measurements in Result 2 by Schmidt decomposition.

$$|\psi_1\rangle_{AB} = \frac{1}{\sqrt{2+2t^2}}(|00\rangle + t|01\rangle + t|10\rangle + |11\rangle). \tag{A39}$$

The coefficient matrix of $|\psi_1\rangle$ is

$$A = \frac{1}{\sqrt{2+2t^2}}\begin{pmatrix} 1 & t \\ t & 1 \end{pmatrix}, \tag{A40}$$

which has the Schmidt decomposition $A = USV$, where

$$S = \begin{pmatrix} \frac{1+t}{\sqrt{2+2t^2}} & 0 \\ 0 & \frac{|1-t|}{\sqrt{2+2t^2}} \end{pmatrix} \tag{A41}$$

and

$$\begin{cases} U = V = \begin{pmatrix} \frac{1}{\sqrt{2}} & \frac{1}{\sqrt{2}} \\ \frac{1}{\sqrt{2}} & -\frac{1}{\sqrt{2}} \end{pmatrix} & \text{if } t<1 \\ U = \begin{pmatrix} \frac{1}{\sqrt{2}} & \frac{1}{\sqrt{2}} \\ \frac{1}{\sqrt{2}} & -\frac{1}{\sqrt{2}} \end{pmatrix}, V = \begin{pmatrix} \frac{1}{\sqrt{2}} & \frac{1}{\sqrt{2}} \\ -\frac{1}{\sqrt{2}} & \frac{1}{\sqrt{2}} \end{pmatrix} & \text{if } t>1 \end{cases}. \tag{A42}$$

Hence, if $t<1$, we have

$$\begin{cases} |0'\rangle_A = \frac{1}{\sqrt{2}}(|0\rangle+|1\rangle)_A \\ |1'\rangle_A = \frac{1}{\sqrt{2}}(|0\rangle-|1\rangle)_A \end{cases}, \begin{cases} |0'\rangle_B = \frac{1}{\sqrt{2}}(|0\rangle+|1\rangle)_B \\ |1'\rangle_B = \frac{1}{\sqrt{2}}(|0\rangle-|1\rangle)_B \end{cases}. \tag{A43}$$

If $t>1$,

$$\begin{cases} |0'\rangle_A = \frac{1}{\sqrt{2}}(|0\rangle+|1\rangle)_A \\ |1'\rangle_A = \frac{1}{\sqrt{2}}(|0\rangle-|1\rangle)_A \end{cases}, \begin{cases} |0'\rangle_B = \frac{1}{\sqrt{2}}(|0\rangle+|1\rangle)_B \\ |1'\rangle_B = \frac{1}{\sqrt{2}}(|1\rangle-|0\rangle)_B \end{cases}. \tag{A44}$$

Now we can consider the relation between operators Z' and X' with new bases and Pauli operators for part A,

$$\begin{aligned} Z'_A &= |0'\rangle_A\langle 0'|_A - |1'\rangle_A\langle 1'|_A = |0\rangle_A\langle 1|_A + |1\rangle_A\langle 0|_A = \sigma_x, \\ X'_A &= |0'\rangle_A\langle 1'|_A + |1'\rangle_A\langle 0'|_A = |0\rangle_A\langle 0|_A - |1\rangle_A\langle 1|_A = \sigma_z. \end{aligned} \tag{A45}$$

For part B, if $t<1$,

$$Z'_B = \sigma_x, X'_B = \sigma_z, \tag{A46}$$

and if $t>1$,

$$Z'_B = \sigma_x, X'_B = -\sigma_z. \tag{A47}$$

Hence, if the operators performed by each party are the same as Lemma 1 with new bases, they can be transformed into Pauli matrices

$$\sigma_Z = A_1 = (-1)^{f(t)} \frac{A_2 - A_3}{2\sin\mu}, \sigma_X = A_0 = \frac{A_2 + A_3}{2\cos\mu},$$
$$\sigma_Z = B_1 = (-1)^{f(t)} \frac{B_2 - B_3}{2\sin\mu}, \sigma_X = B_0 = \frac{B_2 + B_3}{2\cos\mu},$$
$$\sigma_Z = C_1 = (-1)^{f(t)} \frac{C_2 - C_3}{2\sin\mu}, \sigma_X = C_0 = \frac{C_2 + C_3}{2\cos\mu},$$
$$\sigma_Z = D_1 = (-1)^{f(t)} \frac{D_2 - D_3}{2\sin\mu}, \sigma_X = D_0 = \frac{D_2 + D_3}{2\cos\mu}.$$
(A48)

References

1. Dowling, J.P.; Milburn, G.J. Quantum technology: The second quantum revolution. *Philos. Trans. R. Soc. A* **2003**, *361*, 1655–1674. [CrossRef] [PubMed]
2. Gisin, N.; Thew, R. Quantum communication. *Nat. Photon.* **2007**, *1*, 165–171. [CrossRef]
3. Georgescu, I.M.; Ashhab, S.; Nori, F. Quantum simulation. *Rev. Mod. Phys.* **2014**, *86*, 153–158. [CrossRef]
4. Degen, C.L.; Reinhard, F.; Cappellaro, P. Quantum sensing. *Rev. Mod. Phys.* **2017**, *89*, 035002. [CrossRef]
5. Yu, C.H.; Gao, F.; Liu, C.; Huynh, D.; Reynolds, M.; Wang, J. Quantum algorithm for visual tracking. *Phys. Rev. A* **2019**, *99*, 022301. [CrossRef]
6. Liu, H.; Wu, Y.; Wan, L.; Pan, S.; Qin, S.; Gao, F.; Wen, Q. Variational quantum algorithm for Poisson equation. *Phys. Rev. A* **2021**, *104*, 022418. [CrossRef]
7. Eisert, J.; Hangleiter, D.; Walk, N.; Roth, I.; Markham, D.; Parekh, R.; Chabaud, U.; Kashefi, E. Quantum certification and benchmarking. *Nat. Rev. Phys.* **2020**, *2*, 382–390. [CrossRef]
8. Cramer, M.; Plenio, M.B.; Flammia, S.T.; Somma, R.; Gross, D.; Bartlett, S.D.; Landon-Cardinal, O.; Poulin, D.; Liu, Y.-K. Efficient quantum state tomography. *Nat. Commun.* **2010**, *1*, 149. [CrossRef]
9. Mayers, D.; Yao, A. Self testing quantum apparatus. *Quant. Inf. Comput.* **2004**, *4*, 273–286. [CrossRef]
10. Gallego, R.; Brunner, N.; Hadley, C.; Acín, A. Device-independent tests of classical and quantum dimensions. *Phys. Rev. Lett.* **2010**, *105*, 230501. [CrossRef]
11. Long, G.; Liu, X. Theoretically efficient high-capacity quantum-key-distribution scheme. *Phys. Rev. A* **2002**, *65*, 032302. [CrossRef]
12. Kwek, L.; Cao, L.; Luo, W.; Wang, Y.; Sun, S.; Wang, X.; Liu, A. Chip-based quantum key distribution. *Assoc. Asia Pac. Phys. Soc. Bull.* **2021**, *31*, 15. [CrossRef]
13. Pironio, S.; Acín, A.; Massar, S.; de la Giroday, A.B.; Matsukevich, D.N.; Maunz, P.; Olmschenk, S.; Hayes, D.; Luo, L.; Manning, T.A.; et al. Random numbers certified by Bell's theorem. *Nature* **2010**, *464*, 1021–1024. [CrossRef] [PubMed]
14. Bancal, J. Device-independent witnesses of genuine multipartite entanglement. *Phys. Rev. Lett.* **2011**, *106*, 250404. [CrossRef]
15. Nielsen, M.A.; Chuang, I.L. *Quantum Computation and Quantum Information*; Cambridge University Press: Cambridge, UK, 2000.
16. Bancal, J.-D.; Navascués, M.; Scarani, V.; Vértesi, T.; Yang, T.H. Physical characterization of quantum devices from nonlocal correlations. *Phys. Rev. A* **2015**, *91*, 022115. [CrossRef]
17. Popescu, S.; Rohrlich, D. Generic quantum nonlocality. *Phys. Rev. A* **1992**, *166*, 293–297. [CrossRef]
18. Horodecki, M.; Horodecki, P.; Horodecki, R. Quantum entanglement. *Rev. Mod. Phys.* **2009**, *81*, 865–942. [CrossRef]
19. Fannes, M.; Lewis, J.T.; Verbeure, A. Symmetric states of composite systems. *Lett. Math. Phys.* **1988**, *15*, 255–260. [CrossRef]
20. Briegel, H.J.; Browne, D.E.; Dür, W.; Raussendorf, R.; Van den Nest, M. Measurement-based quantum computation. *Nat. Phys.* **2009**, *5*, 19–26. [CrossRef]
21. Šupić, I.; Coladangelo, A.; Augusiak, R.; Acín, A. Self-testing multipartite entangled states through projections onto two systems. *New J. Phys.* **2018**, *20*, 083041. [CrossRef]
22. Coladangelo, A.; Goh, K.T.; Scarani, V. All pure bipartite entangled states can be self-tested. *Nat. Commun.* **2017**, *8*, 15485. [CrossRef] [PubMed]
23. Yang, T.H.; Navascués, M. Robust self-testing of unknown quantum systems into any entangled two-qubit states. *Phys. Rev. A* **2013**, *87*, 050102. [CrossRef]
24. Bamps, C.; Pironio, S. Sum-of-squares decompositions for a family of Clauser-Horne-Shimony-Holt-like inequalities and their application to self-testing. *Phys. Rev. A* **2015**, *91*, 052111. [CrossRef]
25. Wang, Y.; Wu, X.; Scarani, V. All the self-testings of the singlet for two binary measurements. *New J. Phys.* **2016**, *18*, 025021. [CrossRef]
26. Navascues, M.; Pironio, S.; Acín, A. A convergent hierarchy of semidefinite programs characterizing the set of quantum correlations. *New J. Phys.* **2008**, *10*, 073013. [CrossRef]
27. Acín, A.; Massar, S.; Pironio, S. Randomness versus nonlocality and entanglement. *Phys. Rev. Lett.* **2012**, *108*, 100402. [CrossRef]
28. Carteret, H.A.; Higuchi, A.; Sudbery, A. Multipartite generalization of the Schmidt decomposition. *J. Math. Phys.* **2000**, *41*, 7932–7939. [CrossRef]

29. Long, G. Collapse-in and collapse-out in partial measurement in quantum mechanics and its wise interpretation. *Sci. China Phys. Mech. Astron.* **2021**, *64*, 280321. [CrossRef]
30. Zhang, X.; Qu, R.; Chang, Z.; Quan, Q.; Gao, H.; Li, F.; Zhang, P. A geometrical framework for quantum incompatibility resources. *Assoc. Asia Pac. Phys. Soc. Bull.* **2022**, *32*, 17. [CrossRef]
31. Wu, X.; Cai, Y.; Yang, T.H.; Le, H.N.; Bancal, J.-D.; Scarani, V. Robust self-testing of the three-qubit W state. *Phys. Rev. A* **2014**, *90*, 042339. [CrossRef]
32. Li, X.; Wang, Y.; Han, Y.; Qin, S.; Gao, F.; Wen, Q. Self-Testing of Symmetric Three-Qubit States. *IEEE J. Sel. Areas Commun.* **2020**, *38*, 589–597. [CrossRef]
33. Bhatia, R.; Davis, C. A Cauchy-Schwarz inequality for operators with applications. *Linear Algebra Appl.* **1995**, *223–224*, 119–129. [CrossRef]
34. McKague, M.; Yang, T.H.; Scarani, V. Robust self-testing of the singlet. *J. Phys. A Math. Theor.* **2012**, *45*, 455304. [CrossRef]

Article

Belavkin–Staszewski Relative Entropy, Conditional Entropy, and Mutual Information

Yuan Zhai, Bo Yang and Zhengjun Xi *

The College of Computer Science, Shaanxi Normal University, Xi'an 710062, China; zhaiyuan@snnu.edu.cn (Y.Z.); byang@snnu.edu.cn (B.Y.)
* Correspondence: xizhengjun@snnu.edu.cn

Abstract: Belavkin–Staszewski relative entropy can naturally characterize the effects of the possible noncommutativity of quantum states. In this paper, two new conditional entropy terms and four new mutual information terms are first defined by replacing quantum relative entropy with Belavkin–Staszewski relative entropy. Next, their basic properties are investigated, especially in classical-quantum settings. In particular, we show the weak concavity of the Belavkin–Staszewski conditional entropy and obtain the chain rule for the Belavkin–Staszewski mutual information. Finally, the subadditivity of the Belavkin–Staszewski relative entropy is established, i.e., the Belavkin–Staszewski relative entropy of a joint system is less than the sum of that of its corresponding subsystems with the help of some multiplicative and additive factors. Meanwhile, we also provide a certain subadditivity of the geometric Rényi relative entropy.

Keywords: Belavkin–Staszewski relative entropy; geometric Rényi relative entropy; conditional entropy; mutual information; classical-quantum setting

Citation: Zhai, Y.; Yang, B.; Xi, Z. Belavkin–Staszewski Relative Entropy, Conditional Entropy, and Mutual Information. *Entropy* **2022**, *24*, 837. https://doi.org/10.3390/e24060837

Academic Editor: Gregg Jaeger

Received: 23 May 2022
Accepted: 16 June 2022
Published: 17 June 2022

Publisher's Note: MDPI stays neutral with regard to jurisdictional claims in published maps and institutional affiliations.

Copyright: © 2022 by the authors. Licensee MDPI, Basel, Switzerland. This article is an open access article distributed under the terms and conditions of the Creative Commons Attribution (CC BY) license (https:// creativecommons.org/licenses/by/ 4.0/).

1. Introduction

Rényi proposed an axiomatic approach to derive the Shannon entropy, and he found a family of entropies with parameter α ($\alpha \in [0, 1) \cup (1, \infty)$), called Rényi entropy. Meanwhile, the same axiomatic approach was extended to relative entropy and obtained Rényi relative entropy [1]. Relative entropy (or Kullback–Leibler divergence [2]) is a special case of Rényi relative entropy, which is an important ingredient for a mathematical framework of information theory. It has operational meaning in information theoretical tasks and can be used to describe the level of closeness between two random variables [3,4]. The axiomatic approach introduced by Rényi can be readily generalized to quantum settings [5,6]. Because of the non-commutativity of the quantum states, there are at least three different and special ways to generalize the classical Rényi relative entropy [6–10], such as Petz-Rényi relative entropy [11,12], sandwiched Rényi relative entropy [6,13] and geometric Rényi relative entropy [14,15]. These quantities are very meaningful in different information-theoretic tasks, including source coding, hypothesis testing, state merging, and channel coding.

The fact is that quantum relative entropy, by taking the limit as $\alpha \to 1$, is a special case of the Petz-Rényi and sandwiched Rényi relative entropies. However, the geometric Rényi relative entropy converges to the Belavkin–Staszewski (BS) relative entropy by taking the same limit. It is noteworthy that both the quantum and BS relative entropies are important variants of the classical relative entropy extension to quantum settings [16–18]. Quantum relative entropy, a direct generalization of the classical relative entropy, has been studied extensively in recent decades. BS relative entropy is also an enticing and crucial entropy used to process quantum information tasks, which can be used to describe the effects of possible noncommutativity of the quantum states (the quantum relative entropy can not work well for this). Additionally, BS relative entropy has recently attracted the attention of researchers. More precisely, Katariya and Wilde employed BS relative entropy to discuss quantum channel estimation and discrimination [19], Bluhm and Capel contributed a strengthened data processing inequality for BS relative entropy [20]. This property was first established by Hiai and Petz [21]. Bluhm et al. produced some weak quasi-factorization results for BS relative entropy [22]. Fang and Fawzi studied quantum channel capacities with respect to geometric Rényi relative entropy [23].

It is commonly known that von Neumann entropy, quantum conditional entropy, and quantum mutual information play vital roles in quantum information theory. Apart from the above entropic measures derived from the quantum relative entropy, however, other useful entropy-like quantities have also been well studied recently, such as max-information [24], collision entropy [25], and min- and max-entropies [26–28]. All of these information measures were generated from quantum Rényi relative entropies by taking different limits.

BS relative entropy can be seen as a fresh and forceful tool to resolve some specific challenges of quantum information-processing tasks. Concurrently, the main use of the geometric Rényi and BS relative entropies is to establish upper bounds on the rates of feedback-assisted quantum communication protocols [29]. To our present knowledge, there is no systematic analysis and research for conditional entropy and mutual information defined from BS relative entropy. Therefore, this paper explores some basic but necessary results for BS relative entropy. More precisely, we first provide a class of new definitions of conditional entropy (called BS conditional entropy, see Definition 2) and new mutual information (called BS mutual information, see Definition 3) via BS relative entropy. Additionally, we showed that von Neumann entropy can be defined by BS relative entropy. Second, we built an order relation between the BS conditional entropy of the bipartite and tripartite quantum systems. Subsequently, since classical-quantum states play an essential role in quantum channel coding and classical data compression with quantum side information, we discussed some valuable properties of BS conditional entropy and BS mutual information in classical-quantum settings. We established the weak concavity of BS conditional entropy and obtained chain rules for BS mutual information. Last but not least, the subadditivity of the geometric Rényi and BS relative entropies is established with the help of some multiplicative and additive factors (the factors are different linear combinations of quantum max-relative entropy [30]), i.e., the geomertric Rényi/BS relative entropy of a joint system is less than the sum of that of its corresponding subsystems.

This paper is organized as follows. In Section 2, we present the mathematical terminology and formal definitions necessary for the formulation of our results. Our results are shown in Section 3. The paper ends with a conclusion.

2. Basic Notations and Definitions

We denote a finite-dimensional Hilbert space by $\mathcal{H}$. Normalized quantum states are in the set $\mathcal{S}_=(\mathcal{H}) := \{\rho \in \mathcal{P}(\mathcal{H}) : \text{Tr}\rho = 1\}$, and subnormalized states are in the set $\mathcal{S}_\leq(\mathcal{H}) := \{\rho \in \mathcal{P}(\mathcal{H}) : 0 < \text{Tr}\rho \leq 1\}$. We use $\mathcal{P}_+(\mathcal{H})$ and $\mathcal{P}(\mathcal{H})$ to denote the set of positive definite operators and the set of positive semi-definite operators on $\mathcal{H}$, respectively. An identity operator is denoted by I. The Hilbert spaces corresponding to different physical systems are distinguished by different capital Latin letters as a subscript. A compound system is modeled using the Hilbert space $\mathcal{H}_{AB} = \mathcal{H}_A \otimes \mathcal{H}_B$. For a bipartite classical-quantum system $\mathcal{H}_{XB}$, the corresponding state ρ_{XB} is formalized as

$$\rho_{XB} = \sum_x p(x)|x\rangle\langle x|_X \otimes \rho_B^x, \tag{1}$$

where $\{|x\rangle\}$ corresponds to an orthonormal basis on the classical system $\mathcal{H}_X$, ρ_B^x is any quantum state on the quantum system $\mathcal{H}_B$, $p(x)$ is the probability distribution, and $\sum_x p(x) = 1$ [17,29]. We also refer to a tripartite classical-quantum state,

$$\rho_{XAB} = \sum_x p(x)|x\rangle\langle x|_X \otimes \rho_{AB}^x, \tag{2}$$

where ρ_{AB}^x is any quantum state on the quantum system $\mathcal{H}_{AB}$.

In quantum information theory, one can generalize Rényi relative entropy to the quantum case, these quantities depend on a parameter $\alpha \in (0,1) \cup (1,\infty)$, and one can evaluate their values at $\alpha \in \{0, 1, \infty\}$ by taking different limits. For Petz-Rényi relative entropy [11,12] and sandwiched Rényi relative entropy [6,13], if one takes the limit as $\alpha \to 1$, we can obtain the well-known quantum relative entropy. For $\rho \in \mathcal{S}_=(\mathcal{H})$ and $\sigma \in \mathcal{S}_\leq(\mathcal{H})$, if supp$(\rho) \subseteq$ supp(σ), the quantum relative entropy of ρ and σ is defined as

$$D(\rho\|\sigma) = \text{Tr}[\rho(\log \rho - \log \sigma)]; \quad (3)$$

otherwise, it is defined as $+\infty$. Throughout this paper, we take the logarithmic function to base 2. The quantum relative entropy is nonnegative and satisfies the data processing inequality, which has good applications in quantum hypothesis testing and quantum resource theory [5,31,32]. We now define the geometric Rényi relative entropy [5,14,15,29].

Definition 1. *For all $\alpha \in (0,1) \cup (1,\infty)$, $\rho \in \mathcal{S}_=(\mathcal{H})$ and $\sigma \in \mathcal{S}_\leq(\mathcal{H})$, the geometric Rényi relative entropy is defined as*

$$\hat{D}_\alpha(\rho\|\sigma) = \frac{1}{\alpha - 1} \log\left[\text{Tr}\left[\sigma(\sigma^{-\frac{1}{2}}\rho\sigma^{-\frac{1}{2}})^\alpha\right]\right]. \quad (4)$$

The term of $\sigma^{\frac{1}{2}}(\sigma^{-\frac{1}{2}}\rho\sigma^{-\frac{1}{2}})^\alpha \sigma^{\frac{1}{2}}$ is called the weighted matrix geometric mean of two positive definite operators ρ and σ, where α is the weight parameter [5,23,33]. The geometric Rényi relative entropy can be shown to be the maximal relative entropy among all quantum Rényi relative entropies satisfying the data processing inequality [5,15], so it is also called maximal quantum Rényi relative entropy [5]. The geometric Rényi relative entropy increases monotonically with respect to the parameter α. Specially, for the limit as $\alpha \to 1$, the geometric Rényi relative entropy converges to the BS relative entropy [15,19,29], i.e.,

$$\hat{D}(\rho\|\sigma) = \lim_{\alpha \to 1} \hat{D}_\alpha(\rho\|\sigma) = \text{Tr}\left[\rho \log(\rho^{\frac{1}{2}}\sigma^{-1}\rho^{\frac{1}{2}})\right], \quad (5)$$

where supp$(\rho) \subseteq$ supp(σ); otherwise, $\hat{D}(\rho\|\sigma) = +\infty$. Here, the inverse σ^{-1} is taken on the support of σ.

Similar to the quantum relative entropy [17], the BS relative entropy is non-negative and satisfies the data processing inequality [15,19,29]. For every quantum channel $\mathcal{E}$, we have

$$\hat{D}(\mathcal{E}(\rho)\|\mathcal{E}(\sigma)) \leq \hat{D}(\rho\|\sigma). \quad (6)$$

For more properties of the BS and geometric Rényi relative entropies, one can refer to [19,29]. In particular, the quantum relative entropy is never larger than the BS relative entropy [19,21], i.e.,

$$D(\rho\|\sigma) \leq \hat{D}(\rho\|\sigma). \quad (7)$$

Obviously, if ρ and σ can be commuted, the BS relative entropy will reduce to the quantum relative entropy. In this paper, we also need to employ the quantum max-relative entropy [5,6,30,34], which comes from the sandwiched Rényi relative entropy by taking the limit as $\alpha \to \infty$, and

$$D_{\max}(\rho\|\sigma) = \log \inf\{\lambda : \rho \leq \lambda\sigma\}. \quad (8)$$

3. Main Results

Once again, the Petz-/sandwiched and geometric Rényi relative entropies are inconsistent when taking the limit as $\alpha \to 1$, which leads to many differences between the BS relative entropy $\hat{D}(\rho\|\sigma)$ (generated from the geometric Rényi relative entropy) and the quantum relative entropy $D(\rho\|\sigma)$ (generated from the Petz-/sandwiched Rényi relative entropy). However, we find that both the quantum relative entropy and the BS relative entropy reduce to the von Neumann entropy for any quantum state ρ when one takes $\sigma = I$, i.e.,

$$\hat{D}(\rho\|I) = \text{Tr}\left[\rho \log(\rho^{\frac{1}{2}} I^{-1} \rho^{\frac{1}{2}})\right]$$
$$= \text{Tr}[\rho \log \rho]$$
$$= -S(\rho).$$

Thus, we have
$$\hat{D}(\rho\|I) = D(\rho\|I) = -S(\rho). \qquad (9)$$

3.1. Belavkin–Staszewski Conditional Entropy

One of the significant properties of the relative entropy is that it can derive the conditional entropy and mutual information in information theory. The quantum relative entropy is the quantum analogue of Kullback–Leibler divergence. We know that there is no similar concept for the joint probability distribution of two variables with different time in quantum mechanics; in other words, there is no real conditional quantum state to process quantum information tasks. Thus, we can consider a formal definition of the quantum conditional entropy [17,31], i.e.,

$$S(A|B)_\rho = S(\rho_{AB}) - S(\rho_B), \qquad (10)$$

where $\rho_B = \text{Tr}_A(\rho_{AB})$ is the reduced state for the bipartite quantum state ρ_{AB}. The quantum conditional entropy $S(A|B)_\rho$ can be denoted as the quantum relative entropy [5,29], i.e.,

$$S(A|B)_\rho = -D(\rho_{AB}\|I_A \otimes \rho_B). \qquad (11)$$

In fact, from the basic properties of the quantum relative entropy, the above equation has another equivalent expression [5,29],

$$S(A|B)_\rho = \max_{\sigma_B} -D(\rho_{AB}\|I_A \otimes \sigma_B), \qquad (12)$$

where the maximum is taken over all sub-normalized states on $\mathcal{H}_B$.

Combining Equation (9) with Equation (10), we have

$$S(A|B)_\rho = -\hat{D}(\rho_{AB}\|I_{AB}) + \hat{D}(\rho_B\|I_B). \qquad (13)$$

However, from the property of Equation (7) and definition of Equation (11), intuitively, we find that conditional entropy defined by the BS relative entropy is different from the quantum conditional entropy of Equation (11) generally. Therefore, we define a new conditional entropy based on the BS relative entropy in the following: the so-called BS conditional entropy.

Definition 2. *For any quantum state $\rho_{AB} \in \mathcal{S}_=(\mathcal{H}_{AB})$, the BS conditional entropy is defined as*

$$\hat{S}(A|B)_\rho = -\hat{D}(\rho_{AB}\|I_A \otimes \rho_B). \qquad (14)$$

Similar to Equation (12), we can also define the alternative BS conditional entropy, i.e.,

$$\hat{S}_m(A|B)_\rho = \max_{\sigma_B} -\hat{D}(\rho_{AB}\|I_A \otimes \sigma_B), \qquad (15)$$

where $\sigma_B \in \mathcal{S}_\leq(\mathcal{H}_B)$. In general, the optimal state is not necessarily the state ρ_B. We further have

$$\hat{S}_m(A|B)_\rho \leq \hat{S}(A|B)_\rho \leq S(A|B)_\rho, \qquad (16)$$

from the relation of Equation (7). Additionally, if one considers the above relations in the bipartite classical-quantum systems, they remain equal, as follows.

Lemma 1. *For any bipartite classical-quantum states ρ_{XB}, we have*

$$\hat{S}_m(B|X)_\rho = \hat{S}(B|X)_\rho = S(B|X)_\rho. \tag{17}$$

Proof. Without a loss of generality, letting $\sigma_X = \sum_x q(x)|x\rangle\langle x|$ and $\rho_X = \sum_x p(x)|x\rangle\langle x|$, using the definition of Equation (1), we have

$$\begin{aligned}
&\operatorname{Tr}\left[\rho_{XB}\log\left(\rho_{XB}^{\frac{1}{2}}I_B \otimes \sigma_X^{-1}\rho_{XB}^{\frac{1}{2}}\right)\right] \\
&= \operatorname{Tr}\left[\sum_x p(x)|x\rangle\langle x|\otimes \rho_B^x \cdot \log\left(\sum_x p(x)q(x)^{-1}|x\rangle\langle x|\otimes \rho_B^x\right)\right] \tag{18}\\
&= \operatorname{Tr}\left[\sum_x p(x)\log p(x)q(x)^{-1}|x\rangle\langle x|\otimes \rho_B^x\right] + \sum_x p(x)\operatorname{Tr}[\rho_B^x \log \rho_B^x] \\
&= D(p(x)\|q(x)) - \sum_x p(x)S(\rho_B^x),
\end{aligned}$$

where the last equality follows from the fact that

$$\operatorname{Tr}\left[\sum_x p(x)\log p(x)q(x)^{-1}|x\rangle\langle x|\otimes \rho_B^x\right] = \operatorname{Tr}\left[\sum_x p(x)\log p(x)q(x)^{-1}|x\rangle\langle x|\right]\cdot \operatorname{Tr}[\rho_B^x]$$

and $\operatorname{Tr}[\rho_B^x] = 1$.

Next, taking the minimization of σ_X for both sides of Equation (18), we have

$$\begin{aligned}
&\min_{\sigma_B}\operatorname{Tr}\left[\rho_{XB}\log\left(\rho_{XB}^{\frac{1}{2}}I_B\otimes \sigma_X^{-1}\rho_{XB}^{\frac{1}{2}}\right)\right] \\
&= \min_{\sigma_B} D(p(x)\|q(x)) - \sum_x p(x)S(\rho_B^x) \tag{19}\\
&= -\sum_x p(x)S(\rho_B^x).
\end{aligned}$$

The optimization of σ_X for the first equality only depends on the first term. For all x, one takes the minimization if and only if $p(x) = q(x)$, which also implies that $D(p(x)\|q(x)) = 0$. Furthermore, combining the definitions of Equation (15) with Equation (5) to Equation (19), it holds that

$$\hat{S}_m(B|X)_\rho = \sum_x p(x)S(\rho_B^x).$$

For $\hat{S}(B|X)_\rho$, we have

$$\begin{aligned}
&\operatorname{Tr}\left[\rho_{XB}\log\left(\rho_{XB}^{\frac{1}{2}}I_B \otimes \rho_X^{-1}\rho_{XB}^{\frac{1}{2}}\right)\right] \\
&= \operatorname{Tr}\left[\sum_x p(x)|x\rangle\langle x|\otimes \rho_B^x \cdot \log\left(\sum_x p(x)p(x)^{-1}|x\rangle\langle x|\otimes \rho_B^x\right)\right] \\
&= -\sum_x p(x)S(\rho_B^x).
\end{aligned}$$

Similarly, we have

$$\hat{S}(B|X)_\rho = \sum_x p(x)S(\rho_B^x).$$

Finally, we can obtain the same result for $S(B|X)_\rho$. We thus complete this proof. □

Since the BS relative entropy satisfies the data processing inequality (6), for any tripartite quantum systems $\mathcal{H}_{ABC}$, it is easy to obtain that conditioning reduces entropy, i.e.,

$$\hat{S}(A|BC)_\rho \leq \hat{S}(A|B)_\rho. \tag{20}$$

This property also holds for the quantum conditional entropy $S(A|B)_\rho$. However, there is not always true for $S(A|B)_\rho \leq S(AC|B)_\rho$ (Problem 11.3(2), in [17]). For the BS conditional entropy, this paper provides another result in the following.

Lemma 2. *For any tripartite quantum states $\rho_{ABC} \in \mathcal{S}_=(\mathcal{H}_{ABC})$, we have*

$$\hat{S}(AB|C)_\rho - \log d_A \leq \hat{S}(B|C)_\rho \tag{21}$$

and

$$\hat{S}_m(AB|C)_\rho - \log d_A \leq \hat{S}_m(B|C)_\rho, \tag{22}$$

where d_A is the dimension of subsystem $\mathcal{H}_A$.

Proof. Since the BS relative entropy satisfies the data-processing inequality (Corollary 4.53 in [29]) and the fact that partial trace is a quantum channel [5], we have

$$\hat{D}(\rho_{ABC}\|I_{AB} \otimes \rho_C) \geq \hat{D}(\mathrm{Tr}_A(\rho_{ABC})\|\mathrm{Tr}_A(I_{AB} \otimes \rho_C)).$$

Furthermore, we have

$$\hat{D}(\mathrm{Tr}_A(\rho_{ABC})\|\mathrm{Tr}_A(I_{AB} \otimes \rho_C)) = \hat{D}(\rho_{BC}\|d_A I_B \otimes \rho_C),$$

where d_A is the dimension of subsystem $\mathcal{H}_A$. Applying the additivity of the BS relative entropy (Proposition 4.54, [29]), we then have

$$\hat{D}(\rho_{BC}\|d_A I_B \otimes \rho_C) = \hat{D}(\rho_{BC}\|I_B \otimes \rho_C) - \log d_A.$$

Recalling the definition of the BS conditional entropy $\hat{S}(A|B)_\rho$ to the above equality, we have

$$\hat{S}(AB|C)_\rho - \log d_A \leq \hat{S}(B|C)_\rho. \tag{23}$$

Similarly, for the alternative definition of the BS conditional entropy $\hat{S}_m(A|B)_\rho$, taking the minimization of σ_X, we have

$$\min_{\sigma_B} \hat{D}(\rho_{ABC}\|I_{AB} \otimes \sigma_C) \geq \min_{\sigma_B} \hat{D}(\rho_{BC}\|I_B \otimes \sigma_C) - \log d_A,$$

which implies that

$$\hat{S}_m(AB|C)_\rho - \log d_A \leq \hat{S}_m(B|C)_\rho.$$

□

The quantum conditional entropy of Equation (10) also satisfies the concavity, which plays an important role in the quantum information processing [5,17,31]. Additionally, for the BS conditional entropy of the tripartite classical-quantum state, we obtain the following result.

Theorem 1. *For any tripartite classical-quantum states ρ_{XAB}, we have*

$$H(X) + \sum_x p(x)\hat{S}(A_x|B)_\rho \leq \hat{S}(A|B)_\rho + \log d_X \tag{24}$$

and

$$H(X) + \sum_x p(x)\hat{S}_m(A_x|B)_\rho \leq \hat{S}_m(A|B)_\rho + \log d_X, \tag{25}$$

where $H(X)$ is the Shannon entropy, and $\hat{S}(A_x|B)_\rho$ is the BS conditional entropy for the quantum state ρ_{AB}^x.

Proof. For any tripartite classical-quantum states ρ_{XAB}, we have

$$\text{Tr}\left[\rho_{XAB}\log\left(\rho_{XAB}^{\frac{1}{2}}I_{XA}\otimes\rho_B^{-1}\rho_{XAB}^{\frac{1}{2}}\right)\right]$$

$$= \text{Tr}\left[\sum_x p(x)|x\rangle\langle x|\otimes\rho_{AB}^x\cdot\log\left(\sum_x p(x)|x\rangle\langle x|\otimes(\rho_{AB}^x)^{\frac{1}{2}}I_A\otimes\rho_B^{-1}(\rho_{AB}^x)^{\frac{1}{2}}\right)\right] \quad (26)$$

$$= \text{Tr}\left[\sum_x p(x)|x\rangle\langle x|\otimes\rho_{AB}^x\cdot\log\left(\sum_x p(x)|x\rangle\langle x|\right)\right]$$

$$+ \text{Tr}\left[\sum_x p(x)|x\rangle\langle x|\otimes\rho_{AB}^x\log\left((\rho_{AB}^x)^{\frac{1}{2}}I_A\otimes\rho_B^{-1}(\rho_{AB}^x)^{\frac{1}{2}}\right)\right].$$

For the first term of the last equality, we have

$$\text{Tr}\left[\sum_x p(x)|x\rangle\langle x|\otimes\rho_{AB}^x\cdot\log\left(\sum_x p(x)|x\rangle\langle x|\right)\right]$$
$$= \sum_x [p(x)\log p(x)\cdot\text{Tr}[\rho_{AB}^x]]$$
$$= -H(X),$$

where the last equality follows from the fact that $\text{Tr}[\rho_{AB}^x] = 1$. Similarly, for the second term, we further have

$$\text{Tr}\left[\sum_x p(x)|x\rangle\langle x|\otimes\rho_{AB}^x\log\left((\rho_{AB}^x)^{\frac{1}{2}}I_A\otimes\rho_B^{-1}(\rho_{AB}^x)^{\frac{1}{2}}\right)\right]$$
$$= \sum_x p(x)\text{Tr}\left[\rho_{AB}^x\log\left((\rho_{AB}^x)^{\frac{1}{2}}I_A\otimes\rho_B^{-1}(\rho_{AB}^x)^{\frac{1}{2}}\right)\right]$$
$$= \sum_x p(x)\hat{D}(\rho_{AB}^x\|I_A\otimes\rho_B)$$
$$= -\sum_x p(x)\hat{S}(A_x|B)_\rho,$$

where $\hat{S}(A_x|B)_\rho$ is the BS conditional entropy for the quantum state ρ_{AB}^x.

Therefore, we can obtain

$$\text{Tr}\left[\rho_{XAB}\log\left(\rho_{XAB}^{\frac{1}{2}}I_{XA}\otimes\rho_B^{-1}\rho_{XAB}^{\frac{1}{2}}\right)\right] = -H(X) - \sum_x p(x)\hat{S}(A_x|B)_\rho.$$

Using the definition of the BS conditional entropy $\hat{S}(XA|B)_\rho$ to the above equality, we have

$$\hat{S}(XA|B)_\rho = H(X) + \sum_x p(x)\hat{S}(A_x|B)_\rho. \quad (27)$$

Applying Lemma 2, we further have

$$\hat{S}(XA|B)_\rho \leq \hat{S}(A|B)_\rho + \log d_X. \quad (28)$$

Substituting Equation (27) into the above inequality (28), we can obtain the first inequality of Theorem 1.

We will replace ρ_B with σ_B to analyze the case of the alternative BS relative entropy in the same way, i.e.,

$$\mathrm{Tr}\left[\rho_{XAB}\log\left(\rho_{XAB}^{\frac{1}{2}}I_{XA}\otimes\sigma_B^{-1}\rho_{XAB}^{\frac{1}{2}}\right)\right]=-H(X)+\sum_x p(x)\hat{D}(\rho_{AB}^x\|I_A\otimes\sigma_B),$$

taking the optimization of σ_B for the above equality and combining the definition of Equation (15). We then obtain the desired result. $\square$

From the above results, we know that there are two additional terms $H(X)$ and $\log d_X$ on each side of the inequality (24), which are different from the concavity of the quantum conditional entropy $S(A|B)_\rho$. To make a distinction, we call it the weak concavity of the BS conditional entropy given by Theorem 1.

Combining the above fact with Theorem 1, we can establish the relationship between $\hat{S}(A|XB)_\rho$ and $\hat{S}(XA|B)_\rho$. Using the direct sum property of the BS relative entropy (Proposition 4.54 in [29]), we have

$$\hat{S}(A|XB)_\rho = -\sum_x p(x)\hat{D}(\rho_{AB}^x\|I_A\otimes\rho_B^x). \tag{29}$$

We cannot determine the order relations between ρ_B^x with ρ_B, but one can always compare $\hat{D}(\rho_{AB}^x\|I_A\otimes\rho_B^x)$ with $\hat{D}(\rho_{AB}^x\|I_A\otimes\rho_B)$. For the case that the former is less than the latter, we have

$$\hat{S}(A|XB)_\rho \geq -\sum_x p(x)\hat{D}(\rho_{AB}^x\|I_A\otimes\rho_B). \tag{30}$$

Applying Equation (26), we can obtain

$$\hat{S}(XA|B)_\rho - \log d_X \leq \hat{S}(A|XB)_\rho. \tag{31}$$

In addition, as a special case of the inequality (20), we can easily obtain that $\hat{S}(A|XB)_\rho \leq \hat{S}(A|B)_\rho$. Therefore, it holds that

$$\hat{S}(XA|B)_\rho - \log d_X \leq \hat{S}(A|XB)_\rho \leq \hat{S}(A|B)_\rho. \tag{32}$$

Otherwise, for the case of $\hat{D}(\rho_{AB}^x\|I_A\otimes\rho_B^x) \geq \hat{D}(\rho_{AB}^x\|I_A\otimes\rho_B)$, we then obtain

$$H(X) + \hat{S}(A|XB)_\rho \leq \hat{S}(XA|B)_\rho. \tag{33}$$

For the quantum conditional entropy of Equation (10), we know that any bipartite pure states are entangled if and only if $S(A|B) < 0$. Here, we are also interested in the BS conditional entropy. Without a loss of generality, let $|\psi\rangle_{AB} = \sum_i \lambda_i |i\rangle_A |i\rangle_B$ be any bipartite pure state, where λ_i represents non-negative real numbers satisfying $\sum_i \lambda_i^2 = 1$, known as Schmidt coefficients, and $|i\rangle_A$ and $|i\rangle_B$ are orthonormal states for A and B, respectively. The number of non-zero values λ_i is called the Schmidt number for the pure state $|\psi\rangle_{AB}$ [17]. We have

$$\begin{aligned}\hat{S}(A|B)_\psi &= -\mathrm{Tr}\left[\psi_{AB}\log\left(\psi_{AB}^{\frac{1}{2}}I_A\otimes\rho_B^{-1}\psi_{AB}^{\frac{1}{2}}\right)\right]\\ &= -\mathrm{Tr}\left[\psi_{AB}\log\left(I_A\otimes\rho_B^{-\frac{1}{2}}\psi_{AB}I_A\otimes\rho_B^{-\frac{1}{2}}\right)\right]\\ &= -\log r,\end{aligned} \tag{34}$$

where r is the Schmidt number of $|\psi\rangle$. We remark that the bipartite pure state is entangled if the Schmidt number is greater than 1.

3.2. Belavkin–Staszewski Mutual Information

The quantum mutual information is another important measure in quantum information theory, which can describe total correlations in the bipartite quantum subsystems, and there are important applications in quantum channel capacity, quantum cryptography, and quantum thermodynamics [17,35]. Based on the property of the quantum relative entropy, there are four equal definitions for the quantum mutual information, i.e.,

$$
\begin{aligned}
I(A;B)_\rho &= D(\rho_{AB}\|\rho_A \otimes \rho_B) \\
&= \min_{\sigma_B} D(\rho_{AB}\|\rho_A \otimes \sigma_B) \\
&= \min_{\sigma_A} D(\rho_{AB}\|\sigma_A \otimes \rho_B) \\
&= \min_{\sigma_A,\sigma_B} D(\rho_{AB}\|\sigma_A \otimes \sigma_B),
\end{aligned}
\tag{35}
$$

where the minimums are taken over all density operators σ_A and σ_B on quantum systems $\mathcal{H}_A$ and $\mathcal{H}_B$, respectively. However, for other general relative entropies, these equalities do not hold in general, such as max-information [24]. In this section, we will consider a new mutual information via the BS relative entropy. Similar to Equation (35), we define four different BS information terms as follows.

Definition 3. *For any quantum state $\rho_{AB} \in \mathcal{S}_=(\mathcal{H}_{AB})$, the BS mutual information terms are defined as*

$$
\hat{I}^1(A;B)_\rho = \hat{D}(\rho_{AB}\|\rho_A \otimes \rho_B), \tag{36}
$$

$$
\hat{I}^2(A;B)_\rho = \min_{\sigma_B} \hat{D}(\rho_{AB}\|\rho_A \otimes \sigma_B), \tag{37}
$$

$$
\hat{I}^{2'}(A;B)_\rho = \min_{\sigma_A} \hat{D}(\rho_{AB}\|\sigma_A \otimes \rho_B), \tag{38}
$$

$$
\hat{I}^3(A;B)_\rho = \min_{\sigma_A,\sigma_B} \hat{D}(\rho_{AB}\|\sigma_A \otimes \sigma_B). \tag{39}
$$

Notice that, for $\hat{I}^2(A;B)_\rho$ and $\hat{I}^{2'}(A;B)_\rho$, they can be thought of as swapping the positions of the optimization operators σ_A and σ_B, so we will consider only one of them. Intuitively, the remaining three definitions of the BS mutual information $\hat{I}^i(A;B)_\rho$ decreases with i, i.e.,

$$
\hat{I}^3(A;B)_\rho \leq \hat{I}^2(A;B)_\rho \leq \hat{I}^1(A;B)_\rho. \tag{40}
$$

Additionally, recalling the inequality (7), we can obtain that there is not less BS mutual information than there is quantum mutual information, i.e.,

$$
I(A;B)_\rho \leq \hat{I}^i(A;B)_\rho. \tag{41}
$$

From the monotonicity of the BS relative entropy, it follows that discarding quantum systems does not increase the BS mutual information, i.e.,

$$
\hat{I}^i(A;B)_\rho \leq \hat{I}^i(A;BC)_\rho. \tag{42}
$$

Subsequently, for the quantum mutual information (35), it holds that

$$
\begin{aligned}
I(A;B)_\rho &= S(\rho_A) - S(A|B)_\rho \\
&= S(\rho_B) - S(B|A)_\rho.
\end{aligned}
\tag{43}
$$

The above two relations are called chain rules for the quantum mutual information. Chain rule can be regarded as a 'bridge' between conditional entropy with mutual information in information theory. We are also interested in exploring chain rules for the BS mutual information for bipartite classical-quantum system $\mathcal{H}_{XB}$ (for all quantum scenarios, further discussion is needed as a remaining issue). It is well-known that the classical-quantum state only possesses classical correlation, and there is no quantum correlation, which leads us to find some significative and interesting results. We first give the following result before discussing the chain rules for the BS mutual information.

Lemma 3. *For any bipartite classical-quantum states ρ_{XB}, we have*

$$\hat{I}^i(X;B)_\rho = \min_{\sigma_B} \sum_x p(x) \hat{D}(\rho_B^x \| \sigma_B), \qquad (44)$$

where $i = 2, 3$.

Proof. The proof is similar to the proof of Lemma 1, thus we omit some calculation steps. We first consider the case $\hat{I}^3(X;B)_\rho$. Let $\sigma_X = \sum_x q(x)|x\rangle\langle x|$, for any quantum state σ_B, we have

$$\begin{aligned}
&\mathrm{Tr}\left[\rho_{XB}\log\left(\rho_{XB}^{\frac{1}{2}}\sigma_X^{-1}\otimes\sigma_B^{-1}\rho_{XB}^{\frac{1}{2}}\right)\right] \\
&= \mathrm{Tr}\left[\sum_x p(x)|x\rangle\langle x|\otimes\rho_B^x \cdot \log\left(\sum_x p(x)q(x)^{-1}|x\rangle\langle x|\otimes(\rho_B^x)^{\frac{1}{2}}\sigma_B^{-1}(\rho_B^x)^{\frac{1}{2}}\right)\right] \qquad (45) \\
&= \mathrm{Tr}\left[\sum_x p(x)\log p(x)q(x)^{-1}|x\rangle\langle x|\otimes\rho_B^x\right] + \sum_x p(x)\mathrm{Tr}\left[\rho_B^x\log(\rho_B^x)^{\frac{1}{2}}\sigma_B^{-1}(\rho_B^x)^{\frac{1}{2}}\right] \\
&= D(p(x)\|q(x)) + \sum_x p(x)\hat{D}(\rho_B^x\|\sigma_B).
\end{aligned}$$

Taking the minimum optimization for both sides of Equation (45) about σ_X and σ_B, respectively, we then have,

$$\begin{aligned}
\hat{I}^3(X;B)_\rho &= \min_{\sigma_X,\sigma_B}\left[D(p(x)\|q(x)) + \sum_x p(x)\hat{D}(\rho_B^x\|\sigma_B)\right] \\
&= \min_{\sigma_X} D(p(x)\|q(x)) + \min_{\sigma_B}\sum_x p(x)\hat{D}(\rho_B^x\|\sigma_B) \\
&= \min_{\sigma_B}\sum_x p(x)\hat{D}(\rho_B^x\|\sigma_B).
\end{aligned}$$

The last equality follows from the fact that the relative entropy $D(p(x)\|q(x))$ is non-negative; i.e., it holds that

$$\min_{\sigma_X} D(p(x)\|q(x)) = 0,$$

for all x, if and only if $p(x) = q(x)$.

For $\hat{I}^2(X;B)_\rho$, only optimization is required for σ_B from its definition, so we directly have

$$\begin{aligned}
\hat{I}^2(X;B)_\rho &= \min_{\sigma_B} \mathrm{Tr}\left[\rho_{XB}\log\left(\rho_{XB}^{\frac{1}{2}}\rho_X^{-1}\otimes\sigma_B^{-1}\rho_{XB}^{\frac{1}{2}}\right)\right] \\
&= \min_{\sigma_B}\sum_x p(x)\hat{D}(\rho_B^x\|\sigma_B).
\end{aligned}$$

□

Notice that the BS mutual information $\hat{I}^1(X;B)_\rho$ does not involve any optimizations, so we have

$$\hat{I}^1(X;B)_\rho = \sum_x p(x)\hat{D}(\rho_B^x\|\rho_B). \qquad (46)$$

This result shows that the BS mutual information $\hat{I}^1(X;B)_\rho$ is identical in form with the quantum mutual information $I(X;B)_\rho$, while the latter is the well-known Holevo information. In addition, if we consider the tripartite classical-quantum state, we can also obtain a sum form of the BS mutual information for $i = 1$, i.e.,

$$\hat{I}^1(XA;B)_\rho = \sum_x p(x)\hat{I}^1(A_x;\rho_B), \tag{47}$$

where $\hat{I}^1(A_x;\rho_B)$ is the BS mutual information between quantum states ρ^x_{AB} and $\rho^x_A \otimes \rho_B$. Other cases of the BS mutual information are similar, so we will not go into detail. Based on the above results, we obtain the chain rules for the BS mutual information for bipartite classical-quantum states as follows.

Theorem 2. *For any bipartite classical-quantum state ρ_{XB}, we have*

$$\hat{I}^i(X;B)_\rho + \hat{S}_m(X|B)_\rho = H(X), \tag{48}$$

where $i = 2, 3$.

Proof. The proof of this theorem is similar to the proof of Theorem 1, so we omit some of the repetition. For any bipartite classical-quantum state ρ_{XB}, we have

$$\hat{D}(\rho_{XB} \| I_X \otimes \sigma_B) = \sum_x p(x)\hat{D}(\rho^x_B \| \sigma_B) - H(X). \tag{49}$$

Employing the definition of Equation (15), we further have

$$\hat{S}_m(X|B)_\rho = H(X) - \min_{\sigma_B} \sum_x p(x)\hat{D}(\rho^x_B \| \sigma_B). \tag{50}$$

Applying Lemma 3 to Equation (50), we can then complete the proof. □

Similarly, for $\hat{I}^1(X;B)_\rho$, we give a chain rule with respect to the definition of the BS conditional entropy $\hat{S}(X|B)_\rho$ as follows.

Corollary 1. *For any bipartite classical-quantum state $\rho_{XB} \in \mathcal{S}_\leq(\mathcal{H}_{XB})$, we have*

$$\hat{I}^1(X;B)_\rho + \hat{S}(X|B)_\rho = H(X). \tag{51}$$

Proof. From Definition 2, we can directly obtain that

$$\begin{aligned}\hat{S}(X|B)_\rho &= -\mathrm{Tr}\left[\rho_{XB}\log\left(\rho_{XB}^{\frac{1}{2}} I_X \otimes \rho_B^{-1} \rho_{XB}^{\frac{1}{2}}\right)\right]\\ &= H(X) - \sum_x p(x)\hat{D}(\rho^x_B \| \rho_B).\end{aligned} \tag{52}$$

Combining Equation (46) with Equation (52), we then obtain the desired result. □

Recalling Holevo information and applying the result of Lemma 1, we further have

$$\begin{aligned}I(X;B)_\rho &= S(\rho_B) - \hat{S}(B|X)_\rho\\ &= S(\rho_B) - \hat{S}_m(B|X)_\rho\\ &= S(\rho_B) - S(B|X)_\rho.\end{aligned} \tag{53}$$

This result shows that the BS conditional entropy with classical side information can be used to describe the Holevo information as well. In addition, employing the inequality (41), we have

$$S(\rho_B) - \hat{S}_m(B|X)_\rho \leq \hat{I}^3(X;B)_\rho. \tag{54}$$

Comparing this to Theorem 2, we find that, when the side information is classical, the equal sign of the chain rule for $\hat{I}^3(X;B)_\rho$ does not hold in general.

3.3. Subadditivity for the BS Relative Entropy

It is necessary to study the relationship of entropic measures between a joint system and its corresponding subsystems, which plays a vital role in estimating channel capacity bounds and analyzing error exponents. The quantum relative entropy satisfies subadditivity and superadditivity, both of which are fundamental properties of the quantum relative entropy [31]. More precisely, for any bipartite quantum states ρ_{AB} and a product state $\sigma_A \otimes \sigma_B$, the superadditivity of the quantum relative entropy is

$$D(\rho_A\|\sigma_A) + D(\rho_B\|\sigma_B) \leq D(\rho_{AB}\|\sigma_A \otimes \sigma_B). \tag{55}$$

This was extended to a more general setting [36]. This paper does not determine whether the BS relative entropy holds the same property. However, the following result shows an opposite relationship for the BS entropy, i.e., the subadditivity. We first give an equivalent definition of the BS relative entropy for obtaining the desired result.

Lemma 4. *For any quantum state $\rho \in \mathcal{S}_=(\mathcal{H})$ and $\sigma \in \mathcal{S}_\leq(\mathcal{H})$, we have*

$$\hat{D}(\rho\|\sigma) = \mathrm{Tr}\left[\sigma(\sigma^{-\frac{1}{2}}\rho\sigma^{-\frac{1}{2}})\log\left(\sigma^{-\frac{1}{2}}\rho\sigma^{-\frac{1}{2}}\right)\right]. \tag{56}$$

Proof. Let Π_σ be the projection onto the support of σ. One can obtain that $\rho = \rho\Pi_\sigma = \Pi_\sigma\rho$ from $\mathrm{supp}(\rho) \subseteq \mathrm{supp}(\sigma)$. From Equation (5), we thus have

$$\begin{aligned}
\hat{D}(\rho\|\sigma) &= \mathrm{Tr}\left[\rho\log(\rho^{\frac{1}{2}}\sigma^{-1}\rho^{\frac{1}{2}})\right] \\
&= \mathrm{Tr}\left[\rho^{\frac{1}{2}}\Pi_\sigma\rho^{\frac{1}{2}}\log(\rho^{\frac{1}{2}}\sigma^{-\frac{1}{2}}\sigma^{-\frac{1}{2}}\rho^{\frac{1}{2}})\right] \\
&= \mathrm{Tr}\left[\rho^{\frac{1}{2}}\sigma^{\frac{1}{2}}\sigma^{-\frac{1}{2}}\rho^{\frac{1}{2}}\log(\rho^{\frac{1}{2}}\sigma^{-\frac{1}{2}}\sigma^{-\frac{1}{2}}\rho^{\frac{1}{2}})\right],
\end{aligned} \tag{57}$$

where the equalities holds from the fact that $\Pi_\sigma = \sigma^{\frac{1}{2}}\sigma^{-\frac{1}{2}}$. Employing Lemma 2.6 in [29], we have

$$\sigma^{-\frac{1}{2}}\rho^{\frac{1}{2}}\log(\rho^{\frac{1}{2}}\sigma^{-\frac{1}{2}}\sigma^{-\frac{1}{2}}\rho^{\frac{1}{2}}) = \log(\sigma^{-\frac{1}{2}}\rho\sigma^{-\frac{1}{2}})\sigma^{-\frac{1}{2}}\rho^{\frac{1}{2}},$$

where $\rho^{\frac{1}{2}}\sigma^{-\frac{1}{2}} = (\sigma^{-\frac{1}{2}}\rho^{\frac{1}{2}})^\dagger$. We then have

$$\begin{aligned}
\hat{D}(\rho\|\sigma) &= \mathrm{Tr}\left[\rho^{\frac{1}{2}}\sigma^{\frac{1}{2}}\log(\sigma^{-\frac{1}{2}}\rho\sigma^{-\frac{1}{2}})\sigma^{-\frac{1}{2}}\rho^{\frac{1}{2}}\right] \\
&= \mathrm{Tr}\left[\log(\sigma^{-\frac{1}{2}}\rho\sigma^{-\frac{1}{2}})\sigma^{-\frac{1}{2}}\rho\sigma^{\frac{1}{2}}\right].
\end{aligned} \tag{58}$$

The equality holds from the cyclic property of the trace. Since

$$\log(\sigma^{-\frac{1}{2}}\rho\sigma^{-\frac{1}{2}})\sigma^{-\frac{1}{2}}\rho\sigma^{-\frac{1}{2}} = \sigma^{-\frac{1}{2}}\rho\sigma^{-\frac{1}{2}}\log(\sigma^{-\frac{1}{2}}\rho\sigma^{-\frac{1}{2}}),$$

we have

$$\begin{aligned}
\hat{D}(\rho\|\sigma) &= \mathrm{Tr}\left[\log(\sigma^{-\frac{1}{2}}\rho\sigma^{-\frac{1}{2}})\sigma^{-\frac{1}{2}}\rho\sigma^{-\frac{1}{2}}\sigma\right] \\
&= \mathrm{Tr}\left[\sigma^{-\frac{1}{2}}\rho\sigma^{-\frac{1}{2}}\log(\sigma^{-\frac{1}{2}}\rho\sigma^{-\frac{1}{2}})\sigma\right].
\end{aligned} \tag{59}$$

Finally, we obtain the desired result by applying the cyclic property of the trace again. □

Theorem 3. *For any quantum state $\rho_{AB} \in \mathcal{S}_=(\mathcal{H}_{AB})$, $\sigma_A \in \mathcal{S}_\leq(\mathcal{H}_A)$, or $\sigma_B \in \mathcal{S}_\leq(\mathcal{H}_B)$, we have*
$$\hat{D}(\rho_{AB}\|\sigma_A \otimes \sigma_B) \leq \lambda[\log\lambda + \hat{D}(\rho_A\|\sigma_A) + \hat{D}(\rho_B\|\sigma_B)], \tag{60}$$
where $\lambda = 2^{D_{\max}(\rho_{AB}\|\rho_A \otimes \rho_B)}$.

Proof. Let $D_{\max}(\rho_{AB}\|\rho_A \otimes \rho_B) = \log\lambda$ for $\operatorname{supp}\rho_{AB} \subseteq \operatorname{supp}(\rho_A \otimes \rho_B)$, which implies that $\rho_{AB} \leq \lambda \rho_A \otimes \rho_B$. For any quantum state σ_A or σ_B that satisfies $\operatorname{supp}\rho_A \subseteq \operatorname{supp}\sigma_B$ and $\operatorname{supp}\rho_A \subseteq \operatorname{supp}\sigma_B$, respectively, applying Lemma 4, we have

$$\hat{D}(\rho_{AB}\|\sigma_A \otimes \sigma_B)$$
$$= \operatorname{Tr}\left[(\sigma_A \otimes \sigma_B)\left(\sigma_A^{-\frac{1}{2}} \otimes \sigma_B^{-\frac{1}{2}} \rho_{AB} \sigma_A^{-\frac{1}{2}} \otimes \sigma_B^{-\frac{1}{2}}\right) \cdot \log\left(\sigma_A^{-\frac{1}{2}} \otimes \sigma_B^{-\frac{1}{2}} \rho_{AB} \sigma_A^{-\frac{1}{2}} \otimes \sigma_B^{-\frac{1}{2}}\right)\right]. \tag{61}$$

Employing the basic operator inequalities of Lemma 2.13 in [29], we have

$$\sigma_A^{-\frac{1}{2}} \otimes \sigma_B^{-\frac{1}{2}} \rho_{AB} \sigma_A^{-\frac{1}{2}} \otimes \sigma_B^{-\frac{1}{2}} \leq \lambda \sigma_A^{-\frac{1}{2}} \otimes \sigma_B^{-\frac{1}{2}} \rho_A \otimes \rho_B \sigma_A^{-\frac{1}{2}} \otimes \sigma_B^{-\frac{1}{2}}.$$

Substituting the above inequality into Equation (61), we then have

$$\hat{D}(\rho_{AB}\|\sigma_A \otimes \sigma_B)$$
$$\leq \operatorname{Tr}\left[(\sigma_A \otimes \sigma_B)\left(\lambda \sigma_A^{-\frac{1}{2}} \rho_A \sigma_A^{-\frac{1}{2}} \otimes \sigma_B^{-\frac{1}{2}} \rho_B \sigma_B^{-\frac{1}{2}}\right) \cdot \log\left(\lambda \sigma_A^{-\frac{1}{2}} \rho_A \sigma_A^{-\frac{1}{2}} \otimes \sigma_B^{-\frac{1}{2}} \rho_B \sigma_B^{-\frac{1}{2}}\right)\right]$$
$$= \lambda \cdot \operatorname{Tr}\left[(\sigma_A \otimes \sigma_B)\left(\sigma_A^{-\frac{1}{2}} \rho_A \sigma_A^{-\frac{1}{2}} \otimes \sigma_B^{-\frac{1}{2}} \rho_B \sigma_B^{-\frac{1}{2}}\right)\right.$$
$$\left. \cdot \left(\log\lambda + \log\left(\sigma_A^{-\frac{1}{2}} \rho_A \sigma_A^{-\frac{1}{2}}\right) + \log\left(\sigma_B^{-\frac{1}{2}} \rho_B \sigma_B^{-\frac{1}{2}}\right)\right)\right]$$
$$\leq \lambda\log\lambda + \lambda\hat{D}(\rho_A\|\sigma_A) + \lambda\hat{D}(\rho_B\|\sigma_B).$$

The equality follows from the linearity of the trace. The last inequality holds based on

$$\operatorname{Tr}\left[(\sigma_A \otimes \sigma_B)\left(\sigma_A^{-\frac{1}{2}} \rho_A \sigma_A^{-\frac{1}{2}} \otimes \sigma_B^{-\frac{1}{2}} \rho_B \sigma_B^{-\frac{1}{2}}\right)\right] \leq 1$$

and

$$\operatorname{Tr}\left[(\sigma_A \otimes \sigma_B)\left(\sigma_A^{-\frac{1}{2}} \rho_A \sigma_A^{-\frac{1}{2}} \otimes \sigma_B^{-\frac{1}{2}} \rho_B \sigma_B^{-\frac{1}{2}}\right) \log\left(\sigma_A^{-\frac{1}{2}} \rho_A \sigma_A^{-\frac{1}{2}}\right)\right]$$
$$= \operatorname{Tr}\left[\sigma_A\left(\sigma_A^{-\frac{1}{2}} \rho_A \sigma_A^{-\frac{1}{2}}\right) \log\left(\sigma_A^{-\frac{1}{2}} \rho_A \sigma_A^{-\frac{1}{2}}\right)\right]$$
$$= \hat{D}(\rho_A\|\sigma_A).$$

Similarly,

$$\operatorname{Tr}\left[(\sigma_A \otimes \sigma_B)\left(\sigma_A^{-\frac{1}{2}} \rho_A \sigma_A^{-\frac{1}{2}} \otimes \sigma_B^{-\frac{1}{2}} \rho_B \sigma_B^{-\frac{1}{2}}\right) \log\left(\sigma_B^{-\frac{1}{2}} \rho_B \sigma_B^{-\frac{1}{2}}\right)\right] = \hat{D}(\rho_B\|\sigma_B).$$

□

As mentioned above, the geometric Rényi relative entropy converges to the BS relative entropy when the limit is $\alpha \to 1$. More generally, we also provide an upper bound for the geometric Rényi relative entropy.

Theorem 4. For any quantum state $\rho_{AB} \in \mathcal{S}_=(\mathcal{H}_{AB})$, $\sigma_A \in \mathcal{S}_\leq(\mathcal{H}_A)$, or $\sigma_B \in \mathcal{S}_\leq(\mathcal{H}_B)$, we have

$$\hat{D}_\alpha(\rho_{AB}\|\sigma_A \otimes \sigma_B) \leq \frac{\alpha}{\alpha-1} D_{\max}(\rho_{AB}\|\rho_A \otimes \rho_B) + \hat{D}_\alpha(\rho_A\|\sigma_A) + \hat{D}_\alpha(\rho_B\|\sigma_B).$$

Proof. Let $D_{\max}(\rho_{AB}\|\rho_A \otimes \rho_B) = \log \lambda$ for $\mathrm{supp}\rho_{AB} \subseteq \mathrm{supp}(\rho_A \otimes \rho_B)$. This implies that $\rho_{AB} \leq \lambda \rho_A \otimes \rho_B$. For σ_A and σ_B with $\mathrm{supp}\rho_A \subseteq \mathrm{supp}\sigma_B$ and $\mathrm{supp}\rho_A \subseteq \mathrm{supp}\sigma_B$, respectively, employing the relation of Eq. (4.6.21) in [29], we have

$$\mathrm{Tr}\left[(\sigma_A \otimes \sigma_B)\left(\sigma_A^{-\frac{1}{2}} \otimes \sigma_B^{-\frac{1}{2}} \rho_{AB} \sigma_A^{-\frac{1}{2}} \otimes \sigma_B^{-\frac{1}{2}}\right)^\alpha\right] = \mathrm{Tr}\left[\rho_{AB}\left(\rho_{AB}^{\frac{1}{2}}\sigma_A^{-1} \otimes \sigma_B^{-1} \rho_{AB}^{\frac{1}{2}}\right)^{\alpha-1}\right].$$

It then holds that

$$\mathrm{Tr}\left[\rho_{AB}\left(\rho_{AB}^{\frac{1}{2}}\sigma_A^{-1} \otimes \sigma_B^{-1}\rho_{AB}^{\frac{1}{2}}\right)^{\alpha-1}\right]$$
$$\leq \mathrm{Tr}\left[\lambda(\rho_A \otimes \rho_B)\left(\lambda \rho_A^{\frac{1}{2}} \otimes \rho_B^{\frac{1}{2}}\sigma_A^{-1} \otimes \sigma_B^{-1}\rho_A^{\frac{1}{2}} \otimes \rho_B^{\frac{1}{2}}\right)^{\alpha-1}\right]$$
$$= \lambda^\alpha \mathrm{Tr}\left[(\rho_A \otimes \rho_B)\left(\rho_A^{\frac{1}{2}} \otimes \rho_B^{\frac{1}{2}}\sigma_A^{-1} \otimes \sigma_B^{-1}\rho_A^{\frac{1}{2}} \otimes \rho_B^{\frac{1}{2}}\right)^{\alpha-1}\right]$$
$$= \lambda^\alpha \mathrm{Tr}\left[\rho_A\left(\rho_A^{\frac{1}{2}}\sigma_A^{-1}\rho_A^{\frac{1}{2}}\right)^{\alpha-1}\right]\mathrm{Tr}\left[\rho_B\left(\rho_B^{\frac{1}{2}}\sigma_B^{-1} \otimes \rho_B^{\frac{1}{2}}\right)^{\alpha-1}\right].$$

Combining the above result with Definition 1, we have

$$\hat{D}_\alpha(\rho_{AB}\|\sigma_A \otimes \sigma_B) \leq \frac{1}{\alpha-1}\log\left[\lambda^\alpha \mathrm{Tr}\left[\rho_A\left(\rho_A^{\frac{1}{2}}\sigma_A^{-1}\rho_A^{\frac{1}{2}}\right)^{\alpha-1}\right]\mathrm{Tr}\left[\rho_B\left(\rho_B^{\frac{1}{2}}\sigma_B^{-1} \otimes \rho_B^{\frac{1}{2}}\right)^{\alpha-1}\right]\right]$$
$$= \frac{\alpha}{\alpha-1}D_{\max}(\rho_{AB}\|\rho_A \otimes \rho_B) + \hat{D}_\alpha(\rho_A\|\sigma_A) + \hat{D}_\alpha(\rho_B\|\sigma_B).$$

□

Similarly, one can define a new mutual information term via the geometric Rényi relative entropy as

$$\hat{I}_\alpha(A;B)_\rho = \min_{\sigma_A,\sigma_B} \hat{D}_\alpha(\rho_{AB}\|\sigma_A \otimes \sigma_B). \tag{62}$$

It is then easy to draw the following conclusion.

Corollary 2. For any quantum state $\rho_{AB} \in \mathcal{S}_=(\mathcal{H}_{AB})$, $\sigma_A \in \mathcal{S}_\leq(\mathcal{H}_A)$, or $\sigma_B \in \mathcal{S}_\leq(\mathcal{H}_B)$, we have

$$\hat{I}_\alpha(A;B)_\rho \leq \frac{\alpha}{\alpha-1}D_{\max}(\rho_{AB}\|\rho_A \otimes \rho_B) + \hat{D}_\alpha(\rho_A\|\sigma_A) + \hat{D}_\alpha(\rho_B\|\sigma_B). \tag{63}$$

Notably, if one considers the classical-quantum state, there is no result as shown in Lemma 3 for the mutual information defined by the geometric Rényi relative entropy. Specifically, for $\alpha \in (0,1)$, we have

$$\hat{D}_\alpha(\rho_{XB}\|\rho_X \otimes \rho_B) = \frac{1}{\alpha-1}\log\left[\sum_x p(x)\mathrm{Tr}\left[\rho_B\left(\rho_B^{-\frac{1}{2}}\rho_B^x\rho_B^{-\frac{1}{2}}\right)^\alpha\right]\right]$$
$$\leq \frac{1}{\alpha-1}\sum_x p(x)\log\left[\mathrm{Tr}\left[\rho_B\left(\sigma_B^{-\frac{1}{2}}\rho_B^x\rho_B^{-\frac{1}{2}}\right)^\alpha\right]\right] \tag{64}$$
$$= \sum_x p(x)\hat{D}_\alpha(\rho_B^x\|\rho_B),$$

where the inequality comes from the Jensen inequality of $-\log t$. For $\alpha \in (1, \infty)$, we obtain the opposite result, i.e.,

$$\hat{D}_\alpha(\rho_{XB} \| \rho_X \otimes \rho_B) \geq \sum_x p(x) \hat{D}_\alpha(\rho_B^x \| \rho_B). \tag{65}$$

Furthermore, if one considers the conditional entropy defined by the geometric Rényi relative entropy, for $\alpha \in (0,1)$, we have

$$\hat{D}_\alpha(\rho_{XB} \| I_X \otimes \rho_B) \leq \sum_x p(x) \hat{D}_\alpha(\rho_B^x \| \rho_B) - H(X). \tag{66}$$

For $\alpha \in (1, \infty)$, we then have

$$\hat{D}_\alpha(\rho_{XB} \| I_X \otimes \rho_B) \geq \sum_x p(x) \hat{D}_\alpha(\rho_B^x \| \rho_B) - H(X). \tag{67}$$

4. Conclusions

This paper investigates the subadditivity of the geometric Rényi and BS relative entropies and explores the indispensable properties of the BS conditional entropy and mutual information, especially in classical-quantum settings. The subadditivity of the geometric Rényi and BS relative entropies can provide new valuable bounds to estimate channel capacity and analyze the error exponent. As mentioned above, the BS relative entropy represents a different quantum generalization of classical relative entropy. The main use of BS relative entropy is in establishing upper bounds for the rates of feedback-assisted quantum communication protocols. The primary goal of further research on BS relative entropy is to explore the intrinsic properties of its relevant conditional entropy and mutual information and to gain a better understanding of their operational relevance. We hope that the formal tools provided in this paper will be useful for this purpose.

One question worth answering is whether there is a chain rule for the mutual information in terms of the geometric Rényi relative entropy, i.e.,

$$\hat{D}_\alpha(\rho_{AB} \| \rho_A \otimes \rho_B) \gtreqless \hat{S}_\alpha(\rho_A) + \hat{D}_\alpha(\rho_{AB} \| I_A \otimes \rho_B),$$

or the other forms, where $\hat{S}_\alpha(\rho_A)$ is the quantum Rényi entropy. Subsequently, the duality of conditional entropy is an important property for a tripartite pure state system, which can be effectively applied in random number extraction and channel coding [26]. Further research will focus on the duality of the BS conditional entropy.

Author Contributions: Conceptualization, Y.Z. and Z.X.; methodology, Y.Z. and Z.X.; formal analysis, Y.Z.; writing—original draft preparation, Y.Z.; writing—review and editing, Y.Z., B.Y. and Z.X.; project administration, B.Y. and Z.X. All authors have read and agreed to the published version of the manuscript.

Funding: This research was funded by the National Natural Science Foundation of China (Nos. 62171266, U2001205) and the Funded Projects for the Academic Leaders and Academic Backbones, Shaanxi Normal University (No. 16QNGG013).

Institutional Review Board Statement: Not applicable.

Informed Consent Statement: Not applicable.

Data Availability Statement: Not applicable.

Acknowledgments: Z.X. is supported by the National Natural Science Foundation of China (No. 62171266) and by the Funded Projects for the Academic Leaders and Academic Backbones, Shaanxi Normal University (No. 16QNGG013). B.Y. is supported by the National Natural Science Foundation of China (No. U2001205).

Conflicts of Interest: The authors declare that there is no conflict of interest. The funders had no role in the design of the study, in the collection, analyses, or interpretation of data, in the writing of the manuscript, or in the decision to publish the results.

References

1. Rényi, A. On measures of information and entropy. *Proc. Symp. Math. Stat. Probab.* **1961**, *4*, 547–561.
2. Kullback, S.; Leibler, R.A. On information and sufficiency. *Ann. Math. Stat.* **1951**, *22*, 79–86. [CrossRef]
3. Cover, T. M.; Thomas, J.A. *Elements of Information Theory*, 2nd ed.; John Wiley Sons, Inc.: Hoboken, NJ, USA, 2006.
4. Csiszár, I.; Körner, J. *Information Theory: Coding Theorems for Discrete Memoryless Systems*; Cambridge University Press: Cambridge, UK, 2011.
5. Tomamichel, M. Quantum information processing with finite resources. *arXiv* **2015**, arXiv:1504.00233v1.
6. Muller-Lennert, M.; Dupuis, F.; Szehr, O.; Fehr, S.; Tomamichel, M. On quamtum Rényi entropies: A new generalization and some properties. *J. Math. Phys.* **2013**, *54*, 122203. [CrossRef]
7. Mosonyi, M.; Ogawa, T. Quantum hypothesis testing and the operational interpretation of the quantum Rényi relative entropies. *Commun. Math. Phys.* **2015**, *334*, 1617–1648. [CrossRef]
8. Audenaert, K.M.R.; Datta, N. α-z-Rényi relative entropies. *J. Math. Phys.* **2015**, *56*, 022202. [CrossRef]
9. Hiai, F.; Mosonyi, M. Different quantum f-divergences and the reversibility of quantum operations. *Rev. Math. Phys.* **2017**, *29*, 1750023. [CrossRef]
10. Capel, Á.; Lucia, A.; Pérez-García, D. Quantum conditional relative entropy and quasifactorization of the relative entropy. *J. Phys. A Math. Theor.* **2018**, *51*, 484001. [CrossRef]
11. Petz, D. Quasi-entropies for states of a von Neumann algebra. *Publ. Res. Inst. Math. Sci.* **1985**, *4*, 787–800. [CrossRef]
12. Petz, D. Quasi-entropies for finite quantum systems. *Rep. Math. Phys.* **1986**, *23*, 57–65. [CrossRef]
13. Wilde, M.M.; Winter, A.; Yang, D. Strong converse for the classical capacity of entanglement-breaking and Hadamard channels via a sandwiched Rényi relative entropy. *Commun. Math. Phys.* **2014**, *331*, 593–622. [CrossRef]
14. Petz, D.; Ruskai, M.B. Contraction of generalized relative entropy under stochastic mappings on matrices. *Infin. Dimens. Anal. Quantum Probab. Relat. Top.* **1998**, *1*, 83–89. [CrossRef]
15. Matsumoto, K. A new quantum version of f-divergence. *arXiv* **2013**, arXiv:1311.4722.
16. Umegaki, H. Conditional expectations in an operator algebra IV (entropy and information). *Kodai Math. J.* **1962**, *14*, 59–85. [CrossRef]
17. Nielsen, M.A.; Chuang, I.L. *Quantum Computation and Quantum Information*; Cambridge University Press: Cambridge, UK, 2000.
18. Belavkin, V.P.; Staszewski, P. C*-algebraic generalization of relative entropy and entropy. *Ann. Inst. Henri Poincare* **1982**, *37*, 51–58.
19. Katariya, V.; Wilde, M.M. Geometric distinguishability measures limit quantum channel estimation and discrimination. *arXiv* **2020**, arXiv:2004.10708.
20. Bluhm, A.; Capel, A. A strengthened data processing inequality for the Belavkin-Staszewski relative entropy. *Rev. Math. Phys.* **2020**, *32*, 2050005. [CrossRef]
21. Hiai, F.; Petz, D. The proper formula for relative entropy and its asymptotics in quantum probability. *Commun. Math. Phys.* **1991**, *143*, 99–114. [CrossRef]
22. Bluhm, A.; Capel, A.; Perez-Hernandez, A. Weak quasi-factorization for the Belavkin-Staszewski relative entropy. In Proceedings of the 2021 IEEE International Symposium on Information Theory (ISIT), Melbourne, Australia, 12–20 July 2021; pp. 118–123.
23. Fang, K.; Fawzi, H. Geometric Rényi divergence and its applications in quantum channel capacities. *Commun. Math. Phys.* **2021**, *384*, 1615–1677. [CrossRef]
24. Ciganović, N.; Beaudry, N.J.; Renner, R. Smooth max-information as one-shot generalization for mutual information. *IEEE Trans. Inform. Theory* **2014**, *60*, 1573–1581. [CrossRef]
25. Watanabe, Y. Randomness Extraction via a Quantum Generalization of the Conditional Collision Entropy. *IEEE Trans. Inform. Theory* **2020**, *66*, 1171–1177. [CrossRef]
26. Tomamichel, M.; Colbeck, R.; Renner, R. Duality between smooth min- and max-entropies. *IEEE Trans. Inf. Theory* **2010**, *56*, 4674–4681. [CrossRef]
27. König, R.; Renner, R.; Schaffner, C. The operational meaning of min- and max-entropy. *IEEE Trans. Inf. Theory* **2009**, *55*, 4337–4347. [CrossRef]
28. Vitanov, A.; Dupuis, F.; Tomamichel, M.; Renner, R. Chain rules for smooth min- and max-entropies. *IEEE Trans. Inf. Theory* **2013**, *59*, 2603–2612. [CrossRef]
29. Khatri, S.; Wilde, M.M. Principles of quantum communication theory: A modern approach. *arXiv* **2020**, arXiv:2011.04672v1.
30. Datta, N. Min- and max-relative entropies and a new entanglement monotone. *IEEE Trans. Inf. Theory* **2009**, *55*, 2816–2826. [CrossRef]
31. Wilde, M.M. *Quantum Information Theory*, 2nd ed.; Cambridge University Press: Cambridge, UK, 2017.
32. Chitambar, E.; Gour, G. Quantum resource theories. *Rev. Mod. Phys.* **2019**, *91*, 025001. [CrossRef]
33. Lawson, J.D.; Lim, Y. The geometric mean, matrices, metrics, and more. *Am. Math. Mon.* **2001**, *108*, 797–812. [CrossRef]
34. Renner, R. Security of Quantum Key Distribution. Ph.D. Thesis, ETH Zurich, Zurich, Switzerland, 2005.
35. Sagawa, T. Entropy, divergence, and majorization in classical and quantum thermodynamics. *arXiv* **2020**, arXiv:2007.09974v1.
36. Capel, Á.; Lucia, A.; Pérez-García, D. Superadditivity of quantum relative entropy for general states. *IEEE Trans. Inf. Theory* **2018**, *64*, 4758–4765. [CrossRef]

where the inequality comes from the Jensen inequality of $-\log t$. For $\alpha \in (1, \infty)$, we obtain the opposite result, i.e.,

$$\hat{D}_\alpha(\rho_{XB} \| \rho_X \otimes \rho_B) \geq \sum_x p(x) \hat{D}_\alpha(\rho_B^x \| \rho_B). \tag{65}$$

Furthermore, if one considers the conditional entropy defined by the geometric Rényi relative entropy, for $\alpha \in (0, 1)$, we have

$$\hat{D}_\alpha(\rho_{XB} \| I_X \otimes \rho_B) \leq \sum_x p(x) \hat{D}_\alpha(\rho_B^x \| \rho_B) - H(X). \tag{66}$$

For $\alpha \in (1, \infty)$, we then have

$$\hat{D}_\alpha(\rho_{XB} \| I_X \otimes \rho_B) \geq \sum_x p(x) \hat{D}_\alpha(\rho_B^x \| \rho_B) - H(X). \tag{67}$$

4. Conclusions

This paper investigates the subadditivity of the geometric Rényi and BS relative entropies and explores the indispensable properties of the BS conditional entropy and mutual information, especially in classical-quantum settings. The subadditivity of the geometric Rényi and BS relative entropies can provide new valuable bounds to estimate channel capacity and analyze the error exponent. As mentioned above, the BS relative entropy represents a different quantum generalization of classical relative entropy. The main use of BS relative entropy is in establishing upper bounds for the rates of feedback-assisted quantum communication protocols. The primary goal of further research on BS relative entropy is to explore the intrinsic properties of its relevant conditional entropy and mutual information and to gain a better understanding of their operational relevance. We hope that the formal tools provided in this paper will be useful for this purpose.

One question worth answering is whether there is a chain rule for the mutual information in terms of the geometric Rényi relative entropy, i.e.,

$$\hat{D}_\alpha(\rho_{AB} \| \rho_A \otimes \rho_B) \overset{\geq}{\underset{\leq}{}} \hat{S}_\alpha(\rho_A) + \hat{D}_\alpha(\rho_{AB} \| I_A \otimes \rho_B),$$

or the other forms, where $\hat{S}_\alpha(\rho_A)$ is the quantum Rényi entropy. Subsequently, the duality of conditional entropy is an important property for a tripartite pure state system, which can be effectively applied in random number extraction and channel coding [26]. Further research will focus on the duality of the BS conditional entropy.

Author Contributions: Conceptualization, Y.Z. and Z.X.; methodology, Y.Z. and Z.X.; formal analysis, Y.Z.; writing—original draft preparation, Y.Z.; writing—review and editing, Y.Z., B.Y. and Z.X.; project administration, B.Y. and Z.X. All authors have read and agreed to the published version of the manuscript.

Funding: This research was funded by the National Natural Science Foundation of China (Nos. 62171266, U2001205) and the Funded Projects for the Academic Leaders and Academic Backbones, Shaanxi Normal University (No. 16QNGG013).

Institutional Review Board Statement: Not applicable.

Informed Consent Statement: Not applicable.

Data Availability Statement: Not applicable.

Acknowledgments: Z.X. is supported by the National Natural Science Foundation of China (No. 62171266) and by the Funded Projects for the Academic Leaders and Academic Backbones, Shaanxi Normal University (No. 16QNGG013). B.Y. is supported by the National Natural Science Foundation of China (No. U2001205).

Conflicts of Interest: The authors declare that there is no conflict of interest. The funders had no role in the design of the study, in the collection, analyses, or interpretation of data, in the writing of the manuscript, or in the decision to publish the results.

References

1. Rényi, A. On measures of information and entropy. *Proc. Symp. Math. Stat. Probab.* **1961**, *4*, 547–561.
2. Kullback, S.; Leibler, R.A. On information and sufficiency. *Ann. Math. Stat.* **1951**, *22*, 79–86. [CrossRef]
3. Cover, T. M.; Thomas, J.A. *Elements of Information Theory*, 2nd ed.; John Wiley Sons, Inc.: Hoboken, NJ, USA, 2006.
4. Csiszár, I.; Körner, J. *Information Theory: Coding Theorems for Discrete Memoryless Systems*; Cambridge University Press: Cambridge, UK, 2011.
5. Tomamichel, M. Quantum information processing with finite resources. *arXiv* **2015**, arXiv:1504.00233v1.
6. Muller-Lennert, M.; Dupuis, F.; Szehr, O.; Fehr, S.; Tomamichel, M. On quamtum Rényi entropies: A new generalization and some properties. *J. Math. Phys.* **2013**, *54*, 122203. [CrossRef]
7. Mosonyi, M.; Ogawa, T. Quantum hypothesis testing and the operational interpretation of the quantum Rényi relative entropies. *Commun. Math. Phys.* **2015**, *334*, 1617–1648. [CrossRef]
8. Audenaert, K.M.R.; Datta, N. α-z-Rényi relative entropies. *J. Math. Phys.* **2015**, *56*, 022202. [CrossRef]
9. Hiai, F.; Mosonyi, M. Different quantum f-divergences and the reversibility of quantum operations. *Rev. Math. Phys.* **2017**, *29*, 1750023. [CrossRef]
10. Capel, Á.; Lucia, A.; Pérez-García, D. Quantum conditional relative entropy and quasifactorization of the relative entropy. *J. Phys. A Math. Theor.* **2018**, *51*, 484001. [CrossRef]
11. Petz, D. Quasi-entropies for states of a von Neumann algebra. *Publ. Res. Inst. Math. Sci.* **1985**, *4*, 787–800. [CrossRef]
12. Petz, D. Quasi-entropies for finite quantum systems. *Rep. Math. Phys.* **1986**, *23*, 57–65. [CrossRef]
13. Wilde, M.M.; Winter, A.; Yang, D. Strong converse for the classical capacity of entanglement-breaking and Hadamard channels via a sandwiched Rényi relative entropy. *Commun. Math. Phys.* **2014**, *331*, 593–622. [CrossRef]
14. Petz, D.; Ruskai, M.B. Contraction of generalized relative entropy under stochastic mappings on matrices. *Infin. Dimens. Anal. Quantum Probab. Relat. Top.* **1998**, *1*, 83–89. [CrossRef]
15. Matsumoto, K. A new quantum version of f-divergence. *arXiv* **2013**, arXiv:1311.4722.
16. Umegaki, H. Conditional expectations in an operator algebra IV (entropy and information). *Kodai Math. J.* **1962**, *14*, 59–85. [CrossRef]
17. Nielsen, M.A.; Chuang, I.L. *Quantum Computation and Quantum Information*; Cambridge University Press: Cambridge, UK, 2000.
18. Belavkin, V.P.; Staszewski, P. C*-algebraic generalization of relative entropy and entropy. *Ann. Inst. Henri Poincare* **1982**, *37*, 51–58.
19. Katariya, V.; Wilde, M.M. Geometric distinguishability measures limit quantum channel estimation and discrimination. *arXiv* **2020**, arXiv:2004.10708.
20. Bluhm, A.; Capel, A. A strengthened data processing inequality for the Belavkin-Staszewski relative entropy. *Rev. Math. Phys.* **2020**, *32*, 2050005. [CrossRef]
21. Hiai, F.; Petz, D. The proper formula for relative entropy and its asymptotics in quantum probability. *Commun. Math. Phys.* **1991**, *143*, 99–114. [CrossRef]
22. Bluhm, A.; Capel, A.; Perez-Hernandez, A. Weak quasi-factorization for the Belavkin-Staszewski relative entropy. In Proceedings of the 2021 IEEE International Symposium on Information Theory (ISIT), Melbourne, Australia, 12–20 July 2021; pp. 118–123.
23. Fang, K.; Fawzi, H. Geometric Rényi divergence and its applications in quantum channel capacities. *Commun. Math. Phys.* **2021**, *384*, 1615–1677. [CrossRef]
24. Ciganović, N.; Beaudry, N.J.; Renner, R. Smooth max-information as one-shot generalization for mutual information. *IEEE Trans. Inform. Theory* **2014**, *60*, 1573–1581. [CrossRef]
25. Watanabe, Y. Randomness Extraction via a Quantum Generalization of the Conditional Collision Entropy. *IEEE Trans. Inform. Theory* **2020**, *66*, 1171–1177. [CrossRef]
26. Tomamichel, M.; Colbeck, R.; Renner, R. Duality between smooth min- and max-entropies. *IEEE Trans. Inf. Theory* **2010**, *56*, 4674–4681. [CrossRef]
27. König, R.; Renner, R.; Schaffner, C. The operational meaning of min- and max-entropy. *IEEE Trans. Inf. Theory* **2009**, *55*, 4337–4347. [CrossRef]
28. Vitanov, A.; Dupuis, F.; Tomamichel, M.; Renner, R. Chain rules for smooth min- and max-entropies. *IEEE Trans. Inf. Theory* **2013**, *59*, 2603–2612. [CrossRef]
29. Khatri, S.; Wilde, M.M. Principles of quantum communication theory: A modern approach. *arXiv* **2020**, arXiv:2011.04672v1.
30. Datta, N. Min- and max-relative entropies and a new entanglement monotone. *IEEE Trans. Inf. Theory* **2009**, *55*, 2816–2826. [CrossRef]
31. Wilde, M.M. *Quantum Information Theory*, 2nd ed.; Cambridge University Press: Cambridge, UK, 2017.
32. Chitambar, E.; Gour, G. Quantum resource theories. *Rev. Mod. Phys.* **2019**, *91*, 025001. [CrossRef]
33. Lawson, J.D.; Lim, Y. The geometric mean, matrices, metrics, and more. *Am. Math. Mon.* **2001**, *108*, 797–812. [CrossRef]
34. Renner, R. Security of Quantum Key Distribution. Ph.D. Thesis, ETH Zurich, Zurich, Switzerland, 2005.
35. Sagawa, T. Entropy, divergence, and majorization in classical and quantum thermodynamics. *arXiv* **2020**, arXiv:2007.09974v1.
36. Capel, Á.; Lucia, A.; Pérez-García, D. Superadditivity of quantum relative entropy for general states. *IEEE Trans. Inf. Theory* **2018**, *64*, 4758–4765. [CrossRef]

where the inequality comes from the Jensen inequality of $-\log t$. For $\alpha \in (1, \infty)$, we obtain the opposite result, i.e.,

$$\hat{D}_\alpha(\rho_{XB} \| \rho_X \otimes \rho_B) \geq \sum_x p(x) \hat{D}_\alpha(\rho_B^x \| \rho_B). \tag{65}$$

Furthermore, if one considers the conditional entropy defined by the geometric Rényi relative entropy, for $\alpha \in (0, 1)$, we have

$$\hat{D}_\alpha(\rho_{XB} \| I_X \otimes \rho_B) \leq \sum_x p(x) \hat{D}_\alpha(\rho_B^x \| \rho_B) - H(X). \tag{66}$$

For $\alpha \in (1, \infty)$, we then have

$$\hat{D}_\alpha(\rho_{XB} \| I_X \otimes \rho_B) \geq \sum_x p(x) \hat{D}_\alpha(\rho_B^x \| \rho_B) - H(X). \tag{67}$$

4. Conclusions

This paper investigates the subadditivity of the geometric Rényi and BS relative entropies and explores the indispensable properties of the BS conditional entropy and mutual information, especially in classical-quantum settings. The subadditivity of the geometric Rényi and BS relative entropies can provide new valuable bounds to estimate channel capacity and analyze the error exponent. As mentioned above, the BS relative entropy represents a different quantum generalization of classical relative entropy. The main use of BS relative entropy is in establishing upper bounds for the rates of feedback-assisted quantum communication protocols. The primary goal of further research on BS relative entropy is to explore the intrinsic properties of its relevant conditional entropy and mutual information and to gain a better understanding of their operational relevance. We hope that the formal tools provided in this paper will be useful for this purpose.

One question worth answering is whether there is a chain rule for the mutual information in terms of the geometric Rényi relative entropy, i.e.,

$$\hat{D}_\alpha(\rho_{AB} \| \rho_A \otimes \rho_B) \gtreqless \hat{S}_\alpha(\rho_A) + \hat{D}_\alpha(\rho_{AB} \| I_A \otimes \rho_B),$$

or the other forms, where $\hat{S}_\alpha(\rho_A)$ is the quantum Rényi entropy. Subsequently, the duality of conditional entropy is an important property for a tripartite pure state system, which can be effectively applied in random number extraction and channel coding [26]. Further research will focus on the duality of the BS conditional entropy.

Author Contributions: Conceptualization, Y.Z. and Z.X.; methodology, Y.Z. and Z.X.; formal analysis, Y.Z.; writing—original draft preparation, Y.Z.; writing—review and editing, Y.Z., B.Y. and Z.X.; project administration, B.Y. and Z.X. All authors have read and agreed to the published version of the manuscript.

Funding: This research was funded by the National Natural Science Foundation of China (Nos. 62171266, U2001205) and the Funded Projects for the Academic Leaders and Academic Backbones, Shaanxi Normal University (No. 16QNGG013).

Institutional Review Board Statement: Not applicable.

Informed Consent Statement: Not applicable.

Data Availability Statement: Not applicable.

Acknowledgments: Z.X. is supported by the National Natural Science Foundation of China (No. 62171266) and by the Funded Projects for the Academic Leaders and Academic Backbones, Shaanxi Normal University (No. 16QNGG013). B.Y. is supported by the National Natural Science Foundation of China (No. U2001205).

Conflicts of Interest: The authors declare that there is no conflict of interest. The funders had no role in the design of the study, in the collection, analyses, or interpretation of data, in the writing of the manuscript, or in the decision to publish the results.

References

1. Rényi, A. On measures of information and entropy. *Proc. Symp. Math. Stat. Probab.* **1961**, *4*, 547–561.
2. Kullback, S.; Leibler, R.A. On information and sufficiency. *Ann. Math. Stat.* **1951**, *22*, 79–86. [CrossRef]
3. Cover, T. M.; Thomas, J.A. *Elements of Information Theory*, 2nd ed.; John Wiley Sons, Inc.: Hoboken, NJ, USA, 2006.
4. Csiszár, I.; Körner, J. *Information Theory: Coding Theorems for Discrete Memoryless Systems*; Cambridge University Press: Cambridge, UK, 2011.
5. Tomamichel, M. Quantum information processing with finite resources. *arXiv* **2015**, arXiv:1504.00233v1.
6. Muller-Lennert, M.; Dupuis, F.; Szehr, O.; Fehr, S.; Tomamichel, M. On quamtum Rényi entropies: A new generalization and some properties. *J. Math. Phys.* **2013**, *54*, 122203. [CrossRef]
7. Mosonyi, M.; Ogawa, T. Quantum hypothesis testing and the operational interpretation of the quantum Rényi relative entropies. *Commun. Math. Phys.* **2015**, *334*, 1617–1648. [CrossRef]
8. Audenaert, K.M.R.; Datta, N. α-z-Rényi relative entropies. *J. Math. Phys.* **2015**, *56*, 022202. [CrossRef]
9. Hiai, F.; Mosonyi, M. Different quantum f-divergences and the reversibility of quantum operations. *Rev. Math. Phys.* **2017**, *29*, 1750023. [CrossRef]
10. Capel, Á.; Lucia, A.; Pérez-García, D. Quantum conditional relative entropy and quasifactorization of the relative entropy. *J. Phys. A Math. Theor.* **2018**, *51*, 484001. [CrossRef]
11. Petz, D. Quasi-entropies for states of a von Neumann algebra. *Publ. Res. Inst. Math. Sci.* **1985**, *4*, 787–800. [CrossRef]
12. Petz, D. Quasi-entropies for finite quantum systems. *Rep. Math. Phys.* **1986**, *23*, 57–65. [CrossRef]
13. Wilde, M.M.; Winter, A.; Yang, D. Strong converse for the classical capacity of entanglement-breaking and Hadamard channels via a sandwiched Rényi relative entropy. *Commun. Math. Phys.* **2014**, *331*, 593–622. [CrossRef]
14. Petz, D.; Ruskai, M.B. Contraction of generalized relative entropy under stochastic mappings on matrices. *Infin. Dimens. Anal. Quantum Probab. Relat. Top.* **1998**, *1*, 83–89. [CrossRef]
15. Matsumoto, K. A new quantum version of f-divergence. *arXiv* **2013**, arXiv:1311.4722.
16. Umegaki, H. Conditional expectations in an operator algebra IV (entropy and information). *Kodai Math. J.* **1962**, *14*, 59–85. [CrossRef]
17. Nielsen, M.A.; Chuang, I.L. *Quantum Computation and Quantum Information*; Cambridge University Press: Cambridge, UK, 2000.
18. Belavkin, V.P.; Staszewski, P. C*-algebraic generalization of relative entropy and entropy. *Ann. Inst. Henri Poincare* **1982**, *37*, 51–58.
19. Katariya, V.; Wilde, M.M. Geometric distinguishability measures limit quantum channel estimation and discrimination. *arXiv* **2020**, arXiv:2004.10708.
20. Bluhm, A.; Capel, A. A strengthened data processing inequality for the Belavkin-Staszewski relative entropy. *Rev. Math. Phys.* **2020**, *32*, 2050005. [CrossRef]
21. Hiai, F.; Petz, D. The proper formula for relative entropy and its asymptotics in quantum probability. *Commun. Math. Phys.* **1991**, *143*, 99–114. [CrossRef]
22. Bluhm, A.; Capel, A.; Perez-Hernandez, A. Weak quasi-factorization for the Belavkin-Staszewski relative entropy. In Proceedings of the 2021 IEEE International Symposium on Information Theory (ISIT), Melbourne, Australia, 12–20 July 2021; pp. 118–123.
23. Fang, K.; Fawzi, H. Geometric Rényi divergence and its applications in quantum channel capacities. *Commun. Math. Phys.* **2021**, *384*, 1615–1677. [CrossRef]
24. Ciganović, N.; Beaudry, N.J.; Renner, R. Smooth max-information as one-shot generalization for mutual information. *IEEE Trans. Inform. Theory* **2014**, *60*, 1573–1581. [CrossRef]
25. Watanabe, Y. Randomness Extraction via a Quantum Generalization of the Conditional Collision Entropy. *IEEE Trans. Inform. Theory* **2020**, *66*, 1171–1177. [CrossRef]
26. Tomamichel, M.; Colbeck, R.; Renner, R. Duality between smooth min- and max-entropies. *IEEE Trans. Inf. Theory* **2010**, *56*, 4674–4681. [CrossRef]
27. König, R.; Renner, R.; Schaffner, C. The operational meaning of min- and max-entropy. *IEEE Trans. Inf. Theory* **2009**, *55*, 4337–4347. [CrossRef]
28. Vitanov, A.; Dupuis, F.; Tomamichel, M.; Renner, R. Chain rules for smooth min- and max-entropies. *IEEE Trans. Inf. Theory* **2013**, *59*, 2603–2612. [CrossRef]
29. Khatri, S.; Wilde, M.M. Principles of quantum communication theory: A modern approach. *arXiv* **2020**, arXiv:2011.04672v1.
30. Datta, N. Min- and max-relative entropies and a new entanglement monotone. *IEEE Trans. Inf. Theory* **2009**, *55*, 2816–2826. [CrossRef]
31. Wilde, M.M. *Quantum Information Theory*, 2nd ed.; Cambridge University Press: Cambridge, UK, 2017.
32. Chitambar, E.; Gour, G. Quantum resource theories. *Rev. Mod. Phys.* **2019**, *91*, 025001. [CrossRef]
33. Lawson, J.D.; Lim, Y. The geometric mean, matrices, metrics, and more. *Am. Math. Mon.* **2001**, *108*, 797–812. [CrossRef]
34. Renner, R. Security of Quantum Key Distribution. Ph.D. Thesis, ETH Zurich, Zurich, Switzerland, 2005.
35. Sagawa, T. Entropy, divergence, and majorization in classical and quantum thermodynamics. *arXiv* **2020**, arXiv:2007.09974v1.
36. Capel, Á.; Lucia, A.; Pérez-García, D. Superadditivity of quantum relative entropy for general states. *IEEE Trans. Inf. Theory* **2018**, *64*, 4758–4765. [CrossRef]

Article

A Fisher Information-Based Incompatibility Criterion for Quantum Channels

Qing-Hua Zhang [1,2,*,†] and Ion Nechita [2,†]

1. School of Mathematical Sciences, Capital Normal University, Beijing 100048, China
2. Laboratoire de Physique Théorique, Université de Toulouse, CNRS, UPS, 31062 Toulouse, France; ion.nechita@univ-tlse3.fr
* Correspondence: 2190501022@cnu.edu.cn
† These authors contributed equally to this work.

Abstract: We introduce a new incompatibility criterion for quantum channels based on the notion of (quantum) Fisher information. Our construction is based on a similar criterion for quantum measurements put forward by H. Zhu. We then study the power of the incompatibility criterion in different scenarios. First, we prove the first analytical conditions for the incompatibility of two Schur channels. Then, we study the incompatibility structure of a tuple of depolarizing channels, comparing the newly introduced criterion with the known results from asymmetric quantum cloning.

Keywords: incompatibility criterion; quantum channels; quantum measurements; Fisher information

1. Introduction

The impossibility of simultaneous realizations of two quantum operations is one of the fundamental features of quantum theory [1,2]. Two of the most famous incarnations of this principle are the *Heisenberg uncertainty principle* (the position and momentum of a quantum particle can not be measured simultaneously [1]) and the *no-cloning theorem* (there is no physical operation producing two identical copies of an unknown, arbitrary, quantum state [3,4]). In general, two (or more) quantum operations, such as measurements, channels, or instruments, are called *compatible* if they can be seen as marginals of a common operation; if there is no physical operation having the original ones as marginals, they are called *incompatible*. As quantum theory is built on Hilbert space, general quantum measurements are considered the positive operator-valued measures (POVMs). In quantum information theory, there are many applications of the notion of incompatibility, such as the robustness of entanglement [5,6], the robustness of measurement incompatibility [7–9], quantum non-locality [10,11], quantum steering [7,12], quantum state discrimination [13–15], quantum resource theory [16], and quantum cryptography [17].

In the modern formalism of quantum theory, the most general description of physical transformations of quantum states is in terms of *quantum channels* [18,19]. The concept of incompatibility of quantum channels has been proposed in terms of the input–output devices [20,21]. In [21], the authors show that the definition of the *incompatibility of quantum channels* is a natural generalization of joint measurability of quantum observables. There exists a large body of work dealing with this notion from various points of view [15,22–24]. Generally speaking, deciding whether a given family of quantum operations is compatible can be formulated as a *semidefinite program* [25]. However, the size of the program grows *exponentially* with the number of operations considered. Hence, this method can be computationally prohibitive even for small system sizes (such as qubits) when the number of systems is moderately large. To cope with this dimensionality problem, (in-)compatibility criteria have been introduced; these are conditions that are only necessary, or sufficient, for the compatibility of the given tuple of channels. As is the case with quantum measurements [20], there exist much more compatibility criteria [26] than incompatibility criteria.

In this work, we introduce a new *incompatibility criterion for quantum channels* based on the notion of (quantum) Fisher information. Our criterion is based on a similar condition put forward by H. Zhu [27,28] in the case of quantum measurements.

After introducing the necessary background on Fisher information and quantum channel compatibility (Sections 2 and 3), we put forward the new incompatibility criterion in Section 4. The statement of the main result of the paper can be found in Theorem 1. We then apply this result to study, for the first time, the incompatibility of Schur channels, an important class of quantum operations with wide-ranging applications; see Section 5. In the final two sections of the paper, we introduce different compatibility structures for assemblages of quantum channels (Section 6), and we study them in the case of generalized depolarizing channels (Section 7).

2. Classical and Quantum Fisher Information

Consider a family of probability distributions $\{p(x|\theta), x \in R\}$ parametrized by θ. A central research direction in statistics is to estimate the accuracy of the value of parameter θ by observing x outcomes sampled from the distributions. Recall that the (classical) *Fisher information* of the model is defined as

$$I(\theta) := \sum_x p(x|\theta) \left(\frac{\partial \log p(x|\theta)}{\partial \theta} \right)^2.$$

when an estimator $\hat{\theta}(x)$ of the parameter θ is unbiased, the inverse of the classical Fisher information gives a lower bound on the *mean square error* (MSE) of the estimator, which is the well-known *Cramér-Rao bound* [29,30]. The notion of the classical Fisher information plays a significant role in the geometrical approach to statistics [31,32] and the information theory approach to physics [33].

In the multiple-parameter scenario, when θ is a vector, the classical Fisher information is considered as a matrix form, which is a real symmetric matrix with matrix elements [34–36]:

$$I_{ij}(\theta) := \sum_x p(x|\theta) \frac{\partial \log p(x|\theta)}{\partial \theta_i} \frac{\partial \log p(x|\theta)}{\partial \theta_j}.$$

In a quantum parameter estimation scenario, we may perform the quantum positive operator-valued measurement (POVM) on a quantum state that depends on a parameter to extract the parameter information. Consider a quantum measurement $\mathbf{M} = \{M_x \geq 0, \sum_x M_x = I_d\}$ acting on the states $\rho(\theta) \in \mathcal{L}(H_d)$. The parameterized probability of outcomes x of the measurement is $p(x|\theta) = \text{Tr}[\rho(\theta) M_x]$. The corresponding measurement-induced Fisher information $I_\mathbf{M}(\theta)$ is then given by

$$I_\mathbf{M}(\theta) = \sum_x p(x|\theta) \text{Tr}\left(\frac{\partial \log \rho(\theta)}{\partial \theta} M_x \right)^2.$$

The *quantum Fisher information* of the model $\rho(\theta)$ is defined as [37]

$$J(\theta) := \text{Tr}[\rho(\theta) L(\theta)^2],$$

where the symmetric logarithmic derivative (SLD) operators $L(\theta)$ for the parameter θ are determined implicitly by

$$\frac{d\rho(\theta)}{\theta} = \frac{1}{2}[\rho(\theta)L(\theta) + L(\theta)\rho(\theta)].$$

In contrast with the classical Cramér-Rao bound, the inverse of quantum Fisher information is also a lower bound for the MSE of an unbiased estimator, which is called the *quantum Cramér-Rao bound* [37].

In quantum multiple-parameter estimation scenarios, both the measure-induced Fisher information and quantum Fisher information are matrices

$$I_{\mathbf{M},ij}(\theta) = \sum_x p(x|\theta) \operatorname{Tr}\left(\frac{\partial \log \rho(\theta)}{\partial \theta_i} M_x\right) \operatorname{Tr}\left(\frac{\partial \log \rho(\theta)}{\partial \theta_j} M_x\right), \quad (1)$$

$$J_{ij}(\theta) = \frac{1}{2} \operatorname{Tr}\{\rho(\theta)[L_i(\theta)L_j(\theta) + L_j(\theta)L_i(\theta)]\}, \quad (2)$$

where L_k is the SLD operator corresponding with θ_k. The measurement-induced Fisher information resembles the classical correlations, while the quantum Fisher information resembles the quantum mutual information. From the Braunstein–Caves theorem [36], the quantum Fisher information, independent of measurement, is an upper bound of the measurement-induced Fisher information in the positive semidefinite order for matrices:

$$I_{\mathbf{M}}(\theta) \leq J(\theta).$$

In this work, we shall consider another relationship proposed by Gill and Massar [38] for any d-dimensional quantum system:

$$\operatorname{Tr}[J^{-1}(\theta) I_{\mathbf{M}}(\theta)] \leq d - 1. \quad (3)$$

This inequality was the main ingredient in the incompatibility criterion invented by Zhu [27], which lies at the foundation of our incompatibility criterion for quantum channels.

3. Compatibility of Quantum Channels

In this section, we review the basic definitions of quantum channel compatibility.

Let H_d and H_D be Hilbert spaces, and $\mathcal{L}(H_d)$ denote the family of linear operators on H_d. In the Schrödinger picture, a *quantum channel* is defined as a linear map $\Phi : \mathcal{L}(H_d) \to \mathcal{L}(H_D)$ having the following two properties:

- *complete positivity*: for any dimension $k \geq 1$, the linear map $\operatorname{id}_k \otimes \Phi : \mathcal{L}(\mathbb{C}^k \otimes H_d) \to \mathcal{L}(\mathbb{C}^k \otimes H_D)$ is a positive operator;
- *trace-preservation*: for all operators $X \in \mathcal{L}(H_d)$, $\operatorname{Tr}\Phi(X) = \operatorname{Tr} X$.

We say that quantum channels are trace-preserving, completely positive (TPCP) maps. In this paper, we shall also consider the Heisenberg picture of quantum mechanics, where channels are seen as acting on observables instead of states. This amounts to considering the adjoint map $\Phi^* : \mathcal{L}(H_D) \to \mathcal{L}(H_d)$, where the adjoint is taken with respect to the Hilbert–Schmidt scalar product on the corresponding matrix spaces [21]:

$$\langle A, \Phi(\rho) \rangle = \langle \Phi^*(A), \rho \rangle,$$

where $\rho \in \mathcal{L}(H_d)$, $A \in \mathcal{L}(H_D)$, and $\langle X, Y \rangle := \operatorname{Tr}(X^* Y)$.

We now recall the definition of the compatibility of quantum channels and refer the reader to the review [20] for further properties.

Definition 1. *Consider two quantum channels $\Phi_1 : \mathcal{L}(H_d) \to \mathcal{L}(H_{d_1})$ and $\Phi_2 : \mathcal{L}(H_d) \to \mathcal{L}(H_{d_2})$ having the same input space. The pair (Φ_1, Φ_2) is said to be compatible, if there exists a joint channel $\Lambda : \mathcal{L}(H_d) \to \mathcal{L}(H_{d_1} \otimes H_{d_2})$ such that $\Phi_{1,2}$ are the marginals of Λ:*

$$\forall X \in \mathcal{L}(H_d), \quad \Phi_1(X) = \operatorname{Tr}_2 \Lambda(X) \quad \text{and} \quad \Phi_2(X) = \operatorname{Tr}_1 \Lambda(X),$$

where $\operatorname{Tr}_{1,2}$ denote the partial trace operations in $\mathcal{L}(H_{d_1} \otimes H_{d_2}) \cong \mathcal{L}(H_{d_1}) \otimes \mathcal{L}(H_{d_2})$.

In the Heisenberg (dual) picture, the condition above reads

$$\forall A \in \mathcal{L}(H_{d_1}), \quad \Phi_1^*(A) = \Lambda^*(A \otimes I_{d_2}), \quad \text{and} \quad \forall B \in \mathcal{L}(H_{d_2}), \quad \Phi_2^*(B) = \Lambda^*(I_{d_1} \otimes B).$$

The (in-)compatibility of more than two channels is defined in a similar manner.

As an example, let us consider the partially depolarizing channel, which is defined as:

$$\Phi_t = t \cdot \mathrm{id} + (1-t)\Delta, \qquad 0 \leq t \leq 1, \tag{4}$$

with $\mathrm{id}(A) = A$ and $\Delta(A) = \mathrm{Tr}(A) I_d/d$ for any operator A; these quantum channels will be discussed at length in Section 7. From the *no-cloning theorem* [3,4], it follows that two copies of the identity channel $(\mathrm{id}, \mathrm{id})$, are incompatible. On the other hand, the completely depolarizing channel Δ is compatible with any other channel. A question is the self-incompatibility of Φ_t. It is well known that the channel Φ_t is self-compatible if $0 \leq t \leq \frac{d+2}{2(d+1)}$ [26,39]. The necessary and sufficient condition for the compatibility of two different depolarizing channels Φ_s and Φ_t were shown in [40–42]:

$$t + s - \frac{2}{d}\sqrt{(1-t)(1-s)} \leq 1. \tag{5}$$

As previously discussed, quantum channel incompatibility is a key phenomenon in quantum theory, being at the heart of fundamental results in quantum information, such as the *no-cloning theorem*. In order to measure the degree of incompatibility of a given set of quantum channels, several definitions of the *robustness of incompatibility* have been considered in the literature [8,26,43]. In this section, we introduce a new such measure for a tuple of channels, which has the merit of taking into consideration the asymmetry between the channels considered. A similar definition was considered in the case of POVMs in [44,45]. We shall consider only channels acting on $\mathcal{L}(H_d)$, and we recall that Δ denotes the fully depolarizing channel $\Delta(X) = (\mathrm{Tr}\, X) I_d/d$.

Definition 2. *Given an N-tuple of quantum channels $\boldsymbol{\Phi} := (\Phi_1, \Phi_2, \ldots, \Phi_N)$, define the compatibility region of $\boldsymbol{\Phi}$ as*

$$\Gamma_{\boldsymbol{\Phi}} := \left\{ s \in [0,1]^N \;:\; \text{the channels } \left[s_i \Phi_i + (1-s_i)\Delta \right]_{i=1}^N \text{ are compatible} \right\}.$$

Note that the definition is a relevant event in the case where the channels Φ_i are identical: $\Phi_i = \Phi$ for all $i \in [N]$, in which case we call $\Gamma_\Phi := \Gamma_{\boldsymbol{\Phi}}$ the *self-compatibility* region (note that the dependence in N is still present since we are consider N copies of the channel Φ).

The following result is a simple exercise.

Proposition 1. *For any N-tuple of quantum channels $\boldsymbol{\Phi} := (\Phi_1, \Phi_2, \ldots, \Phi_N)$, the set $\Gamma_{\boldsymbol{\Phi}}$ is convex and closed (i.e., a convex body). We have $0 \in \Gamma_{\boldsymbol{\Phi}}$, and, for all $i \in [N]$,*

$$e_i := (0, \ldots, 0, \underbrace{1}_{\text{i-th position}}, 0, \ldots, 0) \in \Gamma_{\boldsymbol{\Phi}}.$$

4. Channel Incompatibility via POVM Incompatibility

This is the main section of our paper, where we put forward a new incompatibility criterion for quantum channels in Theorem 1. Our criterion is based on an incompatibility criterion for quantum measurements (POVMs) introduced by H. Zhu and his collaborators [27,28].

Let us start by recalling the definition of compatibility (or joint measurability) of quantum measurements. First, recall that a *quantum measurement* (or POVM) is a k-tuple of operators $\mathbf{A} = (A_1, A_2, \ldots, A_k)$, having the following two properties:

- *positivity*: the operators $A_1, \ldots, A_k \in \mathcal{L}(H_d)$ are positive semidefinite;
- *normalization*: $\sum_{i=1}^k A_i = I_d$.

A POVM gives the most general form of a physical process that produces the probabilities given by the *Born rule*: when measuring a quantum system described by a density matrix ρ, one obtains the result $i \in [k]$ with probability

$$\mathbb{P}[\text{ outcome } i] = \text{Tr}(\rho A_i).$$

Naturally, one can see a POVM **A** as a quantum-to-classical channel

$$\Phi_{\mathbf{A}}(X) = \sum_{i=1}^{k} \text{Tr}(XA_i)|i\rangle\langle i|,$$

where $\{|i\rangle\}_{i=1}^{k}$ denotes the canonical basis of $\mathbb{C}^k$ corresponding to the pointer states of the measurement apparatus.

Whether two (or more) quantum measurements can be performed simultaneously is one of the crucial questions lying at the foundations of quantum theory [1,2]. Mathematically, we have the following important definition (compare with Definition 1).

Definition 3. *Two POVMs $\mathbf{A} = \{A_i\}_{i \in [k]}$ and $\mathbf{B} = \{B_j\}_{k \in [l]}$ are said to be* compatible *(or jointly measurable) if there exists a third POVM $\mathbf{C} = \{C_{ij}\}_{(i,j) \in [k] \times [l]}$, called* joint measurement, *such that*

$$\forall i \in [k], \quad A_i = \sum_{j=1}^{l} C_{ij},$$

$$\forall j \in [l], \quad B_j = \sum_{i=1}^{k} C_{ij}.$$

Otherwise, the measurements $\mathbf{A}$ and $\mathbf{B}$ are called incompatible [46]. *The compatibility of more than two measurements is defined similarly.*

Quantum measurement (in-)compatibility has received a lot of attention in the literature, see, e.g., the excellent reviews [20,47], or the recent perspective on the problem focusing on the post-processing partial order [48]. Importantly for us, in [27], H. Zhu proposed a family of universal *POVM incompatibility criteria* based on the classical Fisher information matrix. Assume a measurement $\mathbf{C}$ is the joint measurement of $\mathbf{A}_i$. According to the Fisher information data-processing inequality, the measurement-induced Fisher information matrix of $\mathbf{A}_i$ should not exceed that of $\mathbf{C}$, that is to say

$$I_{\mathbf{A}_i} \leq I_{\mathbf{C}}$$

for all quantum states θ (θ is omitted in the formula above for convenience); the Fisher information matrix I was defined in Equation (1). Define $\tilde{I}_{\mathbf{A}_i} := J^{-1/2} I_{\mathbf{A}_i} J^{-1/2}$ as the metric-adjusted Fisher information. The following inequality holds for compatible measurements based on the Gill–Massar inequality (3):

$$\min\left\{\text{Tr } H : H \geq \tilde{I}_{\mathbf{A}_i} \quad \forall i \in [N]\right\} \leq d - 1. \tag{6}$$

Otherwise, the *N*-tuple of measurements $(\mathbf{A}_i)_{i \in [N]}$ is incompatible. When the parameter θ (the state around which we compute the Fisher information) corresponds to the maximally mixed state $\theta = I_d/d$, inequality (6) can be rephrased as the following proposition [27,28].

Proposition 2. *For a set of N measurements $\mathbf{A} = (\mathbf{A}_1, \mathbf{A}_2, \ldots, \mathbf{A}_N)$ on $\mathcal{L}(H_d)$, define the operators*

$$\forall i \in [N] \qquad G_{\mathbf{A}_i} := \sum_{s=1}^{k_i} |A_i(s)\rangle\langle A_i(s)| / [\text{Tr}(A_i(s))] \in \mathcal{L}(H_d^{\otimes 2}),$$

where $A_i(1), A_i(2), \ldots, A_i(k_i)$ are the (non-zero) effects of the POVM $\mathbf{A}_i$, having k_i outcomes. Consider now the quantity

$$\begin{aligned} \tau(\mathbf{A}) := \min \quad & \operatorname{Tr} H \\ \text{s.t.} \quad & H \geq G_{\mathbf{A}_i} \quad \forall i \in [N]. \end{aligned} \qquad (7)$$

If $\tau(\mathbf{A}) > d$, then the N-tuple of POVMs $\mathbf{A} = (\mathbf{A}_1, \mathbf{A}_2, \ldots, \mathbf{A}_N)$ is incompatible.

Remark 1. *Note that the function $\tau(\mathbf{A})$ satisfies two basic requirements for a good measure of (in-)compatibility: monotonicity under coarse-graining and global unitary invariance.*

Remark 2. *For any POVM $\mathbf{A}$, the associated matrix $G_\mathbf{A}$ is larger, in the positive semidefinite order, than the maximally entangled state*

$$\omega := \frac{1}{d} \sum_{i,j=1}^{d} |ii\rangle\langle jj|.$$

This fact is a consequence of the important observation that the $\mathbf{A} \mapsto G_\mathbf{A}$ is an order morphism for the post-processing order of quantum measurements [48], and $G_{\{I\}} = \omega$.

A natural question is how to capture the incompatibility of quantum channels using measurements. Let $\{|e_j\rangle\}$ and $\{|f_k\rangle\}$ be any sets of the basis of Hilbert spaces H_{d_1} and H_{d_2}, respectively. Motivated by the definition of incompatibility of quantum channels, we dedicate to research properties of the induced sets $\{\Phi_1^*(|e_j\rangle\langle e_j|)\}$ and $\{\Phi_2^*(|f_k\rangle\langle f_k|)\}$. As we consider the quantum channel is trace-preserving, thus $\{\Phi_1^*(|e_j\rangle\langle e_j|)\}$ and $\{\Phi_2^*(|f_k\rangle\langle f_k|)\}$ can be regarded as POVMs [23], that is to say,

$$\sum_j \Phi_1^*(|e_j\rangle\langle e_j|) = \sum_k \Phi_2^*(|f_k\rangle\langle f_k|) = I_d. \qquad (8)$$

Lemma 1. *[21] If N quantum channels $\Phi_1, \Phi_2, \ldots, \Phi_N$ are compatible, then, for all orthonormal bases $\mathbf{e}^{(1)}, \mathbf{e}^{(2)}, \ldots, \mathbf{e}^{(N)}$ of $\mathbb{C}^d$, the corresponding POVMs*

$$\mathbf{A}_s := \left[\Phi_s^*(|\mathbf{e}_i^{(s)}\rangle\langle \mathbf{e}_i^{(s)}|) \right]_{i=1}^d, \quad \forall s \in [N]$$

are compatible.

Proof. Let Λ be a joint channel for the compatible N-tuple $(\Phi_1, \Phi_2, \ldots, \Phi_N)$. Clearly, $\Lambda : \mathcal{L}(H_d) \to \mathcal{L}(H_d^{\otimes N})$ thus its adjoint is an unital, completely positive map

$$\Lambda^* : \mathcal{L}(H_d^{\otimes N}) \to \mathcal{L}(H_d).$$

Define operators

$$\mathbf{B} := \left[\Lambda^* \Big(\bigotimes_{s=1}^N |\mathbf{e}_{i_s}^{(s)}\rangle\langle \mathbf{e}_{i_s}^{(s)}| \Big) \right]_{i_1,\ldots,i_N \in [d]}.$$

From the fact that Λ^* is a completely positive, unital map, we infer that $\mathbf{B}$ is a POVM (with d^N outcomes). Let us now compute the marginals of this POVM. For some fixed $s \in [N]$ and $i_s \in [d]$, we have

$$\sum_{i_1,\ldots,i_{s-1},i_{s+1},\ldots,i_N \in [d]} B_{i_1 \cdots i_N} = \Lambda^*(I_d \otimes \cdots \otimes |\mathbf{e}_{i_s}^{(s)}\rangle\langle \mathbf{e}_{i_s}^{(s)}| \otimes \cdots \otimes I_d) = \Phi_s^*(|\mathbf{e}_{i_s}^{(s)}\rangle\langle \mathbf{e}_{i_s}^{(s)}|) = \mathbf{A}_s(i_s), \qquad (9)$$

showing that the s-th marginal of $\mathbf{B}$ is $\mathbf{A}_s$. Thus $\mathbf{B}$ is a joint measurement of $\mathbf{A}_1, \mathbf{A}_2, \ldots, \mathbf{A}_N$, proving the claim. □

We leave open the reciprocal question, which we formulate as a conjecture (below for two channels, although the general version, for a N-tuple, can be easily stated).

Conjecture 1. *Consider two quantum channels* $\Phi, \Psi : \mathcal{L}(H_d) \to \mathcal{L}(H_d)$ *such that, for all orthonormal bases* $\mathbf{e} = (e_1, \ldots, e_d)$, $\mathbf{f} = (f_1, \ldots, f_d)$ *of* $\mathbb{C}^d$, *the POVMs*

$$\left[\Phi^*(|e_i\rangle\langle e_i|)\right]_{i=1}^d \quad \text{and} \quad \left[\Psi^*(|f_j\rangle\langle f_j|)\right]_{j=1}^d$$

are compatible. Then, Φ *and* Ψ *are compatible channels.*

We now turn to the main theoretical result of our paper: a criterion for quantum channel incompatibility. Informally, one can formulate it as follows: given an N-tuple of quantum channels, if one can find an N-tuple of orthonormal bases such that the corresponding quantum measurements are incompatible, then the original N-tuple of channels must also be incompatible. Our criterion is important since there are very few useful incompatibility criteria for channel incompatibility. On the other hand, there exist quite numerous incompatibility criteria for quantum measurements, so one can turn those into criteria for channels using Lemma 1. We introduce the following important notation: to a quantum channel $\Phi : \mathcal{L}(H_d) \to \mathcal{L}(H_d)$ and an orthonormal basis $\mathbf{e} = (e_i)_{i=1}^d$ of $\mathbb{C}^d$, we associate the G matrix

$$G_{\Phi, \mathbf{e}} := \sum_{i=1}^d \frac{|\Phi^*(|e_i\rangle\langle e_i|)\rangle\langle\Phi^*(|e_i\rangle\langle e_i|)|}{\operatorname{Tr}\Phi^*(|e_i\rangle\langle e_i|)}, \tag{10}$$

which corresponds to the G matrix associated to the POVM

$$\left[\Phi^*(|e_i\rangle\langle e_i|)\right]_{i=1}^d.$$

Theorem 1. *Let* $\Phi_1, \Phi_2, \ldots, \Phi_N : \mathcal{L}(H_d) \to \mathcal{L}(H_d)$ *be N quantum channels. If there exists orthonormal bases* $\mathbf{e}^{(1)}, \mathbf{e}^{(2)}, \ldots, \mathbf{e}^{(N)}$ *of* $\mathbb{C}^d$ *such that the value of the semidefinite program*

$$\begin{aligned} \min \quad & \operatorname{Tr} H \\ \text{s.t.} \quad & H \geq G_{\Phi_i, \mathbf{e}^{(i)}} \quad \forall i \in [N] \end{aligned} \tag{11}$$

is strictly larger than d, then the n-tuple of channels $\mathbf{\Phi} = (\Phi_1, \Phi_2, \ldots, \Phi_N)$ *is incompatible.*

Proof. The theorem follows directly from Proposition 2 and Lemma 1. □

Remark 3. *If the quantum channel* Φ *is unital, that is to say,* $\Phi(I_d) = I_d$, *the formula* (10) *simplifies, in the sense that the denominator is trivial:*

$$\operatorname{Tr}\Phi^*(|e_i\rangle\langle e_i|) = \langle I_d, \Phi^*(|e_i\rangle\langle e_i|)\rangle = \langle \Phi(I_d), |e_i\rangle\langle e_i|\rangle = \langle I_d, |e_i\rangle\langle e_i|\rangle = \operatorname{Tr}|e_i\rangle\langle e_i| = 1. \tag{12}$$

This will be the case for most of the examples we shall discuss in what follows.

It is important at this point to note that the incompatibility criterion we put forward in the result above is formulated as an SDP (semidefinite program). The usual way of formulating the compatibility of a tuple of quantum channels is also an SDP: one looks for a joint channel, a problem that can be formulated as an SDP thanks to the Choi formalism. However, let us compare the size of the SDPs:

- channel compatibility: the joint channel has a Choi matrix of size d^{N+1}
- incompatibility criterion from Theorem 1: the variable H has size d^2.

Note also that one has, in both cases, N constraints of size d^2. Therefore, we obtain a dramatic reduction in the size of the SDP at the price of having only a necessary compatibility condition (i.e., an incompatibility criterion).

There is, however, a situation when SDP (11) simplifies and can be analytically solved. This is when the matrices G corresponding to the channel are orthogonal (up to the maximally entangled state ω). We formalize this observation below.

Proposition 3. *Consider N quantum channels $\Phi_1, \Phi_2, \ldots, \Phi_N : \mathcal{L}(H_d) \to \mathcal{L}(H_d)$ and orthonormal bases $\mathbf{e}^{(1)}, \mathbf{e}^{(2)}, \ldots, \mathbf{e}^{(N)}$ such that, for all $i, j \in [N]$, $i \neq j$,*

$$G_{\Phi_i, \mathbf{e}^{(i)}} - \omega \perp G_{\Phi_j, \mathbf{e}^{(j)}} - \omega.$$

Then, the value of SDP (11) is

$$1 - N + \sum_{i=1}^{N} \operatorname{Tr} G_{\Phi_i, \mathbf{e}^{(i)}}.$$

Proof. Taking into consideration Remark 2, one can rewrite SDP (11) by subtracting ω everywhere:

$$\begin{aligned} 1 + \min \quad & \operatorname{Tr} \tilde{H} \\ \text{s.t.} \quad & \tilde{H} \geq G_{\Phi_i, \mathbf{e}^{(i)}} - \omega \quad \forall i \in [N] \end{aligned} \tag{13}$$

where $\tilde{H} = H - \omega$. Using the hypothesis and noting that the matrices $G_{\Phi_i, \mathbf{e}^{(i)}} - \omega$ are all positive semidefinite, any feasible $\tilde{H}$ must satisfy

$$\tilde{H} \geq \sum_{i=1}^{N} G_{\Phi_i, \mathbf{e}^{(i)}} - \omega.$$

Hence, the optimal $\tilde{H}$ achieves equality above, and the conclusion follows. □

This idea will be used in Sections 5 and 7 to obtain (analytical) incompatibility criteria for important classes of quantum channels.

As an example, let us work out the G matrix for the identity channel $\operatorname{id}(X) = X$.

$$G_{\operatorname{id}, \mathbf{e}} = \sum_{i=1}^{d} \big| |e_i\rangle\langle e_i| \big\rangle \big\langle |e_i\rangle\langle e_i| \big| = \sum_{i=1}^{d} |e_i \otimes \bar{e}_i\rangle\langle e_i \otimes \bar{e}_i| =: Z_\mathbf{e}. \tag{14}$$

The matrix $Z_\mathbf{e}$ will play an important role in what follows. We gather some useful facts about it below. Recall that two orthonormal bases $\mathbf{e}, \mathbf{f}$ of $\mathbb{C}^d$ are called *unbiased* if

$$\forall i, j \in [d], \quad |\langle e_i, f_j \rangle| = \frac{1}{\sqrt{d}}.$$

Lemma 2. *For any orthonormal basis $\mathbf{e}$, we have*

$$\langle Z_\mathbf{e}, \omega \rangle = 1.$$

Moreover, if $\mathbf{e}$ and $\mathbf{f}$ are unbiased orthonormal bases, then

$$\langle Z_\mathbf{e}, Z_\mathbf{f} \rangle = 1.$$

Let us close this section by mentioning how the matrices G behave when mixing noise into a quantum channel Φ. This property will be very useful in what follows when investigating the compatibility robustness of some classes of quantum channels.

Lemma 3. *Given a quantum channel* $\Phi : \mathcal{L}(H_d) \to \mathcal{L}(H_d)$, *consider its noisy version*

$$\Phi_t := t\Phi + (1-t)\Delta,$$

where $\Delta(X) = (\operatorname{Tr} X)I/d$ *is the completely depolarizing channel, and* $t \in [0,1]$ *is some parameter. Then, for any orthonormal basis* **e**,

$$G_{\Phi_t,\mathbf{e}} = t^2 G_{\Phi,\mathbf{e}} + (1-t^2)\omega,$$

where ω *is the maximally entangled state (note that* $\omega = G_{\Delta,\mathbf{e}}$).

Proof. This can either be proven directly using formula (10) or by using the corresponding result for POVMs, see, e.g., ([48] Proposition 5.3). □

5. Incompatibility of Two Schur Channels

As the first application of our newly introduced incompatibility criterion for quantum channels, we consider *Schur channels*. A Schur map is a linear map of the form

$$\Sigma_B(X) = B \circ X,$$

where B is a $d \times d$ complex matrix and $\circ$ denotes the Hadamard product. The map Σ_B is completely positive if and only if matrix B is positive semidefinite, and it is trace-preserving if the diagonal of B is the identity: $B_{ii} = 1$ for all i. If both conditions are satisfied, we call map Σ_B a Schur channel (sometimes also called a Schur multiplier), see [49–52]. Schur channels have received a lot of attention in operator algebra and quantum information theory, and they contain the identity channel id $= \Sigma_J$, where J is the all 1s matrix, and the dephasing channel (the conditional expectation on the diagonal sub-algebra) diag $= \Sigma_I$ as examples.

For Schur channel Σ_B, we have

$$G_{\Sigma_B,\mathbf{e}} = |\bar{B}\rangle\langle\bar{B}| \circ Z_{\mathbf{e}},$$

for any orthonormal basis **e** (recall the form of the matrix Z from (14)). If **e** is the canonical basis, we have

$$G_{\Sigma_B,\mathrm{can}} = Z_{\mathrm{can}}.$$

Consider now a basis **f** that is unbiased with respect to the canonical basis; in other works, the elements of **f** form the columns of a Hadamard matrix U: $|f_j\rangle = U|j\rangle$ for all j. An important example of such a basis is the *Fourier basis*:

$$f_j(s) = \exp(2\pi i/d)^{js}, \quad \forall j,s \in [d].$$

Lemma 4. *If B and C are two positive semidefinite matrices with unit diagonal, and* **can** *and* **f** *are unbiased, then*

$$G_{\Sigma_B,\mathrm{can}} - \omega \perp G_{\Sigma_C,\mathbf{f}} - \omega.$$

Proof. Expanding the scalar product and using Lemma 2, we need to show that

$$\langle Z_{\mathrm{can}}, |\bar{C}\rangle\langle\bar{C}| \circ Z_{\mathbf{f}}\rangle = \langle \omega, |\bar{C}\rangle\langle\bar{C}| \circ Z_{\mathbf{f}}\rangle.$$

Let us work out the left-hand-side:

$$\langle Z_{\mathrm{can}}, |\bar{C}\rangle\langle\bar{C}| \circ Z_{\mathbf{f}}\rangle = \langle |C\rangle\langle C| \circ Z_{\mathrm{can}}, Z_{\mathbf{f}}\rangle = \langle Z_{\mathrm{can}}, Z_{\mathbf{f}}\rangle = 1,$$

where we have used Lemma 2 and the fact that $|C\rangle\langle C| \circ Z_{\mathrm{can}} = Z_{\mathrm{can}}$, which follows from the fact that C has unit diagonal. The right-hand-side can be dealt with in the same manner. □

For a $d \times d$ matrix B with unit diagonal, define the real parameter $\beta(B)$ as follows:

$$\beta(B) := \frac{1}{d-1}\left(\frac{1}{d}\sum_{i,j=1}^d |B_{ij}|^2 - 1\right) = \frac{1}{d-1}\sum_{i\neq j\in[d]} |B_{ij}|^2. \tag{15}$$

Recall that the torus $\mathbb{T}^d$ is the set of vectors $b \in \mathbb{C}^d$ with $|b_i| = 1$ for all $i = 1, \ldots, d$.

Lemma 5. *If B is a $d \times d$ positive semidefinite matrix with unit diagonal, then*

$$0 \leq \beta(B) \leq 1,$$

with $\beta(B) = 0$ iff $B = I$ and $\beta(B) = 1$ iff $B = |b\rangle\langle b|$ for a vector $b \in \mathbb{T}^d$.

Proof. The non-negativity of β, as well as the equality case, follows directly from definition (15). For the upper bound, use the ordering of the 1, 2-Schatten norms of B to write

$$\sum_{i,j=1}^d |B_{ij}|^2 = \|B\|_2^2 \leq \|B\|_1^2 = (\operatorname{Tr} B)^2 = d^2,$$

proving the inequality. Equality holds if B is rank one, which, together with the condition on the diagonal, proves that $B = |b\rangle\langle b|$ for some vector $b \in \mathbb{T}^d$. □

We can now, using Theorem 1, provide a new incompatibility criterion for Schur channels.

Theorem 2. *Consider two positive semidefinite matrices B and C with unit diagonal, and the corresponding depolarized Schur channels*

$$\Phi_s(X) = s\Sigma_B(X) + (1-s)\Delta(X) = sB \circ X + (1-s)(\operatorname{Tr} X)\frac{I}{d}$$
$$\Psi_t(X) = t\Sigma_C(X) + (1-t)\Delta(X) = tC \circ X + (1-t)(\operatorname{Tr} X)\frac{I}{d}.$$

If $s^2 + \beta(C)t^2 > 1$, then the channels Φ_s and Ψ_t are incompatible. We have, thus, an upper bound for the compatibility region from Definition 2:

$$\Gamma_{\Phi,\Psi} \subseteq \{(s,t) \in [0,1]^2 : s^2 + \beta(C)t^2 \leq 1 \text{ and } \beta(B)s^2 + t^2 \leq 1\}, \tag{16}$$

where $\Phi := \Phi_1$ and $\Psi := \Psi_1$.

Proof. The proof is an application of Theorem 1. To start, let us compute the G matrices associated with these channels, taking, respectively, the canonical basis **can**, and any unbiased base **f** (e.g., the Fourier basis); this choice is inspired by Lemma 4 and Proposition 3. Applying these results, as well as the scaling Lemma 3, we have

$$G_{\Phi_s,\text{can}} = s^2 G_{\Sigma_B,\text{can}} + (1-s^2)\omega = \omega + s^2(Z_{\text{can}} - \omega)$$
$$G_{\Psi_t,\mathbf{f}} = t^2 G_{\Sigma_C,\mathbf{f}} + (1-t^2)\omega = \omega + t^2(|\bar{C}\rangle\langle\bar{C}| \circ Z_{\mathbf{f}} - \omega).$$

Hence, the value of SDP (11) is given by (see Proposition 3)

$$1 - 2 + \operatorname{Tr} G_{\Phi_s,\text{can}} + \operatorname{Tr} G_{\Psi_t,\mathbf{f}} = s^2(d-1) + 1 - t^2 + t^2 \operatorname{Tr}[|\bar{C}\rangle\langle\bar{C}| \circ Z_{\mathbf{f}}].$$

We can evaluate

$$\operatorname{Tr}[|\bar{C}\rangle\langle\bar{C}| \circ Z_{\mathbf{f}}] = \frac{1}{d}\sum_{i,j=1}^d |C_{ij}|^2,$$

and, using parameter $\beta(C)$ from (15), the incompatibility criterion reads

$$s^2 + \beta(C)t^2 > 1,$$

which is the first claim. The second claim follows by swapping the roles of the unbiased bases **can** and **f**. □

Remark 4. *One can not easily generalize the result above to more than two Schur channels. This is due to the fact that one has to fix one of the bases in Theorem 1 to be the canonical basis. This is due to the fact that the Hadamard product used to define Schur channels is adapted to the canonical basis. We leave the generalization of the result (and method) above for three or more Schur channels open.*

We compare, in Figure 1, the criterion from the theorem above with the actual incompatibility thresholds for some particular Schur channels, concluding that the incompatibility criterion is close to being exact.

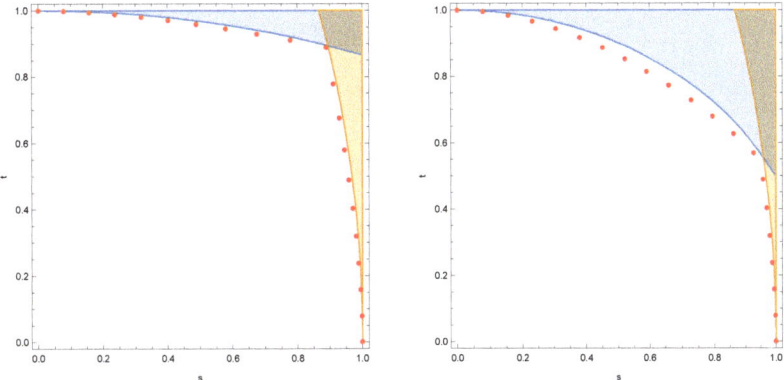

Figure 1. The Fisher information-based incompatibility criterion for Schur channels. In the left panel, we consider two noisy copies of the Schur channel corresponding to $B = \begin{bmatrix} 1 & 1/2 \\ 1/2 & 1 \end{bmatrix}$. In the right panel, we consider noisy versions of Σ_B and Σ_C, where $C = \begin{bmatrix} 1 & \sqrt{3/4} \\ \sqrt{3/4} & 1 \end{bmatrix}$. Shaded regions correspond to the conditions from (16), while the red dots correspond to the maximally compatible channels in the respective directions.

6. Channel Assemblages

The way in which several quantum measurement and quantum channels can be incompatible has been studied extensively in the literature [53–56]. The kind of (in-)compatibility structures that can be found in nature, and their relation to other important manifestations of non-locality (such as Bell inequality violations), is clearly a crucial question at the foundation of quantum theory.

Let $\{\Phi_i\}_{i=1}^N$ be a *channel assemblage* that is an N-tuple of quantum channels. If $\{\Phi_i\}_{i=1}^N$ are incompatible, there does not exist a joint quantum channel for *all* the N channels. However, a joint channel may exist when we consider a certain subset of $\{\Phi_i\}_{i=1}^N$. In other words, some subsets of $\{\Phi_i\}_{i=1}^N$ may be compatible, even though the whole set is incompatible. Obviously, if the whole set of N channels is compatible, then so is any subset: if Λ is a joint channel for the N-tuple. Then, for any subset $S \subseteq [N]$ of the channels, Λ_S, the marginal of Λ corresponding to the output indices in S

$$\Lambda_S : \mathcal{L}(H_d) \to \mathcal{L}\left(\bigotimes_{i \in S} H_d^{(i)}\right)$$

is a joint channel for $\{\Phi_i\}_{i\in S}$; above, we identify the different copies of the output space $\mathcal{L}(H_d)$ by a superscript. Therefore, it is significant to classify the incompatibility of subsets for a given quantum channel assemblage. A *K-subset* of $[N]$ is simply a subset $S \subseteq [N]$ of cardinality $|S| = K$.

Definition 4. *Consider a quantum channel assemblage* $\Phi = \{\Phi_i\}_{i=1}^N$ *and* $1 \leq K \leq N$ *an integer. The N-tuple* Φ *is called:*

- *(N, K)-compatible if all K-subsets of* Φ *are compatible.*
- *(N, K)-incompatible if at least one K-subset of* Φ *is incompatible.*
- *(N, K)-strong incompatible if all K-subsets of* Φ *are incompatible.*
- *(N, K + 1)-genuinely incompatible if it is (N, K)-compatible and (N, K + 1)-incompatible.*
- *(N, K + 1)-genuinely strong incompatible if it is (N, K)-compatible and (N, K + 1)-strong incompatible.*

Note that the assemblage $\{\Phi_i\}_{i=1}^N$ is compatible if and only if it is (N, N)-compatible. The previous definition is strongly inspired by the one from ([56] Section 2) in the case of POVMs. The incompatibility criterion from Theorem 1 can be readily adapted to the previous definition by considering subsets of the PSD constraints in (11). We restate it here for the convenience of the reader. We shall apply it in the next section for assemblages of depolarizing channels.

Theorem 3. *Consider an assemblage* $\Phi = \{\Phi_i\}_{i=1}^N$ *of quantum channels acting on* $\mathcal{L}(H_d)$. *For a K-subset S of* $[N]$, *and K orthonormal bases* $\mathbf{e} = (\mathbf{e}^{(1)}, \mathbf{e}^{(2)}, \ldots, \mathbf{e}^{(K)})$ *of* $\mathbb{C}^d$, *define the value of the following semidefinite program*

$$\mathrm{val}(\Phi, S, \mathbf{e}) := \min \quad \mathrm{Tr}\, H$$
$$\text{s.t.} \quad H \geq G_{\Phi_i, \mathbf{e}^{(i)}} \quad \forall i \in S. \tag{17}$$

If there exists at least one $S \in [N]$ *and a K-tuple of orthonormal bases* $\mathbf{e}$ *such that* $\mathrm{val}(\Phi, S, \mathbf{e}) > d$, *then the assemblage* Φ *is* (N, K)-*incompatible. Moreover, if for all K-subsets* $S \subseteq [N]$, *there exists a K-tuple of bases* $\mathbf{e}_S$ *such that* $\mathrm{val}(\Phi, S, \mathbf{e}_S) > d$, *the assemblage* Φ *is* (N, K)-*strong incompatible.*

7. Assemblages of Depolarizing Channels

In this section, we address the (in-)compatibility properties of an N-tuple of partially depolarizing channels, using the Fisher information-based criterion from Theorem 1. Recall that the *partially depolarizing channel* is the linear map $\Phi_t : \mathcal{L}(H_d) \to \mathcal{L}(H_d)$ given by

$$\Phi_t = t \cdot \mathrm{id} + (1-t)\Delta, \tag{18}$$

where id is the identity channel $\mathrm{id}(X) = X$ and Δ is the fully depolarizing channel $\Delta(X) = (\mathrm{Tr}\, X)I/d$. The parameter $t \in [0, 1]$ interpolates between the identity channel and the fully depolarizing channel.

In this section, we shall study the incompatibility of N partially depolarizing channels $\{\Phi_{t_i}^i\}_{i=1}^N$, for some fixed parameters $t_1, t_2, \ldots, t_N \in [0, 1]$, with the help of the criterion from Theorem 1. To do so, let us first compute the G matrices of depolarizing channels, which are just noisy versions of the identity channel. Recall from Equation (14) that, for the identity channel, we have, for an arbitrary basis $\mathbf{e}$,

$$Z_{\mathbf{e}} = G_{\mathrm{id}, \mathbf{e}} = \sum_{i=1}^d |e_i \otimes \bar{e}_i\rangle\langle e_i \otimes \bar{e}_i|,$$

where $\bar{e}_i$ denotes the (entrywise) complex conjugate of the vector e_i. Hence, by Lemma 3, we have

$$G_{\Phi_t, \mathbf{e}} = t^2 Z_{\mathbf{e}} + (1 - t^2)\omega.$$

As in Section 5, we are going to use the orthogonality of the G matrices in order to put forward analytical incompatibility criteria for depolarizing channels (see Proposition 3). To do so, recall that the $Z_{\mathbf{e}}$ matrices have tractable scalar products for unbiased bases. As it turns out, mutually unbiased bases [57] will play an important role in what follows. Let D_d be the maximal cardinality of a set of mutually unbiased bases of $\mathbb{C}^d$. It is known that $3 \leq D_d \leq d+1$ [58–60]. The upper bounds are attained for all dimensions d, which are prime powers; whether it is always attained is an important open problem in quantum information theory, even the case $d = 6$ being undecided.

We now state the main result of this section, an incompatibility criterion for depolarizing channels.

Proposition 4. *Let N be an integer such that $N \leq D_d$, the maximal number of mutually unbiased bases of $\mathbb{C}^d$. Consider N depolarizing channels $\Phi_{t_1}, \ldots, \Phi_{t_N}$, where $t_1, \ldots, t_N \in [0,1]$ are noise parameters. If*

$$t_1^2 + t_2^2 + \cdots + t_N^2 > 1 \tag{19}$$

then the N depolarizing channels Φ_{t_i} are incompatible.

Proof. Since the number of channels we consider is smaller than D_d, we can choose N mutually unbiased bases $\mathbf{e}^{(1)}, \ldots, \mathbf{e}^{(N)}$. SDP (11) reads

$$\begin{aligned}
\min \quad & \operatorname{Tr} H \\
\text{s.t.} \quad & H \geq t_i^2 Z_{\mathbf{e}^{(i)}} + (1 - t_i^2)\omega \quad \forall i \in [N].
\end{aligned}$$

Proposition 3 applies, so the value of the SDP above is

$$\min \operatorname{Tr} H = 1 + (d-1) \sum_{i=1}^N t_i^2.$$

Hence, if condition (19) holds, by Theorem 1, the N quantum depolarizing channels $\Phi_{t_1}, \ldots, \Phi_{t_N}$ are incompatible. □

As mentioned in the introduction, the compatibility of depolarizing channels is equivalent to approximate quantum cloning: how much noise one needs to add to N copies of the identity channel to render them compatible. In Figure 2, we present the relative performance of the criterion from Proposition 4, with the true values of the noise parameters for $1 \to 2$ asymmetric approximate quantum clonings from Equation (5).

We can specialize the result above to assemblages of depolarizing channels in the spirit of Definition 4.

Corollary 1. *Consider N partially depolarizing channels $\{\Phi_{t_i}\}_{i=1}^N$ acting on $\mathcal{L}(H_d)$ and let $K \leq \min(N, D_d)$ be an integer. If there exists a subset $S \subseteq [N]$ of cardinality K such that*

$$\sum_{i \in S} t_i^2 > 1,$$

then the channels are (N, K)-incompatible. Moreover, if for every subset $S \subseteq [N]$ of cardinality K the condition above holds, the channels are (N, K)-strongly incompatible.

Note that in the statement above, we do not require that the number N of channels must be smaller than the number of mutually unbiased bases in the corresponding Hilbert space; this is required only of the parameter K. This criterion might thus be useful in situations where one has a large number of channels.

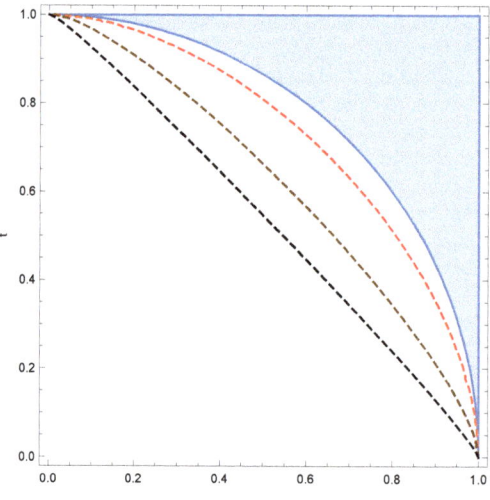

Figure 2. Comparing the incompatibility criterion from Proposition 4 (filled region) with the incompatibility thresholds from Equation (5) (dashed curves) for different values of d: $d = 2$ (red curve), $d = 5$ (brown curve), $d = 20$ (black curve).

We end this section by a similar corollary, in the setting where the channels are identical.

Corollary 2. *If N, K are integers such that $K \leq \min(N, D_d)$, then the partially depolarizing channel Φ_t from Equation (18) is (N, K)-self-(strong) incompatible as soon as $t > 1/\sqrt{K}$.*

Author Contributions: Supervision, I.N.; Writing—original draft, Q.-H.Z.; Writing—review and editing, I.N. All authors have read and agreed to the published version of the manuscript.

Funding: The authors were supported by the ANR project ESQuisses, grant number ANR-20-CE47-0014-01 and by the China Scholarship Council.

Conflicts of Interest: The authors declare no conflict of interest.

References

1. Heisenberg, W. Über den anschaulichen Inhalt der quantentheoretischen Kinematik und Mechanik. *Z. Für Phys.* **1927**, *43*, 172–198. [CrossRef]
2. Bohr, N. The quantum postulate and the recent development of atomic theory. *Nature* **1928**, *121*, 580–590.
3. Dieks, D. Communication by EPR devices. *Phys. Lett. A* **1982**, *92*, 271–272. [CrossRef]
4. Wootters, W.K.; Zurek, W.H. A single quantum cannot be cloned. *Nature* **1982**, *299*, 802–803. [CrossRef]
5. Vidal, G.; Tarrach, R. Robustness of entanglement. *Phys. Rev. A* **1999**, *59*, 141–155. [CrossRef]
6. Steiner, M. Generalized robustness of entanglement. *Phys. Rev. A* **2003**, *67*, 054305. [CrossRef]
7. Uola, R.; Budroni, C.; Gühne, O.; Pellonpää, J.P. One-to-One Mapping between Steering and Joint Measurability Problems. *Phys. Rev. Lett.* **2015**, *115*, 230402. [CrossRef]
8. Uola, R.; Kraft, T.; Shang, J.; Yu, X.D.; Gühne, O. Quantifying Quantum Resources with Conic Programming. *Phys. Rev. Lett.* **2019**, *122*, 130404. [CrossRef]
9. Designolle, S.; Farkas, M.; Kaniewski, J. Incompatibility robustness of quantum measurements: a unified framework. *New J. Phys.* **2019**, *21*, 113053. [CrossRef]
10. Wolf, M.M.; Perez-Garcia, D.; Fernandez, C. Measurements Incompatible in Quantum Theory Cannot Be Measured Jointly in Any Other No-Signaling Theory. *Phys. Rev. Lett.* **2009**, *103*, 230402. [CrossRef]
11. Bene, E.; Vértesi, T. Measurement incompatibility does not give rise to Bell violation in general. *New J. Phys.* **2018**, *20*, 013021. [CrossRef] [PubMed]
12. Quintino, M.T.; Vértesi, T.; Brunner, N. Joint Measurability, Einstein-Podolsky-Rosen Steering, and Bell Nonlocality. *Phys. Rev. Lett.* **2014**, *113*, 160402. [CrossRef] [PubMed]
13. Carmeli, C.; Heinosaari, T.; Toigo, A. Quantum Incompatibility Witnesses. *Phys. Rev. Lett.* **2019**, *122*, 130402. [CrossRef] [PubMed]

14. Skrzypczyk, P.; Šupić, I.; Cavalcanti, D. All Sets of Incompatible Measurements give an Advantage in Quantum State Discrimination. *Phys. Rev. Lett.* **2019**, *122*, 130403. [CrossRef]
15. Mori, J. Operational characterization of incompatibility of quantum channels with quantum state discrimination. *Phys. Rev. A* **2020**, *101*, 032331. [CrossRef]
16. Chitambar, E.; Gour, G. Quantum resource theories. *Rev. Mod. Phys.* **2019**, *91*, 025001. [CrossRef]
17. Brunner, N.; Cavalcanti, D.; Pironio, S.; Scarani, V.; Wehner, S. Bell nonlocality. *Rev. Mod. Phys.* **2014**, *86*, 419–478. [CrossRef]
18. Nielsen, M.A.; Chuang, I.L. *Quantum Computation and Quantum Information: 10th Anniversary Edition*; Cambridge University Press: Cambridge, UK, 2010. [CrossRef]
19. Busch, P.; Grabowski, M.; Lahti, P.J. *Operational Quantum Physics*; Springer: Berlin/Heidelberg, Germany, 1995. [CrossRef]
20. Heinosaari, T.; Miyadera, T.; Ziman, M. An invitation to quantum incompatibility. *J. Phys. Math. Theor.* **2016**, *49*, 123001. [CrossRef]
21. Heinosaari, T.; Miyadera, T. Incompatibility of quantum channels. *J. Phys. Math. Theor.* **2017**, *50*, 135302. [CrossRef]
22. Kuramochi, Y. Quantum incompatibility of channels with general outcome operator algebras. *J. Math. Phys.* **2018**, *59*, 042203. [CrossRef]
23. Carmeli, C.; Heinosaari, T.; Miyadera, T.; Toigo, A. Witnessing incompatibility of quantum channels. *J. Math. Phys.* **2019**, *60*, 122202. [CrossRef]
24. Heinosaari, T.; Kiukas, J.; Reitzner, D.; Schultz, J. Incompatibility breaking quantum channels. *J. Phys. Math. Theor.* **2015**, *48*, 435301. [CrossRef]
25. Boyd, S.; Vandenberghe, L. *Convex Optimization*; Cambridge University Press: Cambridge, UK, 2004. [CrossRef] [PubMed]
26. Girard, M.; Plávala, M.; Sikora, J. Jordan products of quantum channels and their compatibility. *Nat. Commun.* **2021**, *12*, 2129. [CrossRef]
27. Zhu, H. Information complementarity: A new paradigm for decoding quantum incompatibility. *Sci. Rep.* **2015**, *5*, 14317. [CrossRef]
28. Zhu, H.; Hayashi, M.; Chen, L. Universal steering criteria. *Phys. Rev. Lett.* **2016**, *116*, 070403. [CrossRef]
29. Rao, C.R. *Information and the Accuracy Attainable in the Estimation of Statistical Parameters*; Springer: New York, NY, USA, 1992; pp. 235–247. [CrossRef]
30. Cramér, H. *Mathematical Methods of Statistics (PMS-9)*; Princeton University Press: Princeton, NJ, USA, 2016. [CrossRef]
31. Amari, S.i. *Differential-Geometrical Methods in Statistics*; Lecture Notes in Statistics; Springer: New York, NY, USA, 1985. [CrossRef]
32. Nielsen, F. An elementary introduction to information geometry. *Entropy* **2020**, *22*, 1100. [CrossRef]
33. Frieden, B.R. *Physics from Fisher Information: A Unification*; Cambridge University Press: Cambridge, UK, 1998. [CrossRef]
34. Fisher, R.A. Theory of Statistical Estimation. *Math. Proc. Camb. Philos. Soc.* **1925**, *22*, 700–725. [CrossRef]
35. Yuen, H.; Lax, M. Multiple-parameter quantum estimation and measurement of nonselfadjoint observables. *IEEE Trans. Inf. Theory* **1973**, *19*, 740–750. [CrossRef]
36. Braunstein, S.L.; Caves, C.M. Statistical distance and the geometry of quantum states. *Phys. Rev. Lett.* **1994**, *72*, 3439–3443. https://doi.org/10.1103/PhysRevLett.72.3439.
37. Holevo, A.S. *Probabilistic and Statistical Aspects of Quantum Theory*; Springer: Amsterdam, The Netherlands, 1982. [CrossRef]
38. Gill, R.D.; Massar, S. State estimation for large ensembles. *Phys. Rev. A* **2000**, *61*, 042312. [CrossRef]
39. Werner, R.F. Optimal cloning of pure states. *Phys. Rev. A* **1998**, *58*, 1827–1832. [CrossRef]
40. Hashagen, A.L. Universal asymmetric quantum cloning revisited. *Quantum Inf. Comput.* **2017**, *17*, 747–778. [CrossRef]
41. Haapasalo, E. Compatibility of Covariant Quantum Channels with Emphasis on Weyl Symmetry. *Ann. Henri Poincaré* **2019**, *20*, 3163. [CrossRef]
42. Nechita, I.; Pellegrini, C.; Rochette, D. A geometrical description of the universal $1 \to 2$ asymmetric quantum cloning region. *Quantum Inf. Process.* **2021**, *20*, 333. [CrossRef]
43. Haapasalo, E. Robustness of incompatibility for quantum devices. *J. Phys. A Math. Theor.* **2015**, *48*, 255303. [CrossRef]
44. Bluhm, A.; Nechita, I. Joint measurability of quantum effects and the matrix diamond. *J. Math. Phys.* **2018**, *59*, 112202. [CrossRef]
45. Bluhm, A.; Nechita, I. Compatibility of quantum measurements and inclusion constants for the matrix jewel. *SIAM J. Appl. Algebra Geom.* **2020**, *4*, 255–296. [CrossRef]
46. Ali, S.T.; Carmeli, C.; Heinosaari, T.; Toigo, A. Commutative POVMs and Fuzzy Observables. *Found. Phys.* **2009**, *39*, 593. [CrossRef]
47. Gühne, O.; Haapasalo, E.; Kraft, T.; Pellonpää, J.P.; Uola, R. Incompatible measurements in quantum information science. *arXiv* **2021**, arXiv:2112.06784.
48. Heinosaari, T.; Jivulescu, M.A.; Nechita, I. Order preserving maps on quantum measurements. *arXiv* **2022**, arXiv:2202.00725. [CrossRef]
49. Paulsen, V. *Completely Bounded Maps and Operator Algebras*; Cambridge University Press: Cambridge, UK, 2003. [CrossRef]
50. Harris, S.J.; Levene, R.H.; Paulsen, V.I.; Plosker, S.; Rahaman, M. Schur multipliers and mixed unitary maps. *J. Math. Phys.* **2018**, *59*, 112201. [CrossRef]
51. Watrous, J. *The Theory of Quantum Information*; Cambridge University Press: Cambridge, UK, 2018. [CrossRef]
52. Singh, S.; Nechita, I. Diagonal unitary and orthogonal symmetries in quantum theory. *Quantum* **2021**, *5*, 519. [CrossRef]
53. Liang, Y.C.; Spekkens, R.W.; Wiseman, H.M. Specker's parable of the overprotective seer: A road to contextuality, nonlocality and complementarity. *Phys. Rep.* **2011**, *506*, 1–39. [CrossRef]
54. Kunjwal, R.; Heunen, C.; Fritz, T. Quantum realization of arbitrary joint measurability structures. *Phys. Rev. A* **2014**, *89*, 052126.

55. Yadavalli, S.A.; Andrejic, N.; Kunjwal, R. Bell violations from arbitrary joint measurability structures. *arXiv* **2020**, arXiv:2008.10100. [CrossRef]
56. Sun, B.Z.; Wang, Z.X.; Li-Jost, X.; Fei, S.M. A note on the hierarchy of quantum measurement incompatibilities. *Entropy* **2020**, *22*, 161. [CrossRef]
57. Durt, T.; Englert, B.G.; Bengtsson, I.; Życzkowski, K. On mutually unbiased bases. *Int. J. Quantum Inf.* **2010**, *8*, 535–640. [CrossRef]
58. Wootters, W.K.; Fields, B.D. Optimal state-determination by mutually unbiased measurements. *Ann. Phys.* **1989**, *191*, 363–381.
59. Klappenecker, A.; Rötteler, M. Constructions of mutually unbiased bases. In *International Conference on Finite Fields and Applications*; Springer: Berlin/Heidelberg, Germany, 2003; pp. 137–144.
60. Combescure, M. The mutually unbiased bases revisited. *Contemp. Math.* **2007**, *447*, 29.

Article

Quantum Incoherence Based Simultaneously on *k* Bases

Pu Wang, Zhihua Guo * and Huaixin Cao *

School of Mathematics and Statistics, Shaanxi Normal University, Xi'an 710119, China; wangpu@snnu.edu.cn
* Correspondence: guozhihua@snnu.edu.cn (Z.G.); caohx@snnu.edu.cn (H.C.)

Abstract: Quantum coherence is known as an important resource in many quantum information tasks, which is a basis-dependent property of quantum states. In this paper, we discuss quantum incoherence based simultaneously on *k* bases using Matrix Theory Method. First, by defining a correlation function $m(e, f)$ of two orthonormal bases e and f, we investigate the relationships between sets $\mathcal{I}(e)$ and $\mathcal{I}(f)$ of incoherent states with respect to e and f. We prove that $\mathcal{I}(e) = \mathcal{I}(f)$ if and only if the rank-one projective measurements generated by e and f are identical. We give a necessary and sufficient condition for the intersection $\mathcal{I}(e) \cap \mathcal{I}(f)$ to include a state except the maximally mixed state. Especially, if two bases e and f are mutually unbiased, then the intersection has only the maximally mixed state. Secondly, we introduce the concepts of strong incoherence and weak coherence of a quantum state with respect to a set $\mathcal{B}$ of *k* bases and propose a measure for the weak coherence. In the two-qubit system, we prove that there exists a maximally coherent state with respect to $\mathcal{B}$ when $k = 2$ and it is not the case for $k = 3$.

Keywords: strong incoherence; weak coherence; orthonormal basis; mutually unbiased basis

1. Introduction

Quantum coherence is not only a feature of quantum systems which arise due to superposition principle, but also is a kind of fundamental resources in quantum information and computation [1–8]. The resource theory of coherence is formulated with respect to a distinguished basis of a Hilbert space, which defines free states as the states that are diagonal in this basis [3]. Several important quantifiers of quantum coherence have been introduced and assessed [9–19]. Recently, it is shown that quantum coherence can be useful resource in quantum computation [20–24], quantum metrology [25], quantum thermodynamics [26–31] and quantum biology [32–34].

Since the coherence of quantum states depends on the choice of the reference basis, it is natural to study the relationship among the coherence with respect to different bases. Cheng et al. [35] first studied the situation of two specific coherence measures under mutual unbiased basis (MUB): ℓ_1 norm of coherence and relative entropy of coherence. They proposed the complementary relationship of the two coherence measures under any complete MUB set. Rastegin in [36] discussed the uncertainty relation for the geometric measure of coherence under MUBs. Sheng et al. [37] further studied the realization of quantum coherence through skewed information and the geometric measure under mutual unbiased bases. Recently, considered the standard coherence (SC), the partial coherence (PC) [38–40] and the block coherence (BC) [41,42] as variance of quantum states under some quantum channel Φ, Zhang et al. [43] proposed the concept of channel-based coherence of quantum states, called Φ-coherence, which contains the SC, PC and BC, but not contain the POVM-based coherence [44,45], and obtained some interesting results.

Usually, the coherence of an individual quantum state is discussed only when referring to a preferred basis. Considered sets of quantum states, Designolle et al. [46] introduced the concept of set coherence for characterizing the coherence of a set of quantum states in a basis-independent way. Followed a resource-theoretic approach, the authors of [46] defined the free sets of states as sets $\mathcal{F}_n$ of groups of states $\vec{\rho} = \{\rho_j\}_{j=1}^n$ such that there

exists a choice of basis (equivalently, a unitary U) for which all states $U\rho_j U^\dagger$ in the set $U\vec{\rho}U^\dagger$ become diagonal. Clearly, $\vec{\rho} \in \mathcal{F}_n$ if and only if $\{\rho_j\}_{j=1}^n$ is a commutative family of states, i.e., $\rho_i \rho_j = \rho_j \rho_i$ for all $i, j = 1, 2, \ldots, n$.

Different from the discussions above, in this paper, we focus on the quantum incoherence based simultaneously on k bases; equivalently, the coherence of a quantum state with respect to a basis contained in a given set $\mathcal{B}$ of k orthonormal bases. In Section 2, by defining the correlation function of two orthonormal bases e and f, we study the relationships between two sets of incoherent states with respect to e and f, and investigate the maximally coherent states with respect to e and f. In Section 3, we discuss the strong incoherence and the weak coherence of a state with respect to a set of k orthonormal bases and introduce a measure for the weak coherence. In Section 4, we give a summary of this paper.

2. Correlation Function of Two Bases and Quantum Coherence

Let us consider a quantum system X, which is described by a d-dimensional Hilbert space H and let I denote the identity operator on H. We use $\mathcal{B}(H)$ and $\mathcal{D}(H)$ to denote the sets of all linear operators and all density operators (mixed states) on H, respectively. In quantum information theory, a positive operator valued measure (POVM) is a set $M = \{M_i\}_{i=1}^m$ of operators on H with $0 \leq M_i \leq I$ for all $i = 1, 2, \ldots, m$ and $\sum_{i=1}^m M_i = I$. In particular, if $M_i^2 = M_i$ for all i, then the POVM becomes a projective measurement (PM). For a rank-one PM P, there exists an orthonormal basis $e = \{|e_i\rangle\}_{i=1}^d$ such that $P = \{|e_i\rangle\langle e_i|\}_{i=1}^d$. In this case, we denote $P = P_e = \{|e_i\rangle\langle e_i|\}_{i=1}^d$. We use the notation $\bar{z}$ or z^* to denote the conjugate of a complex number z.

For the fixed orthonormal basis $e = \{|e_i\rangle\}_{i=1}^d$ for H, $\mathcal{I}(e)$ denotes the set of incoherent states on H w.r.t. e, i.e., ones that have diagonal matrix representation under the basis e. A quantum operation Φ on $\mathcal{B}(H)$ is said to be an incoherent operation [3] w.r.t e if it admits an incoherent Kraus decomposition, i.e.,

$$\Phi(\rho) = \sum_{i=1}^n K_i \rho K_i^\dagger, \quad \forall \rho \in \mathcal{B}(H)$$

with

$$K_i \rho K_i^\dagger \in \text{tr}(K_i \rho K_i^\dagger) \mathcal{I}(e), \quad \forall \rho \in \mathcal{I}(e), i = 1, 2, \ldots, n.$$

We use $\mathcal{IO}(e)$ to denote the set of incoherent operations w.r.t e on $\mathcal{B}(H)$.

According to Ref. [3], a coherence measure with respect to e, called an e-coherence measure, is a function $C : \mathcal{D}(H) \mapsto \mathbb{R}$ satisfying the following four conditions.

(1) Faithfulness: $C(\rho) \geq 0$ for all $\rho \in \mathcal{D}(H)$; $C(\rho) = 0$ if and only if $\rho \in \mathcal{I}(e)$.
(2) Monotonicity: $C(\Phi(\rho)) \leq C(\rho)$ for any $\Phi \in \mathcal{IO}(e)$.
(3) Strong monotonicity: $\forall \rho \in \mathcal{D}(H)$, $\sum_{i=1}^n p_i C(\rho_i) \leq C(\rho)$ for all operators K_i in $\mathcal{H}$ such that $\sum_{i=1}^n K_i^\dagger K_i = I$ with $K_i \mathcal{I}(e) K_i^\dagger \subset \mathbb{R}^+ \mathcal{I}(e)$, $p_i = \text{tr}(K_i \rho K_i^\dagger)$ and $\rho_i = K_i \rho K_i^\dagger / p_i$ if $p_i > 0$; $\rho_i = \frac{1}{d} I$ if $p_i = 0$.
(4) Convexity: $C(\sum_{i=1}^n p_i \rho_i) \leq \sum_{i=1}^n p_i C(\rho_i)$ for any states $\rho_i \in \mathcal{D}(H) (i = 1, 2, \ldots, n)$ and any probability distribution $\{p_i\}_{i=1}^n$.

A usual ℓ_1-norm coherence measure [3] of a state $\rho \in \mathcal{D}(H)$ with respect to a basis e is defined by

$$\mathcal{C}_{e,\ell_1}(\rho) = 2 \sum_{1 \leq i < j \leq n} |\langle e_i|\rho|e_j\rangle|.$$

Clearly,

$$\mathcal{C}_{e,\ell_1}(\rho) = \sum_{i,j=1}^n |\langle e_i|\rho|e_j\rangle| - 1 \leq d - 1. \tag{1}$$

Especially, $\mathcal{C}_{e,\ell_1}(\rho) = d - 1$ if and only if $|\langle e_i|\rho|e_j\rangle| = \frac{1}{d}$ for all $i, j = 1, 2, \ldots, d$; in that case, ρ is called a *maximally coherent state* with respect to e.

From the review above, we find that quantum coherence relies on the choice of orthonormal bases. In what follows, we discuss the relationship between quantum coherence based on different reference bases. To do this, we let $e = \{|e_i\rangle\}_{i=1}^d$ and $f = \{|f_i\rangle\}_{i=1}^d$ be two orthonormal bases for H and define

$$m(e,f) = \sum_{i,j=1}^d |\langle e_i | f_j \rangle| - d, \qquad (2)$$

called the *correlation function* between two bases e and f.

Recall that [35] two orthonormal bases e and f for H are said to be mutually unbiased if $|\langle e_i | f_j \rangle| = \frac{1}{\sqrt{d}}$ for all $i, j = 1, 2, \ldots, d$. Thus, when e and f for H are mutually unbiased, it holds that $m(e, f) = d^{\frac{3}{2}} - d$. More properties of the correlation function are given in the following theorem.

Theorem 1. *Let e and f be two orthonormal bases for H. Then*
(1) $0 \leq m(e, f) \leq d^{\frac{3}{2}} - d$.
(2) $m(e, f) = 0$ *if and only if* $P_e = P_f$ *if and only if* $\mathcal{I}(e) = \mathcal{I}(f)$.
(3) $m(e, f) = d^{\frac{3}{2}} - d$ *if and only if e and f are mutually unbiased bases.*

Proof. (1) Since $0 \leq |\langle e_i | f_j \rangle| \leq 1$, we get $|\langle e_i | f_j \rangle|^2 \leq |\langle e_i | f_j \rangle|$ for all $i, j = 1, 2, \ldots, d$. So,

$$\sum_{i,j=1}^d |\langle e_i | f_j \rangle| \geq \sum_{i,j=1}^d |\langle e_i | f_j \rangle|^2$$

$$= \sum_{j=1}^d \left(\sum_{i=1}^d |\langle e_i | f_j \rangle|^2 \right)$$

$$= \sum_{j=1}^d \| |f_j\rangle \|^2$$

$$= d.$$

This shows that $m(e, f) \geq 0$. Since $e = \{|e_i\rangle\}_{i=1}^d$ and $f = \{|f_i\rangle\}_{i=1}^d$ are two orthonormal bases for H, there exists a $d \times d$ unitary matrix $U = [\lambda_{ij}]$ such that $(|e_1\rangle, |e_2\rangle, \ldots, |e_d\rangle) = U(|f_1\rangle, |f_2\rangle, \ldots, |f_d\rangle)$; equivalently,

$$|e_i\rangle = \sum_{j=1}^d \lambda_{ij} |f_j\rangle, \ \forall i = 1, 2, \ldots, d. \qquad (3)$$

Hence, $\lambda_{ij} = \langle f_j | e_i \rangle$, and using the Cauchy inequality yields that

$$\sum_{i,j=1}^d |\langle e_i | f_j \rangle| = \sum_{i,j=1}^d |\lambda_{ij}|$$

$$= \sum_{i=1}^d \left(\sum_{j=1}^d 1 \cdot |\lambda_{ij}| \right)$$

$$\leq \sum_{i=1}^d \sqrt{d} \sqrt{\sum_{j=1}^d |\lambda_{ij}|^2}$$

$$= d^{\frac{3}{2}}.$$

Consequently, $m(e, f) \leq d^{\frac{3}{2}} - d$.

(2) We see from Equation (2) that $m(e,f) = 0$ if and only if for any i, there exists a unique i' such that $|\langle e_i|f_{i'}\rangle| = 1$ and $|\langle e_i|f_k\rangle| = 0$ for all $k \neq i'$ if and only if for any i, there exists a unique i' such that $|e_i\rangle = e^{i\theta_{ii'}}|f_{i'}\rangle$, which is equivalent to $P_e = P_f$, i.e., $\mathcal{I}(e) = \mathcal{I}(f)$.

(3) From the proof of (1), we see that $m(e,f) = d^{\frac{3}{2}} - d$ if and only if $|\lambda_{ij}| = \frac{1}{\sqrt{d}}(\forall i,j)$, that is, e and f are mutually unbiased bases.

Suppose that e and f are mutually unbiased bases, then the coefficients λ_{ij} in (3) satisfy $|\lambda_{ij}| = |\langle f_j|e_i\rangle| = \frac{1}{\sqrt{d}}$ for all $i,j = 1,2,\ldots,d$. Let $\rho \in \mathcal{I}(e) \cap \mathcal{I}(f)$. Then it can be written as $\rho = \sum_{n=1}^{d} \mu_n |e_n\rangle\langle e_n|$ with $\mu_n \geq 0$ for all $n = 1,2,\ldots,d$, $\sum_{n=1}^{d} \mu_n = 1$. Using Equation (3) implies that

$$\rho = \sum_{j,k=1}^{d} \sum_{n=1}^{d} \mu_n \overline{\lambda_{nj}} \lambda_{nk} |f_j\rangle\langle f_k|.$$

Since $\rho \in \mathcal{I}(f)$ and $\sum_{n=1}^{d} \mu_n = 1$, we see that

$$\sum_{n=1}^{d} \mu_n \overline{\lambda_{nj}} \lambda_{nk} = \frac{1}{d}\delta_{k,j}, \quad \forall k,j = 1,2,\ldots,d$$

that is,

$$\begin{pmatrix} \overline{\lambda_{11}} & \overline{\lambda_{21}} & \cdots & \overline{\lambda_{d1}} \\ \overline{\lambda_{12}} & \overline{\lambda_{22}} & \cdots & \overline{\lambda_{d2}} \\ \vdots & \vdots & \ddots & \vdots \\ \overline{\lambda_{1d}} & \overline{\lambda_{2d}} & \cdots & \overline{\lambda_{dd}} \end{pmatrix} \begin{pmatrix} \mu_1 & 0 & 0 & 0 \\ 0 & \mu_2 & 0 & 0 \\ \vdots & \vdots & \ddots & \vdots \\ 0 & 0 & 0 & \mu_d \end{pmatrix} \begin{pmatrix} \lambda_{11} & \lambda_{12} & \cdots & \lambda_{1d} \\ \lambda_{21} & \lambda_{22} & \cdots & \lambda_{2d} \\ \vdots & \vdots & \ddots & \vdots \\ \lambda_{d1} & \lambda_{d2} & \cdots & \lambda_{dd} \end{pmatrix} = \begin{pmatrix} \frac{1}{d} & 0 & 0 & 0 \\ 0 & \frac{1}{d} & 0 & 0 \\ \vdots & \vdots & \ddots & \vdots \\ 0 & 0 & 0 & \frac{1}{d} \end{pmatrix}.$$

Since $U = [\lambda_{ij}]$ is a $d \times d$ unitary matrix, we get $\mu_k = \frac{1}{d}$ for all $k = 1,2,\ldots,d$, i.e., $\rho = \frac{1}{d}\sum_{j=1}^{d} |f_j\rangle\langle f_j| = \frac{1}{d}I$. Hence, $\mathcal{I}(e) \cap \mathcal{I}(f) = \left\{\frac{1}{d}I\right\}$.
$\square$

Remark 1. *Suppose that $P_e \neq P_f$, then there exists an i and $j_1, j_2, \ldots, j_k (2 \leq k \leq d)$ such that $\langle e_i|f_{j_s}\rangle \neq 0 (s = 1,2,\ldots,k)$ and*

$$|e_i\rangle = \sum_{s=1}^{k} \langle f_{j_s}|e_i\rangle |f_{j_s}\rangle.$$

Then $|e_i\rangle\langle e_i| \in \mathcal{I}(e)$ and

$$|e_i\rangle\langle e_i| = \sum_{s=1,t=1}^{k} \langle f_{j_s}|e_i\rangle \overline{\langle f_{j_t}|e_i\rangle} |f_{j_s}\rangle\langle f_{j_t}|.$$

Since $\langle f_{j_s}|e_i\rangle \overline{\langle f_{j_t}|e_i\rangle} \neq 0$ for any $s \neq t$, we get that $|e_i\rangle\langle e_i| \notin \mathcal{I}(f)$. This shows that there exists a state $\rho \in \mathcal{I}(e)$ but $\rho \notin \mathcal{I}(f)$. Similarly, there also exists a state $\rho' \in \mathcal{I}(f)$ but $\rho' \notin \mathcal{I}(e)$.

From Theorem 1 and Remark 1, we get relationships between $m(e,f)$ and $\mathcal{I}(e) \cap \mathcal{I}(f)$ as shown by the following Figure 1.

It is clear that $\frac{1}{d}I \in \mathcal{I}(e) \cap \mathcal{I}(f)$ for any bases e and f. Especially, $\mathcal{I}(e) \cap \mathcal{I}(f) = \left\{\frac{1}{d}I\right\}$ if they are mutually unbiased. However, even though e and f are not a pair of mutually unbiased bases, it is possible that $\mathcal{I}(e) \cap \mathcal{I}(f) = \left\{\frac{1}{d}I\right\}$, see the following example.

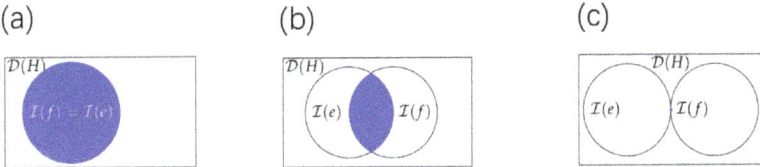

Figure 1. Relationships between $m(e, f)$ and $\mathcal{I}(e) \cap \mathcal{I}(f)$, where subfigures (**a**–**c**) correspond to the cases that $m(e, f) = 0, m(e, f) > 0$ and $m(e, f) = d^{\frac{3}{2}} - d$, respectively.

Example 1. *Let $e = \{|0\rangle, |1\rangle\}$ and $f = \{|f_0\rangle, |f_1\rangle\}$ be two orthonormal bases for $H = \mathbb{C}^2$ with*

$$|f_0\rangle = \frac{1}{\sqrt{3}}|0\rangle + \frac{\sqrt{2}}{\sqrt{3}}|1\rangle, |f_1\rangle = -\frac{\sqrt{2}}{\sqrt{3}}|0\rangle + \frac{1}{\sqrt{3}}|1\rangle.$$

Clearly, e and f are not a pair of mutually unbiased bases while $\mathcal{I}(e) \cap \mathcal{I}(f) = \{\frac{1}{2}I\}$.

This example leads us to study the relationship between two bases e and f for H such that

$$\mathcal{I}(e) \cap \mathcal{I}(f) = \left\{\frac{1}{d}I\right\}.$$

To do this, we let $e = \{|e_i\rangle\}_{i=1}^d$ and $f = \{|f_i\rangle\}_{i=1}^d$ be two bases for H and $\rho = \sum_{i=1}^d x_i |e_i\rangle\langle e_i| \in \mathcal{I}(e) \setminus \{I/d\}$. Since $x_1, \ldots, x_d$ are the eigenvalues of ρ, they can be rearranged as $\lambda_1, \lambda_2, \ldots, \lambda_d$ in decreasing order, say, $\lambda_1 \geq \lambda_2 \geq \ldots \geq \lambda_d$. Thus, there exists a permutation matrix P_1 such that

$$P_1 \begin{pmatrix} x_1 \\ x_2 \\ \vdots \\ x_d \end{pmatrix} = \begin{pmatrix} \lambda_1 \\ \lambda_2 \\ \vdots \\ \lambda_d \end{pmatrix}. \quad (4)$$

Suppose that $\rho \in \mathcal{I}(f)$. Then

$$\rho = \sum_{j=1}^d y_j |f_j\rangle\langle f_j|, \quad (5)$$

where $y_j = \langle f_j|\rho|f_j\rangle$. Using Equation (5) implies that

$$x_i = \langle e_i|\rho|e_i\rangle = \sum_{j=1}^d |\langle e_i|f_j\rangle|^2 y_j (i = 1, 2, \ldots, d),$$

i.e.,

$$\begin{pmatrix} x_1 \\ x_2 \\ \vdots \\ x_d \end{pmatrix} = C \begin{pmatrix} y_1 \\ y_2 \\ \vdots \\ y_d \end{pmatrix}, \quad (6)$$

where

$$C = \begin{pmatrix} |\langle e_1|f_1\rangle|^2 & |\langle e_1|f_2\rangle|^2 & \cdots & |\langle e_1|f_d\rangle|^2 \\ |\langle e_2|f_1\rangle|^2 & |\langle e_2|f_2\rangle|^2 & \cdots & |\langle e_2|f_d\rangle|^2 \\ \vdots & \vdots & \ddots & \vdots \\ |\langle e_d|f_1\rangle|^2 & |\langle e_d|f_2\rangle|^2 & \cdots & |\langle e_d|f_d\rangle|^2 \end{pmatrix}. \quad (7)$$

Since $y_1, \ldots, y_d$ are also the eigenvalues of ρ, they can be also rearranged as $\lambda_1, \lambda_2, \ldots, \lambda_d$ in decreasing order. So, there exists a permutation matrix P_2 such that

$$P_2 \begin{pmatrix} y_1 \\ y_2 \\ \vdots \\ y_d \end{pmatrix} = \begin{pmatrix} \lambda_1 \\ \lambda_2 \\ \vdots \\ \lambda_d \end{pmatrix}. \tag{8}$$

Thus,

$$\begin{pmatrix} \lambda_1 \\ \lambda_2 \\ \vdots \\ \lambda_d \end{pmatrix} = P_1 \begin{pmatrix} x_1 \\ x_2 \\ \vdots \\ x_d \end{pmatrix} = P_1 C \begin{pmatrix} y_1 \\ y_2 \\ \vdots \\ y_d \end{pmatrix} = P_1 C P_2 \begin{pmatrix} \lambda_1 \\ \lambda_2 \\ \vdots \\ \lambda_d \end{pmatrix}. \tag{9}$$

Putting $P_1 C P_2 = [w_{ij}]$ yields that

$$\lambda_i = \sum_{j=1}^{d} w_{ij} \lambda_j \, (i=1,2,\ldots,d). \tag{10}$$

Thus, when $\lambda_1 = \lambda_2 = \ldots = \lambda_r > \lambda_{r+1} \geq \ldots \geq \lambda_d$, we see from Equation (10) that for $1 \leq i \leq r$,

$$\lambda_i = \left(\sum_{j=1}^{r} w_{ij}\right) \lambda_i + \sum_{j=r+1}^{d} w_{ij} \lambda_j$$

and so $\sum_{j=1}^{r} w_{ij} = 1, w_{ij} = 0 (1 \leq i \leq r, r < j \leq d)$. Using Equation (10) again yields that for $1 + r \leq i \leq d$,

$$\lambda_i = \left(\sum_{j=1}^{r} w_{ij}\right) \lambda_1 + \sum_{j=r+1}^{d} w_{ij} \lambda_j$$

and so $\sum_{j=1}^{r} w_{ij} = 0$, implying that $w_{ij} = 0 (r < i \leq d, 1 \leq j \leq r)$. Thus,

$$P_1 C P_2 = \begin{pmatrix} D_1 & 0 & \cdots & 0 \\ 0 & D_2 & \cdots & 0 \\ \vdots & \vdots & \ddots & \vdots \\ 0 & 0 & \cdots & D_k \end{pmatrix}, \tag{11}$$

where k means the number of different eigenvalues $\mu_1 > \mu_2 > \ldots > \mu_k$ of ρ and D_i is an $r_i \times r_i$-doubly stochastic matrix, and r_i denotes the multiplicity of the ith eigenvalue μ_i.

Conversely, suppose that there exist $d \times d$ permutation matrices P_1 and P_2 such that $P_1 C P_2$ is of the form (11) where $k > 1$. Since the matrix $P_1 C P_2$ can be written as

$$P_1 C P_2 = \begin{pmatrix} |\langle e_{s_1}|f_{t_1}\rangle|^2 & |\langle e_{s_1}|f_{t_2}\rangle|^2 & \cdots & |\langle e_{s_1}|f_{t_d}\rangle|^2 \\ |\langle e_{s_2}|f_{t_1}\rangle|^2 & |\langle e_{s_2}|f_{t_2}\rangle|^2 & \cdots & |\langle e_{s_2}|f_{t_d}\rangle|^2 \\ \vdots & \vdots & \ddots & \vdots \\ |\langle e_{s_d}|f_{t_1}\rangle|^2 & |\langle e_{s_d}|f_{t_2}\rangle|^2 & \cdots & |\langle e_{s_d}|f_{t_d}\rangle|^2 \end{pmatrix},$$

where

$$\begin{pmatrix} s_1 \\ s_2 \\ \vdots \\ s_d \end{pmatrix} = P_1 \begin{pmatrix} 1 \\ 2 \\ \vdots \\ d \end{pmatrix}, \begin{pmatrix} t_1 \\ t_2 \\ \vdots \\ t_d \end{pmatrix} = P_2 \begin{pmatrix} 1 \\ 2 \\ \vdots \\ d \end{pmatrix},$$

we see from condition (11) that

$$\langle e_{s_i}|f_{t_j}\rangle = 0 (\forall r_1 < j \leq d, 1 \leq i \leq r_1), \langle e_{s_i}|f_{t_j}\rangle = 0 (\forall r_1 < i \leq d, 1 \leq j \leq r_1). \quad (12)$$

This implies that the subspaces generated by $\{|e_{s_i}\rangle\}_{i=1}^{r_1}$ and $\{|f_{t_j}\rangle\}_{j=1}^{r_1}$ are equal and so

$$\rho := \frac{1}{r_1}\sum_{i=1}^{r_1} |e_{s_i}\rangle\langle e_{s_i}| = \frac{1}{r_1}\sum_{j=1}^{r_1} |f_{t_j}\rangle\langle f_{t_j}|,$$

Clearly, $\rho \in \mathcal{I}(e) \cap \mathcal{I}(f) \setminus \{\frac{1}{d}I\}$.

As a conclusion, we arrive at the following.

Theorem 2. *Let $d \geq 2$, $e = \{|e_i\rangle\}_{i=1}^{d}$ and $f = \{|f_j\rangle\}_{j=1}^{d}$ be two orthonormal bases for H and set $C = [|\langle e_i|f_j\rangle|^2]$. Then there exists a state $\rho \neq \frac{1}{d}I$ in $\mathcal{I}(e) \cap \mathcal{I}(f)$ if and only if there exist two $d \times d$ permutation matrices P_1 and P_2 such that the matrix $P_1 C P_2$ is $k \times k$ block-diagonal for some $k > 1$.*

Example 2. *Let $d > 3$, $e = \{|e_i\rangle\}_{i=1}^{d}$ and $f = \{|f_j\rangle\}_{j=1}^{d}$ be two orthonormal bases for H such that*

$$|\langle f_i|e_j\rangle| = \frac{1}{\sqrt{2}}(i,j = 1,2), |e_i\rangle = |f_i\rangle(i = 3, 4, \ldots, d).$$

Then

$$C = [|\langle e_i|f_j\rangle|^2] = \begin{pmatrix} 0.5 & 0.5 & 0 & \cdots & 0 \\ 0.5 & 0.5 & 0 & \cdots & 0 \\ 0 & 0 & 1 & \cdots & 0 \\ \vdots & \vdots & \vdots & \ddots & \vdots \\ 0 & 0 & \cdots & 0 & 1 \end{pmatrix}.$$

It follows from Theorem 2 that there exists a state $\rho \in \mathcal{I}(e) \cap \mathcal{I}(f) \setminus \{I/d\}$; for example,

$$\rho = \frac{1}{d-2}\sum_{i=3}^{d} |e_i\rangle\langle e_i|.$$

Remark 2. *From Theorem 2, we know that whether $\mathcal{I}(e) \cap \mathcal{I}(f) \setminus \{I/d\} \neq \emptyset$ depends on the structure of the matrix C given by Equation (7). Since this, we call C the correlation matrix of the bases e and f and denote it by $C_{e,f}$. Clearly, it can be written as the Hardamard product of the transition matrix $T_{e,f}$ from e to f and its conjugate matrix $T_{e,f}^*$:*

$$C_{e,f} = T_{e,f} \odot T_{e,f}^*,$$

where

$$T_{e,f} = \begin{pmatrix} \langle e_1|f_1\rangle & \langle e_1|f_2\rangle & \cdots & \langle e_1|f_d\rangle \\ \langle e_2|f_1\rangle & \langle e_2|f_2\rangle & \cdots & \langle e_2|f_d\rangle \\ \vdots & \vdots & \ddots & \vdots \\ \langle e_d|f_1\rangle & \langle e_d|f_2\rangle & \cdots & \langle e_d|f_d\rangle \end{pmatrix}. \quad (13)$$

Theorem 2 also tells us that when $\langle e_i|f_j\rangle \neq 0$ for all i,j, there do not exist permutation matrices P_1 and P_2 such that $P_1 C P_2$ is $r \times r (2 \leq r \leq d)$ block diagonal, so $\mathcal{I}(e) \cap \mathcal{I}(f) = \{I/d\}$. Especially, for a pair of mutually unbiased bases e and f, when $\rho \in \mathcal{I}(e)$ and $\rho \neq \frac{1}{d}I$, we have $\rho \notin \mathcal{I}(f)$. Conversely, when ρ is a maximally coherent state w.r.t. e, a question is: whether ρ is also maximally coherent w.r.t. f. The follow example shows that the answer is negative.

Example 3. Let $e = \{|0\rangle, |1\rangle\}$ and $f = \{|f_0\rangle, |f_1\rangle\}$ be a pair of mutually unbiased bases for $H = \mathbb{C}^2$ where
$$|f_0\rangle = \frac{1}{\sqrt{2}}(|0\rangle + |1\rangle), |f_1\rangle = \frac{1}{\sqrt{2}}(|0\rangle - |1\rangle),$$
choose
$$\rho_1 = \frac{1}{2}(|f_0\rangle\langle f_0| + |f_0\rangle\langle f_1| + |f_1\rangle\langle f_0| + |f_1\rangle\langle f_1|) = |0\rangle\langle 0|.$$
Then ρ_1 is maximally coherent with respect to f but is incoherent w.r.t. e, while for the state
$$\rho_2 = \frac{1}{2}(|f_0\rangle\langle f_0| + i|f_0\rangle\langle f_1| - i|f_1\rangle\langle f_0| + |f_1\rangle\langle f_1|),$$
we have
$$\mathcal{C}_{e,\ell_1}(\rho_2) = \mathcal{C}_{P_f,\ell_1}(\rho_2) = 1.$$
Therefore, ρ_2 is both maximally coherent w.r.t. e and f.

The following theorem shows that there must exist a maximally coherent state w.r.t. any two bases for $\mathbb{C}^2$.

Theorem 3. Let $e = \{|e_i\rangle\}_{i=1}^2$ and $f = \{|f_j\rangle\}_{j=1}^2$ be two orthonormal bases for $\mathbb{C}^2$. Then there exists a state $\rho \in \mathcal{D}(\mathbb{C}^2)$ such that
$$\mathcal{C}_{e,\ell_1}(\rho) + \mathcal{C}_{f,\ell_1}(\rho) = 2.$$

Proof. First, we observe that $\mathcal{C}_{e,\ell_1}(\rho) = 1$ if and only if
$$\rho = \frac{1}{2}(|e_1\rangle\langle e_1| + e^{i\alpha}|e_1\rangle\langle e_2| + e^{-i\alpha}|e_1\rangle\langle e_2| + |e_2\rangle\langle e_2|) \tag{14}$$

and $\mathcal{C}_{P_f,\ell_1}(\rho) = 1$ if and only if
$$\rho = \frac{1}{2}(|f_1\rangle\langle f_1| + e^{i\beta}|f_1\rangle\langle f_2| + e^{-i\beta}|f_2\rangle\langle f_1| + |f_2\rangle\langle f_2|). \tag{15}$$

Suppose that
$$|f_1\rangle = u_{11}|e_1\rangle + u_{12}|e_2\rangle, |f_2\rangle = u_{21}|e_1\rangle + u_{22}|e_2\rangle,$$
then $U := [u_{ij}]$ is a unitary matrix, which is given.

For a state ρ of the form given by (14), then $\mathcal{C}_{e,\ell_1}(\rho) = 1$. We compute that
$$\begin{aligned}
\langle f_1|\rho|f_1\rangle &= (u_{11}^*\langle e_1| + u_{12}^*\langle e_2|)|\rho|(u_{11}|e_1\rangle + u_{12}|e_2\rangle) \\
&= \frac{1}{2}(|u_{11}|^2 + u_{11}^*u_{12}e^{i\alpha} + u_{11}u_{12}^*e^{-i\alpha} + |u_{12}|^2) \\
&= \frac{1}{2} + \operatorname{Re}(u_{11}^*u_{12}e^{i\alpha}),
\end{aligned}$$

$$\begin{aligned}
\langle f_1|\rho|f_2\rangle &= (u_{11}^*\langle e_1| + u_{12}^*\langle e_2|)|\rho|(u_{21}|e_1\rangle + u_{22}|e_2\rangle) \\
&= \frac{1}{2}(u_{11}^*u_{21} + u_{11}^*u_{22}e^{i\alpha} + u_{12}^*u_{21}e^{-i\alpha} + u_{12}^*u_{22}) \\
&= \frac{1}{2}(u_{11}^*u_{22}e^{i\alpha} + u_{12}^*u_{21}e^{-i\alpha}),
\end{aligned}$$

$$\begin{aligned}\langle f_2|\rho|f_2\rangle &= (u_{21}^*\langle e_1| + u_{22}^*\langle e_2|)|\rho|(u_{21}|e_1\rangle + u_{22}|e_2\rangle)\\ &= \frac{1}{2}(|u_{21}|^2 + u_{21}^*u_{22}e^{i\alpha} + u_{21}u_{22}^*e^{-i\alpha} + |u_{22}|^2)\\ &= \frac{1}{2} + \text{Re}(u_{21}^*u_{22}e^{i\alpha}).\end{aligned}$$

Thus, $C_{f,\ell_1}(\rho) = 1$ if and only if

$$\begin{cases} \text{Re}(u_{11}^*u_{12}e^{i\alpha}) = 0;\\ u_{11}^*u_{22}e^{i\alpha} + u_{12}^*u_{21}e^{-i\alpha} = e^{i\beta};\\ \text{Re}(u_{21}^*u_{22}e^{i\alpha}) = 0, \end{cases} \tag{16}$$

if and only if

$$\begin{cases} \text{Re}(u_{11}^*u_{12}e^{i\alpha}) = 0;\\ u_{11}^*u_{22}e^{i\alpha} + u_{12}^*u_{21}e^{-i\alpha} = e^{i\beta} \end{cases} \tag{17}$$

since $u_{11}^*u_{12} = -u_{21}^*u_{22}$.

Since U is a unitary matrix, it can be represented as

$$U = \begin{pmatrix} u_{11} & u_{12} \\ u_{21} & u_{22} \end{pmatrix} = \begin{pmatrix} re^{i\theta_1} & \sqrt{1-r^2}e^{i\theta_2} \\ \sqrt{1-r^2}e^{i\theta_3} & re^{i\theta_4} \end{pmatrix}$$

where $0 \leq r \leq 1$, and $\theta_k \in \mathbb{R}$ s.t. $e^{i(\theta_1-\theta_3)} + e^{i(\theta_2-\theta_4)} = 0$. The last condition implies that $-\theta_1 + \theta_2 + \theta_3 - \theta_4 = (2n+1)\pi$ for some integer n. Taking $\alpha = (\theta_1 - \theta_2 + \theta_3 - \theta_4)/2$ implies that $|u_{11}^*u_{22}e^{i\alpha} + u_{12}^*u_{21}e^{-i\alpha}| = 1$ and so there exists a real number β such that second equation in (17) holds. Since $-\theta_1 + \theta_2 + \alpha = n\pi + \pi/2$, the first equation in (17) holds too. Hence, $C_{f,\ell_1}(\rho) = 1$.

This shows that the state ρ defined by Equation (14) with $\alpha = (\theta_1 - \theta_2 + \theta_3 - \theta_4)/2$ satisfies

$$C_{e,\ell_1}(\rho) = C_{f,\ell_1}(\rho) = 1,$$

that is, $C_{e,\ell_1}(\rho) + C_{f,\ell_1}(\rho) = 2$. □

3. Weak Coherence

In this section, we turn to discuss the weak coherence of quantum states. To this, we use $\mathcal{B}$ to denote a set of k orthonormal bases $e^1, e^2, \ldots, e^k$ for H, i.e., $\mathcal{B} = \{e^1, e^2, \ldots, e^k\}$.

Definition 1. *We say that $\rho \in \mathcal{D}(H)$ is strongly incoherent (S-incoherent) w.r.t. $\mathcal{B}$ if ρ is incoherent w.r.t. any basis in $\mathcal{B}$. Otherwise, we say that ρ is weakly coherent (W-coherent) w.r.t. $\mathcal{B}$.*

Denoted by $\mathcal{SI}(\mathcal{B})$ the set of all S-incoherent states of H w.r.t. $\mathcal{B}$. Clearly,

$$\frac{1}{d}I \in \mathcal{SI}(\mathcal{B}) = \bigcap_{i=1}^{k}\mathcal{I}(e^i).$$

Definition 2. *Let Φ be a quantum operation on $\mathcal{B}(H)$. Then Φ is said to be an S-incoherent operation (SIO) w.r.t. $\mathcal{B}$ (or $\mathcal{B}$-incoherent operation (BIO)) if $\Phi \in \mathcal{IO}(e^i)$ for all $i = 1, 2, \ldots, k$, that is, for each $i = 1, 2, \ldots, k$, Φ has a family of Kraus operators $\{E_{in}\}_{n=1}^{m_i}$ such that*

$$E_{in}(\mathcal{I}(e^i))E_{in}^\dagger \subset \mathbb{R}^+\mathcal{I}(e^i), \quad \forall n = 1, 2, \ldots, m_i.$$

Denoted by $\mathcal{IO}(\mathcal{B})$ the set of all SIOs w.r.t. $\mathcal{B}$, then

$$\mathcal{IO}(\mathcal{B}) = \bigcap_{i=1}^{k}\mathcal{OI}(e^i).$$

Similar to the definition of the standard coherence measure, let us introduce the concept of a $\mathcal{B}$-coherence measure.

Definition 3. *A function $\mathcal{C}_\mathcal{B} : \mathcal{D}(H) \to \mathbb{R}$ is said to be a $\mathcal{B}$-coherence measure if the following four conditions are satisfied:*

(1) *Faithfulness:* $\forall \rho \in \mathcal{D}(H), \mathcal{C}_\mathcal{B}(\rho) \geq 0; \mathcal{C}_\mathcal{B}(\rho) = 0$ *if and only if* $\rho \in \mathcal{SI}(\mathcal{B})$.

(2) *Monotonicity:* $\mathcal{C}_\mathcal{B}(\Phi(\rho)) \leq \mathcal{C}_\mathcal{B}(\rho)$ *for every* $\Phi \in \mathcal{IO}(\mathcal{B})$ *and for every* $\rho \in \mathcal{D}(H)$.

(3) *Strong monotonicity: for each* $i = 1, 2, \ldots, k$, $\sum_{n=1}^{m_i} p_{in} \mathcal{C}_\mathcal{B}(\rho_{in}) \leq \mathcal{C}_\mathcal{B}(\rho)$ *for every* $\rho \in \mathcal{D}(H)$ *and every* $\Phi \in \mathcal{IO}(\mathcal{B})$ *with a family Kraus operators* $\{E_{in}\}_{n=1}^{m_i}$, *where* $p_{in} = \text{tr}(E_{in}\rho E_{in}^\dagger)$ *and* $\rho_{in} = \frac{1}{p_{in}} E_{in}\rho E_{in}^\dagger$ *for* $p_{in} > 0$, *and* $\rho_{in} = \frac{1}{d} I$ *for* $p_{in} = 0$.

(4) *Convexity:* $\mathcal{C}_\mathcal{B}(\sum_{n=1}^{m} p_n \rho_n) \leq \sum_{n=1}^{m} p_n \mathcal{C}_\mathcal{B}(\rho_n)$, *where* $\rho_n \in \mathcal{D}(H)(n = 1, 2, \ldots, m)$ *and* $\{p_n\}_{n=1}^{m}$ *is a probability distribution.*

The following theorem gives a method for constructing a $\mathcal{B}$-coherence measure from k e^i-coherence measures ($i = 1, 2, \ldots, k$).

Theorem 4. *Let $\mathcal{C}_{e^i}(i = 1, 2, \ldots, k)$ be e^i-coherence measures. Then the function $\mathcal{C}_\mathcal{B} : \mathcal{D}(H) \to \mathbb{R}$ defined by*

$$\mathcal{C}_\mathcal{B}(\rho) = \sum_{i=1}^{k} \mathcal{C}_{e^i}(\rho) (\forall \rho \in \mathcal{D}(H)) \tag{18}$$

is a $\mathcal{B}$-coherence measure.

Proof. (1) Let $\rho \in \mathcal{D}(H)$. Since $\mathcal{C}_{e^i}(\rho) \geq 0$ for all $e^i(i = 1, 2, \ldots, k)$, we have $\mathcal{C}_\mathcal{B}(\rho) = \sum_{i=1}^{k} \mathcal{C}_{e^i}(\rho) \geq 0$. Furthermore,

$$\sum_{i=1}^{k} \mathcal{C}_{e^i}(\rho) = 0 \Leftrightarrow \mathcal{C}_{e^i}(\rho) = 0 (i = 1, 2, \ldots, k) \Leftrightarrow \rho \in \mathcal{SI}(\mathcal{B}).$$

(2) Let $\Phi \in \mathcal{IO}(\mathcal{B})$. For each $i = 1, 2 \ldots, k$, since $\mathcal{C}_{e^i}$ is an e^i-coherence measure and $\Phi \in \mathcal{IO}(e^i)$, we get

$$\mathcal{C}_{e^i}(\Phi(\rho)) \leq \mathcal{C}_{e^i}(\rho)$$

for all $\rho \in \mathcal{D}(H)$, and so

$$\mathcal{C}_\mathcal{B}(\Phi(\rho)) = \sum_{i=1}^{k} \mathcal{C}_{e^i}(\Phi(\rho)) \leq \sum_{i=1}^{k} \mathcal{C}_{e^i}(\rho) = \mathcal{C}_\mathcal{B}(\rho).$$

(3) Let $\rho \in \mathcal{D}(H)$, $\Phi \in \mathcal{IO}(\mathcal{B})$ with families of Kraus operators $\{E_{in}\}_{n=1}^{m_i} (i = 1, 2, \ldots, k)$. Put $p_{in} = \text{tr}(E_{in}\rho E_{in}^\dagger)$ and $\rho_{in} = \frac{1}{p_{in}} E_{in}\rho E_{in}^\dagger$ for $p_{in} > 0$, and $\rho_{in} = \frac{1}{d} I$ for $p_{in} = 0$. For each $j = 1, 2, \ldots, k$, since $\mathcal{C}_{e^j}$ is an e^j-coherence measure and $\Phi \in \mathcal{IO}(e^j)$, we get

$$\sum_{n=1}^{m_i} p_{in} \mathcal{C}_{e^j}(\rho_{in}) \leq \mathcal{C}_{e^j}(\rho) (i, j = 1, 2, \ldots, k).$$

This implies that for each $i = 1, 2, \ldots, k$,

$$\sum_{n=1}^{m_i} p_{in} \mathcal{C}_\mathcal{B}(\rho_{in}) = \sum_{n=1}^{m_i} p_{in} \left(\sum_{j=1}^{k} \mathcal{C}_{e^j}(\rho_{in}) \right) = \sum_{j=1}^{k} \left(\sum_{n=1}^{m_i} p_{in} \mathcal{C}_{e^j}(\rho_{in}) \right) \leq \sum_{j=1}^{k} \mathcal{C}_{e^j}(\rho) = \mathcal{C}_\mathcal{B}(\rho).$$

(4) Let $\rho_n \in \mathcal{D}(H)(n = 1, 2, \ldots, m)$ and let $\{p_n\}_{n=1}^m$ be a probability distribution. Since $\mathcal{C}_{e^i}$ is an e^i-coherence measure, we have

$$\sum_{n=1}^m p_n \mathcal{C}_{e^i}(\rho_n) \geq \mathcal{C}_{e^i}\left(\sum_{n=1}^m p_n \rho_n\right)$$

for all $i = 1, 2, \ldots, k$, and therefore,

$$\sum_{n=1}^m p_n \mathcal{C}_{\mathcal{B}}(\rho_n) = \sum_{i=1}^k \left(\sum_{n=1}^m p_n \mathcal{C}_{e^i}(\rho_n)\right) \geq \sum_{i=1}^k \mathcal{C}_{e^i}\left(\sum_{n=1}^m p_n \rho_n\right) = \mathcal{C}_{\mathcal{B}}\left(\sum_{n=1}^m p_n \rho_n\right).$$

Using Definition 3 yields that the function $\mathcal{C}_{\mathcal{B}}$ defined by Equation (18) becomes a $\mathcal{B}$-coherence measure. □

Using Theorem 4 yields that the function $\mathcal{C}_{\mathcal{B}} : \mathcal{D}(H) \to \mathbb{R}$ defined by

$$\mathcal{C}_{\mathcal{B},\ell_1}(\rho) = \sum_{i=1}^k \mathcal{C}_{e^i,\ell_1}(\rho)(\forall \rho \in \mathcal{D}(H)) \qquad (19)$$

is a $\mathcal{B}$-coherence measure. We see from property (1) that $\mathcal{C}_{\mathcal{B},\ell_1}(\rho) \leq k(d-1)$ for all states ρ of the system. A state ρ is said to be *maximally coherent* w.r.t. $\mathcal{C}_{\mathcal{B},\ell_1}$ if $\mathcal{C}_{\mathcal{B},\ell_1}(\rho) = k(d-1)$. Clearly, a state ρ is maximally coherent $\mathcal{C}_{\mathcal{B},\ell_1}$ if and only if it is maximally coherent w.r.t. each $\mathcal{C}_{e^i,\ell_1}$.

Remark 3. (1) $\frac{I}{d} \in \mathcal{SI}(\mathcal{B})$; Especially, if there exist two mutually unbiased bases in $\mathcal{B}$, then $\mathcal{SI}(\mathcal{B}) = \{\frac{I}{d}\}$, that is, $\mathcal{C}_{\mathcal{B},\ell_1}(\rho) = 0$ if and only if $\rho = \frac{I}{d}$.
(2) Theorem 3 implies when $d = 2$ and $\mathcal{B} = \{e, f\}(e \neq f)$, there exists a maximally coherent state ρ w.r.t. $\mathcal{C}_{\mathcal{B},\ell_1}$, that is, $\mathcal{C}_{\mathcal{B},\ell_1}(\rho) = 2$.
(3) The following theorem means that when $d = 2$ and $\mathcal{B} = \{e, f, g\}$ is a complete set of mutually unbiased bases, there does not exist necessarily a maximally coherent state w.r.t. $\mathcal{C}_{\mathcal{B},\ell_1}$.

It was proved in [47] that the maximal number $MUB(H)$ of mutually unbiased bases for H is $d + 1$ if the dimension d of H is a prime-power. Thus, $MUB(\mathbb{C}^2) = 3$, i.e., there exists a complete set of three mutually unbiased bases for $\mathbb{C}^2$.

Theorem 5. Let $\mathcal{B} = \{e, f, g\}$ where $e = \{|e_1\rangle, |e_2\rangle\}$ be any orthonormal basis for $\mathbb{C}^2$, $f = \{|f_1\rangle, |f_2\rangle\}$ and $g = \{|g_1\rangle, |g_2\rangle\}$ with

$$|f_1\rangle = \frac{1}{\sqrt{2}}(|e_1\rangle + |e_2\rangle), |f_2\rangle = \frac{1}{\sqrt{2}}(|e_1\rangle - |e_2\rangle),$$

$$|g_1\rangle = \frac{1}{\sqrt{2}}(|e_1\rangle + i|e_2\rangle), |f_2\rangle = \frac{1}{\sqrt{2}}(|e_1\rangle - i|e_2\rangle).$$

Then e, f and g are mutually unbiased bases pairwise for $\mathbb{C}^2$ and $\mathcal{C}_{\mathcal{B},\ell_1}(\rho) < 3$ for all states ρ of $\mathbb{C}^2$, that is, there does not exist a state ρ such that

$$\mathcal{C}_{e,\ell_1}(\rho) = \mathcal{C}_{f,\ell_1}(\rho) = \mathcal{C}_{g,\ell_1}(\rho) = 1. \qquad (20)$$

Proof. Obviously, e, f and g are mutually unbiased bases pairwise for $\mathbb{C}^2$. Suppose that there exists a state ρ such that Equation (20) holds, i.e.,

$$|\langle e_1|\rho|e_2\rangle| = |\langle f_1|\rho|f_2\rangle| = |\langle g_1|\rho|g_2\rangle| = \frac{1}{2}. \qquad (21)$$

Then under the three bases, we have

$$\rho = a|e_1\rangle\langle e_1| + \frac{1}{2}e^{i\theta_1}|e_1\rangle\langle e_2| + \frac{1}{2}e^{-i\theta_1}|e_2\rangle\langle e_1| + (1-a)|e_2\rangle\langle e_2|, \tag{22}$$

$$\rho = b|f_1\rangle\langle f_1| + \frac{1}{2}e^{i\theta_2}|f_1\rangle\langle f_2| + \frac{1}{2}e^{-i\theta_2}|f_2\rangle\langle f_1| + (1-b)|f_2\rangle\langle f_2|, \tag{23}$$

$$\rho = c|g_1\rangle\langle g_1| + \frac{1}{2}e^{i\theta_3}|g_1\rangle\langle g_2| + \frac{1}{2}e^{-i\theta_3}|g_2\rangle\langle g_1| + (1-c)|g_2\rangle\langle g_2|, \tag{24}$$

where $a, b, c \in [0, 1], 0 \le \theta_k < 2\pi (k = 1, 2, 3)$. Since $\rho \ge 0$, we conclude from Equation (21) that $a = b = c = \frac{1}{2}$. Substituting $2|f_i\rangle\langle f_j|$ in Equation (23) with

$$2|f_1\rangle\langle f_1| = |e_1\rangle\langle e_1| + |e_1\rangle\langle e_2| + |e_2\rangle\langle e_1| + |e_2\rangle\langle e_2|,$$

$$2|f_1\rangle\langle f_2| = |e_1\rangle\langle e_1| - |e_1\rangle\langle e_2| + |e_2\rangle\langle e_1| - |e_2\rangle\langle e_2|,$$

$$2|f_2\rangle\langle f_1| = |e_1\rangle\langle e_1| + |e_1\rangle\langle e_2| - |e_2\rangle\langle e_1| - |e_2\rangle\langle e_2|,$$

$$2|f_2\rangle\langle f_2| = |e_1\rangle\langle e_1| - |e_1\rangle\langle e_2| - |e_2\rangle\langle e_1| + |e_2\rangle\langle e_2|,$$

and comparing the coefficient of $|e_1\rangle\langle e_2|$ in Equations (22) and (23), we find that

$$e^{i\theta_1} = -i\sin\theta_2 \text{ and so } \cos\theta_1 = 0. \tag{25}$$

Similarly, substituting $2|g_i\rangle\langle g_j|$ in Equation (24) with

$$2|g_1\rangle\langle g_1| = |e_1\rangle\langle e_1| - i|e_1\rangle\langle e_2| + i|e_2\rangle\langle e_1| + |e_2\rangle\langle e_2|,$$

$$2|g_1\rangle\langle g_2| = |e_1\rangle\langle e_1| + i|e_1\rangle\langle e_2| + i|e_2\rangle\langle e_1| - |e_2\rangle\langle e_2|,$$

$$2|g_2\rangle\langle g_1| = |e_1\rangle\langle e_1| - i|e_1\rangle\langle e_2| - i|e_2\rangle\langle e_1| - |e_2\rangle\langle e_2|,$$

$$2|g_2\rangle\langle g_2| = |e_1\rangle\langle e_1| + i|e_1\rangle\langle e_2| - i|e_2\rangle\langle e_1| + |e_2\rangle\langle e_2|,$$

and comparing the coefficient of $|e_1\rangle\langle e_2|$ in Equations (22) and (24), we find that

$$e^{i\theta_1} = -\sin\theta_3 \text{ and so } \sin\theta_1 = 0. \tag{26}$$

Combining Equations (25) and (26) yields that $\cos\theta_1 = \sin\theta_1 = 0$, a contradiction. □

4. Conclusions

In this paper, we have introduced a correlation function $m(e, f)$ of two orthonormal bases e and f with the property that $0 \le m(e, f) \le d^{\frac{3}{2}} - d$, and proved that $m(e, f) = 0$ if and only if the rank-one projective measurements generated by e and f are identical if and only if $\mathcal{I}(e) = \mathcal{I}(f)$, where $\mathcal{I}(e)$ and $\mathcal{I}(f)$ denote the sets of incoherent states with respect to e and f, respectively. We have also shown that $m(e, f)$ reaches the maximum $d^{\frac{3}{2}} - d$ if and only if the bases e and f are mutually unbiased; in that case, the intersection $\mathcal{I}(e) \cap \mathcal{I}(f)$ includes only the maximally mixed state. We have observed that even though two bases e and f are not mutually unbiased, $\mathcal{I}(e) \cap \mathcal{I}(f)$ may include only the maximally mixed state. We have obtained a necessary and sufficient condition for $\mathcal{I}(e) \cap \mathcal{I}(f) = \frac{I}{d}$. We have introduced the concepts of strong incoherence and weak coherence of a quantum state w.r.t. a set $\mathcal{B}$ of k orthonormal bases and proposed a measure $\mathcal{C}_\mathcal{B}$ for the weak coherence. In the two-qubit system, we have proved that there exists a maximally coherent state w.r.t. the measure $\mathcal{C}_{\mathcal{B},\ell_1}$ when $\mathcal{B}$ consists of any two bases and observed that there exist does not a maximally coherent state w.r.t. the measure $\mathcal{C}_{\mathcal{B},\ell_1}$ when $\mathcal{B}$ consists of some three mutually unbiased bases.

Author Contributions: The work of this paper was accomplished by P.W., Z.G. and H.C. Moreover, all authors have read the paper carefully and approved the research contents that were written in the final manuscript. All authors have read and agreed to the published version of the manuscript.

Funding: This work was supported by the National Natural Science Foundation of China (Nos. 11871318, 11771009, 12001480), the Fundamental Research Fund for the Central Universities (GK20200 7002, GK202103003) and the Special Plan for Young Top-notch Talent of Shaanxi Province (1503070117).

Institutional Review Board Statement: Not applicable.

Informed Consent Statement: Not applicable.

Data Availability Statement: Data are contained within the article.

Acknowledgments: The authors would like to thank the anonymous reviewers for their invaluable and constructive comments.

Conflicts of Interest: The authors declare no conflict of interest.

References

1. Nielsen, M.A.; Chuang, I.L. Quantum Computation and Quantum Information. *Contemrary Phys.* **2011**, *52*, 604–605.
2. Åberg, J. Quantifying superposition. *arXiv* **2006**, arXiv:quant-ph/0612146.
3. Baumgratz, T.; Cramer, M.; Plenio, M.B. Quantum coherence. *Phys. Rev. Lett.* **2014**, *113* 140401. [CrossRef] [PubMed]
4. Streltsov, A.; Adesso, G.; Plenio, M.B. Colloquium: Quantum coherence as a resource. *Rev. Mod. Phys.* **2017**, *89*, 041003. [CrossRef]
5. Winter, A.; Yang, D. Operational resource theory of coherence. *Phys. Rev. Lett.* **2016**, *116*, 120404. [CrossRef]
6. Hu, M.L.; Hu, X.Y.; Wang, J.C.; Peng, Y.; Zhang, Y.R.; Fan, H. Quantum coherence and geometric quantum discord. *Phys. Rep.* **2018**, *762–764*, 1–100. [CrossRef]
7. Yang, C.; Guo, Z.H.; Zhang, C.Y.; Cao, H.X. Broadcasting coherence via incoherent operations. *Linear Mult. Alg.* **2021**. [CrossRef]
8. Guo, Z.H.; Cao, H.X. Creating quantum correlation from coherence via incoherent quantum operations. *J. Phys. A Math. Theor.* **2019**, *52*, 265301. [CrossRef]
9. Girolami, D. Observable measure of quantum coherence in finite dimensional systems. *Phys. Rev. Lett.* **2014**, *113*, 170401. [CrossRef]
10. Streltsov, A.; Singh, U.; Dhar, H.S.; Bera, M.N.; Adesso, G. Measuring quantum coherence with entanglement. *Phys. Rev. Lett.* **2015**, *115*, 020403. [CrossRef]
11. Lostaglio, M.; Korzekwa, K.; Jennings, D.; Rudolph, T. Quantum coherence, time-translation symmetry, and thermodynamics. *Phys. Rev. X* **2015**, *5*, 021001. [CrossRef]
12. Shao, L.H.; Xi, Z.J.; Fan, H.; Li, Y.M. Fidelity and trace-norm distances for quantifying coherence. *Phys. Rev. A* **2015**, *91*, 042120. [CrossRef]
13. Pires, D.P.; Céleri, L.C.; Soares-Pinto, D.O. Geometric lower bound for a quantum coherence measure. *Phys. Rev. A* **2015**, *91*, 042330. [CrossRef]
14. Yao, Y.; Xiao, X.; Ge, L.; Sun, C.P. Quantum coherence in multipartite systems. *Phys. Rev. A* **2015**, *92*, 022112. [CrossRef]
15. Napoli, C.; Bromley, T.R.; Cianciaruso, M.; Piani, M.; Johnston N.; Adesso G. Robustness of coherence: An operational and observable measure of quantum coherence. *Phys. Rev. Lett.* **2016**, *116*, 150502. [CrossRef]
16. Rana, S.; Parashar, P.; Lewenstein, M. Trace-distance measure of coherence. *Phys. Rev. A* **2016**, *93*, 012110. [CrossRef]
17. Rastegin, A.E. Quantum-coherence quantifiers based on the Tsallis relative α entropies. *Phys. Rev. A* **2016**, *93*, 032136. [CrossRef]
18. Luo, S.; Sun, Y. Quantum coherence versus quantum uncertainty. *Phys. Rev. A* **2017**, *96*, 022130. [CrossRef]
19. Xi, Z.J.; Hu, M.L.; Li, Y.M.; Fan, H. Entropic cohering power in quantum operations. *Quantum Inf. Proc.* **2018**, *17*, 34. [CrossRef]
20. Shi, H.L.; Liu, S.Y.; Wang, X.H.; Yang, W.L.; Yang, Z.Y.; Fan H. Coherence depletion in the Grover quantum search algorithm. *Phys. Rev. A* **2017**, *95*, 032307. [CrossRef]
21. Anand, N.; Pati, A.K. Coherence and entanglement monogamy in the discrete analogue of analog grover search. *arXiv* **2016**, arXiv:1611.04542.
22. Rastegin, A.E. On the role of dealing with quantum coherence in amplitude amplification. *Quantum Inf. Proc.* **2018**, *17*, 179. [CrossRef]
23. Hillery, M. Coherence as a resource in decision problems: The Deutsch-Jozsa algorithm and a variation. *Phys. Rev. A* **2016**, *93*, 012111. [CrossRef]
24. Matera, J.M.; Egloff, D.; Killoran, N.; Plenio, M.B. Coherent control of quantum systems as a resource theory. *Quantum Sci. Technol.* **2016**, *1*, 01LT01. [CrossRef]
25. Giovannetti, V.; Lloyd, S.; Maccone, L. Advances in quantum metrology. *Nat. Photonics* **2011**, *5*, 222–229. [CrossRef]
26. Rodríguez-Rosario, C.A.; Frauenheim, T.; Aspuru-Guzik, A. Thermodynamics of quantum coherence. *arXiv* **2013**, arXiv:1308.1245.
27. Lostaglio, M.; Jennings, D.; Rudolph, T. Description of quantum coherence in thermodynamic processes requires constraints beyond free energy. *Nat. Commun.* **2015**, *6*, 6383. [CrossRef]

28. Brandão, F.; Horodecki, M.; Ng, N.; Oppenheim J.; Wehner, S. The second laws of quantum thermodynamics. *Proc. Natl. Acad. Sci. USA* **2015**, *112*, 3275. [CrossRef]
29. Narasimhachar, V.; Gour, G. Low-temperature thermodynamics with quantum coherence. *Nat. Commun.* **2015**, *6*, 7689. [CrossRef]
30. Ćwikliński, P.; Studziński, M.; Horodecki, M.; Oppenheim J. Limitations on the evolution of quantum coherences: Towards fully quantum second laws of thermodynamics. *Phys. Rev. Lett.* **2015**, *115*, 210403. [CrossRef]
31. Misra, A.; Singh, U.; Bhattacharya, S.; Pati, A.K. Energy cost of creating quantum coherence. *Phys. Rev. A* **2016**, *93*, 052335. [CrossRef]
32. Plenio, M.B.; Huelga, S.F. Dephasing-assisted transport: Quantum networks and biomolecules. *New J. Phys.* **2008**, *10*, 113019. [CrossRef]
33. Lloyd, S. Quantum coherence in biological systems. *J. Phys. Conf. Ser.* **2011**, *302*, 012037. [CrossRef]
34. Levi, F.; Mintert, F. A quantitative theory of coherent delocalization. *New J. Phys.* **2014**, *16*, 033007. [CrossRef]
35. Cheng, S.M.; Hall, M.J.W. Complementarity relations for quantum coherence. *Phys. Rev. A* **2015**, *92*, 042101. [CrossRef]
36. Rastegin, A.E. Uncertainty relations for quantum coherence with respect to mutually unbiased bases. *Front. Phys.* **2017**, *13*, 130304. [CrossRef]
37. Sheng, Y.H.; Zhang, J.; Tao, Y.H.; Fei, S.M. Applications of quantum coherence via skew information under mutually unbiased bases. *Quantum Inf. Proc.* **2021**, *20*, 82. [CrossRef]
38. Luo, S.; Sun, Y. Partial coherence with application to the monotonicity problem of coherence involving skew information. *Phys. Rev. A* **2017**, *96*, 022136. [CrossRef]
39. Kim, S.; Li, L.; Kumar, A.; Wu, J. Interrelation between partial coherence and quantum correlations. *Phys. Rev. A* **2018**, *98*, 022306. [CrossRef]
40. Xiong, C.; Kumar, A.; Huang, M.; Das, S.; Sen, U.; Wu, J. Partial coherence and quantum correlation with fifidelity and affifinity distances. *Phys. Rev. A* **2019**, *99*, 032305. [CrossRef]
41. Bischof, F.; Kampermann, H.; Bruß, D. Resource theory of coherence based on positive-operator-valued measures. *Phys. Rev. Lett.* **2019**, *123*, 110402. [CrossRef] [PubMed]
42. Bischof, F.; Kampermann, H.; Bruß, D. Quantifying coherence with respect to general quantum measurements. *Phys. Rev. A* **2021**, *103*, 032429. [CrossRef]
43. Zhang, C.Y.; Wang, P.; Bai, L.H.; Guo, Z.H.; Cao, H.X. Channel-based coherence of quantum states. *Int. J. Quantum Inf.* **2022**. [CrossRef]
44. Xu, J.W. Coherence of quantum channels. *Phys. Rev. A* **2019**, *100*, 052311. [CrossRef]
45. Xu, J.W.; Shao, L.H.; Fei, S.M. Coherence measures with respect to general quantum measurements. *Phys. Rev. A* **2020**, *102*, 012411. [CrossRef]
46. Designolle, S.; Uola, R.; Luoma, K.; Brunner N. Set coherence: Basis-independent quantification of quantum coherence. *Phys. Rev. Lett.* **2021**, *126*, 220404. [CrossRef]
47. Wootters, W.K.; Fields, B.D. Optimal state-determination by mutually unbiased measurements. *Ann. Phys.* **1989**, *191*, 363. [CrossRef]

Article

When Is a Genuine Multipartite Entanglement Measure Monogamous?

Yu Guo

Institute of Quantum Information Science, School of Mathematics and Statistics, Shanxi Datong University, Datong 037009, China; guoyu@sxdtdx.edu.cn

Abstract: A crucial issue in quantum communication tasks is characterizing how quantum resources can be quantified and distributed over many parties. Consequently, entanglement has been explored extensively. However, there are few genuine multipartite entanglement measures and whether it is monogamous is so far unknown. In this work, we explore the complete monogamy of genuine multipartite entanglement measure (GMEM) for which, at first, we investigate a framework for unified/complete GMEM according to the unified/complete multipartite entanglement measure we proposed in 2020. We find a way of inducing unified/complete GMEM from any given unified/complete multipartite entanglement measure. It is shown that any unified GMEM is completely monogamous, and any complete GMEM that is induced by given complete multipartite entanglement measure is completely monogamous. In addition, the previous GMEMs are checked under this framework. It turns out that the genuinely multipartite concurrence is not as good of a candidate as GMEM.

Keywords: genuine entanglement; entanglement measure; complete monogamy

Citation: Guo, Y. When Is a Genuine Multipartite Entanglement Measure Monogamous? *Entropy* **2022**, *24*, 355. https://doi.org/10.3390/e24030355

Academic Editors: Rosario Lo Franco, Shunlong Luo, Ming Li and Shao-Ming Fei

Received: 5 February 2022
Accepted: 25 February 2022
Published: 28 February 2022

Publisher's Note: MDPI stays neutral with regard to jurisdictional claims in published maps and institutional affiliations.

Copyright: © 2022 by the authors. Licensee MDPI, Basel, Switzerland. This article is an open access article distributed under the terms and conditions of the Creative Commons Attribution (CC BY) license (https://creativecommons.org/licenses/by/4.0/).

1. Introduction

Entanglement is a quintessential manifestation of quantum mechanics and is often considered to be a useful resource for tasks like quantum teleportation or quantum cryptography [1–4], etc. There has been a tremendous amount of research in the literature aimed at characterizing entanglement in the last three decades [1–9]. In an effort to contribute to this line of research, however, the genuine multiparty entanglement, which represents the strongest form of entanglement in many body systems, still remains unexplored or less studied in many facets.

A fundamental issue in this field is to quantify the genuine multipartite entanglement and then analyze the distribution among the different parties. In 2000 [10], Coffman et al. presented a measure of genuine three-qubit entanglement, called "residual tangle", and discussed the distribution relation for the first time. In 2011, Ma et al. [11] established postulates for a quantity to be a GMEM and gave a genuine measure, called genuinely multipartite concurrence (GMC), by the origin bipartite concurrence. The GMC is further explored in Ref. [12], the generalized geometric measure is introduced in Refs. [13,14], and the average of "residual tangle" and GMC, i.e., $(\tau + C_{gme})/2$ [15], is shown to be genuine multipartite entanglement measures. Another one is the divergence-based genuine multipartite entanglement measure presented in [16,17]. Recently, Ref. [18] introduced a new genuine three-qubit entanglement measure, called *concurrence triangle*, which is quantified as the square root of the area of a triangle deduced by concurrence. Consequently, we improved and supplemented the method in [18] and proposed a general way of defining GMEM in Ref. [19].

The distribution of entanglement is believed to be monogamous, i.e., a quantum system entangled with another system limits its entanglement with the remaining others [20]. There are two methods used in this research. The first one is analyzing monogamy relation based on bipartite entanglement measure, and the second one is based on multipartite entanglement measure. For the former one, considerable efforts have been made in the last two decades [10,21–40]. It is shown that almost all bipartite entanglement measures we know by now are monogamous. In 2020, we established a framework for multipartite entanglement measure and discussed its monogamy relation, which is called complete monogamy relation and tight complete monogamy relation [22]. Under this framework, the distribution of entanglement becomes more clear since it displays a complete hierarchy relation of different subsystems. We also proposed several multipartite entanglement measures and showed that they are completely monogamous.

The situation becomes much more complex when we deal with genuine entanglement, since it associates with not only multiparty system but also the most complex entanglement structure. The main purpose of this work is to establish the framework of unified/complete GMEM, by which we then present the definition of complete monogamy and tight complete monogamy of unified and complete GMEM, respectively. Another aim is to find an approach of deriving GMEM from the multipartite entanglement measure introduced in Ref. [22]. In the next section we list some necessary concepts and the associated notations. In Section 3 we discuss the framework of unified/complete GMEM and give several illustrated examples. Then, in Section 4, we investigate the complete monogamy relation and tight complete monogamy relation for GMEM accordingly. A summary is concluded in the last section.

2. Preliminary

For convenience, in this section, we recall the concepts of genuine entanglement, complete multipartite entanglement measure, monogamy relation, complete monogamy relation, and genuine multipartite entanglement measure. In the first subsection, we introduce the coarser relation of multipartite partition by which the following concepts can be easily processed. For simplicity, throughout this paper, we denote by $\mathcal{H}^{A_1A_2\cdots A_m} := \mathcal{H}^{A_1} \otimes \mathcal{H}^{A_2} \otimes \cdots \otimes \mathcal{H}^{A_m}$ an m-partite Hilbert space with finite dimension and by $\mathcal{S}^X$ we denote the set of density operators acting on $\mathcal{H}^X$.

2.1. Coarser Relation of Multipartite Partition

Let $X_1|X_2|\cdots|X_k$ be a partition (or called k-partition) of $A_1A_2\cdots A_m$, i.e., $X_s = A_{s(1)}A_{s(2)}\cdots A_{s(f(s))}$, $s(i) < s(j)$ whenever $i < j$, and $s(p) < t(q)$ whenever $s < t$ for any possible p and q, $1 \leq s,t \leq k$. For instance, partition $AB|C|DE$ is a 3-partition of $ABCDE$. Let $X_1|X_2|\cdots|X_k$ and $Y_1|Y_2|\cdots|Y_l$ be two partitions of $A_1A_2\cdots A_n$ or subsystem of $A_1A_2\cdots A_n$. $Y_1|Y_2|\cdots|Y_l$ is said to be *coarser* than $X_1|X_2|\cdots|X_k$, denoted by

$$X_1|X_2|\cdots|X_k \succ Y_1|Y_2|\cdots|Y_l, \tag{1}$$

if $Y_1|Y_2|\cdots|Y_l$ can be obtained from $X_1|X_2|\cdots|X_k$ by one or some of the following ways (the coarser relation was also introduced in Ref. [41], but the the third case in Ref. [41] is a little different from the third item below):

- (C1) Discarding some subsystem(s) of $X_1|X_2|\cdots|X_k$;
- (C2) Combining some subsystems of $X_1|X_2|\cdots|X_k$;
- (C3) Discarding some subsystem(s) of some subsystem(s) X_k provided that $X_k = A_{k(1)}A_{k(2)}\cdots A_{k(f(k))}$ with $f(k) \geq 2$.

For example, $A|B|C|D|E \succ A|B|C|DE \succ A|B|C|D \succ AB|C|D \succ AB|CD$, $A|B|C|DE \succ A|B|DE$. Clearly, $X_1|X_2|\cdots|X_k \succ Y_1|Y_2|\cdots|Y_l$ and $Y_1|Y_2|\cdots|Y_l \succ Z_1|Z_2|\cdots|Z_s$ imply $X_1|X_2|\cdots|X_k \succ Z_1|Z_2|\cdots|Z_s$.

Furthermore, if $X_1|X_2|\cdots|X_k \succ Y_1|Y_2|\cdots|Y_l$, we denote by $\Xi(X_1|X_2|\cdots|X_k - Y_1|Y_2|\cdots|Y_l)$ the set of all the partitions that are coarser than $X_1|X_2|\cdots|X_k$ and either exclude any subsystem of $Y_1|Y_2|\cdots|Y_l$ or include some but not all subsystems of $Y_1|Y_2|\cdots|Y_l$. We take the five-partite system $ABCDE$ for example, $\Xi(A|B|CD|E - A|B) = \{CD|E, A|CD|E, B|CD|E, A|CD, A|E, B|E, A|C, A|D, B|C, B|D\}$.

For more clarity, we fix the following notations. Let $X_1|X_2|\cdots|X_k$ and $Y_1|Y_2|\cdots|Y_l$ be partitions of $A_1A_2\cdots A_n$ or subsystem of $A_1A_2\cdots A_n$. We denote by

$$X_1|X_2|\cdots|X_k \succ^a Y_1|Y_2|\cdots|Y_l \tag{2}$$

for the case of (C1), by

$$X_1|X_2|\cdots|X_k \succ^b Y_1|Y_2|\cdots|Y_l \tag{3}$$

for the case of of (C2), and in addition by

$$X_1|X_2|\cdots|X_k \succ^c Y_1|Y_2|\cdots|Y_l \tag{4}$$

for the case of of (C2). For example, $A|B|C|D \succ^a A|B|D \succ^a B|D$, $A|B|C|D \succ^b AC|B|D \succ^b AC|BD$, $A|BC \succ^c A|B$, $A|BC \succ^c A|C$.

2.2. Multipartite Entanglement

An m-partite pure state $|\psi\rangle \in \mathcal{H}^{A_1A_2\cdots A_m}$ is called biseparable if it can be written as $|\psi\rangle = |\psi\rangle^X \otimes |\psi\rangle^Y$ for some bipartition of $A_1A_2\cdots A_m$. $|\psi\rangle$ is said to be k-separable if $|\psi\rangle = |\psi\rangle^{X_1}|\psi\rangle^{X_2}\cdots|\psi\rangle^{X_k}$ for some k-partition of $A_1A_2\cdots A_m$. $|\psi\rangle$ is called fully separable if it is m-separable. It is clear that whenever a state is k-separable, it is automatically also l-separable for all $1 < l < k \leq m$. An m-partite mixed state ρ is biseparable if it can be written as a convex combination of biseparable pure states $\rho = \sum_i p_i|\psi_i\rangle\langle\psi_i|$, wherein the contained $\{|\psi_i\rangle\}$ can be biseparable with respect to different bipartitions (i.e., a mixed biseparable state does not need to be separable with respect to any particular bipartition). Otherwise it is called genuinely m-partite entangled (or called genuinely entangled briefly). We denote by $\mathcal{S}_g^{A_1A_2\cdots A_m}$ the set of all genuinely entangled states in $\mathcal{S}^{A_1A_2\cdots A_m}$. Throughout this paper, for any $\rho \in \mathcal{S}^{A_1A_2\cdots A_m}$ and any given k-partition $X_1|X_2|\cdots|X_k$ of $A_1A_2\cdots A_m$, we denote by $\rho^{X_1|X_2|\cdots|X_k}$ the state for which we consider it as a k-partite state with respect to the partition $X_1|X_2|\cdots|X_k$.

2.3. Complete Multipartite Entanglement Measure

A function $E^{(m)} : \mathcal{S}^{A_1A_2\cdots A_m} \to \mathbb{R}_+$ is called an m-partite entanglement measure in literatures [3,42,43] if it satisfies:

- **(E1)** $E^{(m)}(\rho) = 0$ if ρ is fully separable;
- **(E2)** $E^{(m)}$ cannot increase under m-partite LOCC.

An m-partite entanglement measure $E^{(m)}$ is said to be an m-partite entanglement monotone if it is convex and does not increase on average under m-partite stochastic LOCC. For simplicity, throughout this paper, if E is an entanglement measure (bipartite, or multipartite) for pure states, we define

$$E_F(\rho) := \min \sum_i p_i E^{(m)}(|\psi_i\rangle) \tag{5}$$

and call it the convex-roof extension of E, where the minimum is taken over all pure-state decomposition $\{p_i, |\psi_i\rangle\}$ of ρ (Sometimes, we use E^F to denote E_F hereafter). When we take into consideration an m-partite entanglement measure, we need discuss whether it is defined uniformly for any k-partite system at first, $k < m$. Let $E^{(m)}$ be a multipartite entanglement measure (MEM). If $E^{(k)}$ is uniquely determined by $E^{(m)}$ for any $2 \leq k < m$, then we call $E^{(m)}$ a *uniform* MEM. For example, GMC, denoted by C_{gme} [11], is uniquely defined for any k, thus it is a uniform GMEM. Recall that,

$$C_{gme}(|\psi\rangle) := \min_{\gamma_i \in \gamma} \sqrt{2\left[1 - \text{Tr}(\rho^{A_{\gamma_i}})^2\right]}$$

for pure state $|\psi\rangle \in \mathcal{H}^{A_1A_2\cdots A_m}$, where $\gamma = \{\gamma_i\}$ represents the set of all possible bipartitions of $A_1A_2\cdots A_m$, and via the convex-roof extension for mixed states [11]. All the unified MEMs presented in Ref. [22] are uniform MEM. That is, a uniform MEM is series of MEMs that have uniform expressions definitely. A uniform MEM $E^{(m)}$ is called a *unified* multipartite entanglement measure if it also satisfies the following condition [22]:

- **(E3)** *the unification condition*, i.e., $E^{(m)}$ is consistent with $E^{(k)}$ for any $2 \leqslant k < m$.

The unification condition should be comprehended in the following sense [22]. Let $|\psi\rangle^{A_1A_2\cdots A_m} = |\psi\rangle^{A_1A_2\cdots A_k}|\psi\rangle^{A_{k+1}\cdots A_m}$, then

$$E^{(m)}(|\psi\rangle^{A_1A_2\cdots A_m}) = E^{(k)}(|\psi\rangle^{A_1A_2\cdots A_k}) + E^{(m-k)}|\psi\rangle^{A_{k+1}\cdots A_m}.$$

And

$$E^{(m)}(\rho^{A_1A_2\cdots A_m}) = E^{(m)}(\rho^{\pi(A_1A_2\cdots A_m)})$$

for any $\rho^{A_1A_2\cdots A_m} \in \mathcal{S}^{A_1A_2\cdots A_m}$, where π is a permutation of the subsystems. In addition,

$$E^{(k)}(X_1|X_2|\cdots|X_k) \geqslant E^{(l)}(Y_1|Y_2|\cdots|Y_l)$$

for any $\rho^{A_1A_2\cdots A_m} \in \mathcal{S}^{A_1A_2\cdots A_m}$ whenever $X_1|X_2|\cdots|X_k \succ^a Y_1|Y_2|\cdots|Y_l$, where the vertical bar indicates the split across which the entanglement is measured. A uniform MEM $E^{(m)}$ is called a *complete* multipartite entanglement measure if it satisfies both **(E3)** above and the following [22]:

- **(E4)** $E^{(m)}(X_1|X_2|\cdots|X_k) \geqslant E^{(k)}(Y_1|Y_2|\cdots|Y_l)$ holds for all $\rho \in \mathcal{S}^{A_1A_2\cdots A_m}$ whenever $X_1|X_2|\cdots|X_k \succ^b Y_1|Y_2|\cdots|Y_l$.

We need to remark here that, although the partial trace is in fact a special trace-preserving completely positive map, we cannot derive $\rho^{Y_1|Y_2|\cdots|Y_l}$ from $\rho^{X_1|X_2|\cdots|X_k}$ by any k-partite LOCC for any given $X_1|X_2|\cdots|X_k \succ Y_1|Y_2|\cdots|Y_l$. Namely, different from that of bipartite case, the unification condition cannot be induced by the m-partite LOCC. For any bipartite measure E, $E(A|BC) \geq E(AB)$ for any ρ^{ABC} since $\rho^{AB} = \text{Tr}_C \rho^{ABC}$ can be obtained by partial trace on part C and such a partial trace is in fact a bipartite LOCC acting on $A|BC$. However, ρ^{AB} cannot be derived from any tripartite LOCC acting on ρ^{ABC}. Thus, whether $E^{(3)}(A|BC) \geq E^{(2)}(AB)$ is unknown.

Several unified tripartite entanglement measures were proposed in Ref. [22]:

$$E_f^{(3)}(|\psi\rangle) = \frac{1}{2}\left[S(\rho^A) + S(\rho^B) + S(\rho^C)\right],$$

$$\tau^{(3)}(|\psi\rangle) = 3 - \text{Tr}(\rho^A)^2 - \text{Tr}(\rho^B)^2 - \text{Tr}(\rho^C)^2,$$

$$C^{(3)}(|\psi\rangle) = \sqrt{\tau^{(3)}(|\psi\rangle)},$$

$$N^{(3)}(|\psi\rangle) = \text{Tr}^2\sqrt{\rho^A} + \text{Tr}^2\sqrt{\rho^B} + \text{Tr}^2\sqrt{\rho^C} - 3,$$

$$T_q^{(3)}(|\psi\rangle) = \frac{1}{2}\left[T_q(\rho^A) + T_q(\rho^B) + T_q(\rho^C)\right], q > 1,$$

$$R_\alpha^{(3)}(|\psi\rangle) = \frac{1}{2}R_\alpha(\rho^A \otimes \rho^B \otimes \rho^C), 0 < \alpha < 1$$

for pure state $|\psi\rangle \in \mathcal{H}^{ABC}$, and then by the convex-roof extension for mixed state $\rho^{ABC} \in \mathcal{S}^{ABC}$ (for mixed state, $N^{(3)}$ is replaced with $N_F^{(3)}$), where $T_q(\rho) := (1-q)^{-1}[\text{Tr}(\rho^q) - 1]$ is the Tsallis q-entropy, $R_\alpha(\rho) := (1-\alpha)^{-1}\ln(\text{Tr}\rho^\alpha)$ is the Rényi α-entropy. In addition [22],

$$N^{(3)}(\rho) = \|\rho^{T_a}\|_{\text{Tr}} + \|\rho^{T_b}\|_{\text{Tr}} + \|\rho^{T_c}\|_{\text{Tr}} - 3 \qquad (6)$$

for any $\rho \in \mathcal{S}^{ABC}$. $E_f^{(3)}, C^{(3)}, \tau^{(3)}$ and $T_q^{(3)}$ are shown to be complete tripartite entanglement measures while $R_\alpha^{(3)}$, $N^{(3)}$ and $N_F^{(3)}$ are proved to be unified but not complete tripartite entanglement measures [22].

In Ref. [44], we introduce three unified tripartite entanglement measures (but not complete tripartite entanglement measures) in terms of fidelity:

$$E_{\mathcal{F}}^{(3)}(|\psi\rangle) := 1 - \mathcal{F}\left(|\psi\rangle\langle\psi|, \rho^A \otimes \rho^B \otimes \rho^C\right), \tag{7}$$

$$E_{\mathcal{F}'}^{(3)}(|\psi\rangle) := 1 - \sqrt{\mathcal{F}}\left(|\psi\rangle\langle\psi|, \rho^A \otimes \rho^B \otimes \rho^C\right), \tag{8}$$

$$E_{A\mathcal{F}}^{(3)}(|\psi\rangle) := 1 - \mathcal{F}_A\left(|\psi\rangle\langle\psi|, \rho^A \otimes \rho^B \otimes \rho^C\right), \tag{9}$$

for any pure state $|\psi\rangle$ in $\mathcal{H}^{ABC}$, where $\mathcal{F}$ is the Uhlmann-Jozsa fidelity $\mathcal{F}$ [45,46], which is defined as

$$\mathcal{F}(\rho, \sigma) := \left(\text{Tr}\sqrt{\sqrt{\rho}\sigma\sqrt{\rho}}\right)^2, \tag{10}$$

$\sqrt{\mathcal{F}}$ is defined by [47–49]

$$\sqrt{\mathcal{F}}(\rho, \sigma) := \sqrt{\mathcal{F}(\rho, \sigma)}, \tag{11}$$

and the *A-fidelity*, $\mathcal{F}_A$, is the square of the quantum affinity $A(\rho, \sigma)$ [50,51], i.e.,

$$\mathcal{F}_A(\rho, \sigma) := [\text{Tr}(\sqrt{\rho}\sqrt{\sigma})]^2. \tag{12}$$

For mixed states, $E_{\mathcal{F},F}^{(3)}$, $E_{\mathcal{F}',F}^{(3)}$, and $E_{A\mathcal{F},F}^{(3)}$ are defined by the convex-roof extension as in Equation (5).

2.4. Monogamy Relation

For a given bipartite measure Q (such as entanglement measure and other quantum correlation measure), Q is said to be monogamous (we take the tripartite case for example) if [10,26]

$$Q(A|BC) \geq Q(AB) + Q(AC). \tag{13}$$

However, Equation (13) is not valid for many entanglement measures [10,24,52,53] but some power function of Q admits the monogamy relation (i.e., $Q^\alpha(A|BC) \geq Q^\alpha(AB) + Q^\alpha(AC)$ for some $\alpha > 0$). In Ref. [23], we address this issue by proposing an improved definition of monogamy (without inequalities) for entanglement measure: A bipartite measure of entanglement E is monogamous if for any $\rho \in \mathcal{S}^{ABC}$ that satisfies the *disentangling condition*, i.e.,

$$E(\rho^{A|BC}) = E(\rho^{AB}), \tag{14}$$

we have that $E(\rho^{AC}) = 0$, where $\rho^{AB} = \text{Tr}_C \rho^{ABC}$. With respect to this definition, a continuous measure E is monogamous according to this definition if and only if there exists $0 < \alpha < \infty$ such that

$$E^\alpha(\rho^{A|BC}) \geq E^\alpha(\rho^{AB}) + E^\alpha(\rho^{AC}) \tag{15}$$

for all ρ acting on the state space $\mathcal{H}^{ABC}$ with fixed dim $\mathcal{H}^{ABC} = d < \infty$ (see Theorem 1 in Ref. [23]). Notice that, for these bipartite measures, only the relation between $A|BC$, AB and AC are revealed, and the global correlation in ABC and the correlation contained in part BC are missed [22]. That is, the monogamy relation in such a sense is not "complete".

For a unified tripartite entanglement measure $E^{(3)}$, it is said to be *completely monogamous* if for any $\rho \in \mathcal{S}^{ABC}$ that satisfies [22]

$$E^{(3)}(\rho^{ABC}) = E^{(2)}(\rho^{AB}) \tag{16}$$

we have that $E^{(2)}(\rho^{AC}) = E^{(2)}(\rho^{BC}) = 0$. If $E^{(3)}$ is a continuous unified tripartite entanglement measure. Then, $E^{(3)}$ is completely monogamous if and only if there exists $0 < \alpha < \infty$ such that [22]

$$E^{\alpha}(\rho^{ABC}) \geqslant E^{\alpha}(\rho^{AB}) + E^{\alpha}(\rho^{AC}) + E^{\alpha}(\rho^{BC}) \tag{17}$$

for all $\rho^{ABC} \in \mathcal{S}^{ABC}$ with fixed dim $\mathcal{H}^{ABC} = d < \infty$, here we omitted the superscript $^{(2,3)}$ of $E^{(2,3)}$ for brevity. Let $E^{(3)}$ be a complete MEM. $E^{(3)}$ is defined to be tightly complete monogamous if for any state $\rho^{ABC} \in \mathcal{S}^{ABC}$ that satisfies [22]

$$E^{(3)}(\rho^{ABC}) = E^{(2)}(\rho^{A|BC}) \tag{18}$$

we have $E^{(2)}(\rho^{BC}) = 0$, which is equivalent to

$$E^{\alpha}(\rho^{ABC}) \geqslant E^{\alpha}(\rho^{A|BC}) + E^{\alpha}(\rho^{BC})$$

for some $\alpha > 0$. Here we omitted the superscript $^{(2,3)}$ of $E^{(2,3)}$ for brevity. For the general case of $E^{(m)}$, one can similarly follow with the same spirit.

2.5. Genuine Entanglement Measure

A function $E_g^{(m)} : \mathcal{S}^{A_1 A_2 \cdots A_m} \to \mathbb{R}_+$ is defined to be a measure of genuine multipartite entanglement if it admits the following conditions [11]:

- **(GE1)** $E_g^{(m)}(\rho) = 0$ for any biseparable $\rho \in \mathcal{S}^{A_1 A_2 \cdots A_m}$;
- **(GE2)** $E_g^{(m)}(\rho) > 0$ for any genuinely entangled state $\rho \in \mathcal{S}^{A_1 A_2 \cdots A_m}$. This item can be weakened as: $E_g^{(m)}(\rho) \geqslant 0$ for any genuinely entangled state $\rho \in \mathcal{S}^{A_1 A_2 \cdots A_m}$. That is, maybe there exists some state that is genuinely entangled such that $E_g^{(m)}(\rho) = 0$. In such a case, the measure is called not faithful. Otherwise, it is called faithful. For example, the "residual tangle" is not faithful since it is vanished for the W state;
- **(GE3)** $E_g^{(m)}(\sum_i p_i \rho_i) \leqslant \sum_i p_i E_g^{(m)}(\rho_i)$ for any $\{p_i, \rho_i\}$, $\rho_i \in \mathcal{S}^{A_1 A_2 \cdots A_m}$, $p_i > 0$, $\sum_i p_i = 1$;
- **(GE4)** $E_g^{(m)}(\rho) \geqslant E_g^{(m)}(\rho')$ for any m-partite LOCC ε, $\varepsilon(\rho) = \rho'$.

Note that **(GE4)** implies that $E_g^{(m)}$ is invariant under local unitary transformations. $E_g^{(m)}$ is said to be a genuine multipartite entanglement monotone if it does not increase on average under m-partite stochastic LOCC. For example, C_{gme} is a GMEM.

3. Complete Genuine Multipartite Entanglement Measure

Analogous to that of unified/complete multipartite entanglement measure established in Ref. [22], we discuss the unification condition and the hierarchy condition for genuine multipartite entanglement measure in this section. We start out with an observation of the examples. Let $|\psi\rangle$ be an m-partite pure state in $\mathcal{H}^{A_1 A_2 \cdots A_m}$. Recall that, the multipartite entanglement of formation $E_f^{(m)}$ is defined as [22]

$$E_f^{(m)}(|\psi\rangle) := \frac{1}{2} \sum_{i=1}^m S(\rho_{A_i}),$$

where $\rho_X := \text{Tr}_{\bar{X}}(|\psi\rangle\langle\psi|)$. We define

$$E_{g-f}^{(m)}(|\psi\rangle) := \frac{1}{2}\delta(|\psi\rangle)\sum_{i=1}^{m} S(\rho_{A_i}), \quad (19)$$

where $\delta(\rho) = 0$ if ρ is biseparable up to some bi-partition and $\delta(\rho) = 1$ if ρ is not biseparable up to any bi-partition. For mixed state, it is defined by the convex-roof extension. Obviously, $E_{g-f}^{(m)}$ is a uniform GMEM since $I(A_1 : A_2 : \cdots : A_n) \geq 0$ for any n [54], where $I(A_1 : A_2 : \cdots : A_n) := \sum_{k=1}^{n} S(\rho_{A_k}) - S(A_1 A_2 \cdots A_n) = S(\rho^{A_1 A_2 \cdots A_n} \| \rho^{A_1} \otimes \rho^{A_2} \otimes \cdots \rho^{A_n}) \geq 0$. The following properties are straightforward: For any $\rho^{A_1 A_2 \cdots A_m} \in \mathcal{S}_g^{A_1 A_2 \cdots A_m}$,

$$E_{g-f}^{(k)}(X_1|X_2|\cdots|X_k) > E_{g-f}^{(l)}(Y_1|Y_2|\cdots|Y_l)$$

for any $X_1|X_2|\cdots|X_k \succ^b Y_1|Y_2|\cdots|Y_l$. It is worth noting that, for any uniform GMEM $E_g^{(m)}$, we cannot require $E_g^{(k)}(X_1|X_2|\cdots|X_k) = E_g^{(l)}(Y_1|Y_2|\cdots|Y_l)$ for any $\rho \in \mathcal{S}_g^{A_1 A_2 \cdots A_m}$ and any $X_1|X_2|\cdots|X_k \succ^a Y_1|Y_2|\cdots|Y_l$. For example, if $E_g^{(4)}(\rho^{ABCD}) = E_g^{(3)}(\rho^{ABC})$ for some $\rho^{ABCD} \in \mathcal{S}_g^{ABCD}$, then the entanglement between part ABC and part D is zero, which means that ρ^{ABCD} is biseparable with respect to the partition $ABC|D$—a contradiction. In addition, let $|\psi\rangle^{ABC}$ be a tripartite genuine entangled state in $\mathcal{H}^{ABC}$, then $|\psi\rangle^{ABC}|\psi\rangle^D$ is not a four-partite genuine entangled state, i.e.,

$$E_g^{(4)}(|\psi\rangle^{ABC}|\psi\rangle^D) = 0,$$

but $E_g^{(3)}(\psi)^{ABC}) > 0$ provided that $E_g^{(3)}$ is faithful. That is, the genuine multipartite entanglement measure is not necessarily decreasing under the discarding of the subsystem. However, for the genuine entangled state, it is decreasing definitely. From these observations, we give the following definition.

Definition 1. *Let $E_g^{(m)}$ be a uniform genuine entanglement measure. If it satisfies the unification condition, i.e.,*

$$E_g^{(m)}(A_1 A_2 \cdots A_m) = E_g^{(m)}(\pi(A_1 A_2 \cdots A_m)) \quad (20)$$

and

$$E_g^{(k)}(X_1|X_2|\cdots|X_k) > E_g^{(l)}(Y_1|Y_2|\cdots|Y_l) \quad (21)$$

for any $\rho \in \mathcal{S}_g^{A_1 A_2 \cdots A_m}$ whenever $X_1|X_2|\cdots|X_k \succ^a Y_1|Y_2|\cdots|Y_l$, we call $E_g^{(m)}$ a unified genuine multipartite entanglement measure, where $\pi(\cdot)$ denotes the permutation of the subsystems.

For any $\rho \in \mathcal{S}_g^{A_1 A_2 \cdots A_m}$, if $X_1|X_2|\cdots|X_k \succ^b Y_1|Y_2|\cdots|Y_l$, We expect any unified GMEM satisfies $E_g^{(k)}(X_1|X_2|\cdots|X_k) \geq E_g^{(l)}(Y_1|Y_2|\cdots|Y_l)$ since 'some amount of entanglement' may be hided in the combined subsystem. For example, the quantity $E_g^{(3)}(AB|C|D)$ cannot report the entanglement contained between subsystems A and B. We thus present the following definition.

Definition 2. *Let $E_g^{(m)}$ be a unified GMEM. If $E_g^{(m)}$ admits the hierarchy condition, i.e.,*

$$E_g^{(k)}(X_1|X_2|\cdots|X_k) \geq E_g^{(l)}(Y_1|Y_2|\cdots|Y_l) \quad (22)$$

for any $\rho \in \mathcal{S}_g^{A_1 A_2 \cdots A_m}$ whenever $X_1|X_2|\cdots|X_k \succ^b Y_1|Y_2|\cdots|Y_l$, then it is said to be a complete genuine multipartite entanglement measure.

We remark here that, for any given uniform GMEM $E_g^{(m)}$,

$$E_g^{(k)}(X_1|X_2|\cdots|X_k) \geqslant E_g^{(k)}(X_1'|X_2'|\cdots|X_k') \tag{23}$$

holds for any $\rho \in \mathcal{S}_g^{A_1 A_2 \cdots A_m}$ whenever $X_1|X_2|\cdots|X_k \succ^c X_1'|X_2'|\cdots|X_k'$ since $\rho^{X_1'|X_2'|\cdots|X_k'}$ is obtained from $\rho^{X_1|X_2|\cdots|X_k}$ by partial trace and such a partial trace is indeed a k-partite LOCC, $2 \leq k \leq m$. That is, a complete GMEM is a series of GMEMs that are compatible in the following sense: Not only the genuine entanglement contained in the global system and that of any subsystem or new partition of the global system are comparable but also the genuine entanglement in any subsystems with the coarser relation can be compared with each other. Of course, the genuine entanglement should be decreasing whenever the system is coarsening, as one may expect. By definition, $E_{g-f}^{(m)}$ is a complete GMEM. We just take $E_{g-f}^{(m)}$ for example. For the three-qubit GHZ state $|GHZ\rangle = \frac{1}{\sqrt{2}}(|000\rangle + |111\rangle)$,

$$E_{g-f}^{(3)}(|GHZ\rangle) = \frac{3}{2} > E_{g-f}^{(2)}(|GHZ\rangle^{A|BC}) = 1 > E_{g-f}^{(2)}(\rho^{AB}) = 0,$$

and for the W state $|W\rangle = \frac{1}{\sqrt{3}}(|100\rangle + |010\rangle + |001\rangle)$, it is straightforward that

$$E_{g-f}^{(3)}(|W\rangle) = \frac{3}{2}\log_2 3 - 1 > E_{g-f}^{(2)}(|W\rangle^{A|BC}) = \log_2 3 - \frac{2}{3} > E_{g-f}^{(2)}(\rho^{AB}) = \frac{2}{3}.$$

In general, the equality in Equation (23) does not hold, i.e., the genuine entanglement decreases strictly under coarser relation (C3). For example, if $E(|\psi\rangle^{A|BC}) = E(\rho^{AB})$, then $|\psi\rangle^{ABC}$ is biseparable for almost all bipartite entanglement measures E so far [36].

It is clear that C_{gme} is not a complete GMEM since it does not satisfy the hierarchy condition (22). We take a four-partite state for example. Let

$$|\psi\rangle = \frac{\sqrt{5}}{4}|0000\rangle + \frac{1}{4}|1111\rangle + \frac{\sqrt{5}}{4}|0100\rangle + \frac{\sqrt{5}}{4}|1010\rangle,$$

then $C_{gme}(|\psi\rangle) = C(|\psi\rangle^{ABC|D}) = \frac{\sqrt{15}}{8} < C(|\psi\rangle^{AB|CD}) = \frac{\sqrt{65}}{8}$. In general, C_{gme} is not even a unified GMEM since we can not guarantee that unification condition (21) holds true.

We now turn to find unified/complete GMEM. $E_{g-f}^{(m)}$ is derived from unified/complete multipartite entanglement measures $E_f^{(m)}$. This motivates us to obtain unified/complete GMEMs from the unified/complete MEMs.

Proposition 1. *Let $E^{(m)}$ be a unified/complete multipartite entanglement measure (resp. monotone), and define*

$$E_{g-F}^{(m)}(\rho) := \min_{\{p_i, |\psi_i\rangle\}} \sum p_i \delta(|\psi_i\rangle) E^{(m)}(|\psi_i\rangle) \tag{24}$$

whenever $E_F^{(m)} = \min_{\{p_i, |\psi_i\rangle\}} \sum p_i E^{(m)}(|\psi_i\rangle)$ and

$$E_g^{(m)}(\rho) := \delta(\rho) E^{(m)}(\rho) \tag{25}$$

whenever $E^{(m)}$ is not defined by the convex-roof extension for mixed state, where the minimum is taken over all pure-state decomposition $\{p_i, |\psi_i\rangle\}$ of $\rho \in \mathcal{S}^{A_1 A_2 \cdots A_m}$, $\delta(\rho) = 1$ whenever ρ is genuinely entangled and $\delta(\rho) = 0$ otherwise. Then, $E_g^{(m)}$ is a unified/complete genuine multipartite entanglement measure (resp. monotone).

Proof. It is clear that $E_{g-F}^{(m)}$ and $E_g^{(m)}$ satisfy the unification condition (resp. hierarchy condition) on $\mathcal{S}_g^{A_1 A_2 \cdots A_m}$ whenever $E^{(m)}$ satisfies the unification condition (resp. hierarchy condition) on $\mathcal{S}^{A_1 A_2 \cdots A_m}$. □

Consequently, according to Proposition 1, we get

$$\tau_g^{(3)}(|\psi\rangle) = \delta(|\psi\rangle)\left[3 - \text{Tr}(\rho^A)^2 - \text{Tr}(\rho^B)^2 - \text{Tr}(\rho^C)^2\right],$$

$$C_g^{(3)}(|\psi\rangle) = \sqrt{\tau_g^{(3)}(|\psi\rangle)},$$

$$N_g^{(3)}(|\psi\rangle) = \delta(|\psi\rangle)\left[\text{Tr}^2\sqrt{\rho^A} + \text{Tr}^2\sqrt{\rho^B} + \text{Tr}^2\sqrt{\rho^C} - 3\right],$$

$$T_{g-q}^{(3)}(|\psi\rangle) = \frac{1}{2}\delta(|\psi\rangle)\left[T_q(\rho^A) + T_q(\rho^B) + T_q(\rho^C)\right], q > 1,$$

$$R_{g-\alpha}^{(3)}(|\psi\rangle) = \frac{1}{2}\delta(|\psi\rangle)R_\alpha(\rho^A \otimes \rho^B \otimes \rho^C), 0 < \alpha < 1,$$

$$E_{g-\mathcal{F}}^{(3)}(|\psi\rangle) = \delta(|\psi\rangle)\left[1 - \mathcal{F}\left(|\psi\rangle\langle\psi|, \rho^A \otimes \rho^B \otimes \rho^C\right)\right],$$

$$E_{g-\mathcal{F}'}^{(3)}(|\psi\rangle) = \delta(|\psi\rangle)\left[1 - \sqrt{\mathcal{F}}\left(|\psi\rangle\langle\psi|, \rho^A \otimes \rho^B \otimes \rho^C\right)\right],$$

$$E_{g-A\mathcal{F}}^{(3)}(|\psi\rangle) = \delta(|\psi\rangle)\left[1 - \mathcal{F}_A\left(|\psi\rangle\langle\psi|, \rho^A \otimes \rho^B \otimes \rho^C\right)\right],$$

for pure states, and define by the convex-roof extension for the mixed states (for mixed state, where $N_g^{(3)}$ is replaced with the convex-roof extension of $N_g^{(3)}$, $N_{g-F}^{(3)}$), and

$$N_g^{(3)}(\rho) = \delta(\rho)\left(\|\rho^{T_a}\|_{\text{Tr}} + \|\rho^{T_b}\|_{\text{Tr}} + \|\rho^{T_c}\|_{\text{Tr}} - 3\right)$$

for any $\rho \in \mathcal{S}^{ABC}$. These tripartite measures, except for $N_g^{(3)}$ are in fact special cases of $\mathcal{E}_{g-123}^F$ in Ref. [19]. Generally, we can define

$$\tau_g^{(m)}(|\psi\rangle) = \delta(|\psi\rangle)\left[m - \sum_i \text{Tr}(\rho^{A_i})^2\right],$$

$$C_g^{(m)}(|\psi\rangle) = \sqrt{\tau_g^{(m)}(|\psi\rangle)},$$

$$N_g^{(m)}(|\psi\rangle) = \delta(|\psi\rangle)\left[\sum_i \text{Tr}^2\sqrt{\rho^{A_i}} - m\right],$$

$$T_{g-q}^{(m)}(|\psi\rangle) = \frac{1}{2}\delta(|\psi\rangle)\sum_i T_q(\rho^{A_i}), q > 1,$$

$$R_{g-\alpha}^{(m)}(|\psi\rangle) = \frac{1}{2}\delta(|\psi\rangle)R_\alpha\left(\bigotimes_i \rho^{A_i}\right), 0 < \alpha < 1,$$

$$E_{g-\mathcal{F}}^{(m)}(|\psi\rangle) = \delta(|\psi\rangle)\left[1 - \mathcal{F}\left(|\psi\rangle\langle\psi|, \bigotimes_i \rho^{A_i}\right)\right],$$

$$E_{g-\mathcal{F}'}^{(m)}(|\psi\rangle) = \delta(|\psi\rangle)\left[1 - \sqrt{\mathcal{F}}\left(|\psi\rangle\langle\psi|, \bigotimes_i \rho^{A_i}\right)\right],$$

$$E_{g-A\mathcal{F}}^{(m)}(|\psi\rangle) = \delta(|\psi\rangle)\left[1 - \mathcal{F}_A\left(|\psi\rangle\langle\psi|, \bigotimes_i \rho^{A_i}\right)\right],$$

for pure states and define by the convex-roof extension for the mixed states (for mixed state, $N_g^{(m)}$ is replaced with $N_{g-F}^{(m)}$), and

$$N_g^{(m)}(\rho) = \delta(\rho)\left(\left\|\sum_i \rho^{T_i}\right\|_{\mathrm{Tr}} - m\right)$$

for any $\rho \in \mathcal{S}^{A_1 A_2 \cdots A_m}$. According to Proposition 1, together with Theorem 5 in Ref. [22], the statement below is straightforward.

Proposition 2. $E_{g-f}^{(m)}$, $\tau_g^{(m)}$, $C_g^{(m)}$, and $T_{g-q}^{(m)}$ are complete genuine multipartite entanglement monotones while $R_{g-\alpha}^{(m)}$, $N_{g-F}^{(m)}$, $N_g^{(m)}$, $E_{g-\mathcal{F}}^{(m)}$, $E_{g-\mathcal{F}'}^{(m)}$, and $E_{g-A\mathcal{F}}^{(m)}$ are unified genuine multipartite entanglement monotones, but not complete genuine multipartite entanglement monotones.

Very recently, we proposed the following genuine four-partite entanglement measures [19]. Let E be a bipartite entanglement measure and let

$$\mathcal{E}_{g-1234(2)}(|\psi\rangle) := \delta(|\psi\rangle)\sum_i x_i^{(2)} \qquad (26)$$

for any given $|\psi\rangle \in \mathcal{H}^{ABCD}$, where $E(|\psi\rangle^{AB|CD}) = x_1^{(2)}$, $E(|\psi\rangle^{A|BCD}) = x_2^{(2)}$, $E(|\psi\rangle^{AC|BD}) = x_3^{(2)}$, $E(|\psi\rangle^{ABC|D}) = x_4^{(2)}$, $E(|\psi\rangle^{AD|BC}) = x_5^{(2)}$, $E(|\psi\rangle^{B|ACD}) = x_6^{(2)}$, $E(|\psi\rangle^{C|ABD}) = x_7^{(2)}$. Then $\mathcal{E}_{g-1234(2)}^F$ is a genuine four-partite entanglement measure. Let $E^{(3)}$ be a tripartite entanglement measure,

$$\mathcal{E}_{g-1234(3)}(|\psi\rangle) = \delta(|\psi\rangle)\sum_i x_i^{(3)} \qquad (27)$$

for any given $|\psi\rangle \in \mathcal{S}^{ABCD}$, where $E^{(3)}(\rho^{A|B|CD}) = x_1^{(3)}$, $E^{(3)}(\rho^{A|BC|D}) = x_2^{(3)}$, $E^{(3)}(\rho^{AC|B|D}) = x_3^{(3)}$, $E^{(3)}(\rho^{AB|C|D}) = x_4^{(3)}$, $E^{(3)}(\rho^{AD|B|C}) = x_5^{(3)}$, $E^{(3)}(\rho^{A|BD|C}) = x_6^{(3)}$. It is clear that $\mathcal{E}_{g-1234(3)}^F$ is a genuine four-partite entanglement measure but not uniform GMEM.

Generally, we can define $\mathcal{E}_{g-1234\cdots m(2)}^F$ by the same way, and it is a uniform GMEM. We check below that $\mathcal{E}_{g-1234\cdots m(2)}^F$ is a complete GMEM whenever E is an entanglement monotone. We only need to discuss the case of $m = 4$, and the general cases can be argued similarly. For any genuine entangled pure state $|\psi\rangle \in \mathcal{H}^{ABCD}$, and any bipartite entanglement monotone E, it is clear that $\mathcal{E}_{g-1234(2)}(|\psi\rangle) > E^F(\rho^{XY})$ for any $\{X,Y\} \in \{A,B,C,D\}$. For any pure state decomposition of ρ^{ABC}, $\rho^{ABC} = \sum_i p_i|\psi_i\rangle\langle\psi_i|$, we have $E(|\psi\rangle^{A|BCD}) \geq \sum_i p_i E(|\psi_i\rangle^{A|BC})$, $E(|\psi\rangle^{AB|CD}) \geq \sum_i p_i E(|\psi_i\rangle^{AB|C})$, and $E(|\psi\rangle^{B|ACD}) \geq \sum_i p_i E(|\psi_i\rangle^{B|AC})$ since any ensemble $\{p_i, |\psi_i\rangle\}$ can be derived by LOCC from $|\psi\rangle$. It follows that $\mathcal{E}_{g-1234(2)}^F(|\psi\rangle) > \mathcal{E}_{g-123(2)}^F(\rho^{ABC})$. By symmetry of the subsystems, we get that the unification condition is valid for pure state. For mixed state $\rho \in \mathcal{S}_g^{ABCD}$, we let

$$\mathcal{E}_{g-1234(2)}^F(\rho) = \sum_j p_j \mathcal{E}_{g-1234(2)}(|\phi_j\rangle)$$

for some decomposition $\rho = \sum_j p_j |\phi_j\rangle\langle\phi_j|$. Then

$$\mathcal{E}_{g-1234(2)}(|\phi_j\rangle) \geq \mathcal{E}_{g-123(2)}^F(\rho_j^{ABC})$$

for any j, where $\rho_j^{ABC} = \mathrm{Tr}_D(|\phi_j\rangle\langle\phi_j|)$. Therefore

$$\mathcal{E}_{g-1234(2)}^F(\rho) = \sum_j p_j \mathcal{E}_{g-1234(2)}^F(|\phi_j\rangle) \geqslant \sum_j p_j \mathcal{E}_{g-123(2)}^F(\rho_j^{ABC}) \geqslant \mathcal{E}_{g-123(2)}^F(\rho^{ABC})$$

as desired. In addition, it is clear that

$$\mathcal{E}_{g-123(2)}^F(\rho^{ABC}) > E^F(\rho^{AB}) \tag{28}$$

for any $\rho \in \mathcal{S}_g^{ABCD}$. That is, $\mathcal{E}_{g-1234\cdots m(2)}^F$ is a unified GMEM. The hierarchy condition is obvious. Thus, $\mathcal{E}_{g-1234\cdots m(2)}^F$ is a complete GMEM whenever E is an entanglement monotone.

Remark 1. *It is clear that, for $\mathcal{E}_{g-1234\cdots m(2)}^F$, the inequality in Equation* (22) *is a strict inequality, i.e.,*

$$E_g^{(k)}(X_1|X_2|\cdots|X_k) > E_g^{(l)}(Y_1|Y_2|\cdots|Y_l) \tag{29}$$

for any $\rho \in \mathcal{S}_g^{A_1 A_2 \cdots A_m}$ whenever $X_1|X_2|\cdots|X_k \succ^b Y_1|Y_2|\cdots|Y_l$. In addition, according to the proof of Proposition 4 in Ref. [22], *Equation* (22) *holds for $E_{g-f}^{(m)}$, $\tau_g^{(m)}$, $C_g^{(m)}$, and $T_{g-q}^{(m)}$. Namely, in general, there does not exist $\rho \in \mathcal{S}_g^{A_1 A_2 \cdots A_m}$ such that $E_g^{(k)}(X_1|X_2|\cdots|X_k) = E_g^{(l)}(Y_1|Y_2|\cdots|Y_l)$ holds, $X_1|X_2|\cdots|X_k \succ^b Y_1|Y_2|\cdots|Y_l$.*

4. Complete Monogamy of Genuine Multipartite Entanglement Measure

We are now ready to discuss the complete monogamy relation of GMEM. By the previous arguments, the genuine multipartite entanglement does not necessarily decrease when discarding the subsystem. However, for the genuine entangled state, it does decrease. We thus conclude the following definition of complete monogamy for genuine entanglement measure.

Definition 3. *Let $E_g^{(m)}$ be a uniform GMEM. We call $E_g^{(m)}$ completely monogamous if for any $\rho \in \mathcal{S}_g^{A_1 A_2 \cdots A_m}$ we have*

$$E_g^{(k)}\left(\rho^{X_1|X_2|\cdots|X_k}\right) > E_g^{(l)}\left(\rho^{Y_1|Y_2|\cdots|Y_l}\right) \tag{30}$$

holds for all $X_1|X_2|\cdots|X_k \succ^a Y_1|Y_2|\cdots|Y_l$.

That is, any unified GMEM is completely monogamous. Moreover, according to the proof of Theorem 1 in Ref. [23], we can get the equivalent statement of complete monogamy for continuous genuine tripartite entanglement measure (the general m-partite case can be followed in the same way).

Proposition 3. *Let $E_g^{(3)}$ be a continuous uniform genuine tripartite entanglement measure. Then, $E_g^{(3)}$ is completely monogamous if and only if there exists $0 < \alpha < \infty$ such that*

$$E_g^\alpha(\rho^{ABC}) > E^\alpha(\rho^{AB}) + E^\alpha(\rho^{AC}) + E^\alpha(\rho^{BC}) \tag{31}$$

for all $\rho^{ABC} \in \mathcal{S}_g^{ABC}$ with fixed $\dim \mathcal{H}^{ABC} = d < \infty$, here we omitted the superscript (3) of $E^{(3)}$ for brevity.

Analogously, for the four-partite case, if $E_g^{(4)}$ is a continuous uniform GMEM, then $E_g^{(4)}$ is completely monogamous if and only if there exist $0 < \alpha, \beta < \infty$ such that

$$E_g^\alpha(\rho^{ABCD}) > E_g^\alpha(\rho^{ABC}) + E_g^\alpha(\rho^{ABD}) + E_g^\alpha(\rho^{ACD}) + E_g^\alpha(\rho^{BCD}), \tag{32}$$

$$E_g^\beta(\rho^{ABCD}) > E^\beta(\rho^{AB}) + E^\beta(\rho^{BC}) + E^\beta(\rho^{AC}) + E^\beta(\rho^{BD}) + E^\beta(\rho^{AD}) + E^\beta(\rho^{CD}) \tag{33}$$

for all $\rho^{ABCD} \in \mathcal{S}_g^{ABCD}$ with fixed dim $\mathcal{H}^{ABC} = d < \infty$, here we omitted the superscript $(3,4)$ of $E^{(3,4)}$ for brevity. Since C_{gme} may not be a unified GMEM, we conjecture that C_{gme} is not completely monogamous.

As a counterpart to the tightly complete monogamous relation of the complete multipartite entanglement measure in Ref. [22], we give the following definition.

Definition 4. *Let $E_g^{(m)}$ be a complete GMEM. We call $E_g^{(m)}$ tightly complete monogamous if it satisfies the genuine disentangling condition, i.e., either for any $\rho \in \mathcal{S}_g^{A_1 A_2 \cdots A_m}$ that satisfies*

$$E_g^{(k)}(X_1|X_2|\cdots|X_k) = E_g^{(l)}(Y_1|Y_2|\cdots|Y_l) \tag{34}$$

we have that

$$E_g^{(*)}(\Gamma) = 0 \tag{35}$$

holds for all $\Gamma \in \Xi(X_1|X_2|\cdots|X_k - Y_1|Y_2|\cdots|Y_l)$, or

$$E_g^{(k)}(X_1|X_2|\cdots|X_k) > E_g^{(l)}(Y_1|Y_2|\cdots|Y_l) \tag{36}$$

holds for any $\rho \in \mathcal{S}_g^{A_1 A_2 \cdots A_m}$, where $X_1|X_2|\cdots|X_k \succ^b Y_1|Y_2|\cdots|Y_l$, and the superscript $(*)$ is associated with the partition Γ, e.g., if Γ is a n-partite partition, then $(*) = (n)$.

Definitions 3 and 4 mean that, if $E_g^{(k)}(X_1|X_2|\cdots|X_k) \approx E_g^{(l)}(Y_1|Y_2|\cdots|Y_l)$, then $E_g^{(*)}(\Gamma) \approx 0$ for any $\Gamma \in \Xi(X_1|X_2|\cdots|X_k - Y_1|Y_2|\cdots|Y_l)$. This fact can make ensure the security of quantum communication tasks, which rely on genuine entanglement as the resource: Whenever $E_g^{(k)}(X_1|X_2|\cdots|X_k) \approx E_g^{(l)}(Y_1|Y_2|\cdots|Y_l)$, the joint information in subsystems $\Gamma \in \Xi(X_1|X_2|\cdots|X_k - Y_1|Y_2|\cdots|Y_l)$ is nearly zero, i.e., we could choose such an entangled state when we would like to prevent subsystem Γ in sharing the information based on the genuine entanglement or from any evegetting information from subsystem Γ.

Remark 2. *According to Remark 1, for $E_{g-f}^{(m)}$, $\tau_g^{(m)}$, $C_g^{(m)}$, $T_{g-q}^{(m)}$, and $\mathcal{E}_{g-1234\cdots m(2)}^F$, the case of Equation (34) cannot occur, so they are tightly complete monogamous. We conjecture that the case of Equation (34) cannot occur for any complete GMEM. In such a sense, any complete GMEM is tightly complete monogamous.*

For example, if $E_g^{(3)}$ is a complete GMEM, then $E_g^{(3)}$ is tightly complete monogamous if for any $\rho^{ABC} \in \mathcal{S}_g^{ABC}$ that satisfies

$$E_g^{(3)}(\rho^{ABC}) = E^{(2)}(\rho^{A|BC}) \tag{37}$$

we have $E^{(2)}(\rho^{BC}) = 0$, and $E_g^{(3)}$ is completely monogamous

$$E_g^{(3)}(\rho^{ABC}) > E^{(2)}(\rho^{AB}) \tag{38}$$

is always correct for any $\rho^{ABC} \in \mathcal{S}_g^{ABC}$. That is, the complete monogamy of $E_g^{(m)}$ refers to it being completely monogamous in the genuine entangled state, and $E_g^{(m)}$ is strictly decreasing under discarding of the subsystem, which is different from that of the complete entanglement measure. Equivalently, if $E_g^{(3)}$ is a continuous complete GMEM, then $E_g^{(3)}$ is tightly complete monogamous if and only if there exists $0 < \alpha < \infty$ such that

$$E_g^\alpha(\rho^{ABC}) \geqslant E^\alpha(\rho^{AB}) + E^\alpha(\rho^{AB|C}) \tag{39}$$

holds for all $\rho^{ABC} \in \mathcal{S}_g^{ABC}$ with fixed dim $\mathcal{H}^{ABC} = d < \infty$, here we omitted the superscript $^{(3)}$ of $E^{(3)}$ for brevity.

By Definition 4, $\mathcal{E}_{g-1234\cdots m(2)}^F$ is tightly complete monogamous since for $\mathcal{E}_{g-1234\cdots m(2)}^F$ the genuine disentangling condition (36) always holds. C_{gme} is not tightly complete monogamous since it violates the genuine disentangling condition. In addition, the tightly complete monogamy of $E_g^{(m)}$ is closely related to that of $E^{(m)}$ whenever $E_g^{(m)}$ is derived from $E^{(m)}$ as in Equations (24) or (25).

Proposition 4. *Let $E^{(m)}$ be a complete multipartite entanglement measure. If $E^{(m)}$ is tightly complete monogamous, then the genuine multipartite entanglement measure $E_g^{(m)}$, induced by $E^{(m)}$ as in Equations (24) or (25), is tightly complete monogamous.*

Together with Proposition 4 in Ref. [22], $R_{g-\alpha}^{(m)}$, $N_{g-F}^{(m)}$ and $N_g^{(m)}$ are completely monogamous but not tightly complete monogamous.

5. Conclusions and Discussion

We have proposed a framework of unified/complete genuine multipartite entanglement measure, from which we established the scenario of complete monogamy and tightly complete monogamy of genuine multipartite entanglement measure. The spirit here is consistent with that of a unified/complete multipartite entanglement measure in Ref. [22]. We also find a simple way of deriving a unified/complete genuine multipartite entanglement measure from the unified/complete multipartite entanglement measure. Under such a framework, the multipartite entanglement becomes more clear, and, in addition, we can judge whether a given genuine entanglement measure is good or not. Compared with other multipartite entanglement measure, the unified genuine entanglement measure is automatically completely monogamous. That is, genuine entanglement displays the monogamy of entanglement more evidently than other measures. These results support that entanglement is monogamous, as we expected. We thus suggest that monogamy should be a necessary requirement for a genuine entanglement measure.

Funding: This work is supported by the National Natural Science Foundation of China under Grant No. 11971277, the Fund Program for the Scientific Activities of Selected Returned Overseas Professionals in Shanxi Province, and the Scientific Innovation Foundation of the Higher Education Institutions of Shanxi Province under Grant No. 2019KJ034.

Data Availability Statement: Not applicable.

Conflicts of Interest: The author declares no conflict of interest.

References

1. Nielsen, M.A.; Chuang, I. *Quantum Computatation and Quantum Information*; Cambridge University Press: Cambridge, UK, 2000.
2. Bennett, C.H.; DiVincenzo, D.P.; Smolin, J.A.; Wootters, W.K. Mixed-state entanglement and quantum error correction. *Phys. Rev. A* **1996**, *54*, 3824. [CrossRef]
3. Horodecki, R.; Horodecki, P.; Horodecki, M.; Horodecki, K. Quantum entanglement. *Rev. Mod. Phys.* **2009**, *81*, 865. [CrossRef]
4. Gühne, O.; Tóth, G. Entanglement detection. *Phys. Rep.* **2009**, *474*, 1. [CrossRef]
5. Burkhart, L.D.; Teoh, J.D.; Zhang, Y.; Axline, C.J.; Frunzio, L.; Devoret, M.H.; Jiang, L.; Girvin, S.M.; Schoelkopf, R.J. Error-Detected State Transfer and Entanglement in a Superconducting Quantum Network. *PRX Quantum* **2021**, *2*, 030321. [CrossRef]

6. Yu, X.-D.; Imai, S.; Gühne, O. Optimal Entanglement Certification from Moments of the Partial Transpose. *Phys. Rev. Lett.* **2021**, *127*, 060504. [CrossRef]
7. Luo, M.X. New Genuinely Multipartite Entanglement. *Adv. Quantum Technol.* **2021**, *4*, 2000123. [CrossRef]
8. Schmid, D.; Fraser, T.C.; Kunjwal, R.; Sainz, A.B.; Wolfe, E.; Spekkens, R.W. Understanding the interplay of entanglement and nonlocality: Motivating and developing a new branch of entanglement theory. *arXiv* **2020**, arXiv:2004.09194v2.
9. Navascués, M.; Wolfe, E.; Rosset, D.; Pozas-Kerstjens, A. Genuine Network Multipartite Entanglement. *arXiv* **2020**, arXiv:2002.02773v3.
10. Coffman, V.; Kundu, J.; Wootters, W.K. Distributed entanglement. *Phys. Rev. A* **2000**, *61*, 052306. [CrossRef]
11. Ma, Z.H.; Chen, Z.H.; Chen, J.L.; Spengler, C.; Gabriel, A.; Huber, M. Measure of genuine multipartite entanglement with computable lower bounds. *Phys. Rev. A* **2011**, *83*, 062325. [CrossRef]
12. Rafsanjani, S.M.H.; Huber, M.; Broadbent, C.J.; Eberly, J.H. Genuinely multipartite concurrence of N-qubit X matrices. *Phys. Rev. A* **2012**, *86*, 062303. [CrossRef]
13. Sen(De), A.; Sen, U. Channel capacities versus entanglement measures in multiparty quantum states. *Phys. Rev. A* **2010**, *81*, 012308. [CrossRef]
14. Sadhukhan, D.; Roy, S.S.; Pal, A.K.; Rakshit, D.; Sen(De), A.; Sen, U. Multipartite entanglement accumulation in quantum states: Localizable generalized geometric measure. *Phys. Rev. A* **2017**, *95*, 022301. [CrossRef]
15. Emary, C.; Beenakker, C.W.J. Relation between entanglement measures and Bell inequalities for three qubits. *Phys. Rev. A* **2004**, *69*, 032317. [CrossRef]
16. Contreras-Tejada, P.; Palazuelos, C.; de Vicente, J.I. Resource theory of entanglement with a unique multipartite maximally entangled state. *Phys. Rev. Lett.* **2019**, *122*, 120503. [CrossRef] [PubMed]
17. Das, S.; Bäuml, S.; Winczewski, M.; Horodecki, K. Universal limitations on quantum key distribution over a network. *arXiv* **2019**, arXiv:1912.03646v3.
18. Xie, S.; Eberly, J.H. Triangle Measure of Tripartite Entanglement. *Phys. Rev. Lett.* **2021**, *127*, 040403. [CrossRef]
19. Guo, Y.; Jia, Y.-P.; Li, X.-P.; Huang, L.-Z. Genuine multipartite entanglement measure. *arXiv* **2021**, arXiv:2108.03638v3.
20. Bennett, C.H.; Bernstein, H.J.; Popescu, S.; Schumacher, B. Concentrating partial entanglement by local operations. *Phys. Rev. A* **1996**, *53*, 2046. [CrossRef]
21. Eltschka, C.; Siewert, J. Distribution of entanglement and correlations in all finite dimensions. *Quantum* **2018**, *2*, 64. [CrossRef]
22. Guo, Y.; Zhang, L. Multipartite entanglement measure and complete monogamy relation. *Phys. Rev. A* **2020**, *101*, 032301. [CrossRef]
23. Gour, G.; Guo, Y. Monogamy of entanglement without inequalities. *Quantum* **2018**, *2*, 81. [CrossRef]
24. Bai, Y.-K.; Xu, Y.-F.; Wang, Z.-D. General monogamy relation for the entanglement of formation in multiqubit systems. *Phys. Rev. Lett.* **2014**, *113*, 100503. [CrossRef] [PubMed]
25. Streltsov, A.; Adesso, G.; Piani, M.; Bruß, D. Are general quantum correlations monogamous? *Phys. Rev. Lett.* **2012**, *109*, 050503. [CrossRef]
26. Koashi, M.; Winter, A. Monogamy of quantum entanglement and other correlations. *Phys. Rev. A* **2004**, *69*, 022309. [CrossRef] [PubMed]
27. Osborne, T.J.; Verstraete, F. General monogamy inequality for bipartite qubit entanglement. *Phys. Rev. Lett.* **2006**, *96*, 220503. [CrossRef] [PubMed]
28. Deng, X.; Xiang, Y.; Tian, C.; Adesso, G.; He, Q.; Gong, Q.; Su, X.; Xie, C.; Peng, K. Demonstration of monogamy relations for Einstein-Podolsky-Rosen steering in Gaussian cluster state. *Phys. Rev. Lett.* **2017**, *118*, 230501. [CrossRef]
29. Camalet, S. Monogamy inequality for any local quantum resource and entanglement. *Phys. Rev. Lett.* **2017**, *119*, 110503. [CrossRef]
30. Karczewski, M.; Kaszlikowski, D.; Kurzyński, P. Monogamy of particle statistics in tripartite systems simulating Bosons and Fermions. *Phys. Rev. Lett.* **2018**, *121*, 090403. [CrossRef]
31. Lancien, C.; DiMartino, S.; Huber, M.; Piani, M.; Adesso, G.; Winter, A. Should entanglement measures be monogamous or faithful? *Phys. Rev. Lett.* **2016**, *117*, 060501. [CrossRef]
32. Ou, Y.-C.; Fan, H. Monogamy inequality in terms of negativity for three-qubit states. *Phys. Rev. A* **2007**, *75*, 062308. [CrossRef] [PubMed]
33. Cheng, S.; Hall, M.J.W. Anisotropic Invariance and the Distribution of Quantum Correlations. *Phys. Rev. Lett.* **2017**, *118*, 010401. [CrossRef]
34. Allen, G.W.; Meyer, D.A. Polynomial Monogamy Relations for Entanglement Negativity. *Phys. Rev. Lett.* **2017**, *118*, 080402. [CrossRef]
35. He, H.; Vidal, G. Disentangling theorem and monogamy for entanglement negativity. *Phys. Rev. A* **2015**, *91*, 012339. [CrossRef]
36. Guo, Y.; Gour, G. Monogamy of the entanglement of formation. *Phys. Rev. A* **2019**, *99*, 042305. [CrossRef]
37. Guo, Y. Strict entanglement monotonicity under local operations and classical communication. *Phys. Rev. A* **2019**, *99*, 022338. [CrossRef]
38. Regula, B.; Osterloh, A.; Adesso, G. Strong monogamy inequalities for four qubits. *Phys. Rev. A* **2016**, *93*, 052338. [CrossRef]
39. Eltschka, C.; Siewert, J. Monogamy Equalities for Qubit Entanglement from Lorentz Invariance. *Phys. Rev. Lett.* **2015**, *114*, 140402. [CrossRef]

40. Eltschka, C.; Huber, F.; Gühne, O.; Siewert, J. Exponentially many entanglement and correlation constraints for multipartite quantum states. *Phys. Rev. A* **2018**, *98*, 052317. [CrossRef]
41. Guo, Y.; Huang, L.; Zhang, Y. Monogamy of quantum discord. *Quantum Sci. Technol.* **2021**, *6*, 045028. [CrossRef]
42. Hong, Y.; Gao, T.; Yan, F. Measure of multipartite entanglement with computable lower bounds. *Phys. Rev. A* **2012**, *86*, 062323. [CrossRef]
43. Hiesmayr, B.C.; Huber, M. Multipartite entanglement measure for all discrete systems. *Phys. Rev. A* **2008**, *78*, 012342. [CrossRef]
44. Guo, Y.; Zhang, L.; Yuan, H. Entanglement measures induced by fidelity-based distances. *Quant. Inf. Process.* **2020**, *19*, 1–17.
45. Jozsa, R. Fidelity for mixed quantum states. *J. Mod. Opt.* **1994**, *41*, 2315–2323. [CrossRef]
46. Uhlmann, A. The 'transition probability' in the state space of a*-algebra. *Rep. Math. Phys.* **1976**, *9*, 273–279. [CrossRef]
47. Zhang, L.; Chen, L.; Bu, K. Fidelity between one bipartite quantum state and another undergoing local unitary dynamics. *Quant. Inf. Process.* **2015**, *14*, 4715–4730. [CrossRef]
48. Fawzi, O.; Renner, R. Quantum conditional mutual information and approximate Markov chains. *Commun. Math. Phys.* **2015**, *340*, 575–611.
49. Luo, S.; Zhang, Q. Informational distance on quantum state space. *Phys. Rev. A* **2004**, *69*, 032106.
50. Ma, Z.; Zhang, F.L.; Chen, J.L. Geometric interpretation for the a fidelity and its relation with the Bures fidelity. *Phys. Rev. A* **2008**, *78*, 064305.
51. Raggio, G.A. *Generalized Transition Probabilities and Applications Quantum Probability and Applications to the Quantum Theory of Irreversible Processes*; Springer: New York, NY, USA, 1984; pp. 327–335.
52. Zhu, X.N.; Fei, S.M. Entanglement monogamy relations of qubit systems. *Phys. Rev. A* **2014**, *90*, 024304.
53. Luo, Y.; Tian, T.; Shao, L.H.; Li, Y. General monogamy of Tsallis q-entropy entanglement in multiqubit systems. *Phys. Rev. A* **2016**, *93*, 062340.
54. Kumar, A. Multiparty quantum mutual information: An alternative definition. *Phys. Rev. A* **2017**, *96*, 012332.

Article

A Characterization of Maximally Entangled Two-Qubit States

Junjun Duan [1], Lin Zhang [1,*], Quan Qian [1] and Shao-Ming Fei [2,3]

[1] School of Sciences, Hangzhou Dianzi University, Hangzhou 310018, China; epochduan@163.com (J.D.); cauchyss@163.com (Q.Q.)
[2] Max Planck Institute for Mathematics in the Sciences, 04103 Leipzig, Germany; feishm@cnu.edu.cn
[3] School of Mathematical Sciences, Capital Normal University, Beijing 100048, China
* Correspondence: godyalin@163.com

Abstract: As already known by Rana's result, all eigenvalues of any partial-transposed bipartite state fall within the closed interval $[-\frac{1}{2}, 1]$. In this note, we study a family of bipartite quantum states where the minimal eigenvalues of partial-transposed states are $-\frac{1}{2}$. For a two-qubit system, we find that the minimal eigenvalue of its partial-transposed state is $-\frac{1}{2}$ if and only if such a two-qubit state is maximally entangled. However this result does not hold in general for a two-qudit system when the dimensions of the underlying space are larger than two.

Keywords: maximally entangled state; positive partial transpose; moment

Citation: Duan, J.; Zhang, L.; Qian, Q.; Fei, S.-M. A Characterization of Maximally Entangled Two-Qubit States. *Entropy* 2022, 24, 247. https://doi.org/10.3390/e24020247

Academic Editor: Giuliano Benenti

Received: 18 January 2022
Accepted: 6 February 2022
Published: 7 February 2022

Publisher's Note: MDPI stays neutral with regard to jurisdictional claims in published maps and institutional affiliations.

Copyright: © 2022 by the authors. Licensee MDPI, Basel, Switzerland. This article is an open access article distributed under the terms and conditions of the Creative Commons Attribution (CC BY) license (https://creativecommons.org/licenses/by/4.0/).

1. Introduction

Let ρ_{AB} be a quantum state in a bipartite quantum system $\mathcal{H}_A \otimes \mathcal{H}_B$ such that the positive partial transpose (PPT) criterion indicates that, for any separable state ρ_{AB}, it must hold $\rho_{AB}^{T_A} \geqslant 0$, where T_A denotes the partial transpose on subsystem A. This PPT condition was first proposed by Peres [1]. Such a condition is not only a necessary one but also a sufficient one for separability in a qubit–qubit, qubit–qutrit or a qutrit–qubit system [2]. The PPT condition can also be verified from the moments of the randomized measurements [3–5].

Recently, Yu et al. [6] found that the PPT condition can be studied by considering the so-called partial transpose moments (PT-moments)

$$p_k := \mathrm{Tr}\left(\left[\rho_{AB}^{T_A}\right]^k\right).$$

In fact, these quantities can be efficiently measured in experiments [4,5]. To see the basic idea behind the PT-moments-based entanglement detection, suppose that we know all the PT-moments $\boldsymbol{p}^{(d)} = (p_1, \ldots, p_d)$, where $d = d_A d_B$ is the dimension of the global system $\mathcal{H}_A \otimes \mathcal{H}_B$, where $d_{A/B} = \dim(\mathcal{H}_{A/B})$. We call $\boldsymbol{p}^{(d)}$ the PT-moment vector of the state ρ_{AB}. All the eigenvalues of $\rho_{AB}^{T_A}$ are denoted by $(x_1, \ldots, x_d)$. As is already known, $(x_1, \ldots, x_d)$ completely determines the elementary symmetric polynomials $(e_1, \ldots, e_d)$, where $e_1 = \sum_{k=1}^d x_k$, $e_2 = \sum_{1 \leqslant i < j \leqslant d} x_i x_j, \ldots$, and $e_d = \prod_{k=1}^d x_k$; and conversely $(e_1, \ldots, e_d)$ can determine $(x_1, \ldots, x_d)$ when ignoring their order. In fact, $(e_1, \ldots, e_d)$ and $(p_1, \ldots, p_d)$, where p_k's are the power sum of x_i's, necessarily identify each other via the following relationship between e_k and p_k [7]:

$$p_k = \begin{vmatrix} e_1 & 1 & 0 & \cdots & 0 \\ 2e_2 & e_1 & 1 & \cdots & 0 \\ \vdots & \vdots & \vdots & \ddots & \vdots \\ (k-1)e_{k-1} & e_{k-2} & e_{k-3} & \cdots & 1 \\ ke_k & e_{k-1} & e_{k-2} & \cdots & e_1 \end{vmatrix} \quad (k \geqslant 1)$$

and

$$e_k = \frac{1}{k!} \begin{vmatrix} p_1 & 1 & 0 & \cdots & 0 \\ p_2 & p_1 & 2 & \cdots & 0 \\ \vdots & \vdots & \vdots & \ddots & \vdots \\ p_{k-1} & p_{k-2} & p_{k-3} & \cdots & k-1 \\ p_k & p_{k-1} & p_{k-2} & \cdots & p_1 \end{vmatrix} \quad (k \geq 1).$$

Therefore $(p_1, \ldots, p_d)$ determines $(x_1, \ldots, x_d)$ up to their order. Then, all eigenvalues of the partial-transposed state $\rho_{AB}^{T_A}$ can be directly obtained. Based on the above observation, the PPT criterion can be verified immediately. For convenience, we always assume that $p_1 = 1$. In addition, p_2 is just the purity due to the fact that $\text{Tr}\left(\left[\rho_{AB}^{T_A}\right]^2\right) = \text{Tr}(\rho_{AB}^2)$. In [6], the authors studied the following problem.

PT-Moment problem: Given the PT-moments of order n, is there a separable state compatible with the data? In more technical language, given the PT-moment vector

$$\boldsymbol{p}^{(n)} = (p_1, \ldots, p_n),$$

is there a separable quantum state ρ_{AB} such that

$$p_k = \text{Tr}\left(\left[\rho_{AB}^{T_A}\right]^k\right), \quad k = 1, \ldots, n?$$

It is natural to consider the detection of entanglement in ρ_{AB} from a few of the PT-moments due to the difficulty in measuring all the PT-moments, such as in [6]. Note that the partial-transposed state $\rho_{AB}^{T_A}$, for $\rho_{AB} \in D(\mathbb{C}^m \otimes \mathbb{C}^n)$, which is the set of all bipartite quantum states acting on $\mathbb{C}^m \otimes \mathbb{C}^n$, cannot have more than $(m-1)(n-1)$ negative eigenvalues and all eigenvalues of $\rho_{AB}^{T_A}$ fall within $[-\frac{1}{2}, 1]$ [8]. Using the second PT-moment to bound the third one is an interesting question. Moreover, we find that this method can be used to get a characterization of maximally entangled two-qubit states, that is, a two-qubit state is maximally entangled if and only if the minimal eigenvalue of its partial-transposed state is $-\frac{1}{2}$. This is also equivalent to the condition that $\boldsymbol{p}^{(4)} = (1, 1, \frac{1}{4}, \frac{1}{4})$, the PT-moment vector of the two-qubit state ρ_{AB}. This amounts to giving the criterion of maximal entanglement to the states using the PT-moment vector, the components of which are measurable quantities.

2. Main Result

In this section, we essentially ask: Is ρ_{AB} maximally entangled if $\rho_{AB} \in D(\mathbb{C}^2 \otimes \mathbb{C}^2)$ and the minimal eigenvalue of its partial-transposed state $\rho_{AB}^{T_A}$ is $\lambda_{\min}\left(\rho_{AB}^{T_A}\right) = -\frac{1}{2}$? We give a positive answer to this question in our main result, i.e., Theorem 1. To that end, we obtained the proof through a series of propositions.

Proposition 1. Let $\rho_{AB}, \sigma_{AB}, \tau_{AB} \in D(\mathbb{C}^m \otimes \mathbb{C}^n)$, where $\rho_{AB} = t\sigma_{AB} + (1-t)\tau_{AB}$ for some $t \in (0, 1)$. If $\lambda_{\min}\left(\rho_{AB}^{T_A}\right) = -\frac{1}{2}$, i.e., the minimal eigenvalue of $\rho_{AB}^{T_A}$, then $\lambda_{\min}\left(\sigma_{AB}^{T_A}\right) = \lambda_{\min}\left(\tau_{AB}^{T_A}\right) = -\frac{1}{2}$.

Proof. Using the main result in [8], we see that, for any bipartite state $\varrho_{AB} \in D(\mathbb{C}^m \otimes \mathbb{C}^n)$, we have

$$\lambda_{\min}(\varrho_{AB}^{T_A}) \in \left[-\frac{1}{2}, 1\right].$$

Thus,
$$\lambda_{\min}(\sigma_{AB}^{T_A}) \geqslant -\frac{1}{2}, \quad \lambda_{\min}(\tau_{AB}^{T_A}) \geqslant -\frac{1}{2}.$$

As is already known, there exists a pure state $|\psi_0\rangle \in \mathbb{C}^m \otimes \mathbb{C}^n$, corresponding to the minimal eigenvalue $\lambda_{\min}\left(\rho_{AB}^{T_A}\right)$, such that

$$\begin{aligned}
-\frac{1}{2} &= \lambda_{\min}\left(\rho_{AB}^{T_A}\right) = \langle\psi_0|\rho_{AB}^{T_A}|\psi_0\rangle = t\langle\psi_0|\sigma_{AB}^{T_A}|\psi_0\rangle + (1-t)\langle\psi_0|\tau_{AB}^{T_A}|\psi_0\rangle \\
&\geqslant t\lambda_{\min}\left(\sigma_{AB}^{T_A}\right) + (1-t)\lambda_{\min}\left(\tau_{AB}^{T_A}\right) \geqslant -\frac{1}{2}.
\end{aligned}$$

We must have that $\lambda_{\min}\left(\sigma_{AB}^{T_A}\right) = \langle\psi_0|\sigma_{AB}^{T_A}|\psi_0\rangle = \lambda_{\min}\left(\tau_{AB}^{T_A}\right) = \langle\psi_0|\tau_{AB}^{T_A}|\psi_0\rangle = -\frac{1}{2}$. □

Corollary 1. *Suppose $\rho_{AB} \in \mathrm{D}(\mathbb{C}^m \otimes \mathbb{C}^n)$ has the pure state decomposition: $\rho_{AB} = \sum_k \lambda_k |\psi_k\rangle\langle\psi_k|$, where $\lambda_k > 0$ for all indices k. If $\lambda_{\min}\left(\rho_{AB}^{T_A}\right) = -\frac{1}{2}$, then*

$$\lambda_{\min}\left(\psi_k^{T_A}\right) = -\frac{1}{2}.$$

Here $\psi_k := |\psi_k\rangle\langle\psi_k|$.

Recall that there is a correspondence between the set $\mathrm{L}(\mathcal{Y},\mathcal{X})$ of all linear operators from a finite-dimensional Hilbert space $\mathcal{Y}$ to another finite-dimensional Hilbert space $\mathcal{X}$. It can be explained immediately. Denote by $\mathcal{X} \otimes \mathcal{Y}$ the tensor space of $\mathcal{X}$ and $\mathcal{Y}$. Let the orthonormal bases of $\mathcal{X}$ and $\mathcal{Y}$ be $\{|i\rangle : i = 1, \ldots, \dim(\mathcal{X})\}$ and $\{|j\rangle : j = 1, \ldots, \dim(\mathcal{Y})\}$, respectively. The mentioned correspondence between $\mathrm{L}(\mathcal{Y},\mathcal{X})$ and $\mathcal{X} \otimes \mathcal{Y}$ is defined by the linear mapping vec : $\mathrm{L}(\mathcal{Y},\mathcal{X}) \to \mathcal{X} \otimes \mathcal{Y}$ via $\mathrm{vec}(|i\rangle\langle j|) = |ij\rangle$ for all i,j [9].

Let $|\psi\rangle \in \mathbb{C}^d \otimes \mathbb{C}^d$ be a bipartite pure state. Then there is an $d \times d$ complex matrix X such that $|\psi\rangle = \mathrm{vec}(X)$. By singular value decomposition (SVD), there are two unitary matrices $U, V \in \mathsf{U}(d)$ such that $X = U\Sigma V^\dagger$, where $\Sigma = \mathrm{diag}(\sigma_1, \ldots, \sigma_r, \ldots, \sigma_d)$ for $\sigma_1 \geqslant \cdots \geqslant \sigma_d \geqslant 0$ and $r = \mathrm{rank}(X) \leqslant d$. Note that $\sum_{j=1}^d \sigma_j^2 = 1$. Then

$$|\psi\rangle\langle\psi| = U \otimes \overline{V} \, \mathrm{vec}(\Sigma) \, \mathrm{vec}(\Sigma)^\dagger (U \otimes \overline{V})^\dagger$$

implying that

$$|\psi\rangle\langle\psi|^{T_A} = \overline{U} \otimes \overline{V} \left(\mathrm{vec}(\Sigma) \, \mathrm{vec}(\Sigma)^\dagger\right)^{T_A} (\overline{U} \otimes \overline{V})^\dagger.$$

Due to the fact that $\Sigma = \sum_{i=1}^d \sigma_i |i\rangle\langle i|$, we see that

$$\mathrm{vec}(\Sigma) \, \mathrm{vec}(\Sigma)^\dagger = \sum_{i,j=1}^d \sigma_i \sigma_j |ij\rangle\langle ij|, \quad \left(\mathrm{vec}(\Sigma) \, \mathrm{vec}(\Sigma)^\dagger\right)^{T_A} = \sum_{i,j=1}^d \sigma_i \sigma_j |ji\rangle\langle ij|$$

Proposition 2. *All eigenvalues of $|\psi\rangle\langle\psi|^{T_A}$ is given by $\{\sigma_1^2, \ldots, \sigma_d^2; \pm\sigma_i\sigma_j \ (1 \leqslant i < j \leqslant d)\}$.*

Proof. Let $F = \left(\text{vec}(\Sigma)\,\text{vec}(\Sigma)^\dagger\right)^{T_A} = \sum_{i,j=1}^d \sigma_i\sigma_j|ji\rangle\langle ij|$. Then

$$\begin{aligned}
FF^\dagger &= \left(\sum_{i,j=1}^d \sigma_i\sigma_j|ji\rangle\langle ij|\right)\left(\sum_{k,l=1}^d \sigma_k\sigma_l|lk\rangle\langle kl|\right)^\dagger = \sum_{i,j,k,l=1}^d \sigma_i\sigma_j\sigma_k\sigma_l|ji\rangle\langle ij|\cdot|kl\rangle\langle lk| \\
&= \sum_{i,j,k,l=1}^d \delta_{ik}\delta_{jl}\sigma_i\sigma_j\sigma_k\sigma_l|ji\rangle\langle lk| = \sum_{i,j=1}^d (\sigma_i\sigma_j)^2|ji\rangle\langle ji|;
\end{aligned}$$

that is, $|F| = \sqrt{FF^\dagger} = \sum_{i,j=1}^d \sigma_i\sigma_j|ji\rangle\langle ji|$. Note that

$$\text{Tr}(F) = \sum_{i=1}^d \sigma_i^2, \quad \text{Tr}(|F|) = \sum_{i,j=1}^d \sigma_i\sigma_j.$$

By using the Jordan decomposition $F = F_+ - F_-$, where $F_\pm^\dagger = F_\pm \geqslant 0$ and $F_+F_- = 0 = F_-F_+$. Then

$$\text{Tr}(F_+) - \text{Tr}(F_-) = \sum_{i=1}^d \sigma_i^2, \quad \text{Tr}(F_+) + \text{Tr}(F_-) = \sum_{i,j=1}^d \sigma_i\sigma_j,$$

and

$$\text{Tr}(F_+) = \sum_{i=1}^d \sigma_i^2 + \sum_{i<j}\sigma_i\sigma_j, \quad \text{Tr}(F_-) = \sum_{i<j}\sigma_i\sigma_j.$$

Therefore, all eigenvalues of F are given by $\{\sigma_1^2,\ldots,\sigma_d^2;\pm\sigma_i\sigma_j\,(1\leqslant i<j\leqslant d)\}$. □

Thus, we need to characterize those bipartite pure states that have the minimal eigenvalue of its partial-transposed state, $-\frac{1}{2}$.

Proposition 3. *If $|\psi\rangle \in \mathbb{C}^2 \otimes \mathbb{C}^2$ is a pure state, then $\lambda_{\min}(\psi^{T_A}) = -\frac{1}{2}$, where $\psi \equiv |\psi\rangle\langle\psi|$, if and only if $|\psi\rangle$ is a maximally entangled state, i.e., $|\psi\rangle$ is proportional to the locally unitarily rotation of the vector $\text{vec}(\mathbb{I}_2)$. Here $\mathbb{I}$ is the identity operator.*

Proof. Let $|\psi\rangle \in \mathbb{C}^2 \otimes \mathbb{C}^2$. Suppose $x = (x_1,x_2,x_3,x_4) \in \mathbb{R}^4$ is the eigenvalues of ψ^{T_A} with $1 \geqslant x_1 \geqslant x_2 \geqslant x_3 \geqslant x_4 \geqslant -\frac{1}{2}$ [8]. Clearly $x_4 = \lambda_{\min}(\psi^{T_A})$.

Now let $x_4 = -\frac{1}{2}$. Again, we see that $x_3 \geqslant 0$ by Rana's result. Let $p_k = \text{Tr}\left([\psi^{T_A}]^k\right)$, where $k = 1, 2, \ldots$. It is easy to see that $p_1 = 1$, $p_2 = 1$. Then

$$\begin{cases} 1 = x_1 + x_2 + x_3 + \left(-\frac{1}{2}\right) \\ 1 = x_1^2 + x_2^2 + x_3^2 + \left(-\frac{1}{2}\right)^2. \end{cases}$$

Due to the constraint $1 \geqslant x_1 \geqslant x_2 \geqslant x_3 \geqslant 0$, the above system of equations has a unique solution: $x_1 = x_2 = x_3 = \frac{1}{2}$.

We have now proved that if $\lambda_{\min}(\psi^{T_A}) = -\frac{1}{2}$ for some pure state $|\psi\rangle \in \mathbb{C}^2 \otimes \mathbb{C}^2$, then all eigenvalues of ψ^{T_A} are $\{\frac{1}{2}, \frac{1}{2}, \frac{1}{2}, -\frac{1}{2}\}$. In fact, if $\lambda_{\min}\left(\rho_{AB}^{T_A}\right) = -\frac{1}{2}$ for some state $\rho_{AB} \in D(\mathbb{C}^2 \otimes \mathbb{C}^2)$, then all eigenvalues of $\rho_{AB}^{T_A}$ is $\{\frac{1}{2}, \frac{1}{2}, \frac{1}{2}, -\frac{1}{2}\}$.

For a pure state $|\psi\rangle \in \mathbb{C}^2 \otimes \mathbb{C}^2$, there exists a 2×2 complex matrix A such that $|\psi\rangle = \text{vec}(A)$. By SVD of A, we get that $A = UDV^\dagger$ where $D = \text{diag}(s_0, s_1)$ with $s_0 \geqslant s_1 \geqslant 0$ and $U, V \in U(2)$. Then

$$\begin{aligned}
|\psi\rangle\langle\psi| &= U \otimes \overline{V}\,\text{vec}(D)\,\text{vec}(D)^\dagger\left(U \otimes \overline{V}\right)^\dagger \\
&= U \otimes \overline{V}\,\text{vec}(D)\,\text{vec}(D)^\dagger U^\dagger \otimes V^T,
\end{aligned}$$

where

$$\text{vec}(D)\text{vec}(D)^\dagger = \text{vec}\left(\sum_i s_i |i\rangle\langle i|\right) \text{vec}\left(\sum_j s_j |j\rangle\langle j|\right)^\dagger = \sum_{i,j=0}^{1} s_i s_j |ii\rangle\langle jj|.$$

Next, we established the equations concerning (s_0, s_1). The first one is $s_0^2 + s_1^2 = 1$ due to the fact that $\text{Tr}(D^2) = \langle \psi, \psi \rangle = 1$. The second one is

$$\begin{aligned}
|\psi\rangle\langle\psi|^{T_A} &= \sum_{i,j=0}^{1} s_i s_j (U|i\rangle\langle j|U^\dagger)^T \otimes \overline{V}|i\rangle\langle j|V^T \\
&= \sum_{i,j=0}^{1} s_i s_j \overline{U}|j\rangle\langle i|U^T \otimes \overline{V}|i\rangle\langle j|V^T \\
&= (\overline{U} \otimes \overline{V}) \sum_{i,j=0}^{1} s_i s_j |j\rangle\langle i| \otimes |i\rangle\langle j| (\overline{U} \otimes \overline{V})^\dagger \\
&= (\overline{U} \otimes \overline{V}) \sum_{i,j=0}^{1} s_i s_j |ji\rangle\langle ij| (\overline{U} \otimes \overline{V})^\dagger.
\end{aligned}$$

Now both $|\psi\rangle\langle\psi|^{T_A}$ and $\sum_{i,j=0}^{1} s_i s_j |ji\rangle\langle ij|$ have the same eigenvalues. That is, all eigenvalues of

$$\sum_{i,j=0}^{1} s_i s_j |ji\rangle\langle ij| = \begin{pmatrix} s_1^2 & 0 & 0 & 0 \\ 0 & 0 & s_1 s_2 & 0 \\ 0 & s_1 s_2 & 0 & 0 \\ 0 & 0 & 0 & s_2^2 \end{pmatrix}$$

are $\{s_0^2, s_1^2, s_0 s_1, -s_0 s_1\} = \{\frac{1}{2}, \frac{1}{2}, \frac{1}{2}, -\frac{1}{2}\}$. This implies that

$$s_0^2 = s_1^2 = s_0 s_1 = \frac{1}{2}.$$

This unique solution is given by $(s_0, s_1) = \left(\frac{1}{\sqrt{2}}, \frac{1}{\sqrt{2}}\right)$. Therefore, $A = \frac{1}{\sqrt{2}} UV^\dagger$. Then

$$|\psi\rangle = \text{vec}(A) = \frac{1}{\sqrt{2}} \text{vec}(UV^\dagger) = \frac{1}{\sqrt{2}} U \otimes \overline{V} \text{vec}(\mathbb{I}_2).$$

We have proven that $|\psi\rangle$ is a maximally entangled state. Conversely, if $|\psi\rangle$ is a maximally entangled state, then the minimal eigenvalue of its partial-transposed state is apparently $-\frac{1}{2}$ [10,11]. □

For the partial-transposed maximally entangled states in $\mathbb{C}^n \otimes \mathbb{C}^n$, the eigenvalues must be $\pm \frac{1}{n}$ where the multiplicities of $\frac{1}{n}$ and $-\frac{1}{n}$ are $\frac{n(n+1)}{2}$ and $\frac{n(n-1)}{2}$, respectively. Thus its PT-moment vector is given by

$$p^{(n^2)} = (p_1, \ldots, p_{n^2}), \quad p_k = \frac{(n+1) + (n-1)(-1)^k}{2n^{k-1}}.$$

In particular, for the case where $n = 2$, the PT-moment vector $p^{(4)} = (1, 1, \frac{1}{4}, \frac{1}{4})$.

Theorem 1. *Let $\rho_{AB} \in D(\mathbb{C}^2 \otimes \mathbb{C}^2)$ be a quantum state, then the following statements are equivalent:*

- *the PT-moment vector of ρ_{AB} is $p^{(4)} = (1, 1, \frac{1}{4}, \frac{1}{4})$.*
- *ρ_{AB} must be maximally entangled.*

Proof. For the implication (ii) $\Longrightarrow$ (i), the proof is trivial. Next, we show that (i) implies (ii). Given (i), let (x_1, x_2, x_3, x_4), where $x_1 \geqslant x_2 \geqslant x_3 \geqslant x_4$, be eigenvalues of the partial-transposed state $\rho_{AB}^{T_A}$, then Rana's result [8] means that $1 \geqslant x_1 \geqslant x_2 \geqslant x_3 \geqslant \begin{cases} 0 \\ x_4 \geqslant -\frac{1}{2} \end{cases}$.
By the given PT-moment vector, we see that

$$\begin{cases} p_1 = x_1 + x_2 + x_3 + x_4 = 1 \\ p_2 = x_1^2 + x_2^2 + x_3^2 + x_4^2 = 1 \\ p_3 = x_1^3 + x_2^3 + x_3^3 + x_4^3 = \frac{1}{4} \\ p_4 = x_1^4 + x_2^4 + x_3^4 + x_4^4 = \frac{1}{4} \end{cases}$$

In fact, note that

$$e_k = \frac{1}{k!} \begin{vmatrix} p_1 & 1 & 0 & \cdots & 0 \\ p_2 & p_1 & 2 & \cdots & 0 \\ \vdots & \vdots & \vdots & \ddots & \vdots \\ p_{k-1} & p_{k-2} & p_{k-3} & \cdots & k-1 \\ p_k & p_{k-1} & p_{k-2} & \cdots & p_1 \end{vmatrix} \quad (k \geqslant 1),$$

and we see that $e_1 = 1, e_2 = 0, e_3 = -\frac{1}{4}, e_4 = -\frac{1}{16}$. The characteristic polynomial of $\rho_{AB}^{T_A}$ is given by

$$\begin{aligned} f(x) &= x^4 - e_1 x^3 + e_2 x^2 - e_3 x + e_4 = x^4 - x^3 + \frac{1}{4}x - \frac{1}{16} \\ &= \frac{1}{16}(2x-1)^3(2x+1). \end{aligned}$$

Solving this system of equations via $f(x) = 0$, we get that $x_1 = x_2 = x_3 = \frac{1}{2}$ and $x_4 = \lambda_{\min}(\rho_{AB}^{T_A}) = -\frac{1}{2}$. Next, if $F = \sum_{i,j=0}^{1} |ji\rangle\langle ij|$, then $F|ij\rangle = |ji\rangle$ and $F^{T_A} = \text{vec}(\mathbb{I})\text{vec}(\mathbb{I})^\dagger$. Note that $F \frac{|01\rangle - |10\rangle}{\sqrt{2}} = -\frac{|01\rangle - |10\rangle}{\sqrt{2}}$. Let $|x\rangle = \frac{|01\rangle - |10\rangle}{\sqrt{2}}$, and we get $\langle x|F|x\rangle = -1 = \lambda_{\min}(F)$.

From the previous discussion, we see that in the pure state decomposition of ρ_{AB}: $\rho_{AB} = \sum_{k=0}^{N-1} \lambda_k |\psi_k\rangle\langle\psi_k|$, where $\lambda_0 \geqslant \lambda_1 \geqslant \cdots \geqslant \lambda_{N-1} \geqslant 0$, all pure state $|\psi_k\rangle$ must be maximally entangled state. Then there exist a pure state $|u\rangle$ such that

$$\left\langle u \left| \psi_k^{T_A} \right| u \right\rangle = -\frac{1}{2} \quad (k = 0, 1, \ldots, N-1).$$

There exist $U_k, V_k \in \mathsf{U}(2)$ such that

$$|\psi_k\rangle = \frac{1}{\sqrt{2}} \text{vec}(U_k V_k^\dagger) = \frac{1}{\sqrt{2}} U_k V_k^\dagger \otimes \mathbb{I} \, \text{vec}(\mathbb{I}) = \frac{1}{\sqrt{2}} W_k \otimes \mathbb{I} \, \text{vec}(\mathbb{I}),$$

where $W_k = U_k V_k^\dagger$, implying that $\psi_k^{T_A} = \frac{1}{2}(\overline{W}_k \otimes \mathbb{I}) F (\overline{W}_k \otimes \mathbb{I})^\dagger$. Now let $|u_k\rangle = W_k^T \otimes \mathbb{I}|u\rangle$. Then

$$-\frac{1}{2} = \left\langle u \left| \psi_k^{T_A} \right| u \right\rangle = \frac{1}{2}\langle u_k | F | u_k \rangle \quad (k = 0, 1, \ldots, N-1).$$

That is,

$$\lambda_{\min}(F) = -1 = \langle u_k | F | u_k \rangle \quad (k = 0, 1, \ldots, N-1).$$

Because -1 is the simple eigenvalue of F, the eigenspace corresponding to -1 is just $\mathbb{C}|x\rangle$. This indicates that all $|u_k\rangle = e^{i\theta_k}|x\rangle$ due to the normalization of $|u_k\rangle$. Furthermore

$$|u\rangle = e^{i\theta_k}(\overline{W}_k \otimes \mathbb{I})|x\rangle \quad (k = 0, 1, \ldots, N-1).$$

In fact, the phase factor $e^{i\theta_k}$ can be absorbed into the unitary matrix W_k. Without loss of generality, we assume that

$$|u\rangle = (\overline{W}_k \otimes \mathbb{I})|x\rangle \quad (k=0,1,\ldots,N-1).$$

Because there is a matrix X such that $|x\rangle = \text{vec}(X)$, then

$$X = \frac{1}{\sqrt{2}}(|0\rangle\langle 1| - |1\rangle\langle 0|) = \frac{1}{\sqrt{2}}\begin{pmatrix} 0 & 1 \\ -1 & 0 \end{pmatrix}.$$

It is easily seen that X is invertible. We see that

$$|u\rangle = \text{vec}(\overline{W}_k X) \quad (k=0,1,\ldots,N-1).$$

implying that $\overline{W}_0 X = \overline{W}_1 X = \cdots = \overline{W}_{N-1} X$, i.e., due to the fact that X is invertible, then $W_0 = W_1 = \cdots = W_{N-1}$, or

$$U_0 V_0^\dagger = U_1 V_1^\dagger = \cdots = U_{N-1} V_{N-1}^\dagger,$$

implying that $\text{vec}(U_0 V_0^\dagger) = \text{vec}(U_1 V_1^\dagger) = \cdots = \text{vec}(U_{N-1} V_{N-1}^\dagger)$; that is, $|\psi_0\rangle = |\psi_1\rangle = \cdots = |\psi_{N-1}\rangle$. Therefore $\rho_{AB} = \sum_k \lambda_k |\psi_k\rangle\langle\psi_k| = |\psi_0\rangle\langle\psi_0|$ is a maximally entangled state. □

In fact, our main result, Theorem 1, tells us that the PT-moment vector of a two-qubit state ρ_{AB} is $(1,1,\frac{1}{4},\frac{1}{4})$ iff the minimal eigenvalue of its partial-transposed state $\rho_{AB}^{T_A}$ is $-\frac{1}{2}$ iff ρ_{AB} is maximally entangled. Naturally, we would expect a similar relation between the magnitude of the lowest negative eigenvalue of the partial-transposed state and the maximally entangled states in higher-dimensional underlying spaces. However, the following result, Proposition 4, indicates that the minimal eigenvalue of the partial-transposed maximally entangled state would approach zero when the dimension of the underlying space becomes larger and larger. Indeed, after tedious computations and induction, we can draw the following conclusion:

Proposition 4. *Let $\rho_{AB} \in D(\mathbb{C}^n \otimes \mathbb{C}^n)$ be a quantum state. If the PT-moment vector of ρ_{AB} is $p^{(n^2)} = (p_1, \ldots, p_{n^2})$, where $p_k = \frac{(n+1)+(n-1)(-1)^k}{2n^{k-1}}$. Then $\lambda_{\min}\left(\rho_{AB}^{T_A}\right) = -\frac{1}{n}$.*

Proof. As an illustration, for a two-qutrit system $\mathbb{C}^3 \otimes \mathbb{C}^3$ as an example, we get $(e_1, \ldots, e_9)$ from $p^{(9)} = (p_1, \ldots, p_9)$, where $p_1 = p_2 = 1, p_3 = p_4 = \frac{1}{9}, p_5 = p_6 = \frac{1}{81}, p_7 = p_8 = \frac{1}{729}$ and $p_9 = \frac{1}{6561}$. That is,

$$e_1 = 1, e_2 = 0, e_3 = -\frac{8}{27}, e_4 = -\frac{2}{27}, e_5 = \frac{2}{81},$$
$$e_6 = \frac{8}{729}, e_7 = 0, e_8 = -\frac{1}{2187}, e_9 = -\frac{1}{19683}.$$

Furthermore, the characteristic polynomial of $\rho_{AB}^{T_A}$ is given by

$$f(x) = x^9 - x^8 + \frac{8x^6}{27} - \frac{2x^5}{27} - \frac{2x^4}{81} + \frac{8x^3}{729} - \frac{x}{2187} + \frac{1}{19683}$$
$$= \frac{(3x-1)^6 (3x+1)^3}{19683}.$$

Thus, we get that

$$x_1 = \cdots = x_6 = \frac{1}{3}, x_7 = x_8 = x_9 = -\frac{1}{3}.$$

Therefore $\lambda_{\min}(\rho_{AB}^{T_A}) = -\frac{1}{3}$. □

From the above result, when $n \to \infty$, $\lambda_{\min}(\rho_{AB}^{T_A}) \to 0$ for a maximally entangled state in $\mathbb{C}^n \otimes \mathbb{C}^n$. Based on the observation, we can conclude that the family of bipartite states with the minimal eigenvalue of their partial-transposed states $(-\frac{1}{2})$ is different from the set of maximally entangled states when the dimensions of the underlying spaces are larger than two. This also indicates that the magnitude of the only lowest negative eigenvalue of the partial-transposed state in higher-dimensional space would not be enough to identify the maximally entangled state when there is more than one negative eigenvalue. In fact, it is known that for higher dimensions the characterization of entanglement can be given by the so-called "negativity" [12], which is defined as the absolute value of the sum of all the negative eigenvalues of the partial-transposed state. That is, the negativity of ρ_{AB} is given by $\mathcal{N}(\rho_{AB}) = \left|\sum_i \min\left\{\lambda_i(\rho_{AB}^{T_A}), 0\right\}\right|$. With this notion, our Theorem 1 can be rewritten: For the two-qubit state ρ_{AB}, $\mathcal{N}(\rho_{AB}) = \frac{1}{2}$ iff ρ_{AB} is maximally entangled. The success of such characterization lies in the possible number of negative eigenvalues being at most one. The reason for the failure of this result in high-dimensional space is that only one negative eigenvalue (the lowest one) would not be enough to characterize entanglement when there could be more than one negative eigenvalue.

3. Concluding Remarks

In this short note, we make an attempt to study the structure of a family of bipartite states with the extreme eigenvalue being $-\frac{1}{2}$ of its partial-transposed states. To characterize the maximally entangled two-qubit states, we employed the approach recently used by Yu et al. to study PT-moments, i.e., PT-moment vectors. In higher dimensional system, we were curious whether the PT-moment vector ($\boldsymbol{p}^{(n^2)} = (p_1, \ldots, p_{n^2})$ where $p_k = \frac{(n+1)+(n-1)(-1)^k}{2n^{k-1}}$) generated by the maximally entangled states, only corresponded to the maximally entangled states. Clearly, a bipartite state in $D(\mathbb{C}^n \otimes \mathbb{C}^n)$ with $\lambda_{\min}(\rho_{AB}^{T_A}) = -\frac{1}{2}$ was, in general, not maximally entangled unless $n = 2$. In future research, we will continue to figure out the structure of this family of states, especially to find out the connection between it and maximally entangled states in a higher dimension. Furthermore, we will study the connection between the entanglement in bipartite states and the number of negative eigenvalues of the corresponding partial-transposed states.

Author Contributions: Writing—original draft, J.D., L.Z. and Q.Q.; Writing—review & editing, S.-M.F. All authors have read and agreed to the published version of the manuscript.

Funding: This work is supported by the National Natural Science Foundation of China under Grant Nos. (11971140, 12075159, 12171044); Beijing Natural Science Foundation (Grant No. Z190005); Academy for Multidisciplinary Studies, Capital Normal University; Shenzhen Institute for Quantum Science and Engineering, Southern University of Science and Technology (No. SIQSE202001), the Academician Innovation Platform of Hainan Province.

Conflicts of Interest: The authors declare no conflict of interest.

Reference

1. Peres, A. Separability criterion for density matrices. *Phys. Rev. Lett.* **1996**, *77*, 1413. [CrossRef] [PubMed]
2. Horodecki, M.; Horodecki, P.; Horodecki, R. Separability of mixed states: Necessary and sufficient conditions. *Phys. Rev. Lett.* **1996**, *223*, 1–8. [CrossRef]
3. Gray, J.; Banchi, L.; Bayat, A.; Bose, S. Machine-learning-assisted many-body entanglement measurement. *Phys. Rev. Lett.* **2018**, *121*, 150503. [CrossRef] [PubMed]
4. Elben, A.; Kueng, R.; Huang, H.-R.; van Bijnen, R.; Kokail, C.; Dalmonte, M.; Calabrese, P.; Kraus, B.; Preskill, J.; Zoller, P.; et al. Mixed-state entanglement from local randomized measurements. *Phys. Rev. Lett.* **2020**, *125*, 200501. [CrossRef] [PubMed]
5. Zhou, Y.; Zeng, P.; Liu, Z. Single-copies estimation of entanglement negativity. *Phys. Rev. Lett.* **2020**, *125*, 200502. [CrossRef] [PubMed]
6. Yu, X.-D.; Imai, S.; Gühne, O. Optimal entanglement certification from moments of the partial transpose. *Phys. Rev. Lett.* **2021**, *127*, 060504. [CrossRef] [PubMed]

7. Macdonald, I.G. *Symmetric Functions and Hall Polynomials*, 2nd ed.; Oxford Unversity Press: Oxford, UK, 1995.
8. Rana, S. Negative eigenvalues of partial transposition of arbitrary bipartite states. *Phys. Rev. A* **2013**, *87*, 054301. [CrossRef]
9. Watrous, J. *The Theory of Quantum Information*; Cambridge University Press: Cambridge, UK, 2018.
10. Li, Z.G.; Zhao, M.J.; Fei, S.M.; Fan, H.; Liu, W.M. Mixed maximally entangled states. *Quant. Inf. Comput.* **2012**, *12*, 63–73. [CrossRef]
11. Zhao, M.J. Maximally entangled states and fully entangled fraction. *Phys. Rev. A* **2015**, *91*, 012310. [CrossRef]
12. Plenio, M. Logarithmic Negativity: A Full Entanglement Monotone That is not Convex. *Phys. Rev. Lett.* **2005**, *95*, 090503. [CrossRef] [PubMed]

Article

Quantum Nonlocality in Any Forked Tree-Shaped Network

Lihua Yang [1,2,†], Xiaofei Qi [1,*,†] and Jinchuan Hou [3,†]

1. School of Mathematical Science, Shanxi University, Taiyuan 030006, China; 201912211008@email.sxu.edu.cn
2. School of Mathematics and Information Technology, Yuncheng University, Yuncheng 044000, China
3. College of Mathematics, Taiyuan University of Technology, Taiyuan 030024, China; houjinchuan@tyut.edu.cn
* Correspondence: qixf1981@sxu.edu.cn
† These authors contributed equally to this work.

Abstract: In the last decade, much attention has been focused on examining the nonlocality of various quantum networks, which are fundamental for long-distance quantum communications. In this paper, we consider the nonlocality of any forked tree-shaped network, where each node, respectively, shares arbitrary number of bipartite sources with other nodes in the next "layer". The Bell-type inequalities for such quantum networks are obtained, which are, respectively, satisfied by all $(t_n - 1)$-local correlations and all local correlations, where t_n denotes the total number of nodes in the network. The maximal quantum violations of these inequalities and the robustness to noise in these networks are also discussed. Our network can be seen as a generalization of some known quantum networks.

Keywords: quantum correlation; nonlocality; Bell inequality; quantum network

1. Introduction

Quantum correlation is one of the main characteristics that distinguishes quantum mechanics from classical mechanics. In the last few decades, quantum nonlocality has been studied extensively both in theory [1–3] and experiment [4–6]. It is found that quantum nonlocality is a powerful resource in quantum information science, such as secure cryptography [7,8], quantum key distribution [9], randomness certification [10], and distributed computing [11]. Bell inequalities are often used to detect quantum nonlocality [12–14]. Violations of Bell inequalities imply the existence of nonlocal correlations.

Different from the usual Bell nonlocality, where entanglement is distributed from one common source, the multi-locality in quantum networks features several independent sources. By performing joint measurements, this leads to stronger correlations throughout the whole network [15], which is fundamental for long-distance quantum communications. Nonlocality of correlations generated in such networks was first observed in a bilocal network [16–18]. Later, the authors in [18] obtained the bilocal inequalities for bilocal networks, and the scholars in [19] explicitly examined quantum violations of the bilocal inequalities for pure states and mixed states, respectively. Since then, the nonlocality of various quantum networks were explored, including chain-shaped networks [20], star-shaped networks [21–23], triangle networks [24], and other networks in [25–32]. Furthermore, stronger forms of network nonlocality were examined in [33–35].

The tree-tensor networks are also important quantum networks. They have wide applications, such as in quantum simulations [36–39], entanglement transitions [40], and quantum-assisted machine learning [41]. Recently, nonlocal correlations of a special class of tree-tensor networks, so-called "two-forked" tree-shaped networks were studied in [42]. In this network, there are $(2^n - 1)$ parties (nodes) distributed in n "layers" ($n \geq 2$), where each layer k ($1 \leq k \leq n$) has 2^{k-1} parties, and each party in the layer k shares a source with another party in the layer $k-1$ and with other two parties in the layer $k+1$. Thus, this network is a $(2^n - 1)$-partite system with $(2^n - 2)$ independent sources.

The purpose of the present paper is to consider the nonlocality of any forked tree-shaped network. In this tree-shaped network, t_n parties are arranged in an n "layer"

Citation: Yang, L.; Qi, X.; Hou, J. Quantum Nonlocality in Any Forked Tree-Shaped Network. *Entropy* 2022, 24, 691. https://doi.org/10.3390/e24050691

Academic Editors: Shao-Ming Fei, Ming Li and Shunlong Luo

Received: 7 April 2022
Accepted: 11 May 2022
Published: 13 May 2022

Publisher's Note: MDPI stays neutral with regard to jurisdictional claims in published maps and institutional affiliations.

Copyright: © 2022 by the authors. Licensee MDPI, Basel, Switzerland. This article is an open access article distributed under the terms and conditions of the Creative Commons Attribution (CC BY) license (https://creativecommons.org/licenses/by/4.0/).

scenario ($n \geq 2$), and the (k, j) party in the layer k, respectively, shares a source with another party in the layer $k-1$ and with other $l_{kj} - l_{k(j-1)}$ parties in the layer $k+1$ ($2 \leq k \leq n-1$, $j \geq 1$), where $l_{k0} = 0$ and $l_{kj} - l_{k(j-1)}$ is an arbitrary positive integer. Denote the total number of parties in layer k by p_k ($k = 1, 2, \cdots, n$), satisfying $p_1 = 1$. Write $t_n = p_1 + \cdots + p_n$. Thus, the whole network is a t_n-partite system with $(t_n - 1)$ independent sources. In particular, if $l_{kj} - l_{k(j-1)} = 2$ for all (k, j), this tree-shaped network reduces to the network in [42].

The rest of this paper is organized as follows. In Section 2, we discuss any forked tree-shaped network with t_n parties and $(t_n - 1)$ independent sources. We explicitly examine the nonlocality of the network for the case of $n = 3$ and generalize the results to arbitrary $n \geq 3$. Moreover, the $(t_n - 1)$-local inequalities of the networks and quantum violations of the corresponding inequalities for pure states and mixed states are obtained. Besides, we also compare this network with some known quantum network scenarios. Some conclusions are presented in Section 3. The detailed proofs of the main results are provided in Appendix A.

2. Nonlocality in Any Forked Tree-Shaped Network Scenario

In this section, we consider the nonlocality of a general tree-shaped network; see Figure 1.

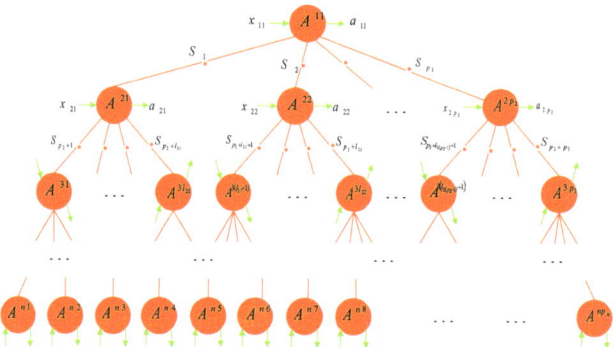

Figure 1. The general any forked tree-shaped network consists of t_n parties (A^{11}, A^{21}, $\cdots$, A^{2p_2}, A^{31}, $\cdots$, A^{3p_3}, $\cdots$, A^{n1}, $\cdots$, A^{np_n}), and $t_n - 1$ independent sources $S_1, \cdots, S_{t_n-1}$. Denote by x_i and a_i the input and output of each party A^i ($i = 11, 21, \cdots, np_n$), respectively.

This general tree-shaped network has n "layers" ($n \geq 2$), where each layer k has p_k parties (nodes) with $p_1 = 1$, say Alice $k1$ (A^{k1}), $\cdots$, Alice kp_k (A^{kp_k}), $1 \leq k \leq n$; each party A^{kj} in the layer k shares one source with another party in the layer $k-1$ and with $l_{kj} - l_{k(j-1)}$ parties in the layer $k+1$, where $l_{kj} - l_{k(j-1)}$ is an arbitrary positive integer, except that $l_{11} = p_2 > 1$, $1 \leq j \leq p_k$, $2 \leq k \leq n-1$, and $l_{k0} = 0$. It is clear that $l_{kp_k} = p_{k+1}$, $k = 1, 2, \cdots, n-1$. Write $t_n = p_1 + p_2 + \cdots + p_n$. Thus, this general tree-shaped quantum network concerns a t_n-partite system with $t_n - 1$ independent sources. In addition, the $t_n - 1$ independent sources $S_1, \cdots, S_{t_n-1}$ are characterized by independent hidden variables $\lambda_1, \cdots, \lambda_{t_n-1}$, respectively. Denote by x_i and a_i the input and output of party A^i ($i = 11, 21, \cdots, np_n$), respectively.

We say that the correlations in the tree-shaped network of Figure 1 are local if the joint probability distribution satisfies

$$\begin{aligned}
&P(a_{11}, a_{21}, \cdots, a_{(n-1)p_{n-1}}, a_{n1}, \cdots, a_{np_n} | x_{11}, x_{21}, \cdots, x_{(n-1)p_{n-1}}, x_{n1}, \cdots, x_{np_n}) \\
&= \int \cdots \int P(\lambda_1, \cdots, \lambda_{t_n-1})[P(a_{11} | x_{11}, \lambda_1, \cdots, \lambda_{p_2}) P(a_{21} | x_{21}, \lambda_1, \lambda_{p_2+1}, \cdots, \lambda_{p_2+l_{21}}) \\
&\cdots P(a_{(n-1)p_{n-1}} | x_{(n-1)p_{n-1}}, \lambda_{t_{n-1}-1}, \lambda_{t_{n-1}+l_{(n-1)(p_{n-1}-1)}}, \cdots, \lambda_{t_n-1}) \\
&\cdot P(a_{n1} | x_{n1}, \lambda_{t_{n-1}}) \cdots P(a_{np_n} | x_{np_n}, \lambda_{t_n-1})] d\lambda_1 \cdots d\lambda_{t_n-1};
\end{aligned} \quad (1)$$

and moreover, if $P(\lambda_1, \cdots, \lambda_{t_n-1})$ in Equation (1) can be decomposed into

$$P(\lambda_1, \cdots, \lambda_{t_n-1}) = P_1(\lambda_1) \cdots P_{t_n-1}(\lambda_{t_n-1}) \text{ with } \int P_i(\lambda_i) d\lambda_i = 1, \ i = 1, 2, \cdots, t_n - 1, \quad (2)$$

then we say that the correlations in the tree-shaped network of Figure 1 are $(t_n - 1)$-local. Under the source independence restriction Equation (2), correlations that cannot be decomposed into Equation (1) are said to be non-$(t_n - 1)$-local.

2.1. $(t_3 - 1)$-Local Network Scenario

If $n = 3$ in Figure 1, then it reduces to the network of Figure 2.

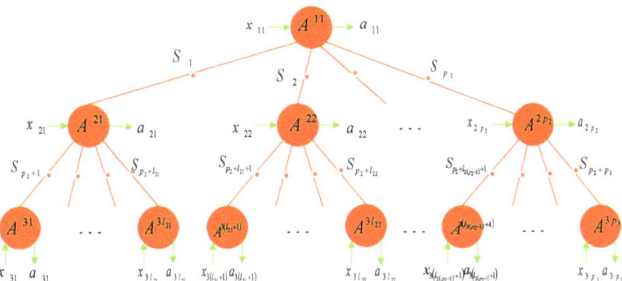

Figure 2. For the case of $n = 3$, the any forked tree-shaped network consists of t_3 parties (A^{11}, A^{21}, $\cdots$, A^{2p_2}, A^{31}, $\cdots$, A^{3p_3}) and $(t_3 - 1)$ independent sources $S_1, \cdots, S_{t_3-1}$. Let $x_{11}, x_{21}, \cdots, x_{2p_2}, x_{31}, \cdots, x_{3p_3}$ and $a_{11}, a_{21}, \cdots, a_{2p_2}, a_{31}, \cdots, a_{3p_3}$ be the corresponding input and output of each party, respectively.

The network of Figure 2 is a t_3-partite system with $t_3 - 1$ independent sources, where party A^{11} shares p_2 sources with parties $A^{21}, A^{22}, \cdots, A^{2p_2}$; party A^{2j} shares $l_{2j} - l_{2(j-1)} + 1$ sources with parties $A^{11}, A^{3(l_{2(j-1)}+1)}, \cdots, A^{3l_{2j}}$, where $j = 1, 2, \cdots, p_2$ and $l_{20} = 0$. Let $l_{2p_2} = p_3$, and then, $t_3 = 1 + p_2 + p_3$.

To illustrate Figure 2, we give a concrete example. Let $p_2 = 2$, $p_3 = l_{22} = 7$, and $l_{21} = 3$. Then, we obtain the network of Figure 3, which is a 10-partite system with nine independent sources.

For the case $n = 3$, the correlations obtained in the network of Figure 2 are called local if the probability distribution can be decomposed as

$$\begin{aligned} & P(a_{11}, a_{21}, \cdots, a_{2p_2}, a_{31}, \cdots, a_{3p_3} | x_{11}, x_{21}, \cdots, x_{2p_2}, x_{31}, \cdots, x_{3p_3}) \\ = & \int \cdots \int d\lambda_1 \cdots d\lambda_{t_3-1} P(\lambda_1, \cdots, \lambda_{t_3-1}) [P(a_{11}|x_{11}, \lambda_1, \cdots, \lambda_{p_2}) \\ & \cdot P(a_{21}|x_{21}, \lambda_1, \lambda_{p_2+1}, \cdots, \lambda_{p_2+l_{21}}) \cdots P(a_{2p_2}|x_{2p_2}, \lambda_{p_2}, \lambda_{p_2+l_{2(p_2-1)}+1}, \cdots, \lambda_{t_3-1}) \\ & \cdot P(a_{31}|x_{31}, \lambda_{p_2+1}) \cdots P(a_{3p_3}|x_{3p_3}, \lambda_{t_3-1})], \end{aligned} \quad (3)$$

and are called $(t_3 - 1)$-local if they have a decomposition form of Equation (3) with the additional restriction

$$P(\lambda_1, \lambda_2, \cdots, \lambda_{t_3-1}) = P_1(\lambda_1) P_2(\lambda_2) \cdots P_{t_3-1}(\lambda_{t_3-1}). \quad (4)$$

Here, the output of every party depends on the corresponding input and all connected sources. Correlations that do not meet Equations (3) and (4) are said to be non-$(t_3 - 1)$-local.

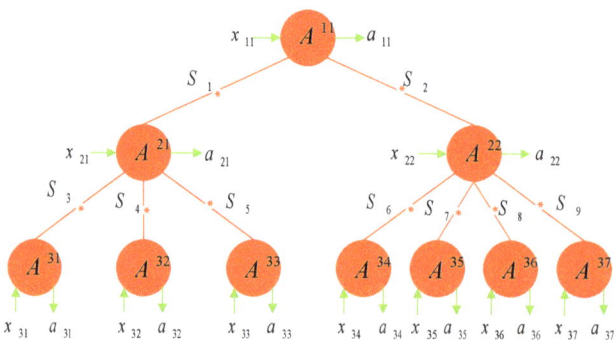

Figure 3. A tree-shaped network involves 10 parties, $A^{11}, A^{21}, A^{22}, A^{31}, \cdots, A^{37}$, and 9 sources, S_1, $\cdots, S_9$. Denote by $x_{11}, x_{21}, x_{22}, x_{31}, \cdots, x_{37}$ and $a_{11}, a_{21}, a_{22}, a_{31}, \cdots, a_{37}$ the input and output of each party, respectively. Here, $l_{11} = 2$, $l_{21} = 3$, $l_{22} = 7$ and $p_2 = 2$, $p_3 = 7$, $t_1 = 1$, $t_2 = 3$, $t_3 = 10$.

2.1.1. $(t_3 - 1)$-Locality Inequality

In what follows, we consider the case that each party A^i ($i = 11, 21, \cdots, 3p_3$) has binary input $x_i (\in \{0,1\})$ with binary output $a_i (\in \{0,1\})$, respectively. We develop inequalities that are fulfilled by all probability distributions satisfying Equations (3) and (4), but which may be violated by measuring quantum states distributed in the tree-shaped network of Figure 2.

Theorem 1. *Any $(t_3 - 1)$-local correlation in the tree-shaped network of Figure 2 must satisfy the following inequalities:*

$$|I_{i_1,\cdots,i_{t_2},0}|^{\frac{1}{p_3}} + |I_{j_1,\cdots,j_{t_2},1}|^{\frac{1}{p_3}} \le 1, \quad \forall i_1,\cdots,i_{t_2},j_1,\cdots,j_{t_2} \in \{0,1\}, \tag{5}$$

where

$$I_{i_1(j_1),\cdots,i_{t_2}(j_{t_2}),k} = \frac{1}{2^{p_3}} \sum_{x_{31},\cdots,x_{3p_3}} (-1)^{kl} \langle A^{11}_{i_1(j_1)} A^{21}_{i_2(j_2)} \cdots A^{2p_2}_{i_{t_2}(j_{t_2})} A^{31}_{x_{31}} \cdots A^{3p_3}_{x_{3p_3}} \rangle,$$

$$\langle A^{11}_{x_{11}} A^{21}_{x_{21}} \cdots A^{2p_2}_{x_{2p_2}} A^{31}_{x_{31}} \cdots A^{3p_3}_{x_{3p_3}} \rangle = \sum_{\substack{a_{11},a_{21},\cdots,a_{2p_2}, \\ a_{31},\cdots,a_{3p_3}}} (-1)^m P(a_{11},a_{21},\cdots,a_{2p_2},a_{31},\cdots,a_{3p_3}|x_{11},x_{21},\cdots,x_{2p_2},x_{31},\cdots,x_{3p_3}),$$

$k \in \{0,1\}$, $l = x_{31} + \cdots + x_{3p_3}$, $m = a_{11} + a_{21} + \cdots + a_{2p_2} + a_{31} + \cdots + a_{3p_3}$, $A^{11}_{x_{11}}$ denotes the observable for binary inputs x_{11} of party A^{11}, and $A^{21}_{x_{21}}, \cdots, A^{2p_2}_{x_{2p_2}}, A^{31}_{x_{31}}, \cdots, A^{3p_3}_{x_{3p_3}}$ are similarly defined.

Note that the subscript t_2 in Ineqs. (5) indicates the total number of parties A^{11}, $A^{21}, \cdots, A^{2p_2}$. By Theorem 1, we see that violation of Ineqs. (5) for at least one possible $(i_1, \cdots, i_{t_2}, j_1, \cdots, j_{t_2})$ guaranteeing the non-$(t_3 - 1)$-local nature of the correlations generated by the network of Figure 2. Besides, each of the above 2^{2t_2} inequalities is tight.

To see this, we give an explicit $(t_3 - 1)$-local decomposition, which is able to saturate the bound. Consider the following strategy:

$$P(a_{11}|x_{11}, \lambda_1, \cdots, \lambda_{p_2}) = \begin{cases} 1, & \text{if } a_{11} = \lambda_1 \oplus \cdots \oplus \lambda_{p_2}, \\ 0, & \text{else,} \end{cases}$$

$$P(a_{21}|x_{21},\lambda_1,\lambda_{p_2+1},\cdots,\lambda_{p_2+l_{21}}) = \begin{cases} 1, & \text{if } a_{21} = (\lambda_1 \oplus \lambda_{p_2+1} \oplus \cdots \oplus \lambda_{p_2+l_{21}-1})\lambda_{p_2+l_{21}}, \\ 0, & \text{else}, \end{cases}$$

......

$$= \begin{cases} P(a_{2p_2}|x_{2p_2},\lambda_{p_2},\lambda_{p_2+l_{2(p_2-1)}+1},\cdots,\lambda_{t_3-1}) \\ \begin{cases} 1, & \text{if } a_{2p_2} = (\lambda_{p_2} \oplus \lambda_{p_2+l_{2(p_2-1)}+1} \oplus \cdots \oplus \lambda_{t_3-2})\lambda_{t_3-1}, \\ 0, & \text{else}, \end{cases} \end{cases}$$

$$P(a_{3j}|x_{3j},\lambda_{p_2+j},\tau_{3j}) = \begin{cases} 1, & \text{if } a_{3j} = \lambda_{p_2+j} \oplus \tau_{3j}x_{3j}, \\ 0, & \text{else}, \end{cases} \quad \forall j = 1,2,\cdots,p_3.$$

Here, λ_m are hidden variables of shared sources S_m with $P_m(\lambda_m = 0) = 1$ ($m = 1,2,\cdots,t_3-1$), and τ_{3j} are sources of local randomness for party A^{3j} with $P_j(\tau_{3j} = 0) = r$ and $P_j(\tau_{3j} = 1) = 1-r$, $r \in [0,1]$ ($j=1,2,\cdots,p_3$). A simple calculation gives $I_{i_1,\cdots,i_{t_2},0} = r^{p_3}$ and $I_{j_1,\cdots,j_{t_2},1} = (1-r)^{p_3}$ for any $i_1,\cdots,i_{t_2},j_1,\cdots,j_{t_2} \in \{0,1\}$. Hence, $|I_{i_1,\cdots,i_{t_2},0}|^{\frac{1}{p_3}} + |I_{j_1,\cdots,j_{t_2},1}|^{\frac{1}{p_3}} = 1$, reaching the bound for all $i_1,\cdots,i_{t_2},j_1,\cdots,j_{t_2} \in \{0,1\}$.

As for the nonlocality correlations in the network of Figure 2, we give a set of Bell-type inequalities.

Theorem 2. *Every local correlation in the tree-shaped network of Figure 2 satisfies the following inequalities:*

$$|I_{i_1,\cdots,i_{t_2},0}| + |I_{j_1,\cdots,j_{t_2},1}| \leq 1, \quad \forall i_1,\cdots,i_{t_2},j_1,\cdots,j_{t_2} \in \{0,1\}, \tag{6}$$

where $I_{i_1,\cdots,i_{t_2},0}$ and $I_{j_1,\cdots,j_{t_2},1}$ are defined as in Theorem 1.

By Theorem 2, the violation of at least one of the 2^{2t_2} Ineqs.(6) guarantees that the corresponding correlations generated by the network are nonlocal. Apparently, the set of (t_3-1)-local correlations is a subset of the set of local correlations in the network of Figure 2.

For the proofs of Theorems 1 and 2, see Appendix A.

2.1.2. Quantum Violations of (t_3-1)-Local Inequalities

Now, we consider the network of Figure 2 involving (t_3-1) independent quantum sources, each generating a bipartite quantum state. Then, the overall quantum state of this network has the form

$$\rho = \rho_{A_1^{11}A_1^{21}} \otimes \cdots \otimes \rho_{A_{p_2}^{11}A_1^{2p_2}} \otimes \rho_{A_2^{21}A^{31}} \otimes \cdots \otimes \rho_{A_{l_{21}+1}^{21}A^{3l_{21}}} \otimes \cdots \otimes \rho_{A_{l_{2p_2}-l_{2(p_2-1)}+1}^{2p_2}A^{3p_3}}$$

with state space $H = H_{A^{11}} \otimes H_{A^{21}} \otimes \cdots \otimes H_{A^{2p_2}} \otimes H_{A^{31}} \otimes \cdots \otimes H_{A^{3p_3}}$, where $H_{A^{11}} = H_{A_1^{11}} \otimes \cdots \otimes H_{A_{p_2}^{11}}$ and $H_{A^{2i}} = H_{A_1^{2i}} \otimes \cdots \otimes H_{A_{l_{2i}-l_{2(i-1)}+1}^{2i}}$, $i = 1,\cdots,p_2$. For simplicity, we write

$$\rho = \rho_{A^{11}A^{21}} \otimes \cdots \otimes \rho_{A^{11}A^{2p_2}} \otimes \rho_{A^{21}A^{31}} \otimes \cdots \otimes \rho_{A^{21}A^{3l_{21}}} \otimes \cdots \otimes \rho_{A^{2p_2}A^{3p_3}}.$$

Once each party receives particles from its all-connecting sources, it performs suitable measurement. The resulting joint probability distribution has the form

$$P(a_{11},a_{21},\cdots,a_{2p_2},a_{31},\cdots,a_{3p_3}|x_{11},x_{21},\cdots,x_{2p_2},x_{31},\cdots,x_{3p_3})$$
$$= \text{tr}[(M_{a_{11}|x_{11}} \otimes M_{a_{21}|x_{21}} \otimes \cdots \otimes M_{a_{3p_3}|x_{3p_3}})(\rho_{A^{11}A^{21}} \otimes \rho_{A^{11}A^{22}} \otimes \cdots \otimes \rho_{A^{2p_2}A^{3p_3}})],$$

where $M_{a_{11}|x_{11}}$ denotes the specific measurement operator of party A^{11} corresponding to the measurement choice x_{11} with the outcome a_{11}, and other measurement operators have similar meanings.

In what follows, we examine quantum violations of the (t_3-1)-local inequalities (5) from pure states and mixed states, respectively.

Non-$(t_3$-1)-local correlations from pure states: Firstly, let all (t_3-1) sources produce any pure entangled states. Then, $\rho_{A^{11}A^{21}}$ can be written in the Schmidt basis as $\rho_{A^{11}A^{21}} = |\psi_{A^{11}A^{21}}\rangle\langle\psi_{A^{11}A^{21}}|$ with $|\psi_{A^{11}A^{21}}\rangle = b_{10}|00\rangle + b_{11}|11\rangle$ and $b_{10}, b_{11} > 0$, the normalized two-qubit pure state shared by the parties A^{11} and A^{21}. Likewise, write $\rho_{A^{11}A^{2i}} = |\psi_{A^{11}A^{2i}}\rangle\langle\psi_{A^{11}A^{2i}}|, \forall i \in \{2, \cdots, p_2\}, \rho_{A^{2j}A^{3k_j}} = |\psi_{A^{2j}A^{3k_j}}\rangle\langle\psi_{A^{2j}A^{3k_j}}|, \forall j \in \{1, 2, \cdots, p_2\}, k_j \in \{l_{2(j-1)}+1, \cdots, l_{2j}\}$, where $|\psi_{A^{11}A^{2i}}\rangle = b_{i0}|00\rangle + b_{i1}|11\rangle$ and $|\psi_{A^{2j}A^{3k_j}}\rangle = c_{k_j0}|00\rangle + c_{k_j1}|11\rangle$ are also written in the Schmidt basis with the corresponding positive coefficients.

For party A^{11}, take the measurement $A_0^{11} = \otimes_{k=1}^{p_2} \sigma_z^k$ and $A_1^{11} = \otimes_{k=1}^{p_2} \sigma_x^k$; for parties A^{2i} ($i = 1, \cdots, p_2$), the corresponding measurement choices are $A_0^{2i} = \otimes_{k=1}^{l_{2i}-l_{2(i-1)}+1} \sigma_z^k$ and $A_1^{2i} = \otimes_{k=1}^{l_{2i}-l_{2(i-1)}+1} \sigma_x^k$. Here, $\sigma_z^k = \sigma_z$ and $\sigma_x^k = \sigma_x$ for all k are Pauli matrices. Let the settings of all parties A^{3q} ($q = 1, \cdots, p_3$) correspond to any projective measurements in the Z-X plane of the Bloch sphere. Thus, each measurement can be characterized by an angle. Write the observables of A^{3q} by $A_0^{3q} = (\sin\alpha_q, 0, \cos\alpha_q)\cdot \vec{\sigma}$, $A_1^{3q} = (\sin\alpha_q', 0, \cos\alpha_q')\cdot\vec{\sigma}$, where $\vec{\sigma} = (\sigma_x, \sigma_y, \sigma_z)$ is the vector of Pauli matrices and $\alpha_q, \alpha_q' \in [0, 2\pi]$ for all $q \in \{1, \cdots, p_3\}$. Note that, if the above Schmidt bases differ from the computational basis, then it would be sufficient to add local unitary rotations to recover the case we discuss here. Then, we have

$$\begin{aligned}
&\langle A_0^{11} A_0^{21} \cdots A_0^{2p_2} A_0^{31} \cdots A_0^{3p_3}\rangle \\
&= \mathrm{tr}\{[\otimes_{k=1}^{p_2}(\sigma_z^k \otimes \sigma_z^k) \otimes (\sigma_z \otimes A_0^{31}) \otimes \cdots \otimes (\sigma_z \otimes A_0^{3p_3})] \\
&\quad \cdot(\rho_{A^{11}A^{21}} \otimes \cdots \otimes \rho_{A^{11}A^{2p_2}} \otimes \rho_{A^{21}A^{31}} \otimes \cdots \otimes \rho_{A^{2p_2}A^{3p_3}})\} \\
&= \prod_{i=1}^{p_2}\mathrm{tr}[(\sigma_z\otimes\sigma_z)\rho_{A^{11}A^{2i}}]\mathrm{tr}[(\sigma_z\otimes A_0^{31})\rho_{A^{21}A^{31}}]\cdots\mathrm{tr}[(\sigma_z\otimes A_0^{3p_3})\rho_{A^{2p_2}A^{3p_3}}] \\
&= \cos\alpha_1 \cos\alpha_2 \cdots \cos\alpha_{p_3}.
\end{aligned}$$

For any $x_{31}, x_{32}, \cdots, x_{3p_3} \in \{0,1\}$, we can follow similar calculations as above for $\langle A_0^{11} A_0^{21} \cdots A_0^{2p_2} A_{x_{31}}^{31} \cdots A_{x_{3p_3}}^{3p_3}\rangle$ and $\langle A_1^{11} A_1^{21} \cdots A_1^{2p_2} A_{x_{31}}^{31} \cdots A_{x_{3p_3}}^{3p_3}\rangle$. Therefore,

$$\begin{aligned}
I_{0,\cdots,0,0} &= \frac{1}{2^{p_3}} \sum_{x_{31},\cdots,x_{3p_3}} \langle A_0^{11} A_0^{21} \cdots A_0^{2p_2} A_{x_{31}}^{31} \cdots A_{x_{3p_3}}^{3p_3}\rangle \\
&= \frac{1}{2^{p_3}} \langle A_0^{11} A_0^{21} \cdots A_0^{2p_2} (A_0^{31} + A_1^{31}) \cdots (A_0^{3p_3} + A_1^{3p_3})\rangle \\
&= \frac{1}{2^{p_3}}(\cos\alpha_1 + \cos\alpha_1') \cdots (\cos\alpha_{p_3} + \cos\alpha_{p_3}')
\end{aligned}$$

and

$$\begin{aligned}
I_{1,\cdots,1,1} &= \frac{1}{2^{p_3}} \sum_{x_{31},\cdots,x_{3p_3}} (-1)^{x_{31}+\cdots+x_{3p_3}} \langle A_1^{11} A_1^{21} \cdots A_1^{2p_2} A_{x_{31}}^{31} \cdots A_{x_{3p_3}}^{3p_3}\rangle \\
&= \frac{1}{2^{p_3}} \langle A_1^{11} A_1^{21} \cdots A_1^{2p_2} (A_0^{31} - A_1^{31}) \cdots (A_0^{3p_3} - A_1^{3p_3})\rangle \\
&= \frac{1}{2^{p_3}} \Delta (\sin\alpha_1 - \sin\alpha_1') \cdots (\sin\alpha_{p_3} - \sin\alpha_{p_3}'),
\end{aligned}$$

where $\Delta = b^{(1)}\cdots b^{(p_2)} c^{(1)}\cdots c^{(p_3)} > 0$, $b^{(i)} = 2b_{i0}b_{i1}$, $i \in \{1, \cdots, p_2\}$, $c^{(q)} = 2c_{q0}c_{q1}$, $q \in \{1, \cdots, p_3\}$. Consequently,

$$\begin{aligned}
S_{(t_3-1)-\mathrm{local}} &= |I_{0,\cdots,0,0}|^{\frac{1}{p_3}} + |I_{1,\cdots,1,1}|^{\frac{1}{p_3}} \\
&= \frac{1}{2}|(\cos\alpha_1 + \cos\alpha_1')\cdots(\cos\alpha_{p_3} + \cos\alpha_{p_3}')|^{\frac{1}{p_3}} \\
&\quad + \frac{1}{2}|\Delta(\sin\alpha_1 - \sin\alpha_1')\cdots(\sin\alpha_{p_3} - \sin\alpha_{p_3}')|^{\frac{1}{p_3}}.
\end{aligned}$$

Write $S_{(t_3-1)-\mathrm{local}} = f(\alpha_1, \alpha_1', \cdots, \alpha_{p_3}, \alpha_{p_3}')$. To derive the maximum of differentiable function $f(\alpha_1, \alpha_1', \cdots, \alpha_{p_3}, \alpha_{p_3}')$, we calculate all the partial derivatives $\frac{\partial f}{\partial \alpha_i} = 0$, $\frac{\partial f}{\partial \alpha_i'} = 0$ for $i = 1, 2, \cdots, p_3$. It follows that the extremal points of f must satisfy the conditions $\alpha_i = -\alpha_i'$ and $|\tan\alpha_i| = \Delta^{1/p_3}$ ($i = 1, 2, \cdots, p_3$). These force $|\cos\alpha_i| = |\cos\alpha_i'| = \frac{1}{\sqrt{1+\Delta^{2/p_3}}}$ and $|\sin\alpha_i| = |\sin\alpha_i'| = \frac{\Delta^{1/p_3}}{\sqrt{1+\Delta^{2/p_3}}}$, $i = 1, 2, \cdots, p_3$. Therefore, the value of f at these extremal points is $|\cos\alpha_1| + \Delta^{1/p_3}|\sin\alpha_1| = \sqrt{1+\Delta^{2/p_3}}$. Comparing this value with the values of f at all boundary points, it is easily seen that the maximum of $S_{(t_3-1)-\text{local}}$ is

$$S^{\max}_{(t_3-1)-\text{local}} = \sqrt{1+\Delta^{2/p_3}} > 1. \tag{7}$$

Notice that $\text{tr}[(\sigma_z \otimes \sigma_x)\rho_i] = \text{tr}[(\sigma_x \otimes \sigma_z)\rho_i] = 0$ hold for all $i = A^{11}A^{21}, \cdots, A^{2p_2}A^{3p_3}$. Thus, other possible nonzero terms for $|I_{i_1,\cdots,i_{t_2},0}|^{\frac{1}{p_3}} + |I_{j_1,\cdots,j_{t_2},1}|^{\frac{1}{p_3}}$ are $|I_{0,\cdots,0,0}|^{\frac{1}{p_3}} + |I_{0,\cdots,0,1}|^{\frac{1}{p_3}}$, $|I_{1,\cdots,1,0}|^{\frac{1}{p_3}} + |I_{1,\cdots,1,1}|^{\frac{1}{p_3}}$, and $|I_{1,\cdots,1,0}|^{\frac{1}{p_3}} + |I_{0,\cdots,0,1}|^{\frac{1}{p_3}}$. However, by similar discussions to the above, one can obtain that these three values are less than 1.

Hence, if all $(t_3 - 1)$ sources in the network of Figure 2 emit pure entangled states, they necessarily violate the $(t_3 - 1)$-local inequalities (5) and, thus, generate non-$(t_3 - 1)$-local correlations.

Non-$(t_3$-1$)$-local correlations from mixed states: Now, we consider the case that all the sources in the network of Figure 2 produce any mixed states.

Assume that the state $\rho_{A^{11}A^{21}}$ shared by the parties A^{11} and A^{21} is a mixed state. Then, it has the following form:

$$\rho_{A^{11}A^{21}} = \frac{1}{4}\left(\mathbb{I} \otimes \mathbb{I} + \vec{r}_{A^{11}} \cdot \vec{\sigma} \otimes \mathbb{I} + \mathbb{I} \otimes \vec{r}_{A^{21}} \cdot \vec{\sigma} + \sum_{i,j} t_{ij}^{A^{11}A^{21}} \sigma_i \otimes \sigma_j\right),$$

where $\vec{\sigma} = (\sigma_x, \sigma_y, \sigma_z)$, $\vec{r}_{A^{11}}$ ($\vec{r}_{A^{21}}$) represents the Bloch vector of the reduced state of subsystem A^{11} (A^{21}), and $T^{A^{11}A^{21}} = (t_{ij}^{A^{11}A^{21}})$ with $i,j \in \{x,y,z\}$ is the correlation matrix. By the polar decomposition, the correlation matrix $T^{A^{11}A^{21}}$ can be written as $T^{A^{11}A^{21}} = U^{A^{11}A^{21}} R^{A^{11}A^{21}}$, where $U^{A^{11}A^{21}}$ is a unitary matrix and $R^{A^{11}A^{21}} = \sqrt{(T^{A^{11}A^{21}})^\dagger T^{A^{11}A^{21}}} \geq 0$. Denote by $\sqrt{\tau_1^{A^{11}A^{21}}} \geq \sqrt{\tau_2^{A^{11}A^{21}}} \geq \sqrt{\tau_3^{A^{11}A^{21}}} \geq 0$ the three non-negative eigenvalues of $R^{A^{11}A^{21}}$.

For the other mixed states $\rho_{A^{11}A^{22}}, \cdots, \rho_{A^{11}A^{2p_2}}, \rho_{A^{21}A^{31}}, \cdots, \rho_{A^{2p_2}A^{3p_3}}$, shared by the corresponding parties, they also have similar expressions to that of $\rho_{A^{11}A^{21}}$, and the corresponding matrices and the eigenvalues are, respectively, represented as

$$R^{A^{11}A^{2i}} = \sqrt{(T^{A^{11}A^{2i}})^\dagger T^{A^{11}A^{2i}}}, \quad \sqrt{\tau_1^{A^{11}A^{2i}}} \geq \sqrt{\tau_2^{A^{11}A^{2i}}} \geq \sqrt{\tau_3^{A^{11}A^{2i}}} \geq 0,$$

$$R^{A^{2j}A^{3k_j}} = \sqrt{(T^{A^{2j}A^{3k_j}})^\dagger T^{A^{2j}A^{3k_j}}}, \quad \sqrt{\tau_1^{A^{2j}A^{3k_j}}} \geq \sqrt{\tau_2^{A^{2j}A^{3k_j}}} \geq \sqrt{\tau_3^{A^{2j}A^{3k_j}}} \geq 0,$$

where $i \in \{1,2,\cdots,p_2\}$, $k_j \in \{l_{2(j-1)}+1, \cdots, l_{2j}\}$, and $j \in \{1,2,\cdots,p_2\}$.

Suppose that party A^{11} performs measurements $A_0^{11} = \otimes_{k=1}^{p_2} \sigma_z^k$, $A_1^{11} = \otimes_{k=1}^{p_2} \sigma_x^k$. We consider the Z and X Bloch directions (on the first subsystem of party A^{11}, connected to the first subsystem of party A^{21}) given by the eigenvectors of the matrix $R^{A^{11}A^{21}}$ corresponding to the two largest eigenvalues $\sqrt{\tau_1^{A^{11}A^{21}}}$ and $\sqrt{\tau_2^{A^{11}A^{21}}}$, respectively [19]. Similarly, we use $R^{A^{11}A^{2i}}$ for aligning the ith subsystem of A^{11}, connected to the first subsystem of A^{2i}, $i = 2, \cdots, p_2$. Note that the Z and X axes used by the parties A^{11} and A^{2i} ($i = 1, \cdots, p_2$) may be different from each other. In this case, party A^{11} can perform different unitary transformations to the p_2 qubits she/he shares with $A^{21}, \cdots, A^{2p_2}$ before performing the measurements. Likewise, we may assume the party A^{2i} ($i = 1, \cdots, p_2$) has measurement choices $A_0^{2i} = \otimes_{k=1}^{l_{2i}-l_{2(i-1)}+1} \sigma_z^k$ and $A_1^{2i} = \otimes_{k=1}^{l_{2i}-l_{2(i-1)}+1} \sigma_x^k$. For party A^{3q} ($q = 1, \cdots, p_3$), he/she performs projective measurements on the Z and X Bloch directions, which are composed of the two eigenvectors with largest eigenvalues of the connected matrix $R^{A^{2j_q}A^{3q}}$ ($1 \leq j_q \leq p_2$). That is, $A_0^{3q} = \vec{c}_q \cdot \vec{\sigma}$ and $A_1^{3q} = \vec{c}_q' \cdot \vec{\sigma}$, where $\vec{c}_q = (\sin\beta_q, 0, \cos\beta_q)$, $\vec{c}_q' = (\sin\beta_q', 0, \cos\beta_q')$, $\beta_q, \beta_q' \in [0, 2\pi]$.

Now, we have

$$
\begin{aligned}
I_{0,\cdots,0,0} &= \frac{1}{2^{p_3}} \sum_{x_{31},\cdots,x_{3p_3}} \langle A_0^{11} A_0^{21} \cdots A_0^{2p_2} A_{x_{31}}^{31} \cdots A_{x_{3p_3}}^{3p_3} \rangle \\
&= \frac{1}{2^{p_3}} \langle A_0^{11} A_0^{21} \cdots A_0^{2p_2} (A_0^{31} + A_1^{31}) \cdots (A_0^{3p_3} + A_1^{3p_3}) \rangle \\
&= \frac{1}{2^{p_3}} \langle (\otimes_{k=1}^{p_2} \sigma_z^k) \otimes (\otimes_{k=1}^{l_{21}+1} \sigma_z^k) \otimes \cdots \otimes (\otimes_{k=1}^{l_{2p_2}-l_{2(p_2-1)}+1} \sigma_z^k) \otimes [(\vec{c_1} + \vec{c_1}') \cdot \vec{\sigma}] \otimes \cdots \\
&\quad \otimes [(\vec{c_{p_3}} + \vec{c_{p_3}}') \cdot \vec{\sigma}] \rangle \\
&= \frac{1}{2^{p_3}} \mathrm{tr}\{[(\otimes_{k=1}^{p_2}(\sigma_z^k \otimes \sigma_z^k)) \otimes (\sigma_z \otimes (\vec{c_1}+\vec{c_1}') \cdot \vec{\sigma}) \otimes \cdots \otimes (\sigma_z \otimes (\vec{c_{p_3}}+\vec{c_{p_3}}') \cdot \vec{\sigma})] \\
&\quad \cdot (\rho_{A^{11}A^{21}} \otimes \cdots \otimes \rho_{A^{11}A^{2p_2}} \otimes \rho_{A^{21}A^{31}} \otimes \cdots \otimes \rho_{A^{2p_2}A^{3p_3}})\} \\
&= \frac{1}{2^{p_3}} \mathrm{tr}[(\sigma_z \otimes \sigma_z)\rho_{A^{11}A^{21}}] \cdots \mathrm{tr}[(\sigma_z \otimes \sigma_z)\rho_{A^{11}A^{2p_2}}] \mathrm{tr}[(\sigma_z \otimes (\vec{c_1}+\vec{c_1}') \cdot \vec{\sigma})\rho_{A^{21}A^{31}}] \\
&\quad \cdots \mathrm{tr}[(\sigma_z \otimes (\vec{c_{p_3}}+\vec{c_{p_3}}') \cdot \vec{\sigma})\rho_{A^{2p_2}A^{3p_3}}] \\
&= \frac{1}{2^{p_3}} \sqrt{\tau_1^{A^{11}A^{21}} \cdots \tau_1^{A^{11}A^{2p_2}} \tau_1^{A^{21}A^{31}} \cdots \tau_1^{A^{2p_2}A^{3p_3}}} \prod_{j=1}^{p_3}(\cos\beta_j + \cos\beta_j')
\end{aligned}
$$

and

$$
\begin{aligned}
I_{1,\cdots,1,1} &= \frac{1}{2^{p_3}} \sum_{x_{31},\cdots,x_{3p_3}} (-1)^{x_{31}+\cdots+x_{3p_3}} \langle A_1^{11} A_1^{21} \cdots A_1^{2p_2} A_{x_{31}}^{31} \cdots A_{x_{3p_3}}^{3p_3} \rangle \\
&= \frac{1}{2^{p_3}} \langle A_1^{11} A_1^{21} \cdots A_1^{2p_2} (A_0^{31} - A_1^{31}) \cdots (A_0^{3p_3} - A_1^{3p_3}) \rangle \\
&= \frac{1}{2^{p_3}} \sqrt{\tau_2^{A^{11}A^{21}} \cdots \tau_2^{A^{11}A^{2p_2}} \tau_2^{A^{21}A^{31}} \cdots \tau_2^{A^{2p_2}A^{3p_3}}} \prod_{j=1}^{p_3}(\sin\beta_j - \sin\beta_j'),
\end{aligned}
$$

and so

$$
\begin{aligned}
S_{(t_3-1)-\mathrm{local}} &= |I_{0,\cdots,0,0}|^{\frac{1}{p_3}} + |I_{1,\cdots,1,1}|^{\frac{1}{p_3}} \\
&= \frac{1}{2}(\tau_1^{A^{11}A^{21}} \cdots \tau_1^{A^{11}A^{2p_2}} \tau_1^{A^{21}A^{31}} \cdots \tau_1^{A^{2p_2}A^{3p_3}})^{\frac{1}{2p_3}} |\prod_{j=1}^{p_3}(\cos\beta_j + \cos\beta_j')|^{\frac{1}{p_3}} \\
&\quad + \frac{1}{2}(\tau_2^{A^{11}A^{21}} \cdots \tau_2^{A^{11}A^{2p_2}} \tau_2^{A^{21}A^{31}} \cdots \tau_2^{A^{2p_2}A^{3p_3}})^{\frac{1}{2p_3}} |\prod_{j=1}^{p_3}(\sin\beta_j - \sin\beta_j')|^{\frac{1}{p_3}}.
\end{aligned}
$$

A calculation gives the maximum

$$
S^{\max}_{(t_3-1)-\mathrm{local}} = \sqrt{\sum_{i=1}^2 (\tau_i^{A^{11}A^{21}} \cdots \tau_i^{A^{11}A^{2p_2}} \tau_i^{A^{21}A^{31}} \cdots \tau_i^{A^{2p_2}A^{3p_3}})^{\frac{1}{p_3}}}. \tag{8}
$$

The detailed proof for Equation (8) is in Appendix A.

It is easily verified that the above Equation (8) reduces to Equation (7) for the case of pure states discussed in the above. In fact, for pure states, we have $\tau_1^{A^{11}A^{21}} = \cdots = \tau_1^{A^{11}A^{2p_2}} = \tau_1^{A^{21}A^{31}} = \cdots = \tau_1^{A^{2p_2}A^{3p_3}} = 1$ and $\tau_2^{A^{11}A^{21}} = (b^{(1)})^2, \cdots, \tau_2^{A^{11}A^{2p_2}} = (b^{(p_2)})^2$, $\tau_2^{A^{21}A^{31}} = (c^{(1)})^2, \cdots, \tau_2^{A^{2p_2}A^{3p_3}} = (c^{(p_3)})^2$, which implies that Equation (8) can be reduced to Equation (7).

From Equation (8), $S^{\max}_{(t_3-1)-\mathrm{local}} > 1$ implies that these states violate the (t_3-1)-locality inequalities (5). Since all these eigenvalues $\tau_i^{A^{11}A^{21}}, \cdots, \tau_i^{A^{2p_2}A^{3p_3}}$ ($i=1,2$) belong to $[0,1]$ ([23] Lemma 3), by [21] Lemma 1, Equation (8) implies

$$
\begin{aligned}
S^{\max}_{(t_3-1)-\mathrm{local}} &\leq \sqrt{\sum_{i=1}^2 (\tau_i^{A^{11}A^{21}} \cdots \tau_i^{A^{11}A^{2p_2}} \tau_i^{A^{21}A^{31}} \cdots \tau_i^{A^{2p_2}A^{3p_3}})^{\frac{1}{p_2+p_3}}} \\
&\leq \left(\sqrt{\tau_1^{A^{11}A^{21}} + \tau_2^{A^{11}A^{21}}} \cdots \sqrt{\tau_1^{A^{11}A^{2p_2}} + \tau_2^{A^{11}A^{2p_2}}} \sqrt{\tau_1^{A^{21}A^{31}} + \tau_2^{A^{21}A^{31}}}\right. \\
&\quad \left. \cdots \sqrt{\tau_1^{A^{2p_2}A^{3p_3}} + \tau_2^{A^{2p_2}A^{3p_3}}}\right)^{\frac{1}{p_2+p_3}} \\
&\doteq (S^{\max}_{A^{11}A^{21}} \cdots S^{\max}_{A^{11}A^{2p_2}} S^{\max}_{A^{21}A^{31}} \cdots S^{\max}_{A^{2p_2}A^{3p_3}})^{\frac{1}{p_2+p_3}},
\end{aligned}
$$

where the expressions $S_{XY}^{max} = \sqrt{\tau_1^{XY} + \tau_2^{XY}}$ represent the maximal CHSH value for the corresponding state ρ_{XY} by the Horodecki criterion in [43]. From the above inequality, we know that once the states altogether violate the $(t_3 - 1)$-locality inequalities, at least one of these states necessarily violates the CHSH inequality. However, for each state violating the CHSH inequality, this does not imply that it necessarily violates the $(t_3 - 1)$-locality inequalities. We illustrate this case by the specific network of Figure 3. For example, let nine sources in Figure 3 all produce the following state:

$$\rho = \frac{3}{4}|\psi^-\rangle\langle\psi^-| + \frac{1}{20}(|\psi^+\rangle\langle\psi^+| + \mathbb{I}) = \begin{pmatrix} 0.05 & 0 & 0 & 0 \\ 0 & 0.45 & -0.35 & 0 \\ 0 & -0.35 & 0.45 & 0 \\ 0 & 0 & 0 & 0.05 \end{pmatrix},$$

where $|\psi^\pm\rangle = (|01\rangle \pm |10\rangle)/\sqrt{2}$. It is easily obtained that $\tau_1 = 0.64$ and $\tau_2 = 0.49$. For this single state, the maximal CHSH value is $S^{max} \simeq 1.06 > 1$. However, through distributing nine copies of this state in the network of Figure 3, the maximal value of the corresponding nine-local inequality is $S_{9-\text{local}}^{max} \simeq 0.98 < 1$.

Remark 1. *To achieve the maximal quantum violation of the $(t_3 - 1)$-local correlation inequalities (5), all possible quantum measurements should be considered. However, this is almost impossible because the calculation is very difficult and complicated. Therefore, for the network of Figure 2, we take separable measurements for parties A^{1j} and A^{2j} and any measurements for parties A^{3j}. In this quantum strategy, the maximal violation $S_{(t_3-1)-\text{local}}^{max}$ is obtained, which gives a sufficient condition that $S_{(t_3-1)-\text{local}}^{max} > 1$ ensures that the state ρ violates the inequality (5) and, thus, is non-$(t_3 - 1)$-local. Of course, there are other strategies of the measurement choices that are computable, and some of them may be better than our strategy, though we have not discovered them yet. This is an interesting problem that is worth being explored later.*

2.1.3. Resistance to White Noise

Now, suppose that each source S_i ($i = 1, \cdots, t_3 - 1$) in Figure 2 produces Bell state $|\phi^+\rangle = (|00\rangle + |11\rangle)/\sqrt{2}$ with white noise of probability $1 - v_i$. Then, the state it actually produces is the Werner state of the form

$$\rho_i(v_i) = v_i|\phi^+\rangle\langle\phi^+| + (1 - v_i)\frac{\mathbb{I}}{4}.$$

Let the input of party A^{11} be $\{A_0^{11} = \otimes_{k=1}^{p_2}\sigma_z^k, A_1^{11} = \otimes_{k=1}^{p_2}\sigma_x^k\}$. For party A^{2j} ($j = 1, \cdots, p_2$), the measurement choices are $\{A_0^{2j} = \otimes_{k=1}^{l_{2j}-l_{2(j-1)}+1}\sigma_z^k, A_1^{2j} = \otimes_{k=1}^{l_{2j}-l_{2(j-1)}+1}\sigma_x^k\}$. Suppose the inputs of each party A^{3q} ($q = 1, 2, \cdots, p_3$) are measurements $\{A_0^{3q} = (\sigma_z + \sigma_x)/\sqrt{2}, A_1^{3q} = (\sigma_z - \sigma_x)/\sqrt{2}\}$. Denoting by $V = \prod_{i=1}^{t_3-1} v_i$ as the overall visibility, we obtain $I_{0,\cdots,0,0} = (\frac{1}{\sqrt{2}})^{p_3}V$, $I_{1,\cdots,1,1} = (\frac{1}{\sqrt{2}})^{p_3}V$, and so,

$$|I_{0,\cdots,0,0}|^{\frac{1}{p_3}} + |I_{1,\cdots,1,1}|^{\frac{1}{p_3}} = \sqrt{2}V^{1/p_3}.$$

That is to say, $V > (\frac{1}{\sqrt{2}})^{p_3}$ implies non-$(t_3 - 1)$-local correlations. Assuming that all the $(t_3 - 1)$ sources emit states with the same noise parameter $v_i = v$, we thus see that a single source necessarily satisfies $v > (\frac{1}{\sqrt{2}})^{\frac{p_3}{t_3-1}}$, which is a little greater than $v' > \frac{1}{\sqrt{2}}$ for the Werner state to violate the CHSH inequality.

2.2. $(t_n - 1)$-Local Network Scenario

In this subsection, we consider the nonlocality of the general tree-shaped network of Figure 1. With similar arguments, if each party A^i ($i = 11, 21, \cdots, np_n$) has binary input

$x_i (\in \{0,1\})$ with binary output $a_i (\in \{0,1\})$, then we obtain the following results for any $n \geq 2$.

Theorem 3. *All $(t_n - 1)$-local correlations generated by the tree-shaped network of Figure 1 necessarily satisfy the following inequalities:*

$$|I_{i_1,\cdots,i_{t_{n-1}},0}|^{\frac{1}{p_n}} + |I_{j_1,\cdots,j_{t_{n-1}},1}|^{\frac{1}{p_n}} \leq 1, \quad \forall i_1,\cdots,i_{t_{n-1}}, j_1,\cdots,j_{t_{n-1}} \in \{0,1\}; \quad (9)$$

and the corresponding local correlations satisfy the following inequalities:

$$|I_{i_1,\cdots,i_{t_{n-1}},0}| + |I_{j_1,\cdots,j_{t_{n-1}},1}| \leq 1, \quad \forall i_1,\cdots,i_{t_{n-1}}, j_1,\cdots,j_{t_{n-1}} \in \{0,1\}. \quad (10)$$

where for $k \in \{0,1\}$,

$$I_{i_1(j_1),\cdots,i_{t_{n-1}}(j_{t_{n-1}}),k}$$
$$= \frac{1}{2^{p_n}} \sum_{x_{n1},\cdots,x_{np_n}} (-1)^{k \cdot (x_{n1}+\cdots+x_{np_n})} \langle A^{11}_{i_1(j_1)} \cdots A^{(n-1)p_{n-1}}_{i_{t_{n-1}}(j_{t_{n-1}})} A^{n1}_{x_{n1}} \cdots A^{np_n}_{x_{np_n}} \rangle,$$

$$\langle A^{11}_{x_{11}} \cdots A^{(n-1)p_{n-1}}_{x_{(n-1)p_{n-1}}} A^{n1}_{x_{n1}} \cdots A^{np_n}_{x_{np_n}} \rangle$$
$$= \sum_{a_{11},\cdots,a_{np_n}} (-1)^m P(a_{11},\cdots,a_{(n-1)p_{n-1}}, a_{n1},\cdots, a_{np_n} | x_{11},\cdots, x_{(n-1)p_{n-1}}, x_{n1},\cdots, x_{np_n}),$$

$m = a_{11} + \cdots + a_{np_n}$, *and $A^i_{x_i}$ denotes the observable for binary inputs x_i of party A^i, $i = 11, 21, 22, \cdots, np_n$.*

Note that the subscript t_{n-1} in Ineqs. (9) and (10) represents the total number of parties $A^{11}, A^{21}, \cdots, A^{2p_2}, \cdots, A^{(n-1)1}, \cdots, A^{(n-1)p_{n-1}}$. In particular, if $n = 3$, then Inequalities (9) and (10) reduce to Inequalities (5) and (6), respectively. By Theorem 3, violating Inequalities (9) for at least one possible $(i_1,\cdots,i_{t_{n-1}}, j_1,\cdots,j_{t_{n-1}})$ implies the non-$(t_n - 1)$-local nature of the general tree-shaped networks in Figure 1. The proof of Theorem 3 is provided in Appendix A.

Next, assume that all sources in Figure 1 produce pure entangled states $|\psi_i\rangle\langle\psi_i|$, $|\psi_i\rangle = b_{i0}|00\rangle + b_{i1}|11\rangle$, written in the Schmidt basis, with positive coefficients b_{i0} and b_{i1}, $i = 1, 2, \cdots, t_n - 1$. Let the measurements of A^{11} be $\{A^{11}_0 = \otimes_{k=1}^{p_2} \sigma^k_z, A^{11}_1 = \otimes_{k=1}^{p_2} \sigma^k_x\}$. For parties A^{ij} with $i = 2, 3, \cdots, n-1$ and $j = 1, 2, \cdots, p_i$, they have the same measurement choices $\{A^{ij}_0 = \otimes_{k=1}^{l_{ij}-l_{i(j-1)}+1} \sigma^k_z, A^{ij}_1 = \otimes_{k=1}^{l_{ij}-l_{i(j-1)}+1} \sigma^k_x\}$. Here, $\sigma^k_z = \sigma_z$ and $\sigma^k_x = \sigma_x$ for any k. For the parties A^{nq} ($q = 1, 2, \cdots, p_n$), they perform projective measurements denoted by $\{A^{nq}_0 = (\sin \alpha_q, 0, \cos \alpha_q) \cdot \vec{\sigma}, A^{nq}_1 = (\sin \alpha'_q, 0, \cos \alpha'_q) \cdot \vec{\sigma}\}$, where $\alpha_q, \alpha'_q \in [0, 2\pi]$. With similar arguments to that of Equation (7), one obtains $I_{0,\cdots,0,0} = \frac{1}{2^{p_n}}(\cos \alpha_1 + \cos \alpha'_1) \cdots (\cos \alpha_{p_n} + \cos \alpha'_{p_n})$ and $I_{1,\cdots,1,1} = \frac{1}{2^{p_n}} \Delta (\sin \alpha_1 - \sin \alpha'_1) \cdots (\sin \alpha_{p_n} - \sin \alpha'_{p_n})$, where

$$\Delta = b^{(1)} b^{(2)} \cdots b^{(t_n - 1)} > 0,$$

$b^{(i)} = 2 b_{i0} b_{i1}$, $i = 1, 2, \cdots, t_n - 1$. Therefore, the maximum of $S_{(t_n-1)-local} = |I_{0,\cdots,0,0}|^{\frac{1}{p_n}} + |I_{1,\cdots,1,1}|^{\frac{1}{p_n}}$ is

$$S^{max}_{(t_n-1)-local} = \sqrt{1 + \Delta^{2/p_n}} > 1. \quad (11)$$

That is to say, all pure entangled states distributed in the network of Figure 1 indicate the non-$(t_n - 1)$-local correlations.

Finally, we consider that all sources in Figure 1 produce any mixed states ρ_i, $i = 1, 2, \cdots, t_n - 1$. Let T^i be the correlation matrix of ρ_i and $\tau^{(i)}_1$, $\tau^{(i)}_2$ the two larger non-negative eigenvalues of $(T^i)^\dagger T^i$, $i = 1, 2, \cdots, t_n - 1$. Let party A^{11} perform measurements $\{A^{11}_0 = \otimes_{k=1}^{p_2} \sigma^k_z, A^{11}_1 = \otimes_{k=1}^{p_2} \sigma^k_x\}$; party A^{ij} perform measurements $\{A^{ij}_0 = \otimes_{k=1}^{l_{ij}-l_{i(j-1)}+1} \sigma^k_z, A^{ij}_1 = \otimes_{k=1}^{l_{ij}-l_{i(j-1)}+1} \sigma^k_x\}$ ($i = 2, 3, \cdots, n-1, j = 1, 2, \cdots, p_i$); and party A^{nq} have measurement choices $\{A_0^{nq} = (\sin\beta_q, 0, \cos\beta_q)\cdot\vec{\sigma}, A_1^{nq} = (\sin\beta'_q, 0, \cos\beta'_q)\cdot\vec{\sigma}\}$ with $\beta_q, \beta'_q \in [0, 2\pi]$ ($q = 1, 2, \cdots, p_n$). By calculations, we obtain

$$I_{0,\cdots,0,0} = \frac{1}{2^{p_n}}\sqrt{\tau_1^{(1)}\tau_1^{(2)}\tau_1^{(3)}\cdots\tau_1^{(t_n-1)}}\prod_{i=1}^{p_n}(\cos\beta_i + \cos\beta'_i)$$

and

$$I_{1,\cdots,1,1} = \frac{1}{2^{p_n}}\sqrt{\tau_2^{(1)}\tau_2^{(2)}\tau_2^{(3)}\cdots\tau_2^{(t_n-1)}}\prod_{i=1}^{p_n}(\sin\beta_i - \sin\beta'_i).$$

Following the analogous proof process of Equation (8), we have that the maximal value of $S_{(t_n-1)-\text{local}} = |I_{0,\cdots,0,0}|^{\frac{1}{p_n}} + |I_{1,\cdots,1,1}|^{\frac{1}{p_n}}$ is

$$S^{\max}_{(t_n-1)-\text{local}} = \sqrt{(\tau_1^{(1)}\tau_1^{(2)}\tau_1^{(3)}\cdots\tau_1^{(t_n-1)})^{1/(p_n)} + (\tau_2^{(1)}\tau_2^{(2)}\tau_2^{(3)}\cdots\tau_2^{(t_n-1)})^{1/(p_n)}}. \quad (12)$$

When $n = 3$, Equations (11) and (12) reduce to Equations (7) and (8). By Equation (12), $S^{\max}_{(t_n-1)-\text{local}} > 1$ implies the non-$(t_n - 1)$-local correlations.

Besides, if all sources in Figure 1, respectively, distribute Werner states with visibilities $v_1, v_2, \cdots, v_{t_n-1}$, then we take the inputs of A^{11} $\{A_0^{11} = \otimes_{k=1}^{p_2}\sigma_z^k, A_1^{11} = \otimes_{k=1}^{p_2}\sigma_x^k\}$; the inputs of A^{ij} $\{A_0^{ij} = \otimes_{k=1}^{l_{ij}-l_{i(j-1)}+1}\sigma_z^k, A_1^{ij} = \otimes_{k=1}^{l_{ij}-l_{i(j-1)}+1}\sigma_x^k\}$ ($i = 2, 3, \cdots, n-1, j = 1, 2, \cdots, p_i$); and the inputs of A^{nq} $\{A_0^{nq} = (\sigma_z + \sigma_x)/\sqrt{2}, A_1^{nq} = (\sigma_z - \sigma_x)/\sqrt{2}\}$. Let the overall visibility be $V = \prod_{i=1}^{t_n-1}v_i$. A calculation gives $I_{0,\cdots,0,0} = (\frac{1}{\sqrt{2}})^{p_n}V$ and $I_{1,\cdots,1,1} = (\frac{1}{\sqrt{2}})^{p_n}V$, and so,

$$|I_{0,\cdots,0,0}|^{\frac{1}{p_n}} + |I_{1,\cdots,1,1}|^{\frac{1}{p_n}} = \sqrt{2}V^{1/p_n}.$$

Hence, if $V > (\frac{1}{\sqrt{2}})^{p_n}$, then the inequalities (9) will be violated, demonstrating non-$(t_n - 1)$-local correlations in Figure 1.

2.3. Comparing Any Forked Tree-Shaped Network with Other Networks

In this subsection, we discuss the relationships of multi-local inequalities between any forked tree-shaped network of Figure 1 and a bilocal network, chain-shaped network, star-shaped network, and two-forked tree-shaped network.

In fact, when $n = 2$ and $p_2 = 2$, the network of Figure 1 reduces to a bilocal network and the (t_n-1)-local Ineq. (5) reduces to the bilocal Ineq. (20) in [18]. When $p_2 = \cdots = p_n = 2$, the network of Figure 1 reduces to the chain-shaped network and Ineq. (5) reduces to the $(2n-2)$-local Ineq. (16) in [20]. When $n = 2$, the network of Figure 1 reduces to a star-shaped network and Ineq. (5) reduces to the p_2-local Ineq. (7) in [21]. Moreover, if $l_{kj} - l_{k(j-1)} = 2$ holds for any (k, j), then the network of Figure 1 reduces to a two-forked tree-shaped network and Ineq. (5) reduces to the $(2^n - 2)$-local Ineq. (16) in [42]. See Table 1. Therefore, from this point of view, any forked tree-shaped network can be seen as a generalization of these networks.

Table 1. Comparison of multi-local inequalities between any forked tree-shaped network and other networks.

Networks	Multi-Local Inequalities	Relations
any forked tree-shaped	$|I_{i_1,\cdots,i_{t_{n-1}},0}|^{\frac{1}{p_n}} + $ $\|I_{j_1,\cdots,j_{t_{n-1}},1}\|^{\frac{1}{p_n}} \leq 1$	
bilocal	$\|I_{i_1,0}\|^{\frac{1}{2}} + \|I_{j_1,1}\|^{\frac{1}{2}} \leq 1$	$n=2, p_2 = 2$
chain-shaped	$|I_{i_1,\cdots,i_{2n-3},0}|^{\frac{1}{2}} + $ $\|I_{j_1,\cdots,j_{2n-3},1}\|^{\frac{1}{2}} \leq 1$	$p_2 = \cdots = p_n = 2$
star-shaped	$\|I_{i_1,0}\|^{\frac{1}{p_2}} + \|I_{j_1,1}\|^{\frac{1}{p_2}} \leq 1$	$n=2$
two-forked tree-shaped	$|I_{i_1,\cdots,i_{2^{n-1}-1},0}|^{\frac{1}{2^{n-1}}} + $ $\|I_{j_1,\cdots,j_{2^{n-1}-1},1}\|^{\frac{1}{2^{n-1}}} \leq 1$	$l_{kj} - l_{k(j-1)} = 2$

3. Discussions

In this work, we discussed the nonlocality of a kind of important quantum network: any forked tree-shaped network, in which each node, respectively, shares an arbitrary number of bipartite sources with other nodes in the next "layer". This network contains $(t_n - 1)$ independent bipartite sources and t_n noninteracting parties ($n \geq 2$). The "two-forked" tree-shaped networks discussed in [42] are special tree-shaped networks. In addition, if $n = 2$, the networks are in fact the p_2-local star networks introduced in [21]. If $p_2 = \cdots = p_n = 2$, the networks are reduced to the chain networks introduced in [20]. We gave a detailed discussion for the case of $n = 3$, i.e., a tree-shaped network scenario with t_3 particles and $(t_3 - 1)$ independent sources. Concretely, we gave the inequalities satisfied by all $(t_3 - 1)$-local correlations, proved that all pure entangled states violate these $(t_3 - 1)$-local inequalities, obtained a necessary condition for mixed states to violate these inequalities, and explored the relation between the $(t_3 - 1)$-locality correlation and locality correlation in this quantum network. Finally, we generalized these results to the general t_n-partite tree-shaped networks. Note that the tree-shaped networks examined here just involve bipartite quantum states. The nonlocality of tree-shaped networks with multipartite states deserves further research.

Author Contributions: Conceptualization, L.Y. and X.Q.; methodology, X.Q. and J.H.; formal analysis, L.Y.; writing—original draft preparation, L.Y.; writing—review and editing, X.Q. and J.H.; visualization, L.Y.; supervision, X.Q.; project administration, X.Q. and J.H. All authors have read and agreed to the published version of the manuscript.

Funding: This work is partially supported by the National Natural Science Foundation of China (12171290, 12071336) and Fund Program for the Scientific Activities of Selected Returned Overseas Professionals in Shanxi Province (20200011).

Conflicts of Interest: The authors declare no conflict of interest.

Appendix A

To prove Theorem 1, the following lemma is needed.

Lemma A1 ([21] Lemma 1). *Assume that x_i^k are non-negative real numbers, $i = 1, 2, \cdots, n$, and $k = 1, 2, \cdots, m$. Then,*

$$\sum_{k=1}^{m} \left(\prod_{i=1}^{n} x_i^k\right)^{1/n} \leq \prod_{i=1}^{n} \left(\sum_{k=1}^{m} x_i^k\right)^{1/n}.$$

Proof of Theorem 1. By the assumption, all joint probability distributions have a $(t_3 - 1)$-local decomposition form satisfying Equations (3) and (4). Firstly, take $i_1 = \cdots = i_{t_2} = j_1 = \cdots = j_{t_2} = 0$. Then,

$$I_{0,\cdots,0,0} = \frac{1}{2^{p_3}} \sum_{x_{31},\cdots,x_{3p_3}} \langle A_0^{11} A_0^{21} \cdots A_0^{2p_2} A_{x_{31}}^{31} \cdots A_{x_{3p_3}}^{3p_3} \rangle$$

and

$$I_{0,\cdots,0,1} = \frac{1}{2^{p_3}} \sum_{x_{31},\cdots,x_{3p_3}} (-1)^{x_{31}+\cdots+x_{3p_3}} \langle A_0^{11} A_0^{21} \cdots A_0^{2p_2} A_{x_{31}}^{31} \cdots A_{x_{3p_3}}^{3p_3} \rangle.$$

Write

$$\langle A_{x_{11}}^{11} \rangle_{\lambda_1,\cdots,\lambda_{p_2}} = \sum_{a_{11}} (-1)^{a_{11}} P(a_{11}|x_{11}, \lambda_1, \cdots, \lambda_{p_2}),$$

$$\langle A_{x_{21}}^{21} \rangle_{\lambda_1, \lambda_{p_2+1}, \cdots, \lambda_{p_2+l_{21}}} = \sum_{a_{21}} (-1)^{a_{21}} P(a_{21}|x_{21}, \lambda_1, \lambda_{p_2+1}, \cdots, \lambda_{p_2+l_{21}}),$$

$$\cdots\cdots$$

$$\langle A_{x_{2p_2}}^{2p_2} \rangle_{\lambda_{p_2}, \lambda_{p_2+l_{2(p_2-1)}+1}, \cdots, \lambda_{t_3-1}} = \sum_{a_{2p_2}} (-1)^{a_{2p_2}} P(a_{2p_2}|x_{2p_2}, \lambda_{p_2}, \lambda_{p_2+l_{2(p_2-1)}+1}, \cdots, \lambda_{t_3-1}),$$

$$\langle A_{x_{3j}}^{3j} \rangle_{\lambda_{p_2+j}} = \sum_{a_{3j}} (-1)^{a_{3j}} P(a_{3j}|x_{3j}, \lambda_{p_2+j}), \quad \forall j = 1, \cdots, p_3.$$

By Equations (3) and (4) and the facts that $|\langle A_0^{11} \rangle_{\lambda_1,\cdots,\lambda_{p_2}}| \leq 1$, $|\langle A_0^{21} \rangle_{\lambda_1, \lambda_{p_2+1}, \cdots, \lambda_{p_2+l_{21}}}| \leq 1$, $\cdots$, $|\langle A_0^{2p_2} \rangle_{\lambda_{p_2}, \lambda_{p_2+l_{2(p_2-1)}+1}, \cdots, \lambda_{t_3-1}}| \leq 1$, we have

$$\begin{aligned}
|I_{0,\cdots,0,0}| &= \tfrac{1}{2^{p_3}} | \int \cdots \int P_1(\lambda_1) \cdots P_{t_3-1}(\lambda_{t_3-1}) \langle A_0^{11} \rangle_{\lambda_1,\cdots,\lambda_{p_2}} \langle A_0^{21} \rangle_{\lambda_1, \lambda_{p_2+1}, \cdots, \lambda_{p_2+l_{21}}} \cdots \\
&\quad \cdot \langle A_0^{2p_2} \rangle_{\lambda_{p_2}, \lambda_{p_2+l_{2(p_2-1)}+1}, \cdots, \lambda_{t_3-1}} \prod_{j=1}^{p_3} (\langle A_0^{3j} \rangle_{\lambda_{p_2+j}} + \langle A_1^{3j} \rangle_{\lambda_{p_2+j}}) d\lambda_1 \cdots d\lambda_{t_3-1}| \\
&\leq \tfrac{1}{2^{p_3}} \int \cdots \int P_1(\lambda_1) \cdots P_{t_3-1}(\lambda_{t_3-1}) |\langle A_0^{11} \rangle_{\lambda_1,\cdots,\lambda_{p_2}}| |\langle A_0^{21} \rangle_{\lambda_1, \lambda_{p_2+1}, \cdots, \lambda_{p_2+l_{21}}}| \cdots \\
&\quad \cdot |\langle A_0^{2p_2} \rangle_{\lambda_{p_2}, \lambda_{p_2+l_{2(p_2-1)}+1}, \cdots, \lambda_{t_3-1}}| \prod_{j=1}^{p_3} |\langle A_0^{3j} \rangle_{\lambda_{p_2+j}} + \langle A_1^{3j} \rangle_{\lambda_{p_2+j}}| d\lambda_1 \cdots d\lambda_{t_3-1} \\
&\leq \tfrac{1}{2^{p_3}} \int \cdots \int P_1(\lambda_1) \cdots P_{t_3-1}(\lambda_{t_3-1}) \prod_{j=1}^{p_3} |\langle A_0^{3j} \rangle_{\lambda_{p_2+j}} + \langle A_1^{3j} \rangle_{\lambda_{p_2+j}}| d\lambda_1 \cdots d\lambda_{t_3-1} \\
&= \prod_{j=1}^{p_3} \frac{\int P_{p_2+j}(\lambda_{p_2+j}) |\langle A_0^{3j} \rangle_{\lambda_{p_2+j}} + \langle A_1^{3j} \rangle_{\lambda_{p_2+j}}| d\lambda_{p_2+j}}{2}.
\end{aligned}$$

Similarly, one has

$$|I_{0,\cdots,0,1}| \leq \prod_{j=1}^{p_3} \frac{\int P_{p_2+j}(\lambda_{p_2+j}) |\langle A_0^{3j} \rangle_{\lambda_{p_2+j}} - \langle A_1^{3j} \rangle_{\lambda_{p_2+j}}| d\lambda_{p_2+j}}{2}.$$

By Lemma A1, we can obtain

$$\begin{aligned}
& |I_{0,\cdots,0,0}|^{\frac{1}{p_3}} + |I_{0,\cdots,0,1}|^{\frac{1}{p_3}} \\
&\leq \prod_{j=1}^{p_3} [\int P_{p_2+j}(\lambda_{p_2+j}) (\frac{|\langle A_0^{3j} \rangle_{\lambda_{p_2+j}} + \langle A_1^{3j} \rangle_{\lambda_{p_2+j}}|}{2} + \frac{|\langle A_0^{3j} \rangle_{\lambda_{p_2+j}} - \langle A_1^{3j} \rangle_{\lambda_{p_2+j}}|}{2}) d\lambda_{p_2+j}]^{\frac{1}{p_3}} \\
&= \prod_{j=1}^{p_3} [\int P_{p_2+j}(\lambda_{p_2+j}) \max\{|\langle A_0^{3j} \rangle_{\lambda_{p_2+j}}|, |\langle A_1^{3j} \rangle_{\lambda_{p_2+j}}|\} d\lambda_{p_2+j}]^{\frac{1}{p_3}} \leq 1.
\end{aligned}$$

With similar discussions, Inequality (5) also holds for any other values of $i_1, \cdots, i_{t_2}, j_1, \cdots, j_{t_2} (\in \{0,1\})$. □

Proof of Theorem 2. For any $i_1, \cdots, i_{t_2}, j_1, \cdots, j_{t_2} \in \{0,1\}$, we can obtain

$$I_{i_1,\cdots,i_{t_2},0} = \frac{1}{2^{p_3}} \langle A_{i_1}^{11} A_{i_2}^{21} \cdots A_{i_{t_2}}^{2p_2} (A_0^{31} + A_1^{31}) \cdots (A_0^{3p_3} + A_1^{3p_3}) \rangle$$

and

$$I_{j_1,\cdots,j_{t_2},1} = \frac{1}{2^{p_3}} \langle A_{j_1}^{11} A_{j_2}^{21} \cdots A_{j_{t_2}}^{2p_2} (A_0^{31} - A_1^{31}) \cdots (A_0^{3p_3} - A_1^{3p_3}) \rangle.$$

Here, we use similar symbols as those in the proof of Theorem 1. Note that $|\langle A_{i_1(j_1)}^{11} \rangle_{\lambda_1,\cdots,\lambda_{p_2}}| \leq 1$, $|\langle A_{i_2(j_2)}^{21} \rangle_{\lambda_1,\lambda_{p_2+1},\cdots,\lambda_{p_2+l_{21}}}| \leq 1, \cdots, |\langle A_{i_{t_2}(j_{t_2})}^{2p_2} \rangle_{\lambda_{p_2},\lambda_{p_2+l_{2(p_2-1)}+1},\cdots,\lambda_{t_3-1}}|$
≤ 1. By Equation (3) and a similar discussion to that in the proof of Theorem 1, we have

$$|I_{i_1,\cdots,i_{t_2},0}| \leq \frac{1}{2^{p_3}} \int \cdots \int P(\lambda_1,\cdots,\lambda_{t_3-1}) \prod_{j=1}^{p_3} |\langle A_0^{3j} \rangle_{\lambda_{p_2+j}} + \langle A_1^{3j} \rangle_{\lambda_{p_2+j}} | d\lambda_1 \cdots d\lambda_{t_3-1}$$

and

$$|I_{j_1,\cdots,j_{t_2},1}| \leq \frac{1}{2^{p_3}} \int \cdots \int P(\lambda_1,\cdots,\lambda_{t_3-1}) \prod_{j=1}^{p_3} |\langle A_0^{3j} \rangle_{\lambda_{p_2+j}} - \langle A_1^{3j} \rangle_{\lambda_{p_2+j}} | d\lambda_1 \cdots d\lambda_{t_3-1}.$$

Consequently,

$$\begin{aligned}
& |I_{i_1,\cdots,i_{t_2},0}| + |I_{j_1,\cdots,j_{t_2},1}| \\
\leq\ & \frac{1}{2^{p_3}} \int \cdots \int P(\lambda_1,\cdots,\lambda_{t_3-1}) \prod_{j=1}^{p_3} (|\langle A_0^{3j} \rangle_{\lambda_{p_2+j}} + \langle A_1^{3j} \rangle_{\lambda_{p_2+j}}| + |\langle A_0^{3j} \rangle_{\lambda_{p_2+j}} - \langle A_1^{3j} \rangle_{\lambda_{p_2+j}}|) \\
& \cdot d\lambda_1 \cdots d\lambda_{t_3-1} \\
=\ & \int \cdots \int P(\lambda_1,\cdots,\lambda_{t_3-1}) \prod_{j=1}^{p_3} \max\{|\langle A_0^{3j} \rangle_{\lambda_{p_2+j}}|, |\langle A_1^{3j} \rangle_{\lambda_{p_2+j}}|\} d\lambda_1 \cdots d\lambda_{t_3-1} \leq 1.
\end{aligned}$$

□

Proof of Equation (8). Note that

$$\begin{aligned}
S_{(t_3-1)-\text{local}} =\ & |I_{0,\cdots,0,0}|^{\frac{1}{p_3}} + |I_{1,\cdots,1,1}|^{\frac{1}{p_3}} \\
=\ & \frac{1}{2} (\tau_1^{A^{11}A^{21}} \cdots \tau_1^{A^{11}A^{2p_2}} \tau_1^{A^{21}A^{31}} \cdots \tau_1^{A^{2p_2}A^{3p_3}})^{\frac{1}{2p_3}} |\prod_{j=1}^{p_3} (\cos \beta_j + \cos \beta_j')|^{\frac{1}{p_3}} \\
& + \frac{1}{2} (\tau_2^{A^{11}A^{21}} \cdots \tau_2^{A^{11}A^{2p_2}} \tau_2^{A^{21}A^{31}} \cdots \tau_2^{A^{2p_2}A^{3p_3}})^{\frac{1}{2p_3}} |\prod_{j=1}^{p_3} (\sin \beta_j - \sin \beta_j')|^{\frac{1}{p_3}}.
\end{aligned}$$

For convenience, write $f(\beta_1, \beta_1', \cdots, \beta_{p_3}, \beta_{p_3}') = S_{(t_3-1)-\text{local}}$. To maximize the function f, calculating all the partial derivatives $\partial_{\beta_j} f = \partial_{\beta_j'} f = 0$ for $j, j' \in \{1, 2, \cdots, p_3\}$, one obtains that the extreme points of f must satisfy

$$\beta_j' = -\beta_j \text{ and } |\tan \beta_j| = \frac{(\tau_2^{A^{11}A^{21}} \cdots \tau_2^{A^{11}A^{2p_2}} \tau_2^{A^{21}A^{31}} \cdots \tau_2^{A^{2p_2}A^{3p_3}})^{\frac{1}{2p_3}}}{(\tau_1^{A^{11}A^{21}} \cdots \tau_1^{A^{11}A^{2p_2}} \tau_1^{A^{21}A^{31}} \cdots \tau_1^{A^{2p_2}A^{3p_3}})^{\frac{1}{2p_3}}}, \quad \forall j = 1, \cdots, p_3.$$

These imply

$$|\cos \beta_j| = \sqrt{\frac{(\tau_1^{A^{11}A^{21}} \cdots \tau_1^{A^{11}A^{2p_2}} \tau_1^{A^{21}A^{31}} \cdots \tau_1^{A^{2p_2}A^{3p_3}})^{\frac{1}{p_3}}}{\sum_{i=1}^{2} (\tau_i^{A^{11}A^{21}} \cdots \tau_i^{A^{11}A^{2p_2}} \tau_i^{A^{21}A^{31}} \cdots \tau_i^{A^{2p_2}A^{3p_3}})^{\frac{1}{p_3}}}}$$

and

$$|\sin\beta_j| = \sqrt{\frac{(\tau_2^{A^{11}A^{21}}\cdots\tau_2^{A^{11}A^{2p_2}}\tau_2^{A^{21}A^{31}}\cdots\tau_2^{A^{2p_2}A^{3p_3}})^{\frac{1}{p_3}}}{\sum_{i=1}^{2}(\tau_i^{A^{11}A^{21}}\cdots\tau_i^{A^{11}A^{2p_2}}\tau_i^{A^{21}A^{31}}\cdots\tau_i^{A^{2p_2}A^{3p_3}})^{\frac{1}{p_3}}}}, \quad \forall j = 1,\cdots,p_3.$$

Hence, the corresponding function value of these extreme points is

$$\sqrt{\sum_{i=1}^{2}(\tau_i^{A^{11}A^{21}}\cdots\tau_i^{A^{11}A^{2p_2}}\tau_i^{A^{21}A^{31}}\cdots\tau_i^{A^{2p_2}A^{3p_3}})^{\frac{1}{p_3}}}.$$

By comparing this function value with those of all endpoints, it follows that the maximum of $f = S_{(t_3-1)-\text{local}}$ is

$$S_{(t_3-1)-\text{local}}^{\max} = \sqrt{\sum_{i=1}^{2}(\tau_i^{A^{11}A^{21}}\cdots\tau_i^{A^{11}A^{2p_2}}\tau_i^{A^{21}A^{31}}\cdots\tau_i^{A^{2p_2}A^{3p_3}})^{\frac{1}{p_3}}}.$$

□

Proof of Theorem 3. Assume that Equation (1) holds. Write

$$\langle A_{x_{11}}^{11}\rangle_{\lambda_1,\cdots,\lambda_{p_2}} = \sum_{a_{11}}(-1)^{a_{11}}P(a_{11}|x_{11},\lambda_1,\cdots,\lambda_{p_2}),$$

$$\cdots\cdots$$

$$\langle A_{x_{(n-1)p_{n-1}}}^{(n-1)p_{n-1}}\rangle_{\lambda_{t_{n-1}-1},\lambda_{t_{n-1}+l_{(n-1)(p_{n-1}-1)}},\cdots,\lambda_{t_n-1}}$$
$$= \sum_{a_{(n-1)p_{n-1}}}(-1)^{a_{(n-1)p_{n-1}}}P(a_{(n-1)p_{n-1}}|x_{(n-1)p_{n-1}},\lambda_{t_{n-1}-1},\lambda_{t_{n-1}+l_{(n-1)(p_{n-1}-1)}},\cdots,\lambda_{t_n-1}),$$

$$\langle A_{x_{nk}}^{nk}\rangle_{\lambda_{t_{n-1}-1+k}} = \sum_{a_{nk}}(-1)^{a_{nk}}P(a_{nk}|x_{nk},\lambda_{t_{n-1}-1+k}), \quad \forall k = 1,\cdots,p_n.$$

By Equation (1), for any $i_1,\cdots,i_{t_{n-1}},j_1,\cdots,j_{t_{n-1}} \in \{0,1\}$, we have

$$|I_{i_1,\cdots,i_{t_{n-1}},0}| = |\tfrac{1}{2^{p_n}}\sum_{x_{n1},\cdots,x_{np_n}}\langle A_{i_1}^{11}\cdots A_{i_{t_{n-1}}}^{(n-1)p_{n-1}}A_{x_{n1}}^{n1}\cdots A_{x_{np_n}}^{np_n}\rangle|$$

$$= |\tfrac{1}{2^{p_n}}\sum_{x_{n1},\cdots,x_{np_n}}\sum_{a_{11},\cdots,a_{np_n}}(-1)^{a_{11}+\cdots+a_{np_n}}\int\cdots\int P(\lambda_1,\cdots,\lambda_{t_n-1})[P(a_{11}|i_1,\lambda_1,\cdots,\lambda_{p_2})\cdots$$
$$\cdot P(a_{(n-1)p_{n-1}}|i_{t_{n-1}},\lambda_{t_{n-1}-1},\lambda_{t_{n-1}+l_{(n-1)(p_{n-1}-1)}},\cdots,\lambda_{t_n-1})P(a_{n1}|x_{n1},\lambda_{t_n-1})\cdots$$
$$\cdot P(a_{np_n}|x_{np_n},\lambda_{t_n-1})]d\lambda_1\cdots d\lambda_{t_n-1}|$$

$$= |\tfrac{1}{2^{p_n}}\sum_{x_{n1},\cdots,x_{np_n}}\int\cdots\int P(\lambda_1,\cdots,\lambda_{t_n-1})\langle A_{i_1}^{11}\rangle_{\lambda_1,\cdots,\lambda_{p_2}}\cdots$$
$$\cdot\langle A_{i_{t_{n-1}}}^{(n-1)p_{n-1}}\rangle_{\lambda_{t_{n-1}-1},\lambda_{t_{n-1}+l_{(n-1)(p_{n-1}-1)}},\cdots,\lambda_{t_n-1}}\langle A_{x_{n1}}^{n1}\rangle_{\lambda_{t_n-1}}\cdots\langle A_{x_{np_n}}^{np_n}\rangle_{\lambda_{t_n-1}}d\lambda_1\cdots d\lambda_{t_n-1}|$$

$$= |\tfrac{1}{2^{p_n}}\int\cdots\int P(\lambda_1,\cdots,\lambda_{t_n-1})\langle A_{i_1}^{11}\rangle_{\lambda_1,\cdots,\lambda_{p_2}}\cdots$$
$$\cdot\langle A_{i_{t_{n-1}}}^{(n-1)p_{n-1}}\rangle_{\lambda_{t_{n-1}-1},\lambda_{t_{n-1}+l_{(n-1)(p_{n-1}-1)}},\cdots,\lambda_{t_n-1}}(\langle A_0^{n1}\rangle_{\lambda_{t_n-1}}+\langle A_1^{n1}\rangle_{\lambda_{t_n-1}})\cdots$$
$$\cdot(\langle A_0^{np_n}\rangle_{\lambda_{t_n-1}}+\langle A_1^{np_n}\rangle_{\lambda_{t_n-1}})d\lambda_1\cdots d\lambda_{t_n-1}|$$

$$\leq \tfrac{1}{2^{p_n}}\int\cdots\int P(\lambda_1,\cdots,\lambda_{t_n-1})|\langle A_{i_1}^{11}\rangle_{\lambda_1,\cdots,\lambda_{p_2}}|\cdots$$
$$\cdot|\langle A_{i_{t_{n-1}}}^{(n-1)p_{n-1}}\rangle_{\lambda_{t_{n-1}-1},\lambda_{t_{n-1}+l_{(n-1)(p_{n-1}-1)}},\cdots,\lambda_{t_n-1}}||\langle A_0^{n1}\rangle_{\lambda_{t_n-1}}+\langle A_1^{n1}\rangle_{\lambda_{t_n-1}}|\cdots$$
$$\cdot|\langle A_0^{np_n}\rangle_{\lambda_{t_n-1}}+\langle A_1^{np_n}\rangle_{\lambda_{t_n-1}}|d\lambda_1\cdots d\lambda_{t_n-1}$$

$$\leq \tfrac{1}{2^{p_n}}\int\cdots\int P(\lambda_1,\cdots,\lambda_{t_n-1})|\langle A_0^{n1}\rangle_{\lambda_{t_n-1}}+\langle A_1^{n1}\rangle_{\lambda_{t_n-1}}|\cdots|\langle A_0^{np_n}\rangle_{\lambda_{t_n-1}}+\langle A_1^{np_n}\rangle_{\lambda_{t_n-1}}|$$
$$\cdot d\lambda_1\cdots d\lambda_{t_n-1}$$

$$= \tfrac{1}{2^{p_n}}\int\cdots\int P(\lambda_1,\cdots,\lambda_{t_n-1})\prod_{k=1}^{p_n}|\langle A_0^{nk}\rangle_{\lambda_{t_{n-1}-1+k}}+\langle A_1^{nk}\rangle_{\lambda_{t_{n-1}-1+k}}|d\lambda_1\cdots d\lambda_{t_n-1}$$

and

$$
\begin{aligned}
|I_{j_1,\cdots,j_{t_{n-1}},1}| &= |\tfrac{1}{2^{p_n}}\sum_{x_{n1},\cdots,x_{np_n}}(-1)^{x_{n1}+\cdots+x_{np_n}}\langle A^{11}_{j_1}\cdots A^{(n-1)p_{n-1}}_{j_{t_{n-1}}}A^{n1}_{x_{n1}}\cdots A^{np_n}_{x_{np_n}}\rangle| \\
&= |\tfrac{1}{2^{p_n}}\sum_{x_{n1},\cdots,x_{np_n}}(-1)^{x_{n1}+\cdots+x_{np_n}}\sum_{a_{11},\cdots,a_{np_n}}(-1)^{a_{11}+\cdots+a_{np_n}}\int\cdots\int P(\lambda_1,\cdots,\lambda_{t_n-1})\\
&\quad\cdot[P(a_{11}|j_1,\lambda_1,\cdots,\lambda_{p_2})\cdots P(a_{(n-1)p_{n-1}}|j_{t_{n-1}},\lambda_{t_{n-1}-1},\lambda_{t_{n-1}+l_{(n-1)(p_{n-1}-1)}},\cdots,\lambda_{t_n-1})\\
&\quad\cdot P(a_{n1}|x_{n1},\lambda_{t_n-1})\cdots P(a_{np_n}|x_{np_n},\lambda_{t_n-1})]d\lambda_1\cdots d\lambda_{t_n-1}|\\
&= |\tfrac{1}{2^{p_n}}\sum_{x_{n1},\cdots,x_{np_n}}(-1)^{x_{n1}+\cdots+x_{np_n}}\int\cdots\int P(\lambda_1,\cdots,\lambda_{t_n-1})\langle A^{11}_{j_1}\rangle_{\lambda_1,\cdots,\lambda_{p_2}}\cdots\\
&\quad\cdot\langle A^{(n-1)p_{n-1}}_{j_{t_{n-1}}}\rangle_{\lambda_{t_{n-1}-1},\lambda_{t_{n-1}+l_{(n-1)(p_{n-1}-1)}},\cdots,\lambda_{t_n-1}}\langle A^{n1}_{x_{n1}}\rangle_{\lambda_{t_n-1}}\cdots\langle A^{np_n}_{x_{np_n}}\rangle_{\lambda_{t_n-1}}d\lambda_1\cdots d\lambda_{t_n-1}|\\
&= |\tfrac{1}{2^{p_n}}\int\cdots\int P(\lambda_1,\cdots,\lambda_{t_n-1})\langle A^{11}_{j_1}\rangle_{\lambda_1,\cdots,\lambda_{p_2}}\cdots\\
&\quad\cdot\langle A^{(n-1)p_{n-1}}_{j_{t_{n-1}}}\rangle_{\lambda_{t_{n-1}-1},\lambda_{t_{n-1}+l_{(n-1)(p_{n-1}-1)}},\cdots,\lambda_{t_n-1}}(\langle A^{n1}_0\rangle_{\lambda_{t_n-1}}-\langle A^{n1}_1\rangle_{\lambda_{t_n-1}})\cdots\\
&\quad\cdot(\langle A^{np_n}_0\rangle_{\lambda_{t_n-1}}-\langle A^{np_n}_1\rangle_{\lambda_{t_n-1}})d\lambda_1\cdots d\lambda_{t_n-1}|\\
&\leq \tfrac{1}{2^{p_n}}\int\cdots\int P(\lambda_1,\cdots,\lambda_{t_n-1})|\langle A^{11}_{j_1}\rangle_{\lambda_1,\cdots,\lambda_{p_2}}|\cdots\\
&\quad\cdot|\langle A^{(n-1)p_{n-1}}_{j_{t_{n-1}}}\rangle_{\lambda_{t_{n-1}-1},\lambda_{t_{n-1}+l_{(n-1)(p_{n-1}-1)}},\cdots,\lambda_{t_n-1}}|\\
&\quad\cdot|\langle A^{n1}_0\rangle_{\lambda_{t_n-1}}-\langle A^{n1}_1\rangle_{\lambda_{t_n-1}}|\cdots|\langle A^{np_n}_0\rangle_{\lambda_{t_n-1}}-\langle A^{np_n}_1\rangle_{\lambda_{t_n-1}}|d\lambda_1\cdots d\lambda_{t_n-1}\\
&\leq \tfrac{1}{2^{p_n}}\int\cdots\int P(\lambda_1,\cdots,\lambda_{t_n-1})|\langle A^{n1}_0\rangle_{\lambda_{t_n-1}}-\langle A^{n1}_1\rangle_{\lambda_{t_n-1}}|\cdots|\langle A^{np_n}_0\rangle_{\lambda_{t_n-1}}-\langle A^{np_n}_1\rangle_{\lambda_{t_n-1}}|\\
&\quad\cdot d\lambda_1\cdots d\lambda_{t_n-1}\\
&= \tfrac{1}{2^{p_n}}\int\cdots\int P(\lambda_1,\cdots,\lambda_{t_n-1})\prod_{k=1}^{p_n}|\langle A^{nk}_0\rangle_{\lambda_{t_{n-1}-1+k}}-\langle A^{nk}_1\rangle_{\lambda_{t_{n-1}-1+k}}|d\lambda_1\cdots d\lambda_{t_n-1}.
\end{aligned}
$$

Therefore,

$$
\begin{aligned}
&|I_{i_1,\cdots,i_{t_{n-1}},0}|+|I_{j_1,\cdots,j_{t_{n-1}},1}|\\
&\leq \tfrac{1}{2^{p_n}}\int\cdots\int P(\lambda_1,\cdots,\lambda_{t_n-1})\prod_{k=1}^{p_n}(|\langle A^{nk}_0\rangle_{\lambda_{t_{n-1}-1+k}}+\langle A^{nk}_1\rangle_{\lambda_{t_{n-1}-1+k}}|\\
&\quad+|\langle A^{nk}_0\rangle_{\lambda_{t_{n-1}-1+k}}-\langle A^{nk}_1\rangle_{\lambda_{t_{n-1}-1+k}}|)d\lambda_1\cdots d\lambda_{t_n-1}\\
&= \int\cdots\int P(\lambda_1,\cdots,\lambda_{t_n-1})\prod_{k=1}^{p_n}\max\{|\langle A^{nk}_0\rangle_{\lambda_{t_{n-1}-1+k}}|,|\langle A^{nk}_1\rangle_{\lambda_{t_{n-1}-1+k}}|\}d\lambda_1\cdots d\lambda_{t_n-1}\leq 1,
\end{aligned}
$$

as desired.

Moreover, if Equation (2) also holds, we have

$$
\begin{aligned}
&|I_{i_1,\cdots,i_{t_{n-1}},0}|\\
&\leq \tfrac{1}{2^{p_n}}\int\cdots\int P_1(\lambda_1)\cdots P_{t_n-1}(\lambda_{t_n-1})\prod_{k=1}^{p_n}|\langle A^{nk}_0\rangle_{\lambda_{t_{n-1}-1+k}}+\langle A^{nk}_1\rangle_{\lambda_{t_{n-1}-1+k}}|d\lambda_1\cdots d\lambda_{t_n-1}\\
&= \prod_{k=1}^{p_n}\int P_{t_{n-1}-1+k}(\lambda_{t_{n-1}-1+k})\tfrac{|\langle A^{nk}_0\rangle_{\lambda_{t_{n-1}-1+k}}+\langle A^{nk}_1\rangle_{\lambda_{t_{n-1}-1+k}}|}{2}d\lambda_{t_{n-1}-1+k}
\end{aligned}
$$

and

$$
\begin{aligned}
&|I_{j_1,\cdots,j_{t_{n-1}},1}|\\
&\leq \tfrac{1}{2^{p_n}}\int\cdots\int P_1(\lambda_1)\cdots P_{t_n-1}(\lambda_{t_n-1})\prod_{k=1}^{p_n}|\langle A^{nk}_0\rangle_{\lambda_{t_{n-1}-1+k}}-\langle A^{nk}_1\rangle_{\lambda_{t_{n-1}-1+k}}|d\lambda_1\cdots d\lambda_{t_n-1}\\
&= \prod_{k=1}^{p_n}\int P_{t_{n-1}-1+k}(\lambda_{t_{n-1}-1+k})\tfrac{|\langle A^{nk}_0\rangle_{\lambda_{t_{n-1}-1+k}}-\langle A^{nk}_1\rangle_{\lambda_{t_{n-1}-1+k}}|}{2}d\lambda_{t_{n-1}-1+k}.
\end{aligned}
$$

Using Lemma A1, we obtain

$$
\begin{aligned}
&|I_{i_1,\cdots,i_{t_{n-1}},0}|^{\frac{1}{p_n}}+|I_{j_1,\cdots,j_{t_{n-1}},1}|^{\frac{1}{p_n}}\\
&\leq \prod_{k=1}^{p_n}[\int P_{t_{n-1}-1+k}(\lambda_{t_{n-1}-1+k})(\tfrac{|\langle A^{nk}_0\rangle_{\lambda_{t_{n-1}-1+k}}+\langle A^{nk}_1\rangle_{\lambda_{t_{n-1}-1+k}}|}{2}\\
&\quad+\tfrac{|\langle A^{nk}_0\rangle_{\lambda_{t_{n-1}-1+k}}-\langle A^{nk}_1\rangle_{\lambda_{t_{n-1}-1+k}}|}{2})d\lambda_{t_{n-1}-1+k}]^{\frac{1}{p_n}}\\
&= \prod_{k=1}^{p_n}[\int P_{t_{n-1}-1+k}(\lambda_{t_{n-1}-1+k})\max\{|\langle A^{nk}_0\rangle_{\lambda_{t_{n-1}-1+k}}|,|\langle A^{nk}_1\rangle_{\lambda_{t_{n-1}-1+k}}|\}d\lambda_{t_{n-1}-1+k}]^{\frac{1}{p_n}}\leq 1,
\end{aligned}
$$

that is, Inequality (9) holds. □

References

1. Einstein, A.; Podolsky, B.; Rosen, N. Can quantum-mechanical description of physical reality be considered complete? *Phys. Rev.* **1935**, *47*, 777. [CrossRef]
2. Bell, J.S. On the Einstein-Podolsky-Rosen paradox. *Physics* **1964**, *1*, 195. [CrossRef]
3. Brunner, N.; Cavalcanti, D.; Pironio, S.; Scarani, V.; Wehner, S. Bell nonlocality. *Rev. Mod. Phys.* **2014**, *86*, 419. [CrossRef]
4. Brendel, J.; Mohler, E.; Martienssen, W. Experimental test of Bell's inequality for energy and time. *Europhys. Lett.* **1992**, *20*, 575. [CrossRef]
5. Gröblacher, S.; Paterek, T.; Kaltenbaek, R.; Brukner, Č.; Żukowski, M.; Aspelmeyer, M.; Zeilinger, A. An experimental test of non-local realism. *Nature* **2007**, *446*, 871. [CrossRef]
6. Giustina, M.; Versteegh, M.A.M.; Wengerowsky, S.; Handsteiner, J.; Hochrainer, A.; Phelan, K.; Steinlechner, F.; Kofler, J.; Larsson, J.A.; Abellán, C.; et al, Significant-Loophole-Free test of Bell's theorem with entangled photons. *Phys. Rev. Lett.* **2015**, *115*, 250401. [CrossRef]
7. Ekert, A.K. Quantum cryptography based on Bell's theorem. *Phys. Rev. Lett.* **1991**, *67*, 661. [CrossRef]
8. Acín, A.; Brunner, N.; Gisin, N.; Massar, S.; Pironio, S.; Scarani, V. Device-independent security of quantum cryptography against collective attacks. *Phys. Rev. Lett.* **2007**, *98*, 230501. [CrossRef]
9. Acín, A.; Gisin, N.; Masanes, L. From Bell's theorem to secure quantum key distribution. *Phys. Rev. Lett.* **2006**, *97*, 120405. [CrossRef]
10. Pironio, S.; Acín, A.; Massar, S.; Boyer de la Giroday, A.; Matsukevich, D.N.; Maunz, P.; Olmschenk, S.; Hayes, D.; Luo, L.; Manning, T.A.; et al. Random numbers certified by Bell's theorem. *Nature* **2010**, *464*, 1021. [CrossRef]
11. Buhrman, H.; Cleve, R.; Massar, S.; de Wolf, R. Nonlocality and communication complexity. *Rev. Mod. Phys.* **2010**, *82*, 665. [CrossRef]
12. Clauser, J.F.; Horne, M.A.; Shimony, A.; Holt, R.A. Proposed experiment to test local hidden-variable theories. *Phys. Rev. Lett.* **1969**, *23*, 880. [CrossRef]
13. Collins, D.; Gisin, N.; Linden, N.; Massar, S.; Popescu, S Bell inequalities for arbitrarily high-dimensional systems. *Phys. Rev. Lett.* **2002**, *88*. 040404. [CrossRef] [PubMed]
14. Cruzeiro, E.Z.; Gisin, N. Complete list of tight Bell inequalities for two parties with four binary settings. *Phys. Rev. A* **2019**, *99*, 022104. [CrossRef]
15. Tavakoli, A.; Pozas-Kerstjens, A.; Luo, M.-X.; Renou, M.-O. Bell nonlocality in networks. *Rep. Prog. Phys.* 2021, in press. [CrossRef]
16. Żukowski, M.; Zeilinger, A.; Horne, M.A.; Ekert, A.K. "Event-Ready-Detectors" Bell experiment via entanglement swapping. *Phys. Rev. Lett.* **1993**, *71*, 4287. [CrossRef]
17. Branciard, C.; Gisin, N.; Pironio, S. Characterizing the nonlocal correlations created via entanglement swapping. *Phys. Rev. Lett.* **2010**, *104*, 170401. [CrossRef]
18. Branciard, C.; Rosset, D.; Gisin, N.; Pironio, S. Bilocal versus nonbilocal correlations in entanglement-swapping experiments. *Phys. Rev. A* **2012**, *85*, 032119. [CrossRef]
19. Gisin, N.; Mei, Q.; Tavakoli, A.; Renou, M.O.; Brunner, N. All entangled pure quantum states violate the bilocality inequality. *Phys. Rev. A* **2017**, *96*, 020304. [CrossRef]
20. Mukherjee, K.; Paul, B.; Sarkar, D. Correlations in n-local scenario. *Quantum Inf. Process.* **2015**, *14*, 2025. [CrossRef]
21. Tavakoli, A.; Skrzypczyk, P.; Cavalcanti, D.; Acín, A. Nonlocal correlations in the star-network configuration. *Phys. Rev. A* **2014**, *90*, 062109. [CrossRef]
22. Tavakoli, A.; Renou, M.O.; Gisin, N.; Brunner, N. Correlations in star networks: From Bell inequalities to network inequalities. *New J. Phys.* **2017**, *19*, 073003. [CrossRef]
23. Andreoli, F.; Carvacho, G.; Santodonato, L.; Chaves, R.; Sciarrino, F. Maximal qubit violation of n-locality inequalities in a star-shaped quantum network. *New J. Phys.* **2017**, *19*, 113020. [CrossRef]
24. Renou, M.-O.; Bäumer, E.; Boreiri, S.; Brunner, N.; Gisin, N.; Beigi, S. Genuine quantum nonlocality in the triangle network. *Phys. Rev. Lett.* **2019**, *123*, 140401. [CrossRef]
25. Luo, M.-X. Computationally efficient nonlinear Bell inequalities for quantum networks. *Phys. Rev. Lett.* **2018**, *120*, 140402. [CrossRef]
26. Frey, M. A Bell inequality for a class of multilocal ring networks. *Quantum Inf. Process* **2017**, *16*, 266. [CrossRef]
27. Fritz, T. Beyond Bell's theorem: Correlation scenarios. *New J. Phys.* **2012**, *14*, 103001. [CrossRef]
28. Tavakoli, A. Quantum correlations in connected multipartite Bell experiments. *J. Phys. A Math. Theor.* **2016**, *49*, 145304. [CrossRef]
29. Chaves, R. Polynomial Bell inequalities. *Phys. Rev. Lett.* **2016**, *116*, 010402. [CrossRef]
30. Luo, M.-X. Nonlocality of all quantum networks. *Phys. Rev. A* **2018**, *98*, 042317. [CrossRef]
31. Mukherjee, K.; Paul, B.; Sarkar, D. Nontrilocality: Exploiting nonlocality from three-particle systems. *Phys. Rev. A* **2017**, *96*, 022103. [CrossRef]
32. Mukherjee, K.; Paul, B.; Roy, A. Characterizing quantum correlations in a fixed-input n-local network scenario. *Phys. Rev. A* **2020**, *101*, 032328. [CrossRef]
33. Bancal, J.-D.; Gisin, N. Nonlocal boxes for networks. *Phys. Rev. A* **2021**, *104*, 052212. [CrossRef]

34. Šupić, I.; Bancal, J.-D.; Cai, Y.; Brunner, N. Genuine network quantum nonlocality and self-testing. *Phys. Rev. A* **2022**, *105*, 022206.
35. Pozas-Kerstjens, A.; Gisin, N.; Tavakoli, A. Full network nonlocality. *Phys. Rev. Lett.* **2022**, *128*, 010403. [CrossRef] [PubMed]
36. Shi, Y.-Y.; Duan, L.-M.; Vidal, G. Classical simulation of quantum many-body systems with a tree tensor network. *Phys. Rev. A* **2006**, *74*, 022320. [CrossRef]
37. Tagliacozzo, L.; Evenbly, G.; Vidal, G. Simulation of two-dimensional quantum systems using a tree tensor network that exploits the entropic area law. *Phys. Rev. B* **2009**, *80*, 235127. [CrossRef]
38. VMurg; Verstraete, F.; Legeza, Ö.; Noack, R.M. Simulating strongly correlated quantum systems with tree tensor networks. *Phys. Rev. B* **2010**, *82*, 205105. [CrossRef]
39. Dumitrescu, E. Tree tensor network approach to simulating Shor's algorithm. *Phys. Rev. A* **2017**, *96*, 062322. [CrossRef]
40. Lopez-Piqueres, J.; Ware, B.; Vasseur, R. Mean-field entanglement transitions in random tree tensor networks. *Phys. Rev. B* **2020**, *102*, 064202. [CrossRef]
41. Wall, M.L.; D'Aguanno, G. Tree-tensor-network classifiers for machine learning: From quantum inspired to quantum assisted. *Phys. Rev. A* **2021**, *104*, 042408. [CrossRef]
42. Yang, L.-H.; Qi, X.-F.; Hou, J.-C. Nonlocal correlations in the tree-tensor-network configuration. *Phys. Rev. A* **2021**, *104*, 042405. [CrossRef]
43. Horodecki, R.; Horodecki, P.; Horodecki, M. Violating Bell inequality by mixed spin-$\frac{1}{2}$ states: Necessary and sufficient condition. *Phys. Lett. A* **1995**, *200*, 340. [CrossRef]

Article

A Distributed Architecture for Secure Delegated Quantum Computation

Shuquan Ma [1], Changhua Zhu [1,2,3,*], Dongxiao Quan [1] and Min Nie [3,4]

[1] State Key Laboratory of Integrated Services Networks, Xidian University, Xi'an 710071, China; msqloveslife@outlook.com (S.M.); dxquan@xidian.edu.cn (D.Q.)
[2] Collaborative Innovation Center of Quantum Information of Shaanxi Province, Xidian University, Xi'an 710071, China
[3] Shaanxi Key Laboratory of Information Communication Network and Security, Xi'an University of Posts & Telecommunications, Xi'an 710121, China; niemin@xupt.edu.cn
[4] School of Communications and Information Engineering, Xi'an University of Posts & Telecommunications, Xi'an 710121, China
* Correspondence: chhzhu@xidian.edu.cn

Abstract: In this paper, we propose a distributed secure delegated quantum computation protocol, by which an almost classical client can delegate a (dk)-qubit quantum circuit to d quantum servers, where each server is equipped with a $2k$-qubit register that is used to process only k qubits of the delegated quantum circuit. None of servers can learn any information about the input and output of the computation. The only requirement for the client is that he or she has ability to prepare four possible qubits in the state of $(|0\rangle + e^{i\theta}|1\rangle)/\sqrt{2}$, where $\theta \in \{0, \pi/2, \pi, 3\pi/2\}$. The only requirement for servers is that each pair of them share some entangled states $(|0\rangle|+\rangle + |1\rangle|-\rangle)/\sqrt{2}$ as ancillary qubits. Instead of assuming that all servers are interconnected directly by quantum channels, we introduce a third party in our protocol that is designed to distribute the entangled states between those servers. This would simplify the quantum network because the servers do not need to share a quantum channel. In the end, we show that our protocol can guarantee unconditional security of the computation under the situation where all servers, including the third party, are honest-but-curious and allowed to cooperate with each other.

Keywords: quantum computation; secure delegated computation; distributed architecture

1. Introduction

Quantum computing has been extensively studied from theory to practice [1,2]. It is widely accepted that noisy intermediate-scale quantum (NISQ) computers may be available in the coming decades [3]. However, the limited quantum memory of NISQ devices means that they may not have the capability to deal with large-scale quantum information processing. This is obviously a severe constraint, as many practical problems, e.g., *machine learning*, usually require immense memory overhead. A feasible way to overcome this obstacle is to utilize *distributed architecture* for quantum computations [4]. That is, using a group of small-scale quantum computers interconnected by classical and quantum networks to implement large-scale quantum computation tasks. However, considering the tremendous cost of building a quantum computer, it is not likely that ordinary consumers will be able to afford an NISQ computer in the foreseeable future. In fact, it is widely believed that the role of quantum computers is similar to today's classical supercomputers, which means only a few organizations or enterprises can have quantum computers at their disposal. Thus, for ordinary customers, a better way to access quantum computers is to delegate their computations to the companies that offer quantum computing as cloud services. Indeed, this computation pattern has been applied in today's Internet, e.g., IBM Quantum platform [5].

Delegated quantum computation is actually closely related to distributed quantum computation [4]. The client-to-server pattern in delegated computation naturally belongs to the category of distributed quantum computation. A class of delegated quantum computation protocols are constructed under the framework of measurement-based quantum computation (MBQC) [6–8], which is driven by a sequence of single-qubit measurements on some specific entangled state, where the entangled resource is also a basic module in the distributed quantum computation. Another class of delegated quantum computation protocols are obtained using the technique *quantum computing on encrypted data* (QCED) [9] or *quantum homomorphic encryption* (QHE) [10]. Although QCED and QHE are distinct concepts, the basic idea behind them is identical. Both of them use the *quantum one-time pad* to encrypt the input and output states but use different the methods to achieve the non-Clifford gates. Nevertheless, most schemes use the entangled states as the ancillary resources, for example [10–12].

Both distributed quantum computation and delegated quantum computation have been investigated broadly; see references [13–21] and [6,11,22–28], respectively. Typically, the distributed architecture for quantum computation makes use of photons as *flying qubits* between computational nodes, where each node is equipped with a quantum computer. The flying qubits are usually used to generate entangle states between distinct servers (i.e., nodes). By means of quantum entanglement, the non-local operations, such as controlled-NOT gate, can be done between two distant servers. Note that the quantum computer in each server is not necessarily an optical quantum computer; it can be made up of some other quantum system [29], such as ion traps or cloud atoms. Related experiments have been successfully demonstrated (see references [30,31]). Recently, researchers also investigated the possibility of simulating large-scale quantum systems in a hybrid quantum-classical manner [32]. That is, using a classical computer combined with a small quantum computer to simulate a large quantum computer [33]. However, the computational model considered in [32,33] is slightly different from the traditional model of circuit-based quantum computation. In this paper, we will not consider the method in [32], but rather the quantum entanglement to implement the non-local operation. In general, delegated quantum computation refers specifically to the *secure delegated quantum computation* (SDQC), which requires that no one except the client can obtain the right input and output of the computation. Typically, the client is required to have some basic quantum capacities, for example, preparing some single qubits or performing single-qubit measurements. In [34], the authors proposed a more rigorous SDQC protocol, which they called *universal blind quantum computation* (UBQC). The new protocol can guarantee that not only the input and output but also the computation itself, i.e., the algorithm, are unknown to the server. Although it seems that UBQC is more secure than SDQC, they are equivalent. That is, SDQC can be converted into UBQC [35]. As delegated quantum computation protocols effectively release the quantum resources in the client side, related experimental demonstrations have rapidly been implemented using the linear optics components (see References [9,25,36,37]).

Based on the above observations, in this paper we formally propose a distributed secure delegated quantum computation protocol that allows a half-classical client who can only prepare special single qubits to implement a large-scale quantum circuit on several quantum servers interconnected by entangled channels. Each server only has a limited quantum memory so that it can only compute a fraction of the delegated circuit. Moreover, during the computation, servers get nothing about the input and output of the computation. We also give a detailed security proof for our protocol. The rest of this paper is organized as follows. Section 2 introduces some basic preliminaries and notation. Section 3 presents the basic modules for delegated quantum computation. Section 4 gives the complete distributed delegated quantum computation protocol. Section 5 analyzes the security of our protocol. The last section discusses some remaining problems in our work.

2. Preliminaries and Notation

We assume that readers are familiar with the basics of quantum computation. In this work, we will use the following basic quantum gates:

$$Z|s\rangle = e^{is\pi}|s\rangle, \tag{1}$$

$$X|s\rangle = |s \oplus 1\rangle, \tag{2}$$

$$H|s\rangle = \frac{1}{\sqrt{2}}(|0\rangle + e^{is\pi}|1\rangle), \tag{3}$$

$$P|s\rangle = e^{i\frac{s}{2}\pi}|s\rangle, \tag{4}$$

$$T|s\rangle = e^{i\frac{s}{4}\pi}|s\rangle, \tag{5}$$

$$CZ|s,t\rangle = e^{ist\pi}|s,t\rangle, \tag{6}$$

where $s,t \in \{0,1\}$ and $i = \sqrt{-1}$; P and T refer to the phase gate and the $\pi/8$ gate, respectively; and CZ denotes the controlled-Z gate. In order to analyze conveniently, we also introduce the Z-rotation operator defined as follows:

$$R_z(\alpha) = \begin{pmatrix} e^{-i\frac{\alpha}{2}} & 0 \\ 0 & e^{i\frac{\alpha}{2}} \end{pmatrix}, \tag{7}$$

where $\alpha \in [0, 2\pi)$ is referred as the *rotation angle*. Regardless of the global phases, we can see that $Z \equiv R_z(\pi)$, $P \equiv R_z(\frac{\pi}{2})$, and $T \equiv R_z(\frac{\pi}{4})$. We use $|+_\varphi\rangle$ to denote the following single qubit:

$$|+_\varphi\rangle = \frac{|0\rangle + e^{i\varphi\pi}|1\rangle}{\sqrt{2}}, \tag{8}$$

where we consider $\varphi \in [0, 2\pi)$. It is clear that, up to an unimportant global phase, $R_z(\alpha)|+_\varphi\rangle \equiv |+_{(\varphi+\alpha)}\rangle$. Thus, φ is also called as the *rotation angle*. By this definition, we can see that $|+\rangle = |+_0\rangle$ and $|-\rangle = |+_\pi\rangle$. Note that for any $\theta \in [0, 2\pi)$ the states $|+_\theta\rangle$ and $|+_{(\theta+\pi)}\rangle$ comprise a basis, thus we can define a single-qubit measurement operator as follows:

$$M(\theta) = \sum_{s \in \{0,1\}} (-1)^s |+_{(\theta+s\pi)}\rangle\langle+_{(\theta+s\pi)}|, \tag{9}$$

where θ is referred as the *measurement angle* in this case, and $s \in \{0,1\}$ denotes the classical measurement outcome. Specifically, $s = 0$ if the post-measurement state is $|+_\theta\rangle$, otherwise $s = 1$. Finally, in this work we will also use a special two-qubit entangled state defined as follows:

$$|H\rangle = \frac{|0\rangle|+\rangle + |1\rangle|-\rangle}{\sqrt{2}}, \tag{10}$$

which can be prepared by applying a CZ gate on two qubits $|+\rangle|+\rangle$.

3. Secure Delegated Quantum Computation

In this work, the delegated quantum computation model we adopt is from [38], in which the authors improved the original QCED protocol [11] in two aspects. First, the quantum capacities of clients are further reduced. In theory, they only need to prepare the qubits $|+_\varphi\rangle$, where $\varphi \in \{0, \frac{\pi}{2}, \pi, \frac{3\pi}{2}\}$. Second, the security of the protocol can be still guaranteed even if some information is leaked to servers.

First of all, we specify that the client's input is encoded in X basis. That is, encoding 0 and 1 as $|+\rangle$ and $|-\rangle$, respectively. Let $x = x_1 x_2 \cdots x_n \in \{0,1\}^n$ be the n-bit classical input string, then the corresponding encoded input state can be expressed as $|+_{x\pi}\rangle \equiv |+_{x_1\pi}\rangle|+_{x_2\pi}\rangle \cdots |+_{x_n\pi}\rangle$. For simplicity, we abbreviate $|+_{x\pi}\rangle$ as $|+_x\rangle$. The universal gate set we consider is $\mathbb{U} = \{X, Z, P, T, H, CZ\}$. Note that this gate set is not minimal because X, Z, and P can be obtained from $\{T, H\}$. Despite that, additional basic gates can effectively decrease the circuit complexity.

Now suppose the client's input state is $|+_x\rangle$, where $x \in \{0,1\}^n$. In [38], the client uses the random operator $X_i^{a_i} Z_i^{b_i} P_i^{c_i}$ to encrypt each qubit $|+_{x_i}\rangle$, where $x_i \in \{0,1\}$, and $a_i, b_i, c_i \in \{0,1\}$ are referred as the *encryption keys*, and for any operator U we define $U^0 = I$ and $U^1 = U$. The subscript i in X_i, Z_i, and P_i is used to denote that the corresponding gate is applied on the ith qubit (hereinafter referred to as qubit i). Similarly, the subscript i in a_i, b_i, c_i is used to denote that the corresponding encryption keys are related to qubit i. We can check that this encryption scheme is a quantum one-time pad (see Equation (11)), thus it provides an information-theoretical security for any qubit ρ.

$$\frac{1}{4} \sum_{a,b,c \in \{0,1\}} X^a Z^b P^c \rho P^{3c} Z^b X^a = \frac{I}{2}. \tag{11}$$

In theory, to achieve this encryption, the client needs to perform random gates P^c, Z^b, and X^a on the state ρ in sequence. However, for the qubit $|+_{x_i}\rangle$, it can be easily verified that

$$X^{a_i} Z^{b_i} P^{c_i} |+_{x_i}\rangle \equiv |+_{\varphi_i}\rangle, \tag{12}$$

where $\varphi_i = (-1)^{a_i}(x_i + b_i + \frac{c_i}{2})\pi \mod 2\pi \in \{0, \frac{\pi}{2}, \pi, \frac{3\pi}{2}\}$. Thus, instead of preparing $|+_{x_i}\rangle$ then encrypting it by $X_i^{a_i} Z_i^{b_i} P_i^{c_i}$, the client can directly generate the encrypted qubit. Specifically, given the ith input bit $x_i \in \{0,1\}$, the client randomly chooses the corresponding encryption keys $a_i, b_i, c_i \in \{0,1\}$, then computes the value $\varphi_i = (-1)^{a_i}(x_i + b_i + \frac{c_i}{2})\pi \mod 2\pi$. Finally, the client prepares the qubit $|+_{\varphi_i}\rangle$ as the encrypted qubit i.

After preparing all encrypted input qubits, the client sends them to the server. The server then performs the delegated quantum circuit U on the encrypted qubits. Here, the circuit U is known to both client and server (they can negotiate in advance via a classical channel). We assume that this circuit has been decomposed into a sequence of basic gates from the gate set $\mathbb{U}$. That is, $U = U_m U_{m-1} \cdots U_2 U_1$, where each $U_i \in \mathbb{U}$ and the positive integer number m is the total number of gates. The following identities, which all hold up to an irrelevant global phase, can be easily verified.

$$X_i(X_i^{a_i} Z_i^{b_i} P_i^{c_i}) \equiv (X_i^{a_i} Z_i^{b_i \oplus c_i} P_i^{c_i}) X_i, \tag{13}$$

$$Z_i(X_i^{a_i} Z_i^{b_i} P_i^{c_i}) \equiv (X_i^{a_i} Z_i^{b_i} P_i^{c_i}) Z_i, \tag{14}$$

$$P_i(X_i^{a_i} Z_i^{b_i} P_i^{c_i}) \equiv (X_i^{a_i} Z_i^{a_i \oplus b_i} P_i^{c_i}) P_i, \tag{15}$$

$$T_i(X_i^{a_i} Z_i^{b_i} P_i^{c_i}) \equiv (X_i^{a_i} Z_i^{a_i \oplus b_i \oplus (a_i c_i)} P_i^{a_i \oplus c_i}) T_i, \tag{16}$$

$$CZ_{i,j}(X_i^{a_i} Z_i^{b_i} P_i^{c_i} X_j^{a_j} Z_j^{b_j} P_j^{c_j}) \equiv (X_i^{a_i} Z_i^{a_j \oplus b_i} P_i^{c_i} X_j^{a_j} Z_j^{a_i \oplus b_j} P_j^{c_j}) CZ_{i,j}. \tag{17}$$

It follows from Equations (13)–(17) that the basic gates X, Z, P, T, CZ are *commutable* with the encryption operator $X^a Z^b P^c$, although the encryption keys may need to be updated. For example, Equation (13) indicates that performing an $X_i^{a_i} Z_i^{b_i} P_i^{c_i}$ followed by an X_i is equivalent to performing an X_i followed by an $X_i^{a_i} Z_i^{b_i \oplus c_i} P_i^{c_i}$. Thus, the client only needs to update the value of b_i such that $b_i := b_i \oplus c_i$. The cases for Z_i, P_i, T_i, and $CZ_{i,j}$ follow the same reason. The related updating rules of encryption keys are shown in Equations (14)–(17). Note, however, that the commutativity noted above is not suited for the Hadamard gate H, as there is no $HP^c \equiv P^{c'} H$ for any $c, c' \in \{0,1\}$. In [38], the authors proposed a quantum teleportation scheme that they called the *H-gadget* (see Figure 1) so as to implement the H gate in a similar manner. Specifically, the client needs to prepare two ancillary qubits $|+_{\alpha_i}\rangle, |+_{\beta_i}\rangle$ and a measurement angle θ_i, where α_i and β_i are chosen randomly, whereas θ_i can be determined by the following way.

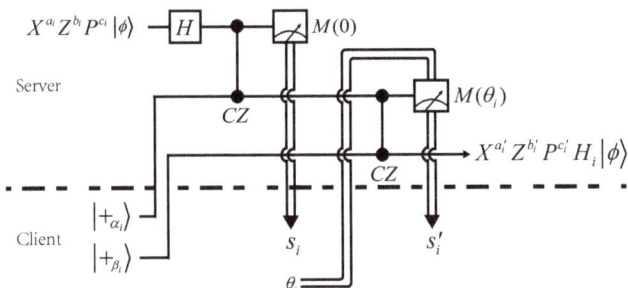

Figure 1. The H-gadget in Ref. [38], which is designed for implementing an H gate on an encrypted qubit i, where $s_i, s'_i \in \{0, 1\}$ are the measurement outcomes and $\alpha_i, \beta_i \in \{0, \frac{\pi}{2}, \pi, \frac{3\pi}{2}\}$ are the rotation angles of two ancillary qubits, and $\theta_i \in \{0, \frac{\pi}{2}, \pi, \frac{3\pi}{2}\}$ is the measurement angle of the second measurement.

Note that for any $\alpha_i, \beta_i \in \{0, \frac{\pi}{2}, \pi, \frac{3\pi}{2}\}$, we can express them uniquely as follows:

$$\alpha_i = (d_i + \frac{e_i}{2})\pi, \beta_i = (f_i + \frac{g_i}{2})\pi, \tag{18}$$

where $d_i, e_i, f_i, g_i \in \{0, 1\}$. Thus, the client can first generate random bits d_i, e_i, f_i, g_i then compute the values of α_i and β_i. To determine θ_i, the client generates a random bit, denoted by $h_i \in \{0, 1\}$, then computes θ_i such that

$$\theta_i = [h_i \oplus b_i \oplus d_i \oplus (a_i c_i) \oplus (s_i c_i) \oplus (c_i e_i)]\pi + \frac{c_i \oplus e_i}{2}\pi. \tag{19}$$

Note also that θ_i is relevant to the measurement outcome s_i, which means it can be determined until the client obtains the first measurement outcome s_i from the server. Nevertheless, in theory, all qubits including ancillary qubits can be sent to the server before the computation begins. Thus, the complete procedure is classically interactive. Finally, the updating rule for H is shown as follows:

$$a'_i = s'_i \oplus h_i, b'_i = a_i \oplus s_i \oplus f_i \oplus [g_i(s'_i \oplus h_i)], c'_i = g_i, \tag{20}$$

where a'_i, b'_i, c'_i denote the updated encryption keys related to qubit i. The correctness of the H-gadget is given in the Appendix A. The detailed security proof of the protocol can be found in [38].

4. Distributed Architecture for Secure Delegated Quantum Computations

In this section, we give a simple scheme to implement the non-local CZ gate between two quantum servers. Our method uses the entangled state $|H\rangle$ (see Equation (10) for its definition) as ancillary qubits. The similar schemes have been studied intensively, for example, in [39,40]. The basic circuit is shown in Figure 2a. In the following content, we first verify the circuit identity shown in Figure 2, then, based on this circuit identity, we construct a distributed architecture for secure delegated quantum computations.

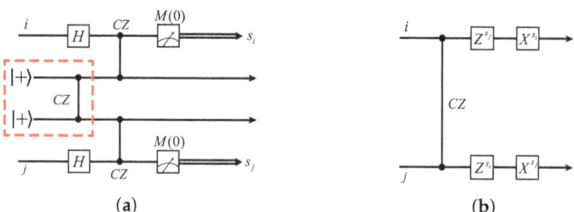

Figure 2. (a) The basic circuit used to implement a non-local CZ gate on two distant qubits i and j, where the partial circuit in the red dotted box is used to generate the entangled state $|H\rangle$. (b) The equivalent quantum circuit for (a).

We start with a circuit named *X-teleportation* [40] (see Figure 3a), which is easy to verify.

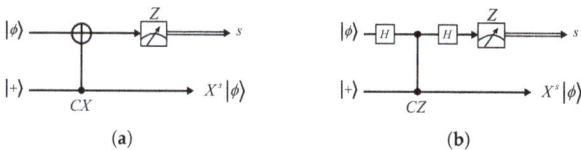

Figure 3. (a) The original X-teleportation in [40]; (b) the X-teleportation that replaces the CX with a CZ and two H gates. In both circuits, the measurement is performed under Z basis.

First, we substitute a CZ and two H gates for the CX gate, obtaining the equivalent circuit, as shown in Figure 3b. We then convert the measurement basis from Z to X by the following identity (see Figure 4), which is also easy to verify. Finally, we obtain a variant of the X-teleportation that consists of H, CZ, and X-basis measurement, as shown in Figure 5.

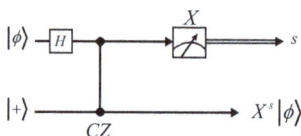

Figure 4. Measurement identity that converts Z-basis to X-basis.

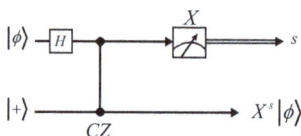

Figure 5. The variant X-teleportation consisting of CZ and H gates, where the measurement basis is X.

We now turn back to Figure 2a. Note first that the CZ gate commutes with itself, thus the circuit can be reorganized, as in Figure 6a. Obviously, the partial circuits in the red-dotted line and blue-dotted line boxes are exactly the same circuit as the one in Figure 5, where $X = M(0)$. Therefore, we can see that, after measuring qubits i, j, the rest qubits and the rest CZ gate comprise the circuit as, in Figure 6b. Finally, we use the following identity to exchange the positions of X and CZ, which can be easily verified:

$$CZ \cdot (X^s \otimes I) = (X^s \otimes Z^s) \cdot CZ, \qquad (21)$$

where $s \in \{0, 1\}$. Substituting the above identity in Figure 6b and considering the symmetry of CZ gate, we immediately obtain the desired circuit, as shown in Figure 2b.

Considering the encryption operators $X_i^{a_i} Z_i^{b_i} P_i^{c_i}$ and $X_j^{a_j} Z_j^{b_j} P_j^{c_j}$ on qubits i and j, we can see from Figure 6b that the non-local CZ can be thought to be performed on qubits i, j, which are encrypted by $X_i^{a_i \oplus s_i} Z_i^{b_i} P_i^{c_i}$ and $X_j^{a_j \oplus s_j} Z_j^{b_j} P_j^{c_j}$, thus according to the updating rule shown in Equation (17), we immediately obtain the updating rule of the non-local CZ gate as follows:

$$\begin{cases} a'_i = a_i \oplus s_i, \\ b'_i = a_j \oplus s_j \oplus b_i, \\ c'_i = c_i, \end{cases} \quad \begin{cases} a'_j = a_j \oplus s_j, \\ b'_j = a_i \oplus s_i \oplus b_j, \\ c'_j = c_j. \end{cases} \quad (22)$$

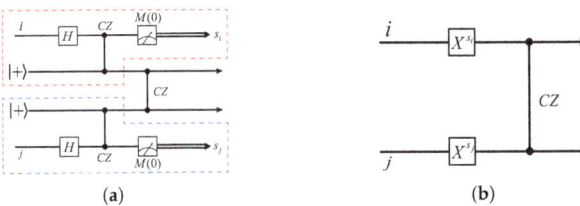

Figure 6. (a) The equivalent form of the circuit shown in Figure 2a. (b) The resulting circuit after measuring qubits i, j.

Based on the above analysis, we construct a distributed architecture for secure delegated quantum computation, where a classical client equipped with some qubit generator can delegate an n-qubit circuit to d small-scale quantum servers. Without loss of generality, we assume that $n = dk$. In this configuration, each server typically needs a $2k$-qubit register to process k input qubits of the n-qubit circuit. That is, for each qubit in the n-qubit circuit, the server needs a 2-qubit register to simulate it. To make sure $2k < n$, it requires that $d > 2$. We show this distributed architecture in Figure 7. Note that there is a special third party in this distributed architecture, which is used to generate and distribute entangled states $|H\rangle$ between all quantum servers. Thus, all servers do not need to be interconnected directly by a quantum (even classical) channel, as there is no information exchange between servers during the computation.

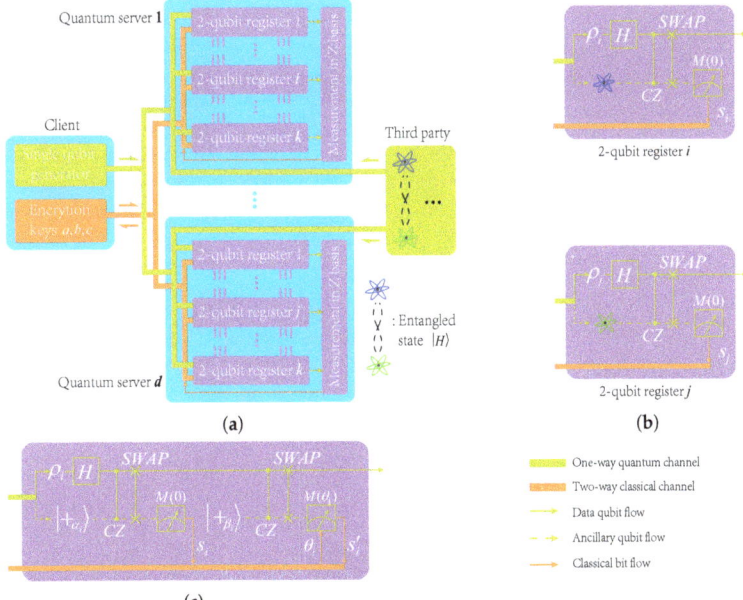

Figure 7. (a) The distributed architecture for secure delegated quantum computations; (b) the circuits for a CZ gate between two nonlocal registers i and j; (c) the circuit for an H gate in any register i.

We give the complete procedure of the protocol in terms of pseudo-code (see Algorithms 1–3). For simplicity, we use $\mathcal{C}$ and $\{\mathcal{S}_q\}_{q=1}^d$ to denote the client and d servers, respectively. That is, the qth quantum server is referred to as $\mathcal{S}_q$. As noted, each server only processes k input qubits of the n-qubit delegated circuit. More specifically, for $\mathcal{S}_q$, it only processes the qubits indexed by $(q-1)k+1, (q-1)k+2, \cdots, qk$. Thus, in the case of no confusion, we also use $\mathcal{S}_q = \{(q-1)k+1, (q-1)k+2, \cdots, qk\}$ to denote the corresponding qubits. In addition, the delegated circuit U is formally expressed as $U = U_m^{p_m} U_{m-1}^{p_{m-1}} \cdots U_1^{p_1}$, where $p_i \subset \{1, 2, \ldots, n\}$ denotes the qubits on which the basic gate U_i is exerted. For example, if $U_i^{p_i}$ is a CZ gate on qubits k and l, then $p_i = \{k, l\}$. By this definition, we can see that there must be $p_i \subset \mathcal{S}_q$ if $U_i^{p_i}$ is a local gate in $\mathcal{S}_q$, otherwise it only can be $p_i \subset \mathcal{S}_q \cup \mathcal{S}_{q'}$ for some $\mathcal{S}_q$ and $\mathcal{S}_{q'}$.

Algorithm 1 Distributed Secure Delegated Quantum Computations
---

Input: $x = x_1 x_2 \cdots x_n$ // private against all $\mathcal{S}_q$
$\qquad\quad U = U_m^{p_m} U_{m-1}^{p_{m-1}} \cdots U_1^{p_1}$ // public for $\mathcal{C}$ and all $\mathcal{S}_q$
Output: $y = y_1 y_2 \cdots y_n$ // private against all $\mathcal{S}_q$

1: $\mathcal{C}$ generates $a, b, c \leftarrow_R \{0,1\}^n$ and computes rotation angles $(\varphi_1, \ldots, \varphi_n)$ according to Equation (12), then prepares $|+_{\varphi_1}\rangle \cdots |+_{\varphi_n}\rangle$ as the encrypted input state, finally sends the qubits $(q-1)k+1, q(k-1)+2, \cdots, qk$ to $\mathcal{S}_q$ where $q = 1, 2, \cdots, d$. Specifically, $\mathcal{C}$ sends the qubits $1, 2, \cdots, k$ to $\mathcal{S}_1$ then sends the qubits $k+1, k+2, \cdots, 2k$ to $\mathcal{S}_2$, and so on
2: **for** $i \leftarrow 1, m$ **do**
3: $\quad$ **if** $U_i^{p_i} \in \{X, Z, P, T, H\}$ and $p_i \subset \mathcal{S}_q$ for some $q \in \{1, 2, \cdots, d\}$ **then**
4: $\quad\quad$ **if** $U_i^{p_i}$ is not H **then**
5: $\quad\quad\quad$ $\mathcal{S}_q$ performs $U_i^{p_i}$ on qubit p_i while $\mathcal{C}$ updates the encryption keys of this qubit according to the updating rules shown in Equations (13)–(16)
6: $\quad\quad$ **else**
7: $\quad\quad\quad$ $\mathcal{C}$ calls the **procedure** HADAMARD(p_i, q) (See Algorithm 2)
8: $\quad\quad$ **end if**
9: $\quad$ **else** // $U_i^{p_i}$ is a CZ gate on qubits p_i
10: $\quad\quad$ **if** $p_i \subset \mathcal{S}_q$ for some $q \in \{1, 2, \cdots, d\}$ **then**
11: $\quad\quad\quad$ $\mathcal{S}_q$ performs $U_i^{p_i}$ on qubits p_i while $\mathcal{C}$ updates the encryption keys of those qubits according to the updating rule shown in Equation (17)
12: $\quad\quad$ **else** // $p_i \subset \mathcal{S}_q \cup \mathcal{S}_{q'}$ for some $q, q' \in \{1, 2, \cdots, d\}$
13: $\quad\quad\quad$ $\mathcal{C}$ calls the **procedure** NONLOCAL-CZ(p_i, q, q') (See Algorithm 3)
14: $\quad\quad$ **end if**
15: $\quad$ **end if**
16: **end for**
17: Each server measures the final k qubits in Z basis, then sends the measurement outcomes to $\mathcal{C}$ // let $\tilde{y} \in \{0,1\}^n$ be the result collected from all servers
18: $\mathcal{C}$ computes the output $y = \tilde{y} \oplus a$. // a is the X encryption keys of the final state

---
Algorithm 2 Implement an H gate on qubit i where i is in $\mathcal{S}_q$

1: **procedure** HADAMARD(i, q) // qubit i is encrypted by $X^{a_i} Z^{b_i} P^{c_i}$
2:     $\mathcal{C}$ generates $d_i, e_i \leftarrow_R \{0,1\}$ and computes the angle α_i according to Equation (18), then prepares and sends the ancillary qubit $|+_{\alpha_i}\rangle$ to $\mathcal{S}_q$
3:     $\mathcal{S}_q$ performs H_i and CZ gates on qubit i and $|+_{\alpha_i}\rangle$, then measures qubit i and sends the measurement outcome s_i to $\mathcal{C}$, finally labels the ancillary qubit as i
4:     $\mathcal{C}$ generates $f_i, g_i, h_i \leftarrow_R \{0,1\}$ and computes the angles β_i and θ_i according to Equations (18) and (19), respectively, then prepares the ancillary qubit $|+_{\beta_i}\rangle$ and sends it with θ_i to $\mathcal{S}_q$
5:     $\mathcal{S}_q$ performs a CZ gate on qubit i and $|+_{\beta_i}\rangle$, then measures qubit i with $M(\theta_i)$ and sends the measurement outcome s'_i to $\mathcal{C}$, finally labels the ancillary qubit as i
6:     $\mathcal{C}$ updates the encryption keys of qubit i according to Equation (20)
7: **end procedure**

Algorithm 3 Implement a nonlocal CZ gate on qubits i and j where i is in $\mathcal{S}_q$ while j is in $\mathcal{S}_{q'}$, that is, $\{i, j\} \subset \mathcal{S}_q \cup \mathcal{S}_{q'}$

1: **procedure** NONLOCAL-CZ$(\{i, j\}, q, q')$ // qubits i and j are encrypted by $X^{a_i} Z^{b_i} P^{c_i}$ and $X^{a_j} Z^{b_j} P^{c_j}$, respectively
2:     $\mathcal{C}$ delegates the third party to prepare an entangled state $|H\rangle$ and distribute it to $\mathcal{S}_q$ and $\mathcal{S}_{q'}$, that is, each server holds one qubit of $|H\rangle$ as the ancillary qubit
3:     $\mathcal{S}_q$ ($\mathcal{S}_{q'}$) performs H_i (H_j) and CZ gates on qubit i (j) and its ancillary qubit, then measures qubit i (j) and sends the measurement outcome s_i (s_j) to $\mathcal{C}$, finally labels its ancillary qubit as i (j)
4:     $\mathcal{C}$ updates the encryption keys of qubits i and j according to Equation (22)
5: **end procedure**

5. The Security of the Distributed Delegated Quantum Computation

We show that our protocol can guarantee the unconditional privacy of the input and output of the computation. We only consider that all servers and the third party who serves as an entanglement resource are *honest-but-curious*, which means they follow the algorithm honestly but try to obtain the information about the input and output. For example, they may record all classical information generated during the computation and cooperate with each other, even with the third party.

For the input, the conclusion is obvious as the client encrypts each input qubit by a quantum one-time pad. Therefore, to complete the proof, we only need to prove that the output state of the computation is also encrypted by a *unbiased* quantum one-time pad. In other words, there is no information leakage about the encryption keys during the computation. From the procedures of Algorithm 1, we can see that only when the client calls the **procedures** HADAMARD and NONLOCAL-CZ will there be an interaction between client and servers. In the other cases, the algorithm is non-interactive, which means there is no information leakage about the encryption keys from client to server as they do not exchange any information. Based on this observation, we infer that to prove the privacy we only need to analyze the procedures that implement the H and the nonlocal CZ gates.

We first consider the **procedure** HADAMARD(i, q). In the following content, we use $\mathcal{S}$ to denote all servers including the *untrusted* third party. According to Algorithm 2, we can see that given the qubit i encrypted by $X^{a_i} Z^{b_i} P^{c_i}$ where $i \subset \mathcal{S}_q$, $\mathcal{S}$ controls two ancillary qubits $Z^{d_i} P^{e_i} |+\rangle$ and $Z^{f_i} P^{g_i} |+\rangle$, and receives a measurement angle θ_i from $\mathcal{C}$, it also generates two measurement outcomes $s_i, s'_i \in \{0, 1\}$ from two independent measurements. We can infer from the below state evolution that the measurement outcomes s_i, s'_i are uniformly random, thus $\mathcal{S}$ can obtain no information gain about any encryption keys according to s_i and s'_i.

$$|\phi\rangle |+\rangle \xrightarrow{H \otimes I} (H|\phi\rangle)|+\rangle \xrightarrow{CZ} \frac{|+\rangle}{\sqrt{2}} |\phi\rangle + \frac{|-\rangle}{\sqrt{2}} X|\phi\rangle . \tag{23}$$

The only available information to $\mathcal{S}$ now is the measurement angle θ_i. Let θ_i be $u_i\pi + \frac{v_i\pi}{2}$, where $u_i, v_i \in \{0, 1\}$, then according to Equation (19), we know that u_i and v_i can be expressed as follows:

$$u_i = h_i \oplus b_i \oplus d_i \oplus (a_ic_i) \oplus (s_ic_i) \oplus (c_ie_i), \tag{24a}$$

$$v_i = c_i \oplus e_i, \tag{24b}$$

where u_i, v_i, and s_i are known to $\mathcal{S}$. Intuitively, given u_i, v_i, and s_i, no server can determine the correct values of $a_i, b_i, c_i, d_i, e_i, h_i$, as there are six variables in two equations. Nevertheless, $\mathcal{S}$ may gain some information utilizing u_i and v_i. For example, if $v_i = 1$, then $\mathcal{S}$ can infer that $c_ie_i = 0$. Substituting this into Equation (24a), $\mathcal{S}$ can obtain a simplified equality $u_i = h_i \oplus b_i \oplus d_i \oplus (a_i \oplus s_i)c_i$. Despite this fact, we can show that there is no information leakage about all variables from a_i to h_i. That is, we prove that in the view of $\mathcal{S}$, the following equality holds true:

$$\Pr[r_i|u_i, v_i] = \Pr[r_i] = \frac{1}{2}, \tag{25}$$

where the random variable r_i represents the possible parameters $\{a_i, b_i, c_i, d_i, e_i, f_i, g_i, h_i\}$. To see that, we need to know the following simple facts.

First, if $x, y \in \{0, 1\}$ and x is uniform, i.e., $x \in_R \{0, 1\}$, then $x \oplus y$ is also uniform. Second, if $x, y \in \{0, 1\}$ are uniform and let $z = x \oplus y$, then $\Pr[x|z] = \Pr[x] = 1/2$. Finally, if $x, y_1, y_2 \in \{0, 1\}$ and x is uniform, let $z = x \oplus (y_1y_2)$, then $\Pr[y_1|z] = \Pr[y_1]$. These three basic facts can be easily verified. With these facts, we can complete our proof. Define $\xi_i = b_i \oplus d_i \oplus (a_ic_i) \oplus (s_ic_i) \oplus (c_ie_i)$ so that $u_i = h_i \oplus \xi_i$. As $b_i, d_i \in_R \{0, 1\}$, we first know that $\xi_i \in_R \{0, 1\}$. Furthermore, as $h_i, \xi_i \in_R \{0, 1\}$, we can get that $\Pr[h_i|u_i] = \Pr[h_i] = 1/2$. Likewise, we can also get $\Pr[b_i|u_i] = \Pr[b_i] = 1/2$ and $\Pr[d_i|u_i] = \Pr[d_i] = 1/2$. For $a_i \in_R \{0, 1\}$, define $\tilde{\xi}_i = h_i \oplus b_i \oplus d_i \oplus (s_ic_i) \oplus (c_ie_i)$ so that $u_i = \tilde{\xi}_i \oplus (a_ic_i)$, from which we can infer that $\Pr[a_i|u_i] = \Pr[a_i] = 1/2$. Note that h_i, b_i, d_i, and a_i are irrelevant to v_i, which means $\Pr[r_i|u_i, v_i] = \Pr[r_i|u_i]$ for any $r_i \in \{h_i, b_i, d_i, a_i\}$. As for $c_i, e_i \in_R \{0, 1\}$, as they are related to both u_i and v_i, in order to simplify our analysis, we define $h'_i = h_i \oplus (a_ic_i)$, $b'_i = b_i \oplus (s_ic_i)$, and $d'_i = d_i \oplus (c_ie_i)$, then obtain that $u_i = h'_i \oplus b'_i \oplus d'_i$. Clearly, $h'_i, b'_i, d'_i \in_R \{0, 1\}$, so c_i and e_i are only related to v_i. By this, we can easily get that $\Pr[c_i|u_i, v_i] = \Pr[c_i|v_i] = \Pr[c_i] = 1/2$ and $\Pr[e_i|u_i, v_i] = \Pr[e_i|v_i] = \Pr[e_i] = 1/2$. Finally, f_i and $g_i \in_R \{0, 1\}$ are obviously irrelevant to u_i and v_i (see Equations (24a) and (24b)), which means $\Pr[f_i|u_i, v_i] = \Pr[f_i] = 1/2$ and $\Pr[g_i|u_i, v_i] = \Pr[g_i] = 1/2$. So far, we have proved the statement in Equation (25), from which we know that the servers can obtain no information gain about $a_i, b_i, c_i, d_i, e_i, f_i, g_i, h_i$ from the θ_i. Thus, after the **procedure** HADAMARD(i, q), the updated keys a'_i, b'_i, c'_i are also secure.

Finally, we consider the **procedure** NONLOCAL-CZ($\{i, j\}, q, q'$), where $\{i, j\} \in \mathcal{S}_q \cup \mathcal{S}_{q'}$. Note that in this procedure, $\mathcal{S}$ can only obtain two independent and uniform measurement outcomes s_i, s_j. According to the updating rules shown in Equation (22), we can see that as long as the encryption keys $\{a_i, b_i, c_i\}$ and $\{a_j, b_j, c_j\}$ are secure then the updated keys will also be secure against the servers. As a result, we conclude that, from the perspective of all servers, the output state of the computation is still encrypted by a sound quantum one-time pad.

6. Discussion

In this work, we proposed a secure distributed delegated quantum computation protocol, which allows clients to delegate their private computation to several quantum servers. We have shown that unconditional security of the input and output of the computation can be guaranteed as long as all servers follow the protocol honestly. Nevertheless, there are some notable problems in our work when we consider it in practice. In the end of this paper, we discuss those practical problems.

First, note that our protocol can only work well in a noise-free environment. To make our protocol fault-tolerant, we assume that each quantum server must be capable of performing *fault-tolerant quantum computation* [41]. However, this would inevitably increase the overhead of ancillary qubits. In addition, we need to consider two channel noises: one is between the client and each server, the other is between the third party and each server. The former will introduce errors in the input state, whereas the latter will introduce errors in the entangled state. There are some methods to remedy this problem. For the input state, the client can utilize some *quantum error-correct code* [42] to protect each qubit. However, it requires that the client can perform additional quantum operations. As for the entangled state, each pair of servers can use some *quantum entanglement distill* [43] protocol to obtain the entangled states with high fidelity. Similarly, it requires additional local operations and classical communications between the servers.

Second, note that our protocol can only protect the security of the input and output of the computation. This is because the model of the delegated quantum computation we used in our work is SDQC protocol instead of UBQC protocol. Nevertheless, we can convert, in principle, a SDQC protocol into a UBQC protocol. To do that, we first encode the delegated circuit U as a binary string denoted by $C(U)$. Next, according to the quantum computation theory [44], there exists a universal quantum circuit $\mathcal{U}$ such that

$$\mathcal{U} |+_{C(U)}\rangle |+_x\rangle = |+_{C(U)}\rangle U |+_x\rangle, \tag{26}$$

where the input of the universal circuit $\mathcal{U}$ consists of two parts: $|+_x\rangle$ is the input state of U and $|+_{C(U)}\rangle$ is the canonical and quantum description of the circuit U. Performing this universal circuit $\mathcal{U}$ in our protocol, we can apparently achieve a blind distributed delegated quantum computation.

Last, we should note that in this work we only consider the honest servers and the third party who perform the protocol as the client desires. However, a real server may not follow the protocol honestly, and an untrusted third party may prepare some other entangled states for the servers. To detect such a malicious server including the untrusted third party, we should introduce a verification mechanics in our protocol. Indeed, verification is an important topic in the quantum computation theory (see [45,46]). There is an easy way to achieve the verification in our protocol. Specifically, given the delegated circuit U, the client can introduce another small quantum circuit V, for example, a permutation circuit [47], which is easy to simulate on a classical computer. The client then randomly inserts the qubits of V into the circuit U and runs this hybrid circuit on the universal quantum circuit $\mathcal{U}$. After the computation, the client check the result of V; if the result does not match the desired, then the client rejects the output.

Author Contributions: Conceptualization, S.M. and C.Z.; formal analysis, S.M.; funding acquisition, C.Z. and D.Q.; methodology, S.M.; supervision, C.Z. and M.N.; validation, C.Z. and D.Q.; writing—original draft, S.M.; writing—review and editing, C.Z. All authors have read and agreed to the published version of the manuscript.

Funding: This work is supported by the National Natural Science Foundation of China (Grant Nos. 62001351, 61372076, 61971348); Natural Science Basic Research Program of Shaanxi, China (Grant No. 2021JM-142); Foundation of Shaanxi Key Laboratory of Information Communication Network and Security (ICNS201802); Key Research and Development Program of Shaanxi Province (2019ZDLGY09-02).

Institutional Review Board Statement: Not applicable.

Informed Consent Statement: Not applicable.

Data Availability Statement: Not applicable.

Conflicts of Interest: The authors declare no conflict of interest.

Appendix A. The Correctness of the H-Gadget

In this section, we briefly prove the correctness of the H-gadget proposed in [38]. We first translate the circuit of this gadget (see Figure 1) into an equivalent form. Note that the ancillary qubits $|+_{\alpha_i}\rangle = R_z(\alpha_i)|+\rangle$, $|+_{\beta_i}\rangle = R_z(\beta_i)|+\rangle$ and any Z-rotation operator is commutable with the controlled-Z gate, thus the circuit of the H-gadget can be expressed equivalently as follows:

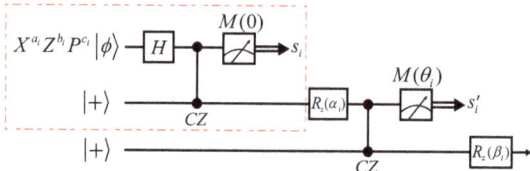

Figure A1. An equivalent circuit of the H-gadget of [38].

In Section 4, we obtained a variant X-teleportation (see Figure 5), which is identical to the above circuit in the red-dotted box. According to this, we can infer immediately that after performing the measurement $M(0)$, the rest circuit is equivalent to the following form, where the operator $R_z(\alpha_i)$ has been absorbed into the input state.

We then use the identity shown in Figure A2, which is easy to verify. Applying this measurement identity to the circuit in Figure A3, we can obtain the following circuit (see Figure A4), where we exchange the positions of $R_z(\theta_i)$ and CZ, and insert a pair of H gates between them. Obviously, the partial circuit in Figure A4 surrounded by the red-dotted box is the variant X-teleportation. Thus, we can infer that after the measurement the remaining qubit will be

$$R_z(\beta_i) X^{s'_i} H R_z(\alpha_i - \theta_i) X^{a_i \oplus s_i} Z^{b_i} P^{c_i} |\phi\rangle \tag{A1}$$

where $R_z(\beta_i)$ is the Z-rotation operator in the end.

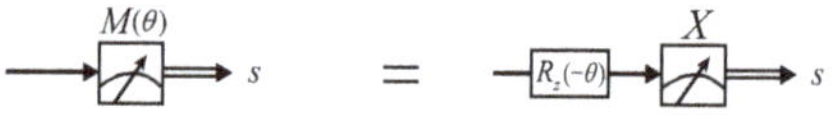

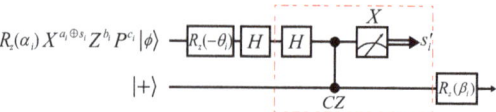

Figure A2. Measurement identity that converts $M(\theta)$ basis to X basis.

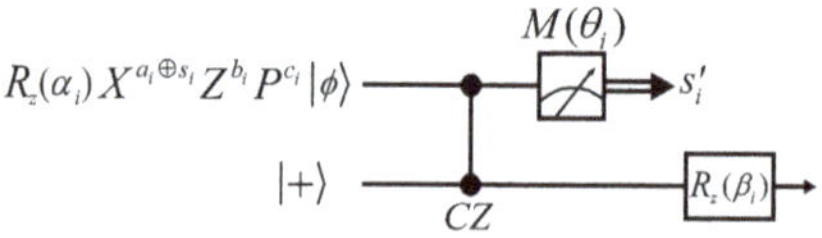

Figure A3. The rest circuit after performing the measurement $M(0)$ on the top line.

Figure A4. The variant X-teleportation where the input qubit is $HR_z(\alpha_i - \theta_i) X^{a_i \oplus s_i} Z^{b_i} P^{c_i} |\phi\rangle$.

In the following content, we simplify this output qubit. For simplicity, we temporarily drop the subscript i and define $R_z(\gamma) \equiv Z^b P^c$, that is, $\gamma = (b + \frac{c}{2})\pi$. It is easy to check that $X^a R_z(\theta) X^a = R_z((-1)^a \theta)$ for any θ. Thus, the output qubit can be rewritten as follows:

$$
\begin{aligned}
&R_z(\beta) X^{s'} H R_z(\alpha - \theta) X^{a \oplus s} R_z(\gamma) |\phi\rangle \\
&= X^{s'} R_z\left((-1)^{s'}\beta\right) H X^{a \oplus s} R_z\left((-1)^{a \oplus s}(\alpha - \theta)\right) R_z(\gamma) |\phi\rangle \\
&= X^{s'} R_z\left((-1)^{s'}\beta\right) Z^{a \oplus s} H R_z\left(\gamma + (-1)^{a \oplus s}(\alpha - \theta)\right) |\phi\rangle \\
&= X^{s'} R_z\left((-1)^{s'}\beta + (a \oplus s)\pi\right) H R_z\left(\gamma + (-1)^{a \oplus s}(\alpha - \theta)\right) |\phi\rangle
\end{aligned}
\tag{A2}
$$

Let $\theta = (-1)^{a \oplus s}\gamma + \alpha + h\pi$, where $h \in \{0,1\}$. Note that θ here is seemingly not the same as the one defined in Equation (19). Despite that, we will show they are exactly the same one. Substitute θ in the above equation, we can easily get the following result:

$$
X^{s'} R_z\left((-1)^{s'}\beta + (a \oplus s)\pi\right) H R_z\left(-(-1)^{a \oplus s} h\pi\right) |\phi\rangle. \tag{A3}
$$

As R_z is an operator with a period of 2π, which means $R_z(\pi) \equiv R_z(-\pi) \equiv Z$, thus the output qubit can be expressed as follows:

$$
\begin{aligned}
&X^{s'} R_z\left((-1)^{s'}\beta + (a \oplus s)\pi\right) H Z^h |\phi\rangle \\
&= X^{s'} R_z\left((-1)^{s'}\beta + (a \oplus s)\pi\right) X^h H |\phi\rangle \\
&= X^{s' \oplus h} R_z\left((-1)^{s' \oplus h}\beta + (-1)^h(a \oplus s)\pi\right) H |\phi\rangle.
\end{aligned}
\tag{A4}
$$

We further express the Z-rotation in Equation (A4) in terms of Z and P. Recalling that $\beta = (f + \frac{g}{2})\pi$ (see Equation (18)) and considering the periodicity of Z-rotation operators, we can get that

$$
\begin{aligned}
&R_z\left((-1)^{s' \oplus h}(f + \frac{g}{2})\pi + (-1)^h(a \oplus s)\pi\right) \\
&\equiv R_z\left((a \oplus s \oplus f)\pi + (-1)^{s' \oplus h}\frac{g}{2}\pi\right) \\
&\equiv R_z\left((a \oplus s \oplus f)\pi + (-1)^{s' \oplus h}\frac{g}{2}\pi + 2(s' \oplus h)g\pi\right) \\
&= R_z\left((a \oplus s \oplus f \oplus [(s' \oplus h)g])\pi + \frac{(-1)^{s' \oplus h} + 2(s' \oplus h)}{2}g\pi\right).
\end{aligned}
\tag{A5}
$$

Note that for any $r \in \{0,1\}$, $(-1)^r + 2r = 1$, so the above Z-rotation operator can be further rewritten as follows:

$$
R_z\left((a \oplus s \oplus f \oplus [g(s' \oplus h)])\pi + \frac{g\pi}{2}\right) \equiv Z^{a \oplus s \oplus f \oplus [g(s' \oplus h)]} P^g. \tag{A6}
$$

Substituting the above equation to Equation (A4), we get the output qubit in the following form:

$$
X^{s' \oplus h} Z^{a \oplus s \oplus f \oplus [g(s' \oplus h)]} P^g H |\phi\rangle \tag{A7}
$$

Finally, we substitute $\gamma = (b + \frac{c}{2})\pi$ and $\alpha = (d + \frac{e}{2})\pi$ in $\theta = (-1)^{a \oplus s}\gamma + \alpha + h\pi$, obtaining

$$\begin{aligned}\theta &= (-1)^{a \oplus s}(b\pi + \frac{c}{2}\pi) + (d\pi + \frac{e}{2}\pi) + h\pi \\ &= b\pi + (-1)^{a \oplus s}\frac{c}{2}\pi + d\pi + \frac{e}{2}\pi + h\pi \\ &= b\pi + c(a \oplus s)\pi + \frac{c}{2}\pi + d\pi + \frac{e}{2}\pi + h\pi \\ &= h \oplus b \oplus d \oplus (ac) \oplus (sc)\pi + \frac{c+e}{2}\pi \\ &= h \oplus b \oplus d \oplus (ac) \oplus (sc) \oplus (ce)\pi + \frac{c \oplus e}{2}\pi. \end{aligned} \quad (A8)$$

where in the last term we use another simple equality: for any $c, e \in \{0, 1\}$, $c + e = 2ce + c \oplus e$. From the above results, the correctness of the H-gadget is obvious.

References

1. Arute, F.; Arya, K.; Babbush, R.; Bacon, D.; Bardin, J.C.; Barends, R.; Biswas, R.; Boixo, S.; Brandao, F.G.; Buell, D.A.; et al. Quantum supremacy using a programmable superconducting processor. *Nature* **2019**, *574*, 505–510. [CrossRef]
2. Harrow, A.W.; Montanaro, A. Quantum computational supremacy. *Nature* **2017**, *549*, 203–209. [CrossRef]
3. Preskill, J. Quantum computing in the NISQ era and beyond. *Quantum* **2018**, *2*, 79. [CrossRef]
4. Campbell, E.T.; Fitzsimons, J. An introduction to one-way quantum computing in distributed architectures. *Int. J. Quantum Inf.* **2010**, *8*, 219–258. [CrossRef]
5. Castelvecchi, D. IBM's quantum cloud computer goes commercial. *Nat. News* **2017**, *543*, 159. [CrossRef]
6. Raussendorf, R.; Briegel, H.J. A One-Way Quantum Computer. *Phys. Rev. Lett.* **2001**, *86*, 5188–5191. [CrossRef] [PubMed]
7. Briegel, H.J.; Browne, D.E.; Dür, W.; Raussendorf, R.; Van den Nest, M. Measurement-based quantum computation. *Nat. Phys.* **2009**, *5*, 19–26. [CrossRef]
8. Morimae, T.; Fujii, K. Blind quantum computation protocol in which Alice only makes measurements. *Phys. Rev. A* **2013**, *87*, 050301. [CrossRef]
9. Fisher, K.A.; Broadbent, A.; Shalm, L.; Yan, Z.; Lavoie, J.; Prevedel, R.; Jennewein, T.; Resch, K.J. Quantum computing on encrypted data. *Nat. Commun.* **2014**, *5*, 3074. [CrossRef] [PubMed]
10. Broadbent, A.; Jeffery, S. Quantum homomorphic encryption for circuits of low T-gate complexity. In Proceedings of the Annual Cryptology Conference, Santa Barbara, CA, USA, 16–20 August 2015; Springer: Berlin/Heidelberg, Germany, 2015; pp. 609–629.
11. Broadbent, A. Delegating private quantum computations. *Can. J. Phys.* **2015**, *93*, 410–413. [CrossRef]
12. Liang, M. Teleportation-Based quantum homomorphic encryption scheme with quasi-compactness and perfect security. *Quantum Inf. Process.* **2020**, *19*, 28. [CrossRef]
13. Jiang, L.; Taylor, J.M.; Sørensen, A.S.; Lukin, M.D. Distributed quantum computation based on small quantum registers. *Phys. Rev. A* **2007**, *76*, 062323. [CrossRef]
14. Moehring, D.L.; Madsen, M.J.; Younge, K.C.; Kohn, R.N., Jr.; Maunz, P.; Duan, L.M.; Monroe, C.; Blinov, B.B. Quantum networking with photons and trapped atoms (Invited). *J. Opt. Soc. Am. B* **2007**, *24*, 300–315. [CrossRef]
15. Li, Y.; Benjamin, S.C. High threshold distributed quantum computing with three-qubit nodes. *New J. Phys.* **2012**, *14*, 093008. [CrossRef]
16. Nickerson, N.H.; Li, Y.; Benjamin, S.C. Topological quantum computing with a very noisy network and local error rates approaching one percent. *Nat. Commun.* **2013**, *4*, 1756. [CrossRef]
17. Monroe, C.; Raussendorf, R.; Ruthven, A.; Brown, K.R.; Maunz, P.; Duan, L.M.; Kim, J. Large-scale modular quantum-computer architecture with atomic memory and photonic interconnects. *Phys. Rev. A* **2014**, *89*, 022317. [CrossRef]
18. Cacciapuoti, A.S.; Caleffi, M.; Tafuri, F.; Cataliotti, F.S.; Gherardini, S.; Bianchi, G. Quantum internet: Networking challenges in distributed quantum computing. *IEEE Netw.* **2019**, *34*, 137–143. [CrossRef]
19. Liu, J.X.; Ye, J.Y.; Yan, L.L.; Su, S.L.; Feng, M. Distributed quantum information processing via single atom driving. *J. Phys. B At. Mol. Opt. Phys.* **2020**, *53*, 035503. [CrossRef]
20. Zhong, Y.; Chang, H.S.; Bienfait, A.; Dumur, É.; Chou, M.H.; Conner, C.R.; Grebel, J.; Povey, R.G.; Yan, H.; Schuster, D.I.; et al. Deterministic multi-qubit entanglement in a quantum network. *Nature* **2021**, *590*, 571–575. [CrossRef]
21. Daiss, S.; Langenfeld, S.; Welte, S.; Distante, E.; Thomas, P.; Hartung, L.; Morin, O.; Rempe, G. A quantum-logic gate between distant quantum-network modules. *Science* **2021**, *371*, 614–617. [CrossRef]
22. Childs, A.M. Secure assisted quantum computation. *Quantum Inf. Comput.* **2005**, *5*, 456–466. [CrossRef]
23. Rohde, P.P.; Fitzsimons, J.F.; Gilchrist, A. Quantum Walks with Encrypted Data. *Phys. Rev. Lett.* **2012**, *109*, 150501. [CrossRef]
24. Dunjko, V.; Fitzsimons, J.F.; Portmann, C.; Renner, R. Composable security of delegated quantum computation. In Proceedings of the International Conference on the Theory and Application of Cryptology and Information Security, Taiwan, China, 7–11 December 2014; Springer: Berlin/Heidelberg, Germany, 2014; pp. 406–425.

25. Marshall, K.; Jacobsen, C.S.; Schäfermeier, C.; Gehring, T.; Weedbrook, C.; Andersen, U.L. Continuous-Variable quantum computing on encrypted data. *Nat. Commun.* **2016**, *7*, 13795. [CrossRef]
26. Zhou, Q.; Lu, S.; Cui, Y.; Li, L.; Sun, J. Quantum search on encrypted data based on quantum homomorphic encryption. *Sci. Rep.* **2020**, *10*, 5135. [CrossRef]
27. Wang, D.; Liu, Y.; Ding, J.; Qiang, X.; Liu, Y.; Huang, A.; Fu, X.; Xu, P.; Deng, M.; Yang, X.; et al. Remote-controlled quantum computing by quantum entanglement. *Opt. Lett.* **2020**, *45*, 6298–6301. [CrossRef]
28. Zhao, X.; Zhao, B.; Wang, Z.; Song, Z.; Wang, X. Practical distributed quantum information processing with LOCCNet. *Npj Quantum Inf.* **2021**, *7*, 159. [CrossRef]
29. Sherson, J.F.; Krauter, H.; Olsson, R.K.; Julsgaard, B.; Hammerer, K.; Cirac, I.; Polzik, E.S. Quantum teleportation between light and matter. *Nature* **2006**, *443*, 557–560. [CrossRef]
30. Olmschenk, S.; Matsukevich, D.N.; Maunz, P.; Hayes, D.; Duan, L.M.; Monroe, C. Quantum Teleportation Between Distant Matter Qubits. *Science* **2009**, *323*, 486–489. [CrossRef]
31. Chou, C.W.; De Riedmatten, H.; Felinto, D.; Polyakov, S.V.; Van Enk, S.J.; Kimble, H.J. Measurement-induced entanglement for excitation stored in remote atomic ensembles. *Nature* **2005**, *438*, 828–832. [CrossRef]
32. Peng, T.; Harrow, A.W.; Ozols, M.; Wu, X. Simulating large quantum circuits on a small quantum computer. *Phys. Rev. Lett.* **2020**, *125*, 150504. [CrossRef]
33. Bravyi, S.; Smith, G.; Smolin, J.A. Trading classical and quantum computational resources. *Phys. Rev. X* **2016**, *6*, 021043. [CrossRef]
34. Broadbent, A.; Fitzsimons, J.; Kashefi, E. Universal blind quantum computation. In Proceedings of the 2009 50th Annual IEEE Symposium on Foundations of Computer Science, Atlanta, GA, USA, 25–27 October 2009; pp. 517–526.
35. Aharonov, D.; Ben-Or, M.; Eban, E.; Mahadev, U. Interactive proofs for quantum computations. *arXiv* **2017**, arXiv:1704.04487.
36. Zeuner, J.; Pitsios, I.; Tan, S.H.; Sharma, A.N.; Fitzsimons, J.F.; Osellame, R.; Walther, P. Experimental quantum homomorphic encryption. *Npj Quantum Inf.* **2021**, *7*, 25. [CrossRef]
37. Barz, S.; Kashefi, E.; Broadbent, A.; Fitzsimons, J.F.; Zeilinger, A.; Walther, P. Demonstration of blind quantum computing. *Science* **2012**, *335*, 303–308. [CrossRef]
38. Ma, S.; Zhu, C.; Nie, M.; Quan, D.; Pei, C. Secure delegated quantum computation based on Z-rotation encryption. *Europhys. Lett.* **2022**, *137*, 38001. [CrossRef]
39. Eisert, J.; Jacobs, K.; Papadopoulos, P.; Plenio, M.B. Optimal local implementation of nonlocal quantum gates. *Phys. Rev. A* **2000**, *62*, 052317. [CrossRef]
40. Zhou, X.; Leung, D.W.; Chuang, I.L. Methodology for quantum logic gate construction. *Phys. Rev. A* **2000**, *62*, 052316. [CrossRef]
41. Gottesman, D. Theory of fault-tolerant quantum computation. *Phys. Rev. A* **1998**, *57*, 127. [CrossRef]
42. Calderbank, A.R.; Shor, P.W. Good quantum error-correcting codes exist. *Phys. Rev. A* **1996**, *54*, 1098. [CrossRef]
43. Rozpędek, F.; Schiet, T.; Thinh, L.P.; Elkouss, D.; Doherty, A.C.; Wehner, S. Optimizing practical entanglement distillation. *Phys. Rev. A* **2018**, *97*, 062333. [CrossRef]
44. Bernstein, E.; Vazirani, U. Quantum complexity theory. *SIAM J. Comput.* **1997**, *26*, 1411–1473. [CrossRef]
45. Fitzsimons, J.F. Private quantum computation: An introduction to blind quantum computing and related protocols. *Npj Quantum Inf.* **2017**, *3*, 23. [CrossRef]
46. Gheorghiu, A.; Kapourniotis, T.; Kashefi, E. Verification of quantum computation: An overview of existing approaches. *Theory Comput. Syst.* **2019**, *63*, 715–808. [CrossRef]
47. Ma, S.; Zhu, C.; Nie, M.; Quan, D. Efficient self-testing system for quantum computations based on permutations. *Chin. Phys. B* **2021**, *30*, 040305. [CrossRef]

Article

Rate-Compatible LDPC Codes for Continuous-Variable Quantum Key Distribution in Wide Range of SNRs Regime

Xiaodong Fan [1], Quanhao Niu [1], Tao Zhao [1] and Banghong Guo [1,2,3,*]

[1] Guangdong Provincial Key Laboratory of Nanophotonic Functional Materials and Devices, Guangdong Provincial Key Laboratory of Quantum Engineering and Quantum Materials, South China Normal University, Guangzhou 510006, China
[2] National Quantum Communication (Guangdong) Co., Ltd., Guangzhou 510700, China
[3] Key Laboratory of Quantum Information, University of Science and Technology of China, Chinese Academy of Sciences, Hefei 230026, China
* Correspondence: guobh@scnu.edu.cn

Abstract: Long block length rate-compatible low-density parity-compatible (LDPC) codes are designed to solve the problems of great variation of quantum channel noise and extremely low signal-to-noise ratio in continuous-variable quantum key distribution (CV-QKD). The existing rate-compatible methods for CV-QKD inevitably cost abundant hardware resources and waste secret key resources. In this paper, we propose a design rule of rate-compatible LDPC codes that can cover all potential SNRs with single check matrix. Based on this long block length LDPC code, we achieve high efficiency continuous-variable quantum key distribution information reconciliation with a reconciliation efficiency of 91.80% and we have higher hardware processing efficiency and lower frame error rate than other schemes. Our proposed LDPC code can obtain a high practical secret key rate and a long transmission distance in an extremely unstable channel.

Keywords: rate compatible; LDPC; continuous-variable quantum key distribution; wide range of SNRs regime

1. Introduction

The cryptosystem based on computational complexity is being challenged by increasingly developed quantum computation. Quantum key distribution (QKD) [1–4], being one-time pad, has been one of the best solutions for its absolute security. QKD enables two remote separated parties named Alice and Bob to extract a symmetrical string of secret keys using a quantum channel.

Currently, there are mainly two types of QKD protocols, called discrete-variable QKD (DV-QKD) [5] and continuous-variable QKD (CV-QKD) [6,7]. In DV-QKD, the information is coded on discrete variables of finite dimensional Hilbert space, such as the polarization or phase of single photon state. In CV-QKD, the information is coded on continuous variables of an infinite-dimensional Hilbert space, including the regular component of coherent state. Compared with the single photon detector used in DV-QKD, homodyne or heterodyne detection techniques, which are used to measure the transmitted quantum states, have already been applied in classical optical communication. Therefore, CV-QKD has great practical advantages for its low cost because of the relatively mature development and being able to transmit in common fiber with classical optical communication. Furthermore, CV-QKD can achieve higher capacity with frequency-multiplexed entanglement source [8].

Due to the imperfection of the quantum channel and potential eavesdropper Eve, the key strings held by Alice and Bob are not consistent, so that a procedure called post-processing is necessary to make them identical. The post-processing of CV-QKD mainly includes four steps: base vector comparison, parameter estimation, information reconciliation and privacy amplification. Information reconciliation is the most important part, whose performance has a direct correlation to the secret key rate. One of the major factors in information reconciliation is reconciliation efficiency β, which is given by $\beta = R/C$. The R is the rate of key and $C = 0.5 log(1 + SNR)$ is the channel compacity. The hardware processing efficiency $\alpha = D_{out}/D_{in}$, where D_{in} represents the data that are input to the hardware device (e.g., Field-programmable Gate Array, FPGA and Graphics Processing Unit, GPU) during information reconciliation and D_{out} represents the output data in unit time [9]. I_{AB} is the mutual information between Alice and Bob. χ_{BE} is the Holevo bound, which is the maximal bound on the information available to the eavesdropper. The factors mentioned above are used to evaluate the performance in a frame, while frame error rate (FER) represents the failure probability of the frames. Ultimately, the practical secret key rate K is given by

$$K = \alpha(1 - FER)(\beta I_{AB} - \chi_{BE}). \tag{1}$$

The parameters mentioned above is related to the error correcting codes, among them low-density parity-compatible (LDPC) code is efficient for CV-QKD [10]. The LDPC code obtained by good degree distribution and reasonable construction method has good error correction performance. The crux of designing a LDPC code is to construct a check matrix which includes check nodes and variable nodes. The degree distribution of check node $\rho(x)$ and variable node $\lambda(x)$ are expressed as:

$$\rho(x) = \sum_{j=2}^{d_c} \rho_i x^{j-1} \tag{2}$$

$$\lambda(x) = \sum_{i=2}^{d_v} \lambda_i x^{i-1}, \tag{3}$$

ρ_i/λ_i is the proportion of the number of edges owned by the check/variable node with degree j/i to the total number of edges in the Tanner graph and d_c/d_v indicates the maximum degree of the check/variable node.

However, quantum is easily influenced in the process of quantum signal preparation and transmission. To realize the free space QKD with satellite [11,12], ship [13], unmanned aerial vehicles [14] or those with orbital angular momentum, we have to take mode distortion, beam wander, weather etc. into account. Therefore, the problems of great variation of quantum channel noise and extremely low signal-to-noise ratio (SNR) have to be solved.

One of the simplest rate-compatible methods for LDPC code is to operate on single-matrix using puncturing, shortening and extending. Furthermore, Gao proposed multi-matrix rate-compatible reconciliation where, in each iteration, multiple matrices produce more useful information to correct errors such that the iteration number falls and the convergence speed increases [15]. However, it inevitably decreases the performance of the original check matrix. Another commonly used way is to construct several check matrices with different code rates to meet the requirements of different SNRs. However, for CV-QKD, the code length has to be longer than 100,000. Base matrices are at least 64,800 long even when we construct the spatially coupled (SC)-LDPC codes or quasi-cyclic (QC)-LDPC codes [16]. As one of the most effective decoding tools of LDPC code, the FPGA has limited hardware resources. To realize high efficiency information reconciliation with FPGA in an extremely unstable channel, it is necessary to construct a single-matrix rate-compatible error correction code. A comparison of the existing works with our proposed LDPC code is shown in Table 1.

In this paper, we first obtain degree distribution with discrete density evolution and differential evolution algorithm. Then we use random construction, progressive edge growth (PEG) algorithm and rate compatible methods of extending and puncturing to construct a check matrix with a code length of 64,800. Finally, we extend the above LDPC code with quasi-cyclic extension to a code length of 648,000. The results show that the proposed codes have a reconciliation efficiency of 91.80%, higher hardware processing efficiency and lower FER than other schemes. Therefore, we can obtain a high practical secret key rate and a longer transmission distance in an extremely unstable channel with wide range of SNRs.

Table 1. Related works comparison in an unstable channel. Transmission distance is 10 km and the number of check matrix changing times N is 3.

Reference	Hardware Resource	Secret Key Rate (bit/pulse)	Abilitiy to Cope with Channel SNR Changing
Single-matrix rate-compatible reconciliation	a, single matrix	0.0021	low
Multimatrix rate-compatible reconciliation [15]	3a, multimatrix	0.0098	low
Multimatrix corresponding to given SNRs [16]	12a, multimatrix	0.0089	low
Our proposed LDPC code	a, single matrix	0.0116	high

The remainder of this paper is organized as follows. In Section 2, we present some preliminaries of LDPC codes and rate-compatibility. In Section 3, we introduce how to construct our rate compatible (RC)-LDPC code. In Section 4, we present the simulation results and comparisons for the proposed scheme and existing schemes. Finally, the conclusions are drawn in Section 5.

2. Preliminaries

In this section, we first briefly introduce the discrete density evolution and differential evolution, which are used to generate degree distribution. Then we introduce the constructions: random construction, PEG algorithm and QC-LDPC extension, with which we can construct the check matrix with the degree distribution ahead. We also introduce the rate compatible methods: puncturing and extending.

2.1. Methods of Obtaining Degree Distribution

2.1.1. Discrete Density Evolution

Compared with continuous density evolution [17] and Gaussian approximation algorithm [18], discrete density evolution [19] has lower complexity and higher accuracy. Therefore, in this paper, we use discrete density evolution to obtain the optimal degree distribution of LDPC codes. The main steps are as follows:

- We firstly define two functions: quantized function Q and probability mass function S.

$$Q(x) = \begin{cases} \lfloor \frac{x}{\Delta} + \frac{1}{2} \rfloor, & x \geq \frac{\Delta}{2} \\ \lceil \frac{x}{\Delta} - \frac{1}{2} \rceil, & x \leq -\frac{\Delta}{2}, \\ 0, & else \end{cases} \quad (4)$$

$\lfloor x \rfloor$ is the largest integer not greater than x; and $\lceil x \rceil$ is the smallest integer not less than x. The value range of decoded message is $[-L, L]$ and evenly divided into $m = 2^q$ intervals; the quantization interval Δ is given by $2L/m$.

$$S(P_a, P_b) = \sum_{(i,j):k\Delta = R(i\Delta, j\Delta)} P_a[i] \cdot P_b[j]. \quad (5)$$

In which two-input operator R is

$$R(a,b) = Q(\tanh^{-1}(\tanh\frac{a}{2}\tanh\frac{b}{2})), \tag{6}$$

where a and b are quantized messages.
- The check node and variable node updating of discrete density evolution is

$$p_{\underline{u}}^{(l)} = \sum_{i=2}^{d_r} \rho_i S^{i-1}\left(p_{\underline{v}}^{(l-1)}\right) \tag{7}$$

$$p_{\underline{v}}^{(l)}(k) = p_{\underline{v}}^{(0)}(k) \cdot \sum_{i=2}^{d_v} \lambda_i \otimes^{i-1}(p_{\underline{u}}^{(l)}(k)), \tag{8}$$

$\otimes$ is discrete convolution and l is the iteration number. The initial value $p_{\underline{v}}^{(0)}$ is

$$p_{\underline{v}}^{(0)} = \frac{\sigma}{8\pi} exp\left(-\frac{(2-\sigma^2 v)^2}{8\sigma^2}\right), v^{(0)} \sim N\left(\frac{2}{\sigma^2}, \frac{4}{\sigma^2}\right). \tag{9}$$

- Finally, we calculate the error rate with

$$p_{\underline{e}}^{(l)} = p_{\underline{v}}^{(l)}(0) + \sum_{k=-m/2}^{-1} p_{\underline{v}}^{(l)}(k). \tag{10}$$

End the procedure when the $p_{\underline{e}}^{(l)}) < 0$ or l reaches the maximum number of iterations. Otherwise, we continue to update the check node and variable node.

Discrete density evolution is first proposed to obtain the noise threshold according to the degree distribution ρ_i and λ_i. In our work, we use it to obtain the degree distribution under specific channel noise.

2.1.2. Differential Evolution

Stom first proposed the differential evolution algorithm in 1995 to solve the optimization problem [20]. It uses differential mutation operator and crossover operator to generate new individuals by the way of survival of the fittest. Based on this method, we can obtain the optimal degree distribution under specific channel noise.

- Set channel noise threshold σ, target error probability P_e, maximum number of iterations l_{max}, maximum degree of variable node d_v and the number of terms of degree distribution polynomial n.
- Randomly generate NP vectors $P_{i,G}, i = 1, 2, \ldots, NP$ for the degree distribution of variable node. Use discretized density to evolve each vector and obtain the respective error probability $P_{e_i,G}$. The vector with the lowest error probability is marked as the best vector $P_{best,G}$ and its error probability is marked as $P_{e_{best},G}$.
- For each i, randomly choose four vectors from set of $P_{i,G}$ and the new vector is updated by

$$v_{i,G+1} = P_{best,G} + 0.5(P_{r_1,G} - P_{r_2,G}) + 0.5(P_{r_3,G} - P_{r_4,G}). \tag{11}$$

Calculate the corresponding error probability $P_{v_i,G+1}$ for each new vector $v_{i,G+1}$.
- For each i, compare $P_{e_i,G}$ with $P_{v_i,G+1}$ and let $P_{i,G+1} = v_{i,G+1}$ if $P_{e_i,G} > P_{v_i,G+1}$. The vector with the lowest error probability is marked as the best vector $P_{best,G+1}$ and its error probability is marked as $P_{e_{best},G+1}$.

- If the error probability corresponding to the best vector $P_{e_{best},G+1} > P_e$, update the vectors again and return to step (4). If $P_{e_{best},G+1} \leq P_e$, the $P_{best,G+1}$ is the ideal vector that we want.

2.2. Constructions

In this work, we use random construction, the PEG algorithm and QC extension for their good results in various situations.

2.2.1. Random Construction

Various random constructions have been proposed based on the same core thought, that is, place non-zero elements in random unfilled positions in the check matrix without violating any set constraint. There are two constraint rules: one is that line l_i contains X_i "1" and column c_i contains Y_i "1" according to the degree distribution of check nodes and variable nodes; the other one is the number of elements "1" at the same position in any two rows or columns is less than or equal to 1. It means that the shortest girth has to be longer than 4.

2.2.2. Progressive-Edge-Growth Algorithm

Before introducing the PEG algorithm, we first introduce a common representation of LDPC codes—the Tanner diagram and several concepts. As shown in Figure 1a, V_i is a variable node, C_j is a check node and the line between them is called an edge. If two nodes are connected with each other, we say these two nodes are adjacent to each other. The girth is defined as the minimum number of lines that comes from a node and back to this node, whose intermediate node is only passed once. As shown in Figure 1a, the shortest girth is 6 and one of them is $V_1 \rightarrow C_1 \rightarrow V_2 \rightarrow C_4 \rightarrow V_5 \rightarrow C_2 \rightarrow V_1$, for instance.

For the PEG algorithm, new edges are added to make the loop girth in the Tanner diagram corresponding to the check matrix as large as possible. As shown in Figure 1b, the steps are as follows:

- Determine the number of check node, variable node and the degree distribution of variable node.
- Randomly choose a variable node V_i and find the check node C_j with the least number of connected edges in the Tanner graph. Then connect the variable node V_i and the check node C_j with an edge and take it as the first edge of the variable node V_i.
- Take the variable node V_i as the root node and expand the current Tanner diagram. When the expansion depth is l, the set of check nodes adjacent to V_i is recorded as $N_{V_i}^l$. The $\overline{N_{V_i}^l}$ is the complement set of $N_{V_i}^l$, where the complete set V_c is the set of all variable nodes. Expand the Tanner graph with the root node and the depth of l. When $\overline{N_{V_i}^l} \neq \varnothing$, $\overline{N_{V_i}^{l+1}} = \varnothing$ and the number of nodes contained in $N_{V_i}^l$ stops increasing but is still less than the number of matrix rows l, connect the check node C_j with the least number of connected edges to the variable node V_i.
- Repeat step (2) to add edges to the selected variable nodes until all of them are added.
- Repeat steps (1) to (3) to add edge for all other variable nodes.

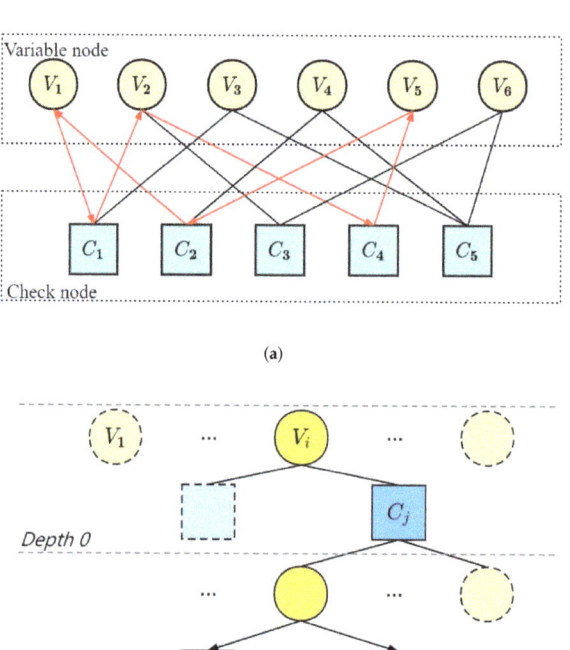

Figure 1. (a) Tanner graph; (b) PEG algorithm.

2.2.3. QC-LDPC Extension

QC-LDPC extension is uniquely determined by the dimension and shift times of the circulant matrix. Its quasi-cyclic characteristics make the process of coding and decoding more efficient. Compared with randomly constructed LDPC codes, QC-LDPC codes have lower error level and are more convenient for storage and hardware implementation. We multiply the corresponding positions of the base matrix H_b and the coefficient matrix H_c and we define this operation as $\odot$, the expression is expressed as follows:

$$H_b \odot H_c = \begin{bmatrix} B_{1,1} & \cdots & B_{1,i} \\ \vdots & \ddots & \vdots \\ B_{j,1} & \cdots & B_{j,i} \end{bmatrix} \odot \begin{bmatrix} C_{1,1} & \cdots & C_{1,i} \\ \vdots & \ddots & \vdots \\ C_{j,1} & \cdots & C_{j,i} \end{bmatrix} = \begin{bmatrix} B_{1,1}C_{1,1} & \cdots & B_{1,i}C_{1,i} \\ \vdots & \ddots & \vdots \\ B_{j,1}C_{j,1} & \cdots & B_{j,i}C_{j,i} \end{bmatrix}. \quad (12)$$

Take lifting size of 3 as an example, the elements of the base matrix are 0 and 1, and the elements of the coefficient matrix are 1, 2 and 3. Then the matrix elements are replaced by the cyclic permutation matrices (CPMs). We replace 0 with zero matrices, 1 with $\begin{bmatrix} 1 & 0 & 0 \\ 0 & 1 & 0 \\ 0 & 0 & 1 \end{bmatrix}$,

2 with $\begin{bmatrix} 0 & 1 & 0 \\ 0 & 0 & 1 \\ 1 & 0 & 0 \end{bmatrix}$ and 3 with $\begin{bmatrix} 0 & 0 & 1 \\ 1 & 0 & 0 \\ 0 & 1 & 0 \end{bmatrix}$.

2.3. Methods of Rate-Compatible

Puncturing is a method that makes the code rate change from low to high. As shown in Figure 2a, the submatrix A are information bits and submatrix B and C are check bits. The initial code rate is $R = L_0/(L_0 + L_1 + L_2)$. By deleting the submatrix C, we can obtain a code rate increasing to $R = L_0/(L_0 + L_1)$.

On the contrary, extending as shown in Figure 2b enables the code rate to change from high to low. We first construct a check matrix A with the high bit rate of $(N_0 - M_0)/N_0$. Moreover, by adding the submatrix A_n, we extend the matrix to make it compatible for the low rate. The code rate is expressed as:

$$R_i = \frac{\sum_0^n N_i - \sum_0^n M_i}{N}. \tag{13}$$

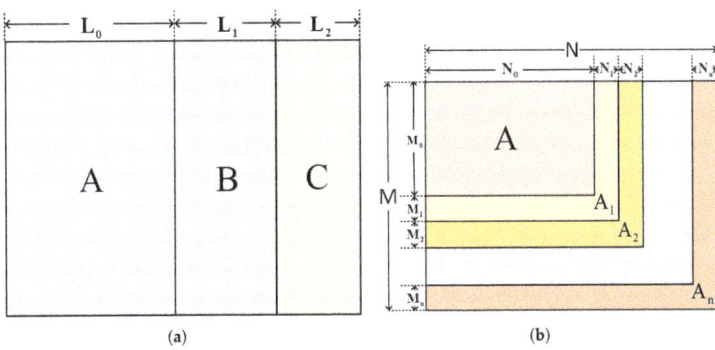

Figure 2. The rate-compatible method: (**a**) puncturing; (**b**) extending.

3. Proposed Check Matrix for RC-LDPC Codes with Wide Range of SNRs Regime

From the Equation (1) we can see that high hardware processing efficiency and reconciliation efficiency result in a good performance of final secret key rate for a given SNR. Proper degree distribution and reasonable construction method lead to good error correction performance.

3.1. Obtaining Degree Distribution

We first obtain the initial optimal degree distribution using discretize density evolution and differential evolution refer to Sections 2.1.1 and 2.1.2. Maximum degree of variable node and the number of terms of degree distribution polynomial are set as 10 and 4, respectively.

From the initial optimal degree distribution, we find that the pairs of degree distribution are distributed nearby λ_3 and λ_7 except of λ_2 and λ_{10}. Therefore, we calculate the average number of λ_3 and λ_7 at rate from 0.3 to 1, i.e., SNR from 0.1 to 3 (the degree distribution is appropriate to the SNR larger than 3 but the maximum rate 1 corresponds to the SNR of 3). The initial values are average number $\overline{\lambda_3}$ and $\overline{\lambda_7}$, and maximum degree of variable node and the number of terms of degree distribution polynomial are still set as 10 and 4. The difference is that the degree distribution of the variable distribution is set on the

λ_2, λ_3, λ_7 and λ_{10} instead of a random distribution. Then we repeat the above operations to obtain the optimal degree distribution in these conditions.

Through the above operations, we obtain the degree, the maximum degree of the variable node, and the number of terms of the degree distribution polynomial. Ultimately, we calculate the optimal degree distribution for proposing our LDPC code with Algorithm 1.

Algorithm 1 Obtaining the ultimate variable degree distribution with density evolution and differential evolution

---

Input: Target error probability P_e, maximum number of iterations l_{max}, population size $NP = 50$, the number of terms of variable node degree distribution polynomial $l = 5$, the highest power of variable node degree distribution, $\lambda_3 = 0.0047$, $\lambda_7 = 0.5072$
Output: Error rate $P_{e_{best}}$, vector P_{best}
1: **for** $i = 1$ to NP **do**
2:     refer to Section 2.1.1 generate vector P_i with λ_2, λ_3, λ_7, λ_8 and λ_{10}, $\lambda_2 + \lambda_8 + \lambda_{10} = 0.4881$;
3:     calculate the error probability P_{e_i};
4:     **if** $P_{e_{best}} > P_{e_i}$ **then**
5:         $P_{e_{best}} \leftarrow P_{e_i}$; $P_{best} \leftarrow P_i$;
6:     **end if**
7: **end for**
8: **for** $j = 1$ to l_{max} **do**
9:     randomly choose four numbers r_1, r_2, r_3, r_4 from 1 to NP;
10:     $v_j = P_{best} + 0.5(P_{r_1} - P_{r_2} + P_{r_3} - P_{r_4})$;
11:     calculate the error probability P_{e_j};
12:     **if** $P_{e_{best}} < P_e$ **then**
13:         output v_j;
14:     **end if**
15:     **if** $P_{e_{best}} > P_{e_j}$ **then**
16:         $P_{e_{best}} \leftarrow P_{e_j}$;
17:     **end if**
18: **end for**

Table 2 is the result of Algorithm 1, whose input signal $X \sim (0, 1)$ and additive white Gaussian noise $Z \sim (0, \sigma^2)$ are random variables that obey Gaussian distribution and independent of each other. The channel noise $SNR = 1/\sigma^2$ and σ represents the maximum allowed value of noise for the additive white Gaussian channel. For $\rho(x) = \lambda(x) = 1$, the check node degree distribution is definite with the constraint condition $r = 1 - \int_0^1 \rho(x)dx / \int_0^1 \lambda(x)dx$. The degree distribution in our scheme especially decreases the difficulty of constructing the check matrix.

Table 2. Variable nodes degree distribution pairs for the code rate from 0.3 to 1.0.

Rate	0.3	0.4	0.5	0.6	0.7	0.8	0.9	1.0 [1]
λ_2	0.0001	0.0001	0.0007	0.0001	0.0002	0.0002	0.0004	0.0005
λ_3				0.0047				
λ_7				0.5072				
λ_8	0.1382	0.1268	0.1044	0.0761	0.0480	0.0367	0.0281	0.0089
λ_{10}	0.3498	0.3612	0.3830	0.4119	0.4399	0.4512	0.4596	0.4787
σ	1.3868	1.1547	1.0000	0.8771	0.7809	0.7001	0.6337	0.5774
SNR	0.52	0.75	1.00	1.30	1.64	2.04	2.49	3.00
C	0.3072	0.4037	0.5000	0.6008	0.7003	0.8020	0.9016	1.0000

[1] The practical rate at 1 is close to but lower than 1.

In order to maximize the use of limited key resources, we still need to fully consider the condition of rate lower than 0.1. Obviously, the secret key rate is low for the low mutual information I_{AB}. Therefore, in order to simplify our work, the degree distribution pairs we choose for the rate lower than 0.1 are directly refer to Appendix A [21,22].

3.2. Constructing Check Matrix for RC-LDPC Code

With the degree distribution we obtained above, we construct a single matrix RC-LDPC code simultaneously with the random construction, the PEG algorithm, and QC-LDPC codes mentioned in Section 2. The structure of the check matrix is shown in Figure 3 and combined with parts A, B and C.

The part A is a shared part for the rate from 0.1 to 1, which is constructed with $\overline{\lambda_3}$ and $\overline{\lambda_7}$. This structure has the advantage of reducing computational complexity and saving the storage resources. Previous work showed that the PEG algorithm has better performance at SNR~3 [23], while random construction exhibits better performance at SNR~1 [24]. Therefore, the construction that we use to construct the sub-matrix A is the PEG algorithm.

The part B is constructed with rest of degree distribution to realize the rate-compatible method of puncturing. In order to further improve the performance of our LDPC code, we construct the check matrix with the thought of puncturing. More specifically, we divide submatrix B_n into two part and construct one part when the R decreases every 0.05. For rate from 0.3 to 0.1, this number is 0.1. We use PEG algorithm to construct B_1 to B_5 and random construction to construct extra part. Moreover, the structure of part B is a lower triangular matrix, which can be directly encoded.

Multi-edge-type (MET)-LDPC codes are employed with low SNRs due to their good error-correcting performances, more amenable decoding complexity and also being able to be rate-compatible at low rates [25]. Based on the check matrix above, we construct part C with degree distribution of the MET-LDPC codes from Appendix A for the rate from 0.01 to 0.1.

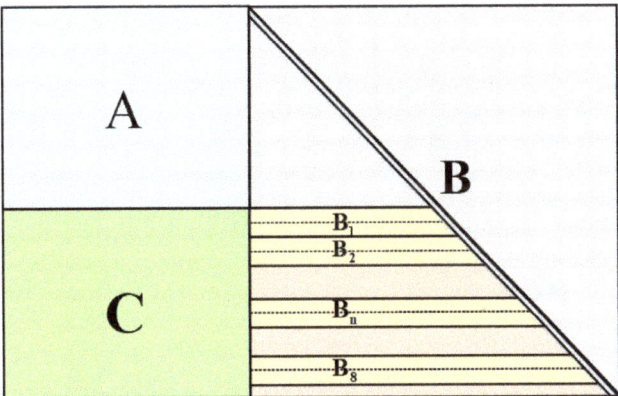

Figure 3. The check matrix for RC-LDPC codes with wide range of SNR.

4. Simulation Experiment

In this section, we summarize the implementation results of the proposed LDPC codes over an unstable channel. Our purpose is to construct a RC-LDPC code with single matrix that can be adapt to the SNR from 0.01 to 15. We show the performance of reconciliation efficiency β, hardware processing efficiency α and FER, which are influenced by the change of SNR. Furthermore, the decoding algorithm is a modified Min-Sum algorithm.

The reconciliation efficiency comes from $\beta = R/C$. Referring to the construction mentioned in Section 3.2, we change the check matrix when R reduces to a certain extent. When R is from 0.3 to 1, C decreases 0.1 to an integer multiple of 0.1. When R is from 0.01 to 0.3, C decreases 0.05 to an integer multiple of 0.05. In Figure 4, assuming that the channel noise is uniformly distributed, the LDPC code we proposed has an average reconciliation efficiency β of 91.80%, and for higher rates from 0.3 to 1 this number is 96.13%. Because the data with rate lower than 0.3 only have a little contribution to reconciliation efficiency, the practical reconciliation efficiency is close to 96.13%. Compared with the existing scheme, the proposed LDPC code has a relatively high reconciliation efficiency.

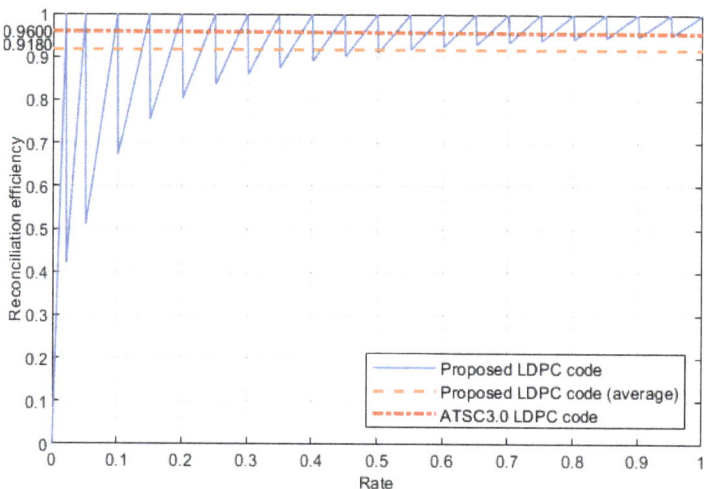

Figure 4. The reconciliation efficiency for different code rate.

From Equation (1), the secret key rate is also related to the hardware processing efficiency α, which is equal to the ratio of D_{out} and D_{in}. More specifically, supposing the times used to load check matrix, load data and decode data are t_{lm}, t_{ld} and t_{dd}, separately. The number of times that check matrix has to be reloaded is n and the number of data blocks that have to be processed is m. Suppose the secret key rate that optical system can provide is M, the number of data blocks m is M/L. The hardware processing efficiency α is

$$\alpha = \frac{1}{nt_{lm} + m(t_{ld} + t_{dd})} \quad (14)$$

Because of the finite-size effects, the block length in the procedure of privacy amplification is at least 10^7, which also takes up abundant hardware resource [26,27], so that not all the check matrices can be stored in advance. The reconciliation efficiency will be reduced quickly even if the SNR changes in a very small range. Therefore, other schemes have to reload the appropriate check matrix and then load and decode data when the rate is higher than the channel capacity. With our proposed LPDC code, we save the time of reloading the check matrix. For the block length of 648,000, the times used to load data and decode data we tested with the FPGA Arria 10 are 13.0 ms and 211.2 ms. Furthermore, the average time we used to load check matrix of ATSC 3.0 LDPC codes is 11.1ms. From the Figure 5, we can see that our work keeps a high hardware processing efficiency α with the number of check matrix changing times n increases. Meanwhile, difference of hardware reconciliation efficiency between our proposed LDPC code and ATSC 3.0 LDPC code also increases.

Frame error rate is the rate that a data block failed to be decoded. It is mainly caused by two reasons: the defect of error correcting code and decoding algorithm; the unadaptable check matrix led by the changing of SNR. The FER caused by the defect of error correcting code and decoding algorithm can be reduced to 3.25×10^{-3}, which is far lower than the FER led by the latter reason [28]. Therefore, we only take the latter reason into account. It can be seen from Figure 6 that with the number of check matrix changes increases, our proposed LDPC code has a lower FER than the other scheme.

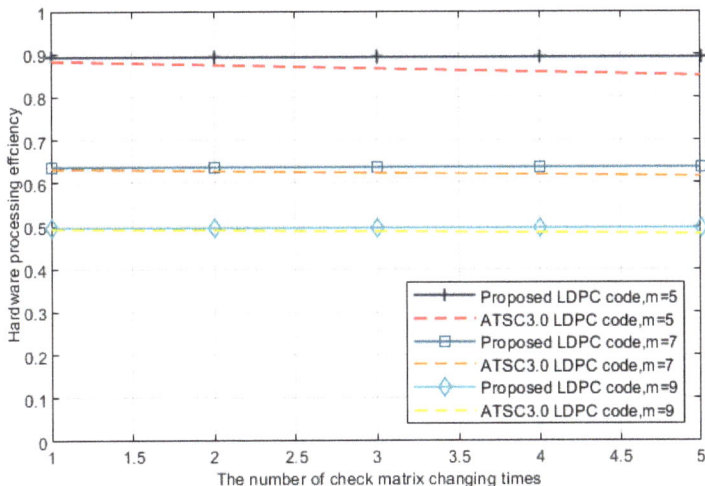

Figure 5. The hardware processing efficiency α influenced by the number of check matrix changing times n.

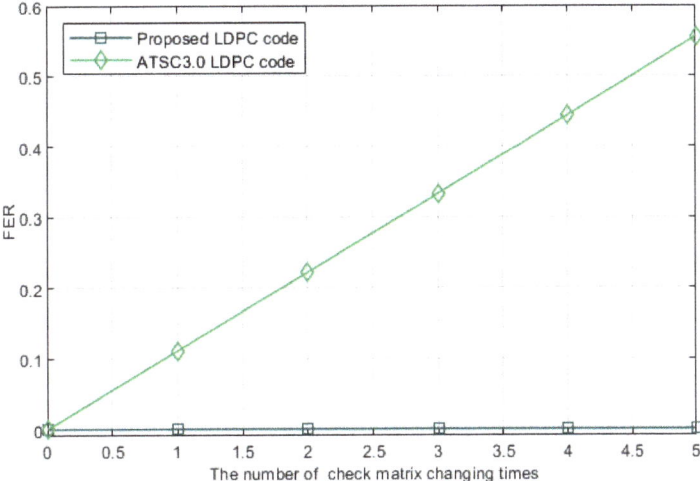

Figure 6. FER influenced by the number of check matrix changing times N. The number of data blocks that have to be processed is nine.

Given the excess noise, efficiency of receiver's detector and electronic noise at Bob's side, we can calculate the practical secret key rate [29]. Figure 7 is the comparison of the practical secret key rate of the proposed LDPC code and ATSC 3.0 LDPC codes. As can be seen in the graph, our scheme has a better performance with same number of check matrix changes N and has a lower performance reduction when the N increases. This comes from the fact that combined action of reconciliation efficiency β, hardware processing efficiency α and FER.

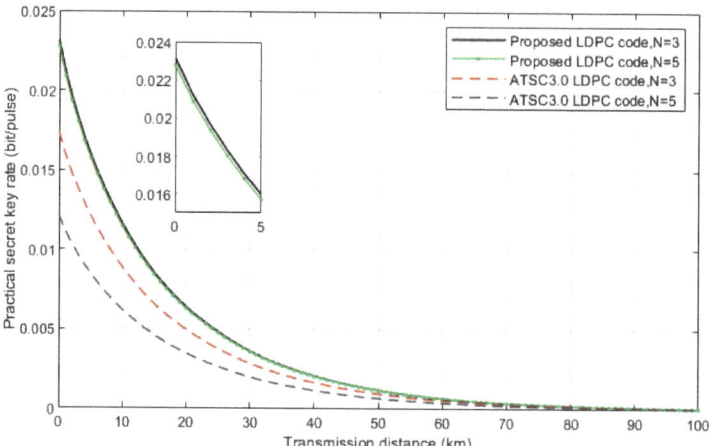

Figure 7. Practical secret key rate with reconciliation efficiency of 91.80% for our proposed LDPC code and 96.00% for ATSC 3.0 LDPC code. The extra parameters $\varepsilon = 0.01$, $\eta = 0.64$ and $V_{el} = 0.1$.

5. Conclusions

In this study, we design a rule of proposing a RC-LDPC code with single matrix for SNRs between 0.01 and 15 to solve the problems of great variation of quantum channel noise and extremely low SNR. First, we use the discretized density evolution algorithm and differential evolution to acquire good node degree distribution pairs of LDPC codes. Then, with construction methods including PEG algorithm, random construction, quasi-cyclic extension and rate-compatible methods including extending and puncturing, we proposed a convenient and efficient construction method for designing a RC-LDPC code. Considering the number of check matrix changing times led by the change of SNR, the result shows that we have a reconciliation efficiency of 91.80%, higher hardware processing efficiency and lower FER. It has a good performance especially in an extremely unstable channel.

Author Contributions: Conceptualization, X.F.; methodology, X.F., Q.N. and T.Z.; software, X.F.; validation, X.F.; formal analysis, X.F.; investigation, X.F.; resources, B.G.; data curation, X.F.; writing—original draft preparation, X.F.; writing—review and editing, X.F., Q.N. and T.Z.; visualization, X.F.; supervision, B.G.; funding acquisition, B.G. All authors have read and agreed to the published version of the manuscript.

Funding: This research was funded by the Key-Area Research and Development Program of Guangdong Province (Grant No. 2018B030325002).

Institutional Review Board Statement: Not applicable.

Informed Consent Statement: Not applicable.

Data Availability Statement: Not applicable.

Acknowledgments: We thank Peng-Cheng Wang, Bo-Wen Dong and Jie Jia for their helpful discussions.

Conflicts of Interest: The authors declare no conflict of interest.

Appendix A

Table A1. Degree distribution pairs of code rate from 0.01 to 0.1.

Rate	Degree Distribution	σ	SNR	C
0.1	$v(r,x) = 0.0775r_1x_1^2x_2^{20} + 0.0475r_1x_1^3x_2^{22} + 0.875r_1x_3$ $\mu(x) = 0.0025x_1^{11} + 0.0225x_1^{12} + 0.03x_2^2x_3 + 0.845x_2^3x_3$	2.541	0.15	0.0488
0.05	$v(r,x) = 0.04r_1x_1^2x_2^{34} + 0.03r_1x_1^3x_2^{34} + 0.93r_1x_3$ $\mu(x) = 0.01x_1^8 + 0.01x_1^9 + 0.41x_2^2x_3 + 0.52x_2^3x_3$	5.91	0.03	0.0213
0.02	$v(r,x) = 0.0225r_1x_1^2x_2^{34} + 0.0175r_1x_1^3x_2^{34} + 0.96r_1x_3$ $\mu(x) = 0.010625x_1^3 + 0.009375x_1^7 + 0.6x_2^2x_3 + 0.36x_2^3x_3$	2.541	0.15	0.1008

References

1. Gisin, N.; Ribordy, G.; Tittel, W.; Zbinden, H. Quantum cryptography. *Rev. Mod. Phys.* **2001**, *74*, 145–195. [CrossRef]
2. Scarani, V.; Bechmann-Pasquinucci, H.; Cerf, N.J.; Dušek, M.; Lütkenhaus, N.; Peev, M. The security of practical quantum key distribution. *Rev. Mod. Phys.* **2009**, *81*, 1301. [CrossRef]
3. Zhu, M.; Hu, M.; Guo, B. Free-Space QKD with Modulating Retroreflectors Based on the B92 Protocol. *Entropy* **2022**, *24*, 204. [CrossRef]
4. Hua X, Hu M, Guo B. Multi-User Measurement-Device-Independent Quantum Key Distribution Based on GHZ Entangled State. *Entropy* **2022**, *24*, 841. [CrossRef] [PubMed]
5. Alia, O.; Tessinari, R.S.; Bahrani, S.; Bradley, T.D.; Sakr, H.; Harrington, K.; Hayes, J.; ; Chen, Y.; Petropoulos, P.; Richardson, D.; et al. DV-QKD Coexistence With 1.6 Tbps Classical Channels Over Hollow Core Fibre. *J. Light. Technol.* **2022**, *40*, 5522–5529. [CrossRef]
6. Weedbrook, C.; Pirola, S.; García-Patrón, R.; Cerf, N.J.; Ralph, T.C.; Shapiro, J.H.; Lloyd, S. Gaussian quantum information. *Rev. Mod. Phys.* **2011**, *84*, 621–669. [CrossRef]
7. Jain, N.; Chin, H.M.; Mani, H.; Lupo, C.; Nikolic, D.S.; Kordts, A.; Pirola, S.; Pedersen, T.B.; Kolb, M.; Omer, B.; et al. Practical continuous-variable quantum key distribution with composable security. *Nat. Commun.* **2022**, *13*, 4740. [CrossRef]
8. Kovalenko, O.; Ra, Y.S.; Cai, Y.; Usenko, V.C.; Fabre, C.; Treps, N.; Filip, R. Frequency-multiplexed entanglement for continuous-variable quantum key distribution. *Photonics Res.* **2021**, *9*, 2351–2359. [CrossRef]
9. Yang, S.; Lu, Z.G.; Li, Y. High-Speed Post-Processing in Continuous-Variable Quantum Key Distribution Based on FPGA Implementation. *J. Light. Technol.* **2020**, *38*, 3935. [CrossRef]
10. Mink, A.; Nakassis, A. LDPC for QKD Reconciliation. *arXiv* **2012**, arXiv:1205.4977.
11. Chen, Y.A.; Zhang, Q.; Chen, T.Y.; Cai, W.Q.; Liao, S.K.; Zhang, J.; Chen, K.; Yin, J.; Ren, J.G.; Chen, Z.; et al. An integrated space-to-ground quantum communication network over 4600 kilometres. *Nature* **2021**, *589*, 214–219. [CrossRef]
12. Yin, J.; Cao, Y.; Li, Y.H.; Liao, S.K.; Zhang, L.; Ren, J.G.; Pan, J.W. Satellite-based entanglement distribution over 1200 kilometers. *Science* **2017**, *356*, 1140–1144. [CrossRef]
13. Zhao, W.; Shi, R.; Ruan, X.; Guo, Y.; Mao, Y.; Feng, Y. Monte Carlo-based security analysis for multi-mode continuous-variable quantum key distribution over underwater channel. *Quantum Inf. Process.* **2022**, *21*, 186. [CrossRef]
14. Liu, H.Y.; Tian, X.H.; Gu, C.; Fan, P.; Ni, X.; Yang, R.; Zhang, J.N.; Hu, M.; Guo, J.; Zhu, S.N.; et al. Drone-based entanglement distribution towards mobile quantum networks. *Natl. Sci. Rev.* **2020**, *5*, 921–928. [CrossRef]
15. Gao, C.H.; Guo, Y.; Jiang, D.; Liu, J.; Chen, L.J. Multimatrix rate-compatible reconciliation for quantum key distribution. *Phys. Rev. A* **2020**, *102*, 022604. [CrossRef]
16. Zhang, K.; Jiang, X.Q.; Feng, Y.; Qiu, R.; Bai, E. High Efficiency Continuous-Variable Quantum Key Distribution Based on ATSC 3.0 LDPC Codes. *Entropy* **2020**, *22*, 1087. [CrossRef]
17. Richardson, T.J. The capacity of low-density parity-check codes under message-passing decoding. *IEEE Trans. Inf. Theory* **2001**, *47*, 599. [CrossRef]
18. Chung, S.Y.; Richardson, T.J.; Urbanke, R.L. Analysis of sum-product decoding of low-density parity-check codes using a Gaussian approximation. *Inf. Theory IEEE Trans.* **2001**, *47*, 657–670. [CrossRef]
19. Chung, S.Y. On the design of low-density parity-check codes within 0.0045 dB of the Shannon limit. *IEEE Commun. Lett.* **2002**, *5*, 58–60. [CrossRef]
20. Storn, R.; Price, K. Differential Evolution—A Simple and Efficient Heuristic for global Optimization over Continuous Spaces. *J. Glob. Optim.* **1997**, *11*, 341–359. [CrossRef]
21. Wang, X.; Zhang, Y.C.; Li, Z.; Xu, B.; Yu, S.; Guo, H. Efficient rate-adaptive reconciliation for continuous-variable quantum key distribution. *arXiv* **2017**, arXiv:1703.04916.
22. Jouguet, P.; Kunz-Jacques, S.; Leverrier, A. Long Distance Continuous-Variable Quantum Key Distribution with a Gaussian Modulation. *Phys. Rev. A* **2011**, *84*, 062317. [CrossRef]
23. Bai, Z.; Wang, X.; Yang, S.; Li, Y. High-efficiency Gaussian key reconciliation in continuous variable quantum key distribution. *Sci. China Phys. Mech. Astron.* **2016**, *59*, 614201. [CrossRef]

24. Bai, Z.; Yang, S.; Li, Y. High-efficiency reconciliation for continuous variable quantum key distribution. *Jpn. J. Appl. Phys.* **2017**, *56*, 044401. [CrossRef]
25. Jeong, S.; Jung, H.; Ha, J. Rate-compatible multi-edge type low-density parity-check code ensembles for continuous-variable quantum key distribution systems. *NPJ Quantum Inf.* **2022**, *8*, 6. [CrossRef]
26. Zhang, C.M.; Li, M.; Huang, J.Z.; Li, H.W.; Li, F.Y.; Wang, C.; Yin, Z.Q.; Chen, W.; Han, Z.F.; Sripimanwat, K.; et al. Fast implementation of length-adaptive privacy amplification in quantum key distribution. *Chin. Phys. B* **2014**, *23*, 090310. [CrossRef]
27. Yan, B.; Li, Q.; Mao, H.; Chen, N. An efficient hybrid hash based privacy amplification algorithm for quantum key distribution. *Quantum Inf. Process.* **2022**, *21*, 130. [CrossRef]
28. Shi, J.J.; Li, B.P.; Huang, D. Reconciliation for CV-QKD using globally-coupled LDPC codes. *Chin. Phys. B* **2020**, *29*, 040301. [CrossRef]
29. Fossier, S.; Diamanti, E.; Debuisschert, T.; Villing, A.; Tualle-Brouri, R.; Grangier, P. Field test of a continuous-variable quantum key distribution prototype. *New J. Phys.* **2009**, *11*, 045023. [CrossRef]

Article

Multi-User Measurement-Device-Independent Quantum Key Distribution Based on GHZ Entangled State

Ximing Hua [1], Min Hu [1,2,*] and Banghong Guo [1,3,*]

[1] Guangdong Provincial Key Laboratory of Nanophotonic Functional Materials and Devices, Guangdong Provincial Key Laboratory of Quantum Engineering and Quantum Materials, South China Normal University, Guangzhou 510006, China; 2019022062@m.scnu.edu.cn
[2] National Quantum Communication (Guangdong) Co., Ltd., Guangzhou 510535, China
[3] Key Laboratory of Quantum Information, University of Science and Technology of China, Chinese Academy of Sciences, Hefei 230026, China
* Correspondence: hmin@scnu.edu.cn (M.H.); guobh@scnu.edu.cn (B.G.)

Abstract: As a multi-particle entangled state, the Greenberger–Horne–Zeilinger (GHZ) state plays an important role in quantum theory and applications. In this study, we propose a flexible multi-user measurement-device-independent quantum key distribution (MDI-QKD) scheme based on a GHZ entangled state. Our scheme can distribute quantum keys among multiple users while being resistant to detection attacks. Our simulation results show that the secure distance between each user and the measurement device can reach more than 280 km while reducing the complexity of the quantum network. Additionally, we propose a method to expand our scheme to a multi-node with multi-user network, which can further enhance the communication distance between the users at different nodes.

Keywords: quantum key distribution; GHZ entangled state; measurement-device-independent; multi-user

1. Introduction

Quantum key distribution (QKD) allows two users, Alice and Bob, to share a secure key privately [1,2]. The first QKD protocol, called the BB84 protocol, was proposed in 1984 by Bennett and Brassard [3]. However, because of the gaps between reality and theory, there exist various loopholes in practical systems through which eavesdroppers can attack the QKD process [4]. Therefore, several investigators have focused on finding ways to resist such attacks [5,6]. In 2012, Lo et al. proposed a measurement-device-independent quantum key distribution (MDI-QKD) protocol [7] to prevent attacks on measurement devices and enhance the communication distance between two users.

QKD research usually begins with a point-to-point scheme. With the development of quantum networks [8–10], multi-user scenarios have become research hotspots. Multi-user QKD, known as quantum cryptography conference (QCC) such as Greenberger–Horne–Zeilinger (GHZ) states [11] based scheme [12] and measurement-device independent scheme [13] or quantum conference key agreement (CKA) such as the intensity-encoded scheme [14] and the scheme based on a W-class state [15], is effective in scenarios where multiple users share common secure keys. Multi-particle entangled states can easily apply in multi-user QKD realization [16], although the communication distance is limited by the stability of entangled states and other issues lead to such schemes being inferior compared to the existing single-photon interference schemes [17].

Ref. [18] proposed an MDI-QKD scheme with an entangled source in the middle and realized ultra-long communication. Inspired by the scheme, we propose a multi-user MDI-QKD scheme based on the GHZ entangled state. We analyze the security of our scheme and derive the secure key rate when users employ an ideal single photon source and a weak coherent source. The simulation results show that a multi-user MDI-QKD system can be realized under this scheme with a reduced number of detectors and quantum channels compared with traditional MDI-QKD, while the distance between each user and the measurement device can reach more than 280 km (more than 560 km between each two users). Additionally, we propose a method to expand our scheme to a multi-node with multi-user network, which can further enhance the communication distance between the users at different nodes. This paper is organized as follows: in Section 2, we introduce the multi-user MDI-QKD based on GHZ entangled state protocol. In Section 3, we estimate the performance of our scheme for an ideal single-photon source and a weak coherent source. In Section 4, we introduce a method to expand our scheme to a multi-node with multi-user network. Finally, a summary is presented in Section 5.

2. Protocol

Before providing details of our protocol, we simply introduce the background knowledge of our scheme. A GHZ entangled state is multi-particle entangled state in which each particle is entangled with other particles. It has maximum output mutual information, and resistance to white noise. The n-particle GHZ entangled state can be expressed as follows [19]:

$$|\phi^+\rangle = \frac{1}{\sqrt{2}}(|000\ldots00\rangle + |111\ldots11\rangle)_N \qquad (1)$$

Based on the distribution of an n-particle GHZ entangled state [16], n users can obtain the common secure key simultaneously. This leads to the generation of a secure key according to the measurement result of the GHZ entangled state.

In MDI-QKD [7], the measurement device utilizes the Hong–Ou–Mandel (HOM) [20] effect to construct the relationship between two input particles. According to the click of the detectors, we obtain the BSM result $|\psi^+\rangle = (|H\rangle|V\rangle + |V\rangle|H\rangle)/\sqrt{2}$ and $|\psi^-\rangle = (|H\rangle|V\rangle - |V\rangle|H\rangle)/\sqrt{2}$. In the Z basis, the successful BSM event ($|\psi^+\rangle$ and $|\psi^-\rangle$) represents the polarization of two particles being different, while the X basis $|\psi^+\rangle$ ($|\psi^-\rangle$) represents the two particles having the same (different) polarization.

Combining the distribution of the GHZ entangled state with the MDI-QKD, we can realize the multi-user QKD by entanglement swapping [21].

As depicted in Figure 1, there is a case of an n-user MDI-QKD system based on GHZ entangled states. The system can divide into four parts: user, measurement device, GHZ entangled state source (GHZ-ESS) and channel. The n-user system includes n users, n measurement devices, a GHZ-ESS, and channel. The user mainly contains a source, a polarization modulator, and an upper computer. In practice, we usually use a weak coherent source with a decoy-state instead of a single photon source. The user uses a polarization modulator to modulate BB84 polarization states. The upper computer control the source, the polarization modulator and the information processing. The information processing includes sifting the efficient data, post-processing, etc. Each user has a corresponding measurement device. The GHZ-ESS connects to all measurement devices. The number of particles in the GHZ entangled state is similar to the number of users. Each particle of the GHZ entangled state will interfere with the polarization state prepared by users in the corresponding measurement device. They will perform Bell state measurement (BSM) in the measurement device. The channel including quantum channel and classical channel. Quantum channels are used to transmit quantum signals. Classical information such as the basis of prepared polarization state is transmitted in classical channel.

As shown in Figure 2, our protocol consists of five main steps:

Step 1: Preparation. Each user randomly prepares one of the BB84 states such as $|+\rangle, |-\rangle$ in the X basis or $|H\rangle, |V\rangle$ in the Z basis, while the GHZ-ESS randomly prepares an n-particle GHZ entangled state. The number of particles in the GHZ entangled state is equal to the number of users (in principle, each user only sends one photon).

Step 2: Transmission. Users (the GHZ-ESS) transmit the BB84 state (the GHZ entangled state) in different quantum channels between each user (the GHZ-ESS) and measurement device.

Step 3: Measurement. The measurement device performs BSM on the BB84 state and the GHZ entangled-state particles. Each particle of the GHZ entangled quantum state can interfere with a particle sent by its corresponding user. If there are only two detectors responding we call it a successful BSM event (a click in D1H and D2V, or in D1V and D2H are $|\psi^-\rangle$; a click in D1H and D1V, or in D2H and D2V are $|\psi^+\rangle$), similar to traditional MDI-QKD.

Step 4: Sifting. All users retain the bits when all the corresponding measurement device generates a successful BSM event. All users announce the basis of the prepared BB84 state, and the GHZ entangled source broadcasts the GHZ state it has prepared through the classical channels. In our scheme, only the states in the Z basis are used to generate a secure key; the states in the X basis are used to estimate the error rate. Hence, users retain the data prepared in the same basis by all users and discard the remaining data. Then, each user should either flip or not flip its local bits according to the BSM result, the GHZ states, and the prepared basis; see following and Appendix A for details. At this point, each user obtains the raw key.

Step 5: Post-processing. Similar to traditional point-to-point QKD protocols, users perform post-processing under the control of upper computer, which includes error correction and privacy amplification. They finally obtain the same secure keys.

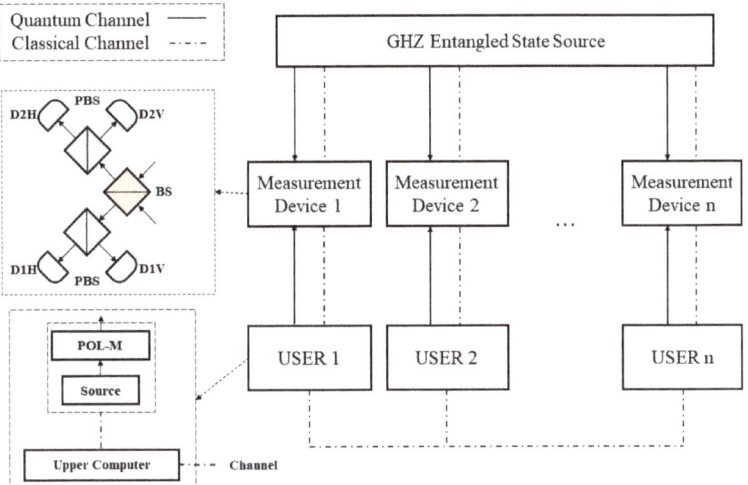

Figure 1. Schematic diagram of n-user MDI-QKD system. **POL-M**: polarization modulator; **BS**: beam splitter; **PBS**: polarization beam splitter; **D1H, D1V, D2H, D2V**: single-photon detector; **Source**: single-photon source or weak coherent source. We use solid line to depict the quantum channel and dotted line to depict the classical channel. The measurement device includes a BS, two PBSs, and four single-photon detectors, and implements the Bell state measurement (BSM) the same as the polarization-based MDI-QKD protocol. The GHZ-ESS can prepare GHZ entangled states with different numbers of particles corresponding to the number of users.

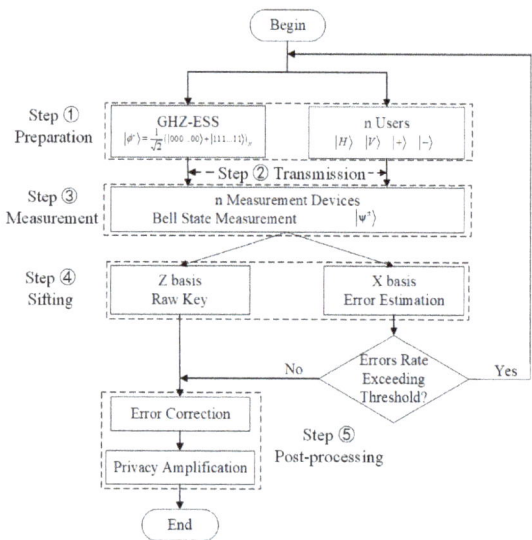

Figure 2. Flow chart of our protocol.

Following the original MDI-QKD protocol [7], users need to operate on their local bits based on the GHZ entangled state and the BSM results to generate secure keys. Taking three users (named Alice, Bob, and Charles) as an example, Table 1 shows the relationship between the prepared GHZ state, the BSM results, and the operations of the three participants. The users can retain the signal to generate a secure key only when all the BSM results are $|\psi^+\rangle$ or $|\psi^-\rangle$.

Table 1. Participants and their operations in the Z basis.

GHZ State	BSM 1	BSM 2	BSM 3	Alice	Bob	Charles
$\frac{1}{\sqrt{2}}(|H\rangle|H\rangle|H\rangle \pm |V\rangle|V\rangle|V\rangle)$	$|\psi^\pm\rangle$	$|\psi^\pm\rangle$	$|\psi^\pm\rangle$	No Flip	No Flip	No Flip
$\frac{1}{\sqrt{2}}(|H\rangle|V\rangle|H\rangle \pm |V\rangle|H\rangle|V\rangle)$	$|\psi^\pm\rangle$	$|\psi^\pm\rangle$	$|\psi^\pm\rangle$	No Flip	Flip	No Flip
$\frac{1}{\sqrt{2}}(|H\rangle|H\rangle|V\rangle \pm |V\rangle|V\rangle|H\rangle)$	$|\psi^\pm\rangle$	$|\psi^\pm\rangle$	$|\psi^\pm\rangle$	No Flip	No Flip	Flip
$\frac{1}{\sqrt{2}}(|H\rangle|V\rangle|V\rangle \pm |V\rangle|H\rangle|H\rangle)$	$|\psi^\pm\rangle$	$|\psi^\pm\rangle$	$|\psi^\pm\rangle$	No Flip	Flip	Flip

For example, when the state prepared by the GHZ-ESS is $\frac{1}{\sqrt{2}}(|H\rangle|H\rangle|H\rangle \pm |V\rangle|V\rangle|V\rangle)$, the message can be retained as a sifted key only if Alice, Bob, and Charles have prepared the same polarization state and all the BSM results are $|\psi^+\rangle$ or $|\psi^-\rangle$.

3. Secure Key Rate

Next, we derive the secure key and error rates to investigate the performance of our scheme with a single-photon source and a weak coherent source.

By combining the MDI-QKD technique [7] and the GLLP method [22], the security key rate is given by

$$R = Q_1^Z[1 - H(e_1^X)] - Q^Z f H(E^{Z*}) \tag{2}$$

where Q^Z and E^{Z*} denote the gain and quantum bit error rate (QBER) in the Z basis, respectively; f is the inefficiency function for the error correction process; Q_1^Z denotes the gain when all users send a single-photon state; e_1^X denotes the phase error rate; and $H(x) = -x\log_2(x) - (1-x)\log_2(1-x)$ is the binary Shannon entropy function. $E^{Z*} = \max\{E_{U_1 U_2}^Z, E_{U_1 U_3}^Z \ldots E_{U_1 U_n}^Z\}$, where $E_{U_1 U_2}^Z \left(E_{U_1 U_3}^Z \ldots E_{U_1 U_n}^Z\right)$ is the marginal quantum bit error rate between user 1 and user 2 (3...n) in the Z basis. In practice, Q^Z and E^{Z*} can be obtained from experimental data.

3.1. Key Rate of Single-Photon Source

For simplicity, we consider the case of three users in our scheme and estimate the secure key rate for a single photon source.

When the users use an ideal single-photon source to prepare the BB84 state, the gain in the Z basis is

$$Q^Z = Q_1^Z = Y_1 \tag{3}$$

where Y_1 denotes the probability of obtaining a successful BSM when all the users send a single-photon state. The yield Y_1 is given by

$$Y_1 = \frac{1}{64}\{(1-P_d)^2[1-(1-P_d)(1-\eta)][1-(1-P_d)(1-\eta_d)] \\ + 2P_d(1-P_d)^2[1-(1-P_d)(1-\eta)(1-\eta_d)]\}^3 \tag{4}$$

where P_d is the dark count, η_d is the detection efficiency, $\eta = \eta_l \times \eta_b = 10^{-\alpha L/10} \times \eta_b$ is the transmittance between the users and measurement device, and η_l represents the channel loss. $\frac{1}{64}$ represents the possibility that users send similar or different polarization states to the particles of the GHZ entangled state in the Z basis.

We assume that our entangled source is perfect; therefore, the error rate contains two main contributions: (1) the error rate e_0 caused by background counts and (2) the error rate e_d corresponding to the misalignment and instability of the optical system. The total error rate is as follows:

$$E^{Z*} = E^Z_{U_1 U_2} = E^Z_{U_1 U_3} = e_0 - \frac{(e_0 - e_d)(\frac{1}{16}\eta^2 \eta_d^2 (1-P_d)^4)}{Y_{U_1 U_2}} \tag{5}$$

where $Y_{U_1 U_2}$ denotes the probability of both measurement devices obtaining a successful BSM when user 1 and user 2 send a single-photon state. Similarly, we obtain the error rate in the X basis as follows:

$$e_1^X = e_0 - \frac{(e_0 - e_d)(\frac{1}{64}\eta^3 \eta_d^3 (1-P_d)^6)}{Y_1} \tag{6}$$

Utilizing the experimental parameters in Table 2 [23], we obtained the simulation results shown in Figure 3. These results show that the communication distance between each user and the GHZ-ESS can exceed 280 km using optical fibers. Using an ideal single-photon source and a perfect GHZ-ESS, the GHZ-ESS can be located at the center to establish a star-configuration quantum network with a radius of 280 km.

Table 2. Experimental parameters used in the simulation. e_d is the system intrinsic bit error rate, P_d is the dark count, f is the error correction inefficiency, and α is the optical fiber transmission loss.

e_d	P_d	f	α
2%	8×10^{-8}	1.16	0.2

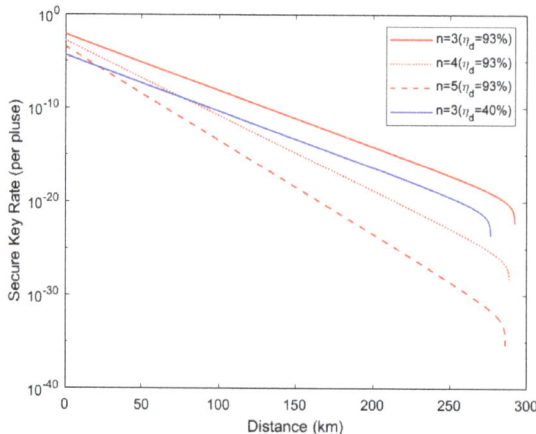

Figure 3. Secure key rate with single-photon state. The red line corresponds to the detection efficiency η_d of 93% [24], and the blue line corresponds to the detection efficiency η_d of 40% [23]. **n** is the number of communication users. The distance refers to the length of the quantum channel between any user and the measurement device.

3.2. Key Rate of Weak Coherent Source with Decoy State

In this section, we analyze the realization of the decoy state using our protocol. Users use the decoy state to resist a photon number splitting (PNS) attack on a weak coherent source. In our protocol, we use the Z basis to generate the secure key and the X basis to detect the error bit. Therefore, we take the quantum state in the Z basis as the signal state (only preparing the signal state) and that in the X basis as the decoy state (preparing both signal state and decoy state).

In our analysis, two decoy-state techniques (signal state v, vacuum state μ_2, decoy-state μ_1) are used, where $v > \mu_1 > \mu_2 = 0$ represents the mean photons of the sources.

We consider the situation consisting of three users as an example to derive the secure key rate. According to the decoy state method [25], in the Z basis, for each measurement device, we can estimate the gain Q_m^Z and error rate E_m^Z as follows:

$$Q_m^Z = \sum_{i=0}^{\infty} e^{-v} Y_{1i} \frac{v^i}{i!} \qquad (7)$$

$$E_m^Z Q_m^Z = \sum_{i=0}^{\infty} e^{-v} e_{1i} Y_{1i} \frac{v^i}{i!} \qquad (8)$$

where Y_{1i} (e_{1i}) represents the yield (error rate) from the GHZ-ESS and the corresponding user. The subscript 1 that different from the traditional MDI-QKD [7] represents the particle of GHZ entangled state in each measurement device. Therefore, we can estimate the total gain and error rate in the Z basis as follows:

$$Q^Z = \sum_{i=0}^{\infty}\sum_{j=0}^{\infty}\sum_{k=0}^{\infty} e^{-3v} Y_{111ijk} \frac{v^{i+j+k}}{i!j!k!} \qquad (9)$$

$$E^Z Q^Z = \sum_{i=0}^{\infty}\sum_{j=0}^{\infty}\sum_{k=0}^{\infty} e^{-3v} e_{111ijk} Y_{111ijk} \frac{v^{i+j+k}}{i!j!k!} \qquad (10)$$

where Y_{111ijk} (e_{111ijk}) represents the overall yield (error rate) in the Z basis. We optimized the formula in the Ref. [26] and added the subscript 111 to describe the influence of GHZ entangled state. We Similarly, we can obtain the total gain and error rate in the X basis.

Because we use the decoy state technique in the X basis, we can obtain the total gain in the Z basis when all users send a single photon pulse as

$$Q_1^Z = v^3 e^{-3v} Y_1^Z \tag{11}$$

where Y_1^Z represents the yield when all users send a single photon pulse.

Next, we need to estimate the lower bound of the yield and the upper bound of the error rate that each user sends for a single-photon pulse in the X basis. According to the decoy-state method [25–27], we can estimate that

$$\begin{aligned} Y_1^X \geq \frac{1}{v^3 \mu_1^3 (v-\mu_1)} [&v^4 (e^{3\mu_1} Q_{111\mu_1\mu_1\mu_1}^X - e^{2\mu_1} Q_{111\mu_1\mu_1 0}^X - e^{2\mu_1} Q_{111\mu_1 0\mu_1}^X - e^{2\mu_1} Q_{1110\mu_1\mu_1}^X \\ &+ e^{\mu_1} Q_{111\mu_1 00}^X + e^{\mu_1} Q_{1110\mu_1 0}^X + e^{\mu_1} Q_{11100\mu_1}^X - Q_{111000}^X) \\ &- \mu_1^4 (e^{3v} Q_{111vvv}^X - e^{2v} Q_{111vv0}^X - e^{2v} Q_{111v0v}^X - e^{2v} Q_{1110vv}^X \\ &+ e^v Q_{111v00}^X + e^v Q_{1110v0}^X + e^v Q_{11100v}^X - Q_{111000}^X) \end{aligned} \tag{12}$$

$$\begin{aligned} e_1^X \leq \frac{1}{\mu_1^3 Y_1^X} (&e^{3\mu_1} E_{111\mu_1\mu_1\mu_1}^X Q_{111\mu_1\mu_1\mu_1}^X - e^{2\mu_1} E_{111\mu_1\mu_1 0}^X Q_{111\mu_1\mu_1 0}^X - e^{2\mu_1} E_{111\mu_1 0\mu_1}^X Q_{111\mu_1 0\mu_1}^X \\ &- e^{2\mu_1} E_{1110\mu_1\mu_1}^X Q_{1110\mu_1\mu_1}^X + e^{\mu_1} E_{111\mu_1 00}^X Q_{111\mu_1 00}^X + e^{\mu_1} E_{1110\mu_1 0}^X Q_{1110\mu_1 0}^X \\ &+ e^{\mu_1} E_{11100\mu_1}^X Q_{11100\mu_1}^X - E_{111000}^X Q_{111000}^X) \end{aligned} \tag{13}$$

where Q_{111ijk}^X ($i,j,k = 0, \mu_1, v$ represent the mean photon number intensities of users' sources) is the overall gain in the X basis when users choose the corresponding intensities. E_{111ijk}^X is the overall error rate in the X basis when users choose corresponding intensities.

Finally, utilizing the experimental parameters in Table 2, we can obtain the performance of our protocol when three users use weak coherent sources as shown in Figure 4. The simulation results show that the communication distance between each user and the GHZ-ESS can reach further than 210 km using optical fibers. Compared with a single photon source, the weak coherent source has a lower secure key rate and shorter communication distance while still realizing a signal transmission of more than 420 km between each two users.

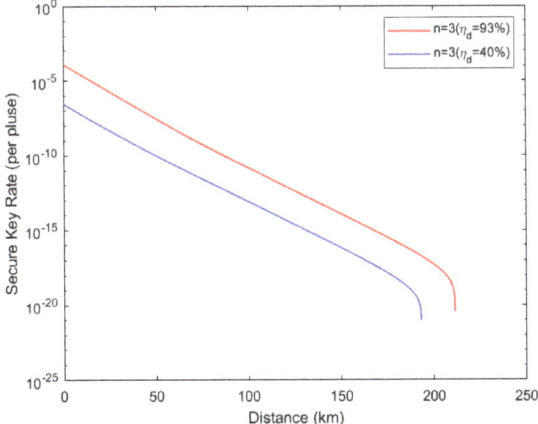

Figure 4. Secure key rate with weak coherent source. The simulation performed for the situation of three users had detection efficiency results of $\eta_d = 93\%$ and $\eta_d = 40\%$. The mean photons of signal state $v = 0.48$, and the mean photons of decoy-state $\mu_1 = 0.05$. The distance refers to the length of the quantum channel between any user and measurement device.

3.3. Security and Discussion

In this section, we will analyze the security of our protocol and compare our protocol with other schemes.

Without loss of generality, we can depict the three-particle GHZ entangled state in eight orthogonal GHZ states as [26]:

$$
\begin{aligned}
|\alpha_1\rangle &= \frac{1}{\sqrt{2}}(|H\rangle|H\rangle|H\rangle + |V\rangle|V\rangle|V\rangle) = \frac{1}{2}(|++\,+\rangle + |+--\rangle + |-+-\rangle + |--+\rangle) \\
|\alpha_2\rangle &= \frac{1}{\sqrt{2}}(|H\rangle|H\rangle|H\rangle - |V\rangle|V\rangle|V\rangle) = \frac{1}{2}(|++-\rangle + |+-+\rangle + |-++\rangle + |---\rangle) \\
|\alpha_3\rangle &= \frac{1}{\sqrt{2}}(|V\rangle|H\rangle|H\rangle + |H\rangle|V\rangle|V\rangle) = \frac{1}{2}(|++\,+\rangle + |+--\rangle - |-+-\rangle - |--+\rangle) \\
|\alpha_4\rangle &= \frac{1}{\sqrt{2}}(|V\rangle|H\rangle|H\rangle - |H\rangle|V\rangle|V\rangle) = \frac{1}{2}(|++-\rangle + |+-+\rangle - |-++\rangle - |---\rangle) \\
|\alpha_5\rangle &= \frac{1}{\sqrt{2}}(|H\rangle|V\rangle|H\rangle + |V\rangle|H\rangle|V\rangle) = \frac{1}{2}(|++\,+\rangle - |+--\rangle + |-+-\rangle - |--+\rangle) \\
|\alpha_6\rangle &= \frac{1}{\sqrt{2}}(|H\rangle|V\rangle|H\rangle - |V\rangle|H\rangle|V\rangle) = \frac{1}{2}(|++-\rangle - |+-+\rangle + |-++\rangle - |---\rangle) \\
|\alpha_7\rangle &= \frac{1}{\sqrt{2}}(|H\rangle|H\rangle|V\rangle + |V\rangle|V\rangle|H\rangle) = \frac{1}{2}(|++\,+\rangle - |+--\rangle - |-+-\rangle + |--+\rangle) \\
|\alpha_8\rangle &= \frac{1}{\sqrt{2}}(|H\rangle|H\rangle|V\rangle - |V\rangle|V\rangle|H\rangle) = \frac{1}{2}(|++-\rangle - |+-+\rangle - |-++\rangle + |---\rangle)
\end{aligned}
\tag{14}
$$

Taking $|\alpha_1\rangle$ as an example, it will randomly collapse into $|\gamma_1\rangle = |H\rangle|H\rangle|H\rangle$ or $|\gamma_2\rangle = |V\rangle|V\rangle|V\rangle$ in the Z basis. In the X basis, any user obtains $|+\rangle$ ($|-\rangle$) when the other obtains the same (different) polarization. We use the character that provides the security of the GHZ entangled sources to generate a secure key in the Z basis and error detection in the X basis.

Based on the principle of MDI-QKD [7], our scheme can resist attacks on the measurement devices. In addition to resisting attacks on the measurement device, our scheme can resist a PNS attack using the decoy state technique [22,25,28,29]. Users can employ weak coherent sources with a decoy-state. The GHZ entangled state is equivalent to an ideal single-photon state in each quantum channel. A PNS attack is ineffective for an ideal single-photon source. Therefore, our scheme can resist PNS attacks.

Compared with traditional MDI-QKD, ref. [30] reported the longest communication record that reached 404 km in experiments, while the simulation result shows that our protocol can be utilized with greater than 560 km between each two users. Four detectors are required to build a traditional MDI-QKD system between two users. Therefore, 2n (n − 1) detectors are required to establish a quantum communication system using the MDI-QKD protocol between n users. However, in our protocol, the number of detectors required to establish communications between n users is reduced to only 4n. Moreover, only 2n channels rather than n (n − 1)/2 channels are required if a traditional point-to-point protocol [7] is used between the users and the measurement device. Thus, the cost and complexity of the network are reduced.

We compare our scheme with other multi-user schemes in Table 3. When we employ a single photon source with $\eta_d = 93\%$, the available distance can reach more than 560 km between each two users. When we employ a weak coherent source with $\eta_d = 93\%$, the available distance can reach more than 420 km between each two users.

Unlike the MDI-QCC based on a post-selection GHZ entangled state [26] and PM-QCC based on a post-selection GHZ entangled state [19], our protocol uses a GHZ entangled state and the polarization state prepared by users to execute BSM and realize multi-user sharing of a common secret key.

Table 3. Comparison of multi-user schemes.

Items	GHZ State MDI-QCC [26]	W State Multi-User MDI-QKD [31]	GHZ State Multi-User MDI-QKD [23]	Our Scheme
Entangled State	GHZ state	W state	GHZ state	GHZ state
Users	≥ 3	≥ 4	≥ 3	≥ 3
Secure Key Rate	10^{-16} ($\eta_d = 93\%$, 400 km between two users, weak coherent)	10^{-16} ($\eta_d = 93\%$, 260 km between two users, single photon)	10^{-21} ($\eta_d = 40\%$, 400 km between two users, single photon)	10^{-15} ($\eta_d = 93\%$, 400 km between two users, single photon)
Available Distance	420 km between two users (weak coherent)	260 km between two users (single photon)	520 km between two users (single photon)	560 km between two users (single photon) 420 km between two users (weak coherent)

CKA schemes [32] based on the principle of twin-field QKD [33] can realize a high secure key rate and long communication distance through the single photon interference. In our scheme, with a more flexible number of users, we can increase the distance between the GHZ-ESS and the measurement device to enhance the communication distance between each two users. In addition, we can expand our scheme further into a multi-node quantum network, as detailed in Section 4.

Because of the coincidence measurement at the measurement device, increasing the number of users will lead to an obvious decrease in the secure key rate. We propose a system that uses an adaptive technique in Appendix B, while we need to investigate the specific performance in our scheme. At the same time, we will consider using asynchronous time multiplexing technology [34,35], which idea is based on adaptive techniques, to further improve our scheme through enhancing the secure key rate under multi-user scenarios.

4. Expansion of Our Protocol

Based on the location-changeable GHZ-ESS, we can expand our scheme further into a multi-node quantum network without quantum memory. An example of two nodes with two users per node is shown in Figure 5, and we can extend the system to n nodes with n users per node.

In the system, we use measurement devices that perform BSM to construct the entangled relationship between two adjacent GHZ entangled sources and extend the communication distance between users in different nodes by increasing the distance between the GHZ-ESS and the measurement device. We use the example shown in Figure 5 to detail the process. In theory, the longest secure communication between user 3 and user 1 can be estimated as follows:

$$L_{U_1U_3} = L_{U_1M_1} + L_{GHZ_1M_1} + L_{GHZ_1M_{GHZ}} + L_{GHZ_2M_{GHZ}} + L_{GHZ_2M_3} + L_{U_3M_3} \quad (15)$$

where $L_{U_1M_1}$ ($L_{U_3M_3}$) is the distance between the user and the corresponding measurement device, $L_{GHZ_1M_1}$ ($L_{GHZ_2M_3}$) is the distance between the GHZ-ESS and the corresponding measurement device, and $L_{GHZ_1M_{GHZ}}$ ($L_{GHZ_2M_{GHZ}}$) is the distance between the GHZ-ESS and the measurement device that is between the adjacent GHZ-ESSs.

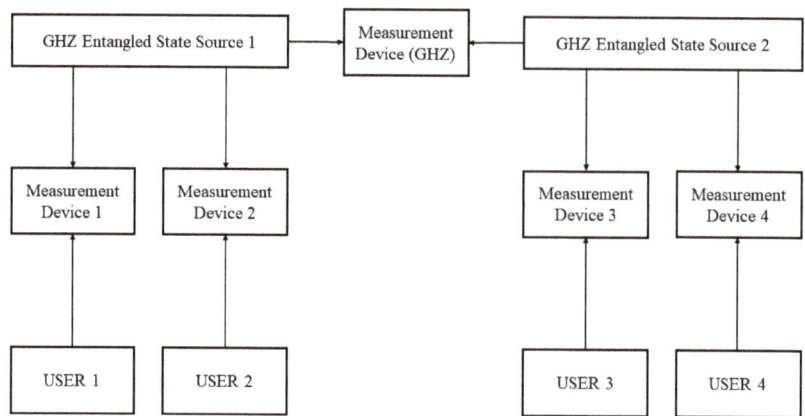

Figure 5. An example of two users per node. The system can help user 1, user 2, user 3, and user 4 to share a common secure key. Unlike our system shown in Figure 1, we build the relationship between two GHZ-ESSs with measurement devices that use BSM like ordinary MDI-QKD devices.

When we assume that two GHZ-ESSs prepare the same GHZ entangled state and all measurement devices obtain successful BSM events ($|\psi^+\rangle$ or $|\psi^-\rangle$), the operations of users in the Z basis are as shown in Table 4.

Table 4. The operations of users in different GHZ states in the Z basis. The operation of bit flip according to user 1 and all measurement devices obtain successful BSM events ($|\psi^+\rangle$ or $|\psi^-\rangle$). We assume that the first particle of the first GHZ is entangled, corresponding to measurement device 1, and the first particle of the second GHZ entangled state corresponds to measurement device 3.

GHZ state	USER 1	USER 2	USER 3	USER 4
$\frac{1}{\sqrt{2}}(|H\rangle|H\rangle|H\rangle \pm |V\rangle|V\rangle|V\rangle)$	No Flip	No Flip	Flip	Flip
$\frac{1}{\sqrt{2}}(|H\rangle|V\rangle|H\rangle \pm |V\rangle|H\rangle|V\rangle)$	No Flip	Flip	Flip	No Flip
$\frac{1}{\sqrt{2}}(|H\rangle|H\rangle|V\rangle \pm |V\rangle|V\rangle|H\rangle)$	No Flip	No Flip	Flip	Flip
$\frac{1}{\sqrt{2}}(|H\rangle|V\rangle|V\rangle \pm |V\rangle|H\rangle|H\rangle)$	No Flip	Flip	Flip	No Flip

5. Conclusions

In this study, we presented a multi-user MDI-QKD scheme based on the GHZ entangled state. We analyzed the security of our scheme and derived the secure key rate when users use an ideal single photon source and a weak coherent source. The MDI-QKD-based scheme is also immune to attacks on the measurement devices, and the communication distance is increased. Furthermore, in contrast to the multi-user quantum network implemented by the original MDI-QKD protocol, the number of detectors required in our scheme is reduced from 2n (n −1) to 4n, and the number of quantum channels is reduced from n (n − 1)/2 to 2n. Our scheme realizes an ultra-long QKD available communication distance that can reach more than 280 km between each user and measurement device (i.e., the longest communication distance between any two users can reach more than 560 km) and further extend by changing the location of the GHZ-ESS. In addition, we can expand our scheme further to a multi-node quantum network without quantum memory, which enhances the communication distance between two users.

Although our scheme can be flexibly applied to QKD networks, there are still two issues remaining to be studied in the future. On one hand, the location of the GHZ entangled source can be changed in our scheme, and we can extend the communication distance between two users by increasing the distance between the GHZ entangled source and the measurement device. Therefore, we will study the influence of GHZ entangled state long-distance division. On the other hand, in our estimation of the secure key rate, we assume that the distance between each user and the corresponding measurement device is similar. Therefore, it will be interesting to consider an asymmetric situation.

Author Contributions: Conceptualization, X.H. and M.H.; methodology, X.H. and M.H.; software, X.H. and M.H.; validation, X.H. and M.H.; formal analysis, X.H.; investigation, X.H. and M.H.; writing—original draft preparation, X.H.; writing—review and editing, X.H. and M.H.; visualization, X.H.; supervision, M.H. and B.G.; funding acquisition, B.G. All authors have read and agreed to the published version of the manuscript.

Funding: This research was funded by the Key-Area Research and Development Program of Guangdong Province (Grant No. 2018B030325002).

Institutional Review Board Statement: Not applicable.

Informed Consent Statement: Not applicable.

Data Availability Statement: Not applicable.

Acknowledgments: We thank Ming-Hao Zhu, Cong Chen, and Fan Yang for their helpful discussions.

Conflicts of Interest: The authors declare no conflict of interest.

Appendix A. Protocol Analysis

In this section, we analyze the generation of the secure key. The key generation in the Z basis in our protocol can be equivalent to the construction shown in Figure A1. The GHZ entangled source distributes a particle of the n-particle GHZ entangled states to each user. Users measure the polarization of the particle and obtain the secure key.

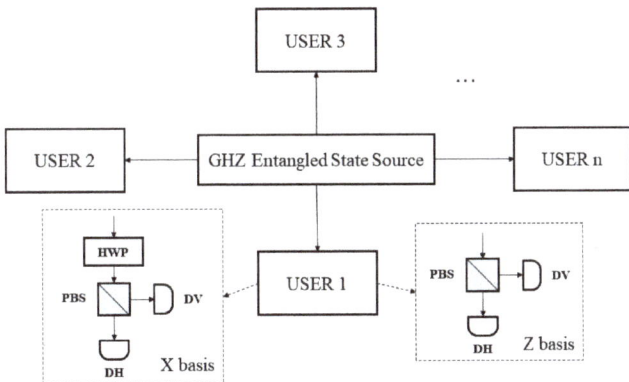

Figure A1. The equivalent topological schematic diagram of the GHZ entangled source distributing a particle of the n-particle GHZ entangled states to each user. **HWP**: half wave plate; **PBS**: polarization beam splitter; **DH, DV**: single photon detector.

We also considered the case of three users. As shown in Table A1, the GHZ-ESS prepares different GHZ states and sends them to users. Users measure the polarization in the Z basis. They obtain value "0" when the measurement result is $|H\rangle$, and value "1" corresponds to $|V\rangle$.

Table A1. Measurement result and value of the secure key. **GHZ entangled state** is the GHZ state sent by the entangled source. **MR1**, **MR2**, and **MR3** are the measurement results of user 1, user 2, and user 3. and **Value1**, **Value2**, and **Value3** are the values of the users' secure keys.

GHZ Entangled State	MR1	Value1	MR2	Value2	MR3	Value3
$\frac{1}{\sqrt{2}}(|H\rangle|H\rangle|H\rangle \pm |V\rangle|V\rangle|V\rangle)$	$|H\rangle$ $|V\rangle$	0 1	$|H\rangle$ $|V\rangle$	0 1	$|H\rangle$ $|V\rangle$	0 1
$\frac{1}{\sqrt{2}}(|V\rangle|H\rangle|H\rangle \pm |H\rangle|V\rangle|V\rangle)$	$|V\rangle$ $|H\rangle$	1 0	$|H\rangle$ $|V\rangle$	0 1	$|H\rangle$ $|V\rangle$	0 1
$\frac{1}{\sqrt{2}}(|H\rangle|V\rangle|H\rangle \pm |V\rangle|H\rangle|V\rangle)$	$|H\rangle$ $|V\rangle$	0 1	$|V\rangle$ $|H\rangle$	1 0	$|H\rangle$ $|V\rangle$	0 1
$\frac{1}{\sqrt{2}}(|H\rangle|H\rangle|V\rangle \pm |V\rangle|V\rangle|H\rangle)$	$|H\rangle$ $|V\rangle$	0 1	$|H\rangle$ $|V\rangle$	0 1	$|V\rangle$ $|H\rangle$	1 0

Compared with the equivalent topological scheme, our protocol can resist attacks on measurement devices and enhance the communication distance between two users. Moreover, if we locate the GHZ entangled source near the measurement device, can we greatly reduce the effect of decoherence of GHZ entangled states. However, we can also increase the distance between the GHZ-ESS and measurement device to increase the communication distance between the two users. Therefore, our protocol can realize multi-user QKD over an ultra-long distance.

Appendix B. Increasing the Secure Key Rate with an Adaptive Technique

According to the idea in [36], we propose our multi-user MDI-QKD system with an adaptive technique as shown in Figure A2.

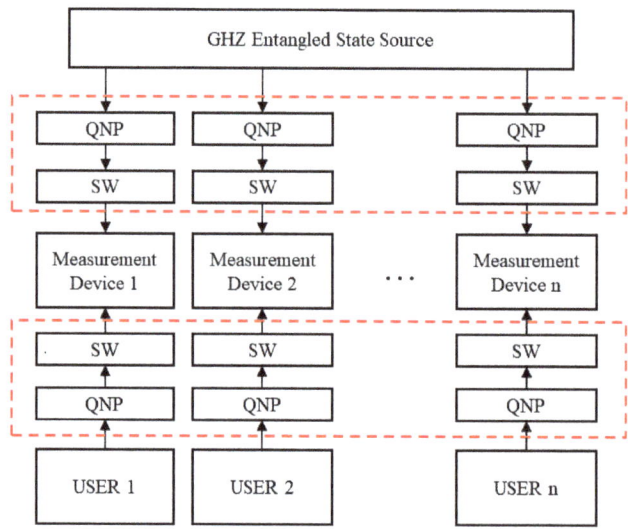

Figure A2. Multi-user MDI-QKD system with adaptive method. **QNP**: quantum non-demolition measurement; **SW**: optical switches. The adaptive technology structures are shown inside the red dashed frames.

The implementation process is as follows. Firstly, all users and GHZ-ESSs send many signal states to the corresponding measurement device; secondly, the QNP performs the quantum non-demolition measurement to detect the arrival of the signal; thirdly, the SW is used to match the arrival signal from the GHZ-ESS and users; fourthly, the measurement device performs BSM between the matched signals and broadcasts the matched result as well as measurement result; lastly, the user keeps the signal data that relate to successful BSM events and other post-processing.

Through the use of an adaptive technique, we can enhance the secure key rate in our multi-user QKD scheme. However, the lack of any particles in the GHZ entangled state will lead to the entire entangled state being unusable, and the GHZ-ESS will need to prepare more signal states than users in principle. We will study the specific performance of using an adaptive technique in future research.

References

1. Xu, F.; Ma, X.; Zhang, Q.; Lo, H.K.; Pan, J.W. Secure quantum key distribution with realistic devices. *Rev. Mod. Phys.* **2020**, *92*, 025002. [CrossRef]
2. Gisin, N.; Ribordy, G.; Tittel, W.; Zbinden, H. Quantum cryptography. *Rev. Mod. Phys.* **2002**, *74*, 145–195. [CrossRef]
3. Bennett, C.H.; Brassard, G. Quantum Cryptography: Public Key distribution and Coin Tossing. In Proceedings of the IEEE International Conference on Computers, Systems and Signal Processing, Bangalore, India, 10–12 December 1984; Institute of Electrical and Electronics Engineers: Bangalore, India, 1984; pp. 174–179.
4. Shor, P.W.; Preskill, J. Simple proof of security of the BB84 quantum key distribution protocol. *Phys. Rev. Lett.* **2000**, *85*, 441–444. [CrossRef] [PubMed]
5. Hwang, W.Y. Quantum Key Distribution with High Loss: Toward Global Secure Communication. *Phys. Rev. Lett.* **2003**, *91*, 057901. [CrossRef] [PubMed]
6. Acín, A.; Brunner, N.; Gisin, N.; Massar, S.; Pironio, S.; Scarani, V. Device-independent security of quantum cryptography against collective attacks. *Phys. Rev. Lett.* **2007**, *98*, 230501. [CrossRef]
7. Lo, H.K.; Curty, M.; Qi, B. Measurement-device-independent quantum key distribution. *Phys. Rev. Lett.* **2012**, *108*, 130503. [CrossRef]
8. Wang, S.; Chen, W.; Yin, Z.Q.; Li, H.W.; He, D.Y.; Li, Y.H.; Zhou, Z.; Song, X.T.; Li, F.Y.; Wang, D.; et al. Field and long-term demonstration of a wide area quantum key distribution network. *Opt. Express* **2014**, *22*, 21739. [CrossRef]
9. Cheng, G.; Guo, B.; Zhang, C.; Guo, J.; Fan, R. Wavelength division multiplexing quantum key distribution network using a modified plug-and-play system. *Opt. Quantum Electron.* **2015**, *47*, 1809–1817. [CrossRef]
10. Chen, Y.A.; Zhang, Q.; Chen, T.Y.; Cai, W.Q.; Liao, S.K.; Zhang, J.; Chen, K.; Yin, J.; Ren, J.G.; Chen, Z.; et al. An integrated space-to-ground quantum communication network over 4,600 kilometres. *Nature* **2021**, *589*, 214–219. [CrossRef]
11. Greenberger, D.M.; Horne, M.A.; Zeilinger, A. Going Beyond Bell's Theorem. In *Bell's Theorem, Quantum Theory and Conceptions of the Universe*; Kafatos, M., Ed.; Springer: Dordrecht, The Netherlands, 1989; pp. 69–72._10. [CrossRef]
12. Multi-partite quantum cryptographic protocols with noisy ghz states. *Quantum Inf. Comput.* **2007**, *7*, 689–715. [CrossRef]
13. Zhang, L.; Hu, M.; Ran, P.; Zeng, H.; Li, J.; Guo, B. Fuzzy Greenberger–Horne–Zeilinger state analyzer and multiparty measurement-device-independent quantum key distribution network. *Opt. Eng.* **2019**, *58*, 016113. [CrossRef]
14. Cao, X.Y.; Gu, J.; Lu, Y.S.; Yin, H.L.; Chen, Z.B. Coherent one-way quantum conference key agreement based on twin field. *New J. Phys.* **2021**, *23*, 043002. [CrossRef]
15. Grasselli, F.; Kampermann, H.; Bruß, D. Conference key agreement with single-photon interference. *New J. Phys.* **2019**, *21*, 123002. [CrossRef]
16. Epping, M.; Kampermann, H.; Macchiavello, C.; Bruß, D. Multi-partite entanglement can speed up quantum key distribution in networks. *New J. Phys.* **2017**, *19*, 093012. [CrossRef]
17. Cao, X.Y.; Lu, Y.S.; Li, Z.; Gu, J.; Yin, H.L.; Chen, Z.B. High Key Rate Quantum Conference Key Agreement with Unconditional Security. *IEEE Access* **2021**, *9*, 128870–128876. [CrossRef]
18. Xu, F.; Qi, B.; Liao, Z.; Lo, H.K. Long distance measurement-device-independent quantum key distribution with entangled photon sources. *Appl. Phys. Lett.* **2013**, *103*, 061101. [CrossRef]
19. Zhao, S.; Zeng, P.; Cao, W.F.; Xu, X.Y.; Zhen, Y.Z.; Ma, X.; Li, L.; Liu, N.L.; Chen, K. Phase-Matching Quantum Cryptographic Conferencing. *Phys. Rev. Appl.* **2020**, *14*, 024010. [CrossRef]
20. Hong, C.K.; Ou, Z.Y.; Mandel, L. Measurement of subpicosecond time intervals between two photons by interference. *Phys. Rev. Lett.* **1987**, *59*, 2044–2046. [CrossRef]
21. Bose, S.; Vedral, V.; Knight, P.L. Multiparticle generalization of entanglement swapping. *Phys. Rev. A At. Mol. Opt. Phys.* **1998**, *57*, 822–829. [CrossRef]
22. Gottesman, D.; Hoi-Kwonglo, L.O.; Lütkenhaus, N.; Preskill, J. Security of quantum key distribution with imperfect devices. *Quantum Inf. Comput.* **2004**, *4*, 325–360. [CrossRef]
23. Cao, W.F.; Zhen, Y.Z.; Zheng, Y.L.; Zhao, S.; Xu, F.; Li, L.; Chen, Z.B.; Liu, N.L.; Chen, K. Open-destination measurement-device-independent quantum key distribution network. *Entropy* **2020**, *22*, 1083. [CrossRef] [PubMed]
24. Marsili, F.; Verma, V.B.; Stern, J.A.; Harrington, S.; Lita, A.E.; Gerrits, T.; Vayshenker, I.; Baek, B.; Shaw, M.D.; Mirin, R.P.; et al. Detecting single infrared photons with 93% system efficiency. *Nat. Photonics* **2013**, *7*, 210–214. [CrossRef]

25. Ma, X.; Qi, B.; Zhao, Y.; Lo, H.K. Practical decoy state for quantum key distribution. *Phys. Rev. A* **2005**, *72*, 012326. [CrossRef]
26. Fu, Y.; Yin, H.L.; Chen, T.Y.; Chen, Z.B. Long-distance measurement-device-independent multiparty quantum communication. *Phys. Rev. Lett.* **2015**, *114*, 090501. [CrossRef]
27. Xu, F.; Curty, M.; Qi, B.; Lo, H.K. Practical aspects of measurement-device-independent quantum key distribution. *New J. Phys.* **2013**, *15*, 113007. [CrossRef]
28. Lütkenhaus, N.; Jahma, M. Quantum key distribution with realistic states: Photon-number statistics in the photon-number splitting attack. *New J. Phys.* **2002**, *4*, 44. [CrossRef]
29. Ma, X.; Razavi, M. Alternative schemes for measurement-device-independent quantum key distribution. *Phys. Rev. A* **2012**, *86*, 062319. [CrossRef]
30. Yin, H.L.; Chen, T.Y.; Yu, Z.W.; Liu, H.; You, L.X.; Zhou, Y.H.; Chen, S.J.; Mao, Y.; Huang, M.Q.; Zhang, W.J.; et al. Measurement-Device-Independent Quantum Key Distribution over a 404 km Optical Fiber. *Phys. Rev. Lett.* **2016**, *117*, 190501. [CrossRef]
31. Zhu, C.; Xu, F.; Pei, C. W-state Analyzer and Multi-party Measurement-device-independent Quantum Key Distribution. *Sci. Rep.* **2015**, *5*, 17449. [CrossRef]
32. Li, Z.; Cao, X.Y.; Li, C.L.; Weng, C.X.; Gu, J.; Yin, H.L.; Chen, Z.B. Finite-key analysis for quantum conference key agreement with asymmetric channels. *Quantum Sci. Technol.* **2021**, *6*, 045019. [CrossRef]
33. Lucamarini, M.; Yuan, Z.L.; Dynes, J.F.; Shields, A.J. Overcoming the rate-distance limit of quantum key distribution without quantum repeaters. *Nature* **2018**, *557*, 400–403. [CrossRef] [PubMed]
34. Xie, Y.M.; Lu, Y.S.; Weng, C.X.; Cao, X.Y.; Jia, Z.Y.; Bao, Y.; Wang, Y.; Fu, Y.; Yin, H.L.; Chen, Z.B. Breaking the Rate-Loss Bound of Quantum Key Distribution with Asynchronous Two-Photon Interference. *Phys. Rev. Appl.* **2021**, *10*, 020315. [CrossRef]
35. Zeng, P.; Zhou, H.; Wu, W.; Ma, X. Quantum key distribution surpassing the repeaterless rate-transmittance bound without global phase locking. *arXiv* **2022**, arXiv:2201.04300.
36. Azuma, K.; Tamaki, K.; Munro, W.J. All-photonic intercity quantum key distribution. *Nat. Commun.* **2015**, *6*, 10171. [CrossRef] [PubMed]

Article

Construction of Binary Quantum Error-Correcting Codes from Orthogonal Array

Shanqi Pang *, Hanxiao Xu and Mengqian Chen

College of Mathematics and Information Science, Henan Normal University, Xinxiang 453007, China;
dm48xuhanxiao@163.com (H.X.); chenmengqian236@163.com (M.C.)
* Correspondence: shanqipang@126.com

Abstract: By using difference schemes, orthogonal partitions and a replacement method, some new methods to construct pure quantum error-correcting codes are provided from orthogonal arrays. As an application of these methods, we construct several infinite series of quantum error-correcting codes including some optimal ones. Compared with the existing binary quantum codes, more new codes can be constructed, which have a lower number of terms (i.e., the number of computational basis states) for each of their basis states.

Keywords: quantum error-correcting codes; k-uniform states; orthogonal array; orthogonal partition

1. Introduction

Errors are inevitable in quantum information processing [1], so quantum error-correcting codes (QECCs) are very important for quantum communication and quantum computing. In 1995, Shor [1] gave the simplest quantum simulation of a classical coding plan and then constructed the first QECC. In 1998, Calderbank et al. provided a close connection between QECCs and classical error correction codes [2], which leads to constructing QECCs from known classical error correction codes. In recent years, the research on QECCs especially on binary QECCs has made great progress. Feng and Ma made a way to obtain good pure stabilizer quantum codes, binary or nonbinary [3]. Li and Li obtained quantum codes of minimum distance three which are optimal or near optimal, and some quantum codes of minimum distance four which are better than previously known codes [4]. Feng and Xing presented a characterization of (binary and non-binary) quantum codes. Based on this characterization, they derived a method to construct pure p-ary quantum codes with dimensions not necessarily equal to powers of p [5]. Some other constructions of non-stabilizer codes, such as CWS codes [6], the codes in [7], and permutation-invariant codes such as in [8–11] have been studied. However, the majority of binary QECCs constructed so far are stabilizer codes [12–14]. The main goal of this work is to link between orthogonal arrays and binary QECCs and to construct more families of new codes.

Orthogonal arrays (OAs) play a more and more important role in quantum information theory [15–22]. An $r \times N$ array A with entries from a set $S = \{0, 1, \ldots, s-1\}$ is said to be an orthogonal array with s levels, strength t (for some t in the range $0 \leq t \leq N$) if every $r \times t$ subarray of A contains each t-tuple based on S as a row with the same frequency. We will denote such an array by $OA(r, N, s, t)$. Recently, many new methods of constructing OAs, especially high strength OAs, have been presented, and many new classes of OAs have been obtained [23–33]. An $OA(r, N, s, t)$ is said to be an irredundant orthogonal array (IrOA) if, in any $r \times (N-t)$ subarray, all of its rows are different [18]. A link between an IrOA with d levels and a t-uniform state was established by Goyeneche et al. [18], i.e., every column and every row of the array correspond to a particular qudit and a linear term of the state, respectively.

Citation: Pang, S.; Xu, H.; Chen, M. Construction of Binary Quantum Error-Correcting Codes from Orthogonal Array. *Entropy* **2022**, *24*, 1000. https://doi.org/10.3390/e24071000

Academic Editors: Shao-Ming Fei, Ming Li and Shunlong Luo

Received: 11 June 2022
Accepted: 16 July 2022
Published: 19 July 2022

Publisher's Note: MDPI stays neutral with regard to jurisdictional claims in published maps and institutional affiliations.

Copyright: © 2022 by the authors. Licensee MDPI, Basel, Switzerland. This article is an open access article distributed under the terms and conditions of the Creative Commons Attribution (CC BY) license (https://creativecommons.org/licenses/by/4.0/).

Connection 1 ([18]). *If* $L = \begin{pmatrix} s_1^1 & s_2^1 & \cdots & s_N^1 \\ s_1^2 & s_2^2 & \cdots & s_N^2 \\ \vdots & \vdots & & \vdots \\ s_1^r & s_2^r & \cdots & s_N^r \end{pmatrix}$ *is an* IrOA(r,N,s,t), *then the superposition of r product states,*

$$|\Phi\rangle = \frac{1}{\sqrt{r}}(|s_1^1 s_2^1 \ldots s_N^1\rangle + |s_1^2 s_2^2 \ldots s_N^2\rangle + \cdots + |s_1^r s_2^r \ldots s_N^r\rangle)$$

is a t-uniform state.

More and more attention has been paid to the construction and characterization of t-uniform states from OAs [15–18,34–39]. Very interestingly, uniform states are closely related to QECCs. Goyeneche and Życzkowski stated $((N,1,k+1))_d$ QECCs are one-to-one connected to k-uniform states of N qudits [18]. Shi et al. also presented the relation between a pure QECC and t-uniform state [40]. It is these new developments in OAs and uniform states that raise the possibility of constructing QECCs from OAs.

In this paper, the Hamming distance and minimal distance (MD) of OAs are applied to the theory of quantum information. By using difference schemes, orthogonal partitions and a replacement method, some new methods to construct pure quantum error-correcting codes are provided from orthogonal arrays. As an application of these methods, we construct several infinite series of quantum error-correcting codes including some optimal ones. Compared with the corresponding binary quantum error-correcting codes in [12,41], more new codes can be constructed, which have fewer terms for each of their basis states.

2. Preliminaries

First, the following concepts and lemmas are needed.

Let A^T be the transposition of matrix A and $(2) = (0,1)^T$. Let 0_r and 1_r denote the $r \times 1$ vectors of 0s and 1s, respectively. If $A = (a_{ij})_{m \times n}$ and $B = (b_{ij})_{u \times v}$ with elements from a Galois field with binary operations (+ and ·), the Kronecker product $A \otimes B$ is defined as $A \otimes B = (a_{ij} \cdot B)_{mu \times nv}$, where $a_{ij} \cdot B$ represents the $u \times v$ matrix with entries $a_{ij} \cdot b_{rs}$ $(1 \le r \le u, 1 \le s \le v)$, and the Kronecker sum $A \oplus B$ is defined as $A \oplus B = (a_{ij} + B)_{mu \times nv}$ where $a_{ij} + B$ represents the $u \times v$ matrix with entries $a_{ij} + b_{rs}$ $(1 \le r \le u, 1 \le s \le v)$ [23,24]. Let $(\mathbb{C}^2)^{\otimes N} = \underbrace{\mathbb{C}^2 \otimes \mathbb{C}^2 \otimes \cdots \otimes \mathbb{C}^2}_{N}$. Let $\mathbb{Z}_2^N = \underbrace{\mathbb{Z}_2 \times \mathbb{Z}_2 \times \cdots \times \mathbb{Z}_2}_{N}$ over ring $\mathbb{Z}_2 = \{0,1\}$.

A matrix A can often be identified with a set of its row vectors if necessary.

Definition 1 ([26]). *Let A be an $OA(r,N,s,t)$ and $\{A_1, A_2, \ldots, A_u\}$ be a set of orthogonal arrays $OA(\frac{r}{u}, N, s, t_1)$ with $t_1 \ge 0$. If $\bigcup_{i=1}^{u} A_i = A$ and $A_i \cap A_j = \emptyset$ for $i \ne j$, then $\{A_1, A_2, \ldots, A_u\}$ is said to be an orthogonal partition of strength t_1 of A.*

Let $\mathcal{A}$ be an abelian group of order s. $\mathcal{A}^t$, $t \ge 1$, denotes the additive group of order s^t consisting of all t-tuples of entries from $\mathcal{A}$ with the usual vector addition as the binary operation. Let $\mathcal{A}_0^t = \{(x_1, \ldots, x_t) : x_1 = \cdots = x_t \in \mathcal{A}\}$. Then, $\mathcal{A}_0^t$ is a subgroup of $\mathcal{A}^t$ of order s, and its cosets will be denoted by $\mathcal{A}_i^t$, $i = 1, \ldots, s^{t-1} - 1$.

Definition 2 ([42]). *An $m \times n$ matrix D based on $\mathcal{A}$ is called a difference scheme of strength t if, for every $m \times t$ submatrix, each set $\mathcal{A}_i^t$, $i = 0, 1, \ldots, s^{t-1} - 1$, is represented equally often when the rows of the submatrix are viewed as elements of $\mathcal{A}^t$. Such a matrix is denoted by $D_t(m,n,s)$. When $t = 2$, $D_t(m,n,s)$ is written as $D(m,n,s)$.*

Definition 3. *Let D be a difference scheme $D_t(m,n,s)$ and $\{D_1, D_2, \ldots, D_u\}$ be a set of difference schemes $D_{t_1}(\frac{m}{u},n,s,)$ with $t_1 \ge 0$. If $\bigcup_{i=1}^{u} D_i = D$ and $D_i \cap D_j = \emptyset$ for $i \ne j$, then $\{D_1, D_2, \ldots, D_u\}$ is said to be a partition of strength t_1 of D.*

Definition 4 ([42]). *Let $S^l = \{(v_1, \ldots, v_l) | v_i \in S, i = 1, 2, \ldots, l\}$. The Hamming distance $\mathrm{HD}(u, v)$ between two vectors $u = (u_1, \ldots, u_l)$, $v = (v_1, \ldots, v_l)$ in S^l is defined as the number of positions in which they differ. The minimal distance $\mathrm{MD}(A)$ of a matrix A is defined to be the minimal Hamming distance between its distinct rows.*

Definition 5 ([43]). *(quantum Singleton bound) Let Q be an $((N, K, d))_s$ QECC. If $K > 1$, then $K \leq s^{N-2d+2}$. A QECC that achieves the equality is said to be optimal.*

Lemma 1 ([42]). *If $s \leq t$ and t is odd, then there exists a difference scheme $D_t(s^{t-1}, t+1, s)$ on S.*

Lemma 2 ([37]). *The minimal distance of an $\mathrm{OA}(s^t, N, s, t)$ is $N - t + 1$ for $s \geq 2$ and $t \geq 1$.*

Lemma 3 ([40]). *Let Q be a subspace of $(\mathbb{C}^s)^{\otimes N}$. If Q is an $((N, K, d))_s$ QECC, then for any $(d-1)$ parties, the reductions of all states in Q to the $(d-1)$ parties are identical. The converse is true. Further, if Q is pure, then any state in Q is a $(d-1)$-uniform state. The converse is also true.*

Lemma 3 can also be viewed as the definition of a QECC. Q is denoted as $((N, K, d))_s$, where N is the length of the code, K is the dimension of the encoding state, d is the minimum Hamming distance, and s is the alphabet size. When $s = 2$, it is simply written as $((N, K, d))$.

Lemma 4 ([44]). *(1) Let D be a difference matrix $D_t(m, n, s)$ and L be an $\mathrm{OA}(r, N, s, t)$ for $t = 2, 3$. Then $D \oplus L$ is an $\mathrm{OA}(mr, nN, s, t)$;*
(2) Let D be a difference matrix $D_t(m, n, s)$ with $t \geq 2$. Then $D \oplus (s)$ is an $\mathrm{OA}(ms, n, s, t)$.

Lemma 5 ([36]). *(Expansive replacement method). Suppose A is an OA of strength t with column 1 having s levels and that B also is an OA of strength t with s rows. After making a one-to-one mapping between the levels of column 1 in A and the rows of B, if each level of column 1 in A is replaced by the corresponding row from B, we can obtain an OA of strength t.*

Lemma 6 ([42]). *If $s \geq 2$ is a prime power then an $\mathrm{OA}(s^t, s+1, s, t)$ of index unity exists whenever $s \geq t - 1 \geq 0$.*

3. Main Results

This section presents some new methods for the construction of QECCs. We begin with a link between OAs and QECCs. There exists a perfect match between the parameters of an $\mathrm{OA}(r, N, s, t)$, A, with an orthogonal partition $\{A_1, A_2, \ldots, A_K\}$ of strength t_1 and the parameters of an $((N, K, d))_s$ QECC, which is listed in Table 1.

Table 1. Correspondence between parameters of OAs and QECCs.

	OAs	QECCs
N	Number of factors	Length of code
K	Number of partitioned blocks	Dimension of code
d	$\min\{t_1 + 1, \mathrm{MD}(A)\}$	MD of code
s	Number of levels	alphabet size

The construction method for a QECC Q with parameter $((N, K, d))$ is summarized in the following Algorithm 1.

Algorithm 1 (OA-QECCs method) OA algorithm for construction of binary QECCs.
Step 1. Find an $OA(r, N, 2, t)$ with minimal distance d' and an orthogonal partition $\{A_1, A_2, \ldots, A_K\}$ of strength t_1 by a difference scheme or a space Z_2^N;
Step 2. Let $d = min\{d', t_1 + 1\}$. Give logical codewords $\varphi_1, \ldots, \varphi_K$, where φ_i is a $(d-1)$-uniform state, by $A_1, A_2, \ldots, A_K$ and Connection 1 in the Introduction;
Step 3. $\{\varphi_1, \ldots, \varphi_K\}$ can be used as a base to form the QECC $Q = ((N, K, d))$.

Theorem 1. *If $t \geq 2$ and t is odd, then we can construct a $((t+1, K, 2))$ QECC for any integer $1 \leq K \leq 2^{t-1}$ including an optimal $((t+1, 2^{t-1}, 2))$ code.*

Proof. Step 1. Find an OA A with minimal distance d' and an orthogonal partition $\{A_1, \ldots, A_K\}$ of strength t_1 by a difference scheme.

By Lemma 1, a difference scheme $D = D_t(2^{t-1}, t+1, 2)$ exists for any odd integer $t \geq 2$. Take $A = D \oplus (2)$. Due to Lemma 4, A is an $OA(2^t, t+1, 2, t)$. Let $D = \begin{pmatrix} d_1 \\ d_2 \\ \vdots \\ d_{2^{t-1}} \end{pmatrix}$.

Then $A_i = d_i \oplus (2)$ is also an $IrOA(2, t+1, 2, 1)$ for $i = 1, 2, \ldots, 2^{t-1}$. It follows from Lemma 2 that $MD(A) = 2$ and $MD(A_i) = t + 1$;

Step 2. Let $d = min\{d', t_1 + 1\}$. Give logical codewords $\varphi_1, \ldots, \varphi_K$, where φ_i is a $(d-1)$-uniform state, generated by $A_1, A_2, \ldots, A_K$ and Connection 1 in the Introduction.

Let $K = 2^{t-1}$. By the relation between irredundant orthogonal arrays and uniform states (Connection 1), $\{A_1, A_2, \ldots, A_{2^{t-1}}\}$ can generate 2^{t-1} one-uniform states $\{\varphi_1, \varphi_2, \ldots, \varphi_{2^{t-1}}\}$;

Step 3. The uniform states $\varphi_1, \ldots, \varphi_K$ are just the logical codewords of a QECC $Q = ((t+1, 2^{t-1}, 2))$.

By Lemma 3 and Definition 5, Q is an optimal code.

Furthermore, if we take Q_K to be the subspace spanned by $\{\varphi_1, \ldots, \varphi_K\}$ for integer $1 \leq K \leq 2^{t-1} - 1$, then it is a $((t+1, K, 2))$ code.

In particular, for $t = 1$, taking $|\varphi\rangle = \frac{1}{\sqrt{2}}(|00\rangle + |11\rangle)$ as a basis state, we have a $((2, 1, 2))$ QECC.

Compared with the binary QECCs in [12], the $((N, K, 2))$ QECCs obtained from Theorem 1 for $N = 4, 6, 8$ have fewer terms for each basis state and more dimensions K not necessarily equal to powers of 2. The comparison is put in Table 2, where "K" denotes the dimension of QECCs and "No." represents the number of terms for each basis state.

Table 2. Comparison of the obtained QECCs with those in [12].

	The QECCs in [12]			The QECCs by Theorem 1		
	$((4, K, 2))$	$((6, K, 2))$	$((8, K, 2))$	$((4, K, 2))$	$((6, K, 2))$	$((8, K, 2))$
K	1, 2, 4	$2^2, 2^3, 2^4$	$2^4, 2^5, 2^6$	1, 2, 3, 4	$1, 2, 3, \ldots, 2^4$	$1, 2, 3, \ldots, 2^6$
No.	4, 4, 2	8, 4, 2	8, 4, 2	2, 2, 2, 2	$2, 2, 2, \ldots, 2$	$2, 2, 2, \ldots, 2$

The following is about construction of QECCs with odd length N and minimum distance 2. □

Theorem 2. *(1) When $N \equiv 1 \pmod 4$, we can construct an $((N, K, 2))$ QECC with $K = 1 + C_N^2 + C_N^4 + \cdots + C_N^{\frac{N-5}{2}} + C_{N-1}^{\frac{N-3}{2}}$;*
(2) When $N \equiv 3 \pmod 4$, there exists an $((N, K, 2))$ QECC with $K = 1 + C_N^2 + C_N^4 + \cdots + C_N^{\frac{N-3}{2}}$.

Proof. (1) Z_2^N has C_N^0 vectors with weight 0, C_N^2 vectors with weight 2, C_N^4 vectors with weight 4, $\cdots$, $C_N^{\frac{N-5}{2}}$ vectors with weight $\frac{N-5}{2}$, and $C_{N-1}^{\frac{N-3}{2}}$ vectors (with the first component equal to 1) with weight $1 + \frac{N-3}{2}$. The above vectors are denoted by $b_1, b_2, b_3, \ldots, b_K$, where $K = 1 + C_N^2 + C_N^4 + \cdots + C_N^{\frac{N-5}{2}} + C_{N-1}^{\frac{N-3}{2}}$. Let $A_i = b_i \oplus (2)$ for $1 \leq i \leq K$. Take
$$A = \begin{pmatrix} A_1 \\ A_2 \\ \vdots \\ A_K \end{pmatrix}.$$
Then A_i and A are strength 1 orthogonal arrays and $\mathrm{MD}(A) = 2$. By Connection 1, $\{A_1, A_2, \ldots, A_K\}$ can generate K one-uniform states, which form an orthogonal basis of a subspace Q of $\mathbb{C}^{2 \otimes N}$. By Lemma 3, Q is an $((N, K, 2))$ QECC;

(2) By arguments similar to those used in the proof of (1), we can obtain the desired QECC. □

Theorem 3. *Let L be an $OA(r, N, 2, 2)$ with $\mathrm{MD}(L) \geq 3$. If there exist vectors $b_1, b_2, \ldots, b_K$ in Z_2^N satisfying $\mathrm{HD}(b_i, b_j) \geq 3$ and $|\mathrm{HD}(b_i, b_j) - \mathrm{HD}(L)| \geq 3$ for $i \neq j$, then there is an $((N, K, 3))$ QECC.*

Proof. Let $M_i = 1_r \otimes b_i + L$ for $1 \leq i \leq K$. Take $M = \begin{pmatrix} M_1 \\ M_2 \\ \vdots \\ M_K \end{pmatrix}$. Both M and M_i are OAs

of strength two. Any two rows of M can be written as $m_1 = b_i + l_1, m_2 = b_j + l_2$, where $b_i, b_j \in \{b_1, b_2, \ldots, b_K\}, l_1, l_2 \in L$.
  (1) When $i = j$, $l_1 \neq l_2$, $\mathrm{HD}(m_1, m_2) = \mathrm{MD}(L) \geq 3$;
  (2) When $i \neq j$, $l_1 = l_2$, $\mathrm{HD}(m_1, m_2) = \mathrm{HD}(b_i, b_j) \geq 3$;
  (3) When $i \neq j$ and $l_1 \neq l_2$, we have $\mathrm{HD}(m_1, m_2) \geq \mathrm{HD}(b_i + l_2, m_2) - \mathrm{HD}(b_i + l_2, m_1)$ or $\mathrm{HD}(m_1, m_2) \geq \mathrm{HD}(b_i + l_2, m_1) - \mathrm{HD}(b_i + l_2, m_2)$, so $\mathrm{HD}(m_1, m_2) \geq |\mathrm{HD}(b_i, b_j) - \mathrm{HD}(L)| \geq 3$.

So $\mathrm{MD}(M) \geq 3$. By Connection 1, $\{M_1, M_2, \ldots, M_K\}$ can generate K states, which form an orthogonal basis of a subspace Q of $\mathbb{C}^{2 \otimes N}$. By Lemma 3, Q is an $((N, K, 3))$ QECC. □

Theorem 4. *There exists a $((3p, 2^{p-n}, 3))$ QECC with $2^{n-1} \leq p \leq 2^n - 1$ for $n \geq 3$. In particular, for $n = 2$, we have a $((9, 2, 3))$ code.*

Proof. Let $D = D(4, 3, 2) = \begin{pmatrix} 0 & 0 & 0 \\ 0 & 0 & 1 \\ 0 & 1 & 0 \\ 0 & 1 & 1 \end{pmatrix}$ be a difference scheme of strength 2. Take

$L_0 = ((2) \otimes 1_{2^{n-1}}, 1_2 \otimes (2) \otimes 1_{2^{n-2}}, \ldots, 1_{2^{n-1}} \otimes (2), L')$ is an $OA(2^n, p, 2, 2)$ for $2^{n-1} \leq p \leq 2^n - 1$ with $n \geq 3$ and $L_i = ((2) \otimes 1_{2^{n-1}}, 1_2 \otimes (2) \otimes 1_{2^{n-2}}, \ldots, 1_{2^{n-1}} \otimes (2), L' + (1_{2^n} \otimes R_i))$ where R_i is the ith row of $\mathbb{Z}_2^{p-n}$ for $i = 1, 2, 3, \ldots, 2^{p-n}$. Then $\{L_1, L_2, \ldots, L_{2^{p-n}}\}$ is an orthogonal partition of strength 2 of $\mathbb{Z}_2^p$. Let

$$M = \begin{pmatrix} D \oplus L_1 \\ D \oplus L_2 \\ \vdots \\ D \oplus L_{2^{p-n}} \end{pmatrix} = \begin{pmatrix} M_1 \\ M_2 \\ \vdots \\ M_{2^{p-n}} \end{pmatrix},$$

By Lemma 4, $M_i = D \oplus L_i$ is an OA of strength 2. Any two rows of M_i can be written as $m_1 = d_1 \oplus l_1, m_2 = d_2 \oplus l_2$, where $d_1, d_2 \in D, l_1, l_2 \in L_i$.
  (1) When $d_1 = d_2$, $\mathrm{HD}(m_1, m_2) = 3 \cdot \mathrm{HD}(l_1, l_2) \geq 3$;
  (2) When $l_1 = l_2$, $\mathrm{HD}(m_1, m_2) = p \cdot \mathrm{HD}(d_1, d_2) \geq 3$;

(3) When $d_1 \neq d_2$ and $l_1 \neq l_2$, we have

$$\text{HD}(m_1, m_2) = (3 - \text{HD}(d_1, d_2)) \cdot \text{HD}(l_1, l_2) + (p - \text{HD}(l_1, l_2)) \cdot \text{HD}(d_1, d_2) \geq 3.$$

So $\text{MD}(M_i) \geq 3$.

Since M can be written as $D(4, 3, 2) \oplus \mathbb{Z}_2^p$ after row permutation, M is an OA of strength 2. Similarly, we also have $\text{MD}(M) \geq 3$. By Connection 1, $\{M_1, M_2, \ldots, M_{2^{p-n}}\}$ can generate 2^{p-n} states, which form an orthogonal basis of a subspace Q of $\mathbb{C}^{2 \otimes 3p}$. By Lemma 3, Q is a $((3p, 2^{p-n}, 3))$ QECC.

Especially, when $n = 2$ and $p = 3$, a $((9, 2, 3))$ QECC exists with logical codewords:

$|\varphi_1\rangle = \frac{1}{4}(|000000000\rangle + |011011011\rangle + |101101101\rangle + |110110110\rangle + |000000111\rangle + |011011100\rangle + |101101010\rangle + |110110001\rangle + |000111000\rangle + |011100011\rangle + |101010101\rangle + |110001110\rangle + |000111111\rangle$
$+ |011100100\rangle + |101010010\rangle + |110001001\rangle)$,

$|\varphi_2\rangle = \frac{1}{4}(|001001001\rangle + |010010010\rangle + |100100100\rangle + |111111111\rangle + |001001110\rangle + |010010101\rangle + |100100011\rangle + |111111000\rangle + |001110001\rangle + |010101010\rangle + |100011100\rangle + |111000111\rangle + |001110110\rangle$
$+ |010101101\rangle + |100011011\rangle + |111000000\rangle)$.

The code is pure, but neither the 9 qubit Shor code in [1] nor the 9 qubit Ruskai code in [11] are pure. □

Theorem 5. *There exists a $((4p, 2^{p-n+1}, 3))$ QECC with $2^{n-1} \leq p \leq 2^n - 1$ for $n \geq 3$. In particular, for $n = 2$, we have a $((12, 4, 3))$ code.*

Proof. Take $D_0 = D(4, 4, 2) = \begin{pmatrix} 0 & 0 & 0 & 0 \\ 0 & 0 & 1 & 1 \\ 0 & 1 & 0 & 1 \\ 0 & 1 & 1 & 0 \end{pmatrix}$ and $D_1 = D(4, 4, 2) = \begin{pmatrix} 0 & 0 & 0 & 1 \\ 0 & 0 & 1 & 0 \\ 0 & 1 & 0 & 0 \\ 0 & 1 & 1 & 1 \end{pmatrix}.$

Then $\{D_0, D_1\}$ is a partition of strength 2 of the difference scheme $D(8, 4, 2) = (0_8, \mathbb{Z}_2^3)$. For $2^{n-1} \leq p \leq 2^n - 1$ and $n \geq 3$, let

$$M = \begin{pmatrix} D_0 \oplus L_1 \\ \vdots \\ D_0 \oplus L_{2^{p-n}} \\ D_1 \oplus L_1 \\ \vdots \\ D_1 \oplus L_{2^{p-n}} \end{pmatrix} = \begin{pmatrix} M_1 \\ \vdots \\ M_{2^{p-n}} \\ M_{2^{p-n}+1} \\ \vdots \\ M_{2^{p-n+1}} \end{pmatrix},$$

where $L_1, L_2, \ldots, L_{2^{p-n}}$ are as in Theorem 5. Similar arguments in Theorem 2 apply to M, we can obtain the desired QECCs.

Especially, when $n = 2$ and $p = 3$, a $((12, 4, 3))$ code can be attained. □

Theorem 6. *There exists a $((4p, 2^{p-n+1}, 4))$ QECC with $2^{n-2} + 1 \leq p \leq 2^{n-1}$ for $n \geq 4$. In particular, for $n = 3$, we have a $((16, 4, 4))$ code.*

Proof. Let $D_0 = D_3(4, 4, 2) = \begin{pmatrix} 0 & 0 & 0 & 0 \\ 0 & 0 & 1 & 1 \\ 0 & 1 & 0 & 1 \\ 0 & 1 & 1 & 0 \end{pmatrix}$ and $D_1 = D_3(4, 4, 2) = \begin{pmatrix} 0 & 0 & 0 & 1 \\ 0 & 0 & 1 & 0 \\ 0 & 1 & 0 & 0 \\ 0 & 1 & 1 & 1 \end{pmatrix}.$

Then $\{D_0, D_1\}$ is a partition of strength 2 of the difference scheme $D(8, 4, 2) = (0_8, \mathbb{Z}_2^3)$. Take $L_0 = ((2) \otimes 1_{2^{n-1}}, 1_2 \otimes (2) \otimes 1_{2^{n-2}}, \ldots, 1_{2^{n-1}} \otimes (2), L')$ is an OA$(2^n, p, 2, 3)$ for $2^{n-2} + 1 \leq p \leq 2^{n-1}$ with $n \geq 4$ and $L_i = ((2) \otimes 1_{2^{n-1}}, 1_2 \otimes (2) \otimes 1_{2^{n-2}}, \ldots, 1_{2^{n-1}} \otimes (2), L' + (1_{2^n} \otimes R_i))$

where R_i is the ith row of $\mathbb{Z}_2^{p-n}$ for $i = 1, 2, 3, \ldots, 2^{p-n}$. Then $\{L_1, L_2, \ldots, L_{2^{p-n}}\}$ is an orthogonal partition of strength 3 of $\mathbb{Z}_2^p$. Let

$$M = \begin{pmatrix} D_0 \oplus L_1 \\ \vdots \\ D_0 \oplus L_{2^{p-n}} \\ D_1 \oplus L_1 \\ \vdots \\ D_1 \oplus L_{2^{p-n}} \end{pmatrix} = \begin{pmatrix} M_1 \\ \vdots \\ M_{2^{p-n}} \\ M_{2^{p-n}+1} \\ \vdots \\ M_{2^{p-n+1}} \end{pmatrix},$$

Similar arguments in Theorem 5 apply to M, we can obtain the desired QECCs. Especially, when $n = 3$ and $p = 4$, a $((16, 4, 4))$ code exists. □

Theorem 7. *Suppose L^N denotes an $OA(r, N, 2, t)$. Let $Y = (0_2 \oplus L^{N_1}, (2) \oplus L^{N-N_1})$. If $MD(Y) \geq t + 1$, then an $((N, 2, t + 1))$ QECC exists.*

Proof. Let $Y_i = (L^{N_1}, i + L^{N-N_1})$ for $i = 0, 1$. Thus $Y = \begin{pmatrix} Y_0 \\ Y_1 \end{pmatrix}$. Obviously, Y_i is an $OA(r, N, 2, t)$ and Y is an $OA(2r, N, 2, t)$. If $MD(Y) \geq t + 1$, then $MD(Y_i) \geq MD(Y) \geq t + 1$. From Lemma 3, there exists an $((N, 2, t + 1))$ QECC. □

Theorem 8. *Let L be an $OA(r, N, 2, t)$ with $MD(L) \geq t + 1$. If there exist vectors $b_1, b_2, \ldots, b_K$ in $\mathbb{Z}_2^N$ such that $MD \begin{pmatrix} 1_r \otimes b_1 + L \\ 1_r \otimes b_2 + L \\ \vdots \\ 1_r \otimes b_K + L \end{pmatrix} \geq t + 1$, then there is an $((N, K, t + 1))$ QECC.*

Proof. Let $M = \begin{pmatrix} M_1 \\ M_2 \\ \vdots \\ M_K \end{pmatrix} = \begin{pmatrix} 1_r \otimes b_1 + L \\ 1_r \otimes b_2 + L \\ \vdots \\ 1_r \otimes b_K + L \end{pmatrix}$. Obviously, M_i is an $OA(r, N, 2, t)$ and $MD(M) \geq t + 1$. From Lemma 3, there exists an $((N, K, t + 1))$ QECC. □

Theorem 9. *There exists a $((2(m_d + 1)(d - 1), 1, d))$ QECC for any integer $d \geq 5$, where m_d is the integer that satisfies $2^{m_d-1} + 2 \leq d \leq 2^{m_d} + 1$. Especially, for $d = 3, 4$, we have three QECCs $((6, 1, 3))$, $((8, 1, 4))$ and $((10, 1, 4))$.*

Proof. Let $s = 2^{m_d} + 1$. From Lemma 6, an $OA(s^{d-1}, s + 1, s, d - 1)$ exists. Obviously, $s + 1 \geq 2d$, then an $OA(s^{d-1}, 2(d - 1), s, d - 1)$ exists and is denoted by A. From Lemma 2, $MD(A) = d$. Replacing the s levels, $0, 1, \ldots, s - 1$, by distinct rows of $\mathbb{Z}_2^{m_d+1}$ respectively, we can get an $IrOA(2^{(m_d+1)(d-1)}, 2(d - 1)(m_d + 1), 2, d - 1)$. By Lemma 3, a $((2(d - 1)(m_d + 1), 1, d))$ QECC exists.

Especially, when $d = 3, 4$, by using Lemma 3 and $IrOA(8, 6, 2, 2)$, $IrOA(16, 8, 2, 3)$, and $IrOA(24, 10, 2, 3)$, three QECCs $((6, 1, 3))$, $((8, 1, 4))$, $((10, 1, 4))$ can be obtained. □

Corollary 1. *For any $d \geq 5$, let m_d be the integer satisfying $2^{m_d-1} + 2 \leq d \leq 2^{m_d}$. Then an $((n_d, 1, d))$ QECC exists for $2(d - 1)(m_d + 1) \leq n_d \leq 2d(m_d + 1) - 1$. In particular, a QECC $((n'_d, 1, 2^{m_d} + 1))$ exists for $(2^{m_d+1})(m_d + 1) \leq n'_d \leq (2^{m_d+1} + 1)(m_d + 1)$.*

Proof. Let $s = 2^{m_d} + 1$. From Lemma 6, an $OA(s^{d-1}, s + 1, s, d - 1)$ exists. Obviously, $B = OA(s^{d-1}, 2d, s, d - 1)$ exists since $s + 1 \geq 2d$. From Lemma 2, $MD(B) = d + 2$. By using the replacement method in Theorem 9, we can get $C = OA(s^{d-1}, 2d(m_d + 1), 2, d - 1)$. Removing the last $1, 2, \ldots, 2m_d + 2$ columns from C, we can get an $OA(s^{d-1}, n_d, 2, d - 1)$

with MD$\geq d$ for $2(d-1)(m_d+1) \leq n_d \leq 2d(m_d+1)-1$. By Lemma 3, the desired $((n_d,1,d))$ QECC exists.

Similarly, from the OA$(s^{d-1}, s+1, s, d-1)$, we can obtain an OA$(s^{d-1}, (s+1)(m_d+1), 2, d-1)$. Then removing the last $0,1,\ldots,m_d+1$ columns, we can have the desired result by Lemma 3. □

4. Examples

In this section, we use examples to illustrate applications of theorems.

Example 1. *Construction of a $((4,K,2))$ QECC for any integer $1 \leq K \leq 4$.*

Let $t = 3$ in Theorem 1. Take $D_3(4,4,2) = \begin{pmatrix} d_1 \\ d_2 \\ d_3 \\ d_4 \end{pmatrix} = \begin{pmatrix} 0 & 0 & 0 & 1 \\ 0 & 0 & 1 & 0 \\ 0 & 1 & 0 & 0 \\ 0 & 1 & 1 & 1 \end{pmatrix}$, $A = D_3(4,4,2) \oplus (2)$ and $A_i = d_i \oplus (2)$ for $1 \leq i \leq 4$. Then A_i $(1 \leq i \leq 4)$ can produce four states, $\varphi_1 = \frac{1}{\sqrt{2}}(|0001\rangle + |1110\rangle)$, $\varphi_2 = \frac{1}{\sqrt{2}}(|0010\rangle + |1101\rangle)$, $\varphi_3 = \frac{1}{\sqrt{2}}(|0100\rangle + |1011\rangle)$, $\varphi_4 = \frac{1}{\sqrt{2}}(|0111\rangle + |1000\rangle)$, which form an orthogonal basis of a subspace Q in $\mathbb{C}^{2\otimes 4}$. Therefore, Q is an optimal $((4,4,2))$ QECC which can be found in [7].

Furthermore, if taking Q_K to be the subspace spanned by $\{\varphi_1,\ldots,\varphi_K\}$ for $1 \leq K \leq 3$, then we obtain a $((4,K,2))$ QECC.

The QECCs in Example 1 are different from and particularly when $K = 1,2$, have less number of items for every basis state than those codes in [12]. To be self-contained, the $((4,K,2))$ QECCs for $K = 1,2,4$ in [12] are provided as follows.

$((4,1,2))$: $|\phi\rangle = \frac{1}{2}(|0000\rangle + |1100\rangle + |0011\rangle + |1111\rangle)$.

$((4,2,2))$: $|\phi_1\rangle = \frac{1}{2}(|0000\rangle + |1010\rangle + |0101\rangle + |1111\rangle)$, $|\phi_2\rangle = \frac{1}{2}(|0011\rangle + |1001\rangle + |0110\rangle + |1100\rangle)$.

$((4,4,2))$: $|\phi_1\rangle = \frac{1}{\sqrt{2}}(|0000\rangle + |1111\rangle)$, $|\phi_2\rangle = \frac{1}{\sqrt{2}}(|0011\rangle + |1100\rangle)$, $|\phi_3\rangle = \frac{1}{\sqrt{2}}(|1010\rangle + |0101\rangle)$, $|\phi_4\rangle = \frac{1}{\sqrt{2}}(|0110\rangle + |1001\rangle)$.

Comparison of the method of code construction with [7].

Both methods can take any classical code to a quantum code. The method proposed in [7] can make it by solving for the amplitudes in the superposition. Since any classical code (N,m,d') is an OA$(m,N,2,t)$, the method in this paper can produce a quantum code $((N,1,d''))$ which is also a $(d''-1)$-uniform state where $d'' = \min\{d', t+1\}$ from Connection 1. Moreover, if the OA$(m,N,2,t)$ with an orthogonal partition $\{A_1, A_2, \ldots, A_K\}$ of strength t_1, this method can produce a quantum code $((N,K,d))$ where $d = \min\{d', t_1+1\}$. The amplitudes in the superposition for each logical codeword are all equal to $\sqrt{\frac{m}{K}}$. For example, the code $((4,4,2))$ in Example 1 after it is normalized is the same as the one constructed using the method proposed in [7]. It is noteworthy that in Example 1 if taking

$D = \begin{pmatrix} 0 & 0 & 0 & 0 \\ 0 & 0 & 1 & 1 \\ 0 & 1 & 0 & 1 \\ 0 & 1 & 1 & 0 \end{pmatrix}$, then we can construct a stabilizer code with parameter $((4,4,2))$

whose logical codewords are $\varphi_1 = \frac{1}{\sqrt{2}}(|0000\rangle + |1111\rangle)$, $\varphi_2 = \frac{1}{\sqrt{2}}(|0011\rangle + |1100\rangle)$, $\varphi_3 = \frac{1}{\sqrt{2}}(|0101\rangle + |1010\rangle)$, $\varphi_4 = \frac{1}{\sqrt{2}}(|0110\rangle + |1001\rangle)$.

Example 2. *(1) For $N = 5$, take $b_1 = (00000)$, $b_2 = (11000)$, $b_3 = (10100)$, $b_4 = (10010)$, and $b_5 = (10001)$. Let $A_i = b_i \oplus (2)$ for $1 \leq i \leq 5$. Then A_i $(1 \leq i \leq 5)$ can produce five states. By Theorem 2, Q is a $((5,5,2))$ QECC;*

(2) For $N = 7$, take $b_1 = (0000000)$, $b_2 = (0000011)$, $b_3 = (0000101)$, $b_4 = (0000110)$, $b_5 = (0001001)$, $b_6 = (0001010)$, $b_7 = (0001100)$, $b_8 = (0010001)$, $b_9 = (0010010)$, $b_{10} = (0010100)$, $b_{11} = (0011000)$, $b_{12} = (0100001)$, $b_{13} = (0100010)$, $b_{14} = (0100100)$,

$b_{15} = (0101000)$, $b_{16} = (0110000)$, $b_{17} = (1000001)$, $b_{18} = (1000010)$, $b_{19} = (1000100)$, $b_{20} = (1001000)$, $b_{21} = (1010000)$, $b_{22} = (1100000)$. Let $A_i = b_i \oplus (2)$. Then A_i $(1 \leq i \leq 22)$ can produce 22 states. With Theorem 2, they yield a $((7,22,2))$ QECC.

Example 3. *Construction of a $((7,2,3))$ QECC.*

Let $r = 8$ and $N = 7$ in Theorem 3. The two vectors $b_1 = (0000000)$ and $b_2 = (1111111)$ can be used to construct a $((7,2,3))$ QECC whose basis states are:

$|\varphi_1\rangle = \frac{1}{2\sqrt{2}}(|0000000\rangle + |0010111\rangle + |0101011\rangle + |0111100\rangle + |1001101\rangle + |1011010\rangle + |1100110\rangle + |1110001\rangle)$ and

$|\varphi_2\rangle = \frac{1}{2\sqrt{2}}(|1111111\rangle + |1101000\rangle + |1010100\rangle + |1000011\rangle + |0110010\rangle + |0100101\rangle + |0011001\rangle + |0001110\rangle)$.

This is in fact equivalent to the Steane code. It can correct one error such as $e = I_2 \otimes I_2 \otimes I_2 \otimes I_2 \otimes I_2 \otimes I_2 \otimes \sigma_x$, $I_2 \otimes I_2 \otimes I_2 \otimes I_2 \otimes I_2 \otimes I_2 \otimes \sigma_y \otimes I_2$ and so on.

Example 4. *Construction of a $((3p, 2^{p-n}, 3))$ QECC with $2^{n-1} \leq p \leq 2^n - 1$ for $n = 3, 4$.*

(1) Let $n = 3$, $p = 4, 5, 6, 7$ in Theorem 4. We can obtain QECCs $((12,2,3))$, $((15,4,3))$, $((18,8,3))$, $((21,16,3))$;

(2) Let $n = 4$, $p = 8, 9, \ldots, 15$ in Theorem 4. One gets QECCs $((24,16,3))$, $((27,32,3))$, $\ldots$, $((45, 2^{11}, 3))$.

Example 5. *Construction of a $((4p, 2^{p-n+1}, 4))$ QECC with $2^{n-2} + 1 \leq p \leq 2^{n-1}$ for $n = 4, 5$.*

For the case $n = 4$ and $2^2 + 1 \leq p \leq 2^3$, Theorem 6 produces QECCs $((20,4,4))$, $((24,8,4))$, $((28,16,4))$, $((32,32,4))$.

For the case $n = 5$ and $2^3 + 1 \leq p \leq 2^4$, Theorem 6 yields QECCs $((36,32,3))$, $((40,64,3))$, $\ldots$, $((64, 2^{12}, 4))$.

Example 6. For $N = 23$ and $N_1 = 16$, take $L^{23} = (a_1, \ldots, a_{23})$ to be the $OA(2048, 23, 2, 6)$ (the first 2048 runs and the first 23 columns from $OA(4096, 24, 2, 7)$ in [45]). Let $L^{16} = (a_1, a_2, \ldots, a_{16})$ and $L^7 = (a_{17}, a_{18}, \ldots, a_{23})$. Then $MD(Y) = 7$. Theorem 7 yields a $((23,2,7))$ QECC.

Example 7. For $r = 512$ and $N = 23$, take L to be the $OA(512, 23, 2, 4)$ (the first 512 runs and the first 23 columns from $OA(1024, 24, 2, 5)$ in [45]). We can get $b_1, b_2, \ldots, b_9 \in Z_2^{23}$ that satisfies the conditions in Theorem 8 where $b_1 = (00000000000000000000000)$, $b_2 = (11111111111111111111111)$, $b_3 = (00000000000000000111011)$, $b_4 = (00000000000000110011101)$, $b_5 = (00000000000001010000111)$, $b_6 = (00000000000011101001011)$, $b_7 = (00000000000011110011110)$, $b_8 = (00000000000100010001010)$, $b_9 = (00000000001100110111110)$. Then we can construct a $((23,9,5))$ QECC.

Example 8. *Comparison of the $((10,1,4))$ QECCs in Theorem 9, [12,46].*

The new quantum state in the QECC $((10,1,4))$ in Theorem 9 has 24 terms. The quantum state in the QECC $((10,1,4))$ in [12] has 1024 terms. The quantum state in the QECC $((10,1,4))$ in [46] with the follow stablizer matrix G has 512 terms where

$$G = \begin{pmatrix} 1100110000 & | & 1111110000 \\ 0110011000 & | & 0111111000 \\ 0011001100 & | & 0011111100 \\ 0001100110 & | & 0001111110 \\ 0000110011 & | & 0000111111 \\ 1111110000 & | & 0011000000 \\ 0111111000 & | & 0001100000 \\ 0011111100 & | & 0000110000 \\ 0001111110 & | & 0000011000 \\ 0000111111 & | & 0000001100 \end{pmatrix}.$$

Compared with the above two codes, it is clear that our construction method has the advantage of a small number of terms.

Example 9. *Some new QECCs with larger minimum distance by Corollary 1.*
Let $d = 94$. Then $m_d = 7$ and we have an $((n_d, 1, 94))$ QECC for $1488 \leq n_d \leq 1503$.
Let $d = 66$. Then $m_d = 7$ and we have an $((n_d, 1, 66))$ QECC for $1040 \leq n_d \leq 1055$.
Let $d = 41$. Then $m_d = 6$ and we have an $((n_d, 1, 41))$ QECC for $560 \leq n_d \leq 573$.
Let $d = 23$. Then $m_d = 5$ and we have an $((n_d, 1, 23))$ QECC for $264 \leq n_d \leq 275$.
Let $d = 129$. Then $m_d = 7$ and we have an $((n'_d, 1, 129))$ QECC for $2048 \leq n'_d \leq 2056$.
Let $d = 33$. Then $m_d = 5$ and we have an $((n'_d, 1, 33))$ QECC for $384 \leq n'_d \leq 390$.

5. Conclusions

In the work, by using OAs, we study the relation between uniform states and binary QECCs. Several methods for constructing QECCs from OAs are presented. Some optimal QECCs are obtained. Our methods have three advantages. The first is to be able to construct an $((N, K_1, d))$ QECC from each $((N, K, d))$ QECC we construct for arbitrary integer $1 \leq K_1 \leq K$. The second is that Theorems 1 and 7–9 can be generalized to construct QECCs $((N, K, d))_q$ for arbitrary d and a prime power q. The third is that for the constructed QECCs, their every basis state has less than or equal to terms compared with the existing binary QECCs in [41] and [12]. A link between an IrOA and the uniform state is established by Connection 1. In fact, from Theorem 1 to Theorem 9 we always make quantum codes by using uniform states generated by orthogonal partitions. On the other hand, when a quantum code is pure we can easily obtain uniform states. For example, each of the logical codewords in the quantum code $((4, 4, 2))$ in [7] is a one-uniform state. When it is not pure it is worth studying how to use quantum codes to make uniform states. In the future, we will also investigate constructing more optimal QECCs with $d > 2$.

Author Contributions: Supervision, S.P.; conceptualization, S.P. and H.X.; investigation, S.P., H.X. and M.C.; methodology, H.X. and M.C.; validation, H.X. and M.C.; writing—original draft, H.X.; writing—review and editing, S.P. and H.X. All authors have read and agreed to the published version of the manuscript.

Funding: This research was funded by the National Natural Science Foundation of China Grant number 11971004.

Institutional Review Board Statement: Not applicable.

Informed Consent Statement: Not applicable.

Data Availability Statement: Not applicable.

Conflicts of Interest: The authors declare no conflict of interest.

References

1. Shor, P.W. Scheme for reducing decoherence in quantum computer memory. *Phys Rev. A* **1995**, *52*, 2493–2496. [CrossRef] [PubMed]
2. Calderbank, A.R.; Rains, E.M.; Shor, P.W.; Sloane, N.J.A. Quantum error correction via codes over GF(4). *IEEE Trans. Inf. Theory* **1998**, *44*, 1369–1387. [CrossRef]
3. Feng, K.; Ma, Z. A finite Gilbert-Varshamov bound for pure stabilizer quantum codes. *IEEE Trans. Inf. Theory* **2004**, *50*, 3323–3325. [CrossRef]
4. Li, R.; Li, X. Binary construction of quantum codes of minimum distance three and four. *IEEE Trans. Inf. Theory* **2004**, *50*, 1331–1335. [CrossRef]
5. Feng, K.; Xing,C. A new construction of quantum error-correcting codes. *Trans. Amer. Math. Soc.* **2008**, *360*, 2007–2019. [CrossRef]
6. Shor, P.W.; Smith, G.; Smolin, J.A.; Zeng, B. High Performance Single-Error-Correcting Quantum Codes for Amplitude Damping. *IEEE Trans. Inf. Theory* **2011**, *57*, 7180–7188. [CrossRef]
7. Movassagh, R.; Ouyang, Y. Constructing quantum codes from any classical code and their embedding in ground space of local hamiltonians. *arXiv* **2020**, arXiv:2012.01453.
8. Ouyang, Y.; Chao, R. Permutation-invariant constant-excitation quantum codes for amplitude damping. *IEEE Trans. Inf. Theory* **2019**, *66*, 2921–2933. [CrossRef]
9. Ouyang, Y.; Permutation-invariant quantum codes. *Phys Rev. A* **2014**, *90*, 062317. [CrossRef]

10. Ouyang, Y. Permutation-invariant qudit codes from polynomials. *Linear Algebra Appl.* **2017**, *532*, 43–59. [CrossRef]
11. Ruskai, M.B. Pauli Exchange Errors in Quantum Computation. *Phys. Rev. Lett.* **2000**, *85*, 194–197. [CrossRef] [PubMed]
12. Grassl, M. Bounds on the Minimum Distance of Additive Quantum Codes. 2022. Available online: http://www.codetables.de (accessed on 1 June 2022).
13. Hu, D.; Tang, W.; Zhao, M.; Chen, Q.; Yu, S.; Oh, C.H. Graphical nonbinary quantum error-correcting codes. *Phys. Rev. A* **2008**, *78*, 012306. [CrossRef]
14. Nebe, G.; Rains, E.M.; Sloane, N.J.A. *Self-Dual Codes and Invariant theory*; Springer: Berlin/Heidelberg, Germany, 2006.
15. Goyeneche, D.; Alsina, D.; Latorre, J.; Riera, A.; Życzkowski, K. Absolutely maximally entangled states, combinatorial designs, and multiunitary matrices. *Phys. Rev. A* **2015**, *92*, 032316. [CrossRef]
16. Goyeneche, D.; Bielawski, J.; Życzkowski, K. Multipartite entanglement in heterogeneous systems. *Phys. Rev. A* **2016**, *94*, 012346. [CrossRef]
17. Goyeneche, D.; Raissi, Z.; Martino, S. Di.; Życzkowski, K. Entanglement and quantum combinatorial designs. *Phys. Rev. A* **2018**, *97*, 062326. [CrossRef]
18. Goyeneche, D.; Życzkowski, K. Genuinely multipartite entangled states and orthogonal arrays. *Phys. Rev. A* **2014**, *90*, 022316. [CrossRef]
19. Pang, S.; Peng, X.; Zhang, X.; Zhang, R.; Yin, C. k-uniform states and quantum combinatorial designs. *IEICE Trans. Fundam.* **2022**, *105*, 975–982. [CrossRef]
20. Pang, S.; Zhang, R.; Zhang, X. Quantum frequency arrangements, quantum mixed orthogonal arrays and entangled states. *IEICE Trans. Fundam.* **2020**, *103*, 1674–1678. [CrossRef]
21. Rötteler, M.; Wocjan, P. Equivalence of decoupling schemes and orthogonal arrays. *IEEE Trans. Inform. Theory* **2006**, *52*, 4171–4181. [CrossRef]
22. Zang, Y.; Facchi, P.; Tian, Z. Quantum combinatorial designs and k-uniform states. *J. Phys. A Math. Theor.* **2021**, *54*, 505204. [CrossRef]
23. Zhang, Y.; Lu, Y.; Pang, S. Orthogonal arrays obtained by orthogonal decomposition of projection matrices. *Statist. Sin.* **1999**, *9*, 595–604.
24. Zhang, Y.; Pang, S.; Wang, Y. Orthogonal arrays obtained by the generalized Hadamard product. *Discrete Math.* **2001**, *238*, 151–170. [CrossRef]
25. Pang, S.; Chen, L. Generalized Latin matrix and construction of orthogonal arrays. *Acta Math. Appl. Sin.* **2017**, *33*, 1083–1092. [CrossRef]
26. Pang, S.; Lin, X.; Wang, J. Construction of asymmetric orthogonal arrays of strength t from orthogonal partition of small orthogonal arrays. *IEICE Trans. Fundam.* **2018**, *101*, 1267–1272. [CrossRef]
27. Pang, S.; Wang, Y.; Chen, G.; Du, J. The existence of a class of mixed orthogonal arrays. *IEICE Trans. Fundam.* **2016**, *99*, 863–868. [CrossRef]
28. Pang, S.; Wang, J.; Lin, D.K.J.; Liu, M. Construction of mixed orthogonal arrays with high strength. *Ann. Statist.* **2021**, *49*, 2870–2884. [CrossRef]
29. Pang, S.; Zhang, Y.; Liu, S. Further results on the orthogonal arrays obtained by generalized Hadamard product. *Statist. Probab. Lett.* **2004**, *68*, 17–25. [CrossRef]
30. Pang, S.; Zhang, X.; Zhang, Q. The Hamming distances of saturated asymmetrical orthogonal arrays with strength 2. *Comm. Statist. Theory Methods* **2020**, *49*, 3895–3910. [CrossRef]
31. Pang, S.; Zhu, Y.; Wang, Y. A class of mixed orthogonal arrays obtained from projection matrix inequalities. *J. Inequal. Appl.* **2015**, *241*, 1–9. [CrossRef]
32. Yin, J.; Wang, J.; Ji, L.; Li, Y. On the existence of orthogonal arrays $OA(3, 5, 4n + 2)$. *J. Combin. Theory Ser. A* **2011**, *118*, 270–276. [CrossRef]
33. Zhang, T.; Deng, Q.; Dey, A. Construction of asymmetric orthogonal arrays of strength three via a replacement Method. *J. Combin. Des.* **2017**, *25*, 339–348.
34. Huber, F.; Ghne, O.; Siewert, J. Absolutely maximally entangled states of seven qubits do not exist. *Phys. Rev. Lett.* **2017**, *118*, 200502. [CrossRef]
35. Pang, S.; Zhang, X.; Du, J.; Wang, T. Multipartite entanglement states of higher uniformity. *J. Phys. A Math. Theor.* **2021**, *54*, 015305. [CrossRef] [PubMed]
36. Pang, S.; Zhang, X.; Fei, S.; Zheng, Z. Quantum k-uniform states for heterogeneous systems from irredundant mixed orthogonal arrays. *Quantum Inf. Process.* **2021**, *20*, 1–46. [CrossRef]
37. Pang, S.; Zhang, X.; Lin, X.; Zhang, Q. Two and three-uniform states from irredundant orthogonal arrays. *npj Quantum Inf.* **2019**, *5*, 1–10. [CrossRef]
38. Scott, A.J. Multipartite entanglement, quantum-error-correcting codes, and entangling power of quantum evolutions. *Phys. Rev. A* **2004**, *69*, 052330. [CrossRef]
39. Chen, G.; Zhang, X.; Guo, Y. New results for 2-uniform states based on irredundant orthogonal arrays. *Quantum Inf. Process.* **2021**, *20*, 1–11. [CrossRef]
40. Shi, F.; Li, M.; Chen, L.; Zhang, X. k-uniform quantum information masking. *Phys. Rev. A* **2021**, *104*, 032601. [CrossRef]

41. Edel, Y. Some Good Quantum Twisted Code [DB/OL]. 2022. Available online: https://www.mathi.uni-heidelberg.de/~yves/Matritzen/QTBCH/QTBCHIndex.html (accessed on 1 June 2022). [CrossRef]
42. Hedayat, A.S.; Sloane, N.J.A.; Stufken, J. *Orthogonal Arrays: Theory and Applications*; Springer: New York, NY, USA, 1999.
43. Rains, E.M. Nonbinary quantum codes. *IEEE Trans. Inform. Theory* **1999**, *45*, 1827–1832.
44. Chen, G.; Lei, J. Constructions of mixed orthogonal arrays of strength three (in Chinese). *Sci. Sin. Math.* **2017**, *47*, 545–564. [CrossRef]
45. Sloane, N.J.A. A Library of Orthogonal Arrays. 2022. Available online: http://neilsloane.com/oadir/index.html (accessed on 1 June 2022).
46. Guan, Q.; Kai, X.; Zhu, S. Hermitian Self-Orthogonal Constacyclic Codes over F_{4^m} *Acta Electron. Sin.* **2017**, *45*, 1469–1474. (In Chinese)

Article

Quantum Linear System Algorithm for General Matrices in System Identification

Kai Li [1], Ming Zhang [2,*], Xiaowen Liu [1], Yong Liu [1], Hongyi Dai [3], Yijun Zhang [1] and Chen Dong [1,*]

[1] College of Information and Communication, National University of Defense Technology, Xi'an 710006, China; likai17@163.com (K.L.); lxw5054@163.com (X.L.); liuyong09@nudt.edu.cn (Y.L.); gfkd_zyj@163.com (Y.Z.)
[2] College of Intelligence Science and Technology, National University of Defense Technology, Changsha 410003, China
[3] College of Liberal Arts and Sciences, National University of Defense Technology, Changsha 410003, China; hydai@nudt.edu.cn
* Correspondence: zhangming@nudt.edu.cn (M.Z.); dongchengfkd@163.com (C.D.); Tel.: +86-18908461616 (M.Z.); +86-17791691216 (C.D.)

Abstract: Solving linear systems of equations is one of the most common and basic problems in classical identification systems. Given a coefficient matrix A and a vector b, the ultimate task is to find the solution x such that $Ax = b$. Based on the technique of the singular value estimation, the paper proposes a modified quantum scheme to obtain the quantum state $|x\rangle$ corresponding to the solution of the linear system of equations in $O(\kappa^2 \sqrt{r}\text{polylog}(mn)/\epsilon)$ time for a general $m \times n$ dimensional A, which is superior to existing quantum algorithms, where κ is the condition number, r is the rank of matrix A and ϵ is the precision parameter. Meanwhile, we also design a quantum circuit for the homogeneous linear equations and achieve an exponential improvement. The coefficient matrix A in our scheme is a sparsity-independent and non-square matrix, which can be applied in more general situations. Our research provides a universal quantum linear system solver and can enrich the research scope of quantum computation.

Keywords: system identification; linear systems of equations; quantum algorithm; time complexity

1. Introduction

System identification [1–3] is a common method to determine the mathematical model describing the behavior of classical systems. Thus, the future evolution of the system can be predicted through the identified system model, which is widely applied to common weather forecast, flood forecast, market trend, etc. The traditional system identification method, namely the classical identification method, mainly includes least squares method [4], impulse response method and maximum likelihood method [5,6]. Existing studies [2,3] found that solving linear systems of equations is the basis of system identification problems. In fact, not only system identification problems, the application of linear equations involves various fields of science and engineering, including machine learning [7], partial differential equations [8], classic control system, and so on. Therefore, solving linear systems of equations for general matrices is of great significance.

Due to the importance of linear systems of equations in various fields, the solution of linear equations has become an enduring issue, and many algorithms derived therefrom. The classical solvers mainly include: matrix elimination method [9] and Kaczmarz method [10]. The most famous one of the former is the Gaussian elimination method, which is often used to solve small linear systems of equations and is suitable for a general coefficient matrix. The Kaczmarz method is generally more practical in the field of large-scale linear equations. The running time for these classical solvers scales as $O(n^3)$, where n is the size of the matrix, which will cost a lot of computing resources in solving large-scale linear systems. However, quantum computation [11–13] is capable of greatly reducing the time complexity for matrix operation and numerical calculation, which can be regarded as a promising attempt as a computing tool to improve the identification efficiency.

Quantum computation is an emerging computing technology that regulates quantum information units to perform high-efficiency calculations based on the laws of quantum mechanics, including coherent superposition and entanglement [14]. In 1994, Shor proposed the algorithm for prime factorization [15] with exponential acceleration over classical algorithms, which shows the potential of quantum computation for the first time. Since then, quantum computation has reached an era of rapid development. In recent years, scholars have also made significant progress in quantum algorithm research, including Grover algorithm [16], quantum simulation [17–19], duality algorithm [20–22], linear systems of equations solver [23–25], matrix multiplication algorithm [26,27], and so on. For the high-dimensional linear systems of equations, there have been breakthroughs in the field of quantum computation. In 2009, Harrow, Hassidim and Lloyd [23] proposed the quantum linear system algorithm (HHL) to obtain the quantum state $|x\rangle = |A^{-1}b\rangle$ corresponding to the solution of $Ax = b$ in time $O(\text{poly} \log(n))$, where the sparse matrix $A \in R^{n \times n}$ and $x, b \in R^n$, which can improve the computational efficiency with an exponential speed-up over classical algorithms. The HHL algorithm is of great significance in the field of quantum information processing and has a wide range of applications in big data, machine learning, numerical computing and other scenarios. In 2018, Wossnig et al. [28] proposed a sparsity-independent quantum linear system algorithm (QLSA) based on a quantum singular value estimation algorithm (QSVE). After that, Shao and Xiang [29] modified the QSVE algorithm to adapt to the non-Hermitian case. Current algorithms for linear systems have been widely applied in the emerging research area of quantum information processing. However, existing quantum algorithms have different restrictions on matrix A, such as the most typical one of HHL algorithm, which requires A to be a sparse Hermitian matrix so that the unitary transformation e^{iAt} [30,31] can be realized in a constant time. At present, the quantum algorithm suitable for arbitrary linear system of equations has not been fully studied.

Without loss of generality, existing quantum algorithms assumed that the coefficient matrix A is Hermitian as it is well known that the general case can be reduced to the Hermitian case by embedding a general rectangular matrix M into a block antidiagonal Hermitian matrix with the elements of $M^\dagger$ and M in the lower and upper half, respectively [28]. Different from previous algorithms, we proposed a modified quantum scheme to solve the cases of general matrices directly, which can reduce the time complexity of solving the linear system of equations. Moreover, it may not be easy to expand A into a Hermitian matrix when A is given as quantum information. However, our scheme does not need such expansion and works well on the original non-Hermitian matrix, and hence it can be implemented more efficiently. Based on this idea, this paper considers three cases of the solution of linear systems and proposes a quantum linear system algorithm for general matrices, where A is not required to be sparse or square, which can effectively improve the computational efficiency and expand the application range of quantum computation. For the homogeneous linear equations, we design the corresponding quantum circuit to ensure the completeness of the solution, which supplies exponential speed-up over classical algorithms. Meanwhile, we modify the quantum phase estimation (QPE) circuit to determine the sign of the phase by setting a sign qubit, which can be widely applied to various quantum algorithms.

The rest of our paper is organized as follows. Section 2 analyzes a general model of classical identification system based on semi-tensor product and shows the detailed process of our quantum algorithms. In Section 3, we make a time complexity comparison between existing algorithms and our algorithms. Then, we perform a numerical simulation to clarify the process of quantum algorithm in Section 4. Finally, we conclude in Section 5.

2. Quantum Algorithms for System Identification

2.1. The Classical System Identification Problem

Consider a general discrete model of system identification as follows:

$$x(i+1) = Ax(i) + Bu(i) \tag{1}$$

where $x(i)$ is an n dimensional system state of the i-th sampling, $u(i)$ is the input with dimension m, A is an $n \times n$ system matrix and B is an $n \times m$ matrix. The goal of system identification is to estimate the matrices A and B from a set of inputs $\{u(i)\}$ and states $\{x(i)\}$.

System identification problems can be expressed in terms of the semi-tensor product method [32]. As a kind of special matrix multiplication, the semi-tensor product generalizes the ordinary matrix multiplication to the general case. $T \otimes S$ denotes the Kronecker product of matrices $T_{m \times n}$ and $S_{p \times q}$, which is expressed as

$$T \otimes S = \begin{bmatrix} t_{1,1}S & t_{1,2}S & \cdots & t_{1,n}S \\ t_{2,1}S & t_{2,2}S & \cdots & t_{2,n}S \\ \vdots & \vdots & \vdots & \vdots \\ t_{m,1}S & t_{m,2}S & \cdots & t_{m,n}S \end{bmatrix} \tag{2}$$

Just as a computational tool for solving the model, $T \ltimes S$ denotes the semi-tensor product of matrices T and S:

$$T \ltimes S = (T \otimes I_{l/n})(S \otimes I_{l/p}) \tag{3}$$

where $l = \text{lcm}(n, p)$ is the least common multiple of n and p. The semi-tensor product is the generalization of matrix multiplication. When $n = p$, there are $l = n = p$ and $T \ltimes S = TS$.

Define $V_C(S) = \begin{bmatrix} s_1 \\ s_2 \\ \vdots \\ s_n \end{bmatrix}$, where s_i is the ith column vector of the matrix S. Therefore, we may estimate A and B from a set of $u(i)$ and $x(i)$.

$$\begin{aligned} x(i+1) &= Ax(i) + Bu(i) \\ &= \begin{bmatrix} a_{11}x_1(i) + \cdots + a_{1n}x_n(i) \\ \vdots \\ a_{n1}x_1(i) + \cdots + a_{nn}x_n(i) \end{bmatrix} + \begin{bmatrix} b_{11}u_1(i) + \cdots + b_{1m}u_m(i) \\ \vdots \\ b_{n1}u_1(i) + \cdots + b_{nm}u_m(i) \end{bmatrix} \\ &= x(i)^T \otimes I_n \cdot V_C(A) + u(i)^T \otimes I_n \cdot V_C(B) \\ &= x(i)^T \ltimes V_C(A) + u(i)^T \ltimes V_C(B) \\ &= (x(i)^T, u(i)^T) \ltimes \begin{bmatrix} V_C(A) \\ V_C(B) \end{bmatrix} \end{aligned} \tag{4}$$

where $x(i)^T$ is a $1 \times n$ matrix and $V_C(A)$ is an $n^2 \times 1$ matrix. According to Equation (3), the least common multiple $\text{lcm}(n, n^2) = n^2$, and $x(i)^T \ltimes V_C(A) = (x(i)^T \otimes I_n)(V_C(A) \otimes I_1)$.

Suppose there are $N + 1$ observed samples, and

$$W = \begin{bmatrix} x(2) \\ \vdots \\ x(N+1) \end{bmatrix}, H = \begin{bmatrix} x(1)^T, u(1)^T \\ \vdots \\ x(N)^T, u(N)^T \end{bmatrix}, Y = \begin{bmatrix} V_C(A) \\ V_C(B) \end{bmatrix}. \tag{5}$$

Then we have

$$H \ltimes Y = W$$
$$\Downarrow \qquad\qquad\qquad\qquad (6)$$
$$(H \otimes I_n)Y = W$$

The Equation (6) is a linear system of equations, and the task is to find the solution Y. In the Equation (6), $H \otimes I_n$ is an $Nn \times (m+n)n$ matrix, where n is the dimension of system states, m is the dimension of the input, and N is the number of samples. For the high-dimensional identification system, the time complexity of classical algorithms is enormous and existing quantum algorithms can not directly solve the non-square linear systems of equations. In order to reduce the cost of computing resources, it is necessary to propose a quantum algorithm for general linear equations.

2.2. The Quantum Linear System Algorithm for General Matrices

Inspired by the singular value estimation algorithm [23,28,29], we propose a quantum algorithm for general linear systems of equations as follows.

Given a general linear equation $Ax = b$, the singular value decomposition is

$$A = \sum_i \sigma_i \mu_i v_i^T \qquad (7)$$

where $A \in R^{m \times n}$, $x \in R^n$ and $b \in R^m$, σ_i is the singular value of A, $\mu_i \in R^m$ and $v_i \in R^n$ are the left and right singular vectors, and $\mu_i^T \mu_i = v_i^T v_i = 1$, $\mu_i^T \mu_j = v_i^T v_j = 0 (i \neq j)$.

Let the rank of A be $r(r \leq m,n)$ and the rank of $[A\ b]$ be q; the relation between the solution vector x of $Ax = b$ and the r, q is:

$$\begin{cases} \text{approximate solution } \hat{x}, & r = n \text{ and } r < q \\ \text{unique solution } x, & r = n = q \\ \text{general solution } \tilde{x}, & r < n. \end{cases} \qquad (8)$$

The linear system of equations $Ax = b$ can be solved by a mathematical optimization technique of minimizing the sum of squares of errors between the solution and the actual data, which is the so-called least squares method

$$e = \|Ax - b\|^2 \qquad (9)$$

In the Equation (7), $\{\mu_i\} \in R^m$ and $\{v_i\} \in R^n$ are a set of basis in m and n dimensional spaces. Therefore, x and b can be expressed as $x = \sum_i^n \alpha_i v_i$, $b = \sum_i^m \beta_i \mu_i$, and

$$\begin{aligned} e &= \|Ax - b\|^2 \\ &= \left\| \sum_{i=1}^r \sigma_i \mu_i v_i^T \sum_{i=1}^n \alpha_i v_i - \sum_{i=1}^m \beta_i \mu_i \right\|^2 \\ &= \left\| \sum_{i=1}^r (\sigma_i \alpha_i - \beta_i) \mu_i - \sum_{i=r+1}^m \beta_i \mu_i \right\|^2 \\ &= \sum_{i=1}^r (\sigma_i \alpha_i - \beta_i)^2 + \sum_{i=r+1}^m \beta_i^2 \end{aligned} \qquad (10)$$

When $\alpha_i = \beta_i / \sigma_i$, $e_m = \min \|Ax - b\|^2 = \sum_{i=r+1}^m \beta_i^2$.

Note that when $r < n$, $\alpha_i (i = r+1, \ldots, n)$ is not assigned, and the equation $Ax = b$ has infinitely many solutions. In engineering, we usually want to find out the lowest energy solution state x with $\langle x|x \rangle$ minimality, that is

$$\begin{cases} \alpha_i = \beta_i / \sigma_i, & i \in [1, r] \\ \alpha_i = 0, & i \in [r+1, n] \end{cases} \qquad (11)$$

The goal is to convert the state $b = \sum_{i=1}^{m} \beta_i \mu_i$ to $x = \sum_{i=1}^{r} \beta_i / \sigma_i v_i$, whose detailed quantum process of our scheme is described as follows.

The following mappings to access to the data structure can be performed in $O(\text{polylog}(mn))$ time.

$$U_P : |\xi\rangle|0\rangle = \sum \xi_i |i\rangle|0\rangle \to \sum \xi_i |i, A_i\rangle$$
$$U_Q : |0\rangle|\xi\rangle = \sum \xi_j |0\rangle|j\rangle \to \sum \xi_j |A_F, j\rangle \qquad (12)$$

The data structure is based on an array of binary trees, each binary tree contains enough leaves that store the squared amplitudes of the corresponding matrix entry, which can be found in [28,33] with a detailed description of such a binary tree memory structure. In order to facilitate mathematical operation, we define two degenerate operators P and Q that operate only on valid input information $|\xi\rangle$, where the dimension of the input state $|\xi\rangle|0\rangle$ is reduced to the dimension of valid information $|\xi\rangle$, so P and Q are called degenerate operators. The maps P and Q append an arbitrary input state $|\xi\rangle$ to a register that encodes:

$$P : |\xi\rangle = \sum \xi_i |i\rangle \to \sum \xi_i |i, A_i\rangle = |P\xi\rangle$$
$$Q : |\xi\rangle = \sum \xi_j |j\rangle \to \sum \xi_j |A_F, j\rangle = |Q\xi\rangle \qquad (13)$$

where $|i, A_i\rangle = \frac{1}{\|A_i\|} \sum_{j=1}^{n} A_{ij} |i, j\rangle$ and $|A_F, j\rangle = \frac{1}{\|A\|_F} \sum_{i=1}^{m} \|A_i\| |i, j\rangle$. That is, $P = \sum_{i=1}^{m} |i\rangle|A_i\rangle\langle i|$ and $Q = \sum_{j=1}^{n} |A_F\rangle|j\rangle\langle j|$.

Based on the above definition, it is easy to obtain $(P^\dagger Q)_{ij} = \langle i, A_i | A_F, j\rangle = \frac{A_{ij}}{\|A_F\|}$. Similarly, it follows that P and Q have orthonormal columns and thus $P^\dagger P = I_m$ and $Q^\dagger Q = I_n$. Let $S = (2PP^\dagger - I)(2QQ^\dagger - I)$, when $m = n$, we can obtain

$$SQ|v_i\rangle = \frac{2\sigma_i}{\|A\|_F} P|\mu_i\rangle - Q|v_i\rangle$$
$$SP|\mu_i\rangle = (\frac{4\sigma_i^2}{\|A\|_F^2} - 1) P|\mu_i\rangle - \frac{2\sigma_i}{\|A\|_F} Q|v_i\rangle \qquad (14)$$

The eigenvalues of S are $e^{\pm 2\pi i \varphi_i}$, and the corresponding eigenvectors are $\omega_i^\pm |w_i^\pm\rangle = -P|\mu_i\rangle + e^{\mp 2\pi i \varphi_i} Q|v_i\rangle$, where φ_i is the phase of eigenvalues and $\omega_i^\pm$ is the norm of eigenvectors. Then, it can be obtained

$$Q|v_i\rangle = \frac{1}{2i\sin(\pi\varphi_i)} (\omega_i^+ |w_i^+\rangle - \omega_i^- |w_i^-\rangle)$$
$$P|\mu_i\rangle = \frac{1}{2i\sin(\pi\varphi_i)} (e^{\pi i \varphi_i} \omega_i^+ |w_i^+\rangle - e^{-\pi i \varphi_i} \omega_i^- |w_i^-\rangle) \qquad (15)$$

Through phase rotation, the process of $\sum_{i=1}^{n} \beta_i |\mu_i\rangle \mapsto \sum_{i=1}^{n} \beta_i |v_i\rangle$ is achievable [28,29]. It is worth noting that the above step is avoidable for the case of the coefficient matrix A being Hermitian. At this point, the singular value decomposition is $A = \sum_i \sigma_i \mu_i \mu_i^T$, and the task is to convert $|b\rangle = \sum_i \beta_i |\mu_i\rangle$ to the solution $|x\rangle = \sum_i \beta_i / \sigma_i |\mu_i\rangle$ such that $Ax = b$. However, for the case of non-Hermitian, it is necessary to realize the transformation of quantum states $|\mu_i\rangle$ to $|v_i\rangle$.

For a general linear system of equations with $m \neq n$, the above derivation will have some changes. For $i \in [1, r]$, Equations (14) and (15) are valid. While $i > r$, $A|v_i\rangle = 0$, $A^\dagger |\mu_i\rangle = 0$, and we can obtain

$$SQ|v_i\rangle = (2PP^\dagger - I)(2QQ^\dagger - I)Q|v_i\rangle$$
$$= (2PP^\dagger - I)Q|v_i\rangle$$
$$= \frac{2}{\|A\|_F} PA|v_i\rangle - Q|v_i\rangle \qquad (16)$$
$$= -Q|v_i\rangle,$$

and

$$\begin{align}SP|\mu_i\rangle &= (2PP^\dagger - I)(2QQ^\dagger - I)P|\mu_i\rangle \\ &= (2PP^\dagger - I)(\frac{2}{\|A\|_F}QA^\dagger|\mu_i\rangle - P|\mu_i\rangle) \\ &= (2PP^\dagger - I)(-P|\mu_i\rangle) \\ &= -P|\mu_i\rangle.\end{align} \tag{17}$$

At this point, $e^{2\pi i\varphi_i} = -1$ is the eigenvalue of S, that is, $\varphi_i = \pm 1/2$, and the corresponding eigenvectors are $Q|v_i\rangle$ and $P|\mu_i\rangle$. In order to achieve $|b\rangle = \sum_{i=1}^m \beta_i|\mu_i\rangle = \sum_{i=1}^r \beta_i|\mu_i\rangle + \sum_{i=r+1}^m \beta_i|\mu_i\rangle \mapsto |x\rangle = \sum_{i=1}^r \beta_i/\sigma_i|v_i\rangle$, we first need to eliminate the formula $\sum_{i=r+1}^m \beta_i|\mu_i\rangle$. Based on these definitions, we show the basic procedure of our algorithm:

1. Preparing the initial quantum state $|b\rangle = \sum_{i=1}^m b_i|i\rangle$, which can be represented as:

$$|b\rangle = \sum_{i=1}^m \beta_i|\mu_i\rangle \tag{18}$$

2. Apply P in the initial state $|b\rangle$

$$\begin{align}P|b\rangle &= \sum_{i=1}^m \beta_i P|\mu_i\rangle \\ &= \sum_{i=1}^r \frac{\beta_i}{2i\sin(\pi\varphi_i)}(e^{\pi i\varphi_i}\omega_i^+|w_i^+\rangle - e^{-\pi i\varphi_i}\omega_i^-|w_i^-\rangle) + \sum_{i=r+1}^m \beta_i P|\mu_i\rangle\end{align} \tag{19}$$

3. Perform phase estimation on input $P|b\rangle$ for $S = (2PP^\dagger - I)(2QQ^\dagger - I)$, as shown in Figure 1, then we obtain the following state

$$\sum_{i=1}^r \frac{\beta_i}{2i\sin(\pi\varphi_i)}(e^{\pi i\varphi_i}\omega_i^+|w_i^+,\varphi_i\rangle - e^{-\pi i\varphi_i}\omega_i^-|w_i^-,-\varphi_i\rangle) + \sum_{i=r+1}^m \beta_i P|\mu_i\rangle|\pm\frac{1}{2}\rangle, \tag{20}$$

where $e^{2\pi i\varphi_i}$ is the eigenvalue of S and $|\frac{1}{2}\rangle = |01000\ldots\rangle, |-\frac{1}{2}\rangle = |11000\ldots\rangle$.

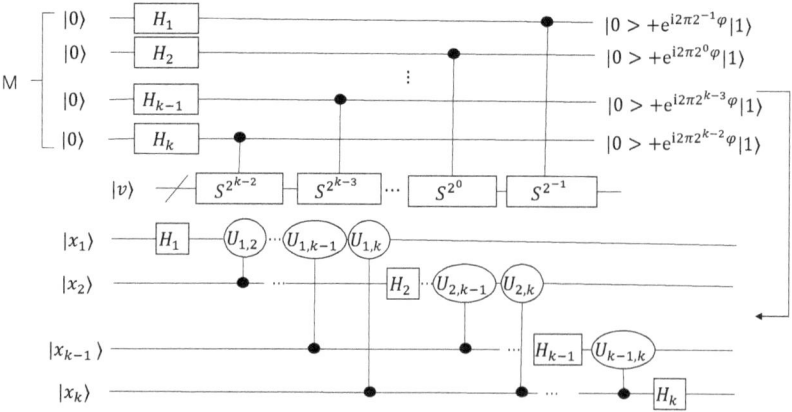

Figure 1. The modified quantum circuit for phase estimation. Set the $|x_1\rangle$ to be the sign bit, $|x_1\rangle = |0\rangle$ means φ_i is a positive value, otherwise it is negative. The state $|\varphi_i\rangle = |x_1\rangle_1|x_2\rangle_2\ldots|x_k\rangle_k$ and the phase value $\varphi_i = \sum_{j=2}^k 2^{-j+1}x_j - x_1$. The quantum circuit can estimate the phase value $\varphi_i \in (-1,1)$.

4. Apply a phase shift operator controlled by the phase φ_i, then we obtain

$$\sum_{i=1}^{r} \frac{\beta_i}{2i\sin(\pi\varphi_i)}(\omega_i^+|w_i^+,\varphi_i\rangle - \omega_i^-|w_i^-,-\varphi_i\rangle) + \sum_{i=r+1}^{m} \beta_i P|\mu_i\rangle| \pm \frac{1}{2}\rangle \quad (21)$$

5. Perform a controlled rotation on the ancillary qubit based on the register storing phase value φ_i and will obtain

$$\sum_{i=1}^{r} \frac{\beta_i}{2i\sin(\pi\varphi_i)}(\omega_i^+|w_i^+,\varphi_i\rangle - \omega_i^-|w_i^-,-\varphi_i\rangle)\left(\frac{t}{\sigma_i}|0\rangle + \sqrt{1-\frac{t^2}{\sigma_i^2}}|1\rangle\right) + \sum_{i=r+1}^{m} \beta_i P|\mu_i\rangle| \pm \frac{1}{2}\rangle|1\rangle, \quad (22)$$

where $\sigma_i = \cos(\pi\varphi_i)\|A\|_F$ and $t = \min_i|\sigma_i|, i \in [1,r]$.

6. Apply the inverse transformation of step 3 to obtain

$$\sum_{i=1}^{r} \frac{\beta_i}{2i\sin(\pi\varphi_i)}(\omega_i^+|w_i^+\rangle - \omega_i^-|w_i^-\rangle)\left(\frac{t}{\sigma_i}|0\rangle + \sqrt{1-\frac{t^2}{\sigma_i^2}}|1\rangle\right) + \sum_{i=r+1}^{m} \beta_i P|\mu_i\rangle|\rangle|1\rangle$$

$$= \sum_{i=1}^{r} \beta_i Q|v_i\rangle\left(\frac{t}{\sigma_i}|0\rangle + \sqrt{1-\frac{t^2}{\sigma_i^2}}|1\rangle\right) + \sum_{i=r+1}^{m} \beta_i P|\mu_i\rangle|1\rangle \quad (23)$$

7. Measure the ancillary register. When the measurement result is $|0\rangle$, the quantum state will collapse to

$$\sum_{i=1}^{r} \beta_i/\sigma_i Q|v_i\rangle \quad (24)$$

8. Apply the inverse of Q and we will obtain the desired state

$$\sum_{i=1}^{r} \beta_i/\sigma_i|v_i\rangle, \quad (25)$$

which is the particular solution of the equation $Ax = b$, that is, the lowest energy solution state.

The quantum gate circuit of our quantum algorithm is shown in Figure 2.

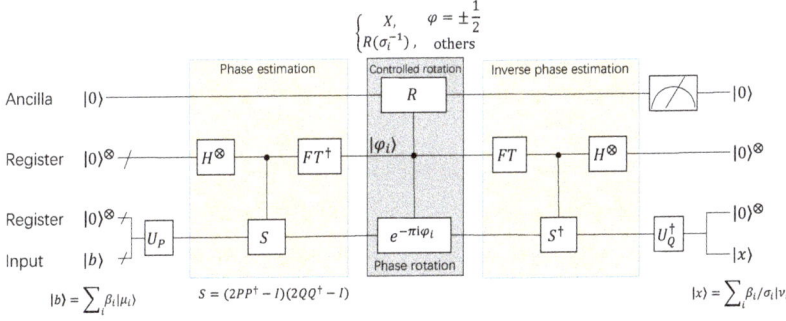

Figure 2. The quantum gate circuit of the particular solution of the equation $Ax = b$. The operator R is a quantum controlled rotation gate. When the phase $\varphi_i = \pm\frac{1}{2}$, R is a NOT gate, otherwise

$$R = R(\sigma_i^{-1}) = \begin{bmatrix} 1/\sigma_i & \sqrt{1-1/\sigma_i^2} \\ \sqrt{1-1/\sigma_i^2} & -1/\sigma_i \end{bmatrix}, \text{ where } \sigma_i = \cos(\pi\varphi_i)\|A\|_F.$$

Note that the actual phase value is $\varphi_i \in (-1,1)$, which serves as the control qubits of the phase shift operation in the step 4, while the previous quantum phase estimation algorithm outputs phase value $\varphi_i \in (0,1)$. Therefore, we design a modified quantum phase estimation circuit to determine the sign of the phase in Figure 1. In the modified QPE circuit, we can estimate the phase value in the range $\varphi \in (-1, 1)$.

For the case of $\varphi \in [0, 1)$, $\varphi = \sum_{j=1}^{k} 2^{-j+1} x_j$. Since $0 \le \varphi < 1$, it is easy to obtain $x_1 = 0$.

While $\varphi \in (-1, 0)$, we can obtain $e^{2\pi i 2^j \varphi} = e^{2\pi i 2^j (2+\varphi)}$, where $j = -1, \ldots, k-1$. Let $\phi = 2 + \varphi \in (1, 2)$, the modified QSV circuit outputs $\phi = \sum_{j=1}^{k} 2^{-j+1} x_j$. It is known that $\phi \in (1, 2)$, thus we obtain $x_1 = 1$ and $\varphi = \sum_{j=1}^{k} 2^{-j+1} x_j - 2 = \sum_{j=2}^{k} 2^{-j+1} x_j - 1$. Therefore, we can obtain

$$\varphi = \begin{cases} \sum_{j=1}^{k} 2^{-j+1} x_j, & x_1 = 0 \\ \sum_{j=2}^{k} 2^{-j+1} x_j - 1, & x_1 = 1 \end{cases} \quad (26)$$

that is, $\varphi = \sum_{j=2}^{k} 2^{-j+1} x_j - x_1$.

2.3. The Quantum Algorithm for Homogeneous Linear Equations

For the condition of $r < n$, the equation $Ax = b$ has infinitely many solutions. Therefore, in order to obtain general solutions of the equation $Ax = b$, we need to solve the homogeneous linear equation $Ax = 0$.

Since $A = \sum_{i=1}^{n} \sigma_i \mu_i v_i^T$ and $x = \sum_{i=1}^{n} \alpha_i v_i$, we can obtain $Ax = \sum_{i=1}^{n} \sigma_i \alpha_i \mu_i$. Let $v_i (i \in [r+1, n])$ be the right singular vector corresponding to $\sigma_i = 0$, when $\sigma_i = 0$ or $\alpha_i = 0$, $Ax = 0$ is valid, that is, $x = \sum_{i=r+1}^{n} \alpha_i v_i$. The description of solving homogeneous linear equations is essentially just finding the projection of a state onto the ground state for an operator [34]. Through the quantum circuit shown in Figure 3, we obtain the combination of the eigenvectors corresponding to $\sigma_i = 0$ and make the solution of homogeneous linear equations complete.

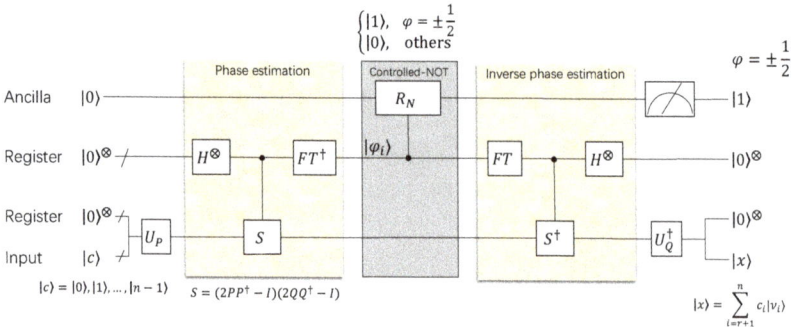

Figure 3. The quantum gate circuit of homogeneous linear equation $Ax = 0$. The input state is $|c\rangle = \sum_{i=1}^{n} c_i |v_i\rangle$ and the output state is $|x\rangle = \sum_{i=r+1}^{n} c_i |v_i\rangle$, where $|x\rangle$ is the combination of right singular vectors corresponding to the singular value 0 of A contained in $|c\rangle$. When the phase $\varphi_i = \pm 1/2$, the output of the controlled-NOT gate R_N is $|1\rangle$, otherwise it outputs $|0\rangle$. We can obtain the solution of the $Ax = 0$ when an arbitrary input $|c\rangle$ contains right singular vectors of A. In order to ensure that the output $|x\rangle$ is complete, we input n linearly independent $|c\rangle = |0\rangle, |1\rangle \ldots |n\rangle$. In addition, the arbitrary r linearly independent x_i can form the solution vector basis of the homogeneous linear equation.

Based on QSVE, our quantum algorithms are sparsity-independent and may be applied to non-square dense matrices.

3. Algorithms Complexity Analysis

Then, we analyse the time complexity of our quantum algorithms.

The time complexity of our scheme includes the following two parts: quantum data generation and the quantum algorithm process. On the one hand, relying on a binary tree memory structure detailed as described in [28,33], where the matrix entries associated with matrix $A_{m \times n}$ are stored as suitable data structure, the oracle from classical data to quantum data can be implemented efficiently in time $O(\log^2 mn)$ and the data structure size is $O(w \log mn)$ where w is the number of non zero entries in A. On the other hand, based on the quantum singular value estimation algorithm, our algorithm achieves a runtime $O(\kappa \, \text{polylog}(mn)/\delta)$, where κ is the condition number of the coefficient matrix A, and δ denotes the precision parameter.

Define that the additive error achieved in output state $\tilde{x}$ is ϵ, which means if x is the exact result and $\tilde{x}$ is the result obtained from quantum algorithms, then $\|x - \tilde{x}\| \leq \epsilon$. In order to achieve accuracy ϵ, the precision parameter of our algorithm needs to reach $\delta = \epsilon/(\kappa \|A\|_F)$. Assuming the spectral norm $\|A\|_*$ is bounded by a constant, since $\|A\|_F \leq \sqrt{r}\|A\|_*$, we have $\|A\|_F = O(\sqrt{r})$, where r is the rank of matrix A. Therefore, our quantum algorithm has the time complexity of $O(\kappa^2 \sqrt{r} \text{polylog}(mn)/\epsilon)$. Remarkably, when A is sparse, exponential acceleration is achievable.

In the quantum algorithm of homogeneous linear equations, the time complexity of QSVE is $O(\text{polylog}(mn)/\epsilon)$. In view of the success probability of the ancillary register collapses to $|1\rangle$, we need to repeat the coherent computation $n/(n-r)$ times on average. Therefore, the runtime of the quantum homogeneous linear equation algorithm is given by $O(n \, \text{polylog}(mn)/((n-r)\epsilon))$.

After obtaining the quantum state $|x\rangle$ corresponding to the solution of $Ax = b$, we need to simulate the subsequent system states through the identified system, where $x = \begin{bmatrix} V_C(A) \\ V_C(B) \end{bmatrix}$. According to Equations (4)–(6), we can obtain

$$x(i+1) = \langle \zeta(i)|x\rangle \tag{27}$$

where $\zeta(i) = [x(i)^T, u(i)^T] \otimes I_n$. The inner product between pairs of states can be implemented in time $O(\text{ploylog}(m+n))$ by the swap text algorithm [35]. Therefore, we can predict the system state at the next moment based on the known system state $x(i)$ and input $u(i)$.

For the case of general matrix $A_{m \times n}$, previous quantum algorithms generally convert A to a Hermitian matrix:

$$H = \begin{bmatrix} 0 & A \\ A^\dagger & 0 \end{bmatrix} \tag{28}$$

Based on QSVE, the quantum algorithm of $H \begin{bmatrix} 0 \\ x \end{bmatrix} = \begin{bmatrix} b \\ 0 \end{bmatrix}$ has the time complexity of $O(\kappa^2 \|H\|_F \, \text{polylog}\,(m+n)^2/\epsilon)$. In addition, the time complexity of our scheme is $O(\kappa^2 \|A\|_F \, \text{polylog}(mn)/\epsilon)$, where $\|H\|_F = \sqrt{2}\|A\|_F$. Let the runtime of our scheme be T, so the runtime of existing SVE-based quantum algorithms is $T' = \sqrt{2}\frac{\text{poly}\log(m+n)^2}{\text{poly}\log(mn)}T$. For the large-scale linear system of equations, there is $T' \approx \sqrt{2}T$. Compared to existing quantum algorithms, our scheme can reduce the time complexity of the linear system of equations with a non-square dense matrix.

4. Numerical Simulation

To clarify the process of our algorithm and prove the feasibility of algorithms, we perform simulation on an illustrative example.

For simplicity, we consider a first-order discrete model of classical system as follows:

$$x(i+1) = ax(i) + du(i) \tag{29}$$

where $x(i)$ is the system state of the i-th sampling and $u(i)$ is the input state. The goal of system identification is to estimate coefficients a and d from a set of $u(i)$ and $x(i)$. Assuming that the initial system state $x(1) = 3$, the input states $u = \{4, 3, 0\}$ and the evolved system states $x(2) = -4, x(3) = x(4) = 0$, the mathematical model can be transformed into a general linear systems of equations $Ax = b$, where $A = \begin{bmatrix} 3 & 4 \\ -4 & 3 \\ 0 & 0 \end{bmatrix}, b = \begin{bmatrix} -4 \\ 0 \\ 0 \end{bmatrix}$. The maps U_P and U_Q append an arbitrary input state to a register that encodes the Equation (12), which can be realized by quantum gate circuits in Figure 4, and matrix forms of these maps are $P = \frac{1}{5}\begin{bmatrix} 3 & 0 & 0 \\ 4 & 0 & 0 \\ 0 & -4 & 0 \\ 0 & 3 & 0 \\ 0 & 0 & \frac{5\sqrt{2}}{2} \\ 0 & 0 & \frac{5\sqrt{2}}{2} \end{bmatrix}, Q = \frac{\sqrt{2}}{2}\begin{bmatrix} 1 & 0 \\ 0 & 1 \\ 1 & 0 \\ 0 & 1 \\ 0 & 0 \\ 0 & 0 \end{bmatrix}$.

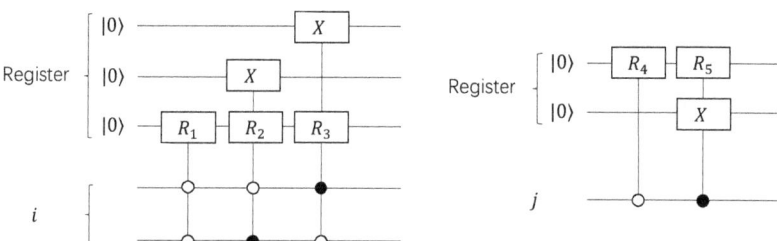

The circuit implementation of U_P The circuit implementation of U_Q

Figure 4. Quantum circuits implementation of U_P and U_Q. The maps U_P and U_Q consist of quantum control gates, where $R_1 = \frac{1}{5}\begin{bmatrix} 3 & 4 \\ 4 & -3 \end{bmatrix}, R_2 = \frac{1}{5}\begin{bmatrix} -4 & 3 \\ 3 & 4 \end{bmatrix}, R_3 = R_4 = R_5 = H = \frac{\sqrt{2}}{2}\begin{bmatrix} 1 & 1 \\ 1 & -1 \end{bmatrix}$ and the $X = \begin{bmatrix} 0 & 1 \\ 1 & 0 \end{bmatrix}$ is the quantum inverse gate.

The following shows the detailed procedure of the numerical simulation:
1. Preparing the initial state $|b\rangle = |0\rangle$.
2. Apply P in the initial state $|b\rangle$, $P|b\rangle = \frac{3}{5}|0\rangle + \frac{4}{5}|1\rangle$.
3. Perform phase estimation on $P|b\rangle$ for $S = (2PP^\dagger - I)(2QQ^\dagger - I) = \frac{1}{25}\begin{bmatrix} 0 & 0 & -7 & 24 & 0 & 0 \\ 0 & 0 & 24 & 7 & 0 & 0 \\ 7 & -24 & 0 & 0 & 0 & 0 \\ -24 & -7 & 0 & 0 & 0 & 0 \\ 0 & 0 & 0 & 0 & 0 & 25 \\ 0 & 0 & 0 & 0 & 25 & 0 \end{bmatrix}$,

then we obtain the following state

$$-\frac{3\sqrt{2}i}{10}\left(e^{\frac{1}{4}\pi i}\omega_1|w_1,\frac{1}{4}\rangle - e^{-\frac{1}{4}\pi i}\omega_2|w_2,-\frac{1}{4}\rangle\right) - \frac{2\sqrt{2}i}{5}\left(e^{\frac{3}{4}\pi i}\omega_3|w_3,\frac{3}{4}\rangle - e^{-\frac{3}{4}\pi i}\omega_4|w_4,-\frac{3}{4}\rangle\right), \quad (30)$$

where the eigenvalues of S are $\lambda_i = i, i, -i, -i, 1, -1$, and $\omega_i|w_i\rangle$ is the corresponding eigenvector.
4. Change the phase, then we obtain

$$-\frac{3\sqrt{2}i}{10}\left(\omega_1|w_1,\frac{1}{4}\rangle - \omega_2|w_2,-\frac{1}{4}\rangle\right) - \frac{2\sqrt{2}i}{5}\left(\omega_3|w_3,\frac{3}{4}\rangle - \omega_4|w_4,-\frac{3}{4}\rangle\right) \quad (31)$$

5. Perform a controlled rotation on the ancillary qubit based on the register storing phase value:

$$-\frac{3\sqrt{2}i}{10}\left(\omega_1|w_1,\tfrac{1}{4}\rangle - \omega_2|w_2,-\tfrac{1}{4}\rangle\right)\left(\tfrac{1}{5}|0\rangle + \tfrac{2\sqrt{6}}{5}|1\rangle\right) - \tfrac{2\sqrt{2}i}{5}\left(\omega_3|w_3,\tfrac{3}{4}\rangle - \omega_4|w_4,-\tfrac{3}{4}\rangle\right)\left(-\tfrac{1}{5}|0\rangle + \tfrac{2\sqrt{6}}{5}|1\rangle\right) \qquad (32)$$

where $\sigma_1 = \cos(\pm\tfrac{1}{4}\pi)\|A\|_F = 5$, $\sigma_2 = \cos(\pm\tfrac{3}{4}\pi)\|A\|_F = -5$.

6. Apply the inverse transformation of step 3 to obtain

$$-\frac{3\sqrt{2}i}{10}(\omega_1|w_1\rangle - \omega_2|w_2\rangle)\left(\tfrac{1}{5}|0\rangle + \tfrac{2\sqrt{6}}{5}|1\rangle\right) - \tfrac{2\sqrt{2}i}{5}(\omega_3|w_3\rangle - \omega_4|w_4\rangle)\left(-\tfrac{1}{5}|0\rangle + \tfrac{2\sqrt{6}}{5}|1\rangle\right) \qquad (33)$$

7. Apply the inverse of Q and we will obtain the desired state

$$\tfrac{3}{5}|0\rangle\left(\tfrac{1}{5}|0\rangle + \tfrac{2\sqrt{6}}{5}|1\rangle\right) - \tfrac{4}{5}|1\rangle\left(-\tfrac{1}{5}|0\rangle + \tfrac{2\sqrt{6}}{5}|1\rangle\right) \qquad (34)$$

8. Measure the ancillary register. When the result is $|0\rangle$, the quantum state will collapse to

$$\tfrac{3}{5}|0\rangle + \tfrac{4}{5}|1\rangle \qquad (35)$$

that is proportional to the solution of the equation $Ax = b$, so we obtain $a = \tfrac{3}{5}C$ and $d = \tfrac{4}{5}C$. Substituting a and d into Equation (29), we obtain $C = -\tfrac{4}{5}$. So far, the first-order discrete identification model is:

$$x(i+1) = -\frac{12}{25}x(i) - \frac{16}{25}u(i) \qquad (36)$$

We simulated a 6-qubit quantum circuit diagram on the Origin Cloud, as shown in Figure 5.

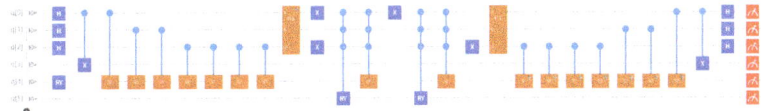

Figure 5. The 6-qubit quantum circuit diagram on the Origin Cloud. The quantum circuit is based on quantum phase estimation, where q[5] is the ancillary qubit and q[4] is the register storing input and output information. From left to right, the controlled rotation gate is $RY_1 = \tfrac{1}{5}\begin{bmatrix} 3 & -4 \\ 4 & 3 \end{bmatrix}$ that generates the initial state $P|b\rangle$, $RY_2 = \tfrac{1}{\sigma_1}\begin{bmatrix} t & -\sqrt{\sigma_1^2 - t^2} \\ \sqrt{\sigma_1^2 - t^2} & t \end{bmatrix}$ and $RY_3 = \tfrac{1}{\sigma_2}\begin{bmatrix} t & -\sqrt{\sigma_2^2 - t^2} \\ \sqrt{\sigma_2^2 - t^2} & t \end{bmatrix}$, where $t = \tfrac{5\sqrt{2}}{2}$. The controlled gates $s_1 = \tfrac{1}{25}\begin{bmatrix} -7 & 24 \\ 24 & 7 \end{bmatrix}$, $s_2 = \tfrac{1}{25}\begin{bmatrix} 7 & -24 \\ -24 & -7 \end{bmatrix}$, $z_1 = \begin{bmatrix} e^{-\tfrac{1}{4}\pi i} & 0 \\ 0 & e^{-\tfrac{1}{4}\pi i} \end{bmatrix}$ and $rz = \begin{bmatrix} e^{-\tfrac{3}{4}\pi i} & 0 \\ 0 & e^{-\tfrac{3}{4}\pi i} \end{bmatrix}$ are applied on the register q[4].

According to the simulation result in Figure 6, when the ancillary qubit q[5] = 0 and the register storing phase information is restored to q[0] = q[1] = q[2] = 0, the probabilities of the output qubit q[4] are $P\{|0\rangle\} = 0.086$ and $P\{|1\rangle\} = 0.16$. Therefore, the amplitudes of q[4] are $A\{|0\rangle\} = \sqrt{P\{|0\rangle\}/(P\{|0\rangle\} + P\{|1\rangle\})} = 0.59$ and $A\{|1\rangle\} = \sqrt{P\{|1\rangle\}/(P\{|0\rangle\} + P\{|1\rangle\})} = 0.81$, and the solution quantum state is q[4] = $0.59|0\rangle + 0.81|1\rangle$, which is consistent with the expected quantum state based on our algorithm.

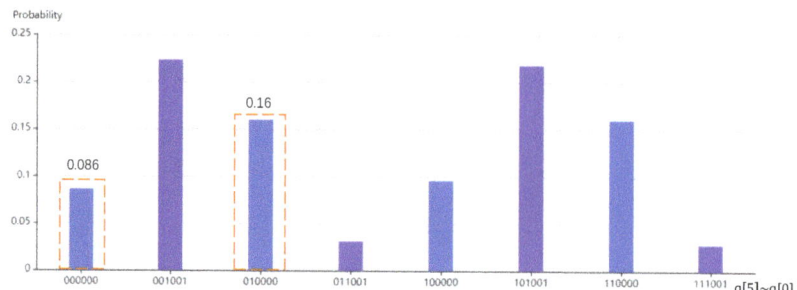

Figure 6. The simulation result of the quantum circuit.

As a comparison, we simulated a second-order discrete system identification model $x(i+1) = A'x(i) + B'u(i)$, where A' is a 2×2 matrix and B' is a 2×1 matrix. Assuming that the initial system state $x(1) = \begin{bmatrix} 1 \\ 0 \end{bmatrix}$, the input $u = \{1, 2, 3\}$ and the evolved system states $x(2) = \begin{bmatrix} 1 \\ 1 \end{bmatrix}$, the mathematical model can be transformed into $Ax = b$, where $A = \begin{bmatrix} 1 & 0 & 0 & 0 & 1 & 0 \\ 0 & 1 & 0 & 0 & 0 & 1 \end{bmatrix}$ and $b = \begin{bmatrix} 1 \\ 1 \end{bmatrix}$. Due to insufficient samples, the linear equation has infinite solutions. Consider the structural features of the coefficient matrix A, which is reduced to $\begin{bmatrix} 1 & 0 & 1 & 0 \\ 0 & 1 & 0 & 1 \end{bmatrix}$.

When the ancillary qubit q[6] = 0 and the register q[5] is restored to 0, the probabilities of the output qubits q[4] and q[3] are shown in the Figure 7. Thus, the solution quantum state is $|x\rangle = 0.493|00\rangle + 0.5|01\rangle + 0.516|10\rangle + 0.485|11\rangle$, which is the lowest energy solution among infinitely many solutions. So far, according to the existing samples, the second-order discrete identification model with the lowest energy is: $x(i+1) = \begin{bmatrix} 0.493 & 0 \\ 0.5 & 0 \end{bmatrix} x(i) + \begin{bmatrix} 0.516 \\ 0.485 \end{bmatrix} u(i)$.

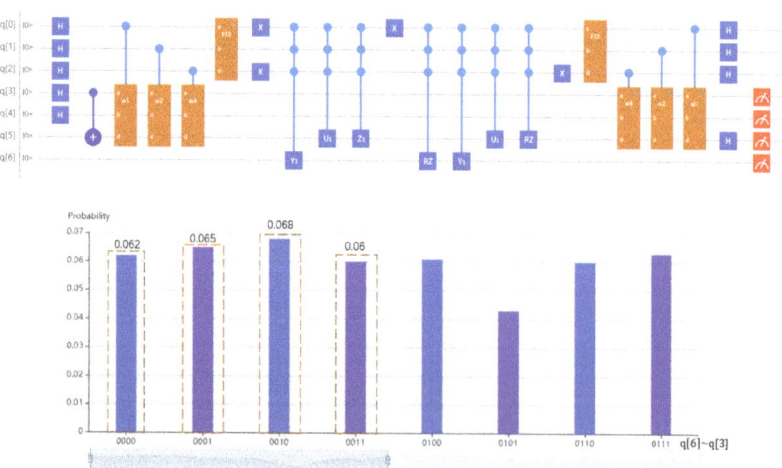

Figure 7. Quantum circuit and simulation result of the two-dimensional discrete system identification model.

5. Conclusions

This paper develops a quantum algorithm of general linear equations for solving classical system identification problems. Our scheme can be finished in time $O(\kappa^2 \sqrt{r} \text{polylog}(mn)/\epsilon)$ for an $m \times n$ dimensional linear systems of equations $Ax = b$, where κ is the condition number of the linear equation, r is the rank of the matrix A and ϵ is the precision parameter, which is superior to existing algorithms. For the linear equation with non-square coefficient matrix, we discuss three cases of solutions, including the unique solution, approximate solution and infinitely many solutions. Our algorithm can obtain the unique solution, the approximate solution with the minimum error and the lowest energy solution among infinitely many solutions, which adapts to all cases of linear systems of equations. For the case of infinitely many solutions, we design a quantum circuit to obtain general solutions in time $O(n \text{ polylog}(mn)/((n-r)\epsilon))$, which can achieve an exponential improvement over classical algorithms. In addition, we design a modified QPE circuit to obtain a wider range of phase values, which can expand the application range of quantum phase estimation.

Based on QSVE, our algorithms is sparsity-independent compared with HHL algorithm. Meanwhile, we have extended the existing quantum linear system algorithms to general equations, which can effectively enrich the application area of linear systems of equations. For large-scale linear systems, such as machine learning, numerical calculation of partial differential equations, etc., our algorithms will have a wider range of applications and is of research significance. In the future work, we will focus on how our algorithms are implemented on quantum computers and how to apply on them to real practical problems.

Author Contributions: Conceptualization, M.Z. and K.L.; methodology, K.L.; validation, X.L., Y.L. and C.D.; investigation, M.Z. and K.L.; resources, M.Z. and C.D.; writing—original draft preparation, M.Z. and K.L.; writing—review and editing, K.L., H.D., C.D. and Y.Z.; supervision, C.D.; project administration, C.D.; funding acquisition, C.D. All authors have read and agreed to the published version of the manuscript.

Funding: This research was funded by the National Natural Science Foundation of China (No.61673389, No. 61273202 and No. 62101559), in part by the National University of Defense Technology under Grant (No.19-QNCXJ and No.ZK21-37), in part by the National Defense Science and technology 173 program technical field Fund (No.2021-JCJQ-JJ-0510), in part by the Innovative Key Projects Promotion in Information and Communication College (No.YJKT-ZD-2105), and in part by the Innovative Talents Promotion in Information and Communication College (No.YJKT-RC-2113).

Institutional Review Board Statement: Not applicable.

Informed Consent Statement: Not applicable.

Data Availability Statement: Data are contained within the article.

Conflicts of Interest: The authors declare no conflict of interest.

References

1. Goodwin, G.; Payne, R. *Dynamic System Identification*; Academic Press: New York, NY, USA, 1977.
2. Mehra, R.K.; Lainiotis, D.G. *System Identification*; Academic Press: New York, NY, USA, 1976.
3. Ljung, L. *System Identification: Theory for The User*; Tsinghua University Press: Beijing, China, 2002.
4. Marquardt, D. An algorithm for least-Squares estimation of nonlinear parameters. *J. Soc. Ind. Appl. Math.* **1963**, *11*, 431–441. [CrossRef]
5. Kohout, R.B. Hedged maximum likelihood quantum state estimation. *Phys. Rev. Lett.* **2010**, *105*, 200504. [CrossRef] [PubMed]
6. Teo, Y.; Zhu, H.; Englert, B.; Rehacekand, J.; Hradil, Z. Quantum-state reconstruction by maximizing likelihood and entropy. *Phys. Rev. Lett.* **2011**, *107*, 020404. [CrossRef]
7. Bishop, C. *Pattern Recognition and Machine Learning*; Springer: New York, NY, USA, 2006; p. 4, ISBN 9780387310732.
8. Childs, A.M.; Liu, J.P.; Ostrander, A. High-precision quantum algorithms for partial differential equations. *arXiv* **2020**, arXiv:2002.07868.
9. Magnus, J.; Neudecker, H. The elimination matrix: Some lemmas and applications. *SIAM J. Algebr. Discret. Methods* **1980**, *1*, 422–449. [CrossRef]
10. Haddock, J.; Needell, D.; Rebrova, E.; Swartworth, W. Quantile-based iterative methods for corrupted systems of linear equations. *arXiv* **2020**, arXiv:2107.05554.

11. Nielsen, M.A.; Chuang, I.L. *Quantum Computation and Quantum Information*; Cambridge University Press: Cambrige, MA, USA, 2000.
12. Emily, G.; Mark, H. *Quantum Computing: Progress and Prospects*; The National Academy Press: Washington, DC, USA, 2018.
13. Adedoyin, A.; Ambrosiano, J.; Anisimov, P.; Bärtschi, A.; Casper, W.; Chennupati, G.; Coffrin, C.; Djidjev, H.; Gunter, D.; Karra, S.; et al. Quantum algorithm implementations for beginners. *arXiv* **2018**, arXiv:1804.03719.
14. Wiebe, N.; Braun, D.; Lloyd, S. Quantum algorithm for data fitting. *Phys. Rev. Lett.* **2012**, *109*, 50505. [CrossRef]
15. Shor, P. Polynomial-time algorithms for prime factorization and discrete logarithms on a quantum computer. *SIAM Rev.* **1999**, *41*, 303–332. [CrossRef]
16. Grover, L.K. A fast quantum mechanical algorithm for database search. In Proceedings of the 28th ACM Symposium on Theory of Computing, Philadelphia, PA, USA, 22–24 May 1996; pp. 212–219.
17. Feynman, R.P. Simulating physics with computers. *Int. J. Theor. Phys.* **1982**, *21*, 467–488. [CrossRef]
18. Lloyd, S. Universal quantum simulators. *Science* **1996**, *273*, 1073–1078. [CrossRef] [PubMed]
19. Berry, D.W.; Childs, A.M. Black-box Hamiltonian simulation and unitary implementation. *Quantum Inf. Comput.* **2012**, *12*, 29–62.
20. Long, G.L. General quantum interference principle and duality computer. *Commun. Theor. Phys.* **2006**, *45*, 825–844.
21. Long, G.L.; Liu, Y. Duality computing in quantum computers. *Commun. Theor. Phys.* **2009**, *50*, 1303.
22. Long, G.L.; Liu, Y.; Wang, C. Allowable generalized quantum gates. *Commun. Theor. Phys.* **2009**, *51*, 65.
23. Harrow, A.W.; Hassidim, A.; Lloyd, S. Quantum algorithm for linear systems of equations. *Phys. Rev. Lett.* **2009**, *103*, 150502. [CrossRef]
24. Kerenidis, I.; Prakash, A. Quantum recommendation system. *Lipics Leibniz Int. Proc. Inform.* **2017**, *49*, 1–21.
25. Li, K.; Dai, H.; Jing, F.; Gao, M.; Xue, B.; Wang, P.; Zhang, M. Quantum algorithms for solving linear regression equation. *J. Phys. Conf. Ser.* **2021**, *1738*, 012063. [CrossRef]
26. Shao, C P. Quantum algorithms to matrix multiplication. *arXiv* **2018**, arXiv:1803.01601.
27. Li, K.; Dai, H.Y.; Zhang, M. Quantum algorithms of state estimators in classical control systems. *Sci. China Inf. Sci.* **2020**, *63*, 1–12. [CrossRef]
28. Wossnig, L.; Zhao, Z.K.; Prakash, A. A quantum linear system algorithm for dense matrices. *Phys. Rev. Lett.* **2018**, *120*, 050502. [CrossRef] [PubMed]
29. Shao, C.P.; Xiang, H. Quantum circulant preconditioner for a linear system of equations. *Phys. Rev. A* **2018**, *98*, 062321. [CrossRef]
30. Childs, A.M.; Wiebe, N. Hamiltonian simulation using linear combinations of unitary operations. *Quantum Inf. Comput.* **2012**, *12*, 901–924. [CrossRef]
31. Berry, D.W.; Ahokas, G.; Cleve, R. Efficient quantum algorithms for simulating sparse Hamiltonians. *Commun. Math. Phys.* **2007**, *270*, 359–371. [CrossRef]
32. Cheng, D.Z. On semi-tensor product of matrices and its applications. *Acta Math. Appl. Sin.* **2003**, *19*, 219–228. [CrossRef]
33. Kerenidis, I.; Prakash, A. Quantum Recommendation Systems. In Proceedings of the 8th Innovations in Theoretical Computer Science Conference, Berkeley, CA, USA, 9–11 January 2017; Schloss Dagstuhl-Leibniz-Zentrum fuer Informatik: Dagstuhl, Germany, 2017.
34. Lin, L.; Tong, Y. Near-Optimal Ground State Preparation. *Quantum* **2020**, *4*, 372. [CrossRef]
35. Buhrman, H.; Cleve, R.; Watrous, J.; Wolf, R. Quantum Fingerprinting. *Phys. Rev. Lett.* **2001**, *87*, 167902. [CrossRef] [PubMed]

Article

Quantum Correlation Swapping between Two Werner States Undergoing Local and Nonlocal Unitary Operations

Chuanmei Xie [1], Zhanjun Zhang [2,*], Jianlan Chen [1] and Xiaofeng Yin [1]

[1] School of Physics and Optoelectronic Engineering, Anhui University, Hefei 230039, China
[2] School of Information and Electronic Engineering, Zhejiang Gongshang University, Hangzhou 310018, China
* Correspondence: zhangzhanjun@zjgsu.edu.cn

Abstract: In this paper, quantum correlation (QC) swapping between two Werner-like states, which are transformed from Werner states undergoing local and nonlocal unitary operations, are studied. Bell states measures are performed in the middle node to realize the QC swapping and correspondingly final correlated sates are obtained. Two different QC quantifiers, i.e., measurement-induced disturbance (MID) and ameliorated MID, are employed to characterize and quantify all the concerned QCs in the swapping process. All QCs in the concerned states are evaluated analytically and numerically. Correspondingly, their characteristics and properties are exposed in detail. It is exposed that, through the QC swapping process, one can obtain the long-distance QC indeed. Moreover, the similarities of monotony features of MID and AMID between the initial states and final states are exposed and analyzed.

Keywords: quantum correlation swapping; werner-like state; measurement-induced disturbance (MID); ameliorated MID (AMID)

PACS: 03.65.Ta; 03.67.-a

Citation: Xie, C.; Zhang, Z.; Chen, J.; Yin, X. Quantum Correlation Swapping between Two Werner States Undergoing Local and Nonlocal Unitary Operations. *Entropy* **2022**, *24*, 1244. https://doi.org/10.3390/e24091244

Academic Editors: Shao-Ming Fei, Ming Li and Shunlong Luo

Received: 3 August 2022
Accepted: 30 August 2022
Published: 4 September 2022

Publisher's Note: MDPI stays neutral with regard to jurisdictional claims in published maps and institutional affiliations.

Copyright: © 2022 by the authors. Licensee MDPI, Basel, Switzerland. This article is an open access article distributed under the terms and conditions of the Creative Commons Attribution (CC BY) license (https:// creativecommons.org/licenses/by/ 4.0/).

1. Introduction

Quantum entanglement swapping is the core technique in quantum entanglement repeaters. Quantum entanglement repeaters are usually employed to realize long-distance quantum entanglements in some quantum tasks in quantum information processing [1–7]. Entanglement swapping can make a null-entanglement bipartite system entangled. Additionally, entanglement swapping can be utilized to enhance quantum entanglement [8].

Today, as is known to all, quantum correlations (QCs) no longer equal to quantum entanglement [9–18]. This recognition was exposed in 2001. Recently, Ollivier and Zurek [19] made a surprising discovery, in that there are indeed existing quantum correlation different from entanglement (QCDE). Later, numerous findings [20–35] about the recognition and applications of QCDEs appeared. Now, QCDE has become a hot field in the research of quantum information and computation.

As the quantum entanglement was generalized to quantum correlation, which can be quantum entanglement or QCDE, quantum entanglement swapping can also be generalized to quantum correlation swapping [36–44]. In quantum correlation swapping, the concerned quantum correlation may be quantum entanglement, QCDE, or both. Obviously, quantum correlation swapping is a general extentson of quantum entanglement swapping. Similarly, the realization of QCDE swapping can be in the same way with entanglement swapping. In many processes, the entanglement swapping and QCDE swapping can be realized simultaneously.

In the studies of quantum correlation swapping, three main aspects are of concern. One is the selection of initial states before QC swapping. Another is the selection of the middle measurement to realize the QC swapping. The last is the QC quantifiers, which are used to quantify the QCs in all the concerned states in the QC swapping process. Hence, one can see that complexities in the QC swapping stem from the above three aspects. Moreover, for the three aspects, one can see that many different selections can be used. Hence, many different properties can be exposed and revealed.

In this paper, a special QC swapping case will be considered. That is to say, two Werner-like states are taken as initial states; the four Bell state measurements are utilized to realize the QC swapping; and measurement-induced disturbance (MID) [20] and ameliorated MID (AMID) [23] are utilized to quantify the QCs in the concerned states.

The following is summarized for the rest of the paper. In Section 2, the Werner-like initial state QC swapping is described in detail. In Section 3, QCs in both the initial states and final states are quantified by MID. In Section 4, QCs in both the initial states and final states are quantified by AMID. In Section 5, QCs in the initial states, MID or AMID, are analyzed, discussed and compared. Lastly, in Section 6, a summary is provided.

2. Swapping QCs in Two Werner States Undergoing Local and Nonlocal Unitary Operations

In the QC swapping process, the two initial states are taken as a special kind of quantum-correlated states. It is called as Werner-like state because it is transformed from the famous Werner state undergoing local and nonlocal unitary operations.

Usually, a two-qubit Werner state can be written as

$$\varrho^W(z) = \frac{1-z}{4}\mathbf{I} + z|\phi^+\rangle\langle\phi^+|, \qquad (1)$$

where $\mathbf{I}$ denotes a unit operator, $|\phi^+\rangle = (|00\rangle + |11\rangle)/\sqrt{2}$, z is real, and $z \in (0,1]$. When $z \leq 1/3$, Werner state $\varrho^W(z)$ is separable, while $z > 1/3$, this state is entangled.

Through unitary operation $U \in U(4)$, one can transform the Werner state $\varrho^W(z)$ to Werner-like state $\sigma(z,c)$, i.e., $\sigma = U\varrho^W U^+$. Correspondingly, the Werner-like state $\sigma_{ab}(z,c)$ can be written as [44]

$$\sigma(z,c) = \frac{1-z}{4}I + z|\psi\rangle\langle\psi|, \qquad (2)$$

where $|\psi\rangle = U|\phi^+\rangle = \sqrt{c}|00\rangle + \sqrt{1-c}|11\rangle$ with $c \in (0,1]$.

As for the QC swapping process in this study, the two initial Werner-like states are respectively written as

$$\sigma_{ab}(z_1,c_1) = \frac{1-z_1}{4}I_{ab} + z_1|\psi_1\rangle_{ab}\langle\psi_1|, \qquad (3)$$

$$\sigma_{cd}(z_2,c_2) = \frac{1-z_2}{4}I_{cd} + z_2|\psi_2\rangle_{cd}\langle\psi_2|, \qquad (4)$$

where $|\psi_i\rangle = \sqrt{c_i}|00\rangle + \sqrt{1-c_i}|11\rangle$, $z_i, c_i \in (0,1]$ characterize the Werner-like states, and I is unit operator. a, b, c and d are four subsystems in the whole system, where a and c are located at a same place.

The QC swapping process can be described as follows. Alice has two particles a and c, Bob has a particle b and David has a particle d. Initially, a and b are in Werner-like state ρ_{ab}, while c and d are in Werner-like state ρ_{cd}. When Alice performs the middle measurement a and c, simultaneously, b and d will be in the final state ρ_{bd}. That is to say, initially, Bob and David have no any correlation. However, after the middle measurement performed by Alice, Bob and David will be correlated.

In the realization of QC swapping, the middle bipartite measurements are needed. In this paper, the following four qubit Bell states are selected as the middle bipartite measurements, i.e.,

$$|\Phi\rangle_{ac}^{\pm} = \frac{1}{\sqrt{2}}(|00\rangle \pm |11\rangle), \qquad (5)$$

$$|\Psi\rangle_{ac}^{\pm} = \frac{1}{\sqrt{2}}(|01\rangle \pm |10\rangle). \qquad (6)$$

By performing one of the middle measurements on the product states of Equations (3) and (4), a final state can be obtained. Corresponding to the four middle measurements, four final states appear. As for the two Bell states in Equation (5), the two final states can be obtained as the following:

$$\sigma_{bd}^{\pm}(z_1, z_2, c_1, c_2) = \frac{1}{N}\{W_0|0\rangle_b\langle 0||0\rangle_d\langle 0| + W_1|0\rangle_b\langle 0||1\rangle_d\langle 1| + W_2|1\rangle_b\langle 1||0\rangle_d\langle 0| + W_3|1\rangle_b\langle 1||1\rangle_d\langle 1|]$$
$$\pm z_1 z_2 \sqrt{c_1 c_2 (1-c_1)(1-c_2)}(|0\rangle_b\langle 1||0\rangle_d\langle 1| + |1\rangle_b\langle 0||1\rangle_d\langle 0|)\}, \qquad (7)$$

where

$$N = W_0 + W_1 + W_2 + W_3, \qquad (8)$$

and

$$W_0 = (\frac{1-z_1}{4} + z_1 c_1)(\frac{1-z_2}{4} + z_2 c_2) + \frac{1-z_1}{4}\frac{1-z_2}{4}, \qquad (9)$$
$$W_1 = (\frac{1-z_1}{4} + z_1 c_1)[\frac{1-z_2}{4}] + [\frac{1-z_2}{4} + z_2(1-c_2)](\frac{1-z_1}{4}),$$
$$W_2 = (\frac{1-z_2}{4} + z_2 c_2)(\frac{1-z_1}{4}) + [\frac{1-z_1}{4} + z_1(1-c_1)][\frac{1-z_2}{4}],$$
$$W_3 = [(\frac{1-z_1}{4} + z_1(1-c_1)][\frac{1-z_2}{4} + z_2(1-c_2)] + \frac{1-z_1}{4}\frac{1-z_2}{4}.$$

Note that the $\pm$ in Equation (7) corresponds to the middle measurements in Equation (5).

As for the two Bell states in Equation (6), the two final states can be obtained as the following:

$$\sigma_{bd}^{\prime\pm}(z_1, z_2, c_1, c_2) = \frac{1}{N'}\{W'_0|0\rangle_b\langle 0||0\rangle_d\langle 0| + W'_1|0\rangle_b\langle 0||1\rangle_d\langle 1| + W'_2|1\rangle_b\langle 1||0\rangle_d\langle 0| + W'_3|1\rangle_b\langle 1||1\rangle_d\langle 1|]$$
$$\pm z_1 z_2 \sqrt{c_1 c_2 (1-c_1)(1-c_2)}(|0\rangle_b\langle 1||0\rangle_d\langle 1| + |1\rangle_b\langle 0||1\rangle_d\langle 0|)\}, \qquad (10)$$

where

$$N' = W'_0 + W'_1 + W'_2 + W'_3, \qquad (11)$$

and

$$W'_0 = (\frac{1-z_1}{4} + z_1 c_1)\frac{1-z_2}{4} + (\frac{1-z_2}{4} + z_2 c_2)\frac{1-z_1}{4}, \qquad (12)$$
$$W'_1 = (\frac{1-z_1}{4} + z_1 c_1)[\frac{1-z_2}{4} + z_2(1-c_2)] + (\frac{1-z_1}{4})(\frac{1-z_2}{4}),$$
$$W'_2 = (\frac{1-z_2}{4} + z_2 c_2)[\frac{1-z_1}{4} + z_1(1-c_1)] + (\frac{1-z_1}{4})(\frac{1-z_2}{4}),$$
$$W'_3 = [(\frac{1-z_1}{4} + z_1(1-c_1)]\frac{1-z_2}{4} + [\frac{1-z_2}{4} + z_2(1-c_2)]\frac{1-z_1}{4}.$$

Here in Equation (10), the $\pm$ correspond to the middle measurements in Equation (6).

3. MID in the Concerned States

Measurement-induced disturbance (MID) is a QC measure [22] that has been attracting considerable attention for its easy computability. MID is defined as the difference between the total correlation and its classical correlation, where, for a given concerned state, the classical correlation is determined by measuring both subsystems with the eigenvectors of marginal states as the measuring bases.

3.1. MIDs in the Two Initial Werner-Like States

For the two initial Werner-like states $\sigma_{ab}(z_1, c_1)$ and $\sigma_{cd}(z_2, c_2)$, their MIDs [45] are

$$\begin{aligned}\mathcal{Q}_M[\sigma_{ab}(z_1,c_1)] &= -(\frac{1-z_1}{4}+z_1c_1)\log_2(\frac{1-z_1}{4}+z_1c_1) - (\frac{1+3z_1}{4}-z_1c_1)\log_2(\frac{1+3z_1}{4}-z_1c_1)\\ &+(\frac{1-z_1}{4})\log_2(\frac{1-z_1}{4})+(\frac{1+3z_1}{4})\log_2(\frac{1+3z_1}{4}),\end{aligned} \quad (13)$$

$$\begin{aligned}\mathcal{Q}_M[\sigma_{cd}(z_2,c_2)] &= -(\frac{1-z_2}{4}+z_2c_2)\log_2(\frac{1-z_2}{4}+z_2c_2) - (\frac{1+3z_2}{4}-z_2c_2)\log_2(\frac{1+3z_2}{4}-z_2c_2)\\ &+(\frac{1-z_2}{4})\log_2(\frac{1-z_2}{4})+(\frac{1+3z_2}{4})\log_2(\frac{1+3z_2}{4}).\end{aligned} \quad (14)$$

3.2. MIDs in the Final States $\sigma_{bd}^{\pm}(z_1, z_2, c_1, c_2)$

Now let us inspect the final state $\sigma_{bd}^{\pm}$ in Equation (7). Obviously, σ_{bd}^{+} and σ_{bd}^{-} are different. However, the difference is minor and it is located at the position $\pm$. In the following calculations, one can find that the MID in σ_{bd}^{+} is equivalent to that in σ_{bd}^{-}. That it to say, in the calculation of MIDs, the position $+$ or $-$ can be ignored. Hence, for convenience, in the following, $\sigma_{bd}^{\pm}$ can be obtained by σ_{bd}.

In the final state $\sigma_{bd}(z_1, z_2, c_1, c_2)$, the total correlation can be obtained as the following

$$\mathcal{I}[\sigma_{bd}(z_1,z_2,c_1,c_2)] = S[\sigma_b(z_1,z_2,c_1,c_2)] + S[\sigma_d(z_1,z_2,c_1,c_2)] - S[\sigma_{bd}(z_1,z_2,c_1,c_2)], \quad (15)$$

where $S[\cdot]$ is von Neumann entropy, $\sigma_b(z_1, z_2, c_1, c_2)$ and $\sigma_d(z_1, z_2, c_1, c_2)$ represent marginal states of $\sigma_{bd}(z_1, z_2, c_1, c_2)$ which take the form as

$$\left.\begin{aligned}\sigma_b(x,y,\kappa) &= \tfrac{1}{4}[(w_0+w_1)|0\rangle_b\langle 0| + (w_2+w_3)|1\rangle_b\langle 1|],\\ \sigma_d(x,y,\kappa) &= \tfrac{1}{4}[(w_0+w_2)|0\rangle_d\langle 0| + (w_1+w_3)|1\rangle_d\langle 1|],\end{aligned}\right\} \quad (16)$$

where $w_0 = \frac{4}{N}W_0$, $w_3 = \frac{4}{N}W_3$, $w_1 = \frac{4}{N}W_1$, $w_2 = \frac{4}{N}W_2$, and W_i's are functions of z_1, z_2, c_1 and c_2 given by Equation (9). Easily, one can obtain

$$S[\sigma_b(z_1,z_2,c_1,c_2)] = \frac{1}{4}[8 - w_{01}\log_2 w_{01} - w_{23}\log_2 w_{23}], \quad (17)$$

$$S[\sigma_d(z_1,z_2,c_1,c_2)] = \frac{1}{4}[8 - w_{02}\log_2 w_{02} - w_{13}\log_2 w_{13}], \quad (18)$$

$$\begin{aligned}S[\sigma_{bd}(z_1,z_2,c_1,c_2)] &= -\frac{1}{4}[w_1\log_2 w_1 + w_2\log_2 w_2 - 2w_{12} - 3w_{03}]\\ &\quad -\frac{1}{8}[(w_{03}+\zeta)\log_2(w_{03}+\zeta) + (w_{03}-\zeta)\log_2(w_{03}-\zeta)],\end{aligned} \quad (19)$$

where $w_{mn} = w_m + w_n$ and $\zeta = \sqrt{(w_3 - w_0)^2 + 16\zeta}$ with $\zeta = 4c_1(1-c_1)c_2(1-c_2)z_1^2 z_2^2 / N^2$.

To calculate MID in the final state $\sigma_{bd}(z_1, z_2, c_1, c_2)$, its marginal states are needed. It is because that the eigenvectors of marginal states are taken as the measuring bases to aquire the classical correlation. Using the marginal states in Equation (16) as measuring bases to measure both subsystems simultaneously, four different outcomes can be obtained. For each outcome, its own probability may be occured. Let $p_{bd}^{(ij)}$ denote its occurrence probability where $|ij\rangle_{bd}$ is the corresponding outcome. It is easy to work out the occurrence probability as

$$p_{bd}^{(00)} = \frac{1}{4}w_0, \quad p_{bd}^{(01)} = \frac{1}{4}w_1, \quad p_{bd}^{(10)} = \frac{1}{4}w_2, \quad p_{bd}^{(11)} = \frac{1}{4}w_3. \tag{20}$$

Integrating above probabilities, the single-partite probability distributions can be obtained:

$$\left.\begin{array}{l} p_b^{(0)} = p_{bd}^{(00)} + p_{bd}^{(01)} = \frac{1}{4}w_{01}, \quad p_b^{(1)} = p_{bd}^{(10)} + p_{bd}^{(11)} = \frac{1}{4}w_{23}, \\ p_d^{(0)} = p_{bd}^{(00)} + p_{bd}^{(10)} = \frac{1}{4}w_{02}, \quad p_d^{(1)} = p_{bd}^{(01)} + p_{bd}^{(11)} = \frac{1}{4}w_{13}. \end{array}\right\} \tag{21}$$

Utilizing Equations (20) and (21), the classical correlation in the final state $\sigma_{bd}(z_1,z_2,c_1,c_2)$ can be obtained, i.e.,

$$\begin{aligned} \mathcal{C}_M[\sigma_{bd}(z_1,z_2,c_1,c_2)] &= \frac{1}{4}(w_0 \log_2 w_0 + w_1 \log_2 w_1 + w_2 \log_2 w_2 + w_3 \log_2 w_3) + 2 \\ &- \frac{1}{4}(w_{01} \log_2 w_{01} + w_{02} \log_2 w_{02} + w_{13} \log_2 w_{13} + w_{23} \log_2 w_{23}), \end{aligned} \tag{22}$$

Finally, MID in the final state $\sigma_{bd}(z_1,z_2,c_1,c_2)$ can be extracted as

$$\begin{aligned} \mathcal{Q}_M[\sigma_{bd}(z_1,z_2,c_1,c_2)] &= I[\sigma_{bd}(z_1,z_2,c_1,c_2)] - \mathcal{C}_M[\sigma_{bd}(z_1,z_2,c_1,c_2)] \\ &= [(w_{03}+\xi)\log_2(w_{03}+\xi) + (w_{03}-\xi)\log_2(w_{03}-\xi) \\ &- 2w_0 \log_2 w_0 - 2w_3 \log_2 w_3 - 2w_{03}]/8. \end{aligned} \tag{23}$$

3.3. MID in the Final States $\sigma_{bd}'^{\pm}(z_1,z_2,c_1,c_2)$

From Equation (10), it is easy to find the difference between $\sigma_{bd}'^{+}(z_1,z_2,c_1,c_2)$ and $\sigma_{bd}'^{-}(z_1,z_2,c_1,c_2)$. It is $+$ or $-$. Similar to that in Section 3.2, MIDs in the two final states are equivalent, i.e., MID in $\sigma_{bd}'^{+}(z_1,z_2,c_1,c_2)$ is equivalent with that in $\sigma_{bd}'^{-}(z_1,z_2,c_1,c_2)$. Hence, for convenience in the context, $\sigma_{bd}'(z_1,z_2,c_1,c_2)$ is considered instead.

Morovere, compare $\sigma_{bd}'^{\pm}(z_1,z_2,c_1,c_2)$ in Equation (10) with $\sigma_{bd}^{\pm}(z_1,z_2,c_1,c_2)$ in Equation (7), one can find that the two kinds of states have similar structure, only parameters in them are different. Hence, according to this similarity and the obtained MID of $\sigma_{bd}(z_1,z_2,c_1,c_2)$ in Equation (22), one can directly accquire MID in $\sigma_{bd}'(z_1,z_2,c_1,c_2)$ as the following

$$\begin{aligned} \mathcal{Q}_M[\sigma_{bd}'(z_1,z_2,c_1,c_2)] &= [(w_{03}'+\xi')\log_2(w_{03}'+\xi') + (w_{03}'-\xi')\log_2(w_{03}'-\xi') \\ &- 2w_0' \log_2 w_0' - 2w_3' \log_2 w_3' - 2w_{03}']/8, \end{aligned} \tag{24}$$

where all the w' are quantities related to those in Equation (23) with W's are replaced by W''s. W's and W''s are listed in Equations (9) and (12), respectively.

4. AMID in the Concerned States

Another QC measure, ameliorated measurement-induced disturbance (AMID), was put forward in 2011, in which the corresponding maximal classical correlation is special. The special aspect is that, to find the maximal classical correlation, optimization procedure to rehearse all joint local measurements is needed. Correspondingly, AMID is defined as the discrepancy between total correlation and the obtained maximal classical correlation.

4.1. AMID in the Two Werner-Like Initial States

For the two initial Werner-like states $\sigma_{ab}(z_1,c_1)$ and $\sigma_{cd}(z_2,c_2)$, their AMIDs [45] are

$$\begin{aligned} \mathcal{Q}_A[\sigma_{ab}(z_1,c_1)] &= -(\frac{1-z_1}{4}+z_1 c_1)\log_2(\frac{1-z_1}{4}+z_1 c_1) - (\frac{1+3z_1}{4}-z_1 c_1)\log_2(\frac{1+3z_1}{4}-z_1 c_1) \\ &+ (\frac{1-z_1}{4})\log_2(\frac{1-z_1}{4}) + (\frac{1+3z_1}{4})\log_2(\frac{1+3z_1}{4}), \end{aligned} \tag{25}$$

$$\mathcal{Q}_A[\sigma_{cd}(z_2,c_2)] = -(\frac{1-z_2}{4}+z_2c_2)\log_2(\frac{1-z_2}{4}+z_2c_2) - (\frac{1+3z_2}{4}-z_2c_2)\log_2(\frac{1+3z_2}{4}-z_2c_2)$$
$$+(\frac{1-z_2}{4})\log_2(\frac{1-z_2}{4}) + (\frac{1+3z_2}{4})\log_2(\frac{1+3z_2}{4}). \quad (26)$$

4.2. AMIDs in the Final States $\sigma_{bd}^{\pm}(z_1,z_2,c_1,c_2)$

In order to evaluate AMID in $\sigma_{bd}^{\pm}(z_1,z_2,c_1,c_2)$, a general joint local measurement should first be parameterized. It can be parameterized as $\{\Omega_b^{(i)}(\alpha_1,\phi_1,\tau_1)\otimes\Lambda_d^{(j)}(\alpha_2,\phi_2,\tau_2), i,j=0,1\}$, where $\Omega^{(k)}$ and $\Lambda^{(k)}$ take the same forms as that of $\Pi^{(k)}$ described as the following three-parameter forms:

$$\{\Pi^{(0)}(\alpha,\phi,\tau) = |0'\rangle\langle 0'|, \quad \Pi^{(1)}(\alpha,\phi,\tau) = |1'\rangle\langle 1'|\} \quad (27)$$

with

$$\begin{pmatrix}|0'\rangle\\|1'\rangle\end{pmatrix} = \begin{pmatrix}\cos\alpha e^{i\phi} & \sin\alpha e^{i\tau}\\-\sin\alpha e^{-i\tau} & \cos\alpha e^{-i\phi}\end{pmatrix}\begin{pmatrix}|0\rangle\\|1\rangle\end{pmatrix}, \quad (28)$$

where $\alpha \in [0,\pi/2]$, $\phi \in [0,2\pi]$ and $\tau \in [0,2\pi]$.

If both subsystems are measured by using the parameterized measuring bases (Appendix A), four different outcomes can be obtained as

$$p_{bd}^{(ij)} = \text{Tr}_{bd}\Omega_b^{(i)}(\alpha_1,\phi_1,\tau_1)\otimes\Lambda_d^{(j)}(\alpha_2,\phi_2,\tau_2)\sigma_{bd} \quad (29)$$

Through some tedious deductions, one can obtain

$$\left.\begin{array}{l}p_{bd}^{(00)} = \mathcal{F}(w_2,w_0,\alpha_1)\cos^2\alpha_2 + \mathcal{F}(w_3,w_1,\alpha_1)\sin^2\alpha_2 + \frac{1}{2N}\sqrt{c_1c_2(1-c_1)(1-c_2)}z_1z_2\sin 2\alpha_1\sin 2\alpha_2\cos\omega,\\ p_{bd}^{(01)} = \mathcal{F}(w_2,w_0,\alpha_1)\sin^2\alpha_2 + \mathcal{F}(w_3,w_1,\alpha_1)\cos^2\alpha_2 - \frac{1}{2N}\sqrt{c_1c_2(1-c_1)(1-c_2)}z_1z_2\sin 2\alpha_1\sin 2\alpha_2\cos\omega,\\ p_{bd}^{(10)} = \mathcal{F}(w_0,w_2,\alpha_1)\cos^2\alpha_2 + \mathcal{F}(w_1,w_3,\alpha_1)\sin^2\alpha_2 - \frac{1}{2N}\sqrt{c_1c_2(1-c_1)(1-c_2)}z_1z_2\sin 2\alpha_1\sin 2\alpha_2\cos\omega,\\ p_{bd}^{(11)} = \mathcal{F}(w_0,w_2,\alpha_1)\sin^2\alpha_2 + \mathcal{F}(w_1,w_3,\alpha_1)\cos^2\alpha_2 + \frac{1}{2N}\sqrt{c_1c_2(1-c_1)(1-c_2)}z_1z_2\sin 2\alpha_1\sin 2\alpha_2\cos\omega,\end{array}\right\} \quad (30)$$

where $\mathcal{F}(s_1,s_2,s_3) \equiv \frac{1}{4}(s_1\sin^2 s_3 + s_2\cos^2 s_3)$ and $\omega = \phi_1+\phi_2-\tau_1-\tau_2$. Combining these bipartite probability distributions, the single-partite probability distributions can be obtained as:

$$\left.\begin{array}{l}p_b^{(0)} = p_{bd}^{(00)} + p_{bd}^{(01)} = \frac{1}{4}(w_{23}\sin^2\alpha_1 + w_{01}\cos^2\alpha_1),\\ p_b^{(1)} = p_{bd}^{(10)} + p_{bd}^{(11)} = \frac{1}{4}(w_{01}\sin^2\alpha_1 + w_{23}\cos^2\alpha_1),\\ p_d^{(0)} = p_{bd}^{(00)} + p_{bd}^{(10)} = \frac{1}{4}(w_{13}\sin^2\alpha_2 + w_{02}\cos^2\alpha_2),\\ p_d^{(1)} = p_{bd}^{(01)} + p_{bd}^{(11)} = \frac{1}{4}(w_{02}\sin^2\alpha_2 + w_{13}\cos^2\alpha_2).\end{array}\right\} \quad (31)$$

Accordingly, the general classical correlation obtained via measure can be expressed as

$$\mathcal{C}[\sigma_{bd}(z_1,z_2,c_1,c_2)] = -\sum_{i=0}^{1}p_b^{(i)}\log_2 p_b^{(i)} - \sum_{i=0}^{1}p_d^{(i)}\log_2 p_d^{(i)} + \sum_{i=0}^{1}\sum_{j=0}^{1}p_{bd}^{(ij)}\log_2 p_{bd}^{(ij)}. \quad (32)$$

Correspondingly, the usual classical correlation is taken as the maximal one:

$$\mathcal{C}_A[\sigma_{bd}(z_1,z_2,c_1,c_2)] = \max_{\{\Omega_b^{(i)}\otimes\Lambda_d^{(j)}\}} \mathcal{C}[\rho_{bd}(z_1,z_2,c_1,c_2)]. \quad (33)$$

In order to obtain the maximal value, the extreme points should first be worked out. That is to say, the derivative equations $\partial\mathcal{C}[\sigma_{bd}(z_1,z_2,c_1,c_2)]/\partial\alpha_1 = \partial\mathcal{C}[\sigma_{bd}(z_1,z_2,c_1,c_2)]/\partial\alpha_2 = \partial\mathcal{C}[\sigma_{bd}(z_1,z_2,c_1,c_2)]/\partial\omega = 0$ should be solved first. However, it is not easy to solve these equations. Fortunately, through observation one can find that the extreme points are $\alpha_1 = \alpha_2 = 0, \pi/4, \pi/2$ and $\omega = 0$. Moreover, through comparing these three points with other points, we find that the value of classical correlation corresponding to this point $\alpha_1 = \alpha_2 = 0, \pi/4, \pi/2$ and $\omega = 0$ is the maximal. Hence, the maximal classical correlation can be expressed

$$\mathcal{C}_A[\sigma_{bd}(z_1, z_2, c_1, c_2)] = \frac{1}{2}[(1 + \frac{2}{N}\sqrt{c_1c_2(1-c_1)(1-c_2)}z_1z_2) \log_2(1 + \frac{2}{N}\sqrt{c_1c_2(1-c_1)(1-c_2)}z_1z_2)$$
$$+ (1 - \frac{2}{N}\sqrt{c_1c_2(1-c_1)(1-c_2)}z_1z_2) \log_2(1 - \frac{2}{N}\sqrt{c_1c_2(1-c_1)(1-c_2)}z_1z_2)]. \quad (34)$$

Finally, AMID can be obtained as the discrepancy between the total correlation (Equation (15)) and the maximal classical correlation (Equation (34)), i.e.,

$$\mathcal{Q}_A[\sigma_{bd}(z_1, z_2, c_1, c_2)] = \mathcal{I}[\sigma_{bd}] - \mathcal{C}_A[\sigma_{bd}]$$
$$= \frac{1}{8}[(w_{03} + \xi) \log_2(w_{03} + \xi) + (w_{03} - \xi) \log_2(w_{03} - \xi)]$$
$$- \frac{1}{4}[w_{01} \log_2 w_{01} + g_{23} \log_2 w_{23} + w_{02} \log_2 w_{02} + w_{13} \log_2 w_{13}]$$
$$- \frac{1}{2}[(1 + \frac{2}{N}\sqrt{c_1c_2(1-c_1)(1-c_2)}z_1z_2) \log_2(1 + \frac{2}{N}\sqrt{c_1c_2(1-c_1)(1-c_2)}z_1z_2)$$
$$+ (1 - \frac{2}{N}\sqrt{c_1c_2(1-c_1)(1-c_2)}z_1z_2) \log_2(1 - \frac{2}{N}\sqrt{c_1c_2(1-c_1)(1-c_2)}z_1z_2)]$$
$$+ \frac{1}{4}[w_1 \log_2 w_1 + w_2 \log_2 w_2 - w_{03}] + 2. \quad (35)$$

4.3. AMIDs in the Final States $\sigma'^{\pm}_{bd}(z_1, z_2, c_1, c_2)$

Similar to Section 4.2, one can find that AMIDs in the two states $\sigma'^{+}_{bd}(z_1, z_2, c_1, c_2)$ and $\sigma'^{-}_{bd}(z_1, z_2, c_1, c_2)$ are equivalent, and hence one can use $\sigma'_{bd}(z_1, z_2, c_1, c_2)$ as the surrogate of $\sigma'^{\pm}_{bd}(z_1, z_2, c_1, c_2)$.

Similar to that in Section 4.3, due to the equivalent structure of $\sigma'^{\pm}_{bd}(z_1, z_2, c_1, c_2)$ and $\sigma^{\pm}_{bd}(z_1, z_2, c_1, c_2)$, one can obtain AMID $\sigma'_{bd}(z_1, z_2, c_1, c_2)$ as

$$\mathcal{Q}_A[\sigma'_{bd}(z_1, z_2, c_1, c_2)] = \frac{1}{8}[(w'_{03} + \xi') \log_2(w'_{03} + \xi') + (w'_{03} - \xi') \log_2(w'_{03} - \xi')]$$
$$- \frac{1}{4}[w'_{01} \log_2 w'_{01} + w'_{23} \log_2 w'_{23} + w'_{02} \log_2 w'_{02} + w'_{13} \log_2 w'_{13}]$$
$$- \frac{1}{2}[(1 + \frac{2}{N}\sqrt{c_1c_2(1-c_1)(1-c_2)}z_1z_2) \log_2(1 + \frac{2}{N}\sqrt{c_1c_2(1-c_1)(1-c_2)}z_1z_2)$$
$$+ (1 - \frac{2}{N}\sqrt{c_1c_2(1-c_1)(1-c_2)}z_1z_2) \log_2(1 - \frac{2}{N}\sqrt{c_1c_2(1-c_1)(1-c_2)}z_1z_2)]$$
$$+ \frac{1}{4}[w'_1 \log_2 w'_1 + w'_2 \log_2 w'_2 - w'_{03}] + 2. \quad (36)$$

where all the w' quantities related to those in Equation (23) with W's are replaced by W''s. W's and W''s that are listed in Equations (9) and (12), respectively.

5. Analyses, Comparisons and Discussion

In the previous two sections, MID and AMID have been respectively utilized to quantify all QCs in the initial and final states. In this section, let us make some analyses, discussions and comparisons.

5.1. Features of QCs in the Initail Werner-Like States

The Werner-like state in Equation (2) is comprised of two terms. They are mingled with the weight z. One is I, a null quantum correlation maximally mixed state. Another state $|\psi\rangle$ is an entangled pure state. QC in the $|\psi\rangle$ increases with $c \in [0, 1/2]$. Hence, for a fixed c, the QC in it is determined. Moreover, the bigger z is, the larger weight of $|\psi\rangle$. Hence, naturally, a larger QC can be induced by the two mixtures. Particularly, the Werner-like state becomes a Werner state when $c = 0.5$.

To be specific, MID and AMID in the initial Werner-like states have the common features: (i) $c = 0.5$ is a symmetrical point of QC; (ii) for given c, MID is an increasing function of z and arrives the maximum at $z = 1$; (iii) for a fixed z, QC increases with c in the region $[0, 1/2]$ and reaches maximum at $c = 1/2$.

5.2. Monotony Features of MIDs in the Final States

5.2.1. Monotony Features of MIDs in the Final State $\sigma_{bd}(z_1, z_2, c_1, c_2)$

Now let us turn to the monotonic properties of the QCs in the final states (see Equations (23), (24), (34) and (35)). As mentioned, QCs in the final state are determined by four parameters, i.e., z_1, z_2, c_1, c_2. Obviously, there are two kinds in the four parameters. One kind is (z_1, z_2) and another is (c_1, c_2). To find the the monotonic properties is not an easy, because it is quite difficult to judge whether the partial derivatives $\partial Q[\sigma_{bd}(z_1, z_2, c_1, c_2)]/\partial v_i$, $v = z, c$ and $i = 1, 2$ are bigger than zero. Hence, we have no choice but to utilize the vast numerical investigations.

To obtain the monotony features of MIDs in the final states, vast numerical calculations have been made. Some typical figures are listed in Figures 1–3. Through the vast numerical calculations, the following properties have been found:

(1) For given (z_1, z_2), $\mathcal{Q}_M[\sigma_{bd}(z_1, z_2, c_1, c_2)]$ is symmetrical regarding c_1 and c_2. To be concrete, $\mathcal{Q}_M[\sigma_{bd}(z_1, z_2, c_1, c_2)]$ is increasing in $c_1 \in (0, 1/2)$ and decreasing in $c_1 \in (1/2, 1)$. Meanwhile, $\mathcal{Q}_M[\sigma_{bd}(z_1, z_2, c_1, c_2)]$ is also increasing in $c_2 \in (0, 1/2)$ and decreasing in $c_2 \in (1/2, 1)$. In other words, $\mathcal{Q}_M[\sigma_{bd}(z_1, z_2, c_1, c_2)]$ is symmetrical regarding $c_1 = c_2 = 0.5$. From Figure 1, one can see that $\mathcal{Q}_M[\sigma_{bd}(z_1, z_2, c_1, c_2)]$ is symmetrical regarding $c_2 = 0.5$ and the maximal point occurs at $c_2 = 0.5$. Moreover, the bigger z_2 is, the bigger the maximal value that can be obtained.

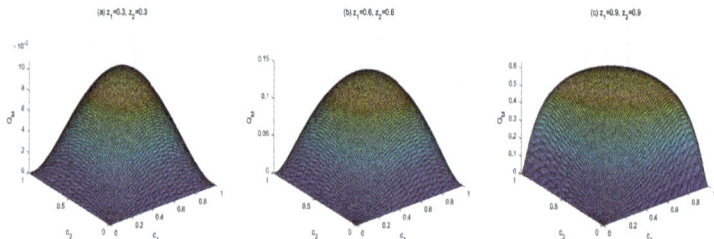

Figure 1. Variation of $\mathcal{Q}_M[\sigma_{bd}]$ with c_1 and c_2 for three sets of z_1 and z_2.

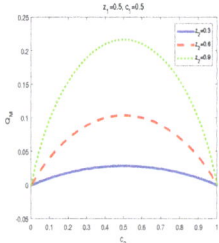

Figure 2. Variation of $\mathcal{Q}_M[\sigma_{bd}]$ with c_2 for $z_1 = 0.5$, $c_1 = 0.5$ and $z_2 = 0.3, 0.6, 0.9$, respectively.

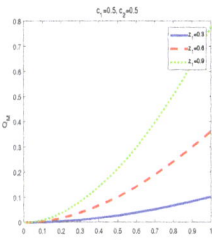

Figure 3. Variation of $\mathcal{Q}_M[\sigma_{bd}]$ with z_2 for $c_1 = 0.5$, $c_2 = 0.5$ and $z_1 = 0.3, 0.6, 0.9$, respectively.

Moreover, a similarity property can be found, i.e., MID in the final state has a similar symmetry property with that in the initial state. That is to say, MIDs in both the two kind states increase in $c_i \in (0, 1/2]$ (i is 1 or 2) and decrease in $c_i \in [1/2, 1)$.

Moreover, One can find that this symmetry property of MID in the final state is similar to that in the initial Werner-like state in Equations (13) and (14). To be concrete, MIDs in both the final state and the initial Werner-like state increase with c_i (i is 1 or 2) in the region $(0, 1/2]$ and decrease with c_i in the region $[1/2, 1)$. Moreover, there exists an obvious symmetry in $c_1 = c_2 = 0.5$. That is to say, taking the final state as example

$$\mathcal{Q}_M[\sigma_{bd}(z_1, z_2, c_1 = 0.5 - \alpha, c_2 = 0.5 - \beta)] = \mathcal{Q}_M[\sigma_{bd}(z_1, z_2, c_1 = 0.5 + \alpha, c_2 = 0.5 + \beta)]. \quad (37)$$

In Equation (37), α and β are both defined in the region $[0, 1/2]$. This property means that the symmetrical property with c_i is unchanged during the QC swapping process. In addition, if z_1 and z_2 are bigger, the quantities of QC are larger.

(2) For given (c_1, c_2), in the final state MID increases with z_1 or z_2 in $z_i \in (0, 1)$, $i = 1, 2$ (see Figure 3). Variations of $\mathcal{Q}_M[\sigma_{bd}(z_1, z_2, c_1, c_2)]$ with z_2 for $c_1 = 0.5, c_2 = 0.5$ and $z_1 = 0.3, 0.6, 0.9$ are plotted respectively in Figure 3. Obviously, one can see that MID in the final state is an increasing function of z_i, $i = 1, 2$.

5.2.2. Monotony Features of MIDs in the Final State

As for $\sigma'_{bd}(z_1, z_2, c_1, c_2)$, QC quantified by MID is expressed in Equation (24). Some features can be exposed through numerical calculations. See Figures 4 and 5.

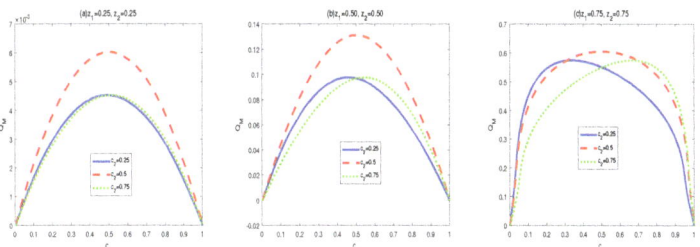

Figure 4. Variation of $\mathcal{Q}_M[\sigma'_{bd}]$ with c_1 and c_2 for three sets of z_1 and z_2.

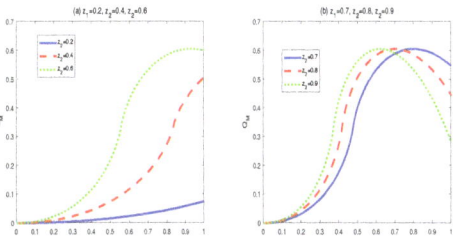

Figure 5. Variation of $\mathcal{Q}_M[\sigma'_{bd}]$ with $c_1 = 0.5, c_2 = 0.5$ for several sets of z_1 and z_2.

(a) For given c_2 and (z_1, z_2), $\mathcal{Q}_M[\sigma'_{bd}]$ first increases then decreases with $c_1 \in (0, 1]$. The maximal points (c_{1m}), i.e., the transition points, vary with parameters. Not only the maximal points and but also the shape of the curves are determined by the value of c_2. To be specific, the smaller the value of $|c_2 - 0.5|$ is, the bigger maximal value of $\mathcal{Q}_M[\sigma'_{bd}]$ is. Moreover, for a given set of (z_1, z_2),

$$\mathcal{Q}_M[\sigma_{bd}(z_1, z_2, c_1 = 0.5 - \alpha, c_2 = 0.5 - \beta)] = \mathcal{Q}_M[\sigma_{bd}(z_1, z_2, c_1 = 0.5 + \alpha, c_2 = 0.5 + \beta)] \quad (38)$$

where $\alpha \in (0, 1/2), \beta \in (0, 1/2)$.

(b) $\mathcal{Q}_M[\sigma'_{bd}]$ is an increasing function of $z_1 \in [0, 1]$ within $z_2 \in [0, 0.58]$. However, when $z_2 \in [0.58, 1]$, $\mathcal{Q}_M[\rho'_{bd}]$ first increases then decreases in $z_1 \in [0, 1]$. Moreover, the bigger $z_2 \in [0.58, 1]$ is, the smaller of transtion point is.

5.3. Monotony Feature of AMIDs in the Final States

5.3.1. Monotony Features of AMIDs in the Final State $\sigma_{bd}(z_1, z_2, c_1, c_2)$

Now let us look at the monotony features of AMIDs in the final states $\sigma_{bd}(z_1, z_2, c_1, c_2)$. Vast numerical calculations have also been made. Some typical figures are listed in Figures 6–8. Through the vast numerical calculations and comparisons, the following properties can be exposed:

(1) $\mathcal{Q}_A[\sigma_{bd}(z_1, z_2, c_1, c_2)]$ is symmetrical regarding c_1 and c_2 for given (z_1, z_2), i.e., $\mathcal{Q}_A[\sigma_{bd}(z_1, z_2, c_1, c_2)]$ is increasing in $c_i \in (0, 1/2)$ and decreasing in $c_i \in (1/2, 1)$, $i = 1, 2$. Moreover, $\mathcal{Q}_A[\sigma_{bd}(z_1, z_2, c_1, c_2)]$ is symmetrical regarding $c_1 = c_2 = 0.5$. and arrives its maximum at this point. From Figure 2, one can see that $\mathcal{Q}_A[\sigma_{bd}(z_1, z_2, c_1, c_2)]$ is symmetrical regarding $c_2 = 0.5$ and the maximal point occurs at $c_2 = 0.5$. Moreover, the bigger z_1 or z_2 is, the bigger maximal value can be obtained.

(2) AMID in the final state $\sigma_{bd}(z_1, z_2, c_1, c_2)$ is an increasing function with z_i in the region $z_i \in (0, 1)$, $i = 1, 2$, for given (c_1, c_2). See Figure 6. In Figure 6, variations of $\mathcal{Q}_A[\sigma_{bd}(z_1, z_2, c_1, c_2)]$ with z_2 for $c_1 = 0.5, c_2 = 0.5$ and $z_1 = 0.3, 0.6, 0.9$ are plotted respectively. Obviously, one can see that MID in the final state increase with z_i, $i = 1, 2$.

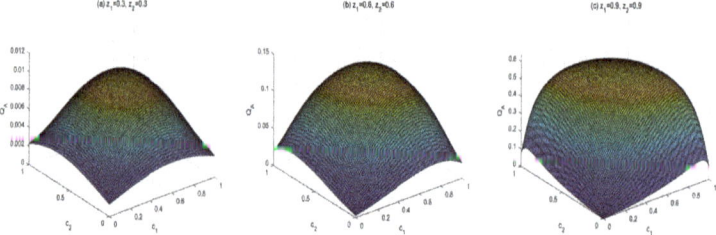

Figure 6. Variation of $\mathcal{Q}_A[\sigma_{bd}]$ with c_1 and c_2 for three sets of z_1 and z_2.

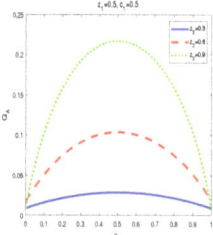

Figure 7. Variation of $\mathcal{Q}_A[\sigma_{bd}]$ with c_2 for $z_1 = 0.5$, $c_1 = 0.5$ and $z_2 = 0.3, 0.6, 0.9$, respectively.

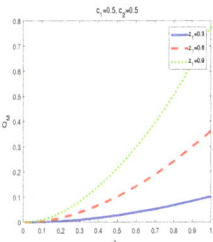

Figure 3. Variation of $\mathcal{Q}_M[\sigma_{bd}]$ with z_2 for $c_1 = 0.5$, $c_2 = 0.5$ and $z_1 = 0.3, 0.6, 0.9$, respectively.

Moreover, a similarity property can be found, i.e., MID in the final state has a similar symmetry property with that in the initial state. That is to say, MIDs in both the two kind states increase in $c_i \in (0, 1/2]$ (i is 1 or 2) and decrease in $c_i \in [1/2, 1)$.

Moreover, One can find that this symmetry property of MID in the final state is similar to that in the initial Werner-like state in Equations (13) and (14). To be concrete, MIDs in both the final state and the initial Werner-like state increase with c_i (i is 1 or 2) in the region $(0, 1/2]$ and decrease with c_i in the region $[1/2, 1)$. Moreover, there exists an obvious symmetry in $c_1 = c_2 = 0.5$. That is to say, taking the final state as example

$$\mathcal{Q}_M[\sigma_{bd}(z_1, z_2, c_1 = 0.5 - \alpha, c_2 = 0.5 - \beta)] = \mathcal{Q}_M[\sigma_{bd}(z_1, z_2, c_1 = 0.5 + \alpha, c_2 = 0.5 + \beta)]. \quad (37)$$

In Equation (37), α and β are both defined in the region $[0, 1/2]$. This property means that the symmetrical property with c_i is unchanged during the QC swapping process. In addition, if z_1 and z_2 are bigger, the quantities of QC are larger.

(2) For given (c_1, c_2), in the final state MID increases with z_1 or z_2 in $z_i \in (0, 1)$, $i = 1, 2$ (see Figure 3). Variations of $\mathcal{Q}_M[\sigma_{bd}(z_1, z_2, c_1, c_2)]$ with z_2 for $c_1 = 0.5, c_2 = 0.5$ and $z_1 = 0.3, 0.6, 0.9$ are plotted respectively in Figure 3. Obviously, one can see that MID in the final state is an increasing function of z_i, $i = 1, 2$.

5.2.2. Monotony Features of MIDs in the Final State

As for $\sigma'_{bd}(z_1, z_2, c_1, c_2)$, QC quantified by MID is expressed in Equation (24). Some features can be exposed through numerical calculations. See Figures 4 and 5.

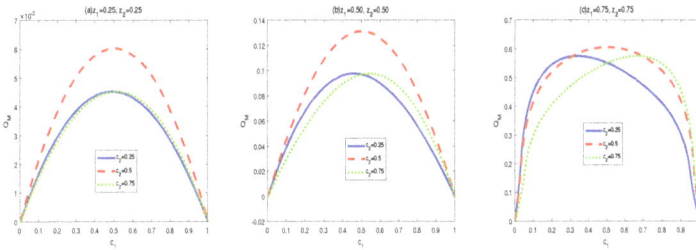

Figure 4. Variation of $\mathcal{Q}_M[\sigma'_{bd}]$ with c_1 and c_2 for three sets of z_1 and z_2.

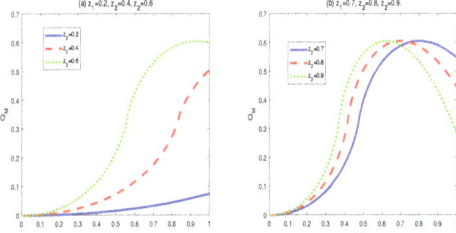

Figure 5. Variation of $\mathcal{Q}_M[\sigma'_{bd}]$ with $c_1 = 0.5, c_2 = 0.5$ for several sets of z_1 and z_2.

(a) For given c_2 and (z_1, z_2), $\mathcal{Q}_M[\sigma'_{bd}]$ first increases then decreases with $c_1 \in (0, 1]$. The maximal points (c_{1m}), i.e., the transition points, vary with parameters. Not only the maximal points and but also the shape of the curves are determined by the value of c_2. To be specific, the smaller the value of $|c_2 - 0.5|$ is, the bigger maximal value of $\mathcal{Q}_M[\sigma'_{bd}]$ is. Moreover, for a given set of (z_1, z_2),

$$\mathcal{Q}_M[\sigma_{bd}(z_1, z_2, c_1 = 0.5 - \alpha, c_2 = 0.5 - \beta)] = \mathcal{Q}_M[\sigma_{bd}(z_1, z_2, c_1 = 0.5 + \alpha, c_2 = 0.5 + \beta)] \quad (38)$$

where $\alpha \in (0, 1/2), \beta \in (0, 1/2)$.

(b) $\mathcal{Q}_M[\sigma'_{bd}]$ is an increasing function of $z_1 \in [0, 1]$ within $z_2 \in [0, 0.58]$. However, when $z_2 \in [0.58, 1]$, $\mathcal{Q}_M[\rho'_{bd}]$ first increases then decreases in $z_1 \in [0, 1]$. Moreover, the bigger $z_2 \in [0.58, 1]$ is, the smaller of transtion point is.

5.3. Monotony Feature of AMIDs in the Final States

5.3.1. Monotony Features of AMIDs in the Final State $\sigma_{bd}(z_1, z_2, c_1, c_2)$

Now let us look at the monotony features of AMIDs in the final states $\sigma_{bd}(z_1, z_2, c_1, c_2)$. Vast numerical calculations have also been made. Some typical figures are listed in Figures 6–8. Through the vast numerical calculations and comparisons, the following properties can be exposed:

(1) $\mathcal{Q}_A[\sigma_{bd}(z_1, z_2, c_1, c_2)]$ is symmetrical regarding c_1 and c_2 for given (z_1, z_2), i.e., $\mathcal{Q}_A[\sigma_{bd}(z_1, z_2, c_1, c_2)]$ is increasing in $c_i \in (0, 1/2)$ and decreasing in $c_i \in (1/2, 1)$, $i = 1, 2$. Moreover, $\mathcal{Q}_A[\sigma_{bd}(z_1, z_2, c_1, c_2)]$ is symmetrical regarding $c_1 = c_2 = 0.5$. and arrives its maximum at this point. From Figure 2, one can see that $\mathcal{Q}_A[\sigma_{bd}(z_1, z_2, c_1, c_2)]$ is symmetrical regarding $c_2 = 0.5$ and the maximal point occurs at $c_2 = 0.5$. Moreover, the bigger z_1 or z_2 is, the bigger maximal value can be obtained.

(2) AMID in the final state $\sigma_{bd}(z_1, z_2, c_1, c_2)$ is an increasing function with z_i in the region $z_i \in (0, 1)$, $i = 1, 2$, for given (c_1, c_2). See Figure 6. In Figure 6, variations of $\mathcal{Q}_A[\sigma_{bd}(z_1, z_2, c_1, c_2)]$ with z_2 for $c_1 = 0.5, c_2 = 0.5$ and $z_1 = 0.3, 0.6, 0.9$ are plotted respectively. Obviously, one can see that MID in the final state increase with $z_i, i = 1, 2$.

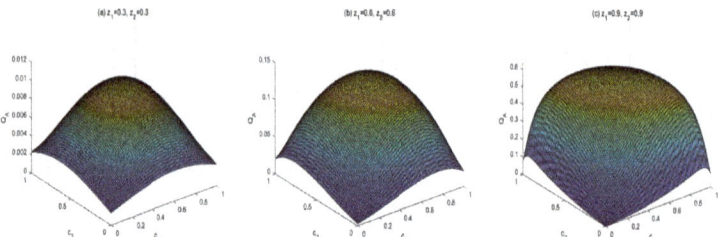

Figure 6. Variation of $\mathcal{Q}_A[\sigma_{bd}]$ with c_1 and c_2 for three sets of z_1 and z_2.

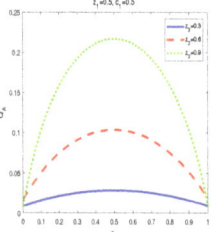

Figure 7. Variation of $\mathcal{Q}_A[\sigma_{bd}]$ with c_2 for $z_1 = 0.5, c_1 = 0.5$ and $z_2 = 0.3, 0.6, 0.9$, respectively.

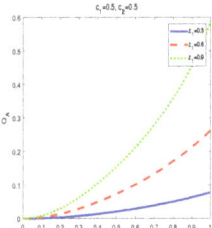

Figure 8. Variation of $\mathcal{Q}_A[\sigma_{bd}]$ with z_2 for $c_1 = 0.5$, $c_2 = 0.5$ and $z_1 = 0.3, 0.6, 0.9$, respectively.

5.3.2. Monotony Features of AMIDs in the Final State $\sigma'_{bd}(z_1, z_2, c_1, c_2)$

To achieve the properties of AMID in the final state $\sigma'_{bd}(z_1, z_2, c_1, c_2)$, we also utilized vast numerical calculations. Some typical figures are listed in Figures 9 and 10. Through the vast numerical calculations and comparisons, the following properties can be exposed.

(a) For given c_2 and (z_1, z_2), $\mathcal{Q}_A[\sigma'_{bd}]$ first increases then decreases with $c_1 \in (0, 1]$. The maximal points (c_{1m}), i.e., the transition points, are changed with different parameters. The maximal points and the shape of the curves are determined by the value of c_2. Concretely, the closer the value of c_1 to 0.5 is, the larger maximal value of $\mathcal{Q}_A[\sigma'_{bd}]$ can be obtained. Moreover, for a given set of (z_1, z_2),

$$\mathcal{Q}_A[\sigma_{bd}(z_1, z_2, c_1 = 0.5 - \alpha, c_2 = 0.5 - \beta)] = \mathcal{Q}_M[\sigma_{bd}(z_1, z_2, c_1 = 0.5 + \alpha, c_2 = 0.5 + \beta)] \quad (39)$$

where $\alpha \in (0, 1/2), \beta \in (0, 1/2)$.

(b) $\mathcal{Q}_A[\sigma'_{bd}]$ is an increasing function of $z_1 \in [0, 1]$ within $z_2 \in [0, 0.58]$. However, when $z_2 \in [0.58, 1]$, $\mathcal{Q}_A[\sigma'_{bd}]$ first increases then decreases in $z_1 \in [0, 1]$. Moreover, the bigger of $z_2 \in [0.58, 1]$, the smaller of transtion point is.

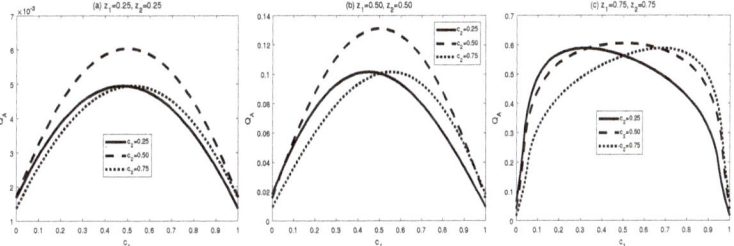

Figure 9. Variation of $\mathcal{Q}_A[\sigma'_{bd}]$ with c_1 and c_2 for three sets of z_1 and z_2.

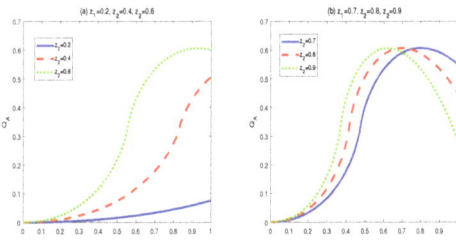

Figure 10. Variation of $\mathcal{Q}_A[\sigma'_{bd}]$ with c_1 and c_2 for three sets of z_1 and z_2.

5.4. Comparisons between MID and AMID in the Final States

In this section, let us make some comparisons between them MID and AMID. From the last sections, through many comparisons, one can obtain the following conclusions:

(i) The properties of MID in the final state σ_{bd} are similar to those of AMID in the final state σ_{bd}. Comparing Figures 1–3 with Figures 6–8, it is easy to obtain this conclusion. Regardless of the QC—MID or AMID—QCs in the final state σ_{bd} are monotonically increasing function of z_i (i = 1,2). Additionally, they increase when $c_i \in [0, 1/2]$ and symmetrically decrease when $c_i \in [1/2, 1]$. These properties are manly due to the middle measurements in Equation (5) during the QC swapping process. In other words, the middle measurements in Equation (5) do not change the QC properties before and after the QC swapping process. To be concrete, the dependent relations of QCs on the parameters (z_i and c_i, $i = 1, 2$) in the initial states are retained in the final states.

(ii) The properties of MID in the final state σ'_{bd} are similar to those of AMID in the final state σ'_{bd}. Comparing Figures 4 and 5 with Figures 9 and 10, one can easily obtain this result. If $c_2 = 0.5$, then QCs (MID or AMID) in the final state σ'_{bd} are symmetrical regarding $c_1 = 0.5$. Moreover, they are increasing in $c_1 \in [0, 1/2]$ and decreasing in $c_1 \in [1/2, 1]$. However, when $c_2 \neq 0.5$, the symmetry disappears. QCs (MID or AMID) in the final state ρ'_{bd} still first increase then decrease, but the transition points are no longer equal to 0.5. As for the dependent relation of QCs (MID or AMID) in the final state σ'_{bd} on z_i, some transitions emerge. For example, if $z_2 \in [0.58, 1]$, QCs (MID or AMID) in the final state σ'_{bd} first increase then decrease. Obviously, the properties of QCs (MID or AMID) in the final state σ'_{bd} on the parameters are no longer similar to those in the two initial states. This is mainly due to the middle measurements in Equation (6). That is to say, the middle measurements in Equation (6) changes the properties during the QC swapping process.

(iii) There are some distinct differences between QCs (MID or AMID) in the final state σ_{bd} and those in the final state σ'_{bd}. From (i) and (ii), one can see the distict differences. Properties in the QCs (MID or AMID) in the final state σ_{bd} are similar to those in the two initial states. However, properties in the QCs (MID or AMID) in the final state σ'_{bd} are no longer similar to those in the two initial states. The distict differences are mainly due to the two kinds of different measurements in Equations (5) and (6).

(iv) The long-distance QC can be realized indeed. From the above discussions, one can find that QCs in the final states are bigger than zero. That is to say, from the two initial states, i.e., two short-QC owners, one can obtain a final state through QC swapping process. Moreover, the final state is a long-distance QC owner.

In addition, let us look at the influences of entanglement of the initial Werner-like states on the QC swapping in this study. For each of the two Werner-like states in Equations (3) and (4), it is entangled, if and only if $1/2 \leq c < 1/2(1 + \sqrt{(z+1)(3z-1)}/2z)$ [44]. Hence, one can see that being entangled or not in each one of the initial Werner-like states is determined by this criterion condition. If the criterion condition is not satisfied, there is no entanglement in the Werner-like state, and thus no entanglement swapping. However, from the conclusions discussed above, one can see that the swapping of QC, MID or AMID, is not influenced by the entanglement criterion condition. That is to say, whether entangled or separable in the initial Werner-like states, it does not affect the quantum correlation swapping in this study.

In [42], we discussed quantum correlation swapping between Werner and separable states. In this paper, we discuss the quantum correlation swapping between two Werner-like states. The differences between the two cases can be listed as the following: (1) In the former case, the two initial states are Werner and separable states. The Werner state can be an entanglement state, the while separable state has no entanglement in it. In the latter case, the Werner-like state can be entangled. Moreover, the Werner-like state is a state from the Werner state undergoing local or nonlocal unitary operations. (2) In the former case, there are only two parameters concerned. One is in the Werner state and another is in the separable state. In the latter case, there are four parameters concerned. A Werner-like state has two parameters, one from the original Werner state and another from the unitary operations. (3) The obtained quantities and properties are distinctly different.

Finally, let us make some simple remarks. In this study, we consider a special case of quantum correlation swapping. The two initial states we considered are two Werner-like states. A Werner-like state is determined by two parameters. For convenience, we select the four Bell states with no parameters in them. Hence, in the final states, there are four parameters. In this work, we respectively study the dependence relations on the four parameters.

6. Summary

In this paper, the QC swapping with two Werner-like states has been considered. MID and AMID have been utilized to quantify all the QCs in the concerned states. Some distinct features about these obtained QCs have been revealed. Especially, it is found that the monotony features of MID and AMID in the two final states are similar to those in the two initial states, while those in two other final states are not. To be specific, the monotony features of MID and AMID in the two final states in Equation (7) are similar to those in the two initial states. However, the monotony features of MID and AMID in the two final states in Equation (9) are different from those in the two initial states. All these obtained distinct properties will be valuable in the field of quantum information processing.

Author Contributions: Data curation, J.C.; Software, X.Y.; Supervision, Z.Z.; Writing—review & editing, C.X. All authors have read and agreed to the published version of the manuscript.

Funding: This work is supported by the National Natural Science Foundation of China (NNSFC) under Grant Nos. 61701002 and 12075205, the Natural Science Foundation of Anhui province under Grant Nos. 1808085MA23, Zhejiang Proivincial Key Laboratory of New Standard and Technologies (NNST) under Grant No. 2013E10012.

Institutional Review Board Statement: Not applicable.

Informed Consent Statement: Not applicable.

Data Availability Statement: Not applicable.

Conflicts of Interest: The author declares no conflict of interest.

Appendix A

In order to evaluate AMID in $\sigma_{bd}^{\pm}(z_1, z_2, c_1, c_2)$, a general joint local measurement can be parameterized as $\{\Omega_b^{(i)}(\alpha_1, \phi_1, \tau_1) \otimes \Lambda_d^{(j)}(\alpha_2, \phi_2, \tau_2), \ i,j = 0,1\}$, where $\Omega^{(k)}$ and $\Lambda^{(k)}$ take the same forms as that in Equations (27) and (28). If the parameterized measuring bases are used to measure both subsystems, then four different outcomes may occur. Those in Equation (29) are occurrence probabilities of different outcomes. After some tedious deductions, one can obtain those in Equation (30).

References

1. Briegel, H.J.; Dür, W.; Cirac, J.I.; Zoller, P. Quantum repeaters: The role of imperfect local operations in quantum communication. *Phys. Rev. Lett.* **1998**, *81*, 5932–5935. [CrossRef]
2. Munro, W.J.; Van, M.R.; Louis, S.G.; Nemoto, K. High-bandwidth hybrid quantum repeater. *Phys. Rev. Lett.* **2008**, *101*, 040502. [CrossRef] [PubMed]
3. Zukowski, M.; Zeilinger, A.; Horne, M.A.; Ekert, A.K. "Event-ready-detectors" Bell experiment via entanglement swapping. *Phys. Rev. Lett.* **1993**, *71*, 4287. [CrossRef]
4. Goebel, A.M.; Wagenknecht, C.; Zhang, Q.; Chen, Y.A.; Chen, K.; Schmiedmayer, J.; Pan, J.W. Multistage entanglement swapping. *Phys. Rev. Lett.* **2008**, *101*, 080403. [CrossRef]
5. Branciard, C.; Gisin, N.; Pironio, S. Characterizing the nonlocal correlations created via entanglement swapping. *Phys. Rev. Lett.* **2010**, *104*, 170401. [CrossRef] [PubMed]
6. Roy, S.M.; Deshpande, A.; Sakharwade, N. Remote tomography and entanglement swapping via von Neumann-Arthurs-Kelly interaction. *Phys. Rev. A* **2014**, *89*, 052107. [CrossRef]
7. Ottaviani, C.; Lupo, C.; Ferraro, A.; Paternostro, M.; Pirandola, S. Multipartite entanglement swapping and mechanical cluster states. *Phys. Rev. A* **2019**, *99*, 030301. [CrossRef]
8. Modlawska, J.; Grudka, A. Increasing singlet fraction with entanglement swapping. *Phys. Rev. A* **2008**, *78*, 032321. [CrossRef]
9. Einstein, A.; Podolsky, B.; Rosen, N. Can quantum-mechanical description of physical reality be considered complete? *Phys. Rev.* **1935**, *47*, 777. [CrossRef]
10. Bohr, N. Can quantum-mechanical description of physical reality be considered complete? *Phys. Rev.* **1935**, *48*, 696. [CrossRef]
11. Ekert, A. Quantum cryptography based on bell's theorem. *Phys. Rev. Lett.* **1991**, *67*, 661. [CrossRef] [PubMed]
12. William, K.W. Entanglement of Formation of an Arbitrary State of Two Qubits. *Phys. Rev. Lett.* **1998**, *80*, 2245.

13. Long, G.L.; Liu, X.S. Theoretically efficient high-capacity quantum-key-distribution scheme. *Phys. Rev. A* **2002**, *65*, 032302. [CrossRef]
14. Cheung, C.Y.; Zhang, Z.J. Criterion for faithful teleportation with an arbitrary multiparticle channel. *Phys. Rev. A* **2009**, *80*, 022327. [CrossRef]
15. Bouwmeester, D.; Pan, J.-W.; Mattle, K.; Eibl, M.; Weinfurter, H.; Zeilinger, A. Experimental quantum teleportation. *Nature* **1997**, *390*, 575–579. [CrossRef]
16. Xiao, L.; Long, G.L.; Deng, F.G.; Pan, J.W. Efficient multiparty quantum-secret-sharing schemes. *Phys. Rev. A* **2004**, *69*, 052307. [CrossRef]
17. Deng, F.G.; Long, G.L.; Liu, X.S. Two-step quantum direct communication protocol using the Einstein-Podolsky-Rosen pair block. *Phys. Rev. A* **2003**, *68*, 042317. [CrossRef]
18. Zhu, A.D.; Xia, Y.; Fan, Q.B.; Zhang, S. Secure direct communication based on secret transmitting order of particles. *Phys. Rev. A* **2006**, *73*, 022338. [CrossRef]
19. Ollivier, H.; Zurek, W.H. Quantum discord: A measure of the quantumness of correlations. *Phys. Rev. Lett.* **2001**, *88*, 017901. [CrossRef]
20. Luo, S.L. Using measurement-induced disturbance to characterize correlations as classical or quantum. *Phys. Rev. A* **2008**, *77*, 022301. [CrossRef]
21. Luo, S.L.; Fu, S.S. Geometric measure of quantum discord. *Phys. Rev. A* **2010**, *82*, 034302. [CrossRef]
22. Zhou, T.; Cui, J.; Long, G.L. Measure of nonclassical correlation in coherence-vector representation. *Phys. Rev. A* **2011**, *84*, 062105. [CrossRef]
23. Girolami, D.; Paternostro, M.; Adesso, G. Faithful nonclassicality indicators and extremal quantum correlations in two-qubit states. *J. Phys. A Math. Theor.* **2011**, *44*, 352002. [CrossRef]
24. Modi, K.; Paterek, T.; Son, W.; Vedral, V.; Williamson, M. Unified view of quantum and classical correlations. *Phys. Rev. Lett.* **2010**, *104*, 080501. [CrossRef]
25. Dakic, B.; Vedral, V.; Brukner, C. Necessary and sufficient condition for nonzero quantum discord. *Phys. Rev. Lett.* **2010**, *105*, 190502. [CrossRef]
26. Rulli, C.C.; Sarandy, M.S. Global quantum discord in multipartite systems. *Phys. Rev. A* **2011**, *84*, 042109. [CrossRef]
27. Zhang, Z.J. Revised definitions of quantum dissonance and quantum discord. *arXiv* **2010**, arXiv:1011.4333.
28. Wei, H.R.; Ren, B.C.; Deng, F.G. Geometric measure of quantum discord for a two-parameter class of states in a qubit-qutrit system under various dissipative channels. *Quantum Inf. Process.* **2013**, *12*, 1109–1124. [CrossRef]
29. Zhang, F.L.; Chen, J.L. Irreducible multiqutrit correlations in Greenberger-Horne-Zeilinger type states. *Phys. Rev. A* **2011**, *84*, 062328. [CrossRef]
30. Radhakrishnan, C.; Laurière, M.; Byrnes, T. Multipartite generalization of quantum Discord. *Phys. Rev. Lett.* **2020**, *124*, 110401. [CrossRef]
31. Kanjilal, S.; Khan, A.; Jebaratnam, C.; Home, D. Remote state preparation using correlations beyond discord. *Phys. Rev. A* **2018**, *98*, 062320. [CrossRef]
32. Carrijo, T.M.; Avelar, A.T. On the continuity of quantum correlation quantifiers. *Quantum Inf. Process.* **2020**, *19*, 214. [CrossRef]
33. Zhu, X.N.; Fei, S.M.; Li-Jost, X.Q. Analytical expression of quantum discord for rank-2 two-qubit states. *Quantum Inf. Process.* **2018**, *17*, 234. [CrossRef]
34. Ye, B.L.; Liu, Y.M.; Chen, J.L.; Liu, X.S.; Zhang, Z.J. Analytic expressions of quantum correlations in qutrit Werner states. *Quantum Inf. Process.* **2013**, *12*, 2335. [CrossRef]
35. Li, G.F.; Liu, Y.M.; Tang, H.J.; Yin, X.F.; Zhang, Z.J. Analytic expression of quantum correlations in qutrit Werner states undergoing local and nonlocal unitary operations. *Quantum Inf. Process.* **2015**, *14*, 559. [CrossRef]
36. Xie, C.M.; Liu, Y.M.; Xing, H.; Chen, J.L.; Zhang, Z.J. Quantum correlation swapping. *Quantum Inf. Process.* **2015**, *14*, 653. [CrossRef]
37. Xie, C.M.; Liu, Y.M.; Chen, J.L.; Zhang, Z.J. Study of quantum correlation swapping with relative entropy methods. *Quantum Inf. Process.* **2016**, *15*, 809. [CrossRef]
38. Xie, C.M.; Liu, Y.M.; Chen, J.L.; Zhang, Z.J. Quantum correlation swapping in parallel and antiparallel two-qubit mixed states. *Quantum Inf. Process.* **2019**, *18*, 106. [CrossRef]
39. Ye, B.L.; Liu, Y.M.; Xu, C.J.; Liu, X.S.; Zhang, Z.J. Quantum correlations in a family of two-qubit separable states. *Commun. Theor. Phys.* **2013**, *60*, 283. [CrossRef]
40. Xie, C.M.; Zhang, Z.J.; Chen, J.L.; Yin, X.F. Analytic expression of quantum discord in Werner states under LQCC. *Entropy* **2020**, *22*, 147. [CrossRef]
41. Xie, C.M.; Zhang, Z.J.; Yuan, H.; Chen, J.L.; Sun, J.; Yin, X.F. Quantum correlation swapping between Werner derivatives. *Laser Phys. Lett.* **2021**, *18*, 125203. [CrossRef]
42. Xie, C.M.; Zhang, Z.J.; Chen, J.L.; Yin, X.F. Quantum correlation swapping between Werner and separable states. *Laser Phys. Lett.* **2021**, *18*, 035203. [CrossRef]
43. Xie, C.M.; Wu, F.Y.; Zhang, Z.J.; Liang, J.W.; Yin, X.F. Increasing quantum correlations based on Measurement-induced disturbance via a swapping procedure with two-qubit mixed states. *Entropy* **2021**, *23*, 147. [CrossRef] [PubMed]

44. Ghiu, I.; Grimaudo, R.; Mihaescu, T.; Isar, A.; Messina, A. Quantum correlation dynamics in controlled two-coupled-qubit system. *Entropy* **2020**, *22*, 785. [CrossRef] [PubMed]
45. Wang, S.F.; Liu,Y.M.; Li, G.F.; Liu, X.S.; Zhang, Z.J. Quantum correlations in Werner derivatives. *Commun. Theor. Phys.* **2013**, *60*, 40. [CrossRef]

MDPI
St. Alban-Anlage 66
4052 Basel
Switzerland
Tel. +41 61 683 77 34
Fax +41 61 302 89 18
www.mdpi.com

Entropy Editorial Office
E-mail: entropy@mdpi.com
www.mdpi.com/journal/entropy

www.ingramcontent.com/pod-product-compliance
Lightning Source LLC
LaVergne TN
LVHW070402100526
838202LV00014B/1374